The City's Defense

In *The City's Defense*, Robert Yee examines how the City of London maintained its status as an international financial center. He traces the role of the Bank of England in restructuring the domestic, imperial, European, and international monetary systems in the aftermath of the First World War. In response to mass unemployment, volatile exchange rates, and competitive devaluations, the Bank expanded its reach into areas outside the traditional scope of central banking, including industrial policy and foreign affairs. It designed a system of economic governance that reinforced the preeminence of sterling as a reserve currency. Drawing on a range of archival evidence from national governments, private corporations, and international organizations, Yee reevaluates our understanding of Britain's impact on the global economic order.

Robert Yee is a lecturer and postdoctoral associate at Yale University.

STUDIES IN MACROECONOMIC HISTORY

The titles in this series investigate themes of interest to economists and economic historians in the rapidly developing field of macroeconomic history. The four areas covered include the application of monetary and finance theory, international economics, and quantitative methods to historical problems; the historical application of growth and development theory and theories of business fluctuations; the history of domestic and international monetary, financial, and other macroeconomic institutions; and the history of international monetary and financial systems. The series amalgamates the former Cambridge University Press series Studies in Monetary and Financial History and Studies in Quantitative Economic History.

Other Books in the Series:

Jon Moen and Mary Tone Rodgers, *Before the Fed: J.P. Morgan, America's Lender of Last Resort* (2025)

Mareike Beck, *Extroverted Financialization: Banking on US Dollar Debt* (2025)

Per H. Hansen, *There Will Be the Devil to Pay: Central Bankers, Uncertainty and Sensemaking in the European Financial Crisis of 1931* (2024)

Simon Amrein, *Capital in Banking: The Role of Capital in Banking in the 19th and 20th Century: The United Kingdom, the United States and Switzerland* (2024)

Stephen Quinn and William Roberds, *How a Ledger Became a Central Bank: A Monetary History of the Bank of Amsterdam* (2023)

Simon Hinrichsen, *When Nations Can't Default: A History of War Reparations and Sovereign Debt* (2023)

Barry Eichengreen and Andreas Kakridis, *The Emergence of the Modern Central Bank and Global Cooperation: 1919–1939* (2023)

Alain Naef, *An Exchange Rate History of the United Kingdom: 1945–1992* (2021)

Barrie A. Wigmore, *The Financial Crisis of 2008: A History of US Financial Markets 2000–2012* (2021)

Max Harris, *Monetary War and Peace: London, Washington, Paris, and the Tripartite Agreement of 1936* (2021)

Kenneth D. Garbade, *After the Accord: A History of Federal Reserve Open Market Operations, the US Government Securities Market, and Treasury Debt Management from 1951 to 1979* (2020)

Harold James, *Making a Modern Central Bank: The Bank of England 1979–2003* (2020)

Claudio Borio, Stijn Claessens, Piet Clement, Robert N. McCauley, and Hyun Song Shin, Editors, *Promoting Global Monetary and Financial Stability: The Bank for International Settlements after Bretton Woods, 1973–2020* (2020)

Patrick Honohan, *Currency, Credit and Crisis: Central Banking in Ireland and Europe* (2019)

William A. Allen, *The Bank of England and the Government Debt: Operations in the Gilt-Edged Market, 1928–1972* (2019)

Eric Monnet, *Controlling Credit: Central Banking and the Planned Economy in Postwar France, 1948–1973* (2018)

Laurence M. Ball, *The Fed and Lehman Brothers: Setting the Record Straight on a Financial Disaster* (2018)

Rodney Edvinsson, Tor Jacobson, and Daniel Waldenström, Editors, *Sveriges Riksbank and the History of Central Banking* (2018)

Peter L. Rousseau and Paul Wachtel, Editors, *Financial Systems and Economic Growth: Credit, Crises, and the Regulation from the 19th Century to the Present* (2017)

Ernst Baltensperger and Peter Kugler, *Swiss Monetary History since the Early 19th Century* (2017)

Øyvind Eitrheim, Jan Tore Klovland, and Lars Fredrik Øksendal, *A Monetary History of Norway, 1816–2016* (2016)

Jan Fredrik Qvigstad, *On Central Banking* (2016)

Michael D. Bordo, Øyvind Eitrheim, Marc Flandreau, and Jan F. Qvigstad, Editors, *Central Banks at a Crossroads: What Can We Learn from History?* (2016)

Michael D. Bordo and Mark A. Wynne, Editors, *The Federal Reserve's Role in the Global Economy: A Historical Perspective* (2016)

Owen F. Humpage, Editor, *Current Federal Reserve Policy Under the Lens of Economic History: Essays to Commemorate the Federal Reserve System's Centennial* (2015)

Michael D. Bordo and William Roberds, Editors, *The Origins, History, and Future of the Federal Reserve: A Return to Jekyll Island* (2013)

Michael D. Bordo and Ronald MacDonald, Editors, *Credibility and the International Monetary Regime: A Historical Perspective* (2012)

Robert L. Hetzel, *The Great Recession: Market Failure or Policy Failure?* (2012)

Tobias Straumann, *Fixed Ideas of Money: Small States and Exchange Rate Regimes in Twentieth-Century Europe* (2010)

Forrest Capie, *The Bank of England: 1950s to 1979* (2010)

Aldo Musacchio, *Experiments in Financial Democracy: Corporate Governance and Financial Development in Brazil, 1882–1950* (2009)

Claudio Borio, Gianni Toniolo, and Piet Clement, Editors, *The Past and Future of Central Bank Cooperation* (2008)

Robert L. Hetzel, *The Monetary Policy of the Federal Reserve: A History* (2008)

Caroline Fohlin, *Finance Capitalism and Germany's Rise to Industrial Power* (2007)

John H. Wood, *A History of Central Banking in Great Britain and the United States* (2005)

Gianni Toniolo (with the assistance of Piet Clement), *Central Bank Cooperation at the Bank for International Settlements, 1930–1973* (2005)

Richard Burdekin and Pierre Siklos, Editors, *Deflation: Current and Historical Perspectives* (2004)

Pierre Siklos, *The Changing Face of Central Banking: Evolutionary Trends since World War II* (2002)

Michael D. Bordo and Roberto Cortés-Conde, Editors, *Transferring Wealth and Power from the Old to the New World: Monetary and Fiscal Institutions in the 17th through the 19th Centuries* (2001)

Howard Bodenhorn, *A History of Banking in Antebellum America: Financial Markets and Economic Development in an Era of Nation-Building* (2000)

Mark Harrison, Editor, *The Economics of World War II: Six Great Powers in International Comparison* (2000)

Angela Redish, *Bimetallism: An Economic and Historical Analysis* (2000)

Elmus Wicker, *Banking Panics of the Gilded Age* (2000)

Michael D. Bordo, *The Gold Standard and Related Regimes: Collected Essays* (1999)

Michele Fratianni and Franco Spinelli, *A Monetary History of Italy* (1997)

Mark Toma, *Competition and Monopoly in the Federal Reserve System, 1914–1951* (1997)

Barry Eichengreen, Editor, *Europe's Postwar Recovery* (1996)

Lawrence H. Officer, *Between the Dollar-Sterling Gold Points: Exchange Rates, Parity and Market Behavior* (1996)

Elmus Wicker, *The Banking Panics of the Great Depression* (1996)

Norio Tamaki, *Japanese Banking: A History, 1859–1959* (1995)

Barry Eichengreen, *Elusive Stability: Essays in the History of International Finance, 1919–1939* (1993)

Michael D. Bordo and Forrest Capie, Editors, *Monetary Regimes in Transition* (1993)

Larry Neal, *The Rise of Financial Capitalism: International Capital Markets in the Age of Reason* (1993)

S. N. Broadberry and N. F. R. Crafts, Editors, *Britain in the International Economy, 1870–1939* (1992)

Aurel Schubert, *The Credit-Anstalt Crisis of 1931* (1992)

Trevor J. O. Dick and John E. Floyd, *Canada and the Gold Standard: Balance of Payments Adjustment under Fixed Exchange Rates, 1871–1913* (1992)

Kenneth Mouré, *Managing the Franc Poincaré: Economic Understanding and Political Constraint in French Monetary Policy, 1928–1936* (1991)

David C. Wheelock, *The Strategy and Consistency of Federal Reserve Monetary Policy, 1924–1933* (1991)

The City's Defense

The Bank of England and the Remaking of Economic Governance, 1914–1939

ROBERT YEE
Yale University

CAMBRIDGE
UNIVERSITY PRESS

CAMBRIDGE
UNIVERSITY PRESS

Shaftesbury Road, Cambridge CB2 8EA, United Kingdom

One Liberty Plaza, 20th Floor, New York, NY 10006, USA

477 Williamstown Road, Port Melbourne, VIC 3207, Australia

314–321, 3rd Floor, Plot 3, Splendor Forum, Jasola District Centre, New Delhi – 110025, India

103 Penang Road, #05–06/07, Visioncrest Commercial, Singapore 238467

Cambridge University Press is part of Cambridge University Press & Assessment, a department of the University of Cambridge.

We share the University's mission to contribute to society through the pursuit of education, learning and research at the highest international levels of excellence.

www.cambridge.org
Information on this title: www.cambridge.org/9781009671880

DOI: 10.1017/9781009671866

When citing this work, please include a reference to the DOI 10.1017/9781009671866

First published 2025

A catalogue record for this publication is available from the British Library

A Cataloging-in-Publication data record for this book is available from the Library of Congress

ISBN 978-1-009-67189-7 Hardback
ISBN 978-1-009-67188-0 Paperback

For my parents

How great the power of the Bank of England is, however, would soon become clear.[1]

Karl Helfferich, 1899

London has held first place because of her prestige and competence, intimate knowledge of international finance, the confidence of the world, and the influence of the B. of E. and its Governor.[2]

Edward Peacock, 1926

[I]f our monetary system is to be managed and our economic life is to be regulated at the source, there can be no possible instrument of this except the Bank of England.[3]

John Maynard Keynes, 1930

[1] Karl Helfferich, "Die Lage der Bank von England," *Neue Freie Presse* 12574, August 25, 1899, 9.

[2] Edward Peacock, "Note Re Bank of England," July 9, 1926, BA Revelstoke Papers 203332.

[3] Committee on Finance and Industry, Notes on Discussion, December 5, 1930, TNA T200/6/7.

Contents

Figures

Tables

Acknowledgments

This book would not exist without the support of numerous people. I owe my greatest intellectual debts to David Cannadine and Harold James, who have both offered me constant encouragement and unwavering support over the years. They taught me how to think critically and broadly about historical research, and their advice has steered my interests in new directions.

At Princeton University, I am particularly grateful to Michael Blaakman, Leah Boustan, Linda Colley, Sheldon Garon, Meg Jacobs, Beth Lew-Williams, Yair Mintzker, and Natasha Wheatley. Special thanks are due to Haris Durrani, Casey Eilbert, Julia Marino, Pablo Pryluka, and Stephanie Zgouridi, who read numerous chapters of the manuscript and offered their enduring support. I also enjoyed engaging conversations with Friedrich Asschenfeldt, Michael Brill, Jin-Woo Choi, Liane Hewitt, Midori Kawaue, Jonathan Raspe, Johanna Rozakis-Siu, Keely Smith, Neel Thakkar, and Constantine Theodoridis.

On both sides of the Atlantic, I have had the opportunity to learn from many colleagues. At Oxford, I wish to thank the Warden and Fellows of Wadham College, who elected me to the David Richards Junior Research Fellowship in Economic History. Sincere thanks are due to Jose Maria Andres Porras, Norman Aselmeyer, Lynn Featherstone, Jane Garnett, Matthew Kempshall, Matt Myers, Tehila Sasson, George Southcombe, and Cecilia Tarruell.

The intellectual community fostered by workshops and seminars at the Faculty of History is similarly unparalleled. Patricia Clavin first welcomed me to Oxford and has since given me insightful feedback on many versions of this manuscript. Catherine Schenk has been a constant source of knowledge and expertise. I have also learned much from my conversations with Raphael Adès, Stephen Broadberry, Martin Conway, Aled Davies, Victoria Gierok, Uziel González-Aliaga, Jane Humphries, Christopher McKenna, Patrick O'Brien, Avner Offer, Sheilagh Ogilvie, and Rebecca Simson.

A Chateaubriand Fellowship from the Embassy of France allowed me to spend a semester at the Paris School of Economics in early 2023. I am grateful to Éric Monnet for sponsoring the visit and offering me helpful guidance on this project. Seminars at the François-Simiand Centre for Economic and Social History and the Banque de France were the site of lively discussions. Alain Naef offered meticulous comments on the manuscript in its early stages. For their perspectives on monetary and banking history, I also wish to thank Pamfili Antipa, Vincent Bignon, Pierre-Cyrille Hautcœur, Raphaël Orange-Leroy, and Miklos Vari.

During my research stays in Berlin, I attended seminars organized by the Centre for British Studies and the Institute for Economic History. I thank Alexander Nützenadel, Sebastian Teupe, and Nikolaus Wolf for the invitation to present at the Colloquium in Economic and Social History. Equally as engaging was a summer I spent at the Kiel Institute for the World Economy, where I had many fruitful discussions with Moritz Hauschulz, Sebastian Horn, Henry Minör, and Christoph Trebesch.

Elsewhere, I have had the opportunity to meet scholars who offered valuable feedback: Maylis Avaro, Grace Ballor, Alexis Drach, Madeleine Dungy, Matthias Kemmerer, Nathan Marcus, Jamie Martin, Juan Ignacio Mercatante, Stefanie Middendorf, Johanna Gautier Morin, Víctor Pérez-Sánchez, Sabine Pitteloud, Claudia Rei, Charlotte Robertson, Kurt Schuler, Judy Stephenson, John Turner, Sean Vanatta, and Paula Vedoveli. I am particularly indebted to Duncan Needham and Peter Sloman at the University of Cambridge for their helpful comments. At Vanderbilt University, David Blackbourn, William Caferro, Thomas Schwartz, Samira Sheikh, and Frank Wcislo were all formative to my undergraduate education.

I would like to thank the prize committee of the Economic History Society for awarding me the 2024 Thirsk–Feinstein Dissertation Prize. My research further benefited from the support of the Anglo-Austrian Society, the Center for International Security Studies at Princeton, the Centre for History and Economics at Cambridge, the German Academic Exchange Service (DAAD), the German History Society, Harvard Business School, the Henry Kaufman Financial History Fellowship, the History of Economics Society, the Jennie Churchill Fund, the Kiel Institute for the World Economy, and the Prussian Privy State Archives. I am especially thankful to Pallavi Nuka and Nancy Turco for fostering a vibrant intellectual atmosphere at the Julis-Rabinowitz Center for Public Policy and Finance.

Countless librarians and archivists have helped me identify material relevant. I would like to acknowledge the assistance of all those at the Bank of England, including Michael Anson, Grace Freeman, Lara Garrett, Kat Harrington, Margherita Orlando, and Evie Stevenson. The Baring Archive, the Churchill Archives Centre, and the Reserve Bank of Australia generously allowed me to reproduce images from their archives.

It was a pleasure to work with Cambridge University Press during the publication process. I am grateful to Michael Bordo for being the skilled editor of this book series, to Robert Dreesen and Sable Gravesandy for their professionalism and responsiveness throughout the publication process, and to the three anonymous reviewers for their incisive and critical comments.

Finally, I would like to express my deepest gratitude to those closest to me. My friends from Vanderbilt, especially Mack Clair, Joshua Hamburger, Eli McDonald, Dylan Rosenfield, and Nate Wasserman, have been the greatest sources of motivation and humor over the years. Above all, I owe the most to my parents, Terri and Howard, to whom this book is dedicated. They, along with my sister, Kristina, have been a source of constant love and encouragement, with unrelenting support at every step of the journey. I thank them for everything.

and the Panic of 1907, a rise in the Bank Rate aimed to curb speculative capital outflows and guard the Bank's reserves.[6] These reactions ensured the continuance of gold convertibility, as well as the broader stability of the liberal economic order.

Over the ensuing century, the Bank prioritized the interests of the domestic banking sector.[7] The succeeding calamities of the First World War and the Great Depression might have dealt a decisive strike to the primacy of the City as the world's financial center, but the central bank's role in the international financial system remained unparalleled. After the Second World War, the British authorities continued to promote the status of sterling as a world reserve currency.[8] Amidst major upheavals in the postwar years, from decolonization to devaluations, the Bank contended with repeated challenges to its authority. Indeed, the central bank, far from the apolitical body it may have wanted to be, often found itself beholden to party politics. As Chancellor of the Exchequer, Winston Churchill clashed with the Bank over its controversial

Respectable Banking: The Search for Stability in London's Money and Credit Markets since 1695 (Cambridge: Cambridge University Press, 2017), 94–110; Stefano Ugolini, *The Evolution of Central Banking: Theory and History* (London: Palgrave Macmillan, 2017), 7–13, 131–143; Ulrich Bindseil, *Central Banking before 1800: A Rehabilitation* (Oxford: Oxford University Press, 2019), 184–194.

[6] On both November 7, 1890 and October 19, 1906, the Bank raised its discount rate to 6 percent; George H. Pownall, "Bank Reserves, the Central Stock of Gold, and £1 Notes," January 27, 1892, in *Transactions of the Manchester Statistical Society* (London: John Heywood, 1891–1892), 39; Robert F. Bruner and Sean D. Carr, *The Panic of 1907: Lessons Learned from the Market's Perfect Storm* (Hoboken: John Wiley & Sons, 2007), 14–15.

[7] See, for instance, the Bank's responses to different financial crises in John Clapham, *The Bank of England: A History, 1694–1797, vol. 1* (Cambridge: Cambridge University Press, 1944), 224–236, 245–272; R.S. Sayers, *The Bank of England, 1891–1944, vol. 2* (Cambridge: Cambridge University Press, 1976), 387–415; John Fforde, *The Bank of England and Public Policy, 1941–1958* (Cambridge: Cambridge University Press, 1992), 141–164; Forrest Capie, *The Bank of England, 1950s to 1979* (Cambridge: Cambridge University Press, 2010), 531–545, 740–759; David Kynaston, *Till Time's Last Sand: A History of the Bank of England, 1694–2013* (London: Bloomsbury, 2017), 164–172, 513–527, 652–659; Harold James, *Making a Modern Central Bank: The Bank of England, 1979–2003* (Cambridge: Cambridge University Press, 2020), 300–309; Alain Naef, *An Exchange Rate History of the United Kingdom, 1945–1992* (Cambridge: Cambridge University Press, 2022), 128–144, 213–218. On the study of central banks as institutions, see Olivier Feiertag, ed., *Mesurer la monnaie : banques centrales et construction de l'autorité monétaire, XIXe–XXe siècle* (Paris: Albin Michel, 2005); Vincent Duchaussoy and Olivier Feiertag, "L'invention des banques centrales : organisation et gouvernance," *Histoire, économie & société* 4, no. 35 (2016): 4–7.

[8] Philip L. Cottrell, "The Bank of England in its International Setting, 1918–1972," in *The Bank of England: Money, Power and Influence, 1694–1994*, ed. Richard Roberts and David Kynaston (Oxford: Clarendon Press, 1995), 119–139; Catherine R. Schenk, *The Decline of Sterling: Managing the Retreat of an International Currency, 1945–1992* (Cambridge: Cambridge University Press, 2010); Sarah Stockwell, *The British End of the British Empire* (Cambridge: Cambridge University Press, 2018), 144–148, 173–177; Maylis Avaro, "Zombie International Currency: The Pound Sterling 1945–1971," *The Journal of Economic History* 84, no. 3 (2024), 919–920.

FIGURE I.1 The Bank of England and the Royal Exchange, 1800
Source: James H. Kernot, Bank of England [and the] Royal Exchange, Yale Center for British Art, Paul Mellon Collection, B1977.14.15256.

refused to acknowledge their advantageous position.[4] From 1844 onward, the central bank maintained an exclusive monopoly on the issuance of notes in England and Wales. A separation between its issue and banking departments also allowed it to maintain its dual position as a public authority and a private bank. The Bank thereafter emerged as the de facto leader of the London money market, overseeing an intricate network of financial institutions that included acceptance houses, discount houses, joint-stock banks, and merchant banks.

By the 1870s, the Bank had become an integral part in the functioning of the classical gold standard, a monetary regime that bound countries together in a system of fixed exchange rates. Adjustments to its main interest rate, the Bank Rate, helped to maintain parity between the British pound and a set amount of gold.[5] During severe global disruptions, including the Baring Crisis of 1890

4 Peter Mathias, *The First Industrial Nation: The Economic History of Britain, 1700–1914* (London: Methuen & Co., 1969), 353–358.

5 Walter Leaf, *Banking* (New York: Henry Holt and Company, 1927), 29–34. On the role of central banks in promoting financial stability, see Charles Goodhart, *The Evolution of Central Banks* (Cambridge, MA, and London: The MIT Press, 1988), 85–102; John D. Turner, *Banking in Crisis: The Rise and Fall of British Banking Stability, 1800 to the Present* (Cambridge: Cambridge University Press, 2014), 174–177, 201–203; Anthony C. Hotson,

world's major commercial and industrial nation.[1] Economic historians have also used quantitative evidence, such as data on debt, trade deficits, and reserves held by central banks, to pinpoint exactly when the US dollar might have overtaken the British pound.[2] Yet beyond the statistical tools lies a narrative of resilience. Britain continually adapted to the changing conditions of global geopolitics, and the Bank constructed the financial architecture that preserved London's prestige throughout the twentieth century. With its reputation established over the prior century, the City benefited from many of its existing trade and commercial links, both within and outside an empire that had reached its territorial apex. Contextualizing these events in the broader history of the international order, *The City's Defense* demonstrates the role of the Bank in reshaping national, imperial, European, and global economic governance.

THE BANK REGNANT

In 1694, the Governor and Company of the Bank of England received a royal charter from the English crown. In exchange for a monopoly on the note issue in England, it raised a loan of £1.2 million to support the nation's wars with France. Forty years later, the Bank moved to its current location on Threadneedle Street, across from the Royal Exchange and in the heart of the City of London (Figure I.1). By the eighteenth century, the Bank had become involved in the circulation of Exchequer bills (a form of short-term debt issued by the state), in addition to the management of accounts on behalf of the government.[3]

Although legally a private institution that was owned and operated by shareholders, the Bank adopted a more public-oriented role as the manager of sovereign and the custodian of the nation's gold reserves. Britain's historic status as the "first industrial nation" had given the Bank the responsibility of maintaining confidence in the financial sector during moments of crises, even if its directors

[1] Adam Tooze, *The Deluge: The Great War, America and the Remaking of the Global Order, 1916–1931* (New York: Viking, 2014); Mary Bridges, *Dollars and Dominion: US Bankers and the Making of a Superpower* (Princeton and Oxford: Princeton University Press, 2024); Christopher M. Meissner, *One from the Many: The Global Economy since 1850* (Oxford: Oxford University Press, 2024), 126–131.

[2] Barry Eichengreen and Marc Flandreau, "The Rise and Fall of the Dollar (or When Did the Dollar Replace Sterling as the Leading Reserve Currency?)," *European Review of Economic History* 13, no. 3 (2009), 392–401; Barry Eichengreen, *Exorbitant Privilege: The Rise and Fall of the Dollar* (Oxford: Oxford University Press, 2011), 30–37; Jeremy Green, *The Political Economy of the Special Relationship: Anglo-American Development from the Gold Standard to the Financial Crisis* (Princeton and Oxford: Princeton University Press, 2020), 56–58.

[3] Anne L. Murphy, *Virtuous Bankers: A Day in the Life of the Eighteenth-Century Bank of England* (Princeton and Oxford: Princeton University Press, 2023), 5; Patrick K. O'Brien and Nuno Palma, "Not an Ordinary Bank but a Great Engine of State: The Bank of England and the British Economy, 1694–1844," *The Economic History Review* 76, no. 1 (2023), 309–310.

Introduction

The economic and political devastation of the First World War transformed the international order. Against the backdrop of unprecedented upheavals – the postwar recession, mass unemployment, and the Great Depression; the rise of communism and fascism; disarmament and rearmament – the nations of Europe confronted an array of challenges that hindered overseas trade and commerce. In response, many countries worked to stabilize the global financial system by restoring the old orthodoxy of the prewar era and establishing new institutions in line with the doctrine of liberal internationalism. With the reconciliation of these seemingly disparate goals, Europe witnessed the restructuring of economic governance in an age of war, democracy, and depression.

Building upon the established view that the war led to a drastic shift in the relationship between politics and the economy, *The City's Defense* examines how British institutions adapted to the new realities of the interwar order. It focuses particularly on the centrality of the Bank of England in leading this transformation. As the government grappled with mass unemployment and a high national debt, and as the City's preeminence was increasingly questioned, the Bank began to accept responsibilities that actively advanced British financial interests abroad. Its subsequent policies reflected its continued, if not expanding, influence in the global economic system. Through its interventions, the Bank emerged as a key component of the state apparatus before its 1946 nationalization and altered expectations of what a central bank was meant to do.

The broader implication is to explain how the City maintained its position as an international financial center longer than previously known. Existing accounts have stressed how Britain was threatened, rivaled, or eclipsed as the global hegemonic power in the interwar years. With its economic output and military strength, the United States emerged from the destruction of war as the

Abbreviations

BIDCo	Bankers' Industrial Development Corporation
CBA	Commonwealth Bank of Australia
CBID	Central Banking Information Department
Cd., Cmd., or Cmnd.	command paper
EAC	Economic Advisory Council
EEA	Exchange Equalisation Account
GDP	gross domestic product
GES	Government Economic Service
GFC	global financial crisis of 2007–2008
HSBC	Hongkong and Shanghai Banking Corporation
IMF	International Monetary Fund
LCC	Lancashire Cotton Corporation
MP	Member of Parliament
RM	Reichsmark
SMT	Securities Management Trust
SRO	Statutory Rules and Orders
UDT	United Dominions Trust

Archival abbreviations are listed in the Appendix.

Note on the Text

The Bank of England (hereafter, capitalized as the Bank) refers to the central bank of the United Kingdom. Commercial banks include those that offer loans to and accept deposits from individuals, businesses, or governments. Clearing banks are the largest commercial banks (the Big Five): Barclays, Lloyds, Midland, National Provincial, and Westminster. Merchant banks, including Barings, Kleinworts, and Schroders, primarily deal in overseas trade and the acceptance market.

The City of London (or the City) is used as a metonym for the banking and financial sector in the United Kingdom. It is analogous to Wall Street in the United States or (to a lesser extent) La Défense in France.

Until decimalization in 1971, one pound (£ = 1 l.) was equivalent to 20 shillings (20 s.), which was further divided into 12 pence (12 d.). The sterling bloc (also known as the sterling area by contemporaries) referred to the countries that pegged their currencies, whether de jure or de facto, to the British pound sterling. From the 1930s onward, the sterling area included most nations of the formal empire and some nations of the "informal" empire, with the exceptions of Canada, Newfoundland, and Hong Kong.

Within each footnote, citations are usually listed in chronological order by date of publication.

interest-rate policy in the 1920s. Only in 1997 did the New Labour government, pressured by efforts to uphold the principle of independent monetary policy, grant the Bank operational independence in its day-to-day affairs.[9]

The goal of this book is to examine the Bank from the perspective of economic governance. It seeks to place the interwar central bank at the intersection of multiple spheres related to national, imperial, European, and global economic policy. At all these levels, the exigencies of the First World War challenged and redefined British hegemony. Initially responding to the July Crisis with ad hoc measures, the Bank adopted responsibilities related to wartime finance and economic diplomacy. It built upon the momentum spurred by the conflict to expand its operations into new areas, including imperial relations, foreign policy, and international monetary cooperation. What transpired in the two and a half decades after 1914 was the Bank's transformation from an institution primarily interested in the London money market to one increasingly concerned with the City's place in the global economy.

It is thus evident that any study of the central bank cannot be understood from the perspective of Threadneedle Street, the City of London, or even Britain alone. Recognizing the Bank's relations with other institutions, such as the Treasury, the private banks, or the London Stock Exchange, certainly offers useful insights into the domestic arrangements that once made Britain an economic powerhouse.[10] From an architectural viewpoint as well, the grandeur of its neoclassical façade designed by John Soane represented the wealth of the English (and later British) nation.[11]

[9] Sylvia Maxfield, *Gatekeepers of Growth: The International Political Economy of Central Banking in Developing Countries* (Princeton: Princeton University Press, 1997), 56; Michael Collins and Mae Baker, "Bank of England Autonomy: A Retrospective," in *The Emergence of Modern Central Banking from 1918 to the Present*, ed. Carl-L. Holtfrerich, Jaime Reis, and Gianni Toniolo (Aldershot: Ashgate, 1999), 21–22; John Singleton, *Central Banking in the Twentieth Century* (Cambridge: Cambridge University Press, 2011), 214–216; Graham Wilson, "Governance after the Crisis," in *The Oxford Handbook of Governance*, ed. David Levi-Faur (Oxford: Oxford University Press, 2012), 374; Sylviane de Saint Seine, *La Banque d'Angleterre : une marche erratique vers l'indépendance, 1977–2007* (Paris: Presses de Sciences Po, 2017), 337, 350–351.

[10] Ranald C. Michie, *The City of London: Continuity and Change, 1850–1990* (Basingstoke: Macmillan, 1992); David Kynaston, *The City of London, vol. 3: Illusions of Gold, 1914–1945* (London: Chatto & Windus, 1999); G.C. Peden, *The Treasury and British Public Policy, 1906–1959* (Oxford: Oxford University Press, 2000); Ranald C. Michie, *The London Stock Exchange: A History* (Oxford: Oxford University Press, 2001).

[11] H. Rooksby Steele and F.R. Yerbury, *The Old Bank of England, London* (London: Ernest Benn, 1930); John Michael Lloyd Booker, "The Architecture of Banking: A Study of the Design of British Banks from the 18th Century to Modern Times," (PhD diss., University of York, 1984); Eva Schumann-Bacia, *Die Bank von England und ihr Architekt John Soane* (Zurich and Munich: Verlag für Architektur Artemis, 1989); Iain Black, "Imperial Visions: Building the Bank of England, 1919–39," in *Imperial Cities: Landscape, Display and Identity*, ed. Felix Driver and David Gilbert (Manchester and New York: Manchester University Press, 1999):

Yet even if the Bank embodied an institution of national importance, committed to domestic order and stability, its activities had global implications. Britain's naval and commercial hegemony characterized its "imperial century" (1815–1914).[12] Rather than determined by a singular ideology or grand strategy, the project of empire-building included vastly divergent experiences and different forms of colonial administration.[13] Economic interests underpinned this expansion, with British capital facilitating the construction of railways and canals, the installation of telegraph cables, and the rapid development of new trade routes abroad. By the early twentieth century, these developments allowed Britain to exert an unparalleled amount of influence across the world. With this infrastructure in place, the Bank was able to establish a global network that included officials in Geneva, experts in Paris, bankers in New York, lawyers in Vienna, politicians in Buenos Aires, and economists throughout the British Empire. Archival sources from these and other locations reveal how the City's interests extended beyond formal borders and across disparate regions.

Above all, the Bank's main endeavor was to defend the prestige of the City of London as an international financial center. Prior to the war, the interests of the private banking sector based in the Square Mile had largely determined the relationship between the economy and the state. Merchant banks, clearing banks, discount houses, and the central bank worked in tandem to maintain the pound's parity to gold in the prewar years. Although the revival of this system in the interwar years offered the most direct means of rehabilitating the economy, the central bank's actions were also compatible with a range of goals in the national interest: the maintenance of sterling's value relative to other currencies, the reinvigoration of British industry, the stabilization of prices, the coordination of imperial economic policies, and the restoration of disrupted trade networks across the world. It was the ability to manage all these priorities that confirmed the Bank's definitive status as the *primus inter pares* in the City.

Efforts to protect London's standing in the world formed the core of what may be defined as the Bank View. In this pursuit, the Bank implemented a wide array of interventions related to industrial policy, monetary reform, and intra-imperial cooperation. In many ways, these engagements aligned with the prevailing Treasury View, an ideological doctrine characterized by a fundamental opposition toward unemployment-reduction spending.[14] Both outlooks

96–113; Daniel M. Abramson, *Building the Bank of England: Money, Architecture, Society, 1694–1942* (New Haven and London: Yale University Press, 2005).

[12] Ronald Hyam, *Britain's Imperial Century, 1815–1914: A Study of Empire and Expansion*, 3rd ed. (Basingstoke: Palgrave Macmillan, 2002).

[13] John Darwin, *Unfinished Empire: The Global Expansion of Britain* (New York: Bloomsbury Press, 2012).

[14] While this book's intervention is to coin the term Bank View, the Treasury View has long been part of the historiography. See, for instance, Robert Skidelsky, "Keynes and the Treasury View:

also supported the tenets of classical liberalism based on balanced budgets, free trade, and fixed exchange rates. Yet the usefulness of the Treasury View appears more limited in an analysis of broader economic considerations. Even if the Bank often agreed with the views espoused by the Treasury in the early 1920s, the onset of the Great Depression engendered a growing rift and, later, a significant departure from such ideas. It was true that the readoption of the gold standard in 1925 might have found support at the Bank and the Treasury, but it was only the former that advocated the independence of monetary policy. Further tensions materialized in the debates over the setting of the Bank Rate, a decision that both John Maynard Keynes and the Treasury found to be incomprehensibly opaque.

The Bank View thus comprises policies specific to the City's interests. Although originally a private corporation, the Bank formulated a response to the crises that fundamentally threatened London's place in the international order. Seeking to aid domestic industry, it advocated the rationalization and amalgamation of firms in manufacturing centers throughout the United Kingdom. Doing so might have revitalized Britain's once-prominent export industries in an era of industrial stagnation. As for the financial sector, the intricate network of British multinational banks and corporations had become increasingly vulnerable to domestic and international crises in the decades after 1914. It was, however, only the Bank, rather than the Cabinet or the Treasury, that advocated the implementation of exchange control, which involved restrictions on the convertibility of sterling into other currencies. By the late 1930s, the central bank had designed a set of economic policies that did not align with the views forwarded by the Treasury.

Nor was the Bank beholden to the demands of City bankers. Certainly, the restoration of orthodox principles represented the convergent interests of the Bank, the Treasury, and the City following the recession of the early 1920s. It also resembled the "Basel consensus" that emanated from the Bank for International Settlements in the 1930s.[15] At first glance, the work of all these

The Case for and against an Active Unemployment Policy, 1920–1929," in *The Emergence of the Welfare State in Britain and Germany, 1850–1950*, ed. W.J. Mommsen (London: Croom Helm, 1981): 167–187; G.C. Peden, "The 'Treasury View' on Public Works and Employment in the Interwar Period," *The Economic History Review* 37, no. 2 (1984): 167–181; G.C. Peden, "The Road to and from Gairloch: Lloyd George, Unemployment, Inflation, and the 'Treasury View' in 1921," *Twentieth Century British History* 4, no. 3 (1993): 224–249; Peden, *The Treasury*, 219–231; Mark Blyth, *Austerity: The History of a Dangerous Idea* (Oxford: Oxford University Press, 2013), 122–126; Clara Elisabetta Mattei, "Hawtrey, Austerity, and the 'Treasury View,' 1918–25," *Journal of the History of Economic Thought* 40, no. 4 (2018): 471–492; Clara Elisabetta Mattei, "Treasury View and Post-WWI British Austerity: Basil Blackett, Otto Niemeyer and Ralph Hawtrey," *Cambridge Journal of Economics* 42, no. 4 (2018): 1123–1144.

[15] Gianni Toniolo, *Central Bank Cooperation at the Bank for International Settlements, 1930–1973* (Cambridge: Cambridge University Press, 2005), 139–149; Martin Daunton, *The Economic Government of the World, 1933–2023* (London: Allen Lane, 2023), 32–33.

institutions might have embodied the dominant influence of the financial establishment in determining the economic priorities of many European nations.[16] Yet these arguments belie the stark differences between and the varying objectives of the economic authorities in power. For instance, both the City and the Treasury strongly opposed an independent Bank Rate policy, deemed unfavorable to Britain's economic interests. In the 1920s, it was Reginald McKenna, chairman of Midland Bank, who denounced the central bank's mishandling of the gold standard and called for a close investigation into its operations.[17] While the Bank may have focused its work on maintaining the status of sterling as a world reserve currency, its view on how to achieve this goal greatly diverged from its counterparts in the City and in Westminster.

DEFINING ECONOMIC GOVERNANCE

To make these claims, *The City's Defense* builds on existing scholarship concerned with the history of global orders, liberal internationalism, economic diplomacy, and international relations. Since E.H. Carr's 1939 study, these works have continually reexamined the twenty years after the First World War from new perspectives.[18] In recent years, the study of global governance has undergone a major shift, emphasizing the post-First World War peace settlement as a fundamental turning point.[19] Indeed, when applied to the interwar years, the evolution of the international order remains essential for understanding the ways in which crises and their consequences shape the global economy.

The concept of an international order, as Glenda Sluga has shown, can be traced to the political vicissitudes that followed the Napoleonic Wars.[20] New

16 Scholars have long argued that the goals of the City, Bank, and Treasury considerably overlapped. Cain and Hopkins claimed that the three institutions formed "a dominant gentlemanly capitalist culture," while Ingham has further suggested that the "City–Bank–Treasury nexus" defined the links between the state and economy. According to E.H.H. Green, the Bank acted as both a "quasi-state institution" and a "sounding-board of City opinions." See also Geoffrey Ingham, *Capitalism Divided? The City and Industry in British Social Development* (Basingstoke: Macmillan, 1984), 171; E.H.H. Green, "The Influence of the City over British Economic Policy, c. 1880–1960," in *Finance and Financiers in European History, 1880–1960*, ed. Youssef Cassis (Cambridge: Cambridge University Press, 1992), 203; G.C. Peden, "The Treasury and the City," in *The British Government and the City of London in the Twentieth Century*, ed. Ranald Michie and Philip Williamson (Cambridge: Cambridge University Press, 2004), 117; P.J. Cain and A.G. Hopkins, *British Imperialism, 1688–2015*, 3rd ed. (London and New York: Routledge, 2016), 484.

17 "Transcript of Speech by Mr. McKenna at a Luncheon and Meeting of the British Engineers' Association," June 16, 1927, CAC McKenna Papers 9/21.

18 E.H. Carr, *The Twenty Years' Crisis, 1919–1939: An Introduction to the Study of International Relations* (London: Macmillan, 1939).

19 See, for instance, Peter Jackson, William Mulligan, and Glenda Sluga, eds., *Peacemaking and International Order after the First World War* (Cambridge: Cambridge University Press, 2023).

20 Glenda Sluga, *The Invention of International Order: Remaking Europe after Napoleon* (Princeton and Oxford: Princeton University Press, 2021), 9.

rules and practices concerning diplomatic relations formed the underlying framework of the Concert of Europe. Nearly a century later, the outbreak of the First World War and the ensuing dislocations strained the functioning of the international system. In its aftermath, unresolved tensions presented a significant obstacle to any sustainable peace settlement.[21] For one, the emergence of self-determination as a dominant mode of rule challenged efforts to revive the nineteenth-century order of European imperialism.[22] As international organizations extolled the tenets of liberal internationalism, their ideas, too, had to reconcile existing priorities of national sovereignty and multilateral cooperation with a wave of democratic ideals.[23]

However, only some of this scholarship has addressed economic aspects, even though these elements lay at the heart of many interwar issues. The initial shock of the July Crisis, the subsequent disruption to global supply chains, debilitating levels of national debt, exchange-rate volatility, and demobilization all had long-term effects on the international order. Finance was central to such problems, as inadequate wartime funding and later contentious debates over reparations hampered the prospect of a permanent peace.[24] The mismanagement of food supplies and other raw materials engendered a postwar humanitarian crisis, resulting in the displacement of millions across the

[21] Margaret MacMillan, *Paris 1919: Six Months That Changed the World* (New York: Random House, 2003); Patrick O. Cohrs, *The Unfinished Peace after World War I: America, Britain and the Stabilisation of Europe 1919–1932* (Cambridge: Cambridge University Press, 2006); Eckart Conze, *Die große Illusion. Versailles 1919 und die Neuordnung der Welt* (Munich: Siedler, 2018); Jörn Leonhard, *Der überforderte Frieden. Versailles und die Welt 1918–1923* (Munich: C.H. Beck, 2018); Klaus Schwabe, *Versailles. Das Wagnis eines demokratischen Friedens 1919–1923* (Paderborn: F. Schöningh, 2019); G. John Ikenberry, *A World Safe for Democracy: Liberal Internationalism and the Crises of Global Order* (New Haven and London: Yale University Press, 2020); Patrick O. Cohrs, *The New Atlantic Order: The Transformation of International Politics, 1860–1933* (Cambridge: Cambridge University Press, 2022); Madeleine Lynch Dungy, *Order and Rivalry: Rewriting the Rules of International Trade after the First World War* (Cambridge: Cambridge University Press, 2023).

[22] Erez Manela, *The Wilsonian Moment: Self-Determination and the International Origins of Anticolonial Nationalism* (Oxford: Oxford University Press, 2007); Adom Getachew, *Worldmaking after Empire: The Rise and Fall of Self-Determination* (Princeton and Oxford: Princeton University Press, 2019).

[23] Mark Mazower, *Governing the World: The History of an Idea* (London: Penguin, 2012); Glenda Sluga, *Internationalism in the Age of Nationalism* (Philadelphia: University of Pennsylvania Press, 2013); Glenda Sluga and Patricia Clavin, eds., *Internationalisms: A Twentieth-Century History* (Cambridge: Cambridge University Press, 2016); Madeleine Herren, *Internationale Organisationen seit 1865. Eine Globalgeschichte der internationalen Ordnung* (Darmstadt: Wissenschaftliche Buchgesellschaft, 2009); Daniel Laqua, "Transnational Intellectual Cooperation, the League of Nations, and the Problem of Order," *Journal of Global History* 6, no. 2 (2011): 223–247; Natasha Wheatley, *The Life and Death of States: Central Europe and the Transformation of Modern Sovereignty* (Princeton and Oxford: Princeton University Press, 2023).

[24] Gerald D. Feldman, *The Great Disorder: Politics, Economics, and Society in the German Inflation, 1914–1924* (New York and Oxford: Oxford University Press, 1997).

continent.[25] How the nations of Europe coped with the consequences of the war – the collapse of four major empires, an unprecedented loss of human life, and the end of the old imperial order – opened new possibilities for reform.

After the war, central banks across Europe gained greater prerogatives as independent monetary authorities. While driven by their own national priorities, they forged a temporary alliance to enforce an orthodox agenda, endeavoring to recreate the conditions that underpinned the pre-1914 state of affairs. At one level, their efforts chiefly revolved around returning to the alleged stability of a bygone era, most notably through a regime of fixed exchange rates.[26] Both the operations of the gold standard and the relative openness of Europe to the free movement of people, goods, and capital had seemingly instigated an era of economic and social prosperity. Seeking to suppress the threat of inflation, central banks reaffirmed the benefits of economic orthodoxy at the Brussels (1920) and Genoa (1922) conferences.

Even so, the consequences of the First World War had severely limited the possible configurations of reform and created opportunities for more radical ideas of economic management. According to Charles Maier, stabilization efforts in the 1920s not only served as a means of restoring a prewar system, but they also prompted the fundamental reordering of politico-economic relations. Conservative forces in interwar France, Germany, and Italy extended wartime compacts that determined the balance of power among workers, industrialists, agriculture, and capitalists. In response to radical revolutionary ideas, corporatist agreements aimed to achieve a temporary form of economic stability, albeit at the expense of parliamentary democracy.[27] International organizations, from the League of Nations to the Bank for International Settlements, similarly adapted existing colonial institutions in an

[25] Patricia Clavin, "The Austrian Hunger Crisis and the Genesis of International Organization after the First World War," *International Affairs* 90, no. 2 (2014): 265–278; Mary E. Cox, *Hunger in War and Peace: Women and Children in Germany, 1914–1924* (Oxford: Oxford University Press, 2019); Emily Baughan, *Saving the Children: Humanitarianism, Internationalism, and Empire* (Oakland: University of California Press, 2022); Jamie Martin, "Raw Materials and International Order from the Great War to the Crisis of 1920–21," in *Peacemaking and International Order after the First World War*, ed. Peter Jackson, William Mulligan, and Glenda Sluga (Cambridge: Cambridge University Press, 2023): 266–285; Elisabeth Piller and Neville Wylie, eds., *Humanitarianism and the Greater War, 1914–24* (Manchester: Manchester University Press, 2023).

[26] Beth A. Simmons, *Who Adjusts? Domestic Sources of Foreign Economic Policy during the Interwar Years* (Princeton: Princeton University Press, 1994), 20–29; Barry Eichengreen, *Globalizing Capital: A History of the International Monetary System*, 3rd ed. (Princeton and Oxford: Princeton University Press, 2019), 43–59.

[27] Charles S. Maier, *Recasting Bourgeois Europe: Stabilization in France, Germany, and Italy in the Decade after World War I* (Princeton: Princeton University Press, 1975). See also Charles S. Maier, *In Search of Stability: Explorations in Historical Political Economy* (Cambridge: Cambridge University Press, 1987), 161–168.

era of democracy and mass politics.[28] By reviving old imperial arrangements, these institutions shaped contemporary debates over the meaning of national sovereignty in the post-Versailles order.

The structure of economic governance thus depended on new institutions working alongside old assumptions, existing norms, and inherited ideals. Defined hereafter as the rules, practices, and institutions that influence trade, commerce, industry, and finance, economic governance may refer to the specific set of arrangements that sustained the international order. It can take into account the shifting and conflicting goals of a multitude of stakeholders, including ministries of finance, business associations, multinational corporations, nongovernmental organizations, and international organizations.[29] From this perspective, the study of governance does not necessarily focus on any particular type of policy or state of international affairs. It is instead concerned with the broader roles and responsibilities of institutions that form the foundation of an economic system.

Moreover, the concept of economic governance itself does not ignore the political and social aspects of national autonomy or institutional norms. On the contrary, it seeks to understand these elements by analyzing the economic conditions that underlay them. For although the Bank may have wanted to remain distant from the political apparatus, it was ostensibly unable to do so if it wanted to defend the privileged position of the City. The rise of interwar liberal internationalism – broadly associated with varying definitions of collective security, rule of law, self-determination, democratic ideals, and the market-based economy – forced nations to reconcile their own domestic priorities with increasingly cooperative rhetoric. Meanwhile, the advent of mass democracy, tensions in parliamentary politics, and other electoral weaknesses further limited the ability to control public discourse at home. The Bank's response, nevertheless, raised an array of questions concerning the future of the economic order: To what extent did liberal internationalism, as propounded by the League of Nations, appeal to the conflicting and diverse goals of the Bank, the City, and the Treasury? What did sovereignty truly mean for new European nations navigating the international order? And how did the

[28] Jamie Martin, *The Meddlers: Sovereignty, Empire, and the Birth of Global Economic Governance* (Cambridge, MA, and London: Harvard University Press, 2022), 161.

[29] William K. Tabb, *Economic Governance in the Age of Globalization* (New York: Columbia University Press, 2004); Rodney Bruce Hall, *Central Banking as Global Governance: Constructing Financial Credibility* (Cambridge: Cambridge University Press, 2008); Arie M. Kacowicz, "Global Governance, International Order, and World Order," in *The Oxford Handbook of Governance*, ed. David Levi-Faur (Oxford: Oxford University Press, 2012), 689; Ellen E. Meade, "The Governance of Central Banks," in *The Oxford Handbook of Governance*, ed. David Levi-Faur (Oxford: Oxford University Press, 2012), 401; Manuela Moschella and Catherine Weaver, "Global Economic Governance: Players, Power and Paradigms," in *Handbook of Global Economic Governance*, ed. Manuela Moschella and Catherine Weaver (Abingdon: Routledge, 2014), 5–7.

unresolved exigencies of a world war and a global depression lead to the fundamental transformation of economic governance?

Answering these and other questions requires evaluating the many components of interwar governance. The international order was not governed by a single institution working alone, but rather sustained by a network of various stakeholders. For many historians, the League of Nations has been the primary object of study for understanding interwar governance. It was an international organization that aimed to address disarmament, while also being concerned with a diverse range of affairs related to finance, labor, public health, and more.[30] Its Economic and Financial Organisation, in particular, facilitated numerous stabilization programs across Central and Eastern Europe, in addition to planning several world economic conferences.[31] Through its collaboration with central banks and national governments, the administrative apparatus of bureaucrats – including legal experts, economists, and technical specialists – sought to ensure the stability of the peace settlement imposed by the Treaty of Versailles.

Still, for Britain in particular, the interwar period was one of stark contrasts. At one level, the period heralded an age of mass democracy and popular politics. In the decade after 1918, women's suffrage and the expansion of the franchise promised unprecedented opportunities to groups previously removed from the political process.[32] The decline of the British aristocracy – whose

[30] Susan Pedersen, "Back to the League of Nations," *The American Historical Review* 112, no. 4 (2007): 1091–1117; Susan Pedersen, *The Guardians: The League of Nations and the Crisis of Empire* (Oxford: Oxford University Press, 2015); Sakiko Kaiga, *Britain and the Intellectual Origins of the League of Nations, 1914–1919* (Cambridge: Cambridge University Press, 2021); David Ekbladh, *Plowshares into Swords: Weaponized Knowledge, Liberal Order, and the League of Nations* (Chicago and London: The University of Chicago Press, 2022).

[31] Patricia Clavin, *Securing the World Economy: The Reinvention of the League of Nations, 1920–1946* (Oxford: Oxford University Press, 2013), 2–4. On the League's economic activities, see Éric Bussière, "L'Organisation économique de la SDN et la naissance du régionalisme économique en Europe," *Relations internationales*, no. 75 (1993): 301–313; Marie-Renée Mouton, *La Société des Nations et les intérêts de la France (1920–1924)* (Bern and New York: P. Lang, 1995), 469–475; Louis W. Pauly, *Who Elected the Bankers? Surveillance and Control in the World Economy* (Ithaca and London: Cornell University Press, 1997); Michel Fior, *Institution globale et marchés financiers : la Société des Nations face à la reconstruction de l'Europe, 1918–1931* (Bern: Peter Lang, 2008); Yann Decorzant, *La Société des nations et la naissance d'une conception de la régulation économique internationale* (Brussels: Peter Lang, 2011); Yann Decorzant, "La Société des Nations et l'apparition d'un nouveau réseau d'expertise économique et financière (1914–1923)," *Critique internationale* 52, no. 3 (2011): 35–50; Roser Cussó, "L'activité statistique de l'Organisation économique et financière de la Société des Nations : un nouveau lien entre pouvoir et quantification," *Histoire & mesure* 27, no. 2 (2012): 107–136; Yann Decorzant, "Banques centrales, banques privées et Société des nations (1919–1929)," in *Les banques centrales et l'État-nation*, ed. Olivier Feiertag and Michel Margairaz (Paris: Presses de Sciences Po, 2016): 355–377.

[32] On democracy in interwar Britain, see Helen McCarthy, "Whose Democracy? Histories of British Political Culture between the Wars," *The Historical Journal* 55, no. 1 (2012): 221–238; Julie V. Gottlieb and Richard Toye, eds., *The Aftermath of Suffrage: Women, Gender, and Politics*

fortunes had been diminished by welfare reforms at the turn of the century, the long depression in agricultural prices, and the world wars – correspondingly demonstrated the possibility of social change without a violent revolution.[33] Yet Britain remained a divided society, internally plagued by deep-seated economic and societal inequities. Women, although enfranchised, lacked proportional representation in Parliament and faced severe disadvantages in the workplace. Meanwhile, inherited wealth continued to be concentrated among members of the aristocracy, the nonlanded industrialists, and, most importantly, financiers in the City.[34]

Unsettled problems in the domestic realm compounded issues in international affairs. To be sure, British hegemony had greatly benefited from a private banking sector that had survived the fallout of the global conflict largely unscathed. With new mandates, protectorates, and colonies in the Middle East and Sub-Saharan Africa, the empire had reached its greatest territorial extent after the First World War. However, the unsettled question of inter-Allied debts, the contentious debate over German reparations, and the loss of the status as the workshop of the world hampered efforts to engender a recovery from the slump. Such unresolved instabilities challenged Britain's ability to exert power on both the imperial and the international stage.[35] Amidst heightened competition with the United States, Britain's naval and financial supremacy appeared simultaneously under threat.

At the same time, British institutions strategically adapted to the broader changes in the international order. Foreign policy, for instance, evolved in response to the perceived shift in the balance of power. Similar to the prewar years, the Foreign Office continued to lead decisive negotiations over imperial defense, trade, and collective security.[36] The diplomatic apparatus itself became

in Britain, 1918–1945 (Basingstoke: Palgrave Macmillan, 2013); Helen McCarthy, *The British People and the League of Nations: Democracy, Citizenship and Internationalism, c. 1918–45* (Manchester and New York: Manchester University Press, 2013); Daniel Ziblatt, *Conservative Parties and the Birth of Democracy* (Cambridge: Cambridge University Press, 2017).

33 David Cannadine, *The Decline and Fall of the British Aristocracy* (New Haven and London: Yale University Press, 1990), 702–704.

34 W.D. Rubinstein, *Men of Property: The Very Wealthy in Britain since the Industrial Revolution* (London: Croom Helm, 1981), 61.

35 David Reynolds, *Britannia Overruled: British Policy and World Power in the 20th Century* (London and New York: Longman, 1991), 105–111; T.G. Otte, "Introduction: British World Policy and the White Queen's Memory," in *British World Policy and the Projection of Global Power, c. 1830–1960*, ed. T.G. Otte (Cambridge: Cambridge University Press, 2019), 3–6.

36 Zara Steiner, *The Foreign Office and Foreign Policy, 1898–1914* (Cambridge: Cambridge University Press, 1969); B.J.C. McKercher, "Old Diplomacy and New: The Foreign Office and Foreign Policy, 1919–1939," in *Diplomacy and World Power: Studies in British Foreign Policy, 1890–1950*, ed. Michael Dockrill and Brian McKercher (Cambridge: Cambridge University Press, 1996): 79–114; Fiona Venn, "In Pursuit of National Security: The Foreign Office and Middle Eastern Oil, 1908–39," in *The Foreign Office, Commerce and British Foreign Policy in the Twentieth Century*, ed. John Fisher, Effie G.H. Pedaliu, and Richard Smith (London: Palgrave Macmillan, 2016): 69–87.

steadily more bureaucratic with its reliance on a trained civil service and highly specialized departments. Other government ministries turned to the League as an instrument for managing foreign relations.[37] The result was an economic order that drew on characteristics of the prewar imperial system, while also embracing the new language of liberal democracy and multilateralism.

Yet the multitude of views on the new international order – as envisioned in different ways by the Bank, the Foreign Office, the Treasury, Westminster, and the League – seemed incompatible as the interwar years progressed. The outbreak of the First World War had already compelled European states to experiment with various forms of economic warfare, from punitive sanctions to retaliatory tariffs, which threatened the viability of liberal internationalism.[38] As the remnants of the old order contended with visions of the new one, the interwar political system became increasingly fragile. In Britain, numerous electoral disturbances – the fall of the Liberals, the rise of Labour, and the failure of the Second Labour Government in 1931 – demonstrated the incapacity of party politics to resolve pressing domestic issues. Abroad, too, a virulent backlash against globalization in the form of tariffs, immigration barriers, and contractionary monetary policies destabilized an international state of affairs in which Britain had once maintained unquestioned supremacy.[39] Unable to reconcile obstacles related to debt, trade, and exchange rates with national priorities, the four major capitalist powers – France, Germany, the United Kingdom, and the United States – witnessed a breakdown of diplomatic relations and the emergence of their respective regional blocs.[40]

As a mediator between foreign governments and the banking sector, the Bank emerged as the chief representative of British interests abroad. Its officials praised the benefits of liberal economic orthodoxy in their discussions with their counterparts across Europe and the empire. Discussions over exchange-rate coordination and imperial preference were two contentious areas in which Britain's views were prominently featured. In this sense, the Bank continually adapted to the changing landscape of international relations

[37] Patricia Clavin, "The Ben Pimlott Memorial Lecture 2019: Britain and the Making of Global Order after 1919," *Twentieth Century British History* 31, no. 3 (2020): 340–359.

[38] Nicholas A. Lambert, *Planning Armageddon: British Economic Warfare and the First World War* (Cambridge, MA, and London: Harvard University Press, 2012); Phillip A. Dehne, *After the Great War: Economic Warfare and the Promise of Peace in Paris 1919* (London: Bloomsbury, 2019); Nicholas Mulder, *The Economic Weapon: The Rise of Sanctions as a Tool of Modern War* (New Haven and London: Yale University Press, 2022).

[39] Harold James, *The End of Globalization: Lessons from the Great Depression* (Cambridge, MA, and London: Harvard University Press, 2001); Robert Boyce, *The Great Interwar Crisis and the Collapse of Globalization* (Basingstoke: Palgrave Macmillan, 2009); Tara Zahra, *Against the World: Anti-Globalism and Mass Politics between the World Wars* (New York: W.W. Norton & Company, 2023).

[40] Patricia Clavin, *The Failure of Economic Diplomacy: Britain, Germany, France and the United States, 1931–36* (Basingstoke: Macmillan, 1996); Zara Steiner, *The Lights that Failed: European International History, 1919–1933* (Oxford: Oxford University Press, 2005).

in unparalleled ways. Its ability to work with representatives at the League, throughout the empire, and on both sides of the Atlantic allowed it to maintain influence on a global scale. The concerted attempts to reconcile competing visions of political sovereignty and international cooperation led to the restructuring of the economic order.

THE AGE OF EXPERTISE

Since the end of the Second World War, unelected officials have shaped the architecture of the international monetary system. The 1944 Bretton Woods conference was a key inflection point in the rise of expert opinion and consensus, facilitating the construction of an Anglo-American order.[41] Ensuing negotiations between civil servants and technical advisers determined the priorities of numerous multilateral organizations, including the United Nations, World Bank, and the Organisation for Economic Co-operation and Development.[42]

Even earlier precedents of technical knowledge existed in the nineteenth century, when experts were integral to the development of the administrative state. As government officials throughout Victorian England and Bismarckian Prussia viewed specialized knowledge as a useful tool for the centralization of state capacity, they devised a language of neutrality that legitimized their existing authority.[43] The result was the rapid expansion of the state bureaucracy

[41] G. John Ikenberry, "The Political Origins of Bretton Woods," in *A Retrospective on the Bretton Woods System: Lessons for International Monetary Reform*, ed. Michael D. Bordo and Barry Eichengreen (Chicago and London: The University of Chicago Press, 1993), 157–158; G. John Ikenberry, "A World Economy Restored: Expert Consensus and the Anglo-American Postwar Settlement," *International Organization* 46, no. 1 (2009): 289–321; Benn Steil, *The Battle of Bretton Woods: John Maynard Keynes, Harry Dexter White, and the Making of a New World Order* (Princeton and Oxford: Princeton University Press, 2013), 160–199; Daniel Speich Chassé, "Towards a Global History of the Marshall Plan: European Post-War Reconstruction and the Rise of Development Economic Expertise," in *Industrial Policy in Europe after 1945: Wealth, Power and Economic Development in the Cold War*, ed. Christian Grabas and Alexander Nützenadel (Basingstoke: Palgrave Macmillan, 2014): 187–212; Daniel Susskind and David Vines, "Global Economic Order and Global Economic Governance," *Oxford Review of Economic Policy* 40, no. 2 (2024): 189–219.

[42] Amy L. Sayward, *The Birth of Development: How the World Bank, Food and Agriculture Organization, and World Health Organization Changed the World, 1945–1965* (Kent: The Kent State University Press, 2006); Matthias Schmelzer, *The Hegemony of Growth: The OECD and the Making of the Economic Growth Paradigm* (Cambridge: Cambridge University Press, 2016); Amy C. Offner, *Sorting Out the Mixed Economy: The Rise and Fall of Welfare and Developmental States in the Americas* (Princeton and Oxford: Princeton University Press, 2019); Christy Thornton, *Revolution in Development: Mexico and the Governance of the Global Economy* (Oakland: University of California Press, 2021); Margarita Fajardo, *The World That Latin America Created: The United Nations Economic Commission for Latin America in the Development Era* (Cambridge, MA, and London: Harvard University Press, 2022).

[43] Jill Pellew, "Law and Order: Expertise and the Victorian Home Office," in *Government and Expertise: Specialists, Administrators, and Professionals, 1860–1919*, ed. Roy Macleod (Cambridge: Cambridge University Press, 1988): 59–72; Till Düppe, "Les origines historiques

in such varied areas as imperial governance, diplomacy, medicine, and social welfare.[44] In these areas, experts were able to amass technical information through colonial administrative bodies, thereby further enforcing their model of governance abroad.[45]

Yet expertise underwent an unprecedented, institutionalized, and transformational moment of triumph after the First World War.[46] Although many nineteenth-century forms of expertise aimed to justify imperial expansion, while later postwar variants were associated with globalization and development, the interwar years brought experts to elevated positions at the forefront of critical debates. In the United Kingdom, government departments grappled with their own priorities in the face of a global depression, compelling them

de l'expertise," in *Experts, sciences et sociétés*, ed. François Claveau and Julien Prud'homme (Montreal: Les Presses de l'Université de Montréal, 2018), 27–28.

44 Recent works on the history of expertise include Martin Kohlrausch, Katrin Steffen, and Stefan Wiederkehr, eds., *Expert Cultures in Central and Eastern Europe: The Internationalization of Knowledge and the Transformation of Nation States since World War I* (Osnabrück: Fibre Verlag, 2010); David Edgerton, *Britain's War Machine: Weapons, Resources, and Experts in the Second World War* (Oxford and New York: Oxford University Press, 2011); Martin Kohlrausch and Helmuth Trischler, *Building Europe on Expertise: Innovators, Organizers, Networkers* (Basingstoke: Palgrave Macmillan, 2014); David Kennedy, *A World of Struggle: How Power, Law, and Expertise Shape Global Political Economy* (Princeton and Oxford: Princeton University Press, 2016); Julien Landry, *Les think tanks et le discours expert sur les politiques publiques au Canada (1890–2015)* (Ottawa: Les Presses de l'Université d'Ottawa, 2021); Jens Steffek, *International Organization as Technocratic Utopia* (Oxford: Oxford University Press, 2021).

45 On expertise in European imperial governance, see John Eddy, "The Technique of Government: Governing Mid-Victorian Australia," in *Government and Expertise: Specialists, Administrators, and Professionals, 1860–1919*, ed. Roy Macleod (Cambridge: Cambridge University Press, 1988): 166–181; Timothy Mitchell, *Rule of Experts: Egypt, Techno-Politics, Modernity* (Berkeley: University of California Press, 2002); Joseph Morgan Hodge, *Triumph of the Expert: Agrarian Doctrines of Development and the Legacies of British Colonialism* (Athens: Ohio University Press, 2007); Helen Tilley, *Africa as a Living Laboratory: Empire, Development, and the Problem of Scientific Knowledge, 1870–1950* (Chicago and London: The University of Chicago Press, 2011); Sabine Clarke, *Science at the End of Empire: Experts and the Development of the British Caribbean, 1940–62* (Manchester: Manchester University Press, 2018); Florian Wagner, *Colonial Internationalism and the Governmentality of Empire, 1893–1982* (Cambridge: Cambridge University Press, 2022).

46 This argument echoes the findings of other works on interwar expertise, including Didier Renard, "*Technocracy*, ou la science contre l'économie : un mouvement américain des années 30," in *La question technocratique : de l'invention d'une figure aux transformations de l'action publique*, ed. Vincent Dubois and Delphine Dulong (Strasbourg: Presses universitaires de Strasbourg, 1999): 19–33; Olga Hidalgo-Weber, "Expertise britannique à l'OIT dans l'entre-deux-guerres : enjeux politiques et transferts de savoirs," *Revue d'histoire de la protection sociale* 10, no. 1 (2017): 22–41; Olivier Feiertag, "Le signe des temps : l'invention de l'expert financier international dans l'entre-deux-guerres," in *Experts et expertises en diplomatie : la mobilisation des compétences dans les relations internationales du congrès de Westphalie à la naissance de l'ONU*, ed. Stanislas Jeannesson, Fabrice Jesné, and Éric Schnakenbourg (Rennes: Presses universitaires de Rennes, 2018): 275–289; Erwin Dekker, *Jan Tinbergen (1903–1994) and the Rise of Economic Expertise* (Cambridge: Cambridge University Press, 2021).

to draw on the advice of outside counsel. Expertise proved capable of offering supposedly neutral and apolitical solutions to the economic slump. Exemplified by various authoritative bodies – the Economic Advisory Council, Keynes' Committee on Economic Information, and the Macmillan Committee – the proliferation of expertise demonstrated the growing interdependence between technical analysis and electoral politics.[47] These interwar antecedents expedited the emergence of economics as one of the most prominent social sciences in the postwar years.[48]

Collective problems facing the nations of Europe instigated what may be termed the Age of Expertise. In the era between the two world wars, advisory groups and specialized committees proliferated in response to destabilized markets, social unrest, and inflationary pressures.[49] A dependence on expert knowledge may have spread profusely in Germany, where the government had continually drawn on specialist advice through the Reich Economic Council and other advisory bodies.[50] As Adam Tooze has shown, the collection, analysis,

[47] On interwar economic knowledge, see Susan Howson and Donald Winch, *The Economic Advisory Council, 1930–1939: A Study in Economic Advice during Depression and Recovery* (Cambridge: Cambridge University Press, 1977); Donald Winch, "Economic Knowledge and Government in Britain: Some Historical and Comparative Reflections," in *The State and Economic Knowledge*, ed. Mary O. Furner and Barry Supple (Washington, DC: Woodrow Wilson International Center for Scholars and Cambridge: Cambridge University Press, 1990), 54–60; Knut Borchardt, "Wirtschaftspolitische Beratung in der Krise. Die Rolle der Wissenschaft," in *Die deutsche Staatskrise, 1930–1933. Handlungsspielräume und Alternativen*, ed. Heinrich August Winkler (Munich: R. Oldenbourg Verlag, 1992): 109–132.

[48] Alexander Nützenadel, *Stunde der Ökonomen. Wissenschaft, Politik und Expertenkultur in der Bundesrepublik 1949–1974* (Göttingen: Vandenhoeck & Ruprecht, 2005); Marion Fourcade, *Economists and Societies: Discipline and Profession in the United States, Britain, and France, 1890s to 1990s* (Princeton and Oxford: Princeton University Press, 2009); Lino Wehrheim, *Im Olymp der Ökonomen. Zur öffentlichen Resonanz wirtschaftspolitischer Experten von 1965 bis 2015* (Tübingen: Mohr Siebeck, 2021); Elizabeth Popp Berman, *Thinking Like an Economist: How Efficiency Replaced Equality in U.S. Public Policy* (Princeton and Oxford: Princeton University Press, 2022).

[49] Adam Tooze and Ted Fertik, "The World Economy and the Great War," *Geschichte und Gesellschaft* 40, no. 2 (2014), 232–233.

[50] On the politicization of expert knowledge in Germany, see Ronald Hitzler, Anne Honer, and Christoph Maeder, eds., *Expertenwissen. Die institutionalisierte Kompetenz zur Konstruktion von Wirklichkeit* (Opladen: Westdeutscher Verlag, 1994); Margit Szöllösi-Janze, "Politisierung der Wissenschaften – Verwissenschaftlichung der Politik. Wissenschaftliche Politikberatung zwischen Kaiserreich und Nationalsozialismus," in *Experten und Politik. Wissenschaftliche Politikberatung in geschichtlicher Perspektive*, ed. Stefan Fisch and Wilfried Rudloff (Berlin: Duncker & Humblot, 2004): 79–100; Lutz Raphael, "Zwischen Sozialaufklärung und radikalem Ordnungsdenken. Die Verwissenschaftlichung des Sozialen im Europa der ideologischen Extreme," in *Europäische Wissenschaftskulturen und politische Ordnungen in der Moderne (1890–1970)*, ed. Gangolf Hübinger (Munich: Oldenbourg Verlag, 2014): 29–50; Agnes Laba, "Akademisches Expertenwissen als Ressource für die Politik. Die „Publikationsstelle Berlin-Dahlem“ als Think Tank der nationalsozialistischen Expansions- und Vernichtungspolitik," in *Externe Experten in Politik und Wirtschaft*, ed. Felix Selgert (Berlin: De Gruyter Oldenbourg, 2020): 95–122.

and distribution of statistics, notably through the Institute for Business Cycle Research, were processes fundamentally tied to the expansion of the modern state.[51] Similarly, politicians in France were drawn to the study of economic questions, embodied by the establishment of the National Economic Council in 1925.[52] Yet the particular circumstances in which expertise manifested itself in Britain must be understood not only as a political project in its own national context but also as an institutional phenomenon determined by global developments. Widespread threats to the prevailing order in which the British financial sector once dominated rapidly accelerated the acceptance of technical knowledge.

The Bank itself witnessed an even more profound evolution when it hired its first economic advisers. Distinct from bankers in the City, politicians in Westminster, and civil servants in Whitehall, experts were those from outside the traditional establishment at the Bank. They rarely had direct connections to the political elite, nor did they have familial ties to the premier merchant banks, such as the Barings, Grenfells, Huths, and Rothschilds. Instead, in-house advisers were able to offer technical views due to their experience in academia, the private sector, and international organizations. Their involvement allowed the Bank to assert its authority in areas it would not have otherwise entered. With its emerging interests in industrial intervention, imperial affairs, and foreign relations, the Bank could retain its jurisdiction over the global financial system through expert employment.

In defining the interwar years as the Age of Expertise, this book must also address a counterargument: Were experts simply hired to confirm existing priorities and justify established views? Opposing expert views was certainly a common way to assert power. It was Montagu Norman, the Governor of the Bank from 1920 to 1944, who once told an expert, "we have appointed you as our economic adviser; let me tell you that you are not here to tell us what to do, but to explain to us why we have done it."[53] In making this claim, however, Norman only attempted to give the illusion that he was the individual solely in control and that the employment of advisers was merely a means to an end. The Governor, in reality, depended on his advisers to help him make decisions and advise him on economic policy. He even reluctantly called the gold-exchange standard "a very abstruse and complicated problem which personally I do not pretend to understand."[54]

[51] J. Adam Tooze, "Weimar's Statistical Economics: Ernst Wagemann, the Reich's Statistical Office, and the Institute for Business-Cycle Research, 1925–1933," *Economic History Review* 52, no. 3 (1999): 523–543; J. Adam Tooze, *Statistics and the German State, 1900–1945: The Making of Modern Economic Knowledge* (Cambridge: Cambridge University Press, 2001).

[52] "Conseil national économique," *Journal officiel de la République française*, no. 14, January 17, 1925, 698–700; Alain Chatriot, *La démocratie sociale à la française : l'expérience du Conseil national économique 1924–1940* (Paris: La Découverte, 2013).

[53] Quoted in Kynaston, *Till Time's Last Sand*, 358.

[54] Norman to Strong, November 28, 1927, BoE ADM33/13 and FRBNY Strong Papers 1116.7, Part 2.

Experts subsequently demonstrated their technical knowledge in a wide range of areas. Richard Sayers attributed the arrival of a "new caste of Advisers" to the abandonment of the gold standard in September 1931.[55] That the desire to debate and discuss the future of the pound drove the central bank to accept institutional change is clear from archival sources. Yet unelected officials had already been present in contemporary debates, such as those concerning reconstruction and monetary policy, for much of the 1920s. The Bank continually deployed its advisers to represent the Governor during his regular and sudden bouts of illness, as well as following his confrontational interrogation before the Macmillan Committee in 1930.[56] By acting as translators of economic terminology, experts were more adept at explaining technical topics on behalf of the entire banking establishment. Such contributions led Deputy Governor Ernest Harvey to admit that one of his advisers was "far more competent to give evidence to the [Macmillan] Committee than I am."[57]

This evidence thus challenges existing narratives that regard Norman as an independent source of power. Past historical works have mainly been concerned with the Governor's efforts to foster central bank cooperation and, by extension, influence the contours of financial diplomacy.[58] He holds an infamous and, at times, mystical allure in the public imagination, in light of his consultations with Swiss psychologist Carl Jung, his recurring mental breakdowns, and his links to Nazi-looted gold.[59] However, institutions are composed of more

[55] Sayers, *The Bank of England, vol.* 2, 417. Also quoted in Patricia Clavin, "'The Fetishes of So-Called International Bankers': Central Bank Co-operation for the World Economic Conference, 1932–3," *Contemporary European History* 1, no. 3 (1992), 285.

[56] Harvey to Siepmann, April 1, 1926, BoE OV33/42.

[57] "The Right Hon. Ernest Musgrave Harvey, K.B.E., Deputy Governor of the Bank of England," July 2, 1930, in Macmillan Committee, *Minutes of Evidence Taken before the Committee on Finance and Industry, vol.* 2 (London: H.M. Stationery Office, 1931), 173.

[58] Paul Einzig, *Montagu Norman: A Study in Financial Statesmanship* (London: Kegan Paul, Trench, Trubner & Co., 1932), 7–9; Paul Einzig, *Bankers, Statesmen and Economists* (London: Macmillan, 1935), 37–46; Henry Clay, *Lord Norman* (London: Macmillan, 1957), 474–489; Andrew Boyle, *Montagu Norman: A Biography* (London: Cassell & Company, 1967), 180–186; Lord Robbins, "Montagu Norman: A 'Monarch' in the City," in *The Evolution of Modern Economic Theory and Other Papers on the History of Economic Thought* (London: Palgrave Macmillan, 1970): 234–242; Philip Geddes, *Inside the Bank of England* (London: Boxtree, 1987), 33–36; György Péteri, "Central Bank Diplomacy: Montagu Norman and Central Europe's Monetary Reconstruction after World War I," *Contemporary European History* 1, no. 3 (1992): 233–258; Liaquat Ahamed, *Lords of Finance: The Bankers Who Broke the World* (New York: Penguin, 2009), 145–153, 220–233, 279–289; Piet Clement, "Institutionalizing Central Bank Cooperation: The Norman–Schacht Vision and Early Experience of the Bank for International Settlements, 1929–1933," in *The Spread of the Modern Central Bank and Global Cooperation, 1919–1939*, ed. Barry Eichengreen and Andreas Kakridis (Cambridge: Cambridge: University Press, 2023): 80–102.

[59] David Blaazer, "Finance and the End of Appeasement: The Bank of England, the National Government and the Czech Gold," *Journal of Contemporary History* 40, no. 1 (2005): 25–39; Paul Krugman, "The Curse of Montagu Norman," *The New York Times Blog*, December 18, 2009, https://archive.nytimes.com/krugman.blogs.nytimes.com/2009/12/18/

than just their leaders, and a disproportionate focus on the Governor eludes the complexity of the decision-making processes that occurred behind closed doors.[60] Evidently, the presence of experts at the central bank explains how Norman was able to exert a degree of influence far beyond the capabilities of one individual. While setting overarching policy goals, he regularly consulted those around him on technical matters and relied not simply on the merchant banks in the City, but rather on a group of mid-level advisers who formed the Bank's intellectual inner circle.[61] Whether advising the government on monetary policy in South Africa, restructuring the system of taxation in Austria, or laying the foundation for a new central bank in Argentina, unelected officials had extended British economic power far beyond the Bank's walls.

Among experts, John Maynard Keynes has remained at the center of scholarship on economic theory and policy.[62] The extent to which fiscal policies of the 1930s resembled a demand-driven, Keynesian "managed economy" had once been the focus of such debates.[63] In the realm of monetary policy, Keynes'

the-curse-of-montagu-norman/; Philip Aldrick, "Was Montagu Norman a Nazi sympathiser?," *The Telegraph*, July 13, 2013, www.telegraph.co.uk/finance/bank-of-england/10214541/Was-Montagu-Norman-a-Nazi-sympathiser.html; Ben Quinn, "How Bank of England 'helped Nazis sell gold stolen from Czechs,'" *The Guardian*, July 31, 2013, www.theguardian.com/business/2013/jul/31/bank-of-england-and-nazis-stolen-gold.

60 After one meeting with representatives from the Banque de France and the Reichsbank, Norman tasked Stewart and Siepmann to examine the policies of other central banks; Montagu Norman, Diary, February 25, 1929, BoE ADM34/18.

61 See, for instance, his frequent meetings with Hjalmar Schacht in October 1932; Montagu Norman, Diary, October 4, October 5, October 6, and October 17, 1932, BoE ADM34/21.

62 Keynes' interwar contribution to public policy has been documented in many works, including T.W. Hutchison, *On Revolutions and Progress in Economic Knowledge* (Cambridge: Cambridge University Press, 1978); Peter Clarke, *The Keynesian Revolution in the Making, 1924–1936* (Oxford: Clarendon Press, 1988); G.C. Peden, *Keynes, The Treasury and British Economic Policy* (Basingstoke: Macmillan, 1988); Alan Booth, *British Economic Policy, 1931–49: Was There a Keynesian Revolution?* (Hertfordshire: Harvester Wheatsheaf, 1989); D.E. Moggridge, *Maynard Keynes: An Economist's Biography* (London and New York: Routledge, 1992); Robert Skidelsky, *John Maynard Keynes, vol. 2: The Economist as Saviour, 1920–1937* (London: Macmillan, 1992); Frank Otto, *Die Keynesianische Revolution in Großbritannien (1929–1948). Zur Entwicklung der Finanzpolitik im Spannungsfeld von wirtschaftswissenschaftlicher Herausforderung, politischem Reformwillen und institutioneller Beharrungskraft* (Berlin: Duncker & Humblot, 1996); Matthias Peter, *John Maynard Keynes und die britische Deutschlandpolitik. Machtanspruch und ökonomische Realität im Zeitalter der Weltkriege 1919–1946* (Munich: R. Oldenbourg, 1997); James Ashley Morrison, *England's Cross of Gold: Keynes, Churchill, and the Governance of Economic Beliefs* (Ithaca and London: Cornell University Press, 2021).

63 Derek H. Aldcroft, "The Development of the Managed Economy before 1939," *Journal of Contemporary History* 4, no. 4 (1969): 117–137; Donald Winch, "Britain in the 'Thirties: A Managed Economy?," in *The Managed Economy: Essays in British Economic Policy and Performance since 1929*, ed. Charles Feinstein (Oxford: Oxford University Press, 1983): 47–67; Roger Middleton, *Towards the Managed Economy: Keynes, the Treasury, and the Fiscal Policy Debate of the 1930s* (London and New York: Methuen, 1985); Alan Booth, "Britain in the 1930s: A Managed Economy?," *The Economic History Review* 40, no. 4 (1987): 499–522;

proposals for a managed currency were vital in determining the proper role of a central bank.[64] Through all these contributions, he came to represent the ascent of economic expertise in interwar Britain. From his efforts to reduce inter-Allied debts after the First World War to the negotiations over the Anglo-American loan after the Second World War, the eminent Cambridge economist frequently used technical arguments to promote Britain's national interests. His participation on numerous government commissions and advisory groups was virtually without precedent.

Yet Keynes was only one figure in these contested realms.[65] In many respects, he operated in a different sphere of influence from experts at the Bank. He had become not only an economic expert in his own right but also a public intellectual following the success of *The Economic Consequences of the Peace* (1919) and his later contributions in *The Nation & Athenæum*.[66] This status made him accountable to a mass audience and open to public censure in ways that the Bank's experts were not. Indeed, the central bank evaded publicity when it threatened to undermine its work. The priority in India, for instance, was "not [to] participate in any public enquiry" or appear critical of existing government policy, while in New Zealand, the Deputy Governor suggested that

Roger Middleton, "Britain in the 1930s: A Managed Economy? A Comment," *The Economic History Review* 42, no. 4 (1989): 544–547; G.C. Peden, "Britain in the 1930s: A Managed Economy? A Comment," *The Economic History Review* 42, no. 4 (1989): 538–543; Alan Booth, "Britain in the 1930s: A Managed Economy? A Reply to Peden and Middleton," *The Economic History Review* 42, no. 4 (1989): 548–556; Jim Tomlinson, *Public Policy and the Economy since 1900* (Oxford: Clarendon Press, 1990), 9–13; Roger Middleton, *Government Versus the Market: The Growth of the Public Sector, Economic Management and British Economic Performance, c. 1890–1979* (Cheltenham: Edward Elgar, 1996).

64 D.E. Moggridge, *British Monetary Policy, 1924–1931: The Norman Conquest of $4.86* (Cambridge: Cambridge University Press, 1972), 75; Susan Howson, *Domestic Monetary Management in Britain, 1919–38* (Cambridge: Cambridge University Press, 1975), 4–5; R.S. Sayers, *The Bank of England, 1891–1944, vol. 1* (Cambridge: Cambridge University Press, 1976), 131.

65 For more critical assessments of attributing economic policy to Keynes, see Neil Rollings, "British Budgetary Policy 1945–1954: A 'Keynesian Revolution'?," *The Economic History Review* 41, no. 2 (1988): 283–298; Harold James, "What Is Keynesian about Deficit Financing? The Case of Interwar Germany," in *The Political Power of Economic Ideas: Keynesianism across Nations*, ed. Peter A. Hall (Princeton: Princeton University Press, 1989): 231–262; Mark Blaug, "Second Thoughts on the Keynesian Revolution," *History of Political Economy* 23, no. 2 (1991): 171–192; David Laidler, *Fabricating the Keynesian Revolution: Studies of the Inter-War Literature on Money, the Cycle, and Unemployment* (Cambridge: Cambridge University Press, 1999); Robert W. Dimand, "What Keynesian Revolution? A Reconsideration Seventy Years after *The General Theory*," in *Keynes's General Theory after Seventy Years*, ed. Robert W. Dimand, Robert A. Mundell, and Alessandro Vercelli (Basingstoke: Palgrave Macmillan, 2010): 287–311.

66 For a recent examination of Keynes' influence, see Patricia Clavin, Giancarlo Corsetti, Maurice Obstfeld, and Adam Tooze, eds., *Keynes's Economic Consequences of the Peace after 100 Years: Polemics and Policy* (Cambridge: Cambridge University Press, 2024).

the Bank's interventions should "be kept entirely secret."[67] To establish his legitimacy, Keynes published articles that reached a broad audience, whereas the Bank could use its existing status as a monetary authority to enforce its orthodox policies without resorting to such measures.

The argument presented herein does not imply that the Bank held a monopoly on all matters of economic governance. Officials were unable to impose a sterling-backed currency in South Africa, to halt the creation of a Reserve Bank of India branch in London, or to install one of its officials as the new Governor of the Bank of Canada. Nor were they immune to mistakes. Imperfect information continually hampered their ability to address many of the persistent issues before them. Archival evidence further reveals the extent to which the Bank depended on an intricate network of stakeholders to implement its reforms. It often deferred many public-facing duties, from taxation to rearmament, to the Treasury, whose leading financial experts, including Sir Ralph Hawtrey and Sir Frederick Phillips, turned the government department into an intellectual powerhouse in its own right. Yet in other spheres, such as imperial and foreign relations, the Bank's experts were more adept at establishing their authority. Throughout the 1920s, they took part in debates on reconstruction and currency stabilization alongside League officials. The aftermath of the 1931 crisis, far from seeing the end of the Bank's dominance, led to its expansion into new areas, such as industrial intervention and exchange-rate management. In this sense, the central bank had effectively forged its own version of governance, distinct from the Keynesian and Hawtreian perspectives on government–business relations.

Shifting the focus from Keynes and the Treasury to the Bank sheds additional light on the compatibility of expertise with democracy. In interwar Britain, the changing landscape of electoral politics, particularly with the expansion of the franchise, initiated frequent calls for political reform and a rejection of expert-led rule. "Gone to the experts" was one familiar adage used to indicate when a particular concern would be deferred to nameless and faceless individuals.[68] The Bank, no stranger to secrecy, may have been a national institution that operated outside the formally elected government apparatus. Yet even if it maintained little interest in providing an open or transparent forum for the voting public, the birth of mass democracy forced the institution to grapple with challenges to its disproportionate influence. Experts felt obligated to use technical language and employ statistical tools in its policy recommendations, often under the guise of efficiency and neutrality. This form of governance attempted to depoliticize the idea of the economy by emphasizing its "rational" or "self-regulating" dimensions.[69]

[67] Harvey to Thomas Wilford [High Commissioner of New Zealand to the United Kingdom], June 30, 1930, BoE G1/335; Henry Clay, "Note of Interview," July 14, 1934, BoE G1/308.

[68] "The Place for Experts," *The Times* 45639, October 9, 1930, 12.

[69] Florian Schui, *Austerity: The Great Failure* (New Haven and London: Yale University Press, 2014), 99–105; Clara Mattei, *The Capital Order: How Economists Invented Austerity and*

At the same time, rather than viewing interwar economic policy as guided by a singular ideological force or set of underlying political motivations, this book seeks to engage with the diverse array of views, opinions, and actions of bankers and experts. It highlights the Bank's transformation from an institution ambitious to restore the pre-1914 era of economic liberalism to an entity imperative to the emergence of postwar managed capitalism. The interwar interregnum, in which no single ideology dominated, saw the central bank's responsibilities expand outside the traditional area of monetary management. Experimentation with more interventionist policies aligned with the government's evolving objectives, especially for recently enfranchised voting groups. Industrial rationalization, for instance, indirectly benefited the working classes, whereas general reconstruction aimed to raise the pound's purchasing power overseas. The Bank, to be sure, did not adopt these priorities due to its own inherent altruism, a regard for democratic processes, or a sense of moral obligation. Its goal was neither to open the central bank to a mass audience nor to prohibit its own modernization. Instead, the activities undertaken by the Bank, along with those supported by the City and welcomed by the Treasury, made economic orthodoxy compatible with the new global order. To defend its authority over the monetary system, the Bank inadvertently ended the interwar years as a more publicly engaged institution.

Through its interventions, the central bank emerged as one crucial part of a much broader evolution in global governance. It worked alongside new international organizations, such as the League of Nations and the Bank for International Settlements, to reshape the economic system. These institutions were able to design financial and legal institutions that drew on the prewar structures of imperial governance.[70] As European empires struggled to confront an era of self-determination and mass democracy, they found ways of exerting a degree of influence through debt commissions, development banks, and intergovernmental commodity programs. Still, by the 1930s, conflicting ideas and visions of how to reorganize global capitalism had ostensibly exposed its fragility.[71] The rules and agreements that once shaped the global economy effectively collapsed over the course of the Great Depression, causing many nations to adopt nationalist and protectionist policies.[72]

Yet any examination of governance must not only consider how governments and international organizations espoused different visions of internationalism.

Paved the Way to Fascism (Chicago and London: The University of Chicago Press, 2022), 203–204.

[70] Martin, *The Meddlers*, 11.

[71] On global economic orders and the role of ideas, see Or Rosenboim, *The Emergence of Globalism: Visions of World Order in Britain and the United States, 1939–1950* (Princeton and Oxford: Princeton University Press, 2017); Eric Helleiner, *The Contested World Economy: The Deep and Global Roots of International Political Economy* (Cambridge: Cambridge University Press, 2023).

[72] Daunton, *The Economic Government*, xxi.

Nor should it focus predominantly on the intellectual history of economic thinkers without showing their direct influence on policy or practice. Although many works have described the structural political and economic forces that governed the interwar order, one should simultaneously contextualize such developments within the overlapping domestic, imperial, European, and global spheres. The Bank, as a national central bank in the heart of the City, a facilitator of imperial and European central bank cooperation, and an international monetary authority at the center of a complex economic system, was one such institution that confronted the instabilities of the new era. Its duties were certainly nationally oriented, steadfast in a commitment to maintain the gold-exchange standard. Nevertheless, the realities of the interwar order following the emergence of radical forces – nationalism, anti-imperialism, fascism, and communism – compelled the Bank to reevaluate its role within the global economy.

OUTLINE

Chapter 1 provides the historical context behind the Age of Expertise. It focuses on the development of the City of London during the first age of globalization in the nineteenth and early twentieth centuries. Although the economic order of the prewar years was hardly monolithic, it featured the consolidation of power among relatively few institutions based in the City. Vital to sustaining economic liberalism was the central bank, an authority once dominated by merchant bankers and industrialists. After the First World War, the Bank began to reconsider its position within the national and international financial system, leading many officials to turn to outside experts. To uphold the prestige of the City of London abroad, bankers conceded their own institutional dominance to their advisers.

Following the war, the Bank looked for those who could provide an intellectual defense of its policies. One of its unofficial advisers, Sir Henry Strakosch, is the subject of Chapter 2. As the Austrian-born managing director of a preeminent South African mining corporation, Strakosch endorsed the emerging Bank View in international fora. He defended the benefits of fixed exchange rates and balanced budgets as chair of the League's Financial Committee. He was also able to influence domestic politics by acting as a personal adviser to Jan Smuts and Winston Churchill. Through Strakosch's campaigns, the Bank could administer numerous monetary and fiscal reforms that culminated in the creation of new central banks throughout Central Europe and the British Empire.

These reforms set the precedent for the employment of economists at home. Chapter 3 shows how statistics provided additional legitimacy to the Bank as a monetary authority. The establishment of an in-house research department, the employment of a specialized staff, and the publication of a monthly report all embodied the growing institutional interest in the study of economics.

With the arrival of highly regarded US economists, namely Walter W. Stewart and Oliver M.W. Sprague, the Bank further tested the value of expert opinion in setting monetary policy. As its advisers gained access to direct channels of influence, they were able to act as the interpreters of economic theory for the traditional banking elite.

Chapter 4 examines debates over the viability of the gold standard. Experts, while having little role in the return to or abandonment of the interwar gold standard (1925–1931), were responsible for providing the rationale behind monetary policy. The ideological strength of the Treasury View drove many contemporary concerns over domestic monetary management. In response to criticism forwarded by Keynes and the Treasury, the Bank aimed to defend a system of fixed exchange rates in which it remained at the center. Even after the 1931 crisis called into question the future of exchange-rate priorities, the Bank remained essential for defining a post-gold standard monetary order.

State interventions in industrial affairs also arose from the unresolved economic problems of the First World War. Chapter 5 assesses the contributions of one economist, Henry Clay, who crafted the Bank's industrial policy throughout the 1930s. Similar to Keynes and other contemporaries, Clay aimed to identify a "middle-way" policy between laissez-faire capitalism and socialism that addressed rising unemployment. He was tasked with advising the Bank on its project of rationalization, a process that involved closing unproductive firms and lending to small- and medium-sized businesses. Localized knowledge of regional production capabilities and unemployment, such as those affecting the Lancashire cotton industry, factored into his calculations. Clay's overarching theories on employment and wages thus served as the basis for the central bank's involvement in industrial affairs.

Other advisers attempted to export the British model of economic governance abroad. Sir Otto Niemeyer, a former Treasury official, arrived at the Bank in 1927. He had already acquired a reputation as an international financial expert through his experience as Controller of Finance and as a member of the League's Financial Committee. While employed at the Bank, he conducted a series of overseas missions to Australia, New Zealand, Argentina, and Brazil, where he advised national governments on the implementation of extensive monetary and fiscal reforms. He sought to establish a chain of Empire Central Banks that adopted orthodox policies and supported the global preeminence of the British pound. As described in Chapter 6, the Niemeyer missions upheld the City of London's status as a financial center through a network of independent central banks.

The apex of the Bank's influence followed the 1932 Ottawa Conference. Experts used the abandonment of the gold standard and the global Great Depression to justify the implementation of orthodox policies. Chapter 7 demonstrates how the creation of central banks in India and Canada emerged as a viable solution after Ottawa. The reforms allowed the Bank to enhance the prominence of sterling as a world reserve currency while also acting as concessions to foreign governments eager for economic recovery and national legitimacy. Through the Empire Central Banks, officials could simultaneously appease rising nationalism and advance their own goals. Further motivated by the collapse of the global economy into regional blocs, the Bank institutionalized a distinct form of monetary cooperation along imperial lines.

The enactment of exchange control marked the end of the interwar economic order. Chapter 8 details the role of the Bank in advocating this practice in the mid- to late 1930s. In contrast to Treasury officials and City bankers, the Bank's advisers were the main proponents of the policy. Conceived as a way of protecting the British pound at the outbreak of war, exchange control involved imposing restrictive measures on conversions and holdings of foreign currencies. Newly hired experts, including George Bolton, Henry Clay, and Harry Siepmann, sought to craft a version of exchange-rate management that contrasted with the authoritative policies devised in Germany and Argentina. With their implementation in 1939 and strict enforcement from 1940 onward, exchange control became the Bank's primary intervention on the eve of the Second World War.

Chapter 9 explores the rise of economic advice in the wartime and postwar years. In Britain, experts initially found themselves in a precarious position during the Second World War, partly due to political opposition to unelected officials. Yet following sterling's devaluations and a devastating IMF loan, the Bank again turned to economic advisers, primarily to lead diplomatic negotiations. With the development of economics as the leading social science, international organizations similarly relied on economists to encourage development and financial stability. These changes laid the foundation for a post-1945 order that drew on the precedents set by interwar central banks and the League of Nations. By exporting ideas of orthodoxy and defending the City's status as the world's financial center, the Bank could continue to shape the structures of economic governance throughout the twentieth century.

The Epilogue brings the history of the Bank to the present day. Although the beginning of the century has been characterized as an era of relatively stable growth, the onset of the global financial crisis (GFC) of 2007–2008 witnessed the return of interventionist central banks. The Bank initially responded to the crisis by lowering interest rates in an effort to inject liquidity into the financial system. It also worked alongside the European Central Bank and the Federal Reserve to implement an array of unconventional monetary policies to bolster global financial stability. As central banks have since confronted new challenges, including climate change, digital currencies, and rising inequality, they have continually adapted their policies and reimagined their roles as monetary authorities.

1

The Old Guard

> The mass of the Bank directors are merchants of experience, employing a considerable capital in trades in which they have been brought up, and with which they are well acquainted. ... Many of them, too, are quiet, serious men, who, by habit and nature, watch with some kind of care every kind of business in which they are engaged, and give an anxious opinion on it.[1]
>
> —Walter Bagehot, 1873

> Now come and see the busy, bustling, crowded streets around the Bank of England at noon on week days. Note the eager groups of business men, competing with one another, for at least a living, and at most a fortune.[2]
>
> —The Reverend C.H. Grundy, 1881

> Questions are again coming to the front which are making the study of Political Economy more imperative than ever.[3]
>
> —Felix Schuster, 1905

A stark divide had long separated bankers in the City of London from academic economists. The former relied on practical skills through experience, and the latter on abstract theories and the quantification of economic phenomena. Yet the historical precedent of how and when expertise – a term that includes the application of statistical tools, technical knowledge of a particular subject, and a reputation of the first degree – bridged the gap and entered

[1] Walter Bagehot, *Lombard Street: A Description of the Money Market* (London: Henry S. King & Co., 1873), 214.

[2] C.H. Grundy, "A Plea for the Poor South of the Thames," *The Church of England Pulpit, and Ecclesiastical Review* XI, no. 262 (1881), 231–232.

[3] Felix Schuster, *The Bank of England and the State: A Lecture Delivered on 14th November, 1905* (Manchester: Manchester University Press, 1906), 35.

the banking establishment can be traced to the interwar years. It was then when the Bank of England, a traditionalist, venerable institution dominated by an exclusive elite, became open to outsiders. The Bank originally turned to economists, statisticians, and financial experts who could help them confront the problems wrought by the First World War. Those who had usually been employed at the Bank, including bankers and industrialists, were willing to work alongside newly hired advisers on matters as varied as industrial policy, exchange-rate management, and imperial relations. Tensions and disagreements notwithstanding, the institutional alliance between these two disparate groups strengthened over the course of the interwar period. This chapter provides the historical context behind the Age of Expertise.

THE CITY'S ARISTOCRACY

In the nineteenth century, the central bank was a veritable component of the British financial establishment. Before the First World War, it employed individuals from leading private banks, trading firms, and multinational corporations based in London.[4] This elite formed the core of the City's "banking aristocracy," the members of which gradually began to adopt the prestige and reputation of the landed aristocracy.[5] Their profits were acquired from a globalized system of trade and commerce that allowed them to amass considerable wealth, particularly for those willing to invest in speculative ventures abroad. Inherited family fortunes and social ties

[4] In a sample of thirty-five individuals represented in the Bank's directorship, seventeen came from trading firms (e.g., Ogilvy, Gillanders & Co.) and thirteen came from merchant banks; Youssef Cassis, *Les banquiers de la City à l'époque Édouardienne (1890–1914)* (Geneva: Librairie Droz, 1984), 109. One contemporary study on the City of London found a high degree of overlap between the Bank's directorship and merchant banks; Percy Arnold, *The Bankers of London* (London: The Hogarth Press, 1938), 22–30. Other research has analyzed the occupations of the Bank's directions since its founding, noting the longstanding dominance of commercial City interests; Anthony Howe, "From 'Old Corruption' to 'New Probity': The Bank of England and Its Directors in the Age of Reform," *Financial History Review* 1, no. 1 (1994), 24; Elizabeth Hennessy, "The Governors, Directors and Management of the Bank of England," in *The Bank of England: Money, Power and Influence, 1694–1994*, ed. Richard Roberts and David Kynaston (Oxford: Clarendon Press, 1995), 200–202.

[5] Youssef Cassis, "Bankers in English Society in the Late Nineteenth Century," *The Economic History Review* 38, no. 2 (1985), 219–222; Cain and Hopkins, *British Imperialism*, 130–134; Simon James Arthur, "The Independence of the Bank of England: A Sociological Investigation" (PhD diss., University of Warwick, 2022), 21–29. On the debate over the extent to which the merchant bankers became part of the aristocracy, see S.D. Chapman, "Aristocracy and Meritocracy in Merchant Banking," *The British Journal of Sociology* 37, no. 2 (1986): 180–193; Youssef Cassis, "Merchant Bankers and City Aristocracy," *The British Journal of Sociology* 39, no. 1 (1988): 114–120; Telesca Giuseppe, "Introduction," in *Financial Elites and European Banking: Historical Perspectives*, ed. Youssef Cassis and Giuseppe Telesca (Oxford: Oxford University Press, 2018), 4.

further bound together this group of exclusive bankers, collectively termed hereafter as the Bank's Old Guard.

One feature of the Old Guard was a general distrust in outside views, particularly those forwarded by the leading political economists of the nineteenth century. Following the collapse of Overend, Gurney & Company (then the largest discount house in London) in 1866, Walter Bagehot, editor of *The Economist*, asserted that the central bank had an obligation to the financial sector. In times of crises, it had to be responsible for providing loans "at a very high rate of interest ... [and] on all good banking securities, and as largely as the public ask for them."[6] His writing detailed how the Bank, with its monopoly over the country's gold reserves, needed to adopt a greater interventionist role as a lender of last resort.[7]

In making these claims, Bagehot prompted countercriticism from the Bank's directors. George Warde Norman (grandfather of a future governor, Montagu Norman) and Thomson Hankey (great uncle of a future deputy governor, Ernest Harvey) argued that Bagehot's doctrine would place an undue burden on the Bank.[8] Governor William Lidderdale instead concluded that the shared work of financial stability fell upon the City as a whole: "[T]he banks of this country and the Bank of England were rowing in the same boat, and ... it would be for the common advantage of bankers and the country if the rowers would take their time a little better from the stroke oar."[9] Bank officials, deliberately choosing not to avail themselves of outside opinion, opposed those who questioned their actions. Although ensuing debates in *The Economic Journal* concerned the viability of the gold standard, notably with regard to the role of the central bank and its monopoly of note issue, the Bank – bereft of an interest

6 Bagehot, *Lombard Street*, 197.

7 Michael D. Bordo, "The Lender of Last Resort: Alternative Views and Historical Experience," *Federal Reserve Bank of Richmond Economic Review* 76, no. 1 (1990), 18–20; Forrest H. Capie and Geoffrey E. Wood, "A European Lender of Last Resort? Some Lessons from History," in *International Monetary Systems in Historical Perspective*, ed. Jaime Reis (London: Palgrave Macmillan, 1995), 218–223; C.A.E. Goodhart, "Myths about the Lender of Last Resort," *International Finance* 2, no. 3 (1999), 340–342; Richard S. Grossman, *Unsettled Account: The Evolution of Banking in the Industrialized World since 1800* (Princeton and Oxford: Princeton University Press, 2010), 98–102; Vincent Bignon, Marc Flandreau, and Stefano Ugolini, "Bagehot for Beginners: The Making of Lender-of-Last-Resort Operations in the Mid-Nineteenth Century," *The Economic History Review* 65, no. 2 (2012), 580–583; Samuel Knafo, *The Making of Modern Finance: Liberal Governance and the Gold Standard* (London and New York: Routledge, 2013), 158–159; Turner, *Banking in Crisis*, 144–166; Hotson, *Respectable Banking*, 18; Ugolini, *The Evolution of Central Banking*, 141–143; Bindseil, *Central Banking before 1800*, 149–154; Eichengreen, *Globalizing Capital*, 32–35.

8 Turner, *Banking in Crisis*, 142; Kynaston, *Till Time's Last Sand*, 202–206; Ugolini, *The Evolution of Central Banking*, 137.

9 Quoted in "The Leeds Proposals and the London Plan," *The Bankers' Magazine* LIII, February 1892, 215. Also cited in John Clapham, *The Bank of England: A History, 1797–1914, vol. 2* (Cambridge: Cambridge University Press, 1944), 346; R.S. Sayers, *Central Banking after Bagehot* (Oxford: Clarendon Press, 1957), 18.

in or a capacity for unorthodox ideas – offered little opportunity for such discussions in the aftermath of the crisis.[10]

The dominance of the Old Guard – with Norman, Hankey, and Lidderdale exemplifying the archetype – reached its apex in response to the 1890 Baring Crisis. After the eponymous merchant bank faced delays in repayments from its Argentine investments, which threatened its own solvency, the Bank offered its assistance. It began to import gold, predominantly from France, while maintaining high interest rates to prevent a sudden outflow.[11] With additional assistance from the other merchant banks, Lidderdale established a three-year guarantee fund of £17.1 million to support Barings.[12] Together, the central bank and the joint-stock banks cooperated in an effort to keep one of their own afloat. Regardless of whether this reaction was motivated more by personal profit and less by moral obligation, it nevertheless reflected the prewar strategy of crisis management.

What the response to the 1890 crisis further indicated was the existence of a self-regulated system of informal coordination. Stability in both domestic and global markets could seemingly be achieved without direct government intervention. During the Baring Crisis, the Old Guard was able to tame the spread of financial distress while simultaneously keeping in place the existing regime of "indirect regulation."[13] In its aftermath, the government chose not to intercede, in part because the Chancellor during the crisis, George Goschen (later,

[10] Walter Bagehot, "A New Standard of Value," *The Economic Journal* 2, no. 7 (1892), 475; G.H. Pownall, "The Insufficiency of Our Cash Reserves and of Our Central Stock of Gold," *The Economic Journal* 2, no. 7 (1893), 534.

[11] A. Andréadès, *Histoire de la Banque d'Angleterre : ses origines, sa fondation, son développement, Tome deuxième, 1819–1903* (Paris: Arthur Rousseau, 1904), 185.

[12] Court of Directors, Minutes, November 20, 1890, BoE G4/113; Clapham, *The Bank of England, vol. 2*, 334–335; John Giuseppi, *The Bank of England: A History from Its Foundation in 1694* (London: Evans Brothers, 1966), 128; Philip Ziegler, *The Sixth Great Power: Barings, 1762–1929* (London: William Collins Sons & Co., 1988), 254; Cassis, *Crises and Opportunities*, 12; Richard S. Grossman and Hugh Rockoff, "Fighting the Last War: Economists on the Lender of Last Resort," in *Central Banks at a Crossroads: What Can We Learn from History?*, ed. Michael D. Bordo, Øyvind Eitrheim, Marc Flandreau, and Jan F. Qvigstad (Cambridge: Cambridge University Press, 2016), 238; Turner, *Banking in Crisis*, 154–157; Forrest Capie and Geoffrey Wood, "The Governance of Central Banks: With Some Examples and Some Implications for All," in *The Oxford Handbook of the Economics of Central Banking*, ed. David G. Mayes, Pierre L. Siklos, and Jan-Egbert Sturm (Oxford: Oxford University Press, 2019), 111.

[13] On indirect or informal regulation, see Andreas Busch, *Banking Regulation and Globalization* (Oxford: Oxford University Press, 2012), 219; Turner, *Banking in Crisis*, 174–180; Linda Arch, *The Regulation of the London Clearing Banks, 1946–1971: Stability and Compliance* (Cham: Palgrave Macmillan, 2018), 45–47; Jack Copley, *Governing Financialization: The Tangled Politics of Financial Liberalization in Britain* (Oxford: Oxford University Press, 2022), 133–134; Leon Wansleben, *The Rise of Central Banks: State Power in Financial Capitalism* (Cambridge, MA, and London: Harvard University Press, 2023), 201.

1st Viscount Goschen), was formerly a Bank director. Although the Bank Act of 1892, known informally as the Goschen agreement, might have forced the Bank to continue managing the national debt at a predetermined rate of remuneration, it left unanswered (and therefore, unregulated) the Bank's jurisdiction over domestic money markets.[14] Without a de jure interventionist state, the central bank was effectively given free rein to respond to future crises.

This form of liberal economic governance underpinned the "first age of globalization" (c. 1870–1914), an era broadly characterized by monetary and financial stability among the core countries of Western Europe and the United States.[15] Vital to the growth and prosperity of the *belle époque* was the international adoption of the gold standard. Through a process known as the price–specie flow mechanism, countries running a balance-of-payment surplus would experience an inflow of gold. With this influx, a rise in domestic prices would lead to a subsequent decline in demand for their exports abroad.[16] The arrangement, as well as the fiscal restraint it entailed, brought substantial credibility to many European nations and acted as an ersatz regulatory policy.[17] It stood in contrast to the diverse experiences of overseas colonies, the governments of which were only able to borrow at lower interest rates due to investors' perceptions of lower risk.[18] For Europe, however, the

[14] Bank Act 1892, 55 & 56 Vict. c. 48; Clapham, *The Bank of England, vol.* 2, 340–342, 410.

[15] On the first age of globalization, see Kevin H. O'Rourke and Jeffrey G. Williamson, *Globalization and History: The Evolution of a Nineteenth-Century Atlantic Economy* (Cambridge, MA, and London: The MIT Press, 1999); Marc Flandreau and Frédéric Zumer, *The Making of Global Finance, 1880–1913* (Paris: Development Centre of the Organisation for Economic Co-operation and Development, 2004); Maartje Abbenhuis and Gordon Morrell, *The First Age of Industrial Globalization: An International History, 1815–1918* (London: Bloomsbury, 2020).

[16] Michael D. Bordo, "The Gold Standard: The Traditional Approach," in *A Retrospective on the Classical Gold Standard, 1821–1931*, ed. Michael D. Bordo and Anna J. Schwartz (Chicago and London: The University of Chicago Press, 1984), 33–35.

[17] Michael D. Bordo and Hugh Rockoff, "The Gold Standard as a 'Good Housekeeping Seal of Approval,'" *The Journal of Economic History* 56, no. 2 (1996): 389–428; Maurice Obstfeld and Alan M. Taylor, "Sovereign Risk, Credibility and the Gold Standard: 1870–1913 Versus 1925–31," *The Economic Journal* 113, no. 487 (2003): 241–275; Jeffry A. Frieden, *Global Capitalism: Its Fall and Rise in the Twentieth Century* (New York and London: W.W. Norton, 2006), 18; Martin Daunton, *State and Market in Victorian Britain: War, Welfare and Capitalism* (Woodbridge: The Boydell Press, 2008), 236; Ola Honningdal Grytten and Arngrim Hunnes, "Price Stability in the Periphery during the International Gold Standard: Scandinavia," in *The Gold Standard Peripheries: Monetary Policy, Adjustment and Flexibility in a Global Setting*, ed. Anders Ögren and Lars Fredrik Øksendal (London: Palgrave Macmillan, 2012): 58–80.

[18] On borrowing costs in the empire, see Niall Ferguson and Moritz Schularick, "The Empire Effect: The Determinants of Country Risk in the First Age of Globalization, 1880–1913," *The Journal of Economic History* 66, no. 2 (2006): 283–312; Olivier Accominotti, Marc Flandreau, and Riad Rezzik, "The Spread of Empire: Clio and the Measurement of Colonial Borrowing Costs," *The Economic History Review* 64, no. 2 (2011): 385–407; Nicolas Degive and Kim Oosterlinck, "Independence and the Effect of Empire: The Case of 'Sovereign Debts' Issued by British Colonies," in *Sovereign Debt Diplomacies: Rethinking Sovereign Debt from Colonial*

management of public debt offered tangible benefits for financial elites and political leaders, who benefited from relatively cheap capital. A country's ability to borrow also depended on its levels of domestic unrest, enfranchisement, and democratic institutions.[19]

International in reach, the infrastructure of global finance fell primarily under the jurisdiction of a London-based elite. From the stock exchange to the multinational clearing banks, the British financial sector commanded significant influence over the international economic system. Its prestige derived from its extensive connections in the expanding British Empire, a fact not lost on contemporaries. As one wrote,

> The London of to-day tells the story of the growth of the Empire … . The land frontiers extend over 25,000 miles, bringing the English people into intimate relations with almost all the nations of the world. The development in India and Eastern Asia, in Australia and New Zealand, in South Africa and Egypt, in North America, the West Indies and in South America, has had a great effect upon the life of the people at home. The United Kingdom has become less and less a kingdom and more and more the central portion of a great Empire. And the heart of that central portion of a tremendous Empire is the City of London.[20]

Although to its onlookers, the City may have represented the engine of imperial expansion, it played an even more crucial role in money markets elsewhere. Capital flows to Latin America, the Middle East, Eastern Europe, and East Asia facilitated the integration of financial markets throughout the nineteenth century.[21] Finding higher rates of return abroad than at home, British investors consistently identified new, and often risky, investment opportunities in different regions around the world. By the final decades of the century, London's command over global credit markets, Keynes later described, effectively made the Bank "the conductor of the international orchestra."[22]

Still, it was not the central bank alone that upheld London's status as a financial center. Rather, the late Victorian and Edwardian version of *haute finance* required the participation of a web of interconnected institutions in the

Empires to Hegemony, ed. Pierre Pénet and Juan Flores Zendejas (Oxford: Oxford University Press, 2021): 94–118; Didac Queralt, *Pawned States: State Building in the Era of International Finance* (Princeton and Oxford: Princeton University Press, 2022), 90–122.

19 Flandreau and Zumer, *The Making of Global Finance*, 34–35, 44.

20 Norman Patterson, "London: The Heart of the Empire," *The Canadian Magazine (Toronto)* XXVI, no. 1 (1905), 11.

21 Philip L. Cottrell, *British Overseas Investment in the Nineteenth Century* (London: Macmillan, 1975); Michael Edelstein, *Overseas Investment in the Age of High Imperialism: The United Kingdom, 1850–1914* (New York: Columbia University Press, 1982); Irving Stone, *The Global Export of British Capital, 1865–1914: A Statistical Survey* (Basingstoke: Macmillan, 1999).

22 John Maynard Keynes, *A Treatise on Money, vol.* 2 (London: Macmillan, 1930), 307. Also quoted in Barry Eichengreen, "Conducting the International Orchestra: Bank of England Leadership under the Classical Gold Standard," *Journal of International Money and Finance* 6, no. 1 (1987), 5.

City. Following the collapse of Overend Gurney, the main discount houses that remained were Alexanders & Co., the National Discount Company, and the recently formed Union Discount Company.[23] The Big Three provided liquidity to the market by purchasing (discounting) instruments known as bills of exchange. Through these operations, trading firms were able to acquire goods and avoid dealing with the high transport costs that might be associated with transactions in gold or other specie.

For London's merchant banks, such as Barings, Kleinwort, and Schroders, another major source of revenue came from dealings in the acceptance market.[24] A merchant bank could guarantee to pay (accept) a bill on behalf of a client, who would then make the final payment at a later date. With this endorsement, the sterling-denominated bill of exchange (the "bill on London"), as well as the acceptance houses that traded them, prompted the rise of the City as an international financial center. Around 60 percent of world trade was financed by the bill on London, which had a dual function as a credit instrument and a means of payment for long-distance transactions.[25] By the end of the nineteenth century, the instrument had developed into a highly liquid asset, as it could be sold (discounted) by discount houses and resold (rediscounted) by other discount houses or even the Bank of England itself.[26]

One can learn even more about the fin-de-siècle City through the profiles of bankers themselves. They were certainly distinct from those of the British aristocracy, the historically dominant class in British high society and local government.[27] Lavish inheritances, hereditary titles, and access to venal offices had long characterized the lifestyles of a patrician collection of dukes, marquesses, earls, and viscounts. Members of the old aristocracy might have sought to preserve their inherited wealth by investing in private corporations or serving

[23] W.T.C. King, *History of the London Discount Market* (London: Routledge, 1936), 256–263.

[24] Stanley Chapman, *The Rise of Merchant Banking* (London: George Allen & Unwin, 1984), 121; Richard Roberts, *Schroders: Merchants & Bankers* (Basingstoke: Macmillan, 1992), 123–128; Jehanne Wake, *Kleinwort, Benson: The History of Two Families in Banking* (Oxford: Oxford University Press, 1997), 116–120; Youssef Cassis, "Private Banks and the Onset of the Corporate Economy," in *The World of Private Banking*, ed. Youssef Cassis and Philip L. Cottrell (Farnham: Ashgate, 2009), 46. In contrast, the Rothschilds were more involved in the bond market; Niall Ferguson, *The House of Rothschild, vol. 2: The World's Banker, 1849–1999* (New York: Viking, 1999), 287–295; Marc Flandreau, *Anthropologists in the Stock Exchange: A Financial History of Victorian Science* (Chicago and London: The University of Chicago Press, 2016), 90–93.

[25] Barry Eichengreen, *Elusive Stability: Essays in the History of International Finance, 1919–1939* (Cambridge: Cambridge University Press, 1990), 288; Michie, *British Banking*, 110–111; Mulder, *The Economic Weapon*, 33–34.

[26] Hotson, *Respectable Banking*, 110; Olivier Accominotti, Delio Lucena-Piquero, and Stefano Ugolini, "The Origination and Distribution of Money Market Instruments: Sterling Bills of Exchange during the First Globalization," *The Economic History Review* 74, no. 4 (2021), 893.

[27] Arno J. Mayer, *The Persistence of the Old Regime: Europe to the Great War* (New York: Pantheon, 1981), 88–95; M.J. Daunton, "'Gentlemanly Capitalism' and British Industry 1820–1914," *Past & Present* 122, no. 1 (1989), 146.

on boards of directors in the City.[28] Yet they kept their distance from the professional classes, comprising bankers, merchants, and financiers based in the capital, where fortunes were tied to more lucrative ventures in overseas trade, rather than country estates.

Bankers nevertheless came to enjoy numerous privileges in high society. They included some of London's most prominent dynasties, including the Houses of Baring, Goschen, Grenfell, Hambro, Huth, Rothschild, and Schroder. Concerned with their own societal advancement, rather than an effort to emulate the aristocratic class, the financial elite developed its entrepreneurial culture through bourgeois activities, such as the purchase of country houses and estates.[29] Similar to the members of the aristocracy, many bankers joined gentlemen's clubs, studied at exclusive schools, attended the same social gatherings, and were awarded knighthoods.[30] Philanthropic activities were not due to any direct tax benefits but instead served an important social function in demonstrating wealth, affluence, and connections to those in power.[31] Of the renowned mercantile dynasties in the City, the two most prominent ones were Barings and Rothschild (Figure 1.1).[32] Both Edward Baring (1st Baron Revelstoke) and Nathan Rothschild (1st Baron Rothschild) had secured peerages during William Gladstone's second premiership.[33] They thus came to represent a City-based elite that maintained extensive links to both the central bank and the upper echelons of high society.

Among the many different groups employed at the Bank itself, none was more influential than the merchant bankers. Even though they rarely comprised the absolute majority of directors, they were able to consolidate their power at the Bank through various leadership positions. A rotational system emerged in which the Court of Directors elected a governor and a deputy governor, who

28 Cannadine, *The Decline and Fall of the British Aristocracy*, 407–420.

29 F.M.L. Thompson, *Gentrification and the Enterprise Culture: Britain, 1780–1980* (Oxford: Oxford University Press, 2001), 93–97. On the gentrification thesis, see also Martin J. Wiener, *English Culture and the Decline of the Industrial Spirit, 1850–1980* (Cambridge: Cambridge University Press, 1981); Lawrence Stone and Jeanne C. Fawtier Stone, *An Open Elite? England, 1540–1880* (Oxford: Clarendon Press, 1984).

30 For instance, the London Coliseum hosted a gathering attended by Charles Addis (a Bank director), the Schroders (a merchant bank), and Charles Whigham (a partner at Morgan Grenfell whose brother was a Bank director); Charles Addis, Diary, May 26, 1927, SOAS Addis Papers Box 4. According to one estimate, around 29 percent of the banking community between 1890 and 1914 had a knighthood; Cassis, *Les banquiers de la City*, 306. On the connections among City bankers, see also David Kynaston, *The City of London, vol. 2: Golden Years, 1890–1914* (London: Chatto & Windus, 1995), 422–426.

31 Pat Thane, "Private Bankers and Philanthropy: The City of London, 1880s–1920s," in *The World of Private Banking*, ed. Youssef Cassis and Philip L. Cottrell (Farnham: Ashgate, 2009), 250.

32 Daunton, "'Gentlemanly Capitalism' and British Industry," 142; David Cannadine, "Review Article: The Empire Strikes Back," *Past & Present* 147, no. 1 (1995), 190.

33 Cannadine, *The Decline and Fall of the British Aristocracy*, 199.

FIGURE 1.1 Baring Brothers & Co., 1927
Source: Ambrose McEvoy, Portrait of Messrs Baring Brothers & Co., The Baring Archive PT/045.

each committed to serving two-year (or, in rare instances, three-year) terms.[34] The deputy governor was usually the most senior director who, after his full term, became the governor.[35] Both officials, as well as prior occupants of the posts and select directors, served on the Bank's de facto decision-making body, the Committee of Treasury. Since its establishment in August 1694, the committee, as the name suggests, originally focused on maintaining communication with Treasury officials. Yet because meetings of the governor, the deputy governor, and the twenty-four directors were too unwieldy in size and too infrequent in consultation, the Committee became the main group to set overall policy. With representation from the leading directors, the decisions made

34 Bagehot, *Lombard Street*, 208. Until the Bank's nationalization in 1946, the Governor and Deputy Governor were elected by secret ballot; Bank of England Act 1946, 9 & 10 Geo. 6 c. 27; Giuseppi, *The Bank of England*, 143; Capie, *The Bank of England*, 36.

35 Bagehot, *Lombard Street*, 208–209.

and the advice offered by the Committee of Treasury became synonymous with the Bank View.

The ancestral ties between the Court of Directors and the merchant banks had been well established in the nineteenth century (Table 1.1). Consider, for instance, the connections to Frederick Huth & Co. Founded in 1809 by a German-born banker, the firm had emerged as one of the distinguished institutions in the City by the middle of the century. It fostered international trade, primarily with South America, through the London money market, and its acceptances were effectively guaranteed by the Bank.[36] The founder's son, Charles Frederick Huth (1806–1895), joined the Bank as a director in 1838, where he remained until his death. Meanwhile, the founder's daughter married another partner of Frederick Huth & Co., Daniel Meinertzhagen (1801–1869). One of their grandchildren, Frederick Huth Jackson (1863–1921), served simultaneously as a partner at the firm and as a director at the Bank.[37] Although the latter position did not offer much in terms of financial compensation, namely a modest salary of £500 per year in the 1890s, it instead presented merchant bankers a venue for exerting power in the City.

An even more striking case was the House of Grenfell. A descendant of a wealthy merchant family, Charles Pascoe Grenfell (1790–1867), the chairman of a major railroad company and a Liberal MP, served as a Bank director from 1830 to 1864. He held shares in several silver mining companies and, along with his brother, dominated Swansea's copper industry.[38] Both his son, Henry Riversdale Grenfell (1824–1902), and his grandson, Edward ("Teddy") Grenfell (1870–1941), were elected Bank directors at relatively young ages. The latter was indispensable in sustaining the bank's international connections, culminating in the renaming of J.P. Morgan's London branch to Morgan Grenfell in 1909.[39] Even excluding Edward's father-in-law, who was also a

[36] Mira Wilkins, *The History of Foreign Investment in the United States, 1914–1945* (Cambridge, MA: Harvard University Press, 2005), 177.

[37] Cassis, *Les banquiers de la City*, 56; Youssef Cassis and Philip L. Cottrell, *Private Banking in Europe: Rise, Retreat, and Resurgence* (Oxford: Oxford University Press, 2015), 220. The Bank also offered assistance to Frederick Huth & Co. in the early 1920s; Sayers, *The Bank of England, vol. 1*, 268–271; Richard Roberts, "The Bank of England and the City," in *The Bank of England: Money, Power and Influence, 1694–1994*, ed. Richard Roberts and David Kynaston (Oxford: Clarendon Press, 1995), 179; Kynaston, *The City of London, vol. 3*, 70.

[38] Chris Evans, *Slave Wales: The Welsh and Atlantic Slavery, 1660–1850* (Cardiff: University of Wales Press, 2010), 118; Chris Evans and Louise Miskell, *Swansea Copper: A Global History* (Baltimore: Johns Hopkins University Press, 2020), 80.

[39] Kathleen Burk, *Morgan Grenfell, 1838–1988: The Biography of a Merchant Bank* (Oxford: Oxford University Press, 1989), 64; M.J. Daunton, "Financial Elites and British Society, 1880–1950," in *Finance and Financiers in European History, 1880–1960*, ed. Youssef Cassis (Cambridge: Cambridge University Press, 1992), 135; Kathleen Burk, "Grenfell, Edward Charles, first Baron St Just (1870–1941)," September 23, 2004, ODNB; Susie J. Pak, *Gentlemen Bankers: The World of J.P. Morgan* (Cambridge, MA, and London: Harvard University Press, 2013), 13.

TABLE 1.1 *Sample List of Bank Directors*

- Sir Charles Stewart Addis (Director, 1918–1932), manager at HSBC
- Sir Alan Garrett Anderson (Director, 1918–1925, 1926–1946; Deputy Governor, 1925–1926), director at London, Midland and Scottish Railway
- John Baring, 2nd Baron Revelstoke (Director, 1898–1929), partner at Barings
    - Father, Edward Baring (Director, 1879–1891)
    - Great-uncle, Alexander Baring (Director, 1805–1817)
    - First cousin once removed, Thomas Baring (Director, 1848–1867)
    - Spouse of first cousin once removed, Humphrey St John Mildmay (Director, 1828–1848)
- William Middleton Campbell (Director, 1886–1888, 1889–1891, 1892–1896, 1897–1905, 1909–1919; Deputy Governor, 1905–1907; Governor, 1907–1909)
- Basil Gage Catterns (Director, 1934–1936, 1945–1948; Deputy Governor, 1936–1945), banker at the Manchester & Liverpool District Bank
- Brien Cokayne, 1st Baron Cullen of Ashbourne (Director, 1902–1915, 1920–1932; Deputy Governor, 1915–1918; Governor, 1918–1920), former partner at Antony Gibbs & Sons
    - Uncle, Hucks Gibbs, 1st Baron Aldenham (Governor, 1875–1877)
- Alfred Clayton Cole (Director, 1895–1920; Deputy Governor, 1909–1911; Governor, 1911–1913)
- Walter Cunliffe, 1st Baron Cunliffe (Director, 1895–1911, 1918–1920; Governor, 1913–1918), banker at Cunliffe Brothers
- Edward Charles Grenfell, 1st Baron St Just (Director, 1905–1940), partner at Morgan, Grenfell & Co.
    - Grandfather, Charles Grenfell (Director, 1830–1864)
    - Father, Henry Grenfell (Governor, 1881–1883)
    - Father-in-law, George William Henderson (Director, 1902–1929)
- Charles Hambro (Director, 1928–1963), managing director at Hambros Bank
    - Grandfather, Everard Hambro (Director, 1879–1925)
- Lionel Henry Hanbury (Director, 1908–1935), head of Wood, Hanbury, Rhodes & Jackson
- Sir Ernest Musgrave Harvey (Director, 1928–1929; Deputy Governor, 1929–1936)
    - Great uncle, Thomson Hankey (Deputy Governor, 1849–1851) and governor (1851–1853)

(continued)

TABLE 1.1 (*continued*)

- Frederick Huth Jackson (Director, 1892–1895, 1896–1921), partner at Frederick Huth & Co.
  - Great uncle, Charles Frederick Huth (Director, 1866–1895)
- Charles Hermann Goschen (Director, 1878–1915), banker at Frühling, Goschen & Co.
  - Brother, George Goschen, 1st Viscount Goschen (Director, 1858–1860, 1861–1863, 1864–1865)
  - Son, Kenneth Goschen (Director, 1922–1936)
- Robert Molesworth Kindersley, 1st Baron Kindersley (Director, 1914–1946), chairman of Lazard Brothers
- Cecil Lubbock (Director, 1909–1923, 1925–1927, 1929–1942; Deputy Governor, 1923–1925, 1927–1929)
  - Uncle, Edgar Lubbock (Deputy Governor, 1907)
- Montagu Collet Norman, 1st Baron Norman (Director, 1907–1918; Deputy Governor, 1918–1920; Governor, 1920–1944), former partner at Brown, Shipley & Co.
  - Paternal grandfather, George Warde Norman (Director, 1821–1872)
  - Maternal grandfather, Sir Mark Collet, 1st Baronet (Governor, 1887–1889)
- Edward Robert Peacock (1921–1924, 1929–1946), partner at Barings Bank and director at the Hudson's Bay Company
- David Powell (Director, 1870–1872, 1873–1876, 1877–1881, 1882–1886, 1887–1889, 1895–1897; Deputy Governor, 1889–1892, Governor, 1892–1895)
- Sir Augustus Prevost (Director, 1881–1884, 1885–1888, 1889–1892, 1893–1899, 1903–1913; Deputy Governor, 1899–1901; Governor, 1901–1903)
- Albert George Sandeman (Director, 1866–1868, 1869–1871, 1872–1875, 1876–1879, 1880–1884, 1885–1888, 1889–1892, 1893–1894, 1897–1918; Deputy Governor, 1894–1895; Governor, 1895–1897)
- Hugh Colin Smith (Director, 1876–1910; Deputy Governor, 1895–1897; Governor, 1897–1899)
  - First cousin once removed, Robert L. Newman (Director, 1896–1936)
- Michael Spencer-Smith (Director, 1920–1928), partner at H.S. Lefevre & Co.
- Frank Cyril Tiarks (Director, 1912–1945), banker at J.H. Schroder & Co.
- Henry Alexander Trotter (Director, 1909–1920, 1923–1926, 1927–1934; Deputy Governor, 1920–1923, 1926–1927), director at Alliance Assurance Co.
- Alexander Falconer Wallace (Deputy Governor, 1903–1905; Governor, 1905–1907), partner at Wallace Brothers & Co.
  - Brother, Robert Wallace (Director, 1919–1931)
- Walter Kennedy Whigham (Director, 1919–1946), banker at Robert Fleming & Co.

Source: R.S. Sayers, *The Bank of England, 1891–1944, Appendices* (Cambridge: Cambridge University Press, 1976), 359–364; Cassis, *Les banquiers de la City*, 101–112, 263–288.

Bank director, in the calculation, the record shows a nearly unbroken line of familial representation at the Bank lasting over a century.

Personal connections, not technical expertise, thus characterized the political economy of prewar banking. After a series of crises that exposed the fragility of the British financial system, Bagehot called upon the Bank to hire more trained professionals. As he wrote in *Lombard Street* (1873), "we should diminish the 'amateur' element; we should augment the trained banking element; and we should ensure more constancy in the administration."[40] Hinting at the necessity of comprehensive administrative reform, he argued that the Bank, by virtue of its monopoly of note issue, should employ individuals on the basis of intellect, rather than of character:

> I believe that the appointment of the new permanent and skilled authority at the Bank is the greatest reform which can be made there, and that which is most wanted. I believe that such a person would give to the decision of the Bank that foresight, that quickness, and that consistency in which those decisions are undeniably now deficient. As far as I can judge, this change in the constitution of the Bank is by far the most necessary, and is perhaps more important even than all other changes.[41]

Despite Bagehot's recommendations, no significant change to the central bank's administration followed. As an institution orthodox in outlook and conservative in customs, the Bank had long been dominated by generations of bankers who were reluctant to amend the system that they had long known. Instead, the Old Guard opted to design various tools, such as the lender-of-last-resort function, without the consultation of expert advice or the need for government intervention.

The realities of crisis management after the turn of the century made the Bank increasingly reliant on the employment of a robust staff. When women first joined the Bank in 1893, they were employed as clerks and responsible for sorting banknotes under the oversight of Janet Hogarth (later, Courtney), an Oxford graduate and the first Superintendent of Women Clerks with an annual salary of £157.[42] In her memoir, Hogarth reflected on how the Bank's standard

40 Bagehot, *Lombard Street*, 73. Also quoted in David Kynaston, *The City of London, vol. 1: A World of Its Own, 1815–1890* (London: Chatto & Windus, 1994), 261; John H. Wood, *A History of Central Banking in Great Britain and the United States* (Cambridge: Cambridge University Press, 2005), 109; Kynaston, *Till Time's Last Sand*, 208.

41 Bagehot, *Lombard Street*, 237. Also quoted in Hennessy, "The Governors, Directors and Management of the Bank of England," 192.

42 "Memorandum by Mr. Currie in Regard to Women Clerks," June 21, 1894, BoE ADM33/12; "Extract from the Minutes of the Court of Directors," June 21, 1894, BoE E3/21; W. Marston Acres, *The Bank of England from Within, vol. 2* (London: Oxford University Press, 1931), 560; Gillian Thomas, "Hogarth [married name Courtney], Janet Elizabeth (1865–1954)," September 23, 2004, ODNB; Gillian Sutherland, *In Search of the New Woman: Middle-Class Women and Work in Britain 1870–1914* (Cambridge: Cambridge University Press, 2015), 107; Kynaston, *Till Time's Last Sand*, 241.

policy was to recruit from "the rank and file from the daughters of professional men, with the necessary sprinkling (one in four) of Bank clerks' daughters."[43] Many of them worked in the Cancelled Notes department with a pay of £1 per week.[44] The position required employees to "lay out bank-notes in patterns like Patience cards, learning all about the little marks on them, crossing them up in piles like card-houses, sorting them into numerical order, counting them in sixties and finally entering their numbers in beautiful ledges made of the very best paper, as if intended to last out the ages."[45]

In 1903, the Bank began to recruit women as shorthand typists. Some of the benefits of the post included a higher salary of £84 a year, access to a pension scheme, and up to twenty-seven days of paid leave per year.[46] Yet there were also stringent requirements for employment, such as those that mandated women remain unmarried (or be widowed); pass a medical examination; and be trained in handwriting, orthography, English composition, and arithmetic.[47] Additional rules dictated a specific dress code in the office (navy blue, black, or dark gray), as well as a prohibition on lipstick or "cosmetics in an exaggerated manner."[48] Along with imposing these regulations, the Bank had largely drawn from a pool of female employees who had existing connections with a director.[49] The professionalization of the workforce in the early twentieth century might have brought more women to the Bank, but the lack of administrative reforms in the process prohibited their advancement.

One individual who embodied the City's exclusivity was Montagu Collet Norman (Figure 1.2). Prior to joining the Bank, Norman had attended Eton College and briefly studied at King's College, Cambridge, before becoming a partner at Brown, Shipley & Co., a merchant bank. In 1907, he was elected to the Court of Directors, a position that allowed him to play a more prominent role at the Bank. Despite his recurring episodes of depression and severe psychosis, which led him to consult the Swiss psychologist, Carl Jung, in 1913, Norman was able to establish himself as a leading central banker.[50] His allegiances were tested at the onset of the First World War, whereupon he took part in negotiations with officials from the Treasury and the City to ensure

43 Janet E. Courtney, *Recollected in Tranquility* (London: William Heinemann, 1926), 154.
44 Courtney, *Recollected in Tranquility*, 154.
45 Courtney, *Recollected in Tranquility*, 155. Also cited in Kynaston, *Till Time's Last Sand*, 248.
46 "Women Clerks," June 1903, BoE E3/21.
47 "Women Clerks," June 1903, BoE E3/21.
48 "Women in the Service," March 30, 1971, BoE ADM33/12.
49 Susanne Dohrn, "Pioneers in a Dead-End Profession: The First Women Clerks in Banks and Insurance Companies," in *The White-Blouse Revolution: Female Office Workers since 1870*, ed. Gregory Anderson (Manchester and New York: Manchester University Press, 1988), 54.
50 On Norman's consultation, see Boyle, *Montagu Norman*, 3, 91–95; Arnold T. Mirwis, "Carl Jung and Lord Montagu Norman: A Failed Consultation," *American Imago* 44, no. 2 (1987): 159–169; Patricia Clavin, "Men and Markets: Global Capital and the International Economy," in *Internationalisms: A Twentieth-Century History*, ed. Glenda Sluga and Patricia Clavin (Cambridge: Cambridge University Press, 2017), 104.

FIGURE 1.2 Montagu Norman, November 1919
Source: Philip Alexius de László, The Right Honourable Montagu Collet Norman (1871–1950), Governor of the Bank of England (1920–1944), Bank of England Museum, Accession Number 1988/025.

the continued functioning of the London money market. He also met with foreign bankers and civil servants throughout the war. Along with Governor Walter Cunliffe and Lord Revelstoke, he led the formative discussions over inter-Allied lending with the French central bank in 1916.[51]

Due to his wartime contributions, Norman was elected Deputy Governor in March 1918. Both this appointment and his subsequent one as Governor in April 1920 were, by all accounts, conventional choices. Although he did not yet have the international reputation others at the Bank could have claimed, Norman possessed a background that was "astonishingly orthodox" given that both his grandfathers were Bank directors.[52] He displayed, as one banker expressed, "great knowledge and strength of character," even if he had "a nervous temperament."[53] Instead of technical training, banking experience and family connections were the essential qualifications for City bankers looking to rise through the ranks of the central bank.

Such an employment practice constituted one of the many unspoken rules that all the members of the Old Guard followed. The Bank primarily hired partners from the leading merchant banks, often without regard for "formal

[51] "Procès-verbal de la séance du jeudi 23 mars 1916," BdF 1069201116/49; Martin Horn, *Britain, France, and the Financing of the First World War* (Montreal and Kingston: McGill-Queen's University Press, 2002), 125–127. After negotiations between the Bank of England and Banque de France recommenced on April 13, Norman was invited to join the Committee of Treasury on April 26; Committee of Treasury, Minutes, April 26, 1916, BoE G8/53.

[52] "Lord Norman," *The Old Lady of Threadneedle Street* XXVI, no. 117, March 1950, 294.

[53] Grenfell to Morgan, April 29, 1920, MLM ARC 1195 Box 5, Folder 3.

qualification" or university degrees.[54] Of greater value was "steady and patient attention to the routine and discipline" that supported the work of "a large institution."[55] Given these objectives, the prewar Bank lacked the intellectual capabilities that might have characterized other European central banks of the day.[56] It was an institution "utterly without the scientific knowledge which a Director of the present day would be expected to possess," with many of its officials in possession of a "humbler grade of intellect."[57] When in early 1918 the government sought to appoint an expert committee to assess the impact of recent mergers in the banking sector, Governor Brien Cokayne (later, 1st Baron Cullen of Ashbourne) shied away from offering any support because "he did not think that any formal advice could now be given by the Bank."[58]

The particularities of the Bank's aristocratic inner circle had major implications on monetary policy. In the nineteenth century, the central bank's most important function was setting the Bank Rate, the discount rate on loans to banks.[59] The goal was to target an appropriate interest rate that protected the nation's gold reserves as well as maintained the pound's peg of $4.86. Any change to the Bank Rate was a decision that occurred behind closed doors among private bankers, one of whom was then selected to make the announcement. In their deliberations, pragmatic arguments based on expert advice had an insignificant role, evidenced by the dearth of explanatory reasoning or rationale in the Committee of Treasury's minutes.[60] The idea that bankers should act with sound judgment and reasoning, rather than technical analysis or quantitative metrics, may have represented a source of pride as much as a

[54] Kynaston, *The City of London, vol. 2*, 247–248.

[55] Quoted in Sayers, *The Bank of England, vol. 2*, 610.

[56] In contrast, experts were more involved in discussions at the prewar Banque de France and the Reichsbank; Robert Yee, "Stability in Numbers: Central Banks, Expertise and the Use of Statistics in Interwar Europe," *Contemporary European History* 33, no. 3 (2024): 1038–1059; Maxence Dutilleul, "From Technical to Academic Central Banking: The Scientization of the Banque de France," *Finance and Society* 11, no. 2 (2025).

[57] Quoted in D.P. O'Brien and John Creedy, *Darwin's Clever Neighbour: George Warde Norman and His Circle* (Cheltenham: Edward Elgar, 2010), 244–245; Kynaston, *Till Time's Last Sand*, 115.

[58] Committee of Treasury, Minutes, July 10, 1918, BoE G8/54.

[59] In addition to setting the Bank Rate, the Bank began to buy and sell gold directly in the market; R.S. Sayers, *Bank of England Operations, 1890–1914* (London: P.S. King & Son, 1936), 85–101. On the discount rate, see also R.S. Sayers, *Bank Rate in Keynes's Century: Keynes Lecture in Economics* (London: British Academy, Oxford University Press, 1979); Barry Eichengreen, *Golden Fetters: The Gold Standard and the Great Depression, 1919–1939* (New York and Oxford: Oxford University Press, 1992), 35–37; Alec Cairncross, "The Bank of England and the British Economy," in *The Bank of England: Money, Power and Influence, 1694–1994*, ed. Richard Roberts and David Kynaston (Oxford: Clarendon Press, 1995), 58–60; Guillaume Bazot, Eric Monnet, and Matthias Morys, "Taming the Global Financial Cycle: Central Banks as Shock Absorbers in the First Era of Globalization," *The Journal of Economic History* 82, no. 3 (2022): 801–839.

[60] Sayers, *The Bank of England, vol. 1*, 28–29.

general mistrust in theory. During a series of discussions over the appropriate volume of discounts and advances to provide the market, statistics on the money supply were reported to have "had no place in the Governors' calculations."

Because resolutions generally found agreement among the group of like-minded merchant bankers who wished to offer a public image of unity, it is often possible to frame the prewar Bank as a single entity.[61] The absence of extensive written sources on the Committee of Treasury's (predominantly verbal) deliberations on the Bank Rate is itself telling of the informal process of decision-making. While minutes from the weekly proceedings had been kept since 1797, they were confidential and primarily used as an aide-mémoire for future discussions.[62] Evidently, they only included what the directors had decided to record. "It would be contrary to the Bank's traditions," wrote one financial journalist, "to give any indication to anyone as to its policy, intentions, and wishes. The City is left completely in the dark."[63] Indeed, there were few (if any) minority reports and letters of dissent that followed announcements made by the Bank's many committees, whose decisions appeared to be based on concord and consensus. As any change in the Bank Rate was meant to convey unanimous agreement among City bankers – in particular, those who seemingly understood the behavior of the market – the purpose was to provide legitimacy behind a seemingly unanimous verdict.

THE BANK AT WAR

The July Crisis in 1914 upended the traditional balance of power between the Bank and the City. With links to continental Europe, London's financial institutions had become vulnerable to the conflict. The de facto abandonment of the gold standard in August dealt the initial blow to the City, while the management of wartime loans and national debt further hampered British economic development well into the postwar years. Widespread panic followed the closure of stock exchanges in London, Birmingham, Edinburgh, Glasgow, and Manchester, and subsequent reverberations brought markets across the rest of Europe, North America, and South America to a standstill.[64]

[61] Forrest Capie has noted how even contemporary analyses were inconsistent in their references to the Bank as a singular or a plural noun; Capie, *The Bank of England*, xxi. See also an argument made for the Federal Reserve in Peter Conti-Brown, *The Power and Independence of the Federal Reserve* (Princeton and Oxford: Princeton University Press, 2016), 4–8.

[62] Revelstoke Committee, "Minute of Thursday, 25th October 1917," BA Revelstoke Papers 200022.02; Sayers, *The Bank of England, vol.* 2, 630. There is, for instance, relatively little material available on the Bank's activities in July and August 1914. While conversations between the Bank's directors and governors occurred on a daily basis, few records exist of the personal conversations; J.A.C. Osborne, "The Bank of England, 1914–1921, vol. 1 (Unpublished War History)," 1926, BoE M7/156, 58–59, 79.

[63] Einzig, *Montagu Norman*, 27.

[64] Richard Roberts, *Saving the City: The Great Financial Crisis of 1914* (Oxford: Oxford University Press, 2013), 21.

Part of the explanation for the global reach of the crisis came from the structure of the financial system. Until the outbreak of war, the bulk of international trade had been financed through bills of exchange. Sterling-denominated bills, deemed an "international currency" by one banker, continued to be one of the most liquid investments and the primary means of debt settlement.[65] Yet as the ensuing exchange-rate crisis on European markets prevented foreign borrowers from remitting their funds back to London, clearing banks began facing a drastic shortage of liquidity.[66] Faced with a crisis that resembled the 1866 Overend crisis, the Bank immediately committed its financial resources and used its institutional connections to control the rapidly spreading financial contagion.[67]

Among institutions in the City, the first to experience major difficulties following the July Crisis was the London Stock Exchange. Still larger than its counterparts in New York and Paris combined, the exchange was forced to close in response to severe liquidity issues on July 31, 1914.[68] The Bank, while initially hesitant to intercede and having not consulted authorities at the London Stock Exchange, chose instead to react to the crisis with its standard practice of raising the Bank Rate to 4 percent on July 30, 8 percent on July 31, and 10 percent on August 1.[69] The implementation of these measures was the primary means of preventing a rapid collapse in investors' confidence.

[65] Quoted in Richard Roberts, "'How We Saved the City': The Management of the Financial Crisis of 1914," in *British Financial Crisis since 1825*, ed. Nicholas Dimsdale and Anthony Hotson (Oxford: Oxford University Press, 2014), 95.

[66] Sayers, *The Bank of England, vol. 1*, 70–71.

[67] Among the many works on the Panic of 1866, the more recent ones include: Marc Flandreau and Stefano Ugolini, "Where It All Began: Lending of Last Resort at the Bank of England Monitoring During the Overend-Gurney Panic of 1866," in *The Origins, History, and Future of the Federal Reserve: A Return to Jekyll Island*, ed. Michael D. Bordo and William Roberds (Cambridge: Cambridge University Press, 2013): 113–161; Gary B. Gorton and Ellis W. Tallman, *Fighting Financial Crises: Learning from the Past* (Chicago and London: The University of Chicago Press, 2018), 179–180; Sabine Schneider, "The Politics of Last Resort Lending and the Overend & Gurney Crisis of 1866," *The Economic History Review* 75, no. 2 (2022): 579–600; Chenzi Xu, "Reshaping Global Trade: The Immediate and Long-Run Effects of Bank Failures," *The Quarterly Journal of Economics* 137, no. 4 (2022): 2107–2161; Charles Read, *Calming the Storms: The Carry Trade, the Banking School and British Financial Crises since 1825* (Cham: Palgrave Macmillan, 2023), 199–207.

[68] Sayers, *The Bank of England, vol. 1*, 71; Michie, *The London Stock Exchange*, 145–149; Roberts, *Saving the City*, 16–21; Robert Boyce, "The Bank of England in the First World War and Its Aftermath: The Price of Victory," in *Les banques centrales pendant la Grande Guerre*, ed. Olivier Feiertag (Paris: Presses de Sciences Po, 2019), 235–236.

[69] J.A.C. Osborne, "The Bank of England, 1914–1921, vol. 1 (Unpublished War History)," 1926, BoE M7/156, 6–7; Roberts, *Saving the City*, 50–54; Marie-Claude Esposito, "La Banque d'Angleterre et le financement de la Première Guerre mondiale," in *Les banques centrales pendant la Grande Guerre*, ed. Olivier Feiertag (Paris: Presses de Sciences Po, 2019), 119.

Throughout the summer of 1914, the Bank and the Treasury sought to formulate a collective response to save the City. A meeting on July 29 led to a discussion on the possible measures to be taken at the outbreak of war.[70] With the stock exchange's closure, the authorities intended to craft a robust financial policy. On August 4, the same day as Britain's formal declaration of war on Germany, Chancellor of the Exchequer David Lloyd George convened the first session of the "War Conference" with representatives from the Bank, Treasury, and Cabinet.[71] The Bank chose to dispatch Governor Cunliffe, Deputy Governor Robert Newman, and former Governor Alfred Cole, all of whom came from respected merchant banks. Their ensuing actions prioritized the interests of the City. Because both domestic depositors and foreign investors could have withdrawn their funds at unsustainable levels, a moratorium on bills of exchange and a bank holiday promised to protect the financial system from the threat of insolvency.[72]

Such interim measures bought the monetary authorities additional time to devise an adequate response. Although the gold standard effectively ended with the royal assent of the Currency and Bank Notes Act on August 6, both the Treasury and the Bank envisioned the decision as a temporary wartime expedient.[73] Addressing common goals, the meetings appeared to symbolize a moment of unprecedented coordination and consensus among those in power. To a certain degree, they represented the overlap of public and private interests. As Lloyd George later recorded in his memoirs, "during the whole of our deliberations I was most ably backed up and advised in my position as chairman by all my colleagues."[74]

However, the Treasury–Bank wartime relationship was a partnership of necessity, far from the cordial affair that Lloyd George might have wanted to portray. The Chancellor was certainly aware of the Bank's "deep resentment" of the party's policies, as on August 6, Cunliffe expressed his personal disapproval

[70] Kynaston, *Till Time's Last Sand*, 266–267; Boyce, "The Bank of England in the First World War," 237.

[71] "Conference between the Chancellor of the Exchequer and Representative Bankers and Traders," August 4, 1914, TNA T170/55; "Adjourned Conference between the Chancellor of the Exchequer, Members of the Cabinet and Representatives of the Bankers," August 5, 1914, TNA T170/56; "Adjourned Conference between the Chancellor of the Exchequer, Members of the Cabinet and Representatives of the Bankers," August 6, 1914, TNA T170/57; Roberts, *Saving the City*, 116–118; Kynaston, *Till Time's Last Sand*, 271.

[72] John Maynard Keynes, "War and the Financial System, August, 1914," *The Economic Journal* 24, no. 95 (1914), 468; Partnership Memo Book, Entry Dated Aug. 3rd, 1914, HCA HB/2/E/3; Lloyds Head Office to the Branch Managers, August 8, 1914, LGA HO/S/Gen/3; Lloyd George to Lord Rothschild, August 21 and 28, 1914, TNA T170/25; Peden, "The Treasury and the City," 123; Lambert, *Planning Armageddon*, 189–191; Roberts, *Saving the City*, 129–130; Michie, *British Banking*, 127.

[73] HL Deb, August 6, 1914, vol. 17, cc. 443–448; Currency and Bank Notes (Amendment) Act 1914, 4 & 5 Geo. 5 c. 72.

[74] David Lloyd George, *War Memoirs of David Lloyd George, vol. 1* (London: Ivor Nicholson & Watson, 1933), 106.

of the issuance of Treasury notes ("[t]his arrangement of yours").[75] Because both the Bank and the City aimed to preserve their relative independence vis-à-vis the government, they looked to the Treasury's imposition in financial affairs with a high degree of suspicion. There was a sense that the government would force the City to use all its resources to fund the war. Robert Brand, a director at Lloyds Bank, reported that the government was misguided in its decision to print unbacked banknotes at a time when it was "important that the country's gold reserve should be economised in every possible way."[76]

Moreover, the government's immediate response to the crisis upended the distribution of power among the economic authorities. It was the Treasury that now exerted control over monetary management, reorganized public finance with a revamped system of taxation, and led negotiations over inter-Allied lending.[77] In part, the Treasury's prominent role can be explained by the work of several experts who offered their continued insights and commentary on the dire economic situation. Ralph Hawtrey warned of the threat that excessive borrowing had on general price levels.[78] After the 1915 budget was announced in September 1915, Keynes similarly criticized the government's policies. He was concerned that the rapid increase in the money supply would adversely affect the balance of payments.[79] Although the Chancellor had announced the imposition of new duties on imported luxury goods, the expected surplus was not enough to cover the costs of wartime borrowing or the loans made to the other Allies.[80] Unresolved issues in the realm of public finance undermined overall trust in the currency.

[75] Quoted in J.A.C. Osborne, "The Bank of England, 1914–1921, vol. 1 (Unpublished War History)," 1926, BoE M7/156, 74; Roberts, *Saving the City*, 124–125. In later years, there were heated debates (the so-called "Cunliffe quarrel") between the Governor and Chancellor Andrew Bonar Law; Sayers, *The Bank of England, vol. 1*, 99–109; Alec Cairncross, "The Bank of England: Relationships with the Government, the Civil Service, and Parliament," in *Central Banks' Independence in Historical Perspective*, ed. Gianni Toniolo (Berlin and New York: Walter de Gruyter, 1988), 44; Harry Wilson, "The Governor, the Chancellor and the Secret War of Words That Raged in 1917," *The Times* 71400, January 8, 2015, 43.

[76] Robert Brand, "Memorandum Re Gold Position," April 1915, BLO Brand Papers 35.

[77] John Maynard Keynes, "Note on the Financial Arrangements between the United Kingdom and the Allies," April 9, 1917, in *The Collected Writings of John Maynard Keynes, vol. 16: Activities 1914–1919, The Treasury and Versailles*, ed. Elizabeth Johnson (Cambridge: Cambridge University Press, 1971): 226–238; Kathleen Burk, "The Treasury: From Impotence to Power," in *War and the State: The Transformation of British Government, 1914–1919* (London: George Allen & Unwin, 1982), 86–102; Tomlinson, *Public Policy and the Economy*, 55–57; Peden, *The Treasury*, 80–107; Martin Farr, *Reginald McKenna: Financier among Statesmen, 1863–1916* (London and New York: Routledge, 2008), 291–298.

[78] R.G. Hawtrey, "Inflation," September 1916, CAC Hawtrey Papers 1/11.

[79] John Maynard Keynes, "The Financial Prospectus of this Financial Year," September 9, 1915, TNA T170/90; Robert Skidelsky, *John Maynard Keynes, vol. 1: Hopes Betrayed, 1883–1920* (London: Macmillan, 1983), 307–308.

[80] John Maynard Keynes, "Note for the Prime Minister on the Financial Position," October 30, 1915, BLO Asquith Papers 133.

Precisely because fiscal reform alone proved insufficient, Treasury officials were able to justify expanding their responsibilities into new areas, such as overseas finance. On August 13, representatives from the Bank, accepting houses, and trading firms presented details of a plan to purchase additional bills. The intention was to inject additional liquidity into the system without government regulation. However, the Chancellor opposed the City's collective efforts and instead wanted to dictate wartime measures that the Treasury prioritized. As one observer later recounted, Lloyd George "appeared to announce these [proposals] as a decision already taken by the Treasury in conjunction with the Bank."[81]

Other institutions, however, proved that they were equally as dynamic in adjusting to the exigencies of war. Keynes described how the central bank had quickly responded to the crisis: "The peculiar relation of Great Britain to the international money market has again enabled the Bank of England to accomplish without the support of a large gold reserve what has been beyond the power of the great state banks of Europe in spite of unexampled gold hoards. The Bank of England alone met the catastrophes of August, 1914, without a suspension of specie payment."[82] It was, to be sure, not solely the Bank's activities that prevented what might have otherwise been a complete financial collapse in the early months of the war. Britain had greatly benefited from its prewar status as a creditor nation and drew on its available short-term balances abroad in moments of crisis.[83] With support from the joint-stock banks, the Bank was able to restore confidence in the market, thereby facilitating the reopening of the London Stock Exchange on January 4, 1915.[84]

Logistical difficulties associated with wartime finance, from raising taxes to procuring loans, intensified throughout the conflict.[85] The Bank primarily aimed to hold an adequate volume of reserves that secured the currency's peg to gold. Early in the war, officials had initiated discussions with J.P. Morgan & Co. and the Federal Reserve Bank of New York. A subsequently established Exchange Committee, with representation from both the Bank and the clearing banks, was able to procure a $50 million loan from the United States in June 1915.[86] Yet

81 Austen Chamberlain, *Down the Years* (London: Cassell and Company, 1935), 105.

82 John Maynard Keynes, "The City of London and the Bank of England, August, 1914," *The Quarterly Journal of Economics* 29, no. 1 (1914), 48.

83 Keynes, "The City of London," 50.

84 Michie, *The London Stock Exchange*, 149; Peden, *The Treasury*, 81; Boyce, "The Bank of England in the First World War," 241.

85 Kathleen Burk, *Britain, America and the Sinews of War, 1914–1918* (London: G. Allen & Unwin, 1985), 55–75; Niall Ferguson, *The Pity of War* (London: Penguin, 1998), 118–135, 326–331; Martin Daunton, *Just Taxes: The Politics of Taxation in Britain, 1914–1979* (Cambridge: Cambridge University Press, 2002), 39–59; Horn, *Britain, France, and the Financing of the First World War*, 148–165, 171–176.

86 Asquith to George V, June 8, 1915, BLO Asquith Papers 8; Sayers, *The Bank of England, vol. 1*, 91; Burk, *Britain, America and the Sinews of War*, 67, 265; Jeremy Wormell, *The Management of the National Debt of the United Kingdom, 1900–1932* (London and New York: Routledge, 2000), 173–174. The Exchange Committee included Lord Cunliffe (Bank), Brien Cokayne (Bank),

with the war's progression, more responsibilities were assigned to only a few officials who could be trusted to represent the Bank. Governor Cunliffe, Revelstoke, and Norman were tasked with managing relations with the Treasury and foreign central banks. Under their direction, a web of Allied central banks emerged to facilitate the settlement of cross-border transactions and sustain the wartime economy.[87] Meanwhile, Edward Grenfell used his personal connections with J.P. Morgan & Co. in New York to procure additional loans from the United States. These links demonstrated how the Bank could use its knowledge, network, and resources to maintain considerable influence in both domestic and foreign affairs.

Such wartime activities accelerated the Bank's own internal developments. At the outbreak of war, military conscription had placed an immediate strain on the administration with the departure of nearly half of its male staff members. In October 1914, the Committee of Treasury agreed "to employ Women Clerks permanently" in the Securities Office and Transfer Office, a decision that led to the overall number of female staff members to increase from 65 in 1914 to well over 2,000 by 1920.[88] Yet greater representation at the Bank did not translate into more opportunities. Appointments were often temporary, and the number of more coveted positions (Permanent Women Clerks) itself decreased over the course of the war. The requirement that women had to resign their appointments when married was maintained until the Second World War.[89]

New innovations regarding how information circulated were also a direct consequence of the war. In December 1916, the War Cabinet under Lloyd George, now prime minister, instituted a practice of recording unpublished meeting minutes.[90] His motivation may have been to distance himself from his predecessor, H.H. Asquith, whose indecisive leadership in the early years of the conflict had alienated both Conservatives and Lloyd George Liberals. More open reporting practices, in this regard, provided a way of justifying actions undertaken by the coalition government, in addition to making a once-informal process more standardized and centralized. The Bank similarly followed with its own administrative changes. During the July Crisis, few discussions had been recorded, and the results of internal deliberations were privy only to

Sir Edward Holden (Midland Bank), Reginald McKenna (Midland Bank), and Sir Felix Schuster (National Provincial); Treasury Minute, November 17, 1915, HSBC, Midland Bank UK 0158-0021; London Exchange Committee, Meeting Minutes, December 28, 1915, HSBC, Midland Bank UK 0158-0020; Horn, *Britain, France, and the Financing of the First World War*, 121.

87 Simon James Bytheway and Mark Metzler, *Central Banks and Gold: How Tokyo, London, and New York Shaped the Modern World* (Ithaca and London: Cornell University Press, 2016), 33–38.

88 Committee of Treasury, Minutes, October 28, 1914, BoE G8/53; Committee of Treasury, Minutes, April 21, 1915, BoE G8/53; "Estimated Number of Women Clerks on the Staff, 1893–1943," November 2, 1943, BoE E31/1.

89 "Women Clerks – Permanent Service," October 29, 1918, BoE E31/1; Elizabeth Hennessy, *A Domestic History of the Bank of England, 1930–1960* (Cambridge: Cambridge University Press, 1992), 13.

90 John F. Naylor, *A Man and an Institution: Sir Maurice Hankey, the Cabinet Secretariat and the Custody of Cabinet Secrecy* (Cambridge: Cambridge University Press, 1984), 16–18, 34–39.

the Governor, the Deputy Governor, and the directors. Yet after several exchange-rate crises, including ones in December 1916 and July 1917, officials began to doubt whether the de jure peg to gold could be maintained.[91] They considered the possible advantages of improving the Banks's minute-keeping practices. After an internal investigation, the directors agreed to improve transparency by allowing the Secretary to begin attending meetings.[92] Fuller minutes were available in the meetings thereafter.

The seemingly minute change in record-keeping practices was one component of a much broader institutional evolution at the Bank. While many of its activities, from setting the Bank Rate to discounting bills, had once occurred along ad hoc lines in response to financial crises as they arose, decisions in the later years of the war increasingly depended on technical analysis and calculation. On October 11, 1917, the directors appointed a special committee to propose reforms to the Bank's administration.[93] Under the chairmanship of John Baring (Lord Revelstoke), the committee stressed the need to build even closer links with the City (Figure 1.3). Preliminary discussions considered different ways of inviting more perspectives from the leading merchant banks, acceptance houses, and clearing banks, thereby improving future coordination efforts.[94] One director, Cecil Lubbock, suggested establishing a Bankers Finance Committee to promote a free and open exchange of "important questions concerning the whole Banking Community."[95]

Whether the Bank needed or wanted to follow the recommendations of the Revelstoke Committee became the topic of subsequent debates. Norman, then the Deputy Governor, suggested the possibility of drawing more support from the joint-stock banks, which in contrast to the merchant banks had historically been the most distant from the Old Guard. After a series of mergers, the leaders in this group were the "Big Five" of Barclays, Midland, Lloyds, National Provincial, and Westminster. Their operations were undeniably relevant to the Bank, as their recent large holdings of deposits effectively allowed them to exert oligopolistic dominance over the domestic credit market.[96] As Norman

91 Kathleen Burk, "J.M. Keynes and the Exchange Rate Crisis of July 1917," *The Economic History Review* 32, no. 3 (1979): 405–416; Burk, *Britain, America and the Sinews of War*, 7.

92 "Points in Regard to the Committee of Treasury and the Directorate So Far Agreed to by the Special Committee," October 27, 1917, BA Revelstoke Paper 200022.01.

93 "Special Committee appointed by the Court of 11th October 1917," October 13, 1917, BA Revelstoke Papers 200022.02.

94 Revelstoke Committee, "Tuesday, the 16th October, 1917," BA Revelstoke Papers 200022.01.

95 Lubbock to Revelstoke, October 17, 1917, BA Revelstoke Papers 200022.02.

96 Lucy Newton, "British Retail Banking in the Twentieth Century: Decline and Renaissance in Industrial Lending," in *Business in Britain in the Twentieth Century: Decline and Renaissance?*, ed. Richard Coopey and Peter Lyth (Oxford: Oxford University Press, 2009), 190. The 1918 (Colwyn) Committee on Bank Amalgamations investigated the extent to which banking amalgamations adversely reduced competition and national credit: *Copy of Report of the Treasury Committee on Bank Amalgamations*, Cd. 9052 (London: H.M. Stationery Office, 1918), 7; "Banking Questions," *The Economist* 086, 3889, March 9, 1918, 420; Geoffrey Jones, *British*

FIGURE 1.3 Lord Revelstoke, 1898
Source: Leslie Matthew "Spy" Ward, Vanity Fair – Bankers and Financiers, Yale Center for British Art, Gift of Michael H. LeWitt, Peter A. LeWitt, and Erwin Strasmick, B1979.14.77.

opened in October 1917, the directors might "eventually profit by a judicious selection of the best individuals from this particular circle."[97]

However, the Bank had a tense and difficult relationship with the clearing banks, partly because the latter resented the former's monopoly over the money supply.[98] Additional friction arose during the war when regular meetings between the private banks, the central bank, and the Treasury revealed the divergent views on particular lending arrangements.[99] As a result, the Revelstoke Committee considered enlisting the aid of outside experts who could, while working in an unofficial capacity, support the Governor and Deputy Governor. Initially, the idea of technical advisers served a political

Multinational Banking, 1830–1990 (Oxford: Clarendon Press, 1993), 235–236; Margaret Ackrill and Leslie Hannah, *Barclays: The Business of Banking, 1690–1996* (Cambridge: Cambridge University Press, 2001), 69–72; Mark Billings, Simon Mollan, and Philip Garnett, "Debating Banking in Britain: The Colwyn Committee, 1918," *Business History* 63, no. 6 (2021), 952.

97 "Opinions of the Members of the Special Committee on the Subject of the Eligibility of Directors of Joint Stock Banks for Election on the Court," October 24, 1917, BA Revelstoke Papers 200022.02.

98 Singleton, *Central Banking in the Twentieth Century*, 39.

99 "Report of Proceedings at the Meeting of the Bankers of the United Kingdom and the Colonies," July 9, 1915, HCA HB/7/B/1; "Meeting of the Clearing Bankers' Committee," January 19, 1917, HSBC, Midland Bank UK 0558-0011.

purpose, namely helping the Bank regain its lost position of influence in the City. As the war continued under the Treasury's seemingly hostile leadership, a consensus emerged at the Bank around a new objective: to ensure that the Bank held "sovereign authority" over the financial system and "regain the position and influence which once was theirs."[100] While the directors had seen much of its authority over the London money market transferred to the Treasury during the war, many of them sought to reassert institutional independence by employing experts who could provide additional insights into the central bank's operations and prerogatives.[101] According to the committee's report,

> By unwritten custom the executive power has been largely concentrated in the hands of the Governors, and we recognise that they cannot constantly consult so large a body as the Directorate. But from time immemorial the Court has appointed a Committee with whom they should consult; and we recommend that measures should be taken to ensure that, in future, the Governors shall enjoy the intimate co-operation of certain colleagues who, as members of a Committee, would relieve the Governors of any occasion for the exercise of an autocratic control.[102]

In making this claim, Lord Revelstoke may have also attempted to counter Governor Cunliffe's abuse of executive power. He had frequently failed to consult the other directors on important decisions. The danger of concentrating power in one position, a notion lost on neither the Bank nor the wider financial community, seemed to make the idea of outside advisers even more appealing.[103] As one director stated, "I think the necessity for an Assistant to the Governors will become greater as time goes on, especially after the declaration of peace. He should in my opinion be a permanent Official with a thorough Banking knowledge and should be paid a large salary."[104]

A NEW FINANCIAL ORDER

The collapse of the old European order created a new set of priorities for British institutions. After the war, Britain faced a myriad of issues – exchange-rate

[100] Revelstoke Committee, "Minute of Thursday, 25th October 1917," BA Revelstoke Papers 200022.02.

[101] "Report of the Special Committee Appointed by the Court of the 11th October, 1917," January 23, 1918, BoE G15/112. Also quoted in "The Position of the Court as Regards Duties Outside the Bank Undertaken by Advisers to the Governors," December 16, 1935, BoE G15/276.

[102] "Report of the Special Committee Appointed by the Court of the 11th October, 1917," January 23, 1918, BoE G15/112. Also quoted in "The Position of the Court as Regards Duties Outside the Bank Undertaken by Advisers to the Governors," December 16, 1935, BoE G15/276.

[103] The press, for instance, had reported on the debates over the governorship; "The Bank of England," *The Economist* 85, 3863, September 8, 1917, 3.

[104] "Replies of Mr. Tiarks to the Questionnaire of the 5th November as Given by Him in His Conversation with the Committee on Monday, the 26th November, 1917," BA Revelstoke Papers 200022.02.

instability, industrial stagnation, and national indebtedness – which compelled it to reconsider its own place in the international economic system. The City, to be sure, had retained its important position in supporting international trade and commerce, sustained most notably by the activities of the leading merchant banks.[105] It enjoyed an immensely privileged status as the world's financial center throughout the 1920s.[106] Nevertheless, while London remained the preferred location for raising capital, it now appeared to contend with New York, Paris, and Berlin for continued supremacy.[107]

A trend particularly alarming to British officials was the rising levels of debt amassed by wartime belligerents. Contemporary estimates, although incomplete, showed the accumulation of high wartime debts among the Allied nations, many of whom heavily relied on foreign borrowing (as opposed to debt incurred through domestic channels) as the war progressed (Table 1.2). Increased spending had been the primary reason countries were forced to abandon the peg to gold. At the Treasury, Hawtrey commented on the continued burden of excessive spending among the states of Europe, some of which had no central bank of issue to manage the national debt.[108] Britain itself financed the war through a combination of taxes, collective savings, and war loans, while also selling Treasury bills to cover the remaining budget deficits.[109] Nevertheless, government spending as a percentage of GDP rose from 12.7 percent (1914) to 35.1 percent (1918).[110]

The immediate consequences of inadequate fiscal management were made apparent at the onset of the postwar slump. Preceded by a brief economic boom, a rapid decline in demand for consumer goods and investments instigated a recession.[111] The downturn in the global business cycle led to a

[105] Youssef Cassis, *Les capitales du capital : histoire des places financières internationales, 1780–2005* (Paris: Champion classiques, 2008), 229–233.

[106] Ranald Michie, "A Financial Phoenix: The City of London in the Twentieth Century," in *London and Paris as International Financial Centres in the Twentieth Century*, ed. Youssef Cassis and Éric Bussière (Oxford: Oxford University Press, 2005), 22.

[107] Reynolds, *Britannia Overruled*, 105; Roberts, "The Bank of England and the City," 183; Cassis, *Les capitales du capital*, 218–251; Ranald C. Michie, "The City of London as a Global Financial Centre, 1880–1939: Finance, Foreign Exchange, and the First World War," in *Centres and Peripheries in Banking: The Historical Development of Financial Markets*, ed. Phillip L. Cottrell, Even Lange, and Ulf Olsson (Aldershot: Ashgate, 2007), 43.

[108] R.G. Hawtrey, "La situation monétaire européenne," *Revue de métaphysique et de morale* 28, no. 2 (1921), 205.

[109] T. Balderston, "War Finance and Inflation in Britain and Germany, 1914–1918," *The Economic History Review* 42, no. 2 (1989), 231; Peden, *The Treasury*, 97; Nicolas Delalande, "The Financial Challenges of Total War," in *A World of Public Debts: A Political History*, ed. Nicolas Barreyre and Nicolas Delalande (Cham: Palgrave Macmillan, 2020), 262.

[110] Stephen Broadberry and Mark Harrison, "The Economics of World War I: An Overview," in *The Economics of World War I*, ed. Stephen Broadberry and Mark Harrison (Cambridge: Cambridge University Press, 2005), 15.

[111] Howson, *Domestic Monetary Management*, 10.

TABLE 1.2 *Wartime Borrowing (millions, 1913 US dollars)*

	1914–1916			1917–1919		
Countries	Internal Debts	External Debts	Total	Internal Debts	External Debts	Total
Austria-Hungary	4,073	711	4,784	2,168	---	2,168
Belgium	---	388	388	---	274	274
Britain	9,631	1,408	11,039	6,451	2,568	9,019
British Empire	10,363	1,740	12,103	8,364	2,200	10,564
France	5,156	861	6,017	5,463	1,671	7,134
Germany	9,106	9	9,115	10,303	---	10,303
Italy	1,674	525	2,199	1,640	753	2,393
Portugal	82	6	88	154	34	188
Russia	5,972	2,165	8,137	1,660	360	2,020
Turkey	191	242	433	162	106	268
United States	1,141	---	1,141	11,344	198	11,542

Source: Harvey E. Fisk, *The Inter-Ally Debts: An Analysis of War and Post-War Public Finance 1914–1923* (New York and Paris: Bankers Trust Company, 1924), 333, 335.

contraction in aggregate output, which, as one financial journalist reported, was "inflicted upon mankind by essentially human hands."[112] The Bank's response largely resembled the traditional way of doing business. On April 15, the Committee of Treasury opted to raise the Bank Rate to 7 percent. The hike – the highest since the outbreak of the war – might have resulted in a readjustment to the trade imbalance by attracting additional gold inflows. Although raising interest rates allowed the Bank to delay the debate over institutional change, the policy of "dear money" exacerbated the severity of the ongoing recession.[113]

Abroad, the national governments and central banks of Europe and the United States addressed the threat to the international order in similar ways. In September 1920, civil servants, bankers, and economists convened in Brussels to discuss the prospect of reform. Their deliberations initially appeared to offer little resolution to the prevailing geopolitical tensions and, as one of the Bank's advisers wrote, were "necessarily doomed to disappoint."[114] Focusing instead

[112] Paul Einzig, *World Finance since 1914* (London: Kegan Paul, Trench, Trubner & Co., 1935), 56.

[113] Susan Howson, "The Origins of Dear Money, 1919–20," *The Economic History Review* 27, no. 1 (1974), 106; Charles P. Kindleberger, *A Financial History of Western Europe* (London: George Allen & Unwin, 1984), 330; S.N. Broadberry, *The British Economy between the Wars: A Macroeconomic Survey* (Oxford: Basil Blackwell, 1986), 142–144.

[114] H.A. Siepmann, "The International Financial Conference at Brussels," *The Economic Journal* 30, no. 120 (1920), 442.

on financial concerns, the delegates upheld a form of liberal internationalism based on the supposed conditions of prewar stability: free movement of capital, balanced budgets, and independent central banks.[115] According to Karl Polanyi, there were few truly laissez-faire elements to the market economy, which required active state intervention.[116] Along these lines, European governments envisioned constructing a new financial order based on the supposed self-correcting mechanisms of the gold standard. The gold-exchange standard, as it was conceptualized, modified the prewar version of the gold standard by allowing central banks to hold both gold and gold-backed foreign currencies to meet their budgetary needs. At the Genoa Conference two years later, officials reaffirmed the benefits of independent central banking and economic orthodoxy.[117]

Even if the Bank had not abandoned the de jure parity to gold during the war, a restriction on gold exports and the printing of an unbacked currency had implied the effective demise of the prewar monetary system. For the Old Guard, orthodox measures, in accordance with the Brussels consensus, were necessary for resurrecting the pre-1914 order. The stabilization of sterling emerged as one of the chief priorities of the interwar years. In September 1919, Governor Brien Cokayne (later, Lord Cullen) described how "the Court [of Directors]," the Bank's unelected body of shareholders, "regard the restoration of the gold standard and the resumption of free gold exports at the earliest possible moment as of vital importance to the Country as a whole and consider that it is well worth a temporary sacrifice to secure that end."[118] This view aligned with that of the (Cunliffe) Committee of Currency and Foreign Exchanges after the War, which recommended the return to the prewar gold standard "at an early date."[119]

The adoption of the gold standard alone might have been enough to revive a system of economic governance based on tradition, orthodoxy, and oligarchy. However, many bankers soon came to recognize the unprecedented challenges

[115] James, *The End of Globalization*, 35–38; Eric Helleiner, *The Making of National Money: Territorial Currencies in Historical Perspective* (Ithaca and London: Cornell University Press, 2003), 141; Kenneth Mouré, "Les banques centrales et l'étalon-or dans l'entre-deux-guerres," in *Politiques et pratiques des banques d'émission en Europe (XVIIe–XXe siècle) : le bicentenaire de la Banque de France dans la perspective de l'identité monétaire européenne*, ed. Olivier Feiertag and Michel Margairaz (Paris: Albin Michel, 2003), 348.

[116] Karl Polanyi, *The Great Transformation* (New York and Toronto: Farrar & Rinehart, 1944).

[117] R.G. Hawtrey, "The Genoa Resolutions on Currency," *The Economic Journal* 32, no. 127 (1922), 292; W.H. Mercer and P.H. Ezekiel, "London as a Gold Centre under the Genoa Plan," June 19, 1922, BoE OV37/20.

[118] Quoted in Kynaston, *The City of London, vol. 3*, 61; Kynaston, *Till Time's Last Sand*, 296.

[119] *Final Report of the Committee on Currency and Foreign Exchange Rates after the War*, Cmd. 464 (London: H.M. Stationery Office, 1919), 3–4. The Cunliffe Committee's interim report also found that "the conditions necessary to the maintenance of an effective gold standard should be restored without delay"; *First Interim Report of the Committee on Currency and Foreign Exchange Rates after the War*, Cd. 9182 (London: H.M. Stationery Office, 1918), 11.

facing the new economic order. They were willing to concede institutional power to those who could help them accomplish their goals. One memorandum by Edward Peacock, a partner at Barings and former Bank director, explained the importance of this endeavor:

> It is vital to England that London should maintain her position. The business of the country has suffered in so many ways that but for this financial pre-eminence she would gradually sink to a secondary position with corresponding loss of wealth and power. The centre of the British Empire need not suffer that decline provided the best use is made of all available resources. The first of these is finance, and the leadership of the B. of E. is essential.
>
> ...
>
> It is the duty of the City of London and the B. of E. to do all possible to maintain British prestige: and leadership in International finance is the [keystone] of the arch. The B. of E. is not organized for such work – it must gradually create a highly competent Secretariat … . Three or four quite exceptional men must be secured to start this work … . Under such conditions the Governor must be a man of vision and highly expert knowledge and he should have great prestige. Apart from M[ontagu] N[orman] is there such a man available?[120]

To reassert their authority in the City and retain influence in the international financial system, officials understood that they had to concede power internally. They turned to advisers not for an underlying faith in the economics discipline. Nor was the central bank – owned and operated by its private shareholders – wholly concerned with its public image. Instead, what explains the rise of expertise was the desire to resolve issues most pressing to the authorities when traditional methods failed.

ENTER THE EXPERTS

Much of the initial impetus behind expert employment was related to domestic governance. Prior to the war, the balance of power largely had shifted to the Treasury, which was able to maintain its authority over policymaking.[121] Yet the Bank strove to reclaim some of the power lost during the conflict. In November 1926, the (Trotter) Special Committee on the Government and Administration of the Bank met to consider the institutional changes needed to reassert dominance.[122] During the deliberations, Frank Cyril Tiarks, a private banker and Bank director, argued that experts needed to meet daily and advise

120 Edward Peacock, "Note Re Bank of England," July 9, 1926, BA Revelstoke Papers 203332.

121 Burk, "The Treasury," 84.

122 "Special Committee on Government & Administration of the Bank," 1926, BoE G15/252; "Report of the Special Committee on the Future Government and Administration of the Bank," September 27, 1927, BoE G15/253; Kynaston, *Till Time's Last Sand*, 304–305.

the Court of Directors.[123] The Bank, to his mind, simply could not continue to have "an expert Governor with an inexpert Court."[124]

Nevertheless, opinions widely differed on who should lead the central bank. Whereas Lord Revelstoke believed that the governor "would increasingly require expert and professional knowledge and experience," another merchant banker, Walter Whigham, more forwardly suggested that "[t]he Governor should be an expert or professional."[125] Given the variety of other possible reforms, the controversy surrounding expertise was not lost in the discussion. The directors questioned, for instance, whether they would be able to find someone "in whom complete trust could be placed in view of the exceptionally confidential knowledge which would be in his possession."[126] It would have been a revolutionary break from a centuries-long tradition to employ an individual who did not share their fundamental interests. As one official claimed, "although experts are necessary in many businesses, a business controlled by an expert is generally not as efficiently run as one in which the best of experts are kept severely under control."[127] Another director, Sir Charles Addis, similarly proposed limiting the influence of expert knowledge altogether: "The proper place for an expert is not in the Chair but behind it. It is for him to assist and advise, but it is for the Merchant Directors to determine the policy of the Bank, and it is the belief that that policy is so determined which has won for the Bank its traditional authority and prestige."[128]

Yet securing both the City's preeminence and the Bank's authority could be mutually inclusive goals. The Old Guard understood how the dislocations of the war had increasingly put the City under strain. Inviting outsiders into the Bank and diffusing power throughout the institution would be a worthwhile sacrifice in order to defend the power of British finance at an international level. This argument unexpectedly came from Lord Revelstoke, one of the City's most traditional and elite merchant bankers. From his point of view, the Bank needed to recognize "the necessity of broadening the basis of our executive control," particularly "in view of the growing expert representation

123 "Notes of Evidence Given by Mr. Tiarks before the Special Committee," March 1, 1927, BoE G15/252 and SA Tiarks Papers 1921–1981; Kynaston, *Till Time's Last Sand*, 305. See also "Notes of Evidence Given by Sir Charles Addis Before the Special Committee on Wednesday, the 23rd February 1927," SOAS Addis Papers Box 39, Item 455.

124 "Notes of Evidence Given by Mr. Tiarks before the Special Committee and SA Tiarks Papers 1921–1981," March 1, 1927, BoE G15/252.

125 "Notes on Lord Revelstoke's Evidence," January 11, 1927, BoE G15/252 and BA Revelstoke Papers 203332; "Notes of Mr. Whigham's Evidence Before the Special Committee," February 25, 1927, BoE G15/252.

126 "Memorandum: Exchanges," April 29, 1926, BoE G14/307.

127 Robert Wallace to Ronald Dale, December 22, 1926, BoE G15/252. See also "Notes of Mr. Wallace's Evidence," January 12, 1927, BoE G15/252.

128 Quoted in Roberta Allbert Dayer, *Finance and Empire: Sir Charles Addis, 1861–1945* (Basingstoke: Macmillan, 1988), 175; Kynaston, *The City of London, vol. 3*, 169.

by which we are increasingly surrounded, in this ailing and exhausted Europe, and in the flourishing New World, and in our own Treasury at Whitehall."[129]

With its array of national and international objectives, the Bank searched for ways of bringing in outside perspectives without abandoning its principles. One director reported that the Bank should be careful of inviting too many officials from the Treasury, lest it be perceived as "a Government Institution."[130] It might have also been the case that "the only way to maintain the Bank's independence is to make it an absolutely efficient impersonal 'machine' guided by a Court which is equally impersonal."[131] Proper checks on power would have allowed the Old Guard to reverse any undesirable decisions if they were too hastily made. Another banker claimed to have "the highest opinion of financial experts," but he believed that they would not be able to lead committees or chair discussions.[132] Instead, they should only remain informal advisers.

In the early 1920s, the Bank primarily consulted experts on an ad hoc and irregular basis. Its first unofficial expert, Sir Henry Strakosch, worked in an advisory capacity to Governor Norman, with whom he shaped the contours of postwar reconstruction. There were also experts later recruited from the Treasury and the League of Nations, such as Harry A. Siepmann and Otto Niemeyer. Both provided perspectives on economic policy that justified the Bank's involvement in imperial and foreign affairs. Together, experts and bankers formed an unexpected alliance that sought to validate the Bank's legitimacy, thereby bringing stability to a chaotic economic order.

Behind many of these hiring decisions was Norman himself. He had hoped to see "a group of whole-time professionals" on the Court of Directors, particularly those with university degrees.[133] Often the employment of outside advisers had a strategic element to it. Siepmann, the Bank's first official adviser, had graduated from New College, Oxford, before joining the Treasury. Along with Strakosch, he oversaw the Bank's reconstruction policies across Central Europe and the British Empire after the First World War. In other instances, Norman strove to import more theoretical insights, leading to the employment of two US economists. The contributions of Walter W. Stewart and Oliver M.W. Sprague centered on researching the supposed role of a central bank, thereby defending existing monetary policy. While still a traditionally conservative institution, the Bank could provide the overarching infrastructure in which experts were allowed to operate.

129 Lord Revelstoke, Speech, October 14, 1926, BA Revelstoke Papers 203332.

130 "A Meeting of the Directors at the Bank on Monday, the 21st May, 1928," BA Revelstoke Papers 203251.

131 Brien Cokayne, "Answers to Questionnaire of the Special Committee on the Future Government and Administration of the Bank," January 4, 1927, BoE G15/252.

132 "A Meeting of the Directors at the Bank on Monday, the 21st May, 1928," BA Revelstoke Papers 203251.

133 Norman to Strong, April 17, 1927, FRBNY Strong Papers 1116.7 Part 2. Also quoted in Sayers, *The Bank of England, vol. 2*, 599.

The rise of expertise at the Bank coincided with the decline in relative power of the British aristocracy and landed elite, whose fortunes were tied to country estates, art collections, and other symbols of conspicuous consumption.[134] Their once-extensive involvement in domestic politics and colonial affairs had demonstrated the degree to which inherited wealth had largely determined the paths to power. Yet a series of public reforms around the turn of the century had threatened the aristocratic order. Undermining their authority, both Sir William Harcourt's Estate Duty in 1894 and Lloyd George's People's Budget in 1909 made higher rates of taxation a new standard. The war delivered another devastating blow to the British establishment. Mass democracy, the expansion of the franchise, and the rise of the Labour Party all entailed greater resistance to aristocratic rule. By the early interwar years, the weakening grip on power exerted by the former ruling classes, coupled with the willingness of the state to search for solutions to the immediate postwar instability, created an opportunity for a group of professionals to emerge.

In terms of class, newly hired experts came from a variety of social backgrounds, often distinct from others at the Bank but still usually in the upper-middle class. Around 80 percent had at least some university-level education, in contrast to approximately 40 percent of the Old Guard. More than half of the Bank's experts had studied at Oxford or Cambridge, one-third had worked in academia, and half had experience in government. Still, their families were not considered members of the English gentry, the British aristocracy, or the wider political establishment. Henry Clay and Niemeyer were sons of German merchant émigrés, while Strakosch's family had ties to the Austrian sugar beet industry. Siepmann's father, also born in Germany, taught modern languages at an English secondary school. Educational backgrounds were similarly diverse. Although many were products of prestigious public schools (Eton, Rugby, St Paul's), a few had attended grammar schools.

Equally notable was the heterogeneity in qualifications (Table 1.3). In most cases, those with university-level training could act as experts: Iris Douglas, Humphrey Mynors, W. Brian Reddaway, James Selwyn, Oliver M.W. Sprague, Josiah Stamp, and Walter W. Stewart all held academic degrees in economics. They sought to apply economic principles to their policy recommendations, which led to lengthy reports with more theoretical underpinnings. However, the term "expert" encompasses more than those who studied the dismal science. George Bolton and Evelyn James Bunbury had prior experience in the banking sector, albeit not at one of the reputable merchant banks. Several advisers had experience at the Treasury. Others, such as J.A.C. Osborne, used the title of statistician.

134 Cannadine, *The Decline and Fall of the British Aristocracy*, 112–125, 189–195; David Cannadine, *Aspects of Aristocracy: Grandeur and Decline in Modern Britain* (New Haven and London: Yale University Press, 1994), 25–36.

TABLE 1.3 *The Bank's Experts*[135]

1. Ronald Eric Harrison Allport, Statistical Section (1925–1933), Economics & Statistics Section (1933–1947)
   B.Mus., University of London
2. George Lewis French Bolton, Foreign Exchange Section (1934–1941), Adviser to the Governors (1941–1948), Director (1948–1957)
   Leyton County High School for Boys
3. Charles Bruce-Gardner, Adviser to the Governors (1935–1938)
   St Dunstan's College, Battersea Technical College
4. Evelyn James Bunbury, Adviser to the Governors (1935–1937), Executive Director (1937–1938), Bank of England
   The Oratory School, B.A., Modern History, The Queen's College, Oxford
5. Henry Clay, Adviser to the Governors (1933–1944)
   Bradford Grammar School, B.A., Literae Humaniores, M.A., University College, Oxford
6. Cameron Fromanteel Cobbold, Adviser to the Governors (1933–1938), Executive Director (1938–1945), Deputy Governor (1945–1949), Governor (1949–1961)
   Eton College, King's College, Cambridge
7. Jessie Iris Douglas, Economist (1931–1948)
   Bradford Girls' Grammar School, B.A., Economics, M.A., Girton College, Cambridge
8. Anthony Reay Mackay Geddes, Staff Economist (1932–1935)
   Rugby School, B.A., Economics, King's College, Cambridge
9. Gilbert Edward Jackson, Adviser to the Governors (1935–1939)
   Denstone College, B.A., Economics, St John's College, Cambridge
10. Raymond Newton Kershaw, Adviser to the Overseas and Finance Department (1932–1935), Adviser to the Governors (1935–1953)
    Sydney Boys' High School, B.A., Modern History, New College, Oxford
11. Humphrey Charles Baskerville Mynors, Economics & Statistical Section (1933–1938), Deputy Secretary (1938–1939), Secretary (1939–1944), Adviser to the Governors (1944–1949), Director (1949–1954), Deputy Governor (1954–1964)
    Marlborough College, B.A., Economics, M.A., Corpus Christi College, Cambridge
12. Otto Ernst Niemeyer, Adviser to the Governors (1927–1938), Director (1938–1952)
    St Paul's School, B.A., Literae Humaniores, Balliol College, Oxford
13. John Arundel Caulfeild Osborne, Principal of the Chief Cashier's Office (1929–1931), Principal of the Statistical Section (1931–1934), Secretary (1934), Adviser to the Governors (1938–1945)
    Charterhouse School
14. William Brian Reddaway, Economic and Statistics Section (1934–1936)
    Oundle School, B.A., Economics, King's College, Cambridge
15. Francis James Rennell Rodd, Adviser to the Governors (1929–1932)
    Eton College, Balliol College, Oxford

(*continued*)

[135] See the appendix for additional biographical details.

TABLE 1.3 (*continued*)

16. James Bertram Selwyn, Economics & Statistics Section (1933–1959), Deputy Chief of the Central Banking Information Department (1959–1964), Deputy Chief of the Economic Intelligence Department (1964–1965), Adviser to the Governors (1965–1971)
    B.Sc., Economics, London School of Economics
17. Harry Arthur Siepmann, Adviser to the Governors (1926–1945), Chief of the Overseas and Foreign Department (1932–1935), Executive Director (1945–1954)
    Rugby School, B.A., Literae Humaniores, New College, Oxford
18. Oliver Mitchell Wentworth Sprague, Adviser to the Governors (1930–1933)
    St. Johnsbury Academy, A.B., Political Science, Harvard College, A.M. and Ph.D., Economics, Harvard University
19. Josiah Charles Stamp, Director (1928–1941)
    Bethany House School, B.Sc. in Economics, University of London, D.Sc. in Economics, London School of Economics
20. Walter Winne Stewart, Adviser to the Governors (1927–1930)
    A.B., Economics, University of Missouri
21. Henry Strakosch, unofficial adviser
    Wasagymnasium
22. Lucius Perronet Thompson-McCausland, Assistant Adviser (1941–1949), Adviser to the Governors (1949–1965)
    Repton School, B.A., Literae Humaniores, King's College, Cambridge

Many directors, to be sure, continued to regard experts with great apprehension, even well into the 1930s. One director, Lionel Hanbury, claimed that "the Public, or at least the City Public, much prefer to have City Merchants or Business men of experience rather than expert Financiers or Theoretical Economists."[136] Still, others understood how technical advisers working behind the scenes, and not with a public-facing role, could be used to their advantage. Addis acknowledged that experts were "apt to be biased by an exaggerated view," but he also recognized "the value of expert opinion … for the general policy of the Bank." As he continued, "[t]he real value of expert testimony lies in its highly specialised character. The strength of the Expert may be said to lie in his limitations, in his narrowness of outlook, his capacity to concentrate on details, and his aloofness … . He is at best, in fact, when his mind is applied to analytical and not to synthetic uses."[137]

The official title for the Bank's experts ("Adviser to the Governors of the Bank of England") implied that outsiders would not be considered directors or members of staff. Instead, they were tasked with supporting the Governor, the Deputy Governor, and the Committee of Treasury in an consultative capacity.

[136] "Replies to Questionnaire by Colonel Lionel H. Hanbury, C.M.G.," July 20, 1931, BoE G15/204. Also quoted in Kynaston, *Till Time's Last Sand*, 355.

[137] C.S. Addis, Note, February 17, 1932, BoE G15/204.

As a fundamentally new concept, the "Adviser" was a "non-committal title" that did not fit neatly into the Bank's normal hierarchy of positions and, as a result, permitted appointments to be easily made.[138] In one note, an expert frustratingly described how "[t]he ordinary work of the Bank offers no scope for an Economic Adviser. It is in the hands of experienced officials who take their decisions on the facts of each case in the light of their experience and have no time to discuss theoretical questions with advisers."[139] Nevertheless, the position was itself an unprecedented change in hiring practices at the Bank, an orthodox institution that had long resisted change in response to past crises. The nature of the new position might have been ill-defined, but the uncharted territory that the City had entered in the interwar years had compelled the Old Guard to consider reforms without past precedents. Offering temporary appointments to outsiders would allow the Bank to experiment with expertise without fully committing to the sudden demands of radical opinions.

Further explaining this transformation requires understanding the perceived necessity of economic expertise. Politicians were generally interested in economic reform for electoral reasons, but they unable to debate its technicalities; economists were keen to develop models for shaping public policy, yet they rarely had the institutional channels to implement such changes; and bankers largely (though not always) opposed change, particularly when it seemed to threaten their own work. The result was a situation in which experts could fill both a theoretical and an occupational gap. Governor Norman, along with the Bank's other directors, constructed *ex nihilo* a cohort of experts who would aid in their endeavors.[140] As one economist retroactively described,

> Before the War the Bank had relied for its overseas information on the members of the Court of Directors, three out of four of whom would usually be Merchant Bankers with extensive overseas connections; Mr. Norman himself was an example of this type. Something more systematic and continuous was now needed, and Mr. Norman met the need in two ways. He created a new class of bank official[s], Advisers, expert[s] in the affairs and conditions of overseas countries, who were usually brought in from outside the regular staff and worked in close contact with the Governors; ... At the same time the internal Bank organisation was being changed to bear the greatly increased – and

[138] Clay, *Lord Norman*, 301.

[139] Henry Clay, Note, January 23, 1935, NCO Clay Papers 59/3/28.

[140] Those who have mentioned Governor Norman's reliance on his advisers, often in passing include: R.J. Truptil, *British Banks and the London Money Market* (London: Jonathan Cape, 1936), 41; Giuseppi, *The Bank of England*, 167; Sayers, *The Bank of England, vol. 1*, 200–201; Sayers, *The Bank of England, vol. 2*, 417–418, 620–622; Hennessy, "The Governors, Directors and Management of the Bank of England," 196; Kynaston, *The City of London, vol. 3*, 169, 382; Wood, *A History of Central Banking*, 281; Capie, *The Bank of England*, 37; Kynaston, *Till Time's Last Sand*, 305.

increasing – burden put upon the Bank by the novel difficulties of post-war finance. … A class of Executive Directors, drawn from inside and outside the Bank, was created.[141]

Made possible by the evolution of the economics discipline and the professionalization of the civil service, the Bank's own dependence on experts was fundamentally a product of interwar circumstances. From industrial stagnation and exchange-rate volatility, few domestic economic issues lay outside their purview.

Experts were granted a great deal of autonomy in unprecedented ways. With relative flexibility in their day-to-day affairs, they spent their time attending conferences, consulting foreign governments, and writing reports. Precisely because of their knowledge of technical topics, ranging from the gold standard to exchange control, they were able to determine the future of economic policy. One may consider, for instance, their work in reforming South African finance in the 1920s. Although Norman provided the general endorsement for "the establishment of a Central bank" on "right and only sound" lines, the exact configurations of a reform program – the right to hold the nation's gold reserves, the exchange-rate policy of the South African rand, and the regulation of the private sector – were determined by Strakosch.[142] Following his assessment of the national banking system, he was able to convince bankers and government officials to adopt his recommendations.[143]

In these instances, expertise was a relative term, contingent upon time and place. To be an expert, an individual had to have acquired knowledge or skills from other institutions. Addis, for instance, might have acted as a foreign adviser to the German central bank (the Reichsbank). Yet while he may have been an expert for his work on German monetary reform, he was not considered one at the Bank because his background largely resembled those of the prewar Old Guard. He was the London-based manager of the Hongkong and Shanghai Banking Corporation (HSBC), a position closely tied to the City establishment. A similar argument could be applied to Lord Revelstoke, a partner at Barings Bank. Although he was the British representative at several conferences abroad, notably in the Committee of Experts assigned to renegotiate German reparation payments in Paris, he, too, was not recognized as an outside expert at the Bank because of his familial ties. In this regard, an expert needed to be someone who had a different type of background.

Because of their ability to apply their skills to existing concerns, experts ultimately became the main intellectual voices at the Bank. They provided perspectives on issues that were exceedingly complex to an audience of bankers, who admitted their lack of specialized knowledge, if only in private. Governor

[141] Henry Clay, "Lord Norman: An Appreciation," March 1950, IAS Director's Office Box 22.
[142] Norman to Smuts, February 4, 1921, BoE OV50/1.
[143] Henry Strakosch, "The Principles of Central Banking," May 21, 1921, BoE OV50/1.

Norman admitted that it would have been "impossible" for many of the Bank's officials "to be familiar with the technical questions or with all the business that is going on."[144] Procuring scientific advice soon became necessary for important decisions, such as changes in the interest rate or the implementation of exchange control, which could be translated into simpler terms. There was a growing desire among the Bank's directors to be well versed in such debates, particularly as they confronted criticism from government officials and economists in public and private fora. As several of them reported, "it would be hopeless and almost ridiculous" if the Governor were not "competent to deal with experts in finance as is the practice in other Central Banks."[145]

It may have been an open secret that those at the Bank were able to manage the London money market but did not possess the theoretical knowledge of its overall functioning. When Prime Minister Lloyd George asked Governor Cunliffe how his accepting house (Cunliffe Brothers) determined which bills of exchange to purchase on the London money market, he simply responded, "I smell them."[146] Even the Bank's own officials understood the ironies present. According to Edward Grenfell, a Bank director and partner of Morgan, Grenfell & Co., Cunliffe may have "had an intimate knowledge of banking, bill broking, stock Ex., [and] accepting," although he "had no gift of public speaking" and was certainly "not the greatest expert in all [areas of finance]."[147]

In contrast, experts were able to address many of the pressing concerns involving the City's precarious position through an analysis of economic conditions and trends. Their presence at the Bank created a distinctly new institution from the days of Bagehot, who had once remarked that the administration "is composed of men with a high average of general good sense, with an excellent knowledge of business in general, but without any special knowledge of the particular business in which they are engaged."[148] The wide range of tasks given to advisers might have baffled even the sharpest minds. In one exchange, Keynes probed Deputy Governor Ernest Harvey on the purpose of advisers at the Bank:

KEYNES: The organisation which you have described to us of the Comptroller and Advisers, a sort of higher Civil Service inside the Bank, is a very new thing?

HARVEY: It is. It is a matter of a few years and is still in course of development.

144 Quoted in Joan Bridges, "New Men for a New Age," November 30, 1973, BoE ADM33/13.

145 "A Meeting of the Directors at the Bank on Monday, the 21st May, 1928," BA Revelstoke Papers 203251.

146 Lloyd George, *War Memoirs, vol. 1*, 101. Quoted in Kynaston, *The City of London, vol. 2*, 280; Roberts, *Saving the City*, 55; Kynaston, *Till Time's Last Sand*, 267.

147 Quoted in Kynaston, *The City of London, vol. 3*, 8; Horn, *Britain, France, and the Financing of the First World War*, 35; Roberts, *Saving the City*, 55; Kynaston, *Till Time's Last Sand*, 268.

148 Bagehot, *Lombard Street*, 215.

KEYNES: It is a very important development of the Bank since the War. They have been gradually developing and evolving what you might call a higher Civil Service, which previous to that scarcely existed in the Bank?

HARVEY: There was formerly no need for it. What has brought the need into existence was the intimate relations which we were in the course of establishing with foreign Central Banks, the need of paying frequent visits to them and receiving visits from them.

KEYNES: But I think the duties of the advisers are not limited to foreign affairs, are they?

HARVEY: Primarily foreign affairs, but not entirely; they are also engaged in the matter of statistics and so on, the application of statistics, advising on questions connected with rationalisation of industry and so on. ... After a time we realised that it was necessary to develop this practice much more fully if we were to make a success of it, and we took into the Bank of England ... several people of what he [Keynes] described as of the standing of the Higher Civil Service, who were able men, had knowledge of finance, and in some cases a knowledge, theoretical or practical, of central banking, and who, above all things, had a knowledge of languages. ... That is what we have been aiming at for some time, and, I think, with considerable success.[149]

The conversation indicated the degree to which the employment of technical advisers had been unusual and unprecedented. Experts, in this regard, were defined by what they were not, namely members of an establishment too entrenched in the institution to conceptualize alternative policies. Rather, each adviser could offer specialized insights for the Bank to address different areas of interest. "Such a man," one Bank official reported, "would have a knowledge and experience of the Market which must almost of necessity be lacking in the man who has spent his life in Central Banking."[150]

From a practical standpoint, experts allowed for more efficient and direct communication. They acted as the Governor's eyes and ears on matters of domestic policy, imperial affairs, and foreign relations. This function was particularly useful for Norman, whose time and energy had become increasingly strained. Experts often communicated with business associations, chambers of commerce, and foreign central banks on the Governor's behalf. Such was the case with the Bank's industrial adviser, who understood the technicalities of rationalization.[151] In turn, this method of employment benefited the Bank as it tried to confront multiple problems at once. During the 1931 crisis, the Bank's advisers were simultaneously sent to meet with representatives of the

149 "The Right Hon. Ernest Musgrave Harvey, K.B.E., Deputy Governor of the Bank of England," November 28, 1929, in Macmillan Committee, *Minutes of Evidence Taken before the Committee on Finance and Industry, vol. 1* (London: H.M. Stationery Office, 1931), 10, 34.

150 Special Committee on Organisation, "Questionnaire & Evidence," June 4, 1931, BoE G15/204.

151 "London Chamber of Commerce, Memorandum," November 30, 1931, BoE EID4/102; Lancashire Industrial Development Council to Clay, January 24, 1934, BoE ADM22/27.

London clearing banks via a special committee, to advise the German government on fiscal reform, and to negotiate with officials at the Banque de France on the prospect of a loan.[152] These activities demonstrated the expanded scope of the central bank's work beyond its traditional responsibilities related to public finance and, after the 1844 Bank Charter Act, the issuance of notes.[153] Adopting more interests in industrial policy and foreign relations in the interwar years, the Bank effectively redistributed his workload and diffused power throughout its own institutional apparatus.

The ensuing Age of Expertise instigated a fundamental restructuring of the global order, now reliant on technical advice. In the war's aftermath, a new form of governance proliferated due to a convergence of an array of political and economic forces: the rise of interwar internationalism after Versailles; the onset of the postwar recession, later followed by the Great Depression; the stagnation of British industry, once the dominant "workshop of the world"; and the threats to British imperial hegemony. At a time when many questioned the City's position in the international financial system, beset as much by volatility within the banking sector as geopolitical threats to the interwar liberal order, experts offered solutions to the multitude of problems at hand. With the arrival of advisers into the upper echelons of the Bank's hierarchy, the Old Guard had created its own dependence on economic expertise.

[152] Clément Moret [Banque de France] to Norman, January 29, 1931, BoE OV45/82; "Nr. 420: Ministerbesprechung vom 30. Juli 1931," in *Akten der Reichskanzlei. Die Kabinette Brüning I u. II, Band 2. 30. März 1930 bis 10. Oktober 1931; 10. Oktober 1931 bis 1. Juni 1932*, ed. Tilman Koops (Boppard am Rhein: Harald Boldt Verlag, 1982), 1462–1466; Committee of Treasury, Minutes, August 22, 1931, BoE G8/60; "Meeting of Clearing Bankers at the Bank of England," September 18, 1931, BoE C43/98.

[153] Bank Charter Act 1844, 7 & 8 Vict. c. 32.

2

Henry Strakosch and Reconstruction

> Any law for the establishment of a Central Bank should ... lay down the fundamental conditions which experience has proven to be essential for the successful functioning of a Central Bank, as the banker of the banks and as the guardian of the country's credit.[1]
>
> —Henry Strakosch, 1921

> A man fell into the Danube and got caught in a whirlpool. He soon began to swallow water and screamed for help with all his might. Many people came and saw the struggle for his life. But the drowning man was unable to help himself. Then someone called out to him from the safety of the shore: "Yes, if you cannot help yourself, then you cannot expect us to help you either." That man's name was Strakosch.[2]
>
> —Viennese newspaper, 1922

Reconstruction was a process that took many forms. As the First World War had disrupted networks of trade and finance, the nations of Europe sought to refashion the global economic order along more stable lines. They turned to a multitude of reforms that could reestablish the supposed benefits of a bygone era. For many contemporaries, this restoration would only come from a strict adherence to economic orthodoxy, exemplified by balanced budgets, free trade, and the classical gold standard. Yet more than a policy of simple financial reform, reconstruction involved contentious political disputes over national sovereignty, and it raised additional questions over international law and statehood. The reordering of the international system ultimately required finding solutions compatible with the political objectives of Europe's nations, both old and new.

[1] Henry Strakosch, "The South African Reserve Bank," *The Economic Journal* 31, no. 122 (June 1921), 173.

[2] "Einfälle, so nebenbei," *Deutschösterreichische Tages-Zeitung (Vienna)* 32, no. 242, September 3, 1922, 4.

Determined neither by politicians nor by bankers alone, reconstruction was, as this chapter argues, a product of expert engagement. Those with technical experience – often acquired from universities, ministries of finance, the League of Nations, or private banks – exerted considerable influence in debates over reform. Impartiality was the supposed ideal, as each technical adviser was expected "not [to act] as a representative of his Government," but simply "as an expert."[3] The notion of an expert implied an outsider who had not only extensive knowledge over a particular subject or country, but also the ability to make technical recommendations without overt political biases, even when they secretly existed.

Through their interventions, experts played an integral role in the construction of the interwar economic order.[4] Central to this effort were initiatives undertaken by the Bank of England, an institution with a vested interest in promoting economic recovery and defending the City of London's position as the international financial center.[5] Its reconstruction projects were led by an unofficial adviser, Sir Henry Strakosch (Figure 2.1). He led rehabilitation efforts throughout Central Europe (Austria and Hungary) and the British Empire (South Africa and India), in addition to smaller engagements in Bulgaria, Czechoslovakia, Greece, and Romania. Using his connections, the central bank was able to shape the prospect and define the limits of reconstruction abroad.

Strakosch was privy to discussions on monetary reform and often had the ear of those in power. According to one League official, his presence in reconstruction debates was "absolutely indispensable from every point of

[3] Provisional Economic and Financial Committee, Finance Section, "Ninth Session. Nineteenth Meeting Held on Friday, September 29, 1922, at 9 a.m.," LoN C36/36/6/5a.

[4] On European reconstruction in the 1920s, see Denise Artaud, *La reconstruction de l'Europe (1919–1929)* (Paris: Presses universitaires de France, 1973); Stephen V.O. Clarke, "The Reconstruction of the International Monetary System: The Attempts of 1922 and 1933," *Princeton Studies in International Finance*, no. 33 (1973); Anne Orde, *British Policy and European Reconstruction after the First World War* (Cambridge: Cambridge University Press, 1990); Steiner, *The Lights that Failed*, 278–284; Dragan Bakić, "Diplomacy and Loans: The Foreign Office, Economic Reconstruction, and Security in South-Eastern Europe in the 1920s," *The International History Review* 34, no. 4 (2012): 631–653; Nathan Marcus, "Les conseillers étrangers à la Banque nationale d'Autriche 1923–1929 : contrôle ou coopération ?," *Histoire, économie & société* 35, no. 4 (2016): 8–20; Christophe Farquet, "'Le comité financier ne pense et ne travaille que pour le bien de l'Autriche.' Théories et pratiques budgétaires du comité financier de la Société des Nations lors de la stabilisation monétaire autrichienne des années 1920," in *Les crises de la dette publique : XVIIIe–XXIe siècle*, ed. Gérard Béaur and Laure Quennouëlle-Corre (Paris: Comité pour l'histoire économique et financière de la France, 2019): 345–364.

[5] Sayers, *The Bank of England, vol. 1*, 111; Robert Boyce, "Government–City of London Relations under the Gold Standard 1925–1931," in *The British Government and the City of London in the Twentieth Century*, ed. Ranald Michie and Philip Williamson (Cambridge: Cambridge University Press, 2004), 215–216; Ranald Michie, "The City of London and the British Government: The Changing Relationship," in *The British Government and the City of London in the Twentieth Century*, ed. Ranald Michie and Philip Williamson (Cambridge: Cambridge University Press, 2004), 36.

FIGURE 2.1 Sir Henry Strakosch, 1924
Source: Sir Henry Strakosch du comité financier de la Ligue des nations, Photographies de l'Agence Rol, 92806.

view."[6] While not officially employed at the Bank, he shared its orthodox views and conveyed such interests in international fora throughout the early 1920s. As Governor Montagu Norman himself admitted,

> I rely for information from the outside about such a subject as this not, as you might suppose, on McKenna or Keynes, but on Sir Henry Strakosch ... . Austrian origin: many years in Johannesburg: 20 years in this country: a student of economics: a gold producer with general financial interests: perhaps the main stay in setting up the South African Reserve Bank: a member of the Financial Committee of the League and of the Indian Currency Commission: full of public spirit, genial and helpful.[7]

[6] Arthur Salter to Strakosch, February 22, 1924, LoN R298/10/33627/2920.

[7] Norman to Strong, November 28, 1927, BoE ADM33/13 and FRBNY Strong Papers 1116.7, Part 2. Also quoted in Robert W.D. Boyce, *British Capitalism at the Crossroads, 1919–1932: A Study in Politics, Economics, and International Relations* (Cambridge: Cambridge University Press, 1987), 160; Philip L. Cottrell, "Norman, Strakosch and the Development of Central Banking: From Conception to Practice, 1919–1924," in *Rebuilding the Financial System in Central and Eastern Europe, 1918–1994*, ed. Philip L. Cottrell (Aldershot: Ashgate, 1997), 30; Boyce, *The Great Interwar Crisis*, 216.

Strakosch was, indeed, connected to a multitude of professional spheres, both public and private. Born to an Austrian-Jewish family in Hohenau, he had experience in the financial sector (the Anglo-Austrian Bank) and the mining industry (the Union Corporation). Becoming a naturalized British citizen in June 1907, he formed one part of a growing network of financial experts. Strakosch financially supported Churchill throughout his many bankruptcies. Upon his death in 1943, he bequeathed £20,000 to the prime minister "as a token of friendship and gratitude," and his entire estate was valued at nearly £2.5 million.[8]

His wealth seemed to match only his extensive experience. Strakosch had established a reputation from his work at a wide range of institutions: as managing director of the Union Corporation, as a member of the Advisory Committee of the South African government, as chairman of the Financial Committee, as chairman of *The Economist*, as an adviser to the Secretary of State for India, and as the Bank's de facto expert.[9] Although "[n]ot allowed to desert Union Corp," likely due to the earnings generated for him, Strakosch informally advised the Bank and the League throughout the 1920s.[10] He remained a valued expert for orthodox institutions until the publication of an interim report in 1930 on the abandonment of the gold standard.[11]

Furthermore, Strakosch was not appointed a director at the Bank, nor had he ever been formally employed there in any capacity. At the Bank, there

[8] "Sir Henry Strakosch," in *The Annual Register: A Review of Public Events at Home and Abroad for the Year 1943*, ed. M. Epstein (London: Longmans, Green & Co., 1944), 441. See also Cannadine, *The Decline and Fall of the British Aristocracy*, 339; Cannadine, *Aspects of Aristocracy*, 146; Roy Jenkins, *Churchill: A Biography* (New York: Farrar, Straus and Giroux, 2001), 517–518; David Lough, *No More Champagne: Churchill and His Money* (London: Head of Zeus, 2015), 262–265. His posthumous bequests included £20,000 to Churchill, £10,000 to Smuts, and £20,000 to the Union Corporation; Joan Bridges, "Strakosch, Sir Henry," May 26, 1972, BoE ADM33/13.

[9] On Strakosch, see Sayers, *The Bank of England, vol. 1*, 202–204; Cottrell, "Norman, Strakosch and the Development of Central Banking," 58–62; Frank Beyersdorf, "'Credit or Chaos'? The Austrian Stabilisation Programme of 1923 and the League of Nations," in *Internationalism Reconfigured: Transnational Ideas and Movements between the World Wars*, ed. Daniel Laqua (London: I.B. Tauris, 2011), 135–158; Bradley Bordiss and Vishnu Padayachee, "'A Superior Practical Man': Sir Henry Strakosch, the Gold Standard and Monetary Policy Debates in South Africa, 1920–23," *Economic History of Developing Regions* 26, no. 1 (2011), 118–121; Zoltán Peterecz, "Hungary and the League of Nations," in *Remaking Central Europe: The League of Nations and the Former Habsburg Lands*, ed. Peter Becker and Natasha Wheatley (Oxford: Oxford University Press, 2020), 156; Ian Kumekawa, "Imperial Schemes: Empire and the Rise of the British Business-State, 1914–1939" (PhD diss., Harvard University, 2020), 191–197.

[10] Quoted in Montagu Norman, Diary, October 2, 1925, BoE ADM34/14.

[11] Patricia Clavin and Jens-Wilhelm Wessels, "Another Golden Idol? The League of Nations' Gold Delegation and the Great Depression, 1929–1932," *The International History Review* 26, no. 4 (2004), 785, 790–792; Clavin, *Securing the World Economy*, 54, 61–62; Boyce, *The Great Interwar Crisis*, 215–216.

had been no Jewish directors since the abrupt resignation of Alfred Charles de Rothschild over a controversial art deal in 1889. When the Committee of Treasury briefly considered Strakosch for a directorship in 1928, it was Sir Charles Addis who opposed the appointment, writing in his diary that "His name is against him."[12] No record of a discussion on Strakosch was subsequently recorded in the meeting minutes. His Jewish background alienated Addis and the Bank's other directors, with anti-Semitism proliferating throughout the British financial establishment. Even Governor Norman, while in support of Strakosch's candidacy for the directorship (but happened to be absent on the day of the meeting), harbored anti-Semitic views.[13]

Although Strakosch's position remained that of an unofficial adviser, he and other financial experts were able to influence policy by working outside the realm of electoral politics. They espoused a vision of economic orthodoxy based on deregulated markets (the self-correcting mechanisms of the gold standard), classical liberalism (free trade), and apolitical solutions (an independent central bank). Reconstruction thus aligned with the principles of interwar internationalism, a movement that reimagined and restructured the global order, most notably through the League's apparatus.[14] While experts highlighted the "neutral" aspects of monetary and fiscal reform, their interventions were always political and contributed to the state-building process of the interwar years. To establish their authority, states were willing to cede some national sovereignty and draw on expert knowledge for the legitimacy it conferred. Far from being a characteristic of weak states, the dependence on expertise can be explained by both the practical economic needs of reconstruction and the political legitimacy needed for forging a nation-state.[15] In other words, expert opinion legitimized national sovereignty in accordance with the new rules of market capitalism.

FROM PARIS TO BRUSSELS

When the Paris Peace Conference convened in 1919, the Allies envisioned rebuilding a continent devastated by war. Although the delegations might have shared a collective victory, each was beholden to its own national interests, fervently defended by its respective leaders. The Big Four – Georges Clemenceau (France), David Lloyd George (United Kingdom), Vittorio

[12] Charles Addis, Diary, February 22, 1928, SOAS Addis Papers Box 5. Also quoted in Kynaston, *The City of London, vol. 3*, 169.

[13] Norman to Strong, November 28, 1927, BoE ADM33/13 and FRBNY Strong Papers 1116.7, Part 2. On Norman's anti-Semitism, see Kynaston, *The City of London, vol. 3*, 337.

[14] See, for instance, Nicole Piétri, *La Société des Nations et la reconstruction financière de l'Autriche, 1921–1926* (Geneva: Centre européen de la Dotation Carnegie pour la paix internationale, 1970); Decorzant, *La Société des nations*; Clavin, *Securing the World Economy*; Martin, *The Meddlers*.

[15] Feiertag, "Le signe des temps," 278.

Emanuele Orlando (Italy), and Woodrow Wilson (United States) – had different priorities and an even more distinct collection of personalities.[16] Added to the individual tensions were the broader geopolitical ones that pervaded ongoing discussions. The collapse of four major empires; the devastating toll on civilian populations; and the disruption to global trade, finance, and migration all threatened to undermine any long-term prospect of peace.

Central bankers closely followed the events in Paris. Despite the lack of direct representation, they were concerned with the implications of the conference for global finance. Such questions primarily revolved around war debts and reparations, but the British delegation also emphasized resolving the more structural issues facing the European economy: "By far the greatest difficulty is the financial one. The problem is unparalleled. Europe is without working capital. Who is to provide her with it?"[17] The Bank was particularly interested in the outcome of this discussion. A month before the conference commenced, Norman wrote to Benjamin Strong, the Governor of the Federal Reserve Bank of New York, that "a cloud of uncertain bulk is hovering in the shape of the Peace Conference."[18] He, in part, suspected that the conference would not be able to address the pressing economic situation unique to Britain. As he continued,

> Our business has been much more disorganised by the War than yours and will therefore come round more slowly; our floating and unfunded debt is large and may be difficult to handle; our need of raw materials is great and immediate; our foreign debtors (as a whole) are good only in the long run, if at all; our debts abroad are large and do not tend to ease the exchange position … . But whatever is to be the outcome, you are abundantly right in saying that the conditions which are soon to govern the world depend very much on the conditions which exist between our two countries. If it is to be economic peace, we … can go a long way towards completing it and making it real.[19]

The Bank had offered only a theoretical proposal for collaboration, rather than a well-defined plan of action. Yet by the 1920s, it began to use its resources and influence to lead the so-called "Norman conquest" of Central Europe.[20] To some extent, the City's interests had already aligned with those of European

[16] Macmillan, *Paris 1919*, 26–43.

[17] "Financial Situation," April 5, 1919, BLO Brand Papers 18. Also quoted from the published version in Jennifer Siegel, "Planning for International Financial Order: The Call for Collective Responsibility at the Paris Peace Conference," in *Peacemaking and International Order after the First World War*, ed. Peter Jackson, William Mulligan, and Glenda Sluga (Cambridge: Cambridge University Press, 2023), 250.

[18] Norman to Strong, December 11, 1918, FRBNY 1116.1, Part 2.

[19] Norman to Strong, December 11, 1918, FRBNY 1116.1, Part 2.

[20] Theodore Gregory, "The 'Norman Conquest' Reconsidered," *Lloyds Bank Review*, no. 46 (1957), 6, 12–13; Gábor Bátonyi, *Britain and Central Europe, 1918–1933* (Oxford: Clarendon Press, 1999), 49; Steiner, *The Lights that Failed*, 281; Barbara Susan Warnock, "The First Bailout: The Financial Reconstruction of Austria 1922–1926," (PhD diss., Birkbeck College, University of London, 2015), 62.

officials, both keen on addressing the threat of inflation. The dual burden of high debts and unstable exchange rates seemed to necessitate monetary reform. As one group of experts at the conference reported, "[t]he currency question is of great importance. The first necessity for the normal resumption of internal and external trade is a sound currency and a sound system of government finance."[21]

If Paris laid the political foundations of the interwar order, Brussels determined its economic arrangements. In September and October 1920, the International Financial Conference convened in the Belgian capital to resolve the systemic problems of inflation and unstable exchange rates.[22] Under the auspices of the League, the conference included delegates from thirty-nine countries, including Strakosch as one of the representatives of South Africa. He had already gained a reputation as a financial expert with his defense of the gold standard. "The functions of gold," he had written in November 1918, "are primarily to form the solid and immediately available backing of our currency and credit."[23] Strakosch reiterated these views while serving on the Sub-Committee of the Committee on Currency and Exchanges, which concluded in its final report that "[i]t is of the utmost importance that the growth of inflation should be stopped."[24] For many countries, including the United Kingdom, wartime spending, rising wages, and excess bank credits had engendered a period of postwar inflation in 1919. Thus, Strakosch claimed that only the "sound methods" of fixed exchange rates could restore confidence in the global economy.[25]

What emerged from the conference was a defined plan for reconstruction based on the "Brussels consensus" of balanced budgets, fixed exchange rates, and independent central banking.[26] The unanimous decision reached by the Commission on Public Finance, for instance, centered on sweeping financial changes: the reduction in military expenditures, the servicing of wartime debts, and the defense of sound finance.[27] Strakosch echoed many of these views, further convinced that the surest means of curbing inflation was to curb uncontrolled

21 Robert Brand, Alexander Legge, Joseph Avenol, and Bernardo Attolico, "Memorandum," May 12, 1919, BLO Brand Papers 18.

22 Sayers, *The Bank of England, vol. 1*, 153–154; Charles P. Kindleberger, *The World in Depression, 1929–1939*, 2nd ed. (Berkeley: University of California Press, 1986), 46–47; Fior, *Institution globale et marchés financiers*, 126–134; Decorzant, *La Société des nations*, 233–290.

23 Henry Strakosch, *The Value of Gold in Our Economic System* (London: Crowther & Goodman, 1918), 5. Reprinted in *The Mining Magazine* 19, no. 5 (November 1918): 251–253.

24 Committee on Currency and Exchange, "Report," n.d., LoN R502/10A/392/392.

25 League of Nations, *International Financial Conference, vol. 2: Verbatim Record of the Debates* (Brussels: League of Nations, 1920), 79.

26 Fior, *Institution globale et marchés financiers*, 245.

27 "Resolutions Proposed by the Commission on Public Finance and Adopted Unanimously by the Conference," in League of Nations, *International Financial Conference, vol. 1: Report of the Conference* (Brussels: League of Nations, 1920), 14–15; League of Nations, *International Financial Conference, vol. 2*, 139–144.

government spending.[28] Fiscal austerity, he surmised, could work alongside other strategies to restore the supposed stability found in prewar Europe.

Yet a general alignment in ideological views meant little if countries were unable or unwilling to abide by the views of experts. Given the global shortage of gold, a return to a system of fixed exchange rates through a modified gold standard became the new priority. Under these arrangements, countries were permitted to hold either gold or gold-backed currencies (such as sterling). They could then ensure the proper functioning of the system if they adhered to the "rules of the game": those that ran a trade deficit would have to export gold, which required them to raise interest rates and lower their money supply. However, it would have been difficult to enforce these rules if independent central banks chose to hoard gold reserves. Recognizing this issue, Strakosch portended difficulties due to the proliferation of gold-hoarding practices, coupled with the gradual decline in gold production, averaging £5.5 million per year over the past five years.[29]

Among the many possible avenues for immediate change – from the reduction of inter-Allied and German reparation payments to the resolution of territorial disputes – the reform of central banking emerged as one of the mutually acceptable policies at the conference.[30] In countries where there was "no central bank of issue," the final report asserted, "one should be established."[31] Monetary authorities could have corrected the trade imbalances of countries with undervalued exchange rates.[32] Moreover, the gold standard, by its nature, forced countries to restrict their spending. Because a currency had to be backed by gold, a central bank was only permitted to issue currency up to the volume of gold reserves in its possession. To address the inflationary patterns arising from wartime spending and postwar debts, the delegates envisioned a restoration of the prewar financial order along such orthodox lines.

Strakosch therefore advocated the adoption of an international monetary standard: "Gold, as the standard of value and as the foundation of the currency and credit organizations of the civilised world, has proved so efficient that it cannot well be supposed that it will be abandoned in the future."[33] While at the Brussels Conference, he found himself representing the interests of a financial establishment (the City) and of a sovereign country (South Africa). Rather than exposing his conflict of interest, he instead used both positions to bolster his credibility. His network in London provided him with direct

[28] Sub-Committee of the Committee on Currency and Exchange, "First Meeting: Progress Report," October 1, 1920, LoN R502/10A/393/392.

[29] "Europe's Financial Ills," *The Times* 42529, September 30, 1920, 9.

[30] Fior, *Institution globale et marchés financiers*, 321–325.

[31] Conférence financière internationale, *Rapport de la conférence* (Brussels: League of Nations, 1920), 13.

[32] Hawtrey, "La situation monétaire européenne," 214.

[33] Henry Strakosch, "The Future of Gold as a Standard of Value," *The Economic World* XX, no. 23, December 18, 1920, 874, League of Nations, *International Financial Conference, vol.* 2, 76.

connections to those in political positions of influence, and his reputation was further enhanced by South Africa's brief and coincidental postwar economic recovery. Due to his contributions, Strakosch was appointed a Knight Bachelor, as part of the 1921 New Year Honours. His influence earned him an invitation to serve as the first chairman of the League's Financial Committee.[34]

AUSTRIA IN CRISIS

One of the Bank's first interwar forays into economic diplomacy was in Austria. After the war had dissolved the Austro-Hungarian Empire, the disruption of existing trade networks and the collapse of an internal market plagued the economies of its successor states. The Republic of Austria, itself ravaged by the First World War and beset with a war debt of nearly 65 billion Austrian kronen (crowns), had projected an additional deficit of more than 12.5 billion kronen in 1920–1921.[35] Under the terms of Article 206 of the Treaty of Saint-Germain (1919), the Allies mandated the dissolution of its central bank (the Austro-Hungarian Bank) without provisions for establishing a new one. Economic dislocations also engendered a humanitarian crisis. With the borders redrawn, the Austrian successor state now produced less than one-third of its prewar food supplies domestically and was too indebted to pay for additional imports.[36]

Many officials recognized the urgency of Austrian reconstruction. As Sir William Goode, the British representative on the Austrian Section of the Reparation Commission, wrote, "it is impossible for Austria to continue to exist without external assistance."[37] Restoring Austria's position as a commercial center was vital for social stability not only in Central Europe but also in Southeastern Europe, where Vienna-based banks had once facilitated trade and commerce.[38] These factors had largely determined Allied strategic interests in the region.[39] Still, political unwillingness hampered Western European

[34] Paul Hymans [League of Nations] to Strakosch, October 28, 1920, LoN S136/86/8/2/11; Strakosch to the Secretariat General [League of Nations], November 8, 1920, LoN S136/86/8/2/11.

[35] Richard Reisch, "Austria: Financial Situation," in League of Nations, *International Financial Conference, vol. 3: Proceedings of the Conference* (Brussels: League of Nations, 1920), 69.

[36] Arthur Salter, "The Reconstruction of Austria," *Foreign Affairs* 2, no. 4 (1924), 631; Clavin, "The Austrian Hunger Crisis," 270.

[37] William Goode and A. Klobukowski, "Report by the Austrian Section of the Reparation Commission," November 1, 1920, TNA CAB 24/115/39.

[38] Boyce, *British Capitalism*, 39; Alice Teichova, "Banking and Industry in Central-East Europe in the First Decades of the 20th Century," in *Bank Austria Creditanstalt. 150 Jahre österreichische Bankengeschichte im Zentrum Europas*, ed. Oliver Rathkolb, Theodor Venus, and Ulrike Zimmerl (Vienna: Paul Zsolnay Verlag, 2005), 152–153.

[39] Alice Teichova and Penelope Ratcliffe, "British Interests in Danube Navigation after 1918," *Business History* 27, no. 3 (1985): 283–300; György Péteri, *Global Monetary Regime and*

involvement in the domestic affairs of a newly sovereign nation. The French Ministry of Finance claimed that French banks were likely unable to offer the credits needed, while the UK Foreign Office declined the Austrian request for British coal and trade credits.[40] Meanwhile, Chancellor of the Exchequer Austen Chamberlain might have once advocated the extension of foreign credits, but by November 1920, he instead noted, "the British Government cannot place further burdens on the British taxpayer for the benefit of Austria."[41] The government continued to affirm its own national priorities in the ensuing months. Following a discussion on the Austrian situation, the Cabinet concluded that it was important to "resist these constant appeals to assume external financial burdens."[42] Even if assistance in the form of a foreign loan might offer a temporary solution to Austria's plight, the ministers ultimately agreed that it would be impossible to give any support.[43]

As a result, reconstruction efforts were initially deferred to the League. Its Financial Committee was tasked with addressing debt, taxation, and monetary issues. As chairman, Strakosch acted as an unofficial spokesperson of the Bank in international negotiations. The Bank benefited from this arrangement, allowing it to avoid any potential backlash against its direct interference in political matters and distancing itself from the League's interventions if the policies failed.[44] In February, Strakosch met with the Austrian Minister to the Court of St. James's to discuss the challenges associated with acquiring £12 million in credits from British bankers.[45] Subsequently tasked with identifying an alternative plan for delivering credits to countries in need of credit, he circulated

National Central Banking: The Case of Hungary, 1921–1929, trans. Mario D. Fenyo (Boulder: Social Science Monographs, 2002), 38; Dragan Bakić, *Britain and Interwar Danubian Europe: Foreign Policy and Security Challenges, 1919–1936* (London: Bloomsbury, 2017), 12; Kumekawa, "Imperial Schemes," 159–166.

40 Orde, *British Policy and European Reconstruction*, 124; Philip L. Cottrell, "Austrian Reconstruction, 1920–1921: A Matter for Private Business or the League of Nations?," in *Business in the Age of Extremes: Essays in Modern German and Austrian Economic History*, ed. Hartmut Berghoff, Jürgen Kocka, and Dieter Ziegler (Cambridge: Cambridge University Press, 2013), 63.

41 "No. 5: Financial Sub-Committee. Notes of a Meeting held at the Treasury on Friday, February 13, 1920, at 5.30 p.m.," in *Documents on British Foreign Policy, 1919–1939, First Series, vol. 7*, ed. Rohan Butler and J.P.T. Bury (London: H.M. Stationery Office, 1958), 40–42; Austen Chamberlain, "Financial Position of Austria," November 23, 1920, in "C.P. 2139," TNA CAB24/115.

42 "Conclusions of a Conference of Ministers," November 25, 1920, TNA CAB23/38.

43 "Cabinet 72(20)," December 17, 1920, TNA CAB23/23.

44 Patricia Clavin, "Habit Not Heredity: Central Banks and Global Order," in *The Spread of the Modern Central Bank and Global Cooperation, 1919–1939*, ed. Barry Eichengreen and Andreas Kakridis (Cambridge: Cambridge University Press, 2023), 64–65.

45 Georg von und zu Franckenstein [Embassy of Austria in London] to Alfred Grünberger [Bundesministerium für Aeusseres], "Unterredung mit Sir Henry Strakosch dem Vorsitzenden des Finanzkomitees des Völkerbundrates," February 19, 1921, OeStA BKA-AA VR/41, ff. 48–49.

two notes concerning a scheme for helping procure foreign credits from other sources.[46] The first was a draft invitation for countries, such as Austria, to take part in a new scheme for accessing lines of credit that would allow them to pay for essential imports.[47] A second, more detailed outline provided assurance for creditors who subscribed to the loan program. Countries that took part in the lending scheme would have to pledge "specific assets" as collateral, the value for which was determined by their value in gold.[48]

These memoranda served as the basis for a long-term strategy of credit provisioning throughout Central and Eastern Europe. On March 2, 1921, the Financial Committee approved the ter Meulen plan, a co-written report by C.E. ter Meulen (a Dutch banker), Joseph Avenol (French Ministry of Finance), and Strakosch.[49] In line with Strakosch's earlier suggestions, the ter Meulen plan allowed countries to raise funds by issuing bonds backed by state collateral.[50] The initiative initially gained the support of politicians, in part because it did not commit them to an electorally unfavorable foreign-aid package. As Chamberlain opined, any "control of the finances of Austria would draw the Powers into the internal politics of Austria."[51] With the conclusion of a subsequent conference in London, the Allied Powers of Britain, France, Italy, and Japan agreed to postpone the repayment of Austrian war debts for an undetermined period of time.[52] This decision bought Austria and the League additional time to arrive at a less politically controversial decision regarding the provisions of a loan.

The prospect of foreign credits, however, was contingent on the Austrian government accepting some form of foreign intervention. In late March, the Financial Committee convened again, this time in Paris, to discuss the possible

46 Henry Strakosch, "Memorandum," n.d., LoN R348/10/12020/12019.

47 Henry Strakosch, "International Credits," n.d., LoN R348/10/12020/12019.

48 Henry Strakosch, "International Credits Scheme," n.d., LoN R348/10/12020/12019.

49 League of Nations, "Report of the Financial Committee to the Council," December 1921, LoN R333/10/20643/11519; Mouton, *La Société des Nations*, 480; Orde, *British Policy and European Reconstruction*, 106–107, 118; Cottrell, "Austrian Reconstruction," 62–67; Hans Kernbauer, "Central Bank Policy under Foreign Control: The Austrian National Bank in the 1920s," in *The Spread of the Modern Central Bank and Global Cooperation, 1919–1939*, ed. Barry Eichengreen and Andreas Kakridis (Cambridge: Cambridge University Press, 2023), 109.

50 Cottrell, "Austrian Reconstruction," 66–69; Nathan Marcus, *Austrian Reconstruction and the Collapse of Global Finance, 1921–1931* (Cambridge, MA, and London: Harvard University Press, 2018), 86–87; Martin, *The Meddlers*, 81.

51 "No. 62: British Secretary's Draft Notes of a Meeting of Financial Experts, held in the Board Room, Treasury, on Saturday, March 12, 1921, at 3 p.m.," in *Documents on British Foreign Policy, 1919–1939, First Series, vol. 15*, ed. Rohan Butler, J.P.T. Bury, and M.E. Lambert (London: H.M. Stationery Office, 1967), 421.

52 Austen Chamberlain, "Statement to the Austrian Ministers," March 17, 1921, in League of Nations, *Financial Reconstruction of Austria: Report of the Financial Committee of the Council* (London: Constable & Co., League of Nations, 1921), 11; "Déclaration faite aux Ministres d'Autriche par M. Austen Chamberlain au nom des Gouvernements Alliés," March 23, 1921, OeStA BKA-AA VR/41, ff. 11–13.

conditions of the loan. The attendance of such high-profile financial experts, including Avenol, ter Meulen, and Strakosch himself, generated much attention.[53] Following their deliberations, the committee recommended the creation of an independent central bank to replace the Austro-Hungarian Bank. As a concession, the committee was willing to consider reserving half of the central bank's board of directors for Austrian nationals.[54] The new entity could also obtain a monopoly of note issue and maintain convertibility of the currency into gold, thereby facilitating the distribution of foreign credits.[55]

At the Bank, Governor Norman recognized that the financial problems facing Austria presented a serious threat to international trade, leading him to suggest the provision of an even larger loan.[56] Yet Strakosch was convinced that the more direct means of stabilizing the currency was with an independent central bank, which would be established before the loan could be extended.[57] It was, he argued, unlikely that investors would subscribe to a foreign loan without certain guarantees imposed on public spending. In response, the Austrian chancellor and finance minister agreed to the tentative measures outlined in the Financial Committee's memorandum, but both requested greater guarantees over a loan, as well as Austrian representation at the new central bank.[58]

By May, the Financial Committee met in London to discuss, among other topics, Austria's eligibility for foreign credits. An estimated 30 billion kronen "would enable Austria to procure all necessaries, including coal for her

[53] Frank Nixon [League of Nations], "Restauration du crédit de l'Autriche," April 11, 1921, OeStA BKA-AA VR/41, ff. 6–7; Jean Monnet [League of Nations] to Addis, May 14, 1921, HBS Lamont Papers Box 82; "Setting Austria on Her Feet," *The Times* 42680, March 29, 1921, 7; "League Body Meets to Assist Austria," *The New York Times* LXX, 23075, March 29, 1921, 2.

[54] "Report of the Delegation Sent to Vienna by the Financial Committee," May 12, 1921, in League of Nations, *Financial Reconstruction of Austria: Report of the Financial Committee of the Council* (London: Constable & Co., League of Nations, 1921), 23; "L'aide financière à l'Autriche," *Le Temps (Paris)* 21789, March 30, 1921, 1.

[55] Michael Mayr and Ferdinand Grimm, "Grundsaetze betreffend Waehrungsreform, Notenbank und Finanzkontrolle in Oesterreich," May 9, 1921, in League of Nations, *Financial Reconstruction of Austria: Report of the Financial Committee of the Council* (London: Constable & Co., League of Nations, 1921), 91–92. An earlier draft is located in OeStA BMF Dept. 17/67.

[56] Norman to Strong, May 14, 1921, FRBNY Strong Papers 1116.2, Part 2.

[57] Provisional Economic and Financial Committee, Finance Section, "4th Session – London, 2nd Meeting," May 24, 1921, LoN R333/10/13130/11519; Provisional Economic and Financial Committee, Finance Section, "4th Session – London, 3rd Meeting," May 25, 1921, LoN R333/10/13130/11519.

[58] "Memorandum abgegeben den 28. April 1921 an den österreichischen Bundesfinanzminister durch die Delegierten der Finanzkommission des Völkerbundes," OeStA BMF Dept. 17/67; Michael Mayr and Ferdinand Grimm, "An die Herren Delegierten des Finanzkomitee des Völkerbundes, M.J. Avenol, Sir Drummond-Fraser und Staats E. Glückstadt," May 9, 1921, OeStA BMF Dept. 17/67.

industries."[59] While such credits might have postponed temporary fiscal problems, a new central bank appeared to promise more structural change. The members of the committee deliberated tying the Austrian krone to the US dollar (Avenol), setting limits on the volume of advances to the government (Albert-Édouard Janssen), or changing the name of the currency altogether (Basil Blackett).[60] They also debated whether they should wait for additional approval from the United States. What they concluded, however, was that while US support for the loan would have undoubtedly been helpful, "it would not be justified in delaying for a moment" the proposed spending cuts.[61]

The League's Council compiled elements from the various reports before them, including one by the Financial Committee from June 28, but a comprehensive stabilization plan failed to materialize.[62] Strakosch's authority was severely limited by the nature of a foreign intervention into the affairs of a sovereign state. For one, the funding for the ter Meulen scheme depended on contributions from private investors, many of whom were unwilling to fund Austrian reconstruction without a clear program of fiscal austerity.[63] As Strakosch reported to the Austrian ambassador, banks in New York were reluctant to support such a credit scheme, partly due to their own lack of knowledge on Austria's economic situation.[64] Moreover, officials in Vienna were still unsure if agreeing to the plan would result in a loss of sovereignty not simply to an international organization or a foreign government, but rather to private bankers.[65] Because the country's economic position seemed relatively stable in the summer of 1921, no general scheme for private credits had been deemed necessary.[66]

Yet a rise in public expenditures and unemployment relief had not been met with a proportional increase in taxation, thereby causing severe budgetary deficits between 1919 and 1922.[67] From the Austrian perspective, the troubles had already been known in August 1921 when the finance minister, Ferdinand

[59] Provisional Economic and Financial Committee, Finance Section, "4th Session – London, 2nd Meeting," May 24, 1921, LoN R333/10/13130/11519.

[60] Provisional Economic and Financial Committee, Finance Section, "4th Session – London, 2nd Meeting," May 24, 1921, LoN R333/10/13130/11519.

[61] Provisional Economic and Financial Committee, Finance Section, "4th Session, 6th Meeting," May 28, 1921, LoN R333/10/13130/11519.

[62] Jean Monnet [League of Nations] to Strakosch, June 30, 1921, LoN S136/86/8/2/11.

[63] Marcus, *Austrian Reconstruction*, 90.

[64] Franckenstein to Alfred Grünberger [Bundesministerium für Aeusseres], "Aussichten der Kreditaktion für Oesterreich," August 4, 1921, OeStA BKA-AA HP/335.

[65] Marcus, *Austrian Reconstruction*, 97.

[66] Arthur Salter, "General Survey," in League of Nations, *The Financial Reconstruction of Austria: General Survey and Principal Documents* (Geneva: League of Nations, 1926), 12–13.

[67] Thomas J. Sargent, "The Ends of Four Big Inflations," in *Inflation: Causes and Effects*, ed. Robert E. Hall (Chicago and London: The University of Chicago Press, 1982), 48–49; Fritz Weber, *Vor dem großen Krach. Österreichs Banken in der Zwischenkriegszeit am Beispiel der Credit-Anstalt für Handel und Gewerbe* (Vienna: Böhlau Verlag, 2016), 26–31.

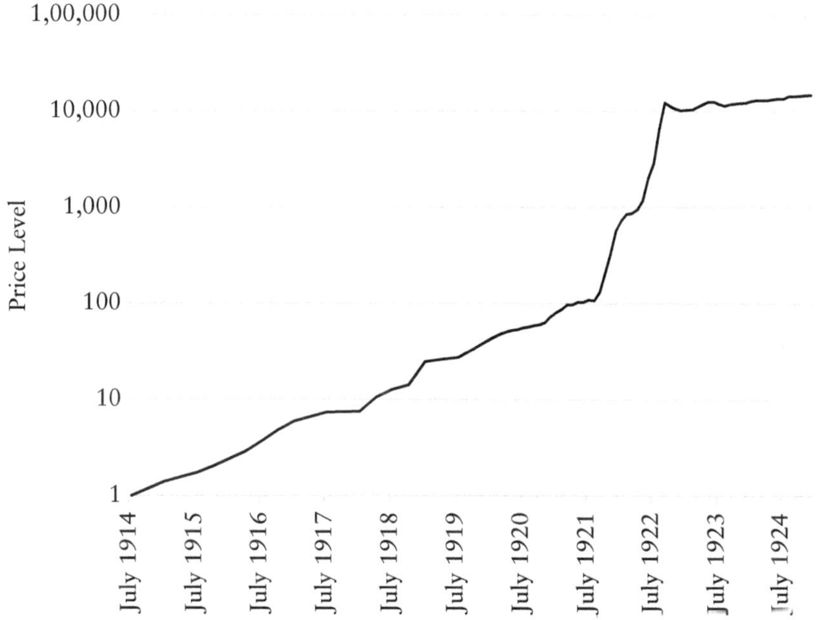

FIGURE 2.2 Consumer Price Index, Log Scale, Monthly Average (July 1914 = 0)
Source: Gerald Hubmann, Clemens Jobst, and Michaela Maier, "Ein neuer langer Verbraucherpreisindex für Österreich, 1800–2018," *Vierteljahrschrift für Sozial- und Wirtschaftsgeschichte* 107, no. 1 (2020): 47–85.

Grimm, warned the Bank of "the serious consequences of the delay in obtaining financial assistance through the League of Nations."[68] Retail prices continued to rise drastically thereafter (Figure 2.2). Further driven by investors' lack of confidence, the rapid depreciation in the currency in the summer of 1922 led individuals to spend much of their earnings, causing prices to spiral even higher.[69]

It was the League's inability to resolve ongoing political and economic concerns that compelled the Bank to intervene. The underlying causes of the Austrian hyperinflation became a highly contested topic of discussion in financial circles. Before the League's Assembly in September 1921, Strakosch asserted that "[t]he disequilibrium in the exchanges is not an ill inherent in the exchanges themselves, but arises from a disequilibrium in economic and monetary conditions generally. Their fluctuations are merely a symptom of a much more deep-seated derangement."[70] In his view, price controls and subsidies

[68] Committee of Treasury, Minutes, August 31, 1921, BoE G8/54.

[69] J. van Walré de Bordes, *The Austrian Crown: Its Depreciation and Stabilization* (London: P.S. King and Son, 1924), 199; Warnock, "The First Bailout," 135; Marcus, *Austrian Reconstruction*, 39–40.

[70] League of Nations, Second Assembly Commission, "Sir Henry Strakosch's Statement," September 19, 1921, OeStA BMF Dept. 17/72. Also quoted in Henry Strakosch, "Exchanges," September 26, 1921, FRBNY Strong Papers 1010.1.

enacted since the First World War had impeded the proper functioning of markets. With this argument, he aimed to use hyperinflation as a pretext for implementing the League's previously failed reform.

Yet as prices continued to rise, Strakosch agreed to tackle another project: creating a central bank in South Africa. Resigning as chairman of the League's Financial Committee, he was due to sail to Pretoria later that year.[71] There, he planned to conduct a thorough examination of the South African monetary system as an adviser to the national government. Concurrent with reconstruction projects in Europe, the Bank aimed to refashion the imperial monetary order along orthodox lines.

SOUTH AFRICA AND GOLD

The Union of South Africa, established in 1910, had begun to play an increasingly prominent role in global economic affairs. Vast deposits of natural resources – and, most importantly, gold – in the Witwatersrand had sustained the profits of mining companies, further financed by capital from London and Paris.[72] During the First World War, South Africa had nominally maintained gold convertibility (until its official abandonment on December 17, 1920), but a strict gold embargo prevented its proper functioning.

Following the conflict, a lack of public confidence in an unbacked currency precipitated debilitating outflows of gold. The wartime issuance of (unbacked) paper money and ensuing depreciation of the South African pound in early 1919 threatened the country with a rise in prices. To address the threat of inflation, the finance minister, Thomas Orr, called for a meeting of economists, politicians, bankers, and industrialists. In October, the Gold Conference convened in Pretoria to address prevailing currency and exchange-rate issues. After outflows of gold put further pressure on the exchange, the members of the conference agreed to implement several reforms: the creation of a mint and refinery for producing gold coins, the enactment of additional restrictions on the export of gold, and the establishment of an independent central bank.[73]

Upon learning of the conference's discussions, Strakosch wrote to John Maynard Keynes, who had recently resigned from the Treasury, on the urgent need for intervention.[74] This reaction indicated one of the ways in which experts viewed the changing landscape of the interwar economy. Observing South Africa's contentious debates over public policy, Strakosch claimed that

[71] Strakosch to H. McKinnon Wood [Economic & Financial Section, League of Nations], November 1, 1921, LoN S136/86/8/2/11.

[72] Charles H. Feinstein, *An Economic History of South Africa: Conquest, Discrimination, and Development* (Cambridge: Cambridge University Press, 2005), 99–106.

[73] *Summarised Report of the Proceedings of the Gold Conference Held at the Union Buildings, Wednesday, 22nd October 1919*, U.G. 18–'20 (Cape Town: Cape Times, 1920), 1.

[74] Strakosch to Keynes, November 14, 1919, KCC Keynes Papers L/ST.

increasing gold production would help stabilize prices in South Africa, which could help expedite the successful return of the gold standard in Britain and other countries.[75] Although Keynes was reluctant to intercede in the country's affairs, Strakosch began negotiating with leading South African officials, including Finance Secretary E.H. Farrer, on the prospect of reform. Through this connection, he was able to gain a position on the Union government's Advisory Committee alongside representatives from the banking, agricultural, and industrial sectors.[76]

Unelected experts who had connections to those in power thereafter determined the contours of reconstruction. In February 1920, Field Marshal Jan Smuts, the recently elected prime minister, personally endorsed Strakosch's application that granted him "facilities to travel to South Africa."[77] During his visit in March and April, Strakosch went to various towns in the province of the Western Cape, including Oudtshoorn, Knysna, and George, before arriving in the legislative capital of Cape Town.[78] After the tour, he was able to draft a plan for a new central bank that would amass the country's metallic reserves.[79] Establishing a free market for gold, ending the embargo on the export of specie, and creating a national mint, to his mind, were additional strategies for combating the rise in price levels.[80] In contrast to Austria, South Africa could also undertake an additional reform: stabilizing exchange rates by tying the currency to the British pound. Strakosch warned Smuts of the "grave danger" in South Africa's return to the gold standard independent of other countries.[81] Instead, he envisioned both South Africa and the United Kingdom together leading the revival of the prewar monetary system by tying their exchange rates to one another.

By late April, the South African government started to take these proposals seriously. The lower house of Parliament, the House of Assembly, called for a select committee to investigate the effects of the gold embargo on the economy.

75 Henry Strakosch, "Gold and the Foreign Exchanges," May 9, 1919, KCC Keynes Papers L/ST and UWA Evans Papers A619-B9, 10; Strakosch to Keynes, November 15, 1919, KCC Keynes Papers L/ST.

76 Farrer to Strakosch, January 28, 1920, NASA TES F53/294/2.

77 Smuts to R.A. Blankenberg [Secretary to the High Commissioner to South Africa], July 16, 1919, NASA BNS 1/7/36 Z605.

78 Strakosch to Farrer, March 19, 1920, NASA TES F53/294/2.

79 Russell Ally, *Gold & Empire: The Bank of England and South Africa's Gold Producers, 1886–1926* (Johannesburg: Witwatersrand University Press, 2001), 117. There had been prior unsuccessful attempts at establishing a central bank, notably in 1911 and 1913; E.H.D. Arndt, *Banking and Currency Development in South Africa (1652–1927)* (Cape Town and Johannesburg: Juta, 1928), 417–420; E.H.D. Arndt and C.S. Richards, "The Banking System of South Africa," in *Foreign Banking Systems*, ed. H. Parker Willis and B.H. Beckhart (New York: H. Holt and Company, 1929), 989.

80 Henry Strakosch, *The South African Currency and Exchange Problem* (Johannesburg: Central News Agency, 1920), 11 12.

81 Strakosch to Smuts, n.d., KCC Keynes Papers L/ST.

Among the witnesses to provide their views, Strakosch was the first and the most persuasive voice.[82] He began his testimony by establishing his legitimacy as a financial expert:

> [A]fter completing my studies, which comprised political economy, I joined one of the important continental exchange banks, the Anglo-Austrian Bank, and I specialized there in foreign exchanges and finally became their foreign exchange manager in London ... . [M]y corporation was in close contact with international finance, as it was originally founded by a group of international bankers in France, England and Germany, and in that way I kept in touch with them ... . I have formulated a scheme for the better realisation of the gold production of the Transvaal, and concurrently with that for establishing extensive dealings in foreign exchanges, and my proposals were considered by Professor Keynes, who I am sure is well known to all of you, and by Mr. McKenna, who used to be Chancellor of the Exchequer, and they have fully endorsed what I suggested.[83]

Following his comments, the Select Committee invited Strakosch to present his ideas on how the monetary system would function under his scheme. Central to his plan was the creation of a reserve bank to manage the country's gold reserves. The new institution would be intentionally designed neither as a state-run enterprise, which would be "subjected to political influences," nor as a commercial bank that competed with other private banks.[84] Instead, it would act as an independent entity dedicated to the stabilization of exchange rates, the money supply, and ultimately price levels.[85]

Expert advice was thus essential for translating technical topics, such as monetary management, into understandable language. To be an expert witness on a government commission meant offering a plan that officials could not have otherwise formulated on their own. The Select Committee relied on such external counsel to address prevailing inflationary concerns. Keenly aware of this dependence, Strakosch used his reputation to his advantage, although he did recognize that the future implementation of currency policy rested solely with the Union government.[86] His involvement stood in contrast to Keynes, who had also been in conversation with Smuts but was unwilling to take part in the reform. Strakosch, however, had no such reservations. While emphasizing his connections to a prominent South African mining company, Strakosch

[82] Arndt and Richards, "The Banking System of South Africa," 966–967; William G. Martin, *South Africa and the World Economy: Remaking Race, State and Region* (Rochester: University of Rochester Press, 2013), 82.

[83] "Minutes of Evidence," April 23, 1920, in *Report of the Select Committee on Embargo on Export of Specie*, S.C. 2–'20 (Cape Town: Government Printers, 1920), 1–2.

[84] "Minutes of Evidence," May 5, 1920, in *Report of the Select Committee on Embargo on Export of Specie*, 158.

[85] "Minutes of Evidence," May 4, 1920, in *Report of the Select Committee on Embargo on Export of Specie*, 129.

[86] Keynes to Strakosch, October 25, 1919, KCC Keynes Papers L/ST.

TABLE 2.1 *Annual Gold Production (Thousands of Ounces)*

	Union of South Africa *% of world*	United States *% of world*	Canada *% of world*	World
1915	9,096 40.3%	4,888 21.6%	918 4.1%	22,594
1923	9,149 51.4%	2,503 14.1%	1,233 6.9%	17,786
1924	9,575 50.3%	2,529 13.3%	1,525 8.0%	19,050
1925	9,598 50.4%	2,412 12.7%	1,736 9.1%	19,031
1926	9,955 51.4%	2,335 12.1%	1,754 9.1%	19,369
1927	10,122 52.1%	2,197 11.3%	1,853 9.5%	19,446
1928	10,354 52.9%	2,233 11.4%	1,891 9.7%	19,583
1929	10,412 53.2%	2,206 11.3%	1,928 9.8%	19,585
1930	10,716 52.8%	2,286 11.3%	2,102 10.4%	20,293
1931	10,878 49.1%	2,396 10.8%	2,694 12.2%	22,168
1932	11,559 48.4%	2,513 10.5%	3,051 12.8%	23,884

Source: Bank for International Settlements, *Third Annual Report: April 1, 1932–March 31, 1933* (Basle: Bank for International Settlements, 1933), 7.

again used the urgency of the inflationary crisis to justify his recommendations to a wider audience.[87]

It was not only the economic rationale that could help instigate structural change. Over the course of his visit, Strakosch's proposal received avid support from South African politicians because it aligned with their particular vision of financial recovery. For many officials, gold had been a symbolic source of pride for the nation and therefore needed to be at the center of monetary reform. At the South African Party Congress, Smuts spoke of gold being "an immense source of strength" for the country.[88] With its abundant deposits in the Witwatersrand fields of the Transvaal province, South Africa was able to produce around half of the world's gold by the early 1920s, outpacing both the United States and Canada combined (Table 2.1).

[87] Strakosch to Farrer, February 10, 1920, NASA TES F53/294/2.

[88] Quoted in Samuel Evans, "The 'Managed Money' Movement in the British Empire as Viewed from South Africa," *The Economic World* 27, no. 17 (April 26, 1924), 581.

Before a government commission in May 1920, Strakosch emphasized the near-unanimous agreement among experts on monetary reform. As he described, "there is no divergence of opinion among all the witnesses – myself included – that it is desirable to restore our currency to a true gold basis at the earliest possible moment. Opinions differ only in regard to the manner and time."[89] Convinced by this line of argument, the chairman of the Select Committee, Finance Minister Henry Burton, introduced a parliamentary bill for the creation of the South African Reserve Bank in July 1920.[90] The proposal for an independent reserve bank aligned with the Bank's goal of defending the preeminence of London abroad. Governor Norman, in particular, was personally invested in the project. In February 1921, he wrote to Prime Minister Smuts on the importance of uniformity within the British Empire:

> A good deal has been said and written about the consolidation of Imperial banking, but I believe the lines upon which you are working to be the right and only sound ones – the establishment of a Central bank within each economic unit of the Empire for the transaction of central banking business within that unit – and I hope the example set by South Africa may be followed by the establishment, in other Dominions, of Central Banks on similar lines.[91]

To prove that Strakosch's proposals on a central bank had additional merit, the Select Committee searched for other experts who could offer additional backing. One such figure was Samuel Evans, a Welsh-born, South African industrialist. Having testified before the Select Committee alongside Strakosch, Evans argued that the persistent threat of inflation necessitated a commitment to fixed exchange rates. He had long argued that during the First World War, the heavy reliance on issuing bank notes had induced a general rise in prices.[92] This inflation – which raised both production costs for businesses and the cost of living for consumers – was "the main stumbling block hindering the recovery of the world from the effects of the Great War."[93] While conceding that it may have been possible to reduce prices by decreasing the money supply or increasing production, he believed that the priority should be to return to "a stable currency … [which] is the condition on which economy and increased production depend."[94]

89 "Minutes of Evidence," May 27, 1920, in *Report of the Select Committee on Embargo on Export of Specie*, 406.

90 "South African Currency," *The Times* 42464, July 16, 1920, 19; Arndt, *Banking and Currency Development in South Africa*, 430–421; Gerhard de Kock, *A History of the South African Reserve Bank (1920–52)* (Pretoria: J.L. van Schaik, 1954), 21–22.

91 Norman to Smuts, February 4, 1921, BoE OV50/1.

92 "Minutes of Evidence," May 27, 1920, in *Report of the Select Committee on Embargo on Export of Specie*, 415; Evans to Cannan, January 21, 1921, LSE Cannan Papers 1026; "Future Course of Gold Values," *The Times* 42733, May 30, 1921, 15.

93 Samuel Evans, *The Gold Premium: Paper Read before the Chemical, Metallurgical and Mining Society of South Africa on Saturday, 15th May, 1920* (Johannesburg: McKowen & Radford, 1920), 9. Also located in UWA Evans Papers A619-A3.

94 Evans, *The Gold Premium*, 9.

Evans and Strakosch, both of whom served on the government's Advisory Committee, found clear benefits to a gold-backed currency. Although not an academic economist, Evans was active in the discipline and had numerous connections to industry. Writing to Smuts on the "Currency Problem" in 1923, he claimed that "every attempt to establish a currency which involves the restriction or the prohibition of the use of gold will not only fail ultimately but will almost certainly do infinite harm in the long run."[95] The best policy for the Union government was to avoid any "[e]xperiments with managed currencies," such as those outlined by Keynes or Hubert Henderson, which "may prove as harmful to England as to South Africa."[96] Evans, however, opposed Strakosch's recommendation to create an independent central bank, urging Smuts instead to "use your great influence" and follow a market-based approach that would include "the removal of all embargoes" and "the free movement of gold."[97]

As a competing adviser, Strakosch took a more practical approach to his advisory work. He knew that Governor Norman believed that creating a central bank in South Africa was "a matter of supreme importance to this Empire, to this Country, and to the Bank of England."[98] Although the Bank may have wanted South Africa to commit to a sterling-based (rather than gold-based) standard, Strakosch understood that a fundamental shift in monetary responsibilities could only be successful if it appealed to a country's particular interests. In Geneva, he sought to rally support for a plan by linking economic reconstruction to the long-term sustainability of peace: "The primary objective of the League of Nations is to avoid future wars … [General Smuts] looks upon the League as an 'ever working organ in the policy of civilisation' an organ which not only attempts the settlement of international disputes after they have arisen, but … deals with the very causes and sources of disputes."[99] By calling Smuts' attention to monetary instability in a public forum, he could expedite the legislative process of reform.

While contending with economic experts and government officials, Strakosch continually faced pushback from various interest groups. He wanted to ensure that a new central bank did not compete with existing commercial banks, which was a major point of contention in Johannesburg's financial sector.[100] Placing certain limits on the prerogatives of the new central bank was

[95] Evans to Smuts, September 26, 1923, PUL Kemmerer Papers Box 217, Folder 2. See also his prior correspondence on procuring foreign expertise; Evans to Smuts, April 27, 1921, NASA TES F53/294.

[96] Evans to Smuts, September 26, 1923, PUL Kemmerer Papers Box 217, Folder 2.

[97] Evans to Smuts, September 26, 1923, PUL Kemmerer Papers Box 217, Folder 2.

[98] Committee of Treasury, Minutes, November 17, 1920, BoE G8/54.

[99] Provisional Economic & Financial Committee, "Memorandum by Sir Henry Strakosch on Elaboration of Organisation," February 21, 1921, LoN R348/10/12020/12019.

[100] Jones, *British Multinational Banking*, 194; Cobus Vermeulen, "One Hundred Years of Private Shareholding in the South African Reserve Bank," *Economic History of Developing Regions* 36, no. 2 (2021), 219.

one way to make the proposal amenable to private bankers. There was also the risk of "commercial banks masquerading as central banks," which would cause "more harm than good."[101] In May 1921, he outlined the principles to which all future central banks should adhere. Key provisions, such as granting the monetary authority a monopoly of note issue or limiting the number of government appointees, were part of the standard part of the Brussels consensus (Table 2.2). The Bank agreed with these proposals, with many officials further arguing that a proper central bank was one that did not profit from the extension of extending loans and managing deposits; instead, it should focus its activities on the stability of the financial system.[102] This plan would effectively replicate the British model of central banking in South Africa.

Due to Strakosch's informal advisory work with the Bank and Prime Minister Smuts, the South African Reserve Bank was formally established on June 30. In passing, the new Governor, W.H. Clegg, credited Strakosch with devising and defending the project.[103] As officials and the press similarly recognized, his testimony before the Select Committee on Embargo on Export of Specie was vital in identifying the responsibilities of the central bank, as later outlined in the Currency and Banking Act of 1920: maintaining relations with commercial banks, issuing notes, establishing the reserve requirement of 40 percent, and making (albeit limited) loans and advances.[104] Thus, the conclusion was that the establishment of an independent central bank, which limited the uncontrolled growth of the money supply, could quell inflationary pressures.[105]

The experimental nature of these reforms was apparent to contemporary observers. When the first meeting of South African Reserve Bank shareholders convened on July 29, Clegg described the pioneering project of central banking in the aftermath of the First World War: "The South African Reserve Bank is the outcome of a conviction that has grown in thoughtful and reflecting minds in the Union during the last few years, that the increasing importance of South Africa in the world of commerce called for some elaboration in her banking machinery."[106] Outside of Britain, no central banks comparable to the British one had

101 Henry Strakosch, "The Principles of Central Banking," May 21, 1921, BoE OV50/1.

102 "Memorandum of Central Banks' Policy for Bank's Internal Use," April 10, 1923, BoE OV50/1; "Memorandum of the Conversation, Held at the Bank of England, Between the Commissioners and the Governor of the Bank of England," November 20, 1924, PUL Kemmerer Papers Box 217, Folder 1.

103 "Imperial Banking: Beginning of a New Era," *Rand Daily Mail (Johannesburg)* 14, 5594, December 21, 1920, 8.

104 "Colonial and Foreign Banking," *The Times* 42475, July 29, 1920, 20; Sydney Buxton [Governor-General of South Africa] to Lord Milner [Colonial Office], August 6, 1920, TNA T160/33/7; "City Notes," *The Times* 42596, December 17, 1920, 18; A.C.L. Day, "The South African Reserve Bank," in *Banking in the British Commonwealth*, ed. R.S. Sayers (Oxford: Clarendon Press, 1952), 373–375.

105 Strakosch, "The South African Reserve Bank," 173.

106 South African Reserve Bank, *First Ordinary General Meeting of Stockholders: Report of Proceedings* (Pretoria: South African Reserve Bank, 1921), 1.

TABLE 2.2 *Excerpt from Henry Strakosch, "The Principles of Central Banking"*

To be genuine central banks[,] they must, it is submitted, observe the following fundamental conditions:

(a) They must be private institutions – i.e., their capital must be subscribed from private funds.
(b) A substantial majority of their boards must be representatives of the economic life of the country, and [they] must be in a position of entire independence politically. The Government nominees must be in the minority.
(c) The bank's business must not be run mainly for profit. Dividends should be limited to a reasonable return on the capital.
(d) Apart from doing its own Government's business, the bank is not to do the ordinary commercial banking business in normal times, but is to act as the banker of banks and to finance the country's business only in times of stress.
(e) It must guide the financial policy by fixing the rate of discount at which it is prepared to discount bankable bills.
(f) It must have the sole right of note issue.
(g) The character of its business must be of the soundest, and should in the main be confined to financing the trade and industry of the country ...
(h) With regard to foreign bills and balances abroad, opinions differ as to whether a Central Bank should be empowered to hold these. I strongly feel that in countries such as the Dominions, with their extensive and intimate trade and financial relations with the Mother Country, it is advisable for them to hold bills and balances on the Mother Country. This is the best safeguard to meet sudden but temporary demands for exchange and thus to prevent violent fluctuations owing to sudden seasonal requirements of exchange.
(i) The reserve requirements should be framed to give elasticity ...
(j) The Bank must publish weekly a clear statement of its position intelligible to the average businessman.

These conditions are indispensable if the Bank is to perform properly the functions of a Central Bank – i.e. to sustain the credit of the country, to guide its financial policy, and to intervene effectively in an emergency.

Source: BoE OV50/1.

yet existed in the British Empire. The dearth of such institutions led Governor Norman to note his sense of the uncharted territories into which the Bank was now headed: "It seems to be a subject on which there is no text book."[107]

EXPORTING ORTHODOXY

Through South Africa's Advisory Committee and the League of Nations, Strakosch had access to numerous channels for influencing public policy. His

[107] Norman to Sir Bernard Hunter [Imperial Bank of India], February 28, 1921, BoE OV50/1.

recommendations, which appeared to end the era of inflation, solidified his reputation as a leading expert. "Strakosch was most helpful to me," Smuts admitted, "and the bill was largely on the lines of his advice."[108]

What followed was the reorganization of the Austrian and the South African financial systems. The establishment of the South African Reserve Bank in 1921 had seemingly proven that extensive changes were possible with the aid of experts. At the subsequent Genoa Conference in April and May 1922, the nations of Europe reaffirmed the tenets of economic orthodoxy established at Brussels and agreed to return their currencies to the prewar parities of gold.[109] Keynes noted the significance of the conference in bringing expert ideas to the forefront of public debates: "The financial experts here assembled could hardly be surpassed in collective experience and intellectual power," and many of them, including Strakosch, "represent[ed] the pick of writers on post-war finance."[110] Again representing South Africa, Strakosch and another banker (Robert Brand) aimed to commit the country to extensive reforms. As they wrote to Smuts,

> We are convinced that the plan laid down in the resolutions ... is the best possible means of securing stability in the European currencies, minimising the fluctuations in the purchasing power of gold, permitting the earliest possible adoption of the gold standard throughout Europe, and therefore assisting in a return to European prosperity. Resting, as they do, on the adoption by all Europe of the gold standard, we are satisfied that the plan is in the interests of South Africa as a whole, including the gold mining industry.[111]

In effect, the League's various commissions sought to stabilize the value of gold to which all European countries would peg their currencies. Strakosch thus argued that South Africa should stabilize its exchange rate by tying its currency to the British pound.[112]

[108] Smuts to Keynes, September 27, 1920, in *Selections from the Smuts Papers, vol. 5: September 1919–November 1934*, ed. Jean van der Poel (Cambridge: Cambridge University Press, 1973), 43. Smuts appointed Strakosch and Robert Brand as his economic advisers; Edgar Walton [High Commissioner to South Africa] to Brand, February 20, 1922, BLO Brand Papers 23.

[109] "No. 109: Second Plenary Session of the Genoa Conference, held at the Palazzo San Giorgio, May 3, 1922, at 10 a.m.," in *Documents on British Foreign Policy, 1919–1939, First Series, vol. 19*, ed. W.N. Medlicott, Douglas Dakin, and M.E. Lambert (London: H.M. Stationery Office, 1974), 706–709. On the Genoa Conference, see Carole Fink, *The Genoa Conference: European Diplomacy, 1921–1922* (Chapel Hill: University of North Carolina Press, 1984); Carole Fink, Axel Frohn, and Jürgen Heideking, eds., *Genoa, Rapallo, and European Reconstruction in 1922* (Washington, DC: German Historical Institute and Cambridge: Cambridge University Press, 1991); Fior, *Institution globale et marchés financiers*, 328–334; Decorzant, *La Société des nations*, 354–361.

[110] John Maynard Keynes, "The Finance Experts at Genoa," April 15, 1922, in *The Collected Writings of John Maynard Keynes, vol. 17: Activities 1920–1922, Treaty Revision and Reconstruction*, ed. Elizabeth Johnson (Cambridge: Cambridge University Press, 1977), 381.

[111] Strakosch and Brand to Smuts, May 11, 1922, BLO Brand Papers 23.

[112] Henry Strakosch, *The South African Currency and Exchange Problem Re-Examined* (Johannesburg: Central News Agency, 1922), 6. An earlier draft of the report is located in NASA TES F53/294/2.

At the same time, South Africa's dominant financial elite continued to object to many of Strakosch's suggestions.[113] Since the mid-nineteenth century, a network of imperial banks had helped finance the growth of major domestic industries.[114] Any legislation forwarded by Strakosch would require their approval. Leading bankers, including James S. Shiel (Standard Bank of South Africa) and H.C. Jorissen (Netherlands Bank of South Africa), were some of the main supporters of the gold embargo as a means of preventing capital outflows.[115] Meanwhile, Edward C. Reynolds (National Bank) similarly believed the government needed to allow the issuance of a nonconvertible paper currency as a temporary solution.[116] While Johannesburg's financial interests were open to many of the early discussions on monetary reform, they also wanted to maintain a seat at the negotiation table.

In response, Strakosch had to assuage their concerns by reaffirming that the central bank would not be motivated by private profits. Rather, its work would "be directed primarily to upholding the credit of the country, and to preparing for helpful intervention in an emergency."[117] The Bank shared this view as well. One internal memorandum indicated the view that the new central bank should not be permitted to interfere in the private sector: "A Central Bank should not compete with other Banks for general business … [and] should not engage in a general Exchange business on its own account with any other country."[118] Compatible with the Bank's orthodox views, this concession ultimately received approval from South African bankers.

Even so, Strakosch wanted to ensure that the United Kingdom – and, above all, the City – remained the principal beneficiary of any modification to the South African banking system. He opposed an existing proposal to create an empire bank, which would perform the functions of a central bank for the whole empire. Coined the "Imperial Bank Fallacy," the flaws of a single central

113 See, for instance Keith Breckenridge, "'Money with Dignity': Migrants, Minelords and the Cultural Politics of the South African Gold Standard Crisis, 1920–33," *The Journal of African History* 36, no. 2 (1995), 272; Admire Mseba, "Beyond Imperial Interests: Settler Regimes, Capital and Africans in Colonial Southern Africa's Currency Politics to 1920," in *Monetary Transitions: Currencies, Colonialism and African Societies*, ed. Karin Pallaver (Cham: Palgrave Macmillan, 2022), 155–157.

114 Bruce Ronald Dalgaard, *South Africa's Impact on Britain's Return to Gold, 1925* (New York: Arno Press, 1981), 35–38; Stuart Jones, *The Great Imperial Banks in South Africa: A Study of the Business of Standard Bank and Barclays Bank, 1861–1961* (Pretoria: University of South Africa, 1996), 75–76; Martin, *South Africa and the World Economy*, 79, 83–84; Grietjie Verhoef, "Financial Intermediaries in Settler Economies: The Role of the Banking Sector Development in South Africa, 1850–2000," in *Settler Economies in World History*, ed. Christopher Lloyd, Jacob Metzer, and Richard Sutch (Leiden and Boston: Brill, 2013), 413–415.

115 Union of South Africa, *Summarised Report of the Proceedings of the Gold Conference*, 14.

116 Union of South Africa, *Summarised Report of the Proceedings of the Gold Conference*, 15.

117 Strakosch, "The South African Reserve Bank," 174.

118 "Central Banks," February 28, 1921, BoE OV50/1.

bank, while alluring in theory, were readily apparent due to the potential coordination problems. A common monetary policy for the Dominions and India would have been difficult to administer, particularly for countries with divergent economic conditions. Because a single central bank appeared neither politically popular nor structurally viable, Strakosch instead envisioned creating a series of imperial banks that aligned both in vision and in ideology.

South Africa demonstrated how economic restructuring could be successfully implemented elsewhere. Upon returning to Geneva, Strakosch applied the lessons that he had learned to the reform of Austria's financial system. On September 9, 1922, the League's Financial Committee officially began its inquiry into the so-called "Austrian question."[119] The two main concerns were whether the country could reach a budget equilibrium and under what conditions it might be able to establish a central bank.[120] While an internal loan raised in Austria was unlikely to succeed owing to inadequate levels of domestic capital, an externally issued loan might be more successful. It could have also quelled inflationary pressures from a rapidly depreciating currency. Still, the prospect of a foreign loan was largely contingent upon budgetary reforms. The committee hoped that through increased taxation and lower government spending, Austria might be able to achieve a balanced budget within two years.

Strakosch recognized the importance of appealing to the commercial bankers, as he had done in South Africa. He intended to cooperate with one of the City's most prominent merchant banks, Rothschild & Co., which had a vested interest in Austria's economic recovery. Its Vienna branch, established in 1820 by Salomon Mayer von Rothschild, had kept close ties to both the Habsburg monarchy and the nation's leading commercial bank, Creditanstalt.[121] From a practical standpoint, raising a loan for Austria also required the backing of international creditors, particularly those in the United States. In March 1922, the New York-based J.P. Morgan & Co. was initially willing to support part of the loan, provided that Governor Norman would "handle [the] British end of such financing."[122] However, following a meeting with representatives from the Bank and the League, its London counterpart (Morgan, Grenfell & Co.)

[119] Financial Committee, "Report to the Council on the Session of the Committee Held at Geneva, September 1922, Communicated to the Assembly in Accordance with the Council's Resolution of September 16th 1922," LoN R323/10/23358/11493.

[120] Provisional Economic and Financial Committee, Finance Section, "Ninth Session. First Meeting held Saturday, September 9th at 12 a.m.," 9 September 1922, LoN C36/36/6/5a; "Reports of the Financial Committee and Resolutions of the Council, with Relevant Papers," September 1922, in League of Nations, *The Financial Reconstruction of Austria: General Survey and Principal Documents* (Geneva: League of Nations, 1926), 176–177.

[121] On the ties between the Rothschilds and Austria, see Niall Ferguson, *The House of Rothschild, vol. 1: Money's Prophets, 1798–1848* (New York: Viking, 1998); Robert Skidelsky, *Money and Government: The Past and Future of Economics* (New Haven and London: Yale University Press, 2018), 90–92.

[122] J.P. Morgan & Co. to Morgan, Grenfell & Co., March 17, 1922, MLM ARC 1221 Box 35, Folder 3.

became increasingly reluctant to offer assistance without greater assurances of repayment.[123] By May, the Rothschilds reported on behalf of the other merchant banks that "we are as yet unable to see any basis such as would justify us in offering upon the investment markets an Austrian Government loan."[124]

Both a commitment to a gold-backed currency and the establishment of a new central bank were reforms that now fell under the oversight of the League. To supervise Austrian public finance, Strakosch suggested the appointment of Alfred R. Zimmerman, a lawyer and the former mayor of Rotterdam, as the League's Commissioner General.[125] An expert in international affairs, Zimmerman was "known as a specialist in financial and economic questions. His knowledge of foreign languages is that of the well educated Dutchmen, that is to say he speaks and writes French, German and English in an intelligible way."[126] Based in Vienna, he could implement far-reaching spending reductions throughout the public sector, notably to universities and railways.[127] However, his post came with limited prerogatives and was mainly used to concentrate public discontent on a single individual. Important decisions would instead be deferred to the independent, Geneva-based Committee of Control.[128] Strakosch's main intervention was to ensure that the Committee of Control would "not be purely and simply a Committee of creditors," but rather a body that upheld economic orthodoxy and was imbued "with the spirit of the League" in mind.[129]

[123] Morgan, Grenfell & Co. to J.P. Morgan & Co., April 4, 1922, MLM ARC 1221 Box 35, Folder 3.

[124] The clearing banks included J.P. Morgan & Co. (New York), N.M. Rothschild & Sons (London), Baring Brothers & Co. (London), and J.H. Schroder & Co. (London); N.M. Rothschild & Sons to Baron Frankenstein [Austrian Legation], May 22, 1922, RAL XI/111/189 and HBS Lamont Papers Box 82.

[125] J.L.J. Bosmans, *De Nederlander. Mr. A.R. Zimmerman als commissaris-generaal van de Volkenbond in Oostenrijk 1922–1926* (Nijmegen: Drukkerij Gebr. Janssen N.V., 1973), 51–65; Orde, *British Policy and European Reconstruction*, 141–142; Pauly, *Who Elected the Bankers?*, 54; Clavin, *Securing the World Economy*, 28; Johannes Feichtinger, "On the Fraught Internationalism of Intellectuals: Alfons Dopsch, Austria, and the League's Intellectual Cooperation Programme," in *Remaking Central Europe: The League of Nations and the Former Habsburg Lands*, ed. Peter Becker and Natasha Wheatley (Oxford: Oxford University Press, 2020), 188.

[126] Adrianus Pelt [Vienna Delegation] to Frank Nixon [League of Nations], February 18, 1922, LoN S103/53/20.

[127] Commission de contrôle, "Troisième session. Annexe I au Procès-verbal de la Première séance. Déclaration du Dr. Zimmermann," n.d., LoN C39/39/6/6c.

[128] Originally, the Austrian government proposed the Committee of Control be composed of three representatives chosen by Austria and three by the Financial Committee. The Financial Committee, however, reserved the right to nominate four representatives; "Report of the Financial Committee," May 31, 1921, in League of Nations, *Financial Reconstruction of Austria: Report of the Financial Committee of the Council* (London: Constable & Co., League of Nations, 1921), 8.

[129] Provisional Economic & Financial Committee, "Ninth Session. 13th Meeting held Tuesday, September 19th, 1922 at 5.30 p.m.," September 19, 1922, LoN C36/36/6/5a.

With the League's support behind it, the project of Austrian reconstruction gained greater momentum. Arthur Balfour, chairman of the Austria Committee, suggested that the government continue to defer to experts who could address many of the pressing financial problems.[130] For Strakosch, this backing was key. On October 17, he traveled to Vienna as the British representative of the Financial Committee to discuss possible measures that would help balance the budget. Reiterating the importance of reducing government spending, he and the Austrian delegation recommended the dismissal of some 100,000 officials from the civil service over the next two years.[131] Their intention was to see Austria achieve a balanced budget by the end of 1924.[132]

Subsequent coverage by the Austrian press noted the adverse consequences of such a foreign intervention. Although born in Austria, Strakosch came to represent the intrusion of British financiers. The liberal *Wiener Allgemeine Zeitung* wrote critically of his proposals: "Sir Henry Strakosch is under the spell of English politics and England is now at the forefront of the states that want to see us completely destroyed."[133] According to these critics, he had seemingly abandoned his Austrian ties and only considered the interests of foreign bankers. Meanwhile, the nationalist *Deutschösterreichische Tages-Zeitung* denounced Strakosch's "dictatorial endeavors" with a plan in which "the standard of living of the population should be ruthlessly reduced until the unviable state structure of Austria created by the Peace Treaty of Saint-Germain should still be able to survive. This is 'the restructuring' that is being imagined in international circles."[134]

Nevertheless, Austrian politicians, themselves more attuned to the country's credit needs, were willing to accept a politically controversial and unpopular policy if they were able to select the central bank's first president. Governor Norman might have been initially keen on selecting one of his own colleagues to fill this position. He first suggested that the position be reserved for Janssen, a director at the National Bank of Belgium, who quickly declined the invitation.[135] Although the Bank believed a Swiss banker was the next likely candidate, it was revealed on December 21 that Richard Reisch, an Austrian lawyer

[130] Arthur Balfour, "Aide-mémoire," November 1, 1921, OeStA BKA-AA HP/331.

[131] "Report by the Provisional Delegation of the League of Nations at Vienna," February 1, 1923, in League of Nations, *The Financial Reconstruction of Austria: General Survey and Principal Documents* (Geneva: League of Nations, 1926), 192.

[132] Piétri, *La Société des Nations*, 70–71.

[133] "Der Partherpfeil. Die englische Politik gegen Oesterreich," *Wiener Allgemeine Zeitung (Vienna)* 13297, August 31, 1922, 3.

[134] "Finanzdiktatur und Wirtschaftsleben," *Deutschösterreichische Tages-Zeitung (Vienna)* 32, no. 242, September 3, 1922, 3; "Notenbankgeheimnis und Sanierungsbluff," *Deutschösterreichische Tages-Zeitung (Vienna)* 32, no. 252, September 23, 1922, 2.

[135] Committee of Treasury, Minutes, December 13 and December 20, 1922, BoE G8/55; Salter to Niemeyer, December 22, 1922, LoN S108/58/8. Strakosch was unable to persuade Janssen

and a former Finance Minister, was to lead the Austrian central bank.[136] With this appointment, Austria was able to retain a degree of national sovereignty throughout the negotiations over a foreign loan. Criticism from Bank officials centered on this appointment. The Committee of Treasury asserted that "this [decision] was opposed to the spirit ... of the agreement with the League of Nations."[137] Both Norman and Strakosch were frustrated by the unwillingness of Austria to commit to an independent central bank. Their views were shared by another Bank official who bluntly remarked that "nothing can be done for Austria."[138]

Although unable to handpick the central bank's new governor, the Bank was able to lay the foundation for a reform that adhered to its vision of economic orthodoxy. In January 1923, the Austrian National Bank was established on the basis of the principles of sovereignty outlined by the 1922 Geneva Protocols.[139] It managed an initial capital base of 30 million gold-backed kronen, amassed from the reserves of both the former Austro-Hungarian Bank and the foreign-exchange office (*Devisenzentrale*).[140] Notes were backed by

to accept the position; Montagu Norman, Diary, December 15, 1922, BoE ADM34/11; Strakosch to Norman, December 30, 1922, BoE OV28/54.

136 Hans Kernbauer, *Währungspolitik in der Zwischenkriegszeit. Geschichte der Österreichischen Nationalbank von 1923 bis 1938* (Vienna: Oesterreichische Nationalbank, 1991), 77; Clemens Jobst and Hans Kernbauer, *Die Bank. Das Geld. Der Staat. Nationalbank und Währungspolitik in Österreich 1816–2016* (Frankfurt am Main: Campus Verlag, 2016), 160; Kernbauer, "Central Bank Policy," 112–113.

137 Committee of Treasury, Minutes, December 27, 1922, BoE G8/55.

138 Quoted in "No. 203: Mr. Akers-Douglas (Vienna) to the Marquess Curzon of Kedleston," December 22, 1922, in *Documents on British Foreign Policy, 1919–1939, First Series, vol.* 24, ed. W.N. Medlicott, Douglas Dakin, and Gillian Bennett (London: H.M. Stationery Office, 1983), 450; Piétri, *La Société des Nations*, 98; Fior, *Institution globale et marchés financiers*, 336.

139 The Geneva Protocols, signed on October 4, 1922, were three separate agreements that reaffirmed Austrian sovereignty, secured an international loan of 650 million gold crowns, and detailed the plans for monetary reconstruction; "Protocols Containing the Scheme for the Financial Reconstruction of Austria, Elaborated by the Council of the League of Nations and Signed at Geneva on October 4th, 1922," in League of Nations, *The Financial Reconstruction of Austria: General Survey and Principal Documents* (Geneva: League of Nations, 1926), 137–150; League of Nations, "Reconstruction de l'Autriche : accords préparés par la Société des Nations et signés à Genève le 4 octobre 1922," OeStA BKA-AA VR/42, ff. 666–694; Austrian National Bank, General Council, Meeting Minutes, April 17, 1923, OeNB I/4b. See also Piétri, *La Société des Nations*, 55–60; Sargent, "The Ends of Four Big Inflations," 52; Kernbauer, *Währungspolitik*, 56–58; Marcus, *Austrian Reconstruction*, 117; Jobst and Kernbauer, *Die Bank*, 157–158; Kernbauer, "Central Bank Policy," 110–111; Martin, *The Meddlers*, 87.

140 "Der erste Ausweis der Nationalbank," *Neue Freie Presse (Vienna)* 20957, January 14, 1923, 16; Austrian National Bank, "Special Memoranda on the Work of Reconstruction," in League of Nations, *The Financial Reconstruction of Austria: General Survey and Principal Documents* (Geneva: League of Nations, 1926), 90. See also Aurel Schubert, "The Emergence of National Central Banks in Central Europe after the Break-Up of the Austro-Hungarian Monarchy," in *The Emergence of Modern Central Banking from 1918 to the Present*, ed.

gold and gold-backed currencies, such as dollars or pounds. The new entity resembled the model of an orthodox central bank in accordance with the Brussels consensus.

With his plan for a central bank remaining largely intact, Strakosch was now able to divide his time between the Bank and the League. That month, he was invited to a meeting in the City to reevaluate the prospect of a loan. Many of the leading merchant bankers in the room, including Lord Revelstoke, Anthony de Rothschild, and Baron Schröder, might have all agreed that a loan was necessary, but they did not want to see the Bank (or British banks, in general) bear the full burden of its issuance. Although London was only able to commit to £1 million, Strakosch was tasked with procuring an additional £1 million from J.P. Morgan & Co. in New York.[141] The successful negotiation of such a loan required not only Austria's commitment to fiscal reform but also expert-led negotiations over a payment plan. Through his correspondence, Strakosch was able to convince the US bank that the Austrian government was in dire need of assistance – particularly to cover an estimated deficit of 457 million kronen – while simultaneously being fiscally capable of repaying any future loan.[142] After Austria announced plans to raise additional revenue from taxation and import duties, the City was able to raise £1.8 million in a short-term loan.[143]

By early March, Norman sought to gauge interest in the issuance of a long-term loan. Conversations with Niemeyer and Strakosch led to the agreement that Austria needed to engage in a publicity campaign with the press to raise confidence in the stabilization program.[144] Acting as the mediator between New York bankers and League officials, Strakosch served as Britain's main representative on the Committee of Control. The group again confronted the issue of how to convince foreign investors that Austria was desperately in need of a loan while also proving that the government was capable of repaying its debts in the future. It debated whether a loan could even be raised under the present circumstances. Initially, Janssen indicated that Belgian banks would probably be willing to support such a plan, contingent upon a guarantee that the central bank would not engage in

Carl-Ludwig Holtfrerich, Jaime Reis, and Gianni Toniolo (Aldershot: Ashgate, 1999), 196; Jobst and Kernbauer, *Die Bank*, 158–161.

141 "Meeting at the Bank," January 15, 1923, BoE OV28/54; Strakosch to Niemeyer, January 15, 1923, BoE OV28/54.

142 Morgan, Grenfell & Co. to J.P. Morgan & Co., January 16, 1923, BoE OV28/54; Marcus, *Austrian Reconstruction*, 162.

143 Franckenstein to Alfred Grünberger [Foreign Minister, Austria], March 1, 1923, OeSTA BKA-AA HP/335; Harvey to Franckenstein, March 2, 1923, OeSTA BKA-AA HP/335; Austrian National Bank, Board of Directors, Meeting Minutes, March 1, 1923, OeNB I/5a; Piétri, *La Société des Nations*, 101–102; Marcus, *Austrian Reconstruction*, 164.

144 Clay, *Lord Norman*, 188; Beyersdorf, "'Credit or Chaos'?," 140.

speculative transactions.[145] Strakosch, however, wanted further assurances from Austria. He convinced the other members of the committee that any successful intervention would need to be "organized in a manner that safeguarded the interests of the guarantor states."[146]

Both expert opinion and promises of fiscal austerity prompted the successful flotation of a long-term loan, with its underwriting completed by June 7 and a public issue made on June 11. The General Council of the Austrian central bank unanimously agreed to list the loan on the Vienna Stock Exchange.[147] Rationalization across the civil service and government administration, coupled with the introduction of a turnover tax (*Umsatzsteuer*), made the plan amenable to the Financial Committee.[148] Before the League's Assembly in September, Strakosch praised the government for implementing a stabilization program that could serve as a model for other nations.[149] He believed that the nation was now better poised to manage its expenditures without experiencing inflation due to the controlled issuance of Treasury bills.[150] With this added confidence, the international community reacted positively to the spending plans, and capital inflows into Austria recommenced shortly thereafter.[151]

CRAFTING A STABILIZATION POLICY

Strakosch's advisory missions to South Africa and Austria set a precedent for future monetary interventions. The relative success of early reconstruction projects appeared to prove the viability of economic orthodoxy, an ideology that defined subsequent reforms in Central Europe, Eastern Europe, and India.

In November 1923, Strakosch attended the Imperial Conference in London, where he represented South Africa on the Committee on Inter-Imperial Exchanges. Chaired by a Bank director, Charles Addis, the committee discussed the potential return to the gold standard throughout the British Empire. The representatives concluded that both the United Kingdom and the Dominions needed to peg their currencies to gold if they wanted to promote intra-imperial trade, further supported by new note-issuing institutions.[152] By extension, the

145 Comité de contrôle des États garants de l'emprunt autrichien, "Troisième session. Procès-verbal de la troisième séance tenue à Genève le dimanche 15 avril 1923, à 11 h," LoN C39/39/6/6c.

146 Comité de contrôle des États garants de l'emprunt autrichien, "Troisième session. Procès-verbal de la quatrième séance, tenue à Genève le dimanche 15 avril 1923, à 16.30 h," LoN C39/39/6/6c.

147 Austrian National Bank, General Council, Meeting Minutes, June 27, 1923, OeNB I/4b.

148 Warnock, "The First Bailout," 161; Marcus, *Austrian Reconstruction*, 158.

149 "Sir H. Strakosch on Austria," *The Times* 43447, September 15, 1923, 15.

150 Commission économique et financière, "12ème session, Londres, Nov. 1923. Troisième séance," November 21, 1923, LoN R335/10/32492/11519.

151 "Lamont Praises Unity on Loan to Austria," *The New York Times* LXXII, 23882, June 14, 1923, 7; Marcus, *Austrian Reconstruction*, 168.

152 Committee on Inter-Imperial Exchanges, "Resolutions Agreed by the Committee at Their Meeting on November 6, 1923," TNA T160/550; "Resolutions Agreed to by the Committee

committee effectively identified a link between reconstruction and British financial interests. If the value of sterling were internationally recognized, then the confidence needed to return to the gold standard could have been assured. Continued fluctuations of the South African pound led Prime Minister Smuts to call again upon the Strakosch's advisory services. "Exchange problems are ever with us in South Africa," he wrote, "[and] I should value your opinion very highly."[153]

Strakosch, concerned about the broader stabilization of the global financial system, focused on institutionalizing orthodox principles elsewhere. He shared ideas of economic reform while serving as a member of the Royal Commission on Indian Currency and Finance. The commission included prominent bankers, industrialists, and experts: Rajendra Mookerjee, a railway and steel industrialist; Norcot Warren, the managing governor of the Imperial Bank of India; and J.C. Coyajee, a professor of political economy. During one discussion on the possible adoption of the gold standard, the representatives considered a proposal written by the UK Treasury on the need for a central bank. Strakosch certainly understood the importance of such an institution for instilling confidence in the currency. Yet there was also a broader question on future governance, namely whether the reformers wanted to establish a completely new institution or to rewrite the statutes of an existing commercial bank, such as the Imperial Bank of India. On this matter, Strakosch brought with him the knowledge of prior experience. An independent central bank in India seemed likely to succeed given that similar types of institutions already existed in Austria, Hungary, Germany, Switzerland, and the United Kingdom.[154] As both a member of the commission and Norman's link to the India Office, Strakosch effectively became the Bank's ambassador abroad.

In other countries, too, orthodoxy had become the core of the Bank's stabilization policy. Beginning in August 1922, the Kingdom of Hungary had experienced its own severe bout of hyperinflation with a rapidly depreciating currency. A subsequent intervention by the League culminated in the establishment of the Hungarian National Bank in May 1924.[155] Throughout the

at Their Meeting on the 6th November, 1923," in *Imperial Economic Conference: Records of Proceedings and Documents*, Cmd. 2009 (London: H.M. Stationery Office, 1924), 479.

153 Smuts to Strakosch, December 11, 1923, UWA Smuts Papers A1337-49.

154 "Mr H Denning," November 27, 1925, in Royal Commission on Indian Currency and Finance, *Minutes of Evidence Taken in India, vol.* 4 (London: H.M. Stationery Office, 1926), 75.

155 On reconstruction in Hungary, see Péteri, "Central Bank Diplomacy," 247–251; Bátonyi, *Britain and Central Europe*, 128–148; Kenneth Mouré, "French Money Doctors, Central Banks, and Politics in the 1920s," in *Money Doctors: The Experience of International Financial Advising, 1850–2000*, ed. Marc Flandreau (London and New York: Routledge, 2005), 143–144; Miklós Lojkó, *Meddling in Middle Europe: Britain and the "Lands Between", 1919–1925* (Budapest and New York: Central European University Press, 2006), 61–126; Fior, *Institution globale et marchés financiers*, 296–299, 338–343; Zoltán Peterecz, *Jeremiah Smith, Jr. and Hungary, 1924–1926: The United States, the League of Nations, and the Financial Reconstruction of Hungary* (London: Versita, 2013); György Péteri, "Sneaking Nationalization: Hungary and the Liberal Monetary Order, 1924–1931," in *The Spread of*

numerous discussions over monetary and fiscal reform, Strakosch had been primarily involved in the contentious loan negotiations, and he had written to the prime minister, Count Bethlen, about the importance of employing a technical expert and the former Finance Minister, Alexander Popovics, to lead the new central bank.[156] Doing so would increase the likelihood of Hungary being able to additional credits in the future. This continued pressure succeeded in facilitating Popovics' appointment as the first president. Through this intervention, Strakosch was able to claim that he had earned the trust of "personages of the official and financial world whose opinions carry the greatest weight."[157]

Still, Strakosch also required additional support from other experts, who could offer him on-the-ground information and additional legitimacy. While in Budapest, he collaborated closely with another financial expert, Harry A. Siepmann, to determine the structural reform needed. As a former Treasury official, Siepmann had been Keynes' personal assistant during the Paris Peace Conference and was later the secretary of the Supreme Economic Council's Financial Committee.[158] In 1924, he joined the National Bank of Hungary as an adviser, a post that allowed him to share details on continental affairs with the Bank. Concerning the League's intervention in Austria, he reported:

> I was in Vienna last weekend and it was like being in a different world. A kind of feudal aristocracy; an insolently bureaucratic and tyrannous Government; incredible incompetence in the administration, and a swarm of vultures, largely indigenous but partly foreign, who demand carrion and putrefaction because they live on it. A press so vile that it defies description and comparison; and a general demoralisation of the national spirit which makes it pretty useless to appeal for support in difficult times.[159]

Siepmann and Strakosch crafted a stabilization plan for Hungary similar to the one enacted in Austria. They took into account the interests of the Bank and the City by seeking to establish an independent central bank. Even so, both were aware of the potential challenges associated with such a plan. Hungary's fiscal issues persisted well after its episode of hyperinflation, leading Norman to conclude, "No one in the world really wants these Hungarian Bonds and the Americans won't even touch them with a barge-pole."[160] Nevertheless, the Governor wanted his experts to amass support for a loan despite the difficulties.

the Modern Central Bank and Global Cooperation, 1919–1939, ed. Barry Eichengreen and Andreas Kakridis (Cambridge: Cambridge University Press, 2023): 139–159.

156 Montagu Norman, Diary, January 23 and May 30, 1924, BoE ADM34/13; "Reconstruction of Hungary," *The Times* 43618, April 4, 1924, 19; Strakosch to Count Bethlen, April 10, 1924, BoE OV33/71; Strakosch to Smith, June 19, 1924, BoE OV33/72; Norman to Strakosch, June 19, 1924, BoE OV33/72.

157 Strakosch to Popovics, April 10, 1924, BoE OV33/71.

158 Harry Siepmann, *Echo of the Guns: Recollections of an Artillery Officer, 1914–18* (London: Robert Hale, 1987), 177.

159 Siepmann to Norman, May 12, 1924, BoE ADM25/14.

160 Norman to Siepmann, May 26, 1924, BoE ADM25/14.

As he pressed Siepmann, "it[']s your job to get here just as soon as you can and mine to give you whatever push or inducement I can."[161]

At its core, European reconstruction may have been primarily concerned with financial matters. Writing to Arthur Salter, the Director of the League's Economic Section, Governor Norman predicted that the countries of Central Europe would continue to experience "periods of temporary strain," similar to the one experienced in Austria.[162] Yet reconstruction was also a politically contentious ordeal that could only work during a moment of ideological convergence among central banks, private banks, and national governments. Advised by Strakosch and Siepmann, the Bank undertook repeated efforts to reduce public spending across Central Europe. In the summer of 1924, Norman wrote to Zimmerman about the worrisome economic conditions in Austria, leading him to recommend whether the central bank could add a permanent clause to introduce "sound principles" into its monetary policy.[163] Strakosch similarly intended to meet with Zimmerman to discuss how to balance the budget later that month.[164]

If Austria intended to continue accepting foreign capital without adequate reform to its public finance, the proportional appreciation of its currency would imply that its exports would not have been able to compete with those of newly stabilized economies, such as Hungary, Germany, and Poland.[165] So, too, would it become necessary to tighten the overall level of credit. Alongside Bank officials, Strakosch criticized the spending practices of the Austrian government, specifically the argument made by the finance minister that budget deficits were a result of the weakened purchasing power of the Austrian krone abroad.[166] He also challenged the Austrian National Bank's claim that cutting interest rates would have helped lower prices.[167] By demonstrating his thorough understanding of the Austrian economy, as well as monetary policy more generally, the distinguished *éminence grise* further solidified the idea of the "impartial" financial expert in contemporary discourse.

While often supported by the League of Nations, stabilization programs represented a novel type of British economic diplomacy. With little experience in international relations, the Old Guard resorted to expert involvement when it suited the Bank's interests. It was thus a strategic choice to employ

161 Norman to Siepmann, May 26, 1924, BoE ADM25/14.

162 Norman to Salter, October 23, 1924, LoN R373/10/40856/19041; "Temporary Borrowing by Central Banks," October 1924, LoN R373/10/40856/19041.

163 Norman to Zimmerman, July 1, 1924, BoE OV9/384.

164 Strakosch to Norman, July 28, 1924, BoE OV9/384.

165 Comité financier, "15ème session. Procès-verbal de la 4ème séance, tenue à Genève, le jeudi 12 juin 1924 à 15 heures 15," June 12, 1924, LoN C37/37/6/5b.

166 Henry Strakosch, "Austria," October 12, 1924, BoE OV28/59. See also Strakosch to Norman, July 1, 1924, BoE OV28/59; Norman to Zimmerman, July 1, 1924, BoE OV28/59; Montagu Norman, Diary, March 16, 1925, BoE ADM34/14.

167 Strakosch to Quesnay, January 23, 1925, ANF Quesnay Papers 374AP/2.

Siepmann, a Treasury official with practical experience. When he arrived at the Bank in July 1926, he took on some of the responsibilities that Strakosch informally had. Throughout the 1920s, Siepmann had visited the central banks of Norway, Czechoslovakia, Poland, and Yugoslavia, and he had been directly involved in currency reform in Estonia, where he drafted statutes for the new central bank.[168]

To ensure that Austria followed a similar path, Norman, Niemeyer, and Strakosch conducted several "interviews" with Reisch, during which they urged him to consider the impact of monetary policy on price levels.[169] These backdoor interrogations allowed the Bank to exert indirect influence over Austrian affairs without spurring public backlash. Although Strakosch argued that credit restrictions and "the adoption of a property monetary policy" were the only ways to control prices, Reisch countered that he was effectively "powerless" to act.[170] However, Strakosch was not convinced of this argument, and he aimed to use his position on the League's Financial Committee to exert additional pressure. After inviting Reisch to Geneva, Strakosch used the legal apparatus of the League, which had facilitated the loan, to reduce Austria's budget.[171] This strategic maneuvering was largely successful. By December 1925, the Council agreed to adopt the Financial Committee's resolutions and work toward limiting Austrian public spending.[172]

RIVAL EXPERTS

Efforts by the Bank and the League to infuse these new institutions with the principles of economic orthodoxy recommenced in the summer of 1924. While on the League's Financial Committee, chaired by ter Meulen, Strakosch had been able to exert considerable influence over Austria's economic policy. He intended to press the government further on addressing its "unfavorable" balance of payments despite the generous loan he had helped facilitate.[173] His

[168] Barry Eichengreen and Andreas Kakridis, "Interwar Central Banks: A Tour d'Horizon," in *The Spread of the Modern Central Bank and Global Cooperation, 1919–1939*, ed. Barry Eichengreen and Andreas Kakridis (Cambridge: Cambridge University Press, 2023), 31.

[169] J.A.C. Osborne, "Second Interview with Dr. Reisch," December 10, 1924, BoE OV28/29; J.A.C. Osborne, "Dr. Reich's 3rd Visit," December 11, 1924, BoE OV28/29; Austrian National Bank, General Council, Meeting Minutes, December 18, 1924, OeNB I/4b.

[170] Quoted in Charles Frederick Whigham [Morgan, Grenfell & Co.] to Lamont, December 16, 1924, HBS Lamont Papers Box 83.

[171] Financial Committee, "Report to the Council on the Seventeenth Session of the Committee," February 14, 1925, LoN R506/10B/42424/24453; "Conversation Between the Governor and Sir Henry Strakosch," February 25, 1925, BoE OV28/29.

[172] Financial Committee, "Resolutions Adopted by the Council at its Thirty-Seventh Session," December 11, 1925, LoN R339/10/48311/11519.

[173] Comité financier, "15ème session. Procès-verbal de la 3ème séance, tenue à Genève, le jeudi 12 juin 1924 à 10 heures," June 12, 1924, LoN C37/37/6/5b.

seemingly simultaneous presence in South Africa remained equally as noticeable. As the *Rand Daily Mail* reported, "Sir Henry Strakosch has been very warmly welcomed in the city, especially in South African mining circles, where Sir Henry's rise to international recognition as a leading economist has been watched with sympathy and appreciation of his sterling abilities."[174]

The Bank envisioned working with Strakosch to impose additional reforms on the South African monetary system. Writing to Smuts, Norman detailed how his experts recommended the adoption of a sterling-exchange standard, as was being simultaneously debated in Australian and New Zealand circles.[175] Yet the limits of the Bank's intervention were determined by those who challenged its legitimacy or claimed greater authority. In late 1924, the Union government decided to invite two "money doctors" to investigate the possibility of returning to the gold standard. Edwin W. Kemmerer, a professor of economics at Princeton University, advocated the adoption of a gold standard due to the continued fluctuations of the British pound.[176] He had previously conducted advisory missions to Mexico (1917), Guatemala (1919), and Colombia (1923). Another expert, Gerald Vissering, former president of the Java Bank (1906–1912) and president of De Nederlandsche Bank (1912–1931), had acquired more practical knowledge of overseas banking and was a close colleague of Smuts.[177]

Over the course of the mission, the two experts conducted hearings and procured evidence from South African officials. Much of the testimony focused on the benefits for South Africa in returning to the gold standard, regardless of the policy adopted in the United Kingdom. Evans, for instance, argued that the establishment of a free market for gold could help combat domestic inflation. In his words, "the importance of gold to this country can hardly be exaggerated."[178] For another South African economist, John E. Holloway (Transvaal University College), deflation was the more likely outcome of inaction due to the country's fundamentally unstable economic conditions. Further informed by the recent bout of hyperinflation in Germany, he believed that drastic fiscal reform needed to accompany the creation of a central bank.[179]

[174] "A Leading Economist," *Rand Daily Mail (Johannesburg)* 15, 6669, July 5, 1924, 8.

[175] Norman to Smuts, January 4, 1924, UWA Smuts Papers A1337-55.

[176] C.S. Richards, "The Kemmerer–Vissering Report and the Position of the Reserve Bank of the Union of South Africa," *The Economic Journal* 35, no. 140 (1925), 563; "Back to Gold: Government's Action Defended," *Rand Daily Mail (Johannesburg)* 15, 6923, April 9, 1925, 12.

[177] Vissering to Smuts, June 23, 1921, UWA Smuts Papers A1337-38.

[178] "Mr. Samuel Evans," December 17, 1924, in *Report Submitted by Dr. Edwin Walter Kemmerer and Dr. Gerard Vissering on the Resumption of Gold Payments by the Union of South Africa*, U.G. 13–'25 (Pretoria: The Government Printing and Stationery Office, 1925), 58.

[179] J.E. Holloway, "The German Currency," 1921, UFS Holloway Papers 6/2/1; "Professor John Edward Holloway, D.Sc.," December 18, 1924, in *Report Submitted by Dr. Edwin Walter Kemmerer and Dr. Gerard Vissering*, 148.

Price stabilization would have been one direct consequence of tying the currency to some stable value, whether gold or sterling. While the Bank may have preferred the latter, it was the exchange of technical views among rival experts that determined the course of future reforms. Kemmerer crafted a plan that centered on the gold-exchange standard, a system in which the South African pound would be backed by both gold and gold-backed currencies. Although gold was not allowed to freely circulate, a stable exchange rate promised to offer South African consumers and importers greater purchasing power on international markets.[180] This reform resembled Kemmerer's prior work in the Philippines, which had adopted the gold-exchange standard in 1905. It was a relevant case study for him of how a country was able to prevent the outflows of gold during a financial panic through fiscal and monetary stabilization.[181]

Based on this advice, the Union Government reversed its policy of maintaining the peg to the pound, instead opting to a return to a gold-backed currency in January 1925. Governor Norman was reportedly irritated at South Africa's decision to reject the idea of a sterling-based standard.[182] Others in leading financial circles, however, were less alarmed. Clegg supported the proposal to tie the currency to gold (not the pound) because of the stability it would entail: "In the disturbed state of Europe, something might happen which would cause her to take retrograde steps. In that event, South Africa should be free to take her own course and so avoid all the worries and woes of another inflation, and subsequent deflation."[183] Strakosch, too, admitted that he was "frankly not displeased with their recommendation" because of the stability offered by a return to gold.[184] For him, other foreign experts had provided a less than optimal solution, yet an acceptable one.

In the years thereafter, Strakosch continued to influence international economic relations.[185] While on the Council of India, and later as an adviser to

[180] "Union of South Africa Report Submitted by Dr. Edwin Walter Kemmerer and Dr. G. Vissering on the Resumption of Gold Payments by the Union of South Africa," January 8, 1925, BoE OV37/21. See also "Kemmerer–Vissering Report on the Resumption of Gold Payments by the Union of South Africa," 1925, PUL Kemmerer Papers Box 343; Edwin Walter Kemmerer, "The Gold Exchange Standard," 1928, PUL Kemmerer Papers Box 251, Folder 3; De Kock, *A History of the South African Reserve Bank*, 67–73; Dalgaard, *South Africa's Impact*, 103–104.

[181] E.W. Kemmerer, "The Establishment of the Gold Exchange Standard in the Philippines," *The Quarterly Journal of Economics* 19, no. 4 (1905): 585–609; Rebeca Gomez Betancourt, "The Political Economy of a Modern Missionary: E.W. Kemmerer in the Philippines," *History of Political Economy* 54, no. 3 (2022): 483–505; Allan E.S. Lumba, *Monetary Authorities: Capitalism and Decolonization in the American Colonial Philippines* (Durham and London: Duke University Press, 2022), 71–87.

[182] Martin, *South Africa and the World Economy*, 85.

[183] W.H. Clegg, "Memorandum on Resumption of Gold Payments," December 15, 1924, PUL Kemmerer Papers Box 217, Folder 1.

[184] Quoted in Ally, *Gold & Empire*, 132.

[185] On Strakosch in the 1930s, see Kenneth Mouré, *Managing the Franc Poincaré: Economic Understanding and Political Constraint in French Monetary Policy, 1928–1936* (Cambridge:

the Secretary of State, he represented the country at several international conferences, including ones in Ottawa (1932) and London (1933). As chairman of *The Economist*, he wrote several articles about the problems plaguing the global world economy.[186] The continued decline in commodity prices, coupled with the high debts incurred by European states, further inhibited a general recovery. This problem led him to design the Convention on Financial Assistance (1930), an agreement signed by thirty countries (but not ratified) to reduce debt obligations.[187] Reforms thus reconciled the various and often divergent goals of commercial banks, national governments, and international organizations. By restructuring national financial systems across Europe and the British Empire, Strakosch upheld the tenets of economic orthodoxy and institutionalized expertise in interwar governance.

Cambridge University Press, 1991), 50–51; Kenneth Mouré, *The Gold Standard Illusion: France, the Bank of France, and the International Gold Standard, 1914–1939* (Oxford: Oxford University Press, 2002), 172–176; Robert Boyce, "La Banque de France et la Banque d'Angleterre dans l'entre-deux-guerres : origines et conséquences d'un conflit," in *Politiques et pratiques des banques d'émission en Europe (XVIIe–XXe siècle) : le bicentenaire de la Banque de France dans la perspective de l'identité monétaire européenne*, ed. Olivier Feiertag and Michel Margairaz (Paris: Albin Michel, 2003), 471–473.

[186] Henry Strakosch, "Gold and the Price Level: A Memorandum on the Economic Consequences of Changes in the Value of Gold," *Supplement to the Economist* 111, 4532, July 5, 1930, 3–11; Henry Strakosch, "The Crisis: A Memorandum," *Supplement to the Economist* 114, 4611, January 9, 1932, 3–8; Henry Strakosch, "Die Krisis. Eine Denkschrift," January 19, 1932, GStA PK, I. HA Rep. 84a; Henry Strakosch, "The Road to Recovery," *Supplement to the Economist* 120, 4767, January 5, 1935, 1–12.

[187] Henry Strakosch, "The Convention on Financial Assistance," *International Affairs* 10, no. 2 (March 1931): 208–222; Mulder, *The Economic Weapon*, 163–164.

3

Economic Statistics

I think one must remember that the collection of statistics is a development of recent years.[1]

—Robert Kindersley, 1930

Exact quantitative knowledge concerning the chief elements of the monetary and financial system is, we consider, of the utmost importance, both to provide the necessary data on which to base the management of the system and also for the purpose of making gradually possible a more definitely scientific treatment of these problems than the existing state of our knowledge of the facts allows.[2]

—Macmillan Committee, 1931

The growing use of statistics in economic discussions involves a danger because so few people yet understand the limits or possibilities of statistics.[3]

—Henry Clay, 1933

The postwar recession of the early 1920s witnessed the largest contraction of the UK economy in over two centuries.[4] Sterling, which had been forced to abandon the gold standard – de facto in August 1914, de jure in March

[1] "Sir Robert M. Kindersley, G.B.E.," January 23, 1930, in Macmillan Committee, *Minutes of Evidence, vol. 1*, 76.

[2] Committee on Finance and Industry, *Report*, Cmd. 3897 (London: H.M. Stationery Office, 1931), 174. Also quoted in Forrest Capie and Alan Webber, *A Monetary History of the United Kingdom, 1870–1982: vol. 1, Data, Sources and Methods* (London: George Allen & Unwin, 1985), 7; Charles A.E. Goodhart and Duncan J. Needham, "Historical Reasons for the Focus on Broad Monetary Aggregates in Post-World War II Britain and the 'Seven Years War' with the IMF," *Financial History Review* 24, no. 3 (2017), 335.

[3] Henry Clay, "Memorandum to Mr. [William] Clegg," July 6, 1933, BoE ADM22/27.

[4] According to present-day estimates, the change in real GDP in 1921 had been the largest single-year decline since the Great Frost of 1709; "A8. Real Compromise/Balanced Estimates of GDP – 'GDP(a),' 1700–2016," in *A Millennium of Macroeconomic Data for the UK: The*

1919 – depreciated against the dollar from its prewar parity of $4.86 to a low of $3.38 in February 1920. Both the unemployment rate and the national debt rose to unprecedented levels. Beyond their immediate consequences, these financial issues served as the catalyst for institutional change. A search for stability, coupled with concurrent developments in the economics discipline, created conditions for experts to obtain prominent positions in government ministries, private corporations, and international organizations.

The Bank was one of the forerunners in the development of economic expertise. It employed its first economist, Walter W. Stewart, a professor at Amherst College and director at the Federal Reserve, in 1927. As officials continued to grapple with the consequences of the war, they began to hire additional advisers who could offer technical insights into monetary policy. By the 1930s, a new cohort of economists – Oliver M.W. Sprague, a professor at Harvard Business School; Henry Clay, an Oxford-educated economist and professor at the University of Manchester; and Humphrey Mynors, a Fellow at Corpus Christi College, Cambridge – reflected the growing importance of specialized knowledge at the central bank.

An institutional interest in data had certainly not been new. Since the eighteenth century, statisticians employed quantitative tools as a way of achieving supposedly objective measurements.[5] Notable advancements in surveying techniques proliferated in the late nineteenth and early twentieth centuries, in part driven by attempts to understand poverty and unemployment.[6] Yet it was primarily the unresolved consequences of the First World War that revealed the fragility of the global economic system and brought the social sciences to the forefront of policy debates. Economists and statisticians pioneered new research in the areas of national-income accounting and business-cycle

Bank of England's Collection of Historical Macroeconomic and Financial Statistics, Version 3.1, 2018, www.bankofengland.co.uk/statistics/research-datasets.

[5] Theodore M. Porter, *The Rise of Statistical Thinking, 1820–1900* (Princeton: Princeton University Press, 1986); Stephen M. Stigler, *The History of Statistics: The Measurement of Uncertainty before 1900* (Cambridge, MA, and London: Harvard University Press, 1986); Theodore M. Porter, *Trust in Numbers: The Pursuit of Objectivity in Science and Public Life* (Princeton: Princeton University Press, 1995); William Deringer, *Calculated Values: Finance, Politics, and the Quantitative Age* (Cambridge, MA, and London: Harvard University Press, 2018).

[6] For instance, Arthur Lyon Bowley conducted extensive studies on national income and inequality in London: A.L. Bowley and A.R. Burnett-Hurst, *Livelihood and Poverty: A Study in the Economic Conditions of Working-Class Households in Northampton, Warrington, Stanley and Reading* (London: G. Bell and Sons, 1915); A.L. Bowley and M.H. Hogg, *Has Poverty Diminished?* (London: P.S. King & Son, 1925); A.L. Bowley and Josiah Stamp, *The National Income, 1924* (Oxford: Clarendon Press, 1927); Tom Crook and Glen O'Hara, "The 'Torrent of Numbers': Statistics and the Public Sphere in Britain, c. 1800–2000," in *Statistics and the Public Sphere: Numbers and the People in Modern Britain, c. 1800–2000*, ed. Tom Crook and Glen O'Hara (New York and London: Routledge, 2011), 13; George R. Boyer, *The Winding Road to the Welfare State: Economic Insecurity and Social Welfare Policy in Britain* (Princeton and Oxford: Princeton University Press, 2019), 170–179.

research.[7] Efforts to standardize economic terminology culminated in several international meetings, including the Conference of Central Bank Statisticians in Paris (1927) and the International Conference on Economic Statistics in Geneva (1928). In these venues, the notion of an "economy" that could be studied or managed had emerged.[8]

To assess the impact of high national debts and volatile exchange rates, the Bank devised new statistical measures that assessed ongoing economic trends. For many of its directors, statistics helped to establish legitimacy and justify decisions taken by the central bank. "When Statistics support conclusions already arrived at," wrote one of the Bank's statisticians, "they provide illustrations and arguments in defence of opinion."[9] At the same time, there was a genuine effort to learn from experts, particularly those with competencies outside the usual realm of knowledge. In 1921, the establishment of the Bank's first research department, the Economic Section, embodied the emerging interest in economic statistics. According to one director, "an improved statistical technique in the handling of social data is absolutely vital to the

[7] Tooze, *Statistics and the German State*; Daniel Speich, "The Use of Global Abstractions: National Income Accounting in the Period of Imperial Decline," *Journal of Global History* 6, no. 1 (2011): 7–28; Diane Coyle, *GDP: A Brief but Affectionate History* (Princeton and Oxford: Princeton University Press, 2014); Walter A. Friedman, *Fortune Tellers: The Story of America's First Economic Forecasters* (Princeton and Oxford: Princeton University Press, 2014); Quinn Slobodian, "How to See the World Economy: Statistics, Maps, and Schumpeter's Camera in the First Age of Globalization," *Journal of Global History* 10, no. 2 (2015): 307–332; Martin Bemmann, "Das Chaos beseitigen. Die internationale Standardisierung forst-und holzwirtschaftlicher Statistiken in den 1920er und 1930er Jahren und der Völkerbund," *Jahrbuch für Wirtschaftsgeschichte* 57, no. 2 (2016): 545–587; Eli Cook, *The Pricing of Progress: Economic Indicators and the Capitalization of American Life* (Cambridge, MA, and London: Harvard University Press, 2017); Quinn Slobodian, *Globalists: The End of Empire and the Birth of Neoliberalism* (Cambridge, MA, and London: Harvard University Press, 2018), 59–73; Jamie Martin, "Time and the Economics of the Business Cycle in Modern Capitalism," in *Power and Time: Temporalities in Conflict and the Making of History*, ed. Dan Edelstein, Stefanos Geroulanos, and Natasha Wheatley (Chicago and London: The University of Chicago Press, 2020): 317–334; Martin Bemmann, *Weltwirtschaftsstatistik. Internationale Wirtschaftsstatistik und die Geschichte der Globalisierung, 1850–1950* (Berlin and Boston: De Gruyter Oldenbourg, 2023).

[8] Timothy Mitchell, "Fixing the Economy," *Cultural Studies* 12, no. 1 (1998): 82–101; J. Adam Tooze, "Imagining National Economies: National and International Economic Statistics, 1900–1950," in *Imagining Nations*, ed. Geoffrey Cubitt (Manchester and New York: Manchester University Press, 1998): 212–228; Margaret Schabas, "Constructing 'the Economy'," *Philosophy of the Social Sciences* 39, no. 1 (2009): 3–19; Timothy Mitchell, "Economists and Economy in the Twentieth Century," in *The Politics of Method in the Human Sciences: Positivism and its Epistemological Other*, ed. George Steinmetz (Durham: Duke University Press, 2005): 126–142; Jim Tomlinson, *Managing the Economy, Managing the People: Narratives of Economic Life in Britain from Beveridge to Brexit* (Oxford: Oxford University Press, 2017), 2; Jonathan Levy, *The Real Economy: History and Theory* (Princeton and Oxford: Princeton University Press, 2025).

[9] J.A.C. Osborne, "Memorandum for the Deputy Governor," November 1925, BoE EID8/1.

further progress of economic science."[10] Even Governor Montagu Norman, who was known for his deep distrust of theory and data, conceded that there was some value in quantitative research at the Bank: "We are in need of a system for the collection and preparation of Statistics and other information on economic questions which may guide us in our financial policy."[11]

It was also true that the Bank remained relatively insulated from contemporary academic debates. The major intellectual theories on economic growth, marginal utility, and the general equilibrium pioneered by leading Cambridge economists – John Maynard Keynes, Arthur Cecil Pigou, Dennis Robertson, Joan Robinson, and Piero Sraffa, among them – fell largely outside the Bank's purview. Instead, the directors were primarily concerned with the study of practical, rather than theoretical, concepts. As one adviser described, "[o]ur present statistical knowledge is very far from reflecting, even with admitted margins for errors ... the full diversity of economic conditions, and I believe if we really guided our affairs by mathematical deductions from such figures as exist we should be both surprised and pained at the result."[12] To contemporaries, quantitative tools and models were supplements, not the driving force, behind policy recommendations.

Statistics, regardless of its limitations, influenced how the Bank viewed the global economy. It affected how officials interpreted rapid changes in the national and international financial system. The quantification of economic phenomena – from exchange rates and prices to unemployment and wages – appeared critical for resolving the multitude of financial and political instabilities arising from the First World War. As the Bank became interested in such methods, it employed statisticians from prominent universities, economists with technical training, and experts with established reputations to lead its in-house research projects. Evolving priorities throughout the Great Depression, coupled with broader efforts to reform domestic governance, created channels for the Bank to shape the study of economic statistics.

EMPLOYING ECONOMISTS

With the collapse of the old European order, the Bank had become an institution with new objectives. Its directors sought to ensure that the central bank would lead future reform efforts, both at home and abroad. Their agenda involved restoring stability to an economic system devastated by war and

[10] Josiah Stamp, "Economics as an Exact Science – An Appeal to Accountancy," October 1921, in *Studies in Current Problems in Finance and Government* (London: P.S. King & Son, 1924), 11.

[11] Norman to Stewart, June 6, 1927, FRBNY Strong Papers 1117.2, Part 1.

[12] Niemeyer to Giblin, October 19, 1932, NLA Copland Papers Series 90.

promoting the orthodox tenets of the gold standard, free trade, and balanced budgets.

It was also in response to these circumstances that a national interest emerged in the study of statistics. As early as 1918, the Bank had begun to promote the study of a more specialized type of education. Governor Norman convinced the Court of Directors to support the University of London's new commerce degree that would train candidates for practical careers in the City.[13] By the 1920s, the Bank's main decision-making body, the Committee of Treasury, endeavored to revive the statistical work that had been abruptly discontinued during the war. There had previously been no full-time research department or body of experts dedicated to the study of economics. Only a few attempts at ad hoc statistical analysis had been made by a single non-economist, Eric Neale Dalton, who had compiled "about a dozen graphs, mostly of the Bank's own figures."[14]

In August 1921, the Committee of Treasury established the Bank's first in-house research department, the Economic Section. Housed within the Chief Cashier's Office, the group initially focused on compiling publicly available statistics. Its work mainly involved collecting information on domestic monetary and banking conditions, "which the Governors and executive departments might require," although often without regard for original insights or in-depth analysis.[15] Still, statistics could offer a better understanding of global economic events as they transpired. In Germany, economic vulnerabilities and political instability, exacerbated further by the Franco-Belgian occupation of the Ruhr, contributed to inflationary pressures in the summer of 1922. At the height of the hyperinflation period, the Committee of Treasury debated different ways of supporting the German economy, such as by issuing a loan, balancing the budget, and facilitating the repayment of war debts.[16] One of the research department's first projects thus involved preparing fifteen charts on imports, exports, and customs data for the Transfer Committee, created after the 1924 Dawes Plan.[17] Those working in the department also added brief comments to select charts they sent abroad.[18]

Administrative innovations at the Bank occurred amidst a broader evolution in governance in Britain. In the early twentieth century, new forms of hierarchical organization, as theorized by Max Weber in *Wirtschaft und*

[13] Committee of Treasury, Minutes, July 31, 1918, BoE G8/54. The Bank offered the university a sum of £6,300 to support commercial education; Sayers, *The Bank of England, vol.* 2, 610.

[14] Quoted in "Some Discursive Notes on the Statistical Section," October 29, 1930, BoE EID8/1.

[15] Quoted in Henry Clay, "Memorandum to Mr. [William] Clegg," July 6, 1933, BoE ADM22/27.

[16] Committee of Treasury, Minutes, October 25, 1922, BoE G8/55; Committee of Treasury, Minutes, January 23, 1924, BoE G8/55. On the Committee of Treasury as an institution, see Hennessy, "The Governors, Directors and Management," 190–191.

[17] "Statistical Section: Charts," November 1925, BoE EID8/1.

[18] J.A.C. Osborne, "Mémoire présenté par M. J.A.C. Osborne (Banque d'Angleterre)," April 12, 1928, BdF 1370200401/1.

Gesellschaft (1922), based on rational frameworks of administration became a seemingly inescapable facet of modern society.[19] This transition characterized the national government's novel hiring practices, embodied by a narrowing gap between upper-class elites and middle-class workers.[20] While an old system of patronage still persisted, the introduction of entrance examinations for the military academies and the civil service (the Home Office, Foreign Office, and Board of Trade) marked the beginning of the decline in aristocratic dominance.[21] Under Sir Warren Fisher, the Head of the Home Civil Service and the Permanent Secretary to the Treasury (1919–1939), the reformed civil service evolved into a bureaucratic apparatus with standardized hiring practices, a regulated allocation of spending throughout the government departments, and a competitive exam.[22] University education and merit-based selection began to symbolize a new turn-of-the-century professional ideal.[23]

Interwar Britain witnessed not only the introduction of increasingly meritocratic practices but also intellectual developments within the economics discipline. Oxford had begun offering courses for its first diploma in economics in 1903, followed by a new degree in philosophy, politics, and economics (PPE) in 1921.[24] Even earlier, at Cambridge, the Economic Tripos, an undergraduate

[19] Max Weber, *Grundriß der Sozialökonomik, III. Abteilung: Wirtschaft und Gesellschaft* (Tübingen: Verlag von J.C.B. Mohr [Paul Siebeck], 1922), 128–129.

[20] C.A.E. Goodhart, "The Bank of England, 1694–2017," in *Sveriges Riksbank and the History of Central Banking*, ed. Rodney Edvinsson, Tor Jacobson, and Daniel Waldenström (Cambridge: Cambridge University Press, 2018), 160.

[21] Cannadine, *The Decline and Fall of the British Aristocracy*, 243–245, 274–280, 294.

[22] On Fisher and the reform of the civil service, see Edward Bridges, *Portrait of a Profession: The Civil Service Tradition* (Cambridge: Cambridge University Press, 1950); John R. Greenaway, "Warren Fisher and the Transformation of the British Treasury, 1919–1939," *Journal of British Studies* 23, no. 1 (1983), 132–137; G.C. Peden, "The Treasury as the Central Department of Government, 1919–1939," *Public Administration* 61, no. 4 (1983), 376; Eunan O'Halpin, *Head of the Civil Service: A Study of Sir Warren Fisher* (London and New York: Routledge, 1989), 46–50; Gail Savage, *The Social Construction of Expertise: The English Civil Service and Its Influence, 1919–1939* (Pittsburgh: University of Pittsburgh Press, 1996), 36–53; Geoffrey K. Fry, "Three Giants of the Inter-War British Higher Civil Service: Sir Maurice Hankey, Sir Warren Fisher and Sir Horace Wilson," in *Bureaucrats and Leadership: Transforming Government*, ed. Kevin Theakston (Basingstoke: Macmillan, 2000), 43–52.

[23] Harold Perkin, *The Rise of Professional Society: England since 1880* (London and New York: Routledge, 1989), 9–17, 116–123.

[24] Lise Arena, "From Economics of the Firm to Business Studies at Oxford: An Intellectual History (1890s–1990s)" (DPhil diss., University of Oxford, 2011), 53; Keith Tribe, *Constructing Economic Science: The Invention of a Discipline, 1850–1950* (Oxford: Oxford University Press, 2022), 177–195. On the study of economics at Oxford, see also Norman Chester, *Economics, Politics and Social Studies in Oxford, 1900–85* (Basingstoke: Macmillan, 1986); Asa Briggs, "Cerberus and the Sphinx: Modern Greats in Oxford," in *Serious Pursuits: Communications and Education: The Collected Essays of Asa Briggs, vol. 3* (Urbana: University of Illinois Press, 1991), 320–326; Warren Young and Frederic S. Lee, *Oxford Economics and Oxford Economists* (Basingstoke: Macmillan, 1993).

examination designed by Alfred Marshall, challenged traditional notions found in classical economics with an abundance of new theories on supply and demand, marginal utility, and elasticity.[25] With new coursework in the dismal science, universities offered training to twentieth-century professionals.

It was with the concurrent changes in the civil service and the economics discipline that the Bank was willing to consider the integration of the new social science into its institutional apparatus. In 1925, the in-house research department was renamed the Statistical Section and obtained a direct line of communication with the Governor.[26] One of its statisticians, John Arundel Caulfeild (J.A.C.) Osborne, wrote to the Deputy Governor on the need for additional support. He argued that a staff of trained technical specialists could assist the Bank in setting interest rates by tracking wholesale prices and employment levels. Doing so would provide "a suitable opportunity for examining outside criticisms of monetary policy, criticisms themselves often largely based on figures of the kind compiled by the Statistical Section."[27] Based on this advice, several employment changes soon followed. Ronald Eric Harrison (R.E.H.) Allport succeeded Dalton as Superintendent of the Statistical Section, while Kenneth W. Cotton from the London School of Economics was appointed to the post of Librarian.[28]

Osborne was one of the early figures at the Bank who recognized the value of technical hires. Since 1921, he had been working as a part-time personal secretary to Governor Norman, who asked him to write a history of the central bank during the First World War.[29] For this project, he traveled to various European central banks to gather information on how their research departments functioned. Following his travels, he concluded that more regular memoranda and reports would help the Bank's directors make informed decisions on matters of economic policy: "It is believed that a service of this kind might possess real value ... [and] the possession of figures and comparisons such as should be forthcoming might assist in furnishing arguments to support such conclusions [made by the Bank]."[30] The apparent value of statistics also lay in its future-oriented approach. Data could offer "an early indication of developments not perhaps unexpected but of which evidence had not yet been

[25] John Maynard Keynes, "Alfred Marshall, 1842–1924," *The Economic Journal* 34, no. 135 (1924), 311, 342–346; John Cunningham Wood, *British Economists and the Empire* (London and Canberra: Croom Helm, 1983), 113–120; John Maloney, *Marshall, Orthodoxy and the Professionalisation of Economics* (Cambridge: Cambridge University Press, 1985), 35–40.

[26] Hennessy, *A Domestic History of the Bank of England*, 314.

[27] J.A.C. Osborne, "Memorandum to the Deputy Governor," August 7, 1925, BoE EID8/1.

[28] Court of Directors, Minutes, November 12, 1925, BoE G4/148; "Some Discursive Notes on the Statistical Section," October 29, 1930, BoE EID8/1.

[29] The personal secretary was a part-time appointment prior to 1929 with the appointment of E. H.D. Skinner, A.C. Darby, "J.A.C. Osborne," *The Old Lady of Threadneedle Street* XLVII, no. 203, September 1971, 196.

[30] J.A.C. Osborne, "Memorandum to the Deputy Governor," August 7, 1925, BoE EID8/1.

forthcoming."[31] The argument appeared to be convincing. By November, the Committee of Treasury invited the directors to begin inspecting the Statistical Section's reports, with a select group of senior officials (Deputy Governor Alan Anderson, Charles Addis, George Macaulay Booth, and Cecil Lubbock) assigned to review the material on a regular basis.[32]

In the development of original statistical research, female staff members played an increasingly important role. Since 1914, women had been recruited at the Bank's various branches in Manchester, Birmingham, and Liverpool.[33] Predominantly working at the main office in London, they soon numbered over 2,000 by the summer of 1919.[34] In the years thereafter, female staff members helped promote the standardization of economic statistics, with their main responsibilities including proofreading, printing materials, and drawing graphs.[35] By 1937, the research department acknowledged that the "recording of regular statistics is done almost entirely by the female routine staff, who also prepare the regular tables and draw all graphs for the Statistical Summary."[36]

With a professional, and often middle-class, army of economists, statisticians, clerks, and typists, the Bank was able to increase the circulation of its monthly report. The *Statistical Summary*, an expanded version of the former *Monthly Report*, was first published for internal use in January 1922.[37] By 1928, the research department distributed a newer version to around thirty central banks, thereby helping to build its reputation as a valuable source of economic data.[38] Even so, the *Statistical Summary* was relatively simple. The January 1927 report amount to only nine pages, seven of which were used to explain the methodology and define key terms.[39] Subsequent reports made references to matters primarily of domestic concern (balances of the Exchequer, unemployment by industry, and wholesale prices calculated by the "'Economist' group") and some foreign trends (foreign trade and monthly foreign-exchange rates).[40] Additionally, the Bank's statisticians wanted to highlight the importance of comparison across previous years. A "Miscellaneous Statistics" section in the report estimated the number of trade

31 J.A.C. Osborne, "Memorandum to the Deputy Governor," August 7, 1925, BoE EID8/1.

32 Committee of Treasury, Minutes, November 25, 1925, BoE G8/56; Committee of Treasury, Minutes, January 15, 1926, BoE G8/56.

33 "The Bank of England: A Career for Women," 1964, BoE 4A156/1.

34 "Estimated Number of Women Clerks on the Staff 1893–1943," November 2, 1943, BoE E31/1.

35 "Regulations Governing the Engagement and Employment of Women Clerks in the Service of the Bank of England," February 18, 1926, BoE E3/21; "Economics & Statistics Section," March 31, 1936, BoE EID8/1.

36 "Economics & Statistics Section – Bank of England," April 9, 1937, BoE EID8/1.

37 "Statistical Section," November 1925, BoE EID8/1.

38 J.A.C. Osborne, "Mémoire présenté par M. J.A.C. Osborne (Banque d'Angleterre)," April 12, 1928, BdF 1370200401/1; "L'organisation et l'œuvre de la section statistique et économique de la Banque d'Angleterre," April 1928, BArch R2501/6857.

39 "Summary of Statistics for the United Kingdom," January 1927, BoE EID2/1.

40 "Summary of Statistics for the United Kingdom," February 1927, BoE EID2/1.

disputes, both in Britain and elsewhere, as well as the number of bankruptcies filed in England, Wales, and Scotland.[41] Meanwhile, imports and exports were not only measured by volume but also listed according to the countries to and from which goods traveled.

It was the lack of original economic information that compelled the Bank to consider hiring those with more technical expertise. Inspired by their counterparts abroad, officials sought "to prepare charts illustrating current economic and financial conditions, modelled on those of the Federal Reserve Bank of New York."[42] In March 1927, Governor Benjamin Strong wrote about the possibility of sending one of its economists, Walter W. Stewart, to conduct "special work" at the Bank, namely building a new research department.[43] The idea was to standardize statistical terminology across central banks as a means of fostering greater cooperation.

Stewart had previously been involved in creating one at the Federal Reserve after his tour of various European central banks in 1925.[44] As the Director of the Division of Analysis and Research at the Federal Reserve Board, he facilitated the consolidation of disparate research projects under a single department, which was now responsible for indices on prices, production, and credit.[45] His early contributions at the Federal Reserve were focused on showcasing the prominence of statistical analysis, most notably in its *Tenth Annual Report* (1923).[46] The nearly 500-page document compiled import and export data across a range of industries and the balance sheets of each of the Federal Reserve banks. As its preface reported,

> Information of this character, as a result of the growing recognition of its value and of the activities in collecting such information both by governmental and private agencies, is now available more currently and in more lines of industry and trade than ever before ... . No statistical analysis can ever be a substitute for judgment in matters of credit administration, but such analyses of economic conditions are indispensable as furnishing the factual basis for credit judgment and for the development of credit policy.[47]

41 "Summary of Statistics for the United Kingdom," March 1927, BoE EID2/1.
42 Clay, *Lord Norman*, 300–301.
43 Strong to Stewart, March 26, 1927, FRBNY Strong Papers 1117.2, Part 1.
44 Lester V. Chandler, *Benjamin Strong, Central Banker* (Washington, DC: The Brookings Institution, 1958), 324.
45 "Meeting Minutes, June 13, 1923," FRBNY Board Minutes Vol. 10, Part 1; Allan H. Meltzer, *A History of the Federal Reserve, 1913–1951, vol. 1* (Chicago and London: The University of Chicago Press, 2003), 141.
46 Milton Friedman and Anna Jacobson Schwartz, *A Monetary History of the United States, 1867–1960* (Princeton: Princeton University Press, 1963), 251; Meltzer, *A History of the Federal Reserve, vol. 1*, 154; Eichengreen, *Golden Fetters*, 251. Strong shared the report with Norman as a model for the Bank's own statistical data; Strong to Norman, February 27, 1925, FRBNY Strong Papers 1116.5, Part 1.
47 Federal Reserve Board, *Tenth Annual Report of the Federal Reserve Board, Covering Operations for the Year 1923* (Washington, DC: Government Printing Office, 1924), 36.

With this information, Stewart was able to show the value of economic theory in informing monetary policy. As he explained, "economists turn toward banking as a means of control because the Reserve Board seems to be the only organization acting in the public interest which has the authority and power to make its decisions effective."[48]

Acknowledging the insights found in the Federal Reserve's *Annual Report*, the Bank agreed to employ Stewart for the "collection and preparation of Statistics ... on economic questions which may guide us in our financial policy."[49] Although hiring a non-British employee was unprecedented, Governor Norman felt that the decision would help the Bank address the "lack of the necessary knowledge and experience" and obtain new insights by paying "whatever was a proper annual fee" for outside counsel.[50] In 1927, Stewart joined the Bank as an adviser with an annual remuneration of £7,000.[51] (By comparison, a 1931 committee proposed that the Governor, Deputy Governor, and directors be paid £7,000 plus a pension of £5,000 per year.[52])

From this perspective, transatlantic cooperation facilitated the development of central bank statistics. The relationship between the United States and the United Kingdom, although contentious at times, converged on the common goal of restabilizing the international economic order.[53] In 1925, negotiations with the Federal Reserve Bank of New York and private banks had helped to raise confidence in sterling through a combined loan of $300 million (even though the credits were not used).[54] With the ensuing readoption of the gold

[48] N.I. Stone, W.C. Schluter, and Walter W. Stewart, "Controlling Business Cycles – Discussion," *The American Economic Review* 12, no. 1 (1922), 41.

[49] Norman to Stewart, June 6, 1927, FRBNY Strong Papers 1117.2, Part 1.

[50] Norman to Strong, March 15, 1927, FRBNY Strong Papers 1116.7, Part 2. On the relationship between Strong and Norman, see Stephen V.O. Clarke, *Central Bank Cooperation, 1924–31* (New York: Federal Reserve Bank of New York, 1967), 29–40, 75–85; Silvano A. Wueschner, *Charting Twentieth-Century Monetary Policy: Herbert Hoover and Benjamin Strong, 1917–1927* (Westport and London: Greenwood Press, 1999), 66–73, 135–142.

[51] Committee of Treasury, Minutes, August 3, 1927, BoE G8/57. Stewart also worked at a Wall Street investment firm, Case, Pomeroy & Co., as its Vice President (1927), Chairman (1930–37), and President (1937–1938); William P. Yohe, "The Mysterious Career of Walter W. Stewart, Especially 1922–1930," *History of Political Economy* 14, no. 4 (1982), 585–587.

[52] "Draft: Notes on Bank Reorganisation," July 1, 1931, BoE G15/205.

[53] On US–UK financial relations, see Frank C. Costigliola, "Anglo-American Financial Rivalry in the 1920s," *The Journal of Economic History* 37, no. 4 (1977): 911–934; Kathleen Burk, "War and Anglo-American Financial Relations in the Twentieth Century," in *Anglo-American Attitudes: From Revolution to Partnership*, ed. Fred M. Leventhal and Roland Quinault (Abingdon: Ashgate, 2000): 243–260; Green, *The Political Economy of the Special Relationship*, 55–72.

[54] Chandler, *Benjamin Strong*, 260–263, 303–319; Clarke, *Central Bank Cooperation*, 81–85; Michael Bordo, Michael Edelstein, and Hugh Rockoff, "Was Adherence to the Gold Standard a 'Good Housekeeping Seal of Approval' during the Interwar Period?," in *Finance, Intermediaries, and Economic Development*, ed. Stanley L. Engerman, Philip T. Hoffman, Jean-Laurent Rosenthal, and Kenneth L. Sokoloff (Cambridge: Cambridge University Press, 2003), 300.

standard, Norman suggested working more closely with his US counterparts in a variety of new areas, including the maintenance of "liquid assets and the employment of such Reserves to secure economy in the use and movement of gold; ... [t]he extension to one another ... of the fullest possible banking facilities consistent with the varying regulations and practice of the several Banks; ... the granting of credit to another Central Bank to meet temporary monetary pressure due to seasonal causes; ... [t]he co-ordination of Credit Policy; ... [and] [t]he free interchange of information and opinions."[55] So cordial was the relationship that rumors even circulated that Stewart's employment was part of a wider Anglo-American cooperation scheme.[56]

As he had done at the Federal Reserve Board, Stewart conducted regular statistical surveys and prepared "seasonal articles for publication" at the Bank.[57] He had arrived at a time when in-house research had been rudimentary, largely focused on tracking changes in prices and interest rates. Initially, he was reported to have "expressed dissatisfaction with the dimensions of the summary and suggested that the dignity of the Bank called for something not only more presentable but also covering a good deal more ground."[58] Yet with the personal backing of the Governor, he was able to "assist in building up the statistical and information Department, to advise as to the material to be collected and to explain how the information obtained might be used to the best advantage."[59] Although his position as an adviser was ill-defined, only broadly assigned to help "guide Central Bank policy," this ambiguity allowed him to undertake a range of different projects at the Bank.[60] One project, for instance, involved the compilation of data on approximately 100 commodities to generate a new price index.

The research department thus developed its statistical capabilities in line with Stewart's vision. In March 1928, the *Statistical Summary* changed its base year – the point of reference and comparison for all other years – from 1913 to 1925. As justified in the report, "the time has now arrived when comparison with some recent year, rather than with a pre-war year, will be more useful, and the year 1925, while not entirely satisfactory as a basis for comparison,

55 Montagu Norman, "Co-Operation between Central Banks: Points for Consideration," November 5, 1925, FRBNY Strong Papers 1116.5, Part 2.

56 Friedrich Sthamer [German Embassy in London] to the German Foreign Office, "Bevorstehende Ernennung eines amerikanischen Beraters bei der Bank von England und eines englischen Beraters bei der Federal Reserve Bank," October 10, 1927, PA AA RZ 207/243954; "Anglo-U.S. Banking Co-Operation," *The Financial Times* 12135, November 14, 1927, 5; Sayers, *The Bank of England, vol. 1*, 376.

57 Committee of Treasury, Minutes, October 24, 1928, BoE G8/58; "Origin of Research Department of the Board," May 3, 1955, FRBNY History Committee Entry 167, Box 2, Folder 5, Item 27.

58 Quoted in "Origin of Statistical Summary," August 26, 1937, BoE EID2/20.

59 Committee of Treasury, Minutes, February 16, 1927, BoE G8/57.

60 J.A.C. Osborne, "Memorandum for the Deputy Governor," November 1925, BoE EID8/1.

has been selected as more nearly representative of post-war conditions than any other recent year."[61] The decision marked the new forward-thinking mindset of economists. According to Osborne, who had become the Principal of the Statistical Section in February 1931, numerical comparisons had to be useful to all potential readers and convey information based on original findings. The *Statistical Summary*, as a result, began publishing figures dating back to 1925, the same year as the return to the gold standard.[62]

Additional economic information helped to explain existing policies. An internal memorandum revealed that the research department planned to keep track of data on foreign production (especially in coal, cotton, iron, and steel), agricultural output (wheat and cotton), foreign capital issues, and unemployment figures.[63] According to one economist, "the Bank stands to gain from a better understanding by economists and others of actual monetary policy, and should therefore do what it can to assist historical research into that subject."[64] In other instances, officials were interested in data on worldwide gold production. As other central banks hoarded gold reserves, the research department prioritized conducting research on gold exports from the abundant mines of South Africa, as well as on the proportion of that gold being imported into the United Kingdom (Figure 3.1). Understanding these trends might help alleviate exchange-rate pressures, as well as justify an adherence to the gold standard.

With the expansion of a research department that demanded more of the Bank's resources and expertise, the Old Guard began to criticize the purpose of technical advisers. Before their arrival, Addis had, in his diary, questioned the necessity of inviting Stewart to the Bank.[65] The subsequent invitation of two economists from the United States seemed to be the next controversial decision, leading Deputy Governor Cecil Lubbock to remark, "the American temperament loves statistical information as much as the English temperament distrusts it."[66] Other central bankers opposed the import of economic theories to what they viewed as a practically minded institution. It was already a revolutionary departure from tradition to employ those from outside the banks in the City, let alone to listen to their ideas. Governor Norman, known for his strong aversion to numerical analyses, admitted to the Macmillan Committee, "I do not attach importance to great elaboration of statistical information."[67]

61 "Summary of Statistics for the United Kingdom," March 1928, BoE EID2/1.

62 J.A.C. Osborne, "Bank of England's Summary of Statistics," November 1928, BoE EID2/20.

63 "S[ummary].O[f].S[tatistics].," July 18, 1931, BoE EID2/20.

64 Clay to Osborne, September 19, 1932, BoE EID8/1.

65 Charles Addis, Diary, March 11, 1927, SOAS Addis Papers Box 4.

66 Quoted in J.A.C. Osborne, "Memorandum for the Deputy Governor," November 1925, BoE EID8/1.

67 "The Right Hon. Montagu Collet Norman, D.S.O., and Sir W. Guy Granet, G.B.E.," February 18, 1931, in Macmillan Committee, *Minutes of Evidence, vol.* 2, 296. Also quoted in Moggridge, *British Monetary Policy*, 244.

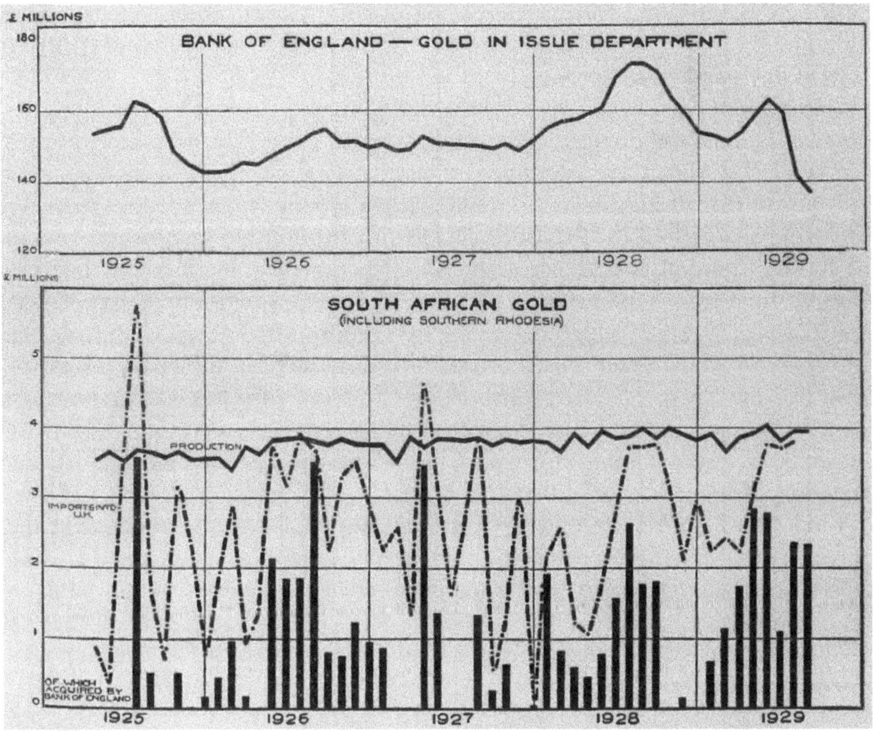

FIGURE 3.1 Gold Reserves at the Bank and in South Africa, 1925–1929
Source: Bank of England Archive, EID2/3.

However, one must also be critical of what central bankers claimed, especially in public fora. In private meetings, such as those held by the Committee of Treasury, Norman and the directors were, at times, willing to acknowledge the benefits of new insights. Stewart appeared to offer a steady stream of data, and the access to "all available facts and figures" helped determine "the position of the Bank and of the market."[68] With the Bank's support, he oversaw the expansion of the division from two staff members (1925) to nine (1929), and, later, to thirteen (1931).[69] Observing these developments, the Governor considered there to be a strategic benefit in employing outsiders, particularly since knowledge of "American affairs" helped promote the goal of central

[68] Committee of Treasury, Minutes, December 21, 1927, BoE G8/57.

[69] In 1929, the staff included Stewart, Osborne (Principal), Allport (Superintendent), two male clerks, and four female clerks. In 1931, it expanded to six male clerks and four female clerks (led by Sprague, Osborne, and Allport); J.A.C. Osborne, "Mémoire présenté par M. J.A.C. Osborne (Banque d'Angleterre)," April 12, 1928, BdF 1370200401/1; L.E. Inman, "Statistical Section," October 15, 1929, BoE EID8/1; "Bank of England," April 1932, BoE EID8/1.

bank cooperation and European reconstruction.[70] Their employment would allow the Bank to gauge the value of expert knowledge before taking concrete steps in any particular direction.

Statistics, in this sense, were not meant to upend the Bank's existing governance. One of the directors, Sir Josiah Stamp (later, Baron Stamp), argued that while "statistics are becoming a main engine of business management and the control of industry," contemporary analysis also needed to incorporate "human nature."[71] "Statistics are no substitution for judgment," one of the Bank's economists similarly asserted.[72] Nevertheless, the Bank intended to continue investing in quantitative research. In preparation for Stewart's departure in 1930, Norman suggested hiring two economists: Henry Clay from the University of Manchester and W. Randolph Burgess from the Federal Reserve Bank of New York.[73] Amidst rumors that the prime minister was planning to organize his own group of advisory economists (later, the Economic Advisory Council), Norman wanted to invite Clay before the government did.[74] Clay, who had previously worked at the Ministry of Labour and New College, Oxford, had been the Stanley Jevons Professor of Political Economy at the University of Manchester since 1922. His reputation in academia as a leading expert on industrial policy and unemployment brought him to the Bank in January 1930.

The Bank envisioned employing a second adviser alongside Clay. Strong proposed one economist named Oliver Mitchell Wentworth Sprague. In both UK and US circles, Sprague was well regarded, particularly because he used less theoretical methods and was more concerned with the practical applications of economics to central banking.[75] Regarded as "one of the best known professors of banking in the United States" by the press, Sprague had conducted extensive research on monetary economics, culminating in his magnum opus, *History of Crises under the National Banking System* (1910).[76] This work served as a point of reference for the members of the National Monetary Commission, whose recommendations led to the creation of the Federal Reserve in 1913.[77]

70 "Statistical Section: Review of the Year 1928," 1929, BoE OV50/4.

71 Josiah Stamp, "Human Nature in Statistics," in *Some Economic Factors in Modern Life* (London: P.S. King & Son, 1929), 255–256.

72 "Production Prices and Depression: Professor Clay on the Trade Outlook," *Evening Sentinel (Stoke-on-Trent)* 20582, October 13, 1930, 5.

73 Committee of Treasury, Minutes, October 2, 1929, BoE G8/58.

74 Committee of Treasury, Minutes, December 11, 1929, BoE G8/58.

75 "Memorandum of [a] Conversation between Governor Strong and Sir Arthur Salter at Hotel George V, Paris – May 25, 1928," FRBNY Strong Papers 1000.9.

76 "Economists at the Bank," *The Economist* 110, 4510, February 1, 1930, 228; O.M.W. Sprague, *History of Crises under the National Banking System* (Washington, DC: Government Printing Office, 1910).

77 O.M.W. Sprague, "Proposals for Strengthening the National Banking System. III.," *The Quarterly Journal of Economics* 25, no. 1 (1910), 71–76; O.M.W. Sprague, "The Aldrich

During the First World War, Sprague had also served on the Council of National Defense, which oversaw the gradual dismantling of wartime controls and the appointment of a reconstruction advisory committee.[78] At war's end, he returned to Harvard to continue giving lectures on banking and finance.

Informally, Norman had already consulted Sprague on his frequent trips to the United States.[79] With Strong's backing, Sprague officially joined the Bank in July 1930 as an Adviser to the Governors of the Bank of England. Given that he was now the second American economist to join the Bank, *The Evening News* critically remarked that there seemed to be "a dearth of sound British economists and statisticians," as "the effort of producing John Maynard Keynes, G.D.H. Cole and Sir Josiah Stamp probably exhausted the nation's capacity."[80] At the same time, the Bank recognized that building a team of advisers required drawing on specialists outside Britain. Doing so would signal its intention to attract "the services of the best economists and financial experts produced in the English-speaking world."[81] As *The Economist* described, the appointments of Sprague and Clay "unquestionably strengthen very greatly the resources of the Bank on the economic side, which, in this respect, challenges comparison with the staff of any other central bank in the world."[82]

Both advisers were thus able to redefine the role of the Bank in economic affairs. Sprague, in particular, believed that its priorities should be neither to restrain credit growth nor to manage foreign-exchange fluctuations but instead to make adjustments to the discount rates that allowed it to maintain adequate gold reserves.[83] In accordance with the "rules of the game" dictated by the gold standard, the central bank needed to set a Bank Rate that ensured the continuation of gold convertibility. Clay, too, was intent on defending the decision to return to gold. As his academic expertise lay in industrial economics, he was particularly convinced that maintaining a stable exchange rate would be vital for an export-based recovery. If the pound became more

Plan for Monetary Legislation," *The American Economic Review* 1, no. 2 (1911), 263–264; O.M.W. Sprague, *Banking Reform in the United States: A Series of Proposals, Including a Central Bank of Limited Scope* (Cambridge, MA: Harvard University Press, 1913), 145–148; Lynn Irvine Schoonover, "O.M.W. Sprague," *Harvard Business School Alumni Bulletin* 7, no. 1 (1930), 17; Hugh Rockoff, "O.M.W. Sprague (The Man Who 'Wrote the Book' on Financial Crises) Meets the Great Depression," *Jahrbuch für Wirtschaftsgeschichte* 63, no. 2 (2022), 528.

78 O.M.W. Sprague, "Memorandum for the Council of National Defense: After the War Economic Reconstruction Problems with Suggestions on Organization," 1918, HBS Faculty Publication Series C.22 GB2.805, Carton 22, Folder 1.

79 Norman to Harvey, March 30, 1931, BoE G1/515; Schoonover, "O.M.W. Sprague," 19.

80 Quoted in "Selection of Sprague Shocks London Paper," *The New York Times* LXXIX, 26304, January 30, 1930, 11.

81 Schoonover, "O.M.W. Sprague," 15.

82 "Economists at the Bank," *The Economist* 110, 4510, February 1, 1930, 228.

83 O.M.W. Sprague, "The Proposal for a Central Bank in the United States: A Critical View," *The Quarterly Journal of Economics* 23, no. 3 (1909), 389–399.

attractive to foreign investors, ensuing capital inflows might further stimulate economic growth.[84]

Through their advisory work, experts offered a bridge between theory and practice. At the Bank, Clay devoted much of his time to improving statistical research, which was now no longer confined to the pages of an internal publication. Instead, he helped it gain broader appeal among members of the international financial community. Over the next several years, the Bank's Statistical Section began publishing more data in its monthly *Statistical Summary*. The report was initially reserved for internal use, with three copies remaining at the Bank, while an additional eight were shared privately with other central banks.[85] Yet its subsequent circulation outside the Bank in the 1930s allowed government officials to be kept informed on the nation's general economic conditions.[86] In addition to this monthly report, the Statistical Section distributed a typewritten summary to several central banks, along with a weekly cable to the National Bank of Hungary and the Federal Reserve Bank of New York.[87]

The Bank's cohort of advisers thus diverged considerably from its traditional group of bankers, both in experience and in background. Although Sprague and Clay had both studied economics at prestigious universities, they had different social upbringings from the Old Guard. Governor Norman was an Eton-educated merchant banker with relatives on both sides of his family who had previously worked at the Bank. He had a social background similar to other key figures at the Bank, including John Baring (Barings Bank), Edward Grenfell (Morgan Grenfell), and Robert Kindersley (Lazard Brothers). In contrast, Sprague had no familial ties to the City's banks, and Clay had attended a grammar school. Their families, instead, had links to the insurance and manufacturing industries, respectively. Employed neither for their personal connections nor for their social status, the Bank's advisers offered technical knowledge in relevant domains.

STATISTICS AND THE MACMILLAN COMMITTEE

More than an instrument for understanding economic trends, statistics also emerged as a political tool. Newly employed economists offered an intellectual

[84] Henry Clay, "The Recent Movement of Prices: Address to be Given to the Birmingham Chamber of Commerce on Thursday, 16th October, 1930," BoE SMT2/60.

[85] "Statistical Section: Charts," November 1925, BoE EID8/1. The research department underwent a series of name changes: the Economic Section (1921), Statistical Section (1925), Economics & Statistics Section (1933), Central Banking Information Department (1959), and Economic Intelligence Department (1964); Bank of England, "The Work of the Economic Intelligence Department," *Bank of England Quarterly Bulletin* 16, Q4 (1976), 439–440; Kynaston, *Till Time's Last Sand*, 328.

[86] "Economics & Statistics Section – Bank of England," April 9, 1937, BoE EID8/1.

[87] "Origin of Statistical Summary," August 26, 1937, BoE EID2/20.

defense of the Bank's policies in response to public criticism, most notably before the Macmillan Committee.

In early November 1929, Chancellor of the Exchequer Philip Snowden announced the creation of the Committee on Finance and Industry to study the state of the British economy, with a particular focus on the relationship between finance and industry.[88] The committee included delegates from various interest groups: Hugh Macmillan, a lawyer who had briefly served as Lord Advocate in Scotland, was appointed the committee's chairman; John Bradbury served in different positions at the Treasury, including as Permanent Secretary to the Treasury (1913–1919); Britain's largest banks were represented by Robert Brand (Lloyds Bank) and Reginald McKenna (Midland Bank), while the interests of trade unions were advocated by Ernest Bevin (General Secretary of the Transport and General Workers' Union); and the two academic economists involved were Arthur Cecil Pigou (Cambridge) and Theodore Gregory (London School of Economics).

The establishment of the Macmillan Committee was itself an experiment in expert-led policymaking. It offered technical advisers a channel to voice their varied perspectives on the Great Depression as it unfolded. According to one contemporary, the proceedings presented an opportunity to assess "the pivotal position occupied by the Bank of England in the financial system of this country" and to understand "the nature and functions of the Bank of England as the Central Bank in this country."[89] Those from the Bank who offered testimony were Norman, Stewart, Sprague, Clay, Stamp, Kindersley, Otto Niemeyer, and Guy Granet. Minutes kept by the Macmillan Committee's secretary revealed the value of technical perspectives, particularly as bankers, politicians, and civil servants often lacked specific knowledge of industrial finance and monetary policy. Brand confessed to having little understanding of the workings of the gold standard – "A man has to have a wet towel over his head to understand the principle of the reserve" – while Bradbury usually deferred to the "professional economists" in the room.[90]

The committee's discussions initially focused on the setting of the Bank's main interest rate. In an attempt to quell outflows of gold, which had been an estimated £11.5 million over the preceding three months, the Committee of

[88] HC Deb, November 4, 1929, vol. 231 c. 615; "Treasury Minute," November 5, 1929, BLO Brand Papers 27/1; Robert Skidelsky, *Politicians and the Slump: The Labour Government of 1929–1931* (London: Macmillan, 1967), 117–118; Sayers, *The Bank of England, vol. 1*, 360–373; Boyce, *British Capitalism*, 280–288; Francesca Carnevali, *Europe's Advantage: Banks and Small Firms in Britain, France, Germany, and Italy since 1918* (Oxford: Oxford University Press, 2005), 26; Kynaston, *Till Time's Last Sand*, 313.

[89] "The Right Hon. Ernest Musgrave Harvey, K.B.E., Deputy Governor of the Bank of England," November 28, 1929, in Macmillan Committee, *Minutes of Evidence, vol. 1*, 1.

[90] Bradbury also repeatedly sought confirmation from economists, namely Keynes and Gregory, while discussing the workings of the gold standard; Committee on Finance and Industry, Notes on Discussion, October 24, 1930, TNA T200/5/3; Committee on Finance and Industry, Notes on Discussion, November 6, 1930, TNA T200/5/5; Committee on Finance and Industry, Notes on Discussion, November 7, 1930, TNA T200/5/5.

Treasury raised the Bank Rate from 4.5 to 5.5 percent on February 6, 1929.[91] The policy, conforming to the standard "rules of the game" view, incited criticism from members of the Macmillan Committee, most notably Keynes. He stipulated that a high Bank Rate alone was insufficient for stopping capital outflows, and its adverse effects on unemployment outweighed any supposed advantages.[92] Stamp and Lubbock, however, rationalized this decision by arguing that the Bank Rate only had a marginal effect on domestic credit. Even though the Bank could have bought additional government securities, thereby providing more credit to the market, it had "no control over how it [the Bank Rate] is used."[93] This argument was primarily an attempt to deflect blame away from the Bank, as changes in the interest rate ostensibly affected both overall credit levels and investors' confidence.

Countering Keynes' remarks, the Bank's advisers sought to defend recent changes in the Bank Rate based on statistical evidence. Sprague's testimony before the committee justified the recent interest-rate hikes, with his response portraying the issue not as a financial problem but instead as an industrial concern: "I do not believe that slight differences in the rates charged have a fundamental effect; ... more liberal supplies of capital would probably have enlarged the production of the things that are now in over-supply."[94] Sprague further showed how the banking sector had not failed industry, as the Macmillan Committee argued. Instead, industry had been at fault for overproducing goods that were no longer needed. Later that year, he reiterated these views before the English-Speaking Union, where he again used quantitative evidence to show how a global disequilibrium in production had emerged between agricultural and manufactured goods.[95]

To confirm the validity of these arguments, the Macmillan Committee needed to acquire more accurate statistics. At the end of the first day of testimony, Keynes asked whether there was "any expert of the Bank who studies prices ... [n]ot merely an official who compiles figures for the use of the Governor, but [one] who interprets them?"[96] Other members of the committee frequently described the need to improve existing, "unsatisfactory" data on capital movements.[97] They were particularly motivated to gather such information before any true evaluation of British industry could be made. Ensuing testimony from

[91] "Summary of Statistics for the United Kingdom," January 1929, BoE EID2/3; Committee of Treasury, Minutes, February 6, 1929, BoE G8/58.

[92] John Maynard Keynes, "The Committee on the Currency," *The Economic Journal* 35, no. 138 (1925), 304.

[93] "Sir Josiah Stamp, G.B.E.," April 3, 1930, in Macmillan Committee, *Minutes of Evidence, vol. 1*, 243.

[94] "The Right Hon. Montagu Collet Norman, D.S.O., and Dr. O.M.W. Sprague," February 18, 1931, in Macmillan Committee, *Minutes of Evidence, vol. 2*, 303.

[95] "Central Banks and the Crisis," *The Economist* 112, 4582, June 20, 1931, 1321.

[96] "The Right Hon. Ernest Musgrave Harvey, K.B.E.," November 28, 1929, in Macmillan Committee, *Minutes of Evidence, vol. 1*, 10.

[97] Committee on Finance and Industry, Notes on Discussion, November 27, 1930, TNA T200/6/4.

leading statisticians, including Emanuel Goldenweiser (Federal Reserve Board) and Dennis Robertson (Cambridge), confirmed the limits of existing statistics, but they offered few immediate solutions. Acknowledging how the lack of such information prevented the committee from making a fair assessment of British industry, Keynes declared, "I am prepared to scrap all the legal reports if I can have my economic statistics."[98]

The shortcomings of publicly available statistics were well known at the Bank. "[A]t present," Stamp asserted, "it is very difficult to know how the Clearing Banks stand."[99] A common and well-known practice of "window dressing" involved banks exchanging funds between one another.[100] This operation allowed the clearing banks to alter their published balance sheets prior to the date of publication by moving cash between one another's accounts.[101] Many commercial banks also planned for a portion of their portfolios to mature in time for the publication of their semiannual and annual reports, thereby causing inflated valuations in June and December.[102] Those that requested additional loans on the money market prior to a reporting day were similarly able to report inflated figures in their accounts held at the Bank. Despite the government's concerted efforts, from the Cunliffe Committee to the Macmillan Committee, to obtain the true daily averages of bank balances, the practice continued well into the postwar years.[103]

Still, for the Bank, the value of statistical evidence derived from its ability to justify central bank independence. In May, Stewart was invited to prepare a statement on the Bank's acquisition of statistics before the Macmillan Committee.[104] Nearing the end of his employment contract, he shared his findings on the main differences between the US and UK banking systems. While the London money market sustained itself through a vast network of financial institutions, such as the discount houses, merchant banks, colonial banks, and the stock market, its New York counterpart relied heavily on the demand for purchases of securities to sustain itself. The implication was that

98 Committee on Finance and Industry, Notes on Discussion, December 5, 1930, TNA T200/6/7.

99 "Sir Josiah C. Stamp, G.B.E.," April 3, 1930, in Macmillan Committee, *Minutes of Evidence, vol. 1*, 243.

100 King, *History of the London Discount Market*, 314–315.

101 R.S. Sayers, *Modern Banking* (London: Oxford University Press, 1938), 36–37; F.W. Paish, "Note on Bank Window-Dressing," *Economica* 6, no. 24 (1939), 456; Moggridge, *British Monetary Policy*, 153–154; Capie and Webber, *A Monetary History of the United Kingdom*, 266–267.

102 Leaf, *Banking*, 214–215; Sayers, *The Bank of England, vol. 1*, 46; Capie and Webber, *A Monetary History of the United Kingdom*, 266.

103 "Macmillan Committee Figures: London Clearing Banks' Current Account and Time Deposits," December 18, 1930, BoE EID1/2; Capie, *The Bank of England*, 503; Hotson, *Respectable Banking*, 112. For estimates of bank deposits, see B.R. Mitchell, *British Historical Statistics* (Cambridge: Cambridge University Press, 1988), 663–665; Capie and Webber, *A Monetary History of the United Kingdom*, 432–454.

104 Committee of Treasury, Minutes, May 7, 1930, BoE G8/59.

the Bank played a much more prominent role in the international financial system, which depended on the proper functioning of the London discount market.[105] As the Bank's actions affected the global economy, its operational independence from the government – and, by extension, its prerogative to set interest rates as it wished – would be imperative for escaping the slump.

Yet the Macmillan Committee's deliberations forced the Bank to confront the flaws with its existing data methods. Its members urged officials to compile average daily balances from the clearing banks in a more standardized manner.[106] Published on July 13, the Macmillan Committee's final report concluded that "the Bank of England should be charged with the duty of collecting these statistics [on foreign balances] to the best of its ability … . Moreover, it is exceedingly desirable that the principal data on which the Bank of England bases its decisions should be generally known."[107] Keynes went further in his criticisms, denouncing the consequences of inadequate statistical information on monetary policy. He claimed that "it seemed that the Bank of England had no statistics as to the aggregate of the notes held by the banks and of their balances … so that the Bank did not know precisely how far they were restricting credit."[108]

Reluctant to make a decision before additional industrial statistics were made available, the committee asked Stewart to provide "evidence as to the monetary policy of the Bank during the past few years."[109] This information would have helped them reach a fairer judgment on the industry–finance debate. To address the problem of window dressing, several members suggested that the Bank also require the clearing banks to share historical data from 1919 to the present.[110] As their final report emphasized, such data would help the government more accurately interpret the ongoing crisis: "If we had a more complete knowledge, both scientific and statistical, of what is going on in our economic system, it might be possible to act sooner with great advantage."[111]

NEW METHODOLOGIES

The findings of the Macmillan Committee demonstrated the importance of statistics for the Bank. Following the proceedings, Osborne noted that the

105 "Dr. W.W. Stewart," July 4, 1930, in Macmillan Committee, *Minutes of Evidence, vol.* 2, 208.

106 Committee on Finance and Industry, *Report*, 157; F.W. Paish, "Note on Bank Window-Dressing," *Economica* 6, no. 24 (1939), 456.

107 Committee on Finance and Industry, *Report*, 177.

108 Committee on Finance and Industry, Notes on Discussion, March 21, 1930, TNA T200/4/4.

109 Committee of Treasury, Minutes, May 7, 1930, BoE G8/59; Committee of Treasury, Minutes, May 14, 1930, BoE G8/59; Committee of Treasury, Minutes, July 9, 1930, BoE G8/59.

110 As reported in George Ismay [Committee on Finance and Industry] to Harvey, August 25, 1930, BoE G1/427.

111 Committee on Finance and Industry, *Report*, 97. Also reported in Josiah Stamp, "The Report of the Macmillan Committee," *The Economic Journal* 41, no. 163 (1931), 431.

committee's final report did not force the Bank to improve its statistical work, but "that was no reason why they [the Committee of Treasury] should not take the initiative."[112] As he expressed elsewhere, "[t]his country has the best banking system in the world. It seems appropriate that it should also have the best body of banking statistics."[113]

In general agreement with the conclusions of the Macmillan Committee on the matter, the Bank invested additional resources into its research department. As Principal of the Statistical Section, Osborne prioritized standardization efforts across the British financial sector.[114] In October 1931, he attended the Conference of Chief Accountants of the Clearing Banks, where he outlined the ideal protocols for reporting: All banks needed to report on the same day of the week (Wednesdays), so as to prevent additional window dressing, and their positions had to distinguish current accounts from deposit accounts.[115] However, as the Bank had soon learned, there existed no uniform definition for relevant financial terms, such as time deposits or advances.[116] Osborne's report offered no definitive resolution to the issue of window dressing, nor did it provide any enforcement mechanism for adhering to the new requirements, ultimately leading the Committee of Clearing Banks to reject the proposal.[117] While the clearing banks informally conceded to adopt some degree of common terminology, they hesitated to change their own practices for the sake of improving the Bank's reports.[118] The data procured from the clearing banks and published in *The Statistical Summary* thus remained largely unchanged throughout the 1930s.

Yet what the Bank could improve was its own collection of economic statistics. The *Statistical Summary* had already become more widely read by foreign central banks and international organizations.[119] It offered direct insights into the operations of the London money market. Throughout the late 1920s, Stewart had emphasized the value of collecting additional information on foreign bank balances, as such data affected the entire

112 J.A.C. Osborne, "Banking Statistics and [the] Macmillan Committee," October 6, 1932, BoE EID4/53.

113 J.A.C. Osborne, "The General Case for Publishing More Statistics of Approximately the Nature and Form Suggested by the Bank," March 28, 1933, BoE EID4/53. Osborne also imagined the research department serving a central role as "a fund of knowledge on the state of banking, Government finance, industry and trade"; J.A.C. Osborne, "The Functions of the Section," February 9, 1932, BoE EID8/5.

114 Court of Directors, Minutes, February 26, 1931, BoE G4/153; J.A.C. Osborne, "The Bank of England, 1914–1921 (Unpublished War History) – Volume 1," 1926, BoE ADM2/1.

115 "Minutes of a Conference of Chief Accountants of the Clearing Banks," October 13, 1931, BoE EID4/53.

116 "Banking Statistics," September 30, 1931, BoE EID4/53.

117 Economics & Statistics Section, "Review of Year 1933," January 12, 1934, BoE EID8/1.

118 Chairman of the Committee of Clearing Bankers to Harvey, April 7, 1933, BoE EID4/53.

119 Ansgar Rosenberg [League of Nations] to Osborne, February 18, 1932, BoE EID4/53; Ansgar Rosenberg to Allport, March 21, 1932, BoE EID4/53.

economy.[120] With its increasingly global network, the research department offered a new goal for the *Statistical Summary*: "to present, in a compact and convenient form, statistics likely to be required by bankers and other students of finance and economics – more particularly statistics relating to this country."[121]

Circulation was key to the Bank's reputation as the definitive source of economic statistics. In late 1931, the research department expanded the *Statistical Summary* to include additional data from foreign and Empire central banks, and its circulation was set to increase severalfold.[122] One plan suggested that circulation should increase to 1,100 copies, while another recommended a more modest run of 850 copies, the latter of which the Committee of Treasury approved.[123] Elsewhere, the *Statistical Summary* was sold commercially with an annual subscription fee of £10 but was complimentary for those the Bank deemed important enough.[124] This "free list" included the newspapers of record based in the United Kingdom, as well as certain ones in the Dominions and the colonies; professors of political economy or statistics at "1st Rank or Specialised Universities"; "Economists of repute" (based on Clay's personal identification); commercial banks; British government departments; insurance companies; and others.[125] Due to rising demand, the report's circulation increased to 1,700 by 1938.[126]

The research department also wanted to choose a more appropriate title for their publication. Prior to the 1930s, the name of the publication had oscillated between *Statistical Summary* and *Summary of Statistics*. A renamed *Bulletin*, Osborne stated in 1928, would only signify "a publication in a standardised form suitable to be used as a work of reference."[127] However, three years later, he made the opposite claim: "The present title 'Summary of Statistics' suggests that the contents of the bulletin are lifted bodily from other publications: however this may have been when the title was first chosen – it is far from being the case now … . A better title would seem to be ~~Bulletin of Statistics~~ Statistical Bulletin."[128] Seeking to avoid adopting a title too similar to the League's *Monthly Bulletin of Statistics*, Osborne decided to maintain the existing title, the *Statistical Summary*.[129]

120 "Summary of Statistics," n.d., BoE EID2/20; Hennessy, *A Domestic History of the Bank of England*, 315–316.
121 "Statistical Summary," January 1932, BoE EID2/20.
122 Committee of Treasury, Minutes, December 9, 1931, BoE G8/60.
123 Note, December 23, 1931, BoE EID2/20.
124 "Bank of England's Statistical Summary: Probable Circulation if Made Public," December 3, 1931, BoE EID2/20; Committee of Treasury, Minutes, February 10, 1932, BoE G8/60; Committee of Treasury, Minutes, March 9, 1932, BoE G8/60.
125 J.A.C. Osborne, "Statistical Summary Free List," February 9, 1932, BoE EID8/5.
126 "Bank of England: May Statistical Summary," *The Financial Times* 13527, May 28, 1932, 4.
127 J.A.C. Osborne, "Bank of England's Summary of Statistics," November 1928, BoE EID2/20.
128 Strikethrough in the original; J.A.C. Osborne, "Summary of Statistics," August 26, 1931, BoE EID2/20.
129 J.A.C. Osborne, "Summary of Statistics," December 18, 1931, BoE EID2/20.

To support this work, the Bank began employing those with more quantitative backgrounds. They looked for specialists who were willing to collect data on foreign bank balances, exchange movements, and balance of payments, information that was often only available in other languages.[130] While the charts and tables of the *Statistical Summary* proved insightful, they still offered little explanation into the qualitative differences among various countries. Before the American Statistical Association, Sprague argued that there was a need for specialists who could thus translate statistics into understandable language:

> In the financial sphere, for example, we have statistical information about changes in velocity of circulation, changes in interest rates, in the price level, and data regarding variations among prices of different commodities ... . [W]e have industrial statistics showing changes in the physical volume of trade and changes in the relative quantities of different goods and services that are being currently produced. Again, we have data about employment, wage rates, pay rolls, and the total money income of the community and its distribution ... . When the economist, the government official, or the business man examines this statistical material he does not find that it explains why changes have taken place and he is particularly at a loss when he is concerned to discover what, in any given situation, it is desirable to do.[131]

Portraying themselves as the ones who could make sense of statistics, experts planned to provide additional context to the data found in the *Statistical Summary*. The goal thereafter was not only to improve existing charts and tables but also to demonstrate the usefulness of experts in interpreting them.

Indeed, the Bank's advisers were far more aware of new statistical methodologies and terminology than the members of the Old Guard. After the abandonment of the gold standard in September 1931, the Statistical Section started to use the term "sterling area" in its monthly reports. The phrase referred to countries that had continued to peg their currencies to sterling, a decision that would promote crossborder trade. One contemporary might have acknowledged that the concept was "extremely loose and may vary at different times and with different writers."[132] Yet believing the sterling area was essential for Britain's economic recovery, the research division began updating its reports with the new terminology. In one of his studies on foreign lending, Clay reported, "[w]e differentiate between Sterling Area and non-Sterling Area countries, because the former keep a large part of their monetary reserves in the form of sterling balances, and are also closely linked commercially and financially with England."[133] Another economist found that a steady recovery

[130] "The Bank of England's Suggestions Not Referred to in the Macmillan Report," February 17, 1933, BoE EID4/53.

[131] O.M.W. Sprague, "Statistics and Economics," *Journal of the American Statistical Association* 29, no. 185 (1934), 162.

[132] Robert B. Stewart, "Instruments of British Policy in the Sterling Area," *Political Science Quarterly* 52, no. 2 (1937), 175.

[133] Henry Clay, "Foreign Lending," February 12, 1936, NCO Clay Papers 67/1/6.

in the sterling area led to the growth in its share of world trade from 26.9 percent in 1931 to 29.9 percent in 1934.[134]

While in 1927, the staff of the Statistical Section included two men and one woman, the number increased to six men and three women the following year.[135] Both male and female workers were tasked with translating foreign reports, often from French or German.[136] Nearly all employees in the Section had university degrees "or some other special qualification," such as relevant industry experience.[137] A degree in economics, while "no substitute for what [one] learns in the Bank," was another one of the preferred qualifications.[138] Beyond those with quantitative backgrounds, new employees had to demonstrate certain qualitative skills. As one Bank report indicated, "All need not be statisticians or mathematics and we do not want mere students ... [but] every member of the staff must be able to express himself clearly in writing."[139]

The research department employed statisticians to support its growing list of responsibilities (Table 3.1). In June 1932, the (Peacock) Special Committee on Organisation recognized the growing importance of advisers at the Bank, affirming that they "shall report direct[ly] to the Governors and shall not be concerned with Departmental Administration."[140] Many of them were not only involved in the study of economic indicators but also engaged in various assignments and ad hoc tasks. The Committee of Treasury envisioned centralizing these efforts among the various departments, in addition to streamlining the determination of promotions, salaries, and pensions.[141] Meanwhile, other officials made the case for the continued expansion of the research department by hiring individuals who had training in both foreign languages and economics.[142] Such qualifications were held by James Bertram Selwyn, a graduate of the London School of Economics, who had a working

134 Humphrey Mynors, "The Sterling Area's Share in World Trade, 1931–4," June 24, 1935, BoE OV21/37.

135 "Statistical Section," February 15, 1929, BoE OV50/4.

136 Another group, the Overseas & Foreign Department (informally called the Central Banking Division), was divided into three branches based on the main language of communication: German (Austria, the Baltic states, Bulgaria, Czechoslovakia, Denmark, Finland, Hungary, the Netherlands and Java, Norway, Sweden, and Russia), French (Belgium, France, Greece, Italy, Latin America, Portugal, and Spain), and English (the Dominions, Japan, and the United States); "Memorandum," November 13, 1925, BoE EID8/1; Pierre Quesnay to Émile Moreau, October 12, 1926, BdF 1064199002/144.

137 "Economics & Statistics Section – Bank of England," April 9, 1937, BoE EID8/1.

138 Clay to H.B.C. Yeomans, November 11, 1932, BoE SMT5/7.

139 Underlining in the original; "Memorandum to the Chief Cashier: Statistical Section," November 15, 1932, BoE EID8/1.

140 "Report of the Special Committee on Organisation, as Approved by the Court of Directors," 1932, BoE G15/205.

141 Committee of Treasury, Minutes, October 26, 1932, BoE G8/61.

142 "Some Discursive Notes on the Statistical Section," October 29, 1930, BoE EID8/1.

TABLE 3.1 *Responsibilities of the Bank's Statistical Section*

1. To prepare the figures and graphs for the monthly Summaries of Statistics for the United Kingdom.
2. To explore possible sources of fresh material for statistical tables.
3. To undertake and carry out special economic research needed by the Governors, Directors, and high Officials of the Bank.
4. To keep in touch with the Statistical Departments of other Central Banks, the League of Nations, etc., by the circulation of the Summary and the exchange of statistical and other information.
5. To keep in touch with certain Government Departments, particularly the Board of Trade, where mutual assistance is possible.
6. To keep up figures and graphs on subjects of general interest, such as Note Circulation, Gold Movements, etc., for the reference of Officials.
7. To coordinate and summarise internal information recorded in different Departments of the Bank.
8. To attempt to forecast actions of the Clearing Banks, needs of [the] Market, etc.
9. To send a weekly summary of the Stock and Commodity markets to the National Bank of Hungary and a weekly cable to the Federal Reserve Bank of New York.
10. To keep up certain graphs for the Central Banking Section.

Source: "Statistical Section," October 15, 1929, BoE EID8/1.

knowledge of Spanish, French, and German. In 1933, he joined the Bank to develop its research on capital markets and national-income accounting.[143] At the age of twenty-two, he was among the youngest of the Bank's statisticians, and he later became principal of the department.

By 1932, the Statistical Section emerged as a highly specialized research department, with tasks distributed according to expertise and experience. It developed a group system in which a head specialist oversaw a particular area of research (Table 3.2).[144] Selwyn worked on financial markets and new statistical measurements; L.E. Inman focused on trade and tariffs, in addition to relaying letters to the central banks of Hungary and the United States; R.T. Nightingale was responsible for wholesale and retail price indices; and all contributed to the Empire Letter that was distributed on a regular basis.[145] Female clerks dealt with the compilation and formatting of the *Statistical Summary* under the direction of W.J. Graham. As the Principal Clerk, she oversaw a subsection that compiled entries, drew graphs, and filed letters and memoranda on behalf of the Statistical Section.[146]

143 "Economics & Statistics Section," March 31, 1936, BoE EID8/1; "Retirements: J.B. Selwyn," *The Old Lady of Threadneedle Street* XLVI, March 1970, 52.

144 R.E.H. Allport, Memorandum, May 6, 1938, BoE EID8/1.

145 "Statistical Section," 1932, BoE EID8/1.

146 J.A.C. Osborne, "The Organisation of the Section," February 9, 1932, BoE EID8/5.

TABLE 3.2 *Administrative Groups of the Bank's Statistical Section*

Group	Head	Research Specialties
I	L.E. Inman	External Trade
		Tariffs, Quotas, Export Credits
		Transport
		Superintendence of the Office
II	A.C. Darby	Banking and Currency
		Foreign Funds
		Distribution of Periodicals, Newspapers, Inward Letters
III	J.B. Selwyn	Company Finance
		Security Markets
		Capital Issues
		National Income and Capital
		Statistical Method
IV	A. Hopkinson	Government Finance
		Gold
		Balance of Payments
		Insurance
V	V.K. Bloomfield	Commodity Prices
		Commodity Markets
VI	R.L. Thomas	State of Trade and Industry
		Finance of and Assistance to Industry
VII	J. Humphry	Employment and Wages
		Social Services
		Agriculture and Building
		Statistical Summary Free List
VIII	J.I. Douglas	Retail and Wholesale Trade
		Retail Prices
IX	W.J. Graham	General Routine

Source: J.A.C. Osborne, "The Organisation of the Section," February 9, 1932, BoE EID8/5.

There were some efforts to hire more women as permanent clerks at the Bank, although only a few were employed.

While the majority of those hired in the research department were employed due to their training in economics or mathematics, personal connections still helped a few obtain employment.[147] W. Brian Reddaway, for instance, was only able to join the Bank due to a letter of recommendation written by Keynes.[148]

[147] J.A.C. Osborne, Memorandum, July 14, 1931, BoE EID8/1; Clay to Robertson, June 14, 1932, BoE SMT5/6.

[148] He later worked at the Board of Trade during the Second World War and as a professor of political economy at Cambridge; Keith Tribe, *Economic Careers: Economics and Economists in Britain 1930–1970* (London: Routledge, 1997), 71; Alex Millmow, "W. Brian Reddaway (1913–2002)," *History of Economics Review* 36, no. 1 (2002), 177.

Reddaway, however, had little interest in the work at the Bank and returned to academia two years later. Another staff member, A.R.M. Geddes, son of the Conservative MP Eric Geddes, completed Part I of the Economic Tripos at Cambridge, where one of his examiners was later an economist at the Bank. In December 1932, Geddes secured one of the several new permanent posts in the research department reserved for those trained in economics, although he left the Bank several years later.[149]

Amidst these changes, the Bank considered employing a permanent, full-time economist to lead its research department. Osborne, while not trained in economics himself, intended to hire someone who was. As he initially wrote in 1925,

> The Economist is there primarily to weigh the "ponderables" … . [A] trained Economist could be consulted whenever the views of an "expert" were considered likely to be of assistance in clearing up obscure points of economics, while the Economist himself would be able occasionally to take the initiative and call attention to developments that he might think worthy of the Court's consideration. … He should be fully "qualified" as far as Degrees, &c., indicate; must not be a crank, and must have the gift of applying economics to practical affairs.[150]

By 1931, Osborne affirmed that "knowledge of Central Banking, general economics, and statistical methods is requisite."[151] Concerted efforts to expand research capabilities directly led to the employment of the first permanent economist. In August 1933, Humphrey Mynors, a Fellow and Lecturer in Economics at Corpus Christi College, Cambridge (and the nephew of Deputy Governor Ernest Harvey), joined the Bank to run the Economics & Statistical Section.[152] As the department's Deputy Principal (and later Principal), Mynors prioritized new research projects, especially those that fostered links with "the statistical departments in Whitehall, those of trade organisations in the commodity markets and so on."[153] He assisted various Bank directors with ad hoc requests. Because of this support, Mynors earned a reputation for being "well informed on affairs in general, especially on the economic side" and was later the first economist to be appointed a director (1949) and deputy governor (1954).[154]

Under Mynors, the research department debated whether to add a new introductory note to its monthly reports. This change "would save the Press

[149] Hennessy, *A Domestic History of the Bank of England*, 346–347; "Sir Reay Geddes," *The Times* 66136, February 27, 1998, 27; Kynaston, *Till Time's Last Sand*, 350–351.

[150] J.A.C. Osborne, "Memorandum for the Deputy Governor," November 1925, BoE EID8/1.

[151] "Notes on Mr. Osborne's Evidence," June 11, 1931, BoE G15/204.

[152] Committee of Treasury, Minutes, July 20, 1932, BoE G8/61; Clay to P. Malcolm Stewart, November 10, 1932, BoE SMT5/9; Hennessy, *A Domestic History of the Bank of England*, 315–316.

[153] H.C.B. Mynors, "Economics and Statistics Section," April 26, 1930, BoE EID8/1.

[154] Norman to Lefeaux, October 10, 1933, BoE G1/339; "An Economist's Economist Comes to Court," *The Financial Times* 23207, January 10, 1964, 12.

and many other readers from the necessity of looking at the Tables ... [and] would afford some opportunity, if one were needed, for the Bank to call attention to developments."[155] Although no such preface was ultimately written, the reports did begin to include more information regarding the sources of various data points. In 1933, the Statistical Section was again renamed, this time to the Economic & Statistics Section, a title that reflected the acceptance of economics as an indispensable component of its research agenda. Both economists and statisticians continued to draw on other studies, such as one by the government's Economic Advisory Council on the effective working hours of iron and steel production in continental Europe.[156] With regard to industrial profits, the researchers noted that *The Economist*'s table "makes a yearly comparison ... of one year with the next," but included no long-term perspectives or insights.[157]

Intending to aggregate disparate sources of data with varying degrees of accuracy, the research department found ways of standardizing data across time and institution. It aimed to address the suggestion raised by the Macmillan Committee on the use of more appropriate labels for graphs, tables, and charts.[158] As one economist suggested, the monthly report needed to explain the difference between "insured" unemployment and "registered" unemployment; the precise definitions of town, metropolitan, country, and provincial banks; and the types of goods that were included in its price indices.[159] Standardization would allow readers to compare reports across countries as well. After inviting Stewart, the Bank adopted language that was more consistent with other central banks, including the same definitions for financial terms (capital issues, bonds) and geographic areas (British Empire, Latin America).[160]

Another area of interest for the Bank was original research. In March 1932, the Bank received a letter from J. Iris Douglas, an economist at the advertising company, J. Walter Thompson & Co. She had been collecting data for a study on retail statistics. Although Clay admitted to not having the time to commit to an additional project, he suggested that Douglas discuss her research with Osborne, the head of the research department, who was also concurrently working on a study of retail trade.[161] As the Bank's first female economist, Douglas joined the Statistical Section on a probationary basis until being offered full-time employment in October 1932.[162] She then began working

155 "Statistical Summary," September 21, 1932, BoE EID2/20.
156 L.E. Inman, "Iron and Steel," September 4, 1930, BoE EID9/23.
157 "Industrial Profits as Reported in 'The Economist,'" August 14, 1929, BoE EID11/4.
158 Humphrey Mynors, "Statistical Summary," September 26, 1935, BoE EID2/20.
159 Humphrey Mynors, Memo, September 13, 1935, BoE EID2/20.
160 "Statistical Section: Review of the Year 1928," February 15, 1929, BoE EID8/1.
161 Clay to Douglas, March 13, 1931, BoE SMT5/1; Hennessy, *A Domestic History of the Bank of England*, 316.
162 Joan Bridges, "The Servants of the House," May 17, 1972, BoE ADM33/13.

with external organizations, such as the Incorporated Association of Retail Distributors, to gather data on retail prices.[163]

The dearth of existing retail information provided the Bank an opportunity to develop its own dataset. In-house economists and statisticians wanted to be able to adjust the basket of retail goods to reflect changing consumer preferences and new goods that appeared on the market. During her time at J. Walter Thompson, Douglas had already begun building a general survey of the retail industry in England.[164] At the Bank, she similarly proposed a way of calculating retail prices that took quality into account.[165] Her project initially focused on creating an index that standardized the basket of goods by which prices could be measured: "Every care is to be taken to leave as little room as possible for any divergence of opinion regarding the size of the quality change."[166] The implication of this work was to use the consumption of retail goods as a proxy for business activity in different parts of the country.

In the summer of 1933, Douglas planned to visit department stores across the United Kingdom to discuss exactly what information she needed in order to create a new companion to the price index: the quality index.[167] While she and a representative from the Board of Trade (Hector Leak) believed that various items could be easily substituted into the new index, Osborne countered their arguments on grounds of continuity: "We want a continuous series, and it seems to me that if a substitute article enters at the departmental average and not at the price relative of its predecessor, you are definitely getting a discontinuity in the series."[168] By November 1934, the economists reached a compromise by adding a graph that indicated the percentage of new goods added to the index.

Improved quantitative metrics had direct implications on economic policy. Seeking to identify a reliable metric that could easily compare retail prices across different regions, Douglas described the work that the research department had recently undertaken: "A compromise appears to be afforded if we confine our Price Index to articles chosen solely from Department Stores ... [which] may very well be fairly representative of changes in retail prices as a

163 Iris Douglas, "The American Census of Distribution, 1930," *Journal of the Royal Statistical Society* 94, no. 3 (1931), 433; Iris Douglas, "Retail Trade Statistics in Different Countries," *Journal of the Royal Statistical Society* 98, no. 3 (1935), 470.

164 Douglas to Clay, May 27, 1930, BoE SMT5/11; Douglas to Clay, March 12, 1931, BoE SMT5/1.

165 "Proposed Index of Retail Prices," May 23, 1933, BoE EID9/37.

166 Iris Douglas, "Retail Price Index," May 24, 1933, BoE EID9/37.

167 Iris Douglas, "Retail Price Index: Participation of Scottish Department Stores," June 22, 1933, BoE EID9/37; Iris Douglas, "Retail Price Index," September 4, 1933, BoE EID9/37.

168 Leak to Douglas, September 29, 1933, BoE EID9/37; Osborne to Leak, September 30, 1933, BoE EID9/37.

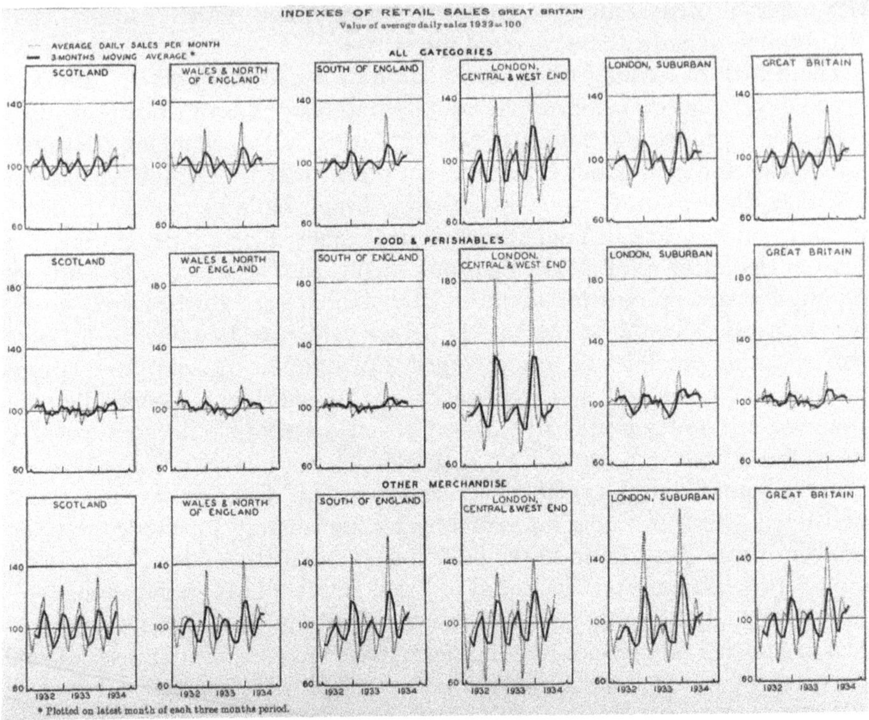

FIGURE 3.2 Retail Price Indices, 1932–1934
Source: Bank of England Archive, EID2/8.

whole."[169] Presented before the Royal Statistical Society, the project aimed to show how small retail shops often had insufficient access to working capital, leading to around 84 percent of business failures in England and Wales.[170] Doing so may have, in part, explained the severity of the Great Depression in certain regions, as well as ascribed blame to regional banks (as opposed to the central bank).

As the Bank's most original research project at the time, the quarterly retail index aggregated data of around 1,000 types of articles (Figure 3.2).[171] It allowed for the substitution of goods that entered the market. This feature gained the attention of economists across the British Empire, including those in Australia and South Africa who requested that the Bank assist with studies of retail trade in their own countries.[172] Subsequent monthly reports on retail

169 Economics & Statistics Section, "Retail Price Index," October 31, 1933, BoE EID9/37.

170 "Too Many Shops? Failures Among Retail Traders," *The Manchester Guardian* 27618, March 20, 1935, 7.

171 "Memorandum to the Chief Cashier: Statistical Section," November 15, 1932, BoE EID8/1.

172 Economics & Statistics Section, "Review of Year 1933," January 12, 1934, BoE EID8/1.

trade, collected by Douglas and published by the Bank, preceded the more institutionalized indices of retail trade by the Census of Distribution and the Board of Trade in the postwar years.[173]

The development of the retail price index indicated one of the ways in which the Bank was willing to experiment. In 1935, Mynors, now the Principal of the Economics & Statistics Section, stated that "it is perhaps true that they add little to what is already available, so far as the statistical position is concerned."[174] At the same time, statistics offered technical advisers a means of interpreting ongoing economic trends and preparing policy recommendations. Over the ensuing years, the *Statistical Summary* continued to be held in high regard, thereby allowing the Bank to elevate its own profile as a trustworthy source of information. Lionel Robbins, a professor at the London School of Economics, remarked that the report "goes from strength to strength. It is extraordinarily good."[175] The findings were published on a monthly basis until 1946 when they were replaced by the *Monthly Digest of Statistics*, later reconstituted as the *Quarterly Bulletin* in 1959.[176]

Economists had thus entered the central bank due to their technical skills. The economics discipline, although still nascent in its development, appeared to offer relevant terminology and conceptual frameworks for many of the leading monetary authorities. Already in 1930, *The Economist* remarked on the Bank's "policy of recent years of recruiting from outside its walls a team of economists of world-wide repute."[177] Indeed, advisers were keen on further enhancing the reputation of both the Bank and its statistics. Before the Royal Statistical Society, Sprague defined the role of the financial expert: "Through appropriate analysis and investigation it is obviously the proper function of the economist and statistician to endeavour to discover not only the appropriate adjustments for meeting a situation like the present of extreme depression, but also to furnish the necessary groundwork for policies designed to secure a more stable industrial future."[178]

By viewing the economy as a topic worthy of study, newly hired advisers had been vital to the development of the interwar central bank. They devised new methodologies that accurately measured changes in the British financial sector, and some of their contributions predated the later research funded by the Bank for International Settlements in the 1930s.[179] The evolution of monetary statistics included the proliferation of new quantitative methodologies, the

[173] Ely Devons, *An Introduction to British Economic Statistics* (Cambridge: Cambridge University Press, 1956), 126–130.

[174] Humphrey Mynors, "Branch Reports," February 20, 1935, BoE EID9/25.

[175] Quoted in Clay to Osborne, December 1, 1932, BoE SMT5/7.

[176] Capie, *The Bank of England*, 131–132.

[177] "Banking and Industry," *The Economist* 110, 4524, May 10, 1930, 8.

[178] O.M.W. Sprague, "Major and Minor Trade Fluctuations," *Journal of the Royal Statistical Society* 94, no. 4 (1931), 545.

[179] Toniolo, *Central Bank Cooperation*, 192.

publication of monthly reports, and collaboration with other economists, both in the United Kingdom and abroad. Although few in number – the Statistical Section employed around a dozen workers throughout the 1920s – the Bank's advisers were able to establish a reputation as financial experts.[180] It was through these changes that statistical research fundamentally shaped the central bank's outlook on the economy.

[180] Sprague, for instance, briefly served on President Roosevelt's Brain Trust in 1933; Committee of Treasury, Minutes, May 17, 1933, BoE G8/61.

4

Defending the Gold Standard

> Lenin and Mussolini have at least explained what they were at. But our despots are dumb. The veiled prophetess of Threadneedle Street speaks in the riddles of Bank rate, the City reverently accepts her word, but no one, it seems, has any idea what the old lady really means.[1]
>
> —John Maynard Keynes, 1925

> [T]he Gold standard has bound together the civilised world for good or evil in the greatest international partnership ever known in history.[2]
>
> —Henry Strakosch, 1930

> The gold standard has emerged triumphantly from the welter of disordered currencies of the World War period and gold has now become more universally than ever before the foundation of the structure of credit throughout the world.[3]
>
> —Oliver Sprague, 1930

On April 28, 1925, Chancellor of the Exchequer Winston Churchill presented a bill before the House of Commons on the return to a system of fixed exchange rates (Figure 4.1).[4] The adoption of the gold-exchange standard, according to

[1] John Maynard Keynes, "Relation of Finance to British Industry," October 15, 1925, in *The Collected Writings of John Maynard Keynes, vol. 19: Activities 1922–1929, The Return to Gold and Industrial Policy*, ed. Donald Moggridge (Cambridge: Cambridge University Press, 1981), 445–446.

[2] Henry Strakosch, "Précis of Evidence to be Submitted to the Committee on Finance and Industry: The Economic Consequences of Changes in the Value of Gold," May 1930, BoE G1/425 and BLO Brand Papers 28/B/2.

[3] O.M.W. Sprague, "The Working of the Gold Standard under Present Conditions," *Proceedings of the Academy of Political Science* 13, no. 4 (1930), 72.

[4] HC Deb, April 28, 1925, vol. 183, cc. 52–58. While the act was first introduced on April 28, it became law on 13 May: The Gold Standard Act 1925, 15 & 16 Geo. 5 c. 29.

FIGURE 4.1 Winston Churchill on Budget Day, 1925
Source: Churchill Archives Centre, Churchill Press Photographs, CHPH 1A/F2/10.

evidence assembled by numerous government commissions, would guarantee future price stability.[5] Through this policy, the Treasury offered a noninflationary approach to economic recovery based on fiscal restraint and credit rationing. Because stable exchange rates might have further raised investors' confidence in the currency, the Chancellor was able to proclaim that "the pound can look the dollar in the face."[6]

An adherence to the prewar rate harkened back to the classical gold standard of the late Victorian and Edwardian eras. The re-stabilization of exchange rates would affirm the centrality of the City of London to the global economy by ensuring investors continued to have faith in sterling. For Churchill, the merits of the gold standard, as well as those of balanced budgets and sound financial practices,

[5] Such were the recommendations of the (Cunliffe) Committee on Currency and Foreign Exchanges (1918–1919) and the (Chamberlain–Bradbury) Committee on the Currency and Bank of England Note Issues (1924–1925); *Final Report of the Committee on Currency and Foreign Exchange Rates after the War*, 3; *Report of the Committee on the Currency and Bank of England Note Issues*, Cmd. 2393 (London: H.M. Stationery Office, 1925).

[6] HC Deb, May 4, 1925, vol. 183, cc. 602–704. Also quoted in David Cannadine, *In Churchill's Shadow: Confronting the Past in Modern Britain* (Oxford and New York: Oxford University Press, 2003), 101.

seemed to be a way to revitalize the British economy.[7] As he justified, the policy had received the endorsement of nearly every prominent financial expert, economist, and civil servant since the end of the First World War.[8] Although there were notable exceptions, such as the former Treasury official John Maynard Keynes who criticized the danger of an overvalued parity and the deflation it entailed, the majority of economic experts lauded its benefits.[9] Neither the Bank nor the Treasury harbored any major doubts about the gold standard, so much so that the only concern appeared to be when, rather than if, to return.

The interwar gold standard acted as a credible commitment for countries willing to commit to price stability.[10] In Britain, its readoption in 1925 may have been influenced by a "false religion" or a "mythologized history" surrounding the glory of the prewar years.[11] Yet what more evidently determined the ensuing changes in monetary policy – and, by extension, the apparent necessity of a stable monetary regime – were the arguments around rationality and reason propounded by experts. Contemporaries frequently extolled the principles of economic orthodoxy, as it seemed to be a legitimate way of promoting recovery. At the same time, an intellectual defense of the gold standard was itself a political tool that deflected blame for Britain's poor economic performance away from the central bank and the financial sector. By identifying other factors – industrial inefficiency, the growth of labor unions, and the actions of foreign central banks –the Bank aimed to confront widespread criticism of the existing monetary system.

This chapter thus examines exchanges among civil servants, politicians, and the Bank's advisers – including Sir Henry Clay, Sir Otto Niemeyer, Harry A. Siepmann, Oliver M.W. Sprague, and Walter W. Stewart – over the operations of the gold standard. Their goal was to ensure the continued status of sterling as an international reserve currency through a system based on fixed

[7] Winston Churchill, "British Financial Policy," *Advocate of Peace through Justice* 87, no. 8 (1925), 494.

[8] Winston Churchill, "Public Expenditure and Revenue," April 28, 1925, CAC Chartwell Papers 9/71.

[9] John Maynard Keynes, *A Tract on Monetary Reform* (London: Macmillan, 1924), 164; D.E. Moggridge, *The Return to Gold, 1925: The Formulation of Economic Policy and Its Critics* (Cambridge: Cambridge University Press, 1969), 25–28; Moggridge, *British Monetary Policy*, 42; Sayers, *The Bank of England, vol. 1*, 134; Michael Collins, *Money and Banking in the UK: A History* (London: Croom Helm, 1988), 279; Skidelsky, *John Maynard Keynes, vol. 2*, 187–191; Jim Tomlinson, *Churchill and Industrial Britain: Liberalism, Empire and Employment, 1900–1929* (London: Bloomsbury, 2024), 175–176.

[10] Bordo and Rockoff, "The Gold Standard," 392; Michael D. Bordo and Finn E. Kydland, "The Gold Standard as a Rule," in *The Gold Standard in Theory and History*, 2nd ed., ed. Barry Eichengreen and Marc Flandreau (London and New York: Routledge, 1997), 106; Kirsten Wandschneider, "The Stability of the Interwar Gold Exchange Standard: Did Politics Matter?," *The Journal of Economic History* 68, no. 1 (2008), 153.

[11] Morrison, *England's Cross of Gold*, 13.

exchange rates. By inviting those from outside the City aristocracy, the Bank was able to respond intelligently and coherently to critics of monetary policy. After the collapse of the gold standard in September 1931, experts were able to craft alternative strategies for protecting sterling in a changing global order. Technical advice, while having little bearing on either the adoption or the abandonment of the gold standard, was imperative for promoting the nation's financial objectives.

More broadly, the Bank's commitment to the gold standard elevated its own status as a monetary authority. From the mid-nineteenth century onward, the central bank had played a prominent role in the national monetary system, partly due to the continued support of the state. The Bank Charter Act of 1844, for instance, had delineated the distinct prerogatives associated with the Issue Department (maintaining a monopoly of note issue) and the Banking Department (accepting deposits and issuing loans).[12] Yet even though exchange-rate management had been an old responsibility, it was one that tackled a fundamentally new set of problems in the interwar years. Inflationary pressures, inter-Allied debts, and a new geopolitical landscape altered the approach to monetary policy. Motivated by these goals, the Bank was able to retain its authority over economic governance not due to the leadership of Governor Norman alone but instead due to the network of institutions in which he and his experts operated. Direct connections to Treasury officials, City bankers, and Westminster politicians allowed it to maintain a voice in discussions over economic policy. Through these links, the Bank was able to emerge as the de facto intellectual authority in both domestic and international monetary affairs.

THE RETURN TO GOLD

The readoption of the gold standard in 1925 was a defining moment in the economic history of interwar Britain. It effectively reversed the 1920 Gold and Silver Export Embargo Act, which had postponed the question over the return to gold by allowing the government to continue issuing wartime paper notes.[13] Long upheld as the goal of the triumvirate of British financial institutions – the City, the Bank, and the Treasury – whose officials praised the decision to return to the prewar rate of $4.865 to the pound, the policy marked a return to a state of financial stability. Churchill surmised that the gold standard could even act as a unifying force for the British Empire.[14]

Restoring the prewar parity was only one component of interwar economic orthodoxy. Other priorities, according to Niemeyer, then the Controller at the Treasury, included balancing the budget, reducing the national debt, and

[12] Bank Charter Act 1844, 7 & 8 Vict. c. 32.
[13] Gold and Silver (Export Control, &c.) Act 1920, 10 & 11 Geo. 5 c. 70.
[14] Churchill to George V, April 23, 1925, CAC Chartwell Papers 18/7.

curtailing future expenditures.[15] As the government resolved to consolidate its debts after the war, it implemented numerous tax reforms and a range of cost-cutting measures across the public sector.[16] The proponents of such policies warned of the debilitating effects that continued liabilities might impose on the economy. "Not only is our debt so heavy as to be almost overwhelming," one Treasury official claimed, "but it includes a very heavy external debt and a very heavy floating debt. Both ... are points of weakness in an emergency ... [and have] an injurious effect upon our financial strength."[17]

Bankers and politicians primarily viewed a return to the gold standard as a way of reversing the economic disorder wrought by the Great War. It aimed to encourage foreign countries and central banks to hold sterling reserves, thereby preserving its value. To those who prioritized price stability, devaluation was an unacceptable policy because it raised the likelihood of inflation. Instead, the stabilization of exchange rates could help bring domestic and foreign prices into equilibrium.[18] In August 1925, Niemeyer noted that any negative consequences that the gold standard might have caused, as its critics warned, had not materialized:

> It was predicted that sterling would return to [the] approximate parity with the gold \$. This has taken place ... . Some feared that we should be called upon to export large quantities of gold. This has not happened. ... Some feared that [the] Bank rate would have to be put up perhaps to very high rates. This has not happened.[19]

Despite the criticism of trade unions and politicians, the 1925 moment was meant to be one of class unity for a divided country. Economic orthodoxy offered a compelling model of financial stability for the nations of Britain, Europe, and the British Empire. As Churchill maintained in his Budget Day speech, "Germany and the United States are already on the gold standard ... Canada is already on the gold standard, South Africa, Australia and New Zealand only await the British signal. The importance of a uniform standard of value to which all transactions can be referred throughout the British Empire

[15] Niemeyer to Baldwin, May 22, 1925, CUA Baldwin Papers D.2, Volume 3; Otto Niemeyer, Memorandum, June 26, 1925, TNA T176/21.

[16] Nicholas Crafts and Terence C. Mills, "Self-Defeating Austerity? Evidence From 1930s' Britain," *European Review of Economic History* 19, no. 2 (2015): 109–127; Mattei, *The Capital Order*, 184–187.

[17] R.G. Hawtrey, "War and Financial Power," March 20, 1925, CAC Hawtrey Papers 1/35.

[18] Frederick Leith-Ross, *Money Talks: Fifty Years of International Finance* (London: Hutchinson & Co., 1968), 91–92; David Williams, "Montagu Norman and Banking Policy in the Nineteen Twenties," *Bulletin of Economic Research* 11, no. 1 (1959), 48–49. On the debate over sterling's valuation, see John Redmond, "The Sterling Overvaluation in 1925: A Multilateral Approach," *The Economic History Review* 37, no. 4 (1984): 520–532; K.G.P. Matthews, "Was Sterling Overvalued in 1925?," *The Economic History Review* 39, no. 4 (1986): 572–587; Susan Wolcott, "Keynes versus Churchill: Revaluation and British Unemployment in the 1920s," *The Journal of Economic History* 53, no. 3 (1993): 601–628.

[19] Niemeyer to Churchill, "Gold Standard Results," August 4, 1925, TNA T208/105.

and through a very large part of the world cannot be over-estimated. It benefits all countries, but it benefits no country more than our crowded island with its vast world trade and finance by which it lives."[20]

At the Bank, the decision was met with equal élan. Governor Norman congratulated Churchill on his speech.[21] From one perspective, the Bank strategically saw its own importance elevated after 1925, as it now had to manage both the parity to gold and general price levels. This shift in power allowed the Bank to claim greater influence over economic affairs from the ever-dominant Treasury. From a strategic point of view as well, Norman assumed that the problems of unemployment and inflation could be simultaneously addressed through the maintenance of a gold-backed currency.[22] Not returning to gold might have left London more economically isolated, thereby conceding its position of power to New York.[23]

However, for all the supposed benefits, the period of celebration was short-lived, as central bankers, private bankers, and government officials began to disagree over the technicalities of monetary management. It was the decision to adopt an overvalued prewar parity to gold that initially faced the most criticism. Sir Reginald McKenna, chairman of Midland Bank, had long described the excessive burden placed on commercial banks for managing levels of credit, while also noting how the Bank's deflationary policies instigated the ongoing slump.[24] A former chancellor, McKenna frequently oscillated in his views on the return to the gold standard. Not opposing it on principle, he denounced the premature return to the old parity, similar to Keynes, even though he also believed that the stability of exchange rates was key to general prosperity.[25] By January 1925, he had contrarily

[20] Churchill to George V, April 23, 1925, CAC Chartwell Papers 18/8.

[21] Norman to Churchill, April 28, 1925, CAC Chartwell Papers 2/141. The Chancellor also received praise from J.P. Morgan & Co.; J.P. Morgan & Co. to Morgan Grenfell & Co., May 1, 1925, CAC Chartwell Papers 18/8; Martin Horn, *J.P. Morgan & Co. and the Crisis of Capitalism: From the Wall Street Crash to World War II* (Cambridge: Cambridge University Press, 2022), 62.

[22] Clay, *Lord Norman*, 170–171.

[23] Costigliola, "Anglo-American Financial Rivalry," 926; Frank C. Costigliola, *Awkward Dominion: American Political, Economic, and Cultural Relations with Europe, 1919–1933* (Ithaca and London: Cornell University Press, 1984), 97.

[24] Reginald McKenna, Speech Notes on the Bank of England, 1920, CAC McKenna Papers 9/15; Midland Bank, "Minutes of Proceedings of the Ordinary General Meeting of Shareholders Held at the Cannon Street [Hotel], London," January 27, 1922, HSBC, Midland Bank UK 0009-0188; Reginald McKenna, "Currency, Credit and Trade: Importance of Monetary Policy," January 25, 1924, in *Post-War Banking Policy: A Series of Addresses* (London: William Heinemann, 1928), 85; "Note of a Second Meeting between the Chancellor of the Exchequer and the Bankers," March 26, 1925, TNA T176/16.

[25] Boyce, *British Capitalism*, 73; Robert Boyce, "Creating the Myth of Consensus: Public Opinion and Britain's Return to the Gold Standard in 1925," in *Money and Power: Essays in Honour of L. S. Pressnell*, ed. P.L. Cottrell and D.E. Moggridge (Basingstoke: Macmillan, 1988), 173–174; Rogério Arthmar and Michael McLure, "On Britain's Return to the Gold Standard: Was There

proclaimed that "the gold standard has in existing circumstances great and striking advances."[26] He then warned Churchill: "There is no escape; you have to go back; but it will be hell."[27]

McKenna, at least prior to his change of heart, was not alone in voicing criticism. Several clearing banks – those that held deposits and extended short-term loans – joined the growing chorus of objections to recent economic policy. Representatives from the Trades Union Congress and the Labour Party had questioned the return to gold, partly because it had appeared as a moment of political triumph and unity for the Conservative Party.[28] Yet even the Federation of British Industries, a group of trade associations, expressed anxieties over the potential problems caused by a return to gold. The relative strengthening of the currency meant that British exports would be more expensive. While its economic adviser, R.G. Glenday, supported the policy in theory, he further believed that the maldistribution of gold reserves, particularly those accumulated in the United States, could hinder the prospect of a stabilization.[29]

Perhaps the most well-known critic of the interwar gold standard was Keynes. His objections to the policy were featured extensively in the Liberal outlet, *The Nation & Athenæum*.[30] Other essays, such as one titled *The Economic Consequences of Mr Churchill* (1925), blamed the Chancellor and the Cabinet for returning to an overvalued rate.[31] Because this rate effectively made exports more expensive, industries were unable to find demand for their goods abroad, leading to lower profits and higher unemployment. Keynes therefore recommended a reduction in the value of sterling by 10 percent. Added to future difficulties was the uncertainty of US monetary policy, which compelled the Bank to respond by raising interest rates to prevent outflows of

a 'Pigou–McKenna School'?," *Economic Record* 92, no. S1 (2016), 4–5; Morrison, *England's Cross of Gold*, 259–261.

26 Reginald McKenna, "Commodity Prices and the Gold Standard," January 27, 1925, in *Post-War Banking Policy: A Series of Addresses* (London: William Heinemann, 1928), 101–102.

27 Quoted in R.S. Sayers, "The Return to Gold, 1925," in *Studies in the Industrial Revolution: Presented to T.S. Ashton*, ed. L.S. Pressnell (London: University of London, The Athlone Press, 1960), 317; Boyce, *British Capitalism*, 76; Moggridge, *Maynard Keynes*, 429.

28 Boyce, "Creating the Myth of Consensus," 192.

29 "Memorandum on the Proposed Return to the Gold Standard (Draft)," February 5, 1925, MRC FBI F/3/E1/4/1/1.

30 See, for instance, John Maynard Keynes, "The Policy of the Bank of England," *The Nation & Athenæum* 35, no. 16, July 19, 1924, 500–501; John Maynard Keynes, "The Return Towards Gold," *The Nation & Athenæum* 36, no. 21, February 21, 1925, 707–709; John Maynard Keynes, "The Problem of the Gold Standard," *The Nation & Athenæum* 36, no. 25, March 21, 1925, 866–870.

31 John Maynard Keynes, *The Economic Consequences of Mr Churchill* (London: The Hogarth Press, 1925), 6. The essay was a compilation of a series of separate articles written for *The Evening Standard* and was later published as *The Economic Consequences of Sterling Parity* in New York.

gold. He therefore condemned the decision to return to the gold standard at the prewar parity. As he wrote,

> If Mr. Churchill had restored gold by fixing the parity lower than the pre-war figure, or if he had waited until our money values were adjusted to the pre-war parity, then these particular arguments would have no force. But in doing what he did in the actual circumstances of last spring, he was just asking for trouble … . Why did he do such a silly thing?[32]

Keynes remained convinced that the United Kingdom did not have the means of operating a system of fixed exchange rates properly, primarily due to the accumulation of gold reserves in the United States, yet also because of the realities of Britain's economic standing in the world. In accordance with the "rules of the Gold Standard game," the Bank was compelled to decrease the volume of public credit and the level of loanable funds in the London money market.[33] Any potential benefit by way of exchange-rate stability for exporting industries seemed to be outweighed by the consequences of an overvalued currency.

DEBATING THE BANK RATE

The main instrument for sustaining the regime of fixed exchange rates was the Bank Rate. Any effective operation of the gold standard depended on this rate, which itself was the product of internal deliberations of the Bank's authoritative body, the Committee of Treasury, behind closed doors. Since the return to the gold standard, all changes to the Bank Rate, as well as the opaque procedure by which it was set, had raised public concerns. In October, Keynes criticized existing monetary policy and, by extension, the authority that the Bank held over the British economy. As he opined, "the Bank of England has seized the opportunity to restrict credit and so organise a depression with a view to lowering prices in the interests of the dollar exchange."[34]

More criticism of the Bank came from the Treasury. As Chancellor, Churchill might have publicly affirmed the independence of the Bank to set its own policy. When asked in Parliament if the Bank Rate needed to be raised prior to the return to gold, he responded, "[t]his is a matter for the decision of the Bank" and "it is not the practice for the Treasury to be formally consulted in these matters."[35] One Treasury official, Otto Niemeyer, affirmed this view: "In pre-war days a change in Bank rate was no more regarded as the business of the Treasury than the colour which the Bank painted its front door."[36] Privately, however,

[32] Keynes, *The Economic Consequences of Mr Churchill*, 10.

[33] Keynes, *The Economic Consequences of Mr Churchill*, 18.

[34] Keynes, "Relation of Finance to British Industry," 445.

[35] "Extracts from Parliamentary Questions," March 4, 1925, in "Relations between the Treasury and the Bank of England: Control of the Bank Rate," 1929, TNA T176/13.

[36] Niemeyer to Phillips, February 18, 1929, TNA T176/13. Also quoted in David Kynaston, "The Bank of England and the Government," in *The Bank of England: Money, Power and Influence,*

the Treasury often tried to exert influence over Bank policy.[37] Churchill wrote to Niemeyer on the need for intervention, famously stating his priority for British businesses: "I would rather see Finance less proud and Industry more content."[38] At his request, Niemeyer urged Norman to consider lowering the Bank Rate in an attempt to support domestic industry. As Churchill's main Treasury expert, he was able to offer a more nuanced interpretation than the Chancellor on the implications of monetary policy. Both the steady decline in prices and the Bank's improved returns in recent weeks demonstrated that a reduction in the Bank Rate was possible and, indeed, necessary.[39]

Another disapproving voice at the Treasury was Ralph Hawtrey (later, Sir Ralph). Since 1919, he had served as the Director of Financial Enquiries, a position created to gather economic intelligence on wartime issues.[40] In this capacity, which itself had no administrative requirements, Hawtrey often criticized the Bank's handling of monetary policy. Because of rising unemployment, he tried to persuade the Bank to lower interest rates in the summer of 1925: "[I]t is of urgent importance that it [the Bank Rate] should be reduced as soon as circumstances allow ... [A]t the present time we are keeping bank rate up to a point high enough practically to prevent <u>any</u> export of gold."[41] For Hawtrey, it was the Bank Rate (and not the money supply itself) that determined overall credit levels, which were also linked to short-term interest rates on bank loans, Treasury bills, and commercial bills.[42] The Bank continued to stall amidst pressure from both Hawtrey and Churchill to adjust interest rates. Only on August 5 did the Committee of Treasury eventually concede and lower the Bank Rate to 4.5 percent the following day.[43]

In late 1925, the Bank tried to reassert its authority and deliberated a proposal to raise the Bank Rate, this time to 5 percent. Circumstances outside the Bank's control seemed to justify this response. Norman wrote to Benjamin

1694–1994, ed. Richard Roberts and David Kynaston (Oxford: Clarendon Press, 1995), 25; Clarke, *The Keynesian Revolution*, 35; Kynaston, *Till Time's Last Sand*, 250; Martin, *The Meddlers*, 108.

37 Howson, *Domestic Monetary Management*, 37.

38 Churchill to Niemeyer, February 22, 1925, CAC CHAR18/12A-B. Also quoted in Moggridge, *British Monetary Policy*, 76; Paul Addison, *Churchill on the Home Front, 1900–1955* (London: Jonathan Cape, 1992), 248; Peter Catterall, "Churchill as Chancellor of the Exchequer (1924–9) and the Return to the Gold Standard," in *Winston Churchill: Politics, Strategy and Statecraft*, ed. Richard Toye (London: Bloomsbury, 2017), 36; Morrison, *England's Cross of Gold*, 263.

39 Niemeyer to Norman, July 21, 1925, TNA T176/13.

40 Alan Gaukroger, "The Director of Financial Enquiries: A Study of the Treasury Career of R.G. Hawtrey, 1919–1939," (PhD diss., University of Huddersfield, 2008), 33–35.

41 R.G. Hawtrey, "Gold and Bank Rate," July 11, 1925, CAC Hawtrey Papers 1/35 and TNA T176/13.

42 Patrick Deutscher, *R.G. Hawtrey and the Development of Macroeconomics* (Basingstoke: Macmillan, 1990), 38.

43 Committee of Treasury, Minutes, August 5, 1925, BoE G8/56; Howson, *Domestic Monetary Management*, 34; Boyce, *British Capitalism*, 92; Sayers, *The Bank of England, vol. 1*, 218.

Strong, the Governor of the Federal Reserve Bank of New York, that the other Federal Reserve banks in the United States had raised their rates, "leaving you alone at the lower rate & I am wondering what you are going to do. Perhaps be forced to do … ."[44] Even though gold outflows had weakened the Bank's position, the Committee of Treasury believed that "it might be possible to avoid raising the Bank Rate" unless the Federal Reserve Bank of New York raised its discount rate.[45] Whereas Strong ultimately decided against raising the New York discount rate, Norman still sought to protect the Bank's gold reserves by raising the Bank Rate from 4 to 5 percent. The Treasury sharply criticized the subsequent decision, with Hawtrey claiming the decision was "nothing less than a national disaster."[46]

CRACKS IN THE SYSTEM

Even if Bank officials might have chosen to remain outwardly unaffected by criticism, they still had to contend with the structural problems of the gold standard itself. In a letter to Niemeyer, Churchill blamed the rigidity of industrial performance on the central bank's policies, describing how "the financial policy of Great Britain since the war has been directed by the Governor of the Bank of England and distinguished Treasury permanent officials who … have pursued inflexibly a strict, rigid, highly particularist line of action … almost entirely unsatisfactory in its reactions upon the wider social, industrial and political spheres."[47]

From 1927 onward, the viability of the gold-exchange standard (the modified form of the gold standard) had come under question. Keynes continued to believe that the main problem lay in the overvaluation of sterling. Both the Bank and the Treasury had chosen to return to the prewar parity, which, from his point of view, required maintaining exceedingly high interest rates to attract gold inflows. Because short-term rates rose without spurring a proportional increase in foreign investments, the prewar parity appeared no longer sustainable.[48] McKenna similarly noted the ongoing complications associated with gold. He called for a public inquiry into the monetary system and, along with many industrialists and trade unionists, became increasingly critical of a high-interest rate policy.[49] The basis of his judgment rested on

[44] Norman to Strong, November 23, 1925, FRBNY Strong Papers 1116.5, Part 2.

[45] Committee of Treasury, Minutes, November 25, 1925, BoE G8/56.

[46] R.G. Hawtrey, "The Credit Situation," December 5, 1925, CAC Hawtrey Papers 1/31 and TNA T176/13; Peden, *The Treasury*, 203; Gaukroger, "The Director of Financial Enquiries," 194.

[47] Churchill to Niemeyer, April 29, 1927, CAC Chartwell Papers 18/71. Also quoted in Boyce, *British Capitalism*, 139; Wood, *A History of Central Banking*, 291.

[48] John Maynard Keynes, "The British Balance of Trade, 1925–27," *The Economic Journal* 37, no. 148 (1927), 559–560.

[49] Boyce, "Government–City of London Relations," 227; Boyce, *The Great Interwar Crisis*, 211.

the assumption that the Bank was responsible for the general level of credit. Without a firm mandate to serve the public interest, the central bank appeared to be an anti-democratic institution.

Following the increase in the Bank Rate, the overall cost of credit rose. High interest rates necessarily limited the volume of loans that businesses were able to obtain, thereby reducing demand for foreign commodities and causing a downward spiral in prices.[50] Although not in full agreement with McKenna's logic, Keynes nevertheless applauded the willingness to join him in denouncing the Bank in public fora: "He has done a service by the persistent efforts to educate the public and his colleagues on the vital importance of some fundamental principles of monetary policy of which the truth is as certain as the day but to which the City is blind as night."[51]

These attacks threatened the Bank's credibility as an institution. The Old Guard had already dealt with contentious attacks from Keynes, Churchill, and the Treasury over the setting of the Bank Rate in 1925. As one Bank official had then claimed, "[t]he raising of our rate to 5%, while disliked by some people whose particular interests may be unfavourably affected by it, is, I think, recognized by all competent judges to be the right thing to do."[52] With the resurgence of criticism after 1925, the directors now sought to defend existing interest-rate policy, but many found themselves ill-prepared to do so. Not yet having consulted any experts, they lacked the theoretical capabilities to respond to fervent criticism. In their search for allies, neither institutional nor intellectual support came from the clearing banks. As Sir Charles Addis recorded in his diary, "McKenna's refusal to join gold pooling with [the] Bank. Governor wants Agitation! I demur."[53]

To counter Keynes and McKenna's assertions on the prewar parity, along with the earlier Treasury's criticism of the proper Bank Rate, the directors began to consider the employment of outside counsel. They wanted to hire those who could speak more intelligently about matters of monetary policy in response to more electorally minded politicians. "Churchill," one director had bluntly written, "is not skilled in Finance."[54] More pressingly, the independent setting of exchange rates had been a key priority for those who remembered the classical gold standard of the prewar era. In May 1926, the Committee of Treasury agreed "to appoint someone from outside the Staff of the Bank who would be

[50] "Ordinary General Meeting," January 28, 1927, CAC Chartwell Papers 18/40; Midland Bank, "Minutes of Proceedings of the Annual Ordinary General Meeting of Shareholders Held at the Cannon Street Hotel, London," January 28, 1927, HSBC, Midland Bank UK 0009-0188.

[51] John Maynard Keynes, "Mr McKenna on Monetary Policy," *The Nation & Athenæum* 40, no. 19, February 12, 1927, 651; John Maynard Keynes, "Mr McKenna on Monetary Policy," February 12, 1927, in *The Collected Writings of John Maynard Keynes, vol. 9: Essays in Persuasion*, ed. Donald Moggridge (Cambridge: Cambridge University Press, 1972), 201.

[52] Lubbock to Lamont, March 7, 1925, HBS Lamont Papers Box 122.

[53] Charles Addis, Diary, May 11, 1927, SOAS Addis Papers Box 4.

[54] Grenfell to Morgan, March 23, 1925, MLM ARC 1195 Box 5, Folder 12.

competent to advise the Bank on questions connected with the Exchanges."[55] The discussion primarily concerned where to find an expert with "a practical knowledge of exchange operations," one who was both "conversant with the reasons for the fluctuations" and able "to speak with great authority."[56] Although some officials questioned the necessity of hiring an outside specialist, particularly an economist, they ultimately conceded that "[n]o official of the Bank has the intimate knowledge or experience required."[57]

Following more discussions, the Bank identified one potential candidate. Keynes' assistant during the 1919 Paris Peace Conference, Harry A. Siepmann, had extensive experience from his time at the Treasury, at a London stockbroker, on the Viceroy's Council of India, and at the National Bank of Hungary. He appeared to be a valuable source of technical knowledge given his connections throughout Europe and the empire. Already in March, Governor Norman had written in his diary that "[Siepmann] might become [an] adviser to BoE and liaison with E. Eastern [central banks]. Partly in London and partly on visits. He likes the idea."[58] Yet concerned with more than central bank cooperation, Siepmann offered a way of challenging Keynes' criticisms. While the Bank's longstanding priority had been to improve international economic relations, officials came to believe there were also pressing challenges to economic recovery in the domestic realm. Ensuring that foreign central banks continued to use sterling for international payments necessitated the stability of the gold standard at home. For this reason, Siepmann, originally an adviser to the German-speaking countries of Europe, was appointed the Bank's first Adviser to the Governors in June 1926.[59]

Debates over the role of experts at the Bank intensified the following year. For many officials, it seemed impractical to assign a single adviser to manage both domestic and foreign affairs. The Bank then considered inviting another expert from the Treasury, an institution that had long shared its support of economic orthodoxy. Before the Committee of Treasury, Norman reiterated, now with greater persistence, "[t]he urgent need for the appointment of an Exchange Expert."[60] As he described to Governor Strong,

> [I]t is clear that they [the Committee of Treasury] will decide in favour of help from outside … . We made a step in this direction last year through the arrangement with Siepmann – which has been very successful. Now there seems every chance that we shall make another step to take effect after the summer. You know Niemeyer: he has an established position, great ability, and is aged about 44. He does not mean to stay much longer at the Treasury and could get a good job any day. So he is to come here,

[55] Committee of Treasury, Minutes, May 19, 1926, BoE G8/57.

[56] "Memorandum: Exchanges," April 29, 1926, BoE G14/307.

[57] "Exchange Expert," November 27, 1926, BoE ADM16/4 and G14/307.

[58] Montagu Norman, Diary, March 1, 1926, BoE ADM34/15.

[59] As reported in "Foreign Business Committee," December 2, 1926, BoE ADM16/4.

[60] Committee of Treasury, Minutes, March 16, 1927, BoE G8/57.

permanently, to do League work in particular and other work in general. I think he will be a great addition and I hope the idea will be carried out this year: so far nothing is definite and everything secret.[61]

After declining an invitation to meet with McKenna and the Chancellor in May to discuss the technicalities of monetary policy, Norman felt even more pressure to protect himself from verbal criticism.[62] Given that the Bank's priority was to launch an intellectual defense of existing policy, the Committee of Treasury approved the appointment of Niemeyer as another adviser in April 1927.[63] He resigned from the Treasury and was hired on equal terms with Siepmann.

Employing those with economic knowledge was important for ongoing debates. The Bank's experts first aimed to challenge Keynes' logic by highlighting the supposed benefits of the gold standard's arrangements. One of its unofficial advisers, Henry Strakosch, had earned a reputation as an international financial expert from his time as chairman of the Union Corporation and as a member of the League's Financial Committee. His past work in the formation of central banks in Austria, Hungary, and South Africa reflected the success of currency-stabilization programs along orthodox lines.

In the years thereafter, the Bank deployed its experts to rally support behind the gold-exchange standard among the central banks of Europe. Because he was not formally employed at the Bank, Strakosch was able to adopt a more public-oriented role. "The economic chaos in the many countries on the Continent of Europe after the war," he wrote in *The Times*, "followed by their spectacular recovery as soon as their currency systems were brought back to the ordered conditions of the gold exchange standard, is eloquent proof of its efficacy."[64] Statistical analysis, in particular, could vindicate the gold-exchange standard. By 1928, Strakosch had developed an index to measure the volatility of European currencies, each weighted according to the population of each country. Normalizing these fluctuations relative to US dollars, the metric showed the success of the gold standard in stabilizing exchange rates. It estimated that overall fluctuations had increased from an annual average of 13 percent (1922) to 2,385 percent (1923) during the period of hyperinflation, before falling to a low of 0.9 percent (1928) after the adoption of the gold-exchange standard. Later published in *The Economist*, these metrics indicated that the Bank's orthodox reconstruction programs implemented in the mid-1920s had brought a great deal of stability.[65]

[61] Norman to Strong, April 8, 1927, FRBNY Strong Papers 1116.7, Part 2.

[62] Committee of Treasury, Minutes, May 11, 1927, BoE G8/57.

[63] Committee of Treasury, Minutes, April 13, 1927, BoE G8/57.

[64] Henry Strakosch, "The Gold Standard," July 31, 1925, *The Times* 44028, 15.

[65] Henry Strakosch, "Monetary Stability and the Gold Standard," May 30, 1928, BoE EID4/102; Henry Strakosch, "Monetary Stability and the Gold Standard," *Supplement to the Economist* 107, 4446, November 10, 1928, 1–7.

Although the Bank occupied a relatively stable position with its gold reserve of £153 million and a secret holding of £42 million, its advisers had to acknowledge the flaws with the gold standard if they hoped to legitimize their authority.[66] In November 1927, Siepmann admitted that, while the prevailing arrangements proved beneficial for its reported stability, they also incentivized countries to hoard gold reserves.[67] The accumulation of reserves in one country prevented a corresponding credit expansion in another. In other words, contemporaries knew that the system could not be self-sustaining given existing circumstances and national interests. Even Strakosch noted that the gold-exchange standard was a delicate apparatus that depended on conditions "entirely fortuitous" to central banks, such as the volume of gold mined and exported.[68] For him, it was solely the actions of the few countries with "relatively abundant gold reserves" that would determine the future of the entire system.[69]

Yet the arguments forwarded by Siepmann and Strakosch were primarily a means of directing blame elsewhere. France was the Bank's main target. At the behest of Premier Raymond Poincaré, the French franc had achieved a de facto stabilization in December 1926. The country had effectively returned to a devalued parity to gold – specifically, a rate of 125 francs = £1, a reduction of 80 percent from the prewar rate.[70] Its central bank then intended to begin purchasing gold in exchange for sterling, initially set at £5 million, a decision that Norman did not oppose.[71] Strakosch, however, was more attuned to the impending problems that came from France's return to the gold standard. Critical of the decision to devalue, he reported that "she [France] is not [on the gold standard], and that is the real root of the trouble."[72] In other words, the Banque de France's accumulation of foreign currencies (and after 1928, gold) had created an imbalance of credit in the world's industrial economies.[73] Its

[66] Sayers, *The Bank of England, vol. 1*, 221.

[67] Siepmann to Strakosch, November 9, 1927, BoE OV48/1.

[68] Strakosch, "Monetary Stability and the Gold Standard," 6.

[69] Strakosch, "Monetary Stability and the Gold Standard," 7.

[70] Boyce, *The Great Interwar Crisis*, 165.

[71] Charles Rist, "Avantages, pour le Trésor, des achats d'or intérieur et politique à suivre par la Banque," September 8, 1926, BdF 1397199403/3; Moreau to Norman, October 21, 1926, BdF 1397199403/3; Norman to Moreau, October 26, 1926, BoE OV45/78 and BdF 1397199403/3; Émile Moreau, *Souvenirs d'un Gouverneur de la Banque de France : histoire de la stabilisation du franc (1926–1928)* (Paris: Librairie de Médicis, 1954), 254–258, 281.

[72] Strakosch to Siepmann, October 12, 1927, BoE OV48/1.

[73] Barry Eichengreen, "The Bank of France and the Sterilization of Gold, 1926–1932," *Explorations in Economic History* 23, no. 1 (1986), 64. On French exchange-rate management, see Humphrey Mynors, "Gold Hoarding by Central Banks," December 13, 1933, BoE EID3/202; Kindleberger, *The World in Depression*, 49–53; Mouré, *Managing the Franc Poincaré*, 49–65; Eichengreen, *Golden Fetters*, 211–216, 253–254; Pierre Sicsic and Bertrand Villeneuve, "L'afflux d'or en France de 1928 à 1934," in *Du franc Poincaré à l'écu : colloque tenu à Bercy les 3 et 4 décembre 1992*, ed. Maurice Lévy-Leboyer, Alain Plessis, Michel Aglietta, and Christian de Boissieu (Paris: Comité pour l'histoire économique et financière de la France, 1993): 21–55; H. Clark Johnson, *Gold, France, and the Great Depression, 1919–1932*

sterilization policy, through which it accepted gold inflows without proportionally increasing the money supply, effectively imposed deflation on other countries on the gold-exchange standard.

Following the de jure return on June 25, 1928, the Governor of the Banque de France, Émile Moreau, and one of his experts, Pierre Quesnay, alerted the Bank that it intended to continue purchasing gold in exchange for sterling. In response, the Bank made no attempt to hide its anti-French sentiments. The Banque de France's actions, Siepmann described, were only "regarded less unfavourably at the Bank of England than a movement of gold from London to America."[74] Even then, it was an operation that seemed to demonstrate the unsustainability of the European economic system. An anticipated accumulation of £4 million in gold before year's end helped the Banque de France consolidate its own position as a monetary authority (and still maintain its minimum 35 percent gold cover). The Bank believed that the gold purchases had been politically motivated: Governor Moreau could report higher profits at the central bank to justify its own independence from the national government.[75] As a result, Siepmann warned his counterpart at the Banque de France of the great dangers that the transaction might have had on sterling, thereby threatening to raise the Bank's own interest rate in the process.[76]

Raising interest rates again, however, would have only exacerbated already high unemployment levels, a fact that the Old Guard knew perfectly well.[77] The Bank, without resorting to its false threat, instead needed to identify unconventional solutions to mitigate the outflow of gold. It was particularly important to stabilize the value of sterling since the "bill on London" remained the primary instrument for financing international trade.[78] In August, while Governor Norman was en route to South Africa, experts devised several proposals for avoiding publicity concerning the Bank's losses. Strakosch initiated the campaign by revising one of his existing plans. Because most European central banks held accounts in London (where they were able to earn interest), the Bank was an important financial connection between the metropole and the rest of Europe. One aspect of this role was being able to manage sudden drains of gold when central banks abroad tried to augment their own reserves. It might have

(New Haven and London: Yale University Press, 1997), 66–69; Mouré, *The Gold Standard Illusion*, 181–191; Douglas A. Irwin, "La France a-t-elle causé la Grande Dépression ?," *Revue française d'économie* XXV, no. 4 (2010), 4–5; Eichengreen, *Globalizing Capital*, 59–62.

[74] Harry A. Siepmann, "Note of a Conversation on the Telephone with Monsieur Quesnay," November 14, 1928, BoE G1/453.

[75] Harry A. Siepmann, "Gold," November 26, 1928, BoE G1/453.

[76] Harry A. Siepmann, "Note of a Conversation on the Telephone with Monsieur Quesnay," November 14, 1928, BoE G1/453.

[77] Lubbock to Harrison, August 3, 1928, BoE G1/453.

[78] R.G. Hawtrey, *The Gold Standard in Theory and Practice* (London: Longmans, Green & Co., 1927), 106.

been possible to subsidize gold imports from New York such that they were no more costly than those out of London. The result, Strakosch imagined, was an equalization of gold prices between the world's two financial centers.[79] Accepting this rationale, Norman agreed to implement the policy.[80]

As the Bank monitored the global movement of gold, it looked to its other experts for additional advice. In August 1928, Siepmann proposed a plan where the Bank could sell gold to the Bank of Poland, which would then act as an intermediary between London and New York. Because Poland kept its account in London, no gold was expected to leave the country physically or be reported as capital outflows.[81] As he concluded, "[t]he destination of the gold which we lose is not disclosed. I very much doubt whether the Financial News will connect together the loss of gold in London with the gain of gold in New York."[82] While managing tensions with the press characterized much of the Bank's external relationships, securing investors' confidence was an even greater concern, since volatile capital flows were subject to public perceptions. "Any movement of gold to New York even in small amounts might have psychological results," Siepmann concluded.[83] Even so, this relatively small transaction had little impact on the central bank's balance sheets, particularly compared to the extensive gold-purchasing campaign undertaken by the Banque de France. By November, the French central bank had reported more than 30 billion francs (£230 million) in gold reserves.[84]

In accordance with conventional wisdom at the Bank, no subsequent change to the Bank Rate came in 1928. Instead, officials continued to identify other measures for mitigating unstable capital outflows. In July, the long-awaited debate over when to merge wartime Treasury notes with the Bank's existing notes concluded with the passing of the 1928 Currency and Bank Notes Act.[85] Future profits derived from these notes were expected to be paid directly to the Treasury. The legislation also raised the fiduciary issue – the total volume of notes not backed by gold – from £19.75 million (set in 1921) to £260 million (1928). By resurrecting the old system of monetary management, administered primarily by the central bank, the Old Guard hoped to secure confidence in the pound and avoid sweeping interventions or direct regulation.[86]

79 Henry Strakosch, "Notes on the 'Scheme for Equalising the New York and London Gold Points of Europe,'" August 19, 1927, BoE ADM16/4.

80 Norman to Addis, August 26, 1927, BoE ADM16/4.

81 Siepmann to Karpinski, August 10, 1928, BoE G1/453.

82 Siepmann to Stewart, August 10, 1928, BoE G1/453.

83 Siepmann to Quesnay, August 15, 1928, ANF Quesnay Papers 374AP/9 and BoE G1/453.

84 Siepmann to Quesnay, November 15, 1928, ANF Quesnay Papers 374AP/9.

85 Currency and Bank Notes Act 1928, 18 & 19 Geo. 5 c. 13; Sayers, *The Bank of England, vol. 1*, 284–290; Peden, *The Treasury*, 204–205; Wormell, *The Management of the National Debt*, 706–707; William A. Allen, *The Bank of England and the Government Debt: Operations in the Gilt-Edged Market, 1928–1972* (Cambridge: Cambridge University Press, 2019), 15.

86 Harry A. Siepmann, "Market Control," August 27, 1928, BoE EID7/5.

CONFRONTING THE BRITISH SLUMP

Despite the efforts to blame France for the problems that undermined domestic finance, there was a pressing need to define the complications at home. It was, indeed, a British slump that transpired. Business leaders issued calls for a public examination into the relationship between industrial and credit policy.[87] In November 1929, Prime Minister Ramsay MacDonald established a commission to assess the state of domestic banking and industry. The Macmillan Committee, as it became known, intended "to hear expert evidence, of an informational character" during its public and private deliberations.[88] Many of the Bank's advisers served as witnesses, but only Lubbock directly represented the central bank on the committee.

Determining how the Bank decided interest rates became a key priority in the months prior to the first meeting of the Macmillan Committee. The process itself was opaque to outsiders, set neither by industrial interests nor prevailing economic theory. According to Walter Bagehot's *Lombard Street* (1873), the traditional practice had been to maintain a Bank Rate above the average market interest rate, which discouraged discount houses from discounting bills at a cheaper rate. Additionally, discount houses (or bill brokers) could act as mediators between the Bank and the rest of the financial sector. Operating in the interbank market, they provided liquidity to the system by discounting short-term obligations, ranging from banker's acceptances to Treasury bills. This highly specialized money market granted London "her supremacy as an international financial centre … . [I]n no other centre in the world can vast financial transactions be carried through with such speed or with so little disturbance of the general credit structure; in no other centre is control by the central bank exercised."[89]

To understand the more elusive workings of the financial system, Keynes, while writing what would become *A Treatise on Money* (1930), sought to procure information from the Bank's experts. In his correspondence with Niemeyer, he inquired about the operation involving discount operations. The Cambridge economist specifically wanted to know if there had ever been a departure from the standard practice in recent years.[90] Niemeyer responded by outlining the central bank's standard obligations in the discount market. Bill brokers did not discount their bills at the Bank but "only received accommodation" from the Bank in the form of loans.[91] In short, the Bank had strictly adhered to the Bagehot doctrine. The exchange itself indicated the degree to which economic expertise had become vital to assessing the origins of the

[87] Alfred Mond and Ben Turner, "Memorandum Submitted on the Gold Reserve and its Relations with Industry," April 12, 1928, CUA Baldwin Papers D.3, Volume 29.

[88] Macmillan to Norman, November 22, 1929, BoE G1/425.

[89] King, *History of the London Discount Market*, xi.

[90] Keynes to Niemeyer, December 18, 1928, BoE OV9/588.

[91] Niemeyer to Keynes, December 28, 1928, BoE OV9/588.

slump. It was nevertheless "extraordinarily difficult to pick up the clues" on "the theory and practice of [the] bank rate as a method of credit control."[92] While Keynes acknowledged his own misreading of Bagehot, he also believed that "the exact facts" of Bank Rate policy were still "not generally known, either to economists or to students of central banking systems."[93]

The Keynes–Niemeyer correspondence, which preceded the more antagonistic quarrels on the Macmillan Committee, revealed the growing controversy surrounding monetary policy. Keynes had been correct in arguing that the practice of setting the Bank Rate had been an imperceptible and inconsistent ritual, decided at the Bank by a combination of private dealings and City anxieties. Shortly after Lubbock had met with Baldwin and Churchill on February 6, 1929, the Committee of Treasury unexpectedly decided to raise the Bank Rate – the first time since 1925 – from 4.5 to 5.5 percent.[94] Tightening the monetary supply counteracted the high volume of bills discounted by the Bank, in addition to curbing speculative investments going. It also served to "check certain movements of gold," particularly outflows to the United States.[95] However, questions arose surrounding whether the Bank should be allowed to set monetary policy at will. The Treasury found that raising interest rates failed to protect "against the persistent drain [of gold] to New York."[96] Yet in response to one Treasury official (Sir Richard Hopkins) on the matter, Lubbock simply avoided the question: The "reasons [for raising the Bank Rate] have been so fully set forth in those newspapers which express and reflect instructed opinion that I do not think that it is necessary for me to elaborate the matter."[97]

Without a proper intellectual rationale behind it, the new Bank Rate appeared to be based on unsound logic. Keynes and his allies intended to take advantage of this weakness and demonstrate how monetary policy was fundamentally incompatible with the needs of British industry. High rates had raised both the costs of production for firms and the overall level of unemployment.[98] In this manner, the Macmillan Committee politicized the Bank's once private affair. In 1929, Philip Snowden, the newly appointed Chancellor of the

[92] Keynes to Niemeyer, January 4, 1929, BoE OV9/588.

[93] Keynes to Niemeyer, January 4 and 29, 1929, BoE OV9/588.

[94] Charles Addis, Diary, February 6 and 7, 1929, SOAS Addis Papers Box 5; Committee of Treasury, Minutes, February 6, 1929, BoE G8/58.

[95] Committee on Finance and Industry, Notes on Discussion, December 5, 1930, TNA T200/6/7.

[96] Hopkins to Churchill, March 18, 1929, TNA T176/13.

[97] Lubbock to Hopkins, February 9, 1929, TNA T176/13.

[98] John Maynard Keynes, *A Treatise on Money, vol. 1* (London: Macmillan, 1930), 206; Barry Eichengreen, Mark W. Watson, and Richard S. Grossman, "Bank Rate Policy under the Interwar Gold Standard: A Dynamic Probit Model," *The Economic Journal* 95, no. 379 (1985), 731; Christine Amsler, "Keynes and Bank Rate Policy: Interest Rates Inconsistent with Full Employment," *Journal of Post Keynesian Economics* 15, no. 3 (1993), 410.

Exchequer, accused the Governor of raising the Bank Rate to such an extent that it provided "no remedy" for improving trade.[99] The Bank may have only felt compelled to raise interest rates to protect its gold and foreign-exchange reserves and, by extension, support sterling's parity. Such had been the case on September 26 when the rate increased to 6.5 percent. While the hike did achieve the Bank's intended goal, it had the effect of making the cost of capital significantly higher. Subsequent censure soon appeared in the press, as many newspapers noted it was the highest Bank Rate in eight years.[100] Only later that year did the Bank's Committee of Treasury resolve to decrease the Bank Rate as "a means of increasing confidence in our position" and reverse its pre-crisis policies, lowering the rate to 6 percent (in October), 5.5 percent (November), and 5 percent (December).

By 1930, the Bank's battle with its critics had reached a new peak. The Macmillan Committee described the inability of British industry to access adequate short-term credits, a deficiency known as the Macmillan gap. In their deliberations, the figure who overwhelmingly dominated the discussion was Keynes.[101] As he argued, the Bank's actions had exacerbated many existing industrial problems. High interest rates had led to severe oversavings, which reduced aggregate demand in the economy.[102] Keynes then insisted:

> [I]n 1925 we put on the Bank Rate policy a task of greater magnitude than it had ever been asked to perform before and which it proved to be incapable of performing. If we make the usual assumptions about perfect markets and absence of friction, Bank Rate policy must always be capable of doing the work asked of it; but humanly and politically it was impossible. The result is that we are left jammed in a position of what I described as spurious equilibrium without applying any alternative policy to Bank Rate policy; and that spurious equilibrium may be gradually ruining us.[103]

It was during these discussions when Keynes began to develop theories on the problem of wage stickiness. This phenomenon, which posited that nominal prices were rigid in the short run, had been the direct consequence of high interest rates required for the return to gold in 1925.[104] His logic also directly implicated the Bank. Although the setting of the Bank Rate had been decided

99 "Note of a Conversation between the Governor and the Chancellor of the Exchequer," September 4, 1929, BoE G14/7.

100 "Rise in Bank Rate," *The Times* 45319, September 27, 1929, 14; "Higher Bank Rate and Government Schemes," *The Daily Telegraph* 23206, September 27, 1929, 11.

101 Lord Macmillan, *A Man of Law's Tale: The Reminiscences of the Rt. Hon. Lord Macmillan* (London: Macmillan, 1952), 196; Moggridge, *Maynard Keynes*, 490–495; Skidelsky, *John Maynard Keynes, vol.* 2, 345, 356; Otto, *Die Keynesianische Revolution*, 78–81; Kynaston, *The City of London, vol.* 3, 216.

102 Committee on Finance and Industry, Notes on Discussion, February 21, 1930, TNA T200/4/3; Alec Cairncross and Barry Eichengreen, *Sterling in Decline: The Devaluations of 1931, 1949 and 1967* (Oxford: Basil Blackwell, 1983), 53.

103 Committee on Finance and Industry, Notes on Discussion, February 21, 1930, TNA T200/4/3.

104 Skidelsky, *John Maynard Keynes, vol.* 2, 347–349.

by "the total monetary receipts that we get from the sale of our goods[,] ... [o]ur wages policy fixes the rate of money wages, and the result is to leave no adequate profits to business men."[105] Keynes therefore concluded that "Bank rate policy, whilst theoretically intact, has broken down as a practical instrument for restoring true equilibrium."[106]

Even so, the recently expanded democratic populace did not have much sway over City bankers. Nor was the national government willing to intervene in the Bank's internal affairs. A brief discussion in the Cabinet on the appropriate Bank Rate led to the conclusion that "His Majesty's Government has no responsibility for the movement of the Bank Rate and does not control the policy of the Bank of England."[107] Instead, it was outside the realm of formal electoral politics where the Bank faced the most threats to its independence. During his time on the Macmillan Committee, McKenna openly denounced the authority maintained by the central bank in managing the currency: "The Bank of England is absolutely free in its control of the variations of the quantity of money in this country. It has got [a] certain limitation on its policy, ... but that does not check its power of limiting the quantity of money."[108] He further argued that the recent deflationary policies, which reduced the money supply by £60 million since 1929, had only taken into account conditions in the money market, while adversely and, perhaps even unknowingly, harming British industry. "Every central bank is more or less an autocracy," stated another member of the committee.[109]

Over the course of its proceedings, the general opinion of the Macmillan Committee began to turn against the Bank. When Chairman Hugh Macmillan mentioned the historical precedents that might have granted the Bank the ability to operate at its own discretion, McKenna retorted, "Very much of a discretion."[110] The right of an unelected body of bankers and experts to dictate the economic affairs of the entire nation spurred much controversy. Other contemporaries were convinced that the Bank had been operating not from a position of strength, but rather one of weakness. According to T.E. Gregory, a professor from the London School of Economics, the Bank had limited capabilities with regard to economic performance. Even if it could adjust interest rates and influence conditions on the local money market, it had relatively little influence on the international financial system.[111] In either case, prevailing expert opinion arrived at the conclusion that the Bank had been either too incapable or too misguided in its policies.

105 Committee on Finance and Industry, Notes on Discussion, February 21, 1930, TNA T200/4/3.
106 Committee on Finance and Industry, Notes on Discussion, February 21, 1930, TNA T200/4/3.
107 "Cabinet 5(29)," February 7, 1929, TNA CAB23/60.
108 Committee on Finance and Industry, Notes on Discussion, March 21, 1930, TNA T200/4/4.
109 Committee on Finance and Industry, Notes on Discussion, October 30, 1930, TNA T200/5/4.
110 Committee on Finance and Industry, Notes on Discussion, November 6, 1930, TNA T200/5/5.
111 Committee on Finance and Industry, Notes on Discussion, November 20, 1930, TNA T200/6/2.

Still, the members of the committee were willing to be generous in their assessment and wanted to hear the first-hand rationale for such decisions. In March 1930, Governor Norman, intending to divert blame away from the Bank for unemployment, agreed to go before the committee to present his views on general credit policy.[112] His defense, however, largely lacked the theoretical underpinnings that many economists would have preferred to hear, instead asserting that the changes to the Bank Rate were simply normal responses to general market conditions.[113] Norman's testimony was, as one financial journalist described, "a study in noncommittal and evasive answers."[114] When asked whether he considered the Bank Rate an effective instrument for protecting the Bank's gold reserves, he simply replied, "It is effective"; when asked again, he repeated, "It is effective in my opinion."[115]

To the Governor, the Bank Rate could correct "an adverse international position" in the Bank's reserves, while only marginally having an effect on domestic unemployment.[116] Yet the Macmillan Committee rightly showed the flawed logic of this view and insisted that the implications of high interest rates extended far beyond the Bank's walls or, for that matter, the City of London. Monetary policy had direct effects on industrial performance and, by extent, the stability of the peacetime economy. Exposing Norman's ineptitude on such matters, Keynes denounced the Bank for its actions in exacerbating the British slump, as well as his assumptions on the self-regulating mechanisms of the gold standard that had characterized the prewar system of governance. In response to a question on whether the gold standard had an adverse effect on industry, Norman answered, "I am not aware that that is a true statement."[117] Probed further on how the Bank Rate curtailed credit, Norman only responded, "I could not dispute it with you."[118]

Following the hearings, the Governor returned to the Bank "in a very depressed state," as Deputy Governor Ernest Harvey reported, because "much that was said by Keynes he scarcely understood, whilst McKenna attacked him in a rather aggressive manner."[119] Norman's poor performance, characterized by an inability to provide adequate rationale for the Bank's actions, even led him

112 Macmillan to Norman, November 22, 1929 and March 13, 1930, BoE G1/425.

113 Montagu Norman, Diary, March 26, 1930, BoE ADM34/19; Clay, *Lord Norman*, 160.

114 Einzig, *Montagu Norman*, 37.

115 "The Right Hon. Montagu Collet Norman, D.S.O.," March 26, 1930, in Macmillan Committee, *Minutes of Evidence, vol. 1*, 212.

116 Clay, *Lord Norman*, 161.

117 "The Right Hon. Montagu Collet Norman, D.S.O.," March 26, 1930, in Macmillan Committee, *Minutes of Evidence, vol. 1*, 215.

118 "The Right Hon. Montagu Collet Norman, D.S.O.," March 26, 1930, in Macmillan Committee, *Minutes of Evidence, vol. 1*, 216; Clarke, *The Keynesian Revolution*, 127; Peter Clarke, "Churchill's Economic Ideas, 1900–1930," in *Churchill: A Major Reassessment of His Life in Peace and War*, ed. Robert Blake and Wm. Roger Louis (Oxford: Clarendon Press, 1996), 84.

119 Harvey to Stewart, April 11, 1930, BoE G1/426.

to admit that he had "found [himself] in some difficulty" during the meeting.[120] The absence of any meaningful insights into the operations of domestic monetary management only confirmed existing views that the Bank failed to serve the national interest. Two months later, Harvey suggested the possibility of assigning several of the Bank's newly hired advisers to go before the Macmillan Committee.[121] Doing so could have at least presented some justification for recent decisions made and salvaged the damage to the Bank's reputation.

Norman could have, in theory, redeemed himself in the months thereafter. His private correspondence with Keynes indicated an attempt to protect the Bank's reputation. After Norman described to Keynes in May 1930 that the central bank's position was "more complicated than you paint it," Keynes wrote a fourteen-page letter that detailed the technicalities of gold production, foreign investment, and the international economy.[122] Yet fearing another moment of humiliation, Norman stalled in his response. Nearly a month later, he simply responded by suggesting that Keynes needed to come to the Bank and talk with two of his experts.[123]

In July, the Bank decided to deploy one of its economists, Walter W. Stewart, to speak before the Macmillan Committee. By all accounts, Stewart was better prepared and far more adept than Norman in responding to Keynes. As one Treasury official reported, the expert was able to answer "questions with imperturbable calm."[124] Stewart first aimed to challenge the argument underpinning the existence of the Macmillan gap, instead identifying a reverse relationship. As he stated, "the state of British industry has imposed a heavy strain upon British finance … . The marvel to me is, not the weakness of sterling, but the capacity of British finance to carry over so long a period an international position which has not been supported by an export of goods."[125] He emphasized other factors behind industrial stagnation in a way that diverted blame away from the Bank. The origins of the slump came not from sterling's own overvaluation, he argued, but rather from the heavy burden that British industry itself had placed on the general economy.

One consequence of expert intervention, beyond a defense of the gold standard, was that the Bank could justify its own role in sustaining the system. In his written evidence presented to the committee in May 1930, Strakosch praised the ability of the gold standard to stabilize both prices and exchange rates, as well as to link countries together with a common goal. As he estimated, "practically the whole of the civilised world inhabited by some 1,200,000,000

120 Norman to Gregory, March 27, 1930, BoE G1/425.

121 Harvey to Stewart, May 16, 1930, BoE G1/426.

122 Norman to Keynes, May 20, 1930, KCC Keynes Papers M/2; Keynes to Norman, May 22, 1930, KCC Keynes Papers M/2.

123 Norman to Keynes, June 19, 1930, KCC Keynes Papers M/2.

124 Leith-Ross, *Money Talks*, 129.

125 "Dr. W.W. Stewart," July 3, 1930, in Macmillan Committee, *Minutes of Evidence, vol.* 2, 195.

people – or 60% of the world's population – were handling money linked to gold."[126] Still, the self-correcting mechanisms of the gold standard could have only worked if countries did not hold excessive gold reserves. While serving on the League's Gold Delegation, Strakosch had published a widely read report on the gold-hoarding problem.[127] In private settings, too, he acknowledged that many central banks had "accumulated gold reserves far in excess of their reasonable needs," which made the Bank correspondingly unable to expand its own money supply.[128] The system had begun to fracture as gold-hoarding countries were "depriving the Gold Standard world of the additional currency and credit it needs."[129]

Disagreements between the Bank on one side and the Macmillan Committee on the other centered on who to blame for the slump. One concern surrounded the so-called "Cunliffe minimum," the amount of gold reserves required to maintain investors' confidence in sterling.[130] As theorized by the Cunliffe Committee's 1918 interim report, the central bank only needed to hold £150 million in reserves at any given point.[131] Contemporaries certainly knew that the Bank, compared to other central banks, worked with a relatively thin holding of gold, partly because the noninterest bearing asset did not appear as a viable investment to the Old Guard. Yet to outsiders, it seemed reasonable to suggest that the central bank could strengthen confidence in the currency by acquiring even more gold. Hawtrey estimated that the world's central banks held around £2,200 million in gold reserves, of which £1,700 million were in only seven countries.[132] Acquiring a larger proportion of these reserves could be the primary means of protecting sterling from a crisis of confidence.

126 Henry Strakosch, "Précis of Evidence to be Submitted to the Committee on Finance and Industry: The Economic Consequences of Changes in the Value of Gold," May 1930, BoE G1/425.

127 League of Nations, *Interim Report of the Gold Delegation of the Financial Committee* (Geneva: League of Nations, 1930). On Strakosch and the Gold Delegation, see Boyce, *British Capitalism*, 288–290; Clavin and Wessels, "Another Golden Idol?," 770–771, 787–792; Toniolo, *Central Bank Cooperation*, 132–133; Clavin, *Securing the World Economy*, 54–61; Boyce, *The Great Interwar Crisis*, 274–275; Daunton, *The Economic Government*, 24.

128 Henry Strakosch, "Précis of Evidence to be Submitted to the Committee on Finance and Industry: The Economic Consequences of Changes in the Value of Gold," May 1930, BoE G1/425.

129 Henry Strakosch, "Précis of Evidence to be Submitted to the Committee on Finance and Industry: The Economic Consequences of Changes in the Value of Gold," May 1930, BoE G1/425.

130 Committee on Finance and Industry, Notes on Discussion, November 21, 1930, TNA T200/6/3; Moggridge, *British Monetary Policy*, 18; Cairncross and Eichengreen, *Sterling in Decline*, 50; Boyce, *British Capitalism*, 172; Boyce, *The Great Interwar Crisis*, 153; Morrison, *England's Cross of Gold*, 53–54.

131 *First Interim Report of the Committee on Currency and Foreign Exchanges after the War*, 10, 12.

132 Cited in Josiah Stamp, "The International Functions of Gold: Introductory Survey," December 5, 1929, in *The International Gold Problem, Collected Papers: A Record of the Discussions of a Study Group of Members of the Royal Institute of International Affairs, 1929–1931*, ed. Royal Institute of International Affairs (London: Oxford University Press, 1931), 8. A draft of the proceedings is located in BLO Brand Papers 117/1.

The Bank dispatched its experts to prove that it was not at fault for the maldistribution of gold, as Hawtrey had suggested, and that it should not be required to hold more gold reserves. In July 1930, Oliver M.W. Sprague, a Harvard Business School professor and leading monetary economist, joined the Bank as an adviser. He had been an early advocate of Britain's return to the gold standard, a decision that was "an essential factor in the maintenance of a reasonable measure of international financial stability for which there is no promising and practical substitute."[133] Eleven months after Norman's initial testimony, Sprague was due to appear before the Macmillan Committee to address ongoing controversies. The members of the committee had expressed their frustration with the Bank's inaction, particularly with regard to the problems facing the industrial sector. "There seems to me," reported Keynes, "to be too much dependence upon the operation of what one might call natural forces instead of getting things done on purpose, by design."[134]

On February 18 and 19, 1931, Sprague defended the rise in the Bank Rate, believing it to have had a negligible effect on the depression.[135] His testimony justified the Bank's policy as a tool for proper exchange-rate management. It was not important how or why the central bank adjusted interest rates if the industrial sector was unwilling or unable to overcome its own inherent problems. He disagreed with Strakosch that the global deflation could primarily be explained by US and French gold hoarding. Instead, Sprague contended that it was the excessive supply of commodities that exacerbated the sudden drop in agricultural prices. Because the "world slump" (not British slump) was primarily a consequence of "the over-development of certain goods," such as coffee, cotton, and wheat, providing more "liberal supplies of credit" would have only exacerbated the problem.[136] Lower prices, meanwhile, yielded few benefits to exporting nations, thereby making a balance-of-payment deficit more difficult to overcome. "Monetary policy alone cannot correct a weak position," he asserted.[137]

After having dismissed Strakosch and Hawtrey's views on the link between the distribution of gold reserves and the depression, Sprague joined an assembly of monetary economists who identified other causes of the slump. In February

[133] Sprague, "The Working of the Gold Standard," 72.

[134] Committee on Finance and Industry, Notes on Discussion, November 28, 1930, TNA T200/6/5.

[135] "The Right Hon. Montagu Collet Norman, D.S.O., and Dr. O.M.W. Sprague," February 18, 1931, in Macmillan Committee, *Minutes of Evidence, vol.* 2, 302–303. See also Clay, *Lord Norman*, 161; Clarke, *The Keynesian Revolution*, 131–135; Peter Temin, *Lessons from the Great Depression: The Lionel Robbins Lectures for 1989* (Cambridge, MA, and London: The MIT Press, 1989), 31.

[136] "The Right Hon. Montagu Collet Norman, D.S.O., and Dr. O.M.W. Sprague," February 18, 1931, in Macmillan Committee, *Minutes of Evidence, vol.* 2, 303.

[137] "The Right Hon. Montagu Collet Norman, D.S.O., and Dr. O.M.W. Sprague," February 18, 1931, in Macmillan Committee, *Minutes of Evidence, vol.* 2, 303.

1931, a meeting of a study group at Chatham House featured a continental perspective on the gold standard. Charles Rist, the former Deputy Governor of the Banque de France, believed that there had been too much focus on gold flows: "The mal-distribution of gold has been very often criticized, but nobody has told us what a good distribution of gold would be."[138] Instead, he felt that additional policy coordination among central banks might "help to make this perplexing problem of the distribution of gold disappear from our minds."[139] His goal may have been to absolve the Banque de France of its responsibility, a consideration not lost on British officials. Hawtrey, despite his earlier praise of Rist's monetarist analysis, countered by saying that France did hold a "redundant supply of gold … . It is in the position of a boa-constrictor which starts swallowing a goat – it cannot stop."[140]

Indeed, the Treasury appeared far more pessimistic in discussions over the future stability of exchange rates. After having spoken with Governor Norman in March 1931, Chancellor Snowden expected the country to "slide off" the gold standard in due course.[141] Yet the Bank, keen on the prolongation of the existing system, offered several proposals for stimulating a recovery. One of its industrial advisers, Henry Clay, understood that a fixed exchange rate regime itself was hardly the proximate cause of economic woes. He attributed the slump not to the specific functioning of the gold standard but instead to the dependency of domestic industry on credit, as well as the price differential between domestic and foreign goods. Economic dislocations in British industries caused by the war contributed far more to the level of unemployment, regardless of the course of monetary policy.[142]

Moreover, both Clay and Sprague were aware of the importance of monetary factors in causing the depression, although both presented different cases for its underlying factors. As Clay then wrote, "the war stimulated an enormous expansion … [and] led to currency inflation, which in turn stimulated over-production. When prices are rising from purely monetary causes, costs tend to lag behind and profits are made out of price, without any necessity of a careful direction of industry to the permanent needs of society."[143] The

[138] Charles Rist, "The International Consequences of the Present Distribution of Gold Holdings," February 11, 1931, in *The International Gold Problem, Collected Papers: A Record of the Discussions of a Study Group of Members of the Royal Institute of International Affairs, 1929–1931*, ed. Royal Institute of International Affairs (London: Oxford University Press, 1931), 203.

[139] Rist, "The International Consequences," 206. See also Charles Rist, "La question de l'or," *Revue d'économie politique* 44, no. 6 (1930), 1490–1491; "The Question of Gold," n.d., BLO Brand Papers 117/1.

[140] Rist, "The International Consequences," 208.

[141] Committee of Treasury, Minutes, March 4, 1931, BoE G8/59.

[142] Skidelsky, *John Maynard Keynes, vol. 2*, 357.

[143] Henry Clay, "Some Aspects of the Trade Depression: Insurance Institute of London," March 2, 1931, BoE SMT2/60.

monetary argument was even more adamantly defended by Sprague. Before the English-Speaking Union in May, he blamed the economic malaise on overproduction, particularly the speculative bubble in the US automobile industry, which had raised the overall price levels of manufactured goods relative to agricultural goods.[144] He subsequently shared these findings with Keynes and the Labour Party.[145]

Throughout these debates, price stability remained a key issue for the Bank's experts. Rather than expanding credit, central banks could enact more contractionary policies that might mitigate inflationary tendencies. In May 1931, Sprague argued that a general wage reduction would be an ideal option for addressing the trade imbalance.[146] Doing so, he further claimed, would allow the country to remain tied to gold. In response, Keynes challenged Sprague's justification for the maintenance of the prewar parity: "A widespread bankruptcy, default, and repudiation of bonds would necessarily ensue. Banks would be in jeopardy … . And what would be the advantage of having caused so much ruin? I do not know. Dr. Sprague did not tell us that."[147]

By showing how monetary policy had little impact on a potential recovery, Sprague had provoked criticism from experts and caused confusion among politicians. Writing to Governor Norman, Prime Minister MacDonald admitted, "I do not pretend to have any technical knowledge of banking and monetary questions." He then asked if Sprague's position was that of the Bank as a whole.[148] Norman, seeking to minimize the divisive nature of his adviser's views even if he personally agreed with them, asserted that "the points of difference are not perhaps in fact as great as you assume" and that the prime minister merely "misunderstood Sprague's opinion."[149] The line of argument worked, as experts were held in high regard by those who were unable or unwilling to engage in debates over monetary policy. As MacDonald later confessed, "it is a subject which I have really never studied and therefore know nothing about."[150] Controversies notwithstanding, the Bank regarded Sprague as "the leading banking Economist of America, not only with general international knowledge which is of great use to us but with a particular

[144] "No Relief in Sight Here, Sprague Says," *The New York Times* LXXX, 26772, May 13, 1931, 4; "Remedy for Trade Depression," *The Times* 45821, May 13, 1931, 18; "The Causes of the Crisis," *The Economist* 112, 4577, May 16, 1931, 1037–1038; Meltzer, *A History of the Federal Reserve, vol. 1*, 277–278.

[145] Sprague to Keynes, July 1, 1930, KCC Keynes Papers TM/1/2; Philip Williamson, *National Crisis and National Government: British Politics, the Economy and Empire, 1926–1932* (Cambridge: Cambridge University Press, 1992), 258.

[146] "The Wages Problem," *The Economist* 112, 4579, May 30, 1931, 1143.

[147] John Maynard Keynes, "An Economic Analysis of Unemployment," June 1931, in *The Collected Writings of John Maynard Keynes, vol. 13: The General Theory and After, Part I: Preparation*, ed. Donald Moggridge (Cambridge: Cambridge University Press, 1973), 361.

[148] MacDonald to Norman, June 18, 1931, BoE G15/7.

[149] Norman to MacDonald, June 25, 1931, BoE G15/7.

[150] MacDonald to Norman, June 29, 1931, BoE G15/7.

knowledge of America and intimacy with the Reserve System which is invaluable: thus his qualification, standing and usefulness are well-nigh unique."[151]

THE SUMMER OF 1931

On July 13, the Macmillan Committee published its final report, detailing the role of a central bank in times of crisis. The Bank's purpose was to make the necessary adjustments to the Bank Rate that promoted financial stability. Managing the sterling–dollar rate, in particular, would have had a demonstrably favorable effect on the balance of payments.[152] Yet the Macmillan Report also conceded that the Bank Rate was only to be used "sparingly for temporary adjustments" and "mainly reserved for occasions when the Bank deliberately wishes to contract or to expand credit," a policy that the Bank had once advocated.[153] Although the Governor's testimony to the committee had been weak, the intervention of his experts helped to convince the Macmillan Committee that interest-rate policy was only one component of a much broader issue.

Whether these arguments could remain convincing depended on the structural sustainability of the gold standard amidst destabilizing events abroad. In May 1931, the prominent Vienna-based bank, Creditanstalt, reported substantial losses on its balance sheet. Its subsequent collapse engendered panic among the foreign investors who had significant holdings of investments in Austria.[154] Hungary, too, suffered from the decline in agricultural prices, and an ensuing banking crisis culminated in a loan of $10 million from a consortium of central banks and the Bank for International Settlements.[155] Above all, it was the instability found within the German banking system, itself relatively unexposed to the Austrian crisis, that reverberated throughout international money markets.[156] Since the implementation of its reconstruction program

[151] Norman to MacDonald, June 25, 1931, BoE G15/7.

[152] Committee on Finance and Industry, *Report*, 96.

[153] Committee on Finance and Industry, *Report*, 153.

[154] On the 1931 crisis in Austria, see Aurel Schubert, *The Credit-Anstalt Crisis of 1931* (Cambridge: Cambridge University Press, 1991); Iago Gil Aguado, "The Creditanstalt Crisis of 1931 and the Failure of the Austro-German Customs Union Project," *The Historical Journal* 44, no. 1 (2001): 199–221; James, *The End of Globalization*, 53–57; Toniolo, *Central Bank Cooperation*, 88–97; Per H. Hansen, "Cooperate or Free Ride? The Scandinavian Central Banks, Bank for International Settlements and the Austrian Financial Crisis of 1931," *Scandinavian Journal of History* 37, no. 1 (2012): 87–107; Flora Macher, "The Austrian Banking Crisis of 1931: A Reassessment," *Financial History Review* 25, no. 3 (2018): 297–321; Marcus, *Austrian Reconstruction*, 298–315.

[155] Gates W. McGarrah [Bank for International Settlements] to Norman, June 20, 1931, BoE OV33/47; Eichengreen, *Golden Fetters*, 270; Toniolo, *Central Bank Cooperation*, 108.

[156] Harold James, "The Causes of the German Banking Crisis of 1931," *The Economic History Review* 37, no. 1 (1984), 71; Harold James, "Financial Flows across Frontiers during the Interwar Depression," *The Economic History Review* 45, no. 3 (1992), 595; Marcus, *Austrian Reconstruction*, 300.

in 1924, Germany had procured large volumes of foreign capital, estimated by the Reichsbank to be 8 billion RM since the hyperinflation (although the exact figure was more difficult to know).[157] Given the short-term nature of these investments, investors could undermine the financial sector if they began withdrawing funds at an unsustainable rate.[158]

On the same day the Macmillan report was published, Germany's second largest bank, the Darmstädter und Nationalbank (Danatbank), closed its doors. Severe liquidity problems and risky investment decisions characterized the activities of the most prominent banks based in Berlin.[159] Structural issues endemic to its domestic banking sector evolved into an even larger "twin" crisis, compounded by the inability to balance the national budget that led to a run on the currency.[160] Although the Reichsbank began suffering major losses, bankers and government officials remained divided over the needed actions, such as whether to impose exchange control or if such measures would only further exacerbate the crisis.[161]

The events that thus befell Germany in the summer of 1931 threatened to undermine the stability of the British banking system. Prior to the crisis, London-based merchant banks had extended short-term credits in the form of bankers' acceptances to foreign merchants, thereby effectively guaranteeing their liabilities. Their portfolios, in contrast to those of the larger clearing banks, had direct exposure to continental European debtors.[162] Another issue was

[157] Statistische Abteilung der Reichsbank, "Zur Entwicklung der gegenwärtigen Finanzkrise Deutschlands," July 25, 1931, BArch R2501/6492, ff. 2–22.

[158] Werner Link, *Die amerikanische Stabilisierungspolitik in Deutschland, 1921–32* (Düsseldorf: Droste Verlag, 1970), 406–411; Clarke, *Central Bank Cooperation*, 23; Stephen A. Schuker, "American Reparations to Germany, 1919–33: Implications for the Third World Debt Crisis," *Princeton Studies in International Finance*, no. 61 (1988), 48; Hans-Georg Glasemann, *Deutschlands Auslandsanleihen, 1924–1945. Rückzahlungen nach der Wiedervereinigung von 1990* (Wiesbaden: Gabler, 1993), 3–5; James, *The End of Globalization*, 59–61; Albrecht Ritschl, *Deutschlands Krise und Konjunktur 1924–1934. Binnenkonjunktur, Auslandsverschuldung und Reparationsproblem zwischen Dawes-Plan und Transfersperre* (Berlin: Akademie Verlag, 2002), 109–120; Tobias Straumann, *1931: Debt, Crisis, and the Rise of Hitler* (Oxford: Oxford University Press, 2019), 29–32, 178–179.

[159] James, "The Causes of the German Banking Crisis," 79; Isabel Schnabel, "The German Twin Crisis of 1931," *The Journal of Economic History* 64, no. 3 (2004), 835–839; Robert Yee, "A State of Supervision: The Political Economy of Banking Regulation in Germany, 1900s–1930s," *Business History Review* 97, no. 1 (2023), 98–111; Natacha Postel-Vinay and Stéphanie Collet, "Hot Money Inflows and Bank Risk-Taking: Germany from the 1920s to the Great Depression," *The Economic History Review* 77, no. 2 (2024): 472–502.

[160] Schnabel, "The German Twin Crisis," 825–827.

[161] Statistische Abteilung der Reichsbank, "Zur Entwicklung der deutschen Devisenkrise," July 10, 1931, BArch R2501/6484, ff. 188–193; "Nr. 377: Chefbesprechung vom 12. Juli 1931, 11.50 Uhr," in *Die Kabinette Brüning I u. II, Band 2*, 1334–1337; "Geschäftsbericht des Centralverbands des Deutschen Bank- und Bankiergewerbes für das Jahr 1931," GStA PK, I. HA Rep. 77, Tit. 587, Nr. 14, Bd. 3.

[162] Burk, *Morgan Grenfell*, 146–156; Roberts, *Schroders*, 250–252; Wake, *Kleinwort, Benson*, 242–245; Ferguson, *The House of Rothschild, vol.* 2, 466; Mark Billings and Forrest Capie,

that the merchant banks (and the acceptance houses) were less geographically diverse in their overseas investments than the clearing banks, often due to historical links to particular regions. The result was a highly exposed group of merchant banks with relatively small and undiversified claims abroad, further weakened by exchange-control restrictions in Central Europe and the Hoover moratorium on foreign debt.[163]

Understanding this cross-border exposure, the Bank's advisers believed it was crucial to support the German financial system if they wanted to ensure stability at home. On July 14, Sprague received an invitation to visit Chancellor Heinrich Brüning, who wanted to be advised by a "neutral" party during the crisis.[164] The following day, he flew to Berlin and recommended to the German cabinet and the Reichsbank that the quickest solution was a devaluation.[165] Effectively suspending the gold standard might have helped Germany address the withdrawals of foreign capital that devalued the Reichsmark. Sprague also proposed a plan to improve the position of the failing Dresdner Bank through a capital issue of 300 million RM in preferred stock.[166] This recommendation, however, did not receive support from members of Brüning's cabinet who favored a much less interventionist approach to avoid raising public alarm. Instead, the Minister of Finance planned to negotiate an international line of credit for the Reichsbank, in addition to enacting the standstill agreements that would prevent further withdrawals on private, short-term, foreign debt.[167]

"Financial Crisis, Contagion, and the British Banking System between the World Wars," *Business History* 53, no. 2 (2011): 193–215; Brian O'Sullivan, *From Crisis to Crisis: The Transformation of Merchant Banking, 1914–1939* (Cham: Palgrave Macmillan, 2018), 200–207.

163 Kindleberger, *The World in Depression*, 148–151; Eichengreen, *Golden Fetters*, 277; Schnabel, "The German Twin Crisis," 852; Olivier Accominotti, "London Merchant Banks, the Central European Panic, and the Sterling Crisis of 1931," *The Journal of Economic History* 72, no. 1 (2012), 6–11; Olivier Accominotti, "International Banking and Transmission of the 1931 Financial Crisis," *Economic History Review* 72, no. 1 (2019), 274; Simon Banholzer and Tobias Straumann, "Why the French Said 'Non': A New Perspective on the Hoover Moratorium of June 1931," *Journal of Contemporary History* 56, no. 4 (2021): 1040–1060.

164 "Nr. 385: Chefbesprechung vom 14. Juli 1931, 16 Uhr," in *Die Kabinette Brüning I u. II, Band* 2, 1356–1359; George Harrison, "Dr. Sprague's Invitation," July 21, 1931, CUL Harrison Papers Box 21, Binder 45; Heinrich Brüning, *Memoiren, 1918–1934* (Stuttgart: Deutsche Verlags-Anstalt, 1970), 320, 323; Gerhard Schulz, *Von Brüning zu Hitler. Der Wandel des politischen Systems in Deutschland 1930–1933* (Berlin and New York: Walter de Gruyter, 1992), 444; Philipp Heyde, *Das Ende der Reparationen. Deutschland, Frankreich und der Youngplan, 1929–1932* (Paderborn: F. Schöningh, 1998), 256; Herbert Hömig, *Brüning – Kanzler in der Krise der Republik. Eine Weimarer Biographie* (Paderborn: F. Schöningh, 2000), 353.

165 Harold James, *The German Slump: Politics and Economics, 1924–1936* (Oxford: Clarendon Press, 1986), 389.

166 "Nr. 419: Besprechung mit Sachverständigen am 30. Juli 1931 nachmittags," in *Die Kabinette Brüning I u. II, Band* 2, 1460–1461; "Nr. 420: Ministerbesprechung vom 30. Juli 1931, 17 Uhr," in *Die Kabinette Brüning I u. II, Band* 2, 1462–1466.

167 "Nr. 390: Chefbesprechung vom 16. Juli 1931," in *Die Kabinette Brüning I u. II, Band* 2, 1370–1371.

It had yet to be decided whether Britain would follow a similar course of action to that in Germany. Through open-market operations, the Bank planned to purchase £30 million in securities over the ensuing weeks.[168] However, a contentious meeting with the clearing banks and acceptance houses on July 16 led to no conclusive decision over whether it was necessary to procure a foreign loan similar to the one Germany had recently obtained.[169] British bankers (chief among them, those from the clearing banks) opposed the acquisition of additional credits, which might have forced the country to export even more gold or reveal its lack of adequate reserves.[170] The Bank had similarly recognized the importance of maintaining public confidence in sterling during its foreign negotiations. Assessing the recent financial calamity in Germany, Deputy Governor Harvey reported how the Reichsbank had been forced to raise rates to 10 percent because attempts to raise foreign credits had continually failed. Such a high rate would have been unthinkable for the Bank. After its deliberations, the Committee of Treasury tentatively decided to raise interest rates to a mere 3.5 percent in July.[171]

Throughout these discussions, the Bank considered both the wisdom of the Old Guard and the insights of its new advisers. On the same day that Sprague had returned from Berlin, Stewart had arrived back from Paris.[172] Although no longer officially employed at the Bank as of 1930, the latter had continued to consult Governor Norman as one of his closely trusted experts. He argued that there was little need to maintain a high Bank Rate since the priority needed to be helping the City's banks maintain adequate levels of liquidity.[173] This strategy would have involved the Bank using its authority to influence City behavior without resorting to direct regulation or the abandonment of fixed exchange rates.

In his related research, Sprague sought to understand the links between the British and the European banking systems. On July 20, he reported to President George Harrison of the Federal Reserve Bank of New York that the ongoing crisis in Germany could only be resolved through political intervention: "The economic and industrial position of the country seems to me comparatively good but of course vulnerable on account of short-term foreign indebtedness. Effective means of checking a flight from the mark seem to have been taken and in any case it does not seem to have been of large proportions."[174] While in Germany, government intervention could "eliminate or at least greatly lessen

168 Accominotti, "London Merchant Banks," 30.

169 Montagu Norman, Diary, July 16, 1931, BoE ADM34/20; Norman to Harrison, July 16, 1931, BoE G1/438.

170 James, *The End of Globalization*, 70.

171 Committee of Treasury, Minutes, July 22, 1931, BoE G8/60.

172 Montagu Norman, Diary, July 20, 1931, BoE ADM34/20.

173 Sayers, *The Bank of England, vol. 2*, 423–424.

174 Sprague to Harrison, July 20, 1931, BoE G1/438.

the danger of failure of other important German Banks," British banks were comparatively better placed to avert a general crisis on their own.[175]

The Bank now had an array of policy options to consider. On July 27, the Committee of Treasury suggested the possibility of procuring a foreign loan following negotiations between Robert Kindersley (later, Lord Kindersley) and Governor Clément Moret of the Banque de France.[176] The goal was to raise investors' confidence by publicly announcing a line of credit, even if it remained unused. That same day, Norman and Harvey met with the City's leading banks to discuss whether they were able to provide the bills necessary for the operation. The clearing banks reluctantly agreed to the terms of the Bank's proposal, while also noting their preference for a loan issued in New York instead of Paris. Partially accepting their request, the Bank negotiated a round of emergency loans from both the French and US central banks, totaling $125 million and 3.1 billion French francs, respectively (equivalent to £25 million each).[177]

Still, the prospective collapse of the gold standard incited much controversy. It later appeared to be a highly suspicious ordeal among those on the far right, some of whom insisted the crisis was orchestrated by British bankers succumbing to the allure of "international socialism."[178] Meanwhile, the left similarly denounced the decision, as Labour politicians spoke of an intentionally engineered "bankers' ramp" that only used the crisis to justify further reductions in public spending, most notably in unemployment benefits.[179] In reality, the chaos that arose in the summer of 1931 was neither a calculated plan nor a conspiratorial plot, but rather an unfortunately timed outcome of both domestic and foreign factors outside any single institution's control.

The publication of the national budget, strained by its projected expenditures, exacerbated fears of a run on the pound. On July 31, the (May) Committee on National Expenditure reported a projected deficit of £120 million for the

[175] Sprague to Harrison, July 20, 1931, BoE G1/438.

[176] "Meeting of Members of the Committee of Treasury Held at 11 a.m. on the 27th July 1931," BoE G1/456; Committee of Treasury, Minutes, July 27, 1931, BoE G8/60; Sayers, *The Bank of England, vol.* 2, 392; Mouré, *Managing the Franc Poincaré*, 66–68.

[177] Committee of Treasury, Minutes, July 30, 1931, BoE G8/60; George Harrison, "Proposed Credit to [the] Bank of England," July 31, 1931, CUL Harrison Papers Box 21, Binder 45; Boyce, *British Capitalism*, 345; Diane B. Kunz, "American Bankers and Britain's Fall from Gold," in *The Role of Banks in the Interwar Economy*, ed. Harold James, Håkan Lindgren, and Alice Teichova (Cambridge: Cambridge University Press, 1991), 41; Eichengreen, *Golden Fetters*, 282–283; William H. Janeway, "The 1931 Sterling Crisis and the Independence of the Bank of England," *Journal of Post Keynesian Economics* 18, no. 2 (1995), 263.

[178] See, for instance, Eric D. Butler, *The Enemy within the Empire: A Short History of the Bank of England* (Melbourne: New Times, 1941), 22–23.

[179] Philip Williamson, "A 'Bankers' Ramp'? Financiers and the British Political Crisis of August 1931," *The English Historical Review* 99, no. 393 (1984), 805–806; Sidney Pollard, "Die Krise des Sozialismus in der Zwischenkriegszeit: Großbritannien," *Geschichte und Gesellschaft* 17, no. 2 (1991), 173; Williamson, *National Crisis and National Government*, 5, 326; Boyce, "Government–City of London Relations," 234.

1932/1933 fiscal year, leading the majority report to advocate reductions in wages and in public services.[180] Of the £97 million in total reductions, the largest cut would be to unemployment benefits, which alone would contribute £66.5 million to the budgetary shortfall.[181] While the recommendations of the report had alone been "unreasonably austere," as Hubert Henderson (Joint Secretary to the Economic Advisory Council) described, the ensuing turmoil revealed the close connections between budgetary policy and the stability of the gold standard.[182]

The May Report turned a financial crisis into a political one. Since Governor Norman had suffered a mental breakdown on July 29 – only to return after the crisis – the Bank's experts had emerged as the chief negotiators with the government and foreign central banks. Discussions with the Treasury, for instance, had made a budgetary solution seem highly unlikely in the short term. Until (and unless) the MacDonald government found a resolution to the budget deficit, Britain would continue to suffer from debilitating outflows of capital. Although the Bank initially had hoped that new foreign credits could have prevented gold losses, by early August such an idea had proven to be unrealistic. Gold outflows, according to one adviser, had now amounted to between £2 and £3 million per week.[183] After using its foreign credits on August 7, the Bank resumed its program of open-market operations and emergency lending to the acceptance houses.[184] It received additional approval from the Treasury to increase the fiduciary issue (the volume of unbacked notes allowed to circulate) from £260 to £275 million.[185]

Yet experts questioned whether another foreign loan would abate the severity of the crisis or merely delay an inevitable outcome. Many were reluctant to believe that temporary exigencies, from open-market operations to changes

[180] Committee on National Expenditure, *Report*, Cmd. 3920 (London: H.M. Stationery Office, 1931), 25–26; Bernard Mallet and C. Oswald George, *British Budgets, Third Series, 1921–22 to 1932–33* (London: Macmillan, 1933), 353; Skidelsky, *Politicians and the Slump*, 344; Kindleberger, *A Financial History of Western Europe*, 378; Middleton, *Towards the Managed Economy*, 99; Eichengreen, *Golden Fetters*, 284; Peden, *The Treasury*, 238; Boyce, *British Capitalism*, 345.

[181] Committee on National Expenditure, *Report*, 217–218; Peden, *The Treasury*, 238; Williamson, *National Crisis and National Government*, 267–268; Kynaston, *The City of London, vol. 3*, 233; Peden, "The Treasury and the City," 126; Giuseppe Telesca, "Myths and Memory: The Crisis of the Pound and the Political Use of the Memory of 1931 in the United Kingdom," in *Remembering and Learning from Financial Crisis*, ed. Youssef Cassis and Catherine R. Schenk (Oxford: Oxford University Press, 2021), 64.

[182] Hubert Henderson, "The Economy Report," August 7, 1931, in *The Inter-War Years and Other Papers: A Selection from the Writings of Hubert Douglas Henderson*, ed. Henry Clay (Oxford: Clarendon Press, 1955), 72.

[183] Harry A. Siepmann, "Note of Conversations with Monsieur Moret on Friday, 7th August 1931," August 10, 1931, BoE G1/456.

[184] Williamson, *National Crisis and National Government*, 286–287; Accominotti, "London Merchant Banks," 31.

[185] Committee of Treasury, Minutes, August 5, 1931, BoE G8/60.

in the fiduciary issue, could have had a lasting impact on the structural problems associated with the financial system. In August, Clay remarked how the "manipulation of credit, ... while it may postpone a breakdown and give time for industry to adjust itself to changed conditions, cannot by itself restore the condition of balance that existed before 1914."[186] Moreover, additional credits could have even had the opposite effect, transforming a liquidity crisis confined to the merchant banks into a calamity that threatened the entire financial sector. It may well have been the Bank's intention to let the merchant banks collapse, to reduce moral hazard, and to stop the contagion from spreading to other banks.[187] The danger that the Bank's Old Guard knew was that an intervention too public, too radical, or too desperate would have done more harm than good.

There was thus little hope that adjustments to the Bank Rate could have prevented the debilitating outflow of gold. Indeed, the central bank, with its historical relationship to the merchant banks and discount houses in the City, had long operated under the assumption that raising interest rates might signal to investors a severe strain on gold and foreign-exchange reserves.[188] Such was the opinion reiterated by the Committee of Treasury in early August.[189] For these reasons, the Bank considered looking outside Britain for assistance. Given his prior research on the valuation of the franc and many past trips to Paris, Siepmann was made responsible for handling subsequent discussions with the Banque de France.[190] Upon arriving in Paris, he spoke with Governor Moret and one of his experts, Robert Lacour-Gayet, on the prospect of cooperation. The discussion did not amount to any useful exchange of knowledge. Instead, Siepmann complained of the "virulence with which the French Press campaign has been conducted against sterling and against the Governor personally: in one instance ... on information which can only have been provided by the Bank of France."[191] The Bank, thereafter convinced of France's deliberate attempts to undermine sterling, deemed the risk of another interest hike to be too high.

While British officials might not have expected the immediate collapse of the gold standard, they made concerted attempts to deter the likelihood of such a scenario. In regular conversation with the Bank's directors – including Harvey, Kindersley, Edward Peacock (later, Sir Edward), Edward Grenfell

[186] On August 6, Clay delivered these remarks, which were later published as: Henry Clay, "Finance and the International Market," *The Banker* XX, no. 69, October 1931, 34.

[187] Accominotti, "London Merchant Banks," 27.

[188] James, *The End of Globalization*, 73.

[189] Committee of Treasury, Minutes, August 6, 1931, BoE G8/60.

[190] Harry A. Siepmann, "Note of a Telephone Conversation with Monsieur Moret," August 5, 1931, BoE OV45/82; Harry A. Siepmann, "Going off the Gold Standard," August 19, 1931, BoE G1/459; Diane Kunz, *The Battle for Britain's Gold Standard in 1931* (London: Croom Helm, 1987), 113; Mouré, *Managing the Franc Poincaré*, 68.

[191] Harry A. Siepmann, "Note of Conversations with Monsieur Moret on Friday, 7th August 1931," August 10, 1931, BoE G1/456.

(later, Lord St Just), and Charles Hambro (later, Sir Charles) – experts were tasked with devising a plan that was both feasible and effective. It might have initially been possible to sustain confidence in sterling without resorting to unconventional policies. By mid-August, however, Siepmann declared that the uncertain "internal situation" had become increasingly "intolerable owing to a world economic depression," the only solution for which was a restoration of trust in the pound.[192] The most extreme course of action would have been a devaluation. Sprague may have been overly generous in assessing the amount of power he had over the Brüning government – "Both Brüning and Luther seemed to think that my advice in this matter was wise" – but he raised even more controversy at the Bank when he claimed that a devalued currency would help abate foreign withdrawals of capital.[193] Not truly considering this option, the Committee of Treasury only authorized Sprague to assess the potential consequences of a departure from the gold standard.[194]

The economic reverberations of the crisis outpaced the speed at which the Bank's advisers could work. They were certainly able to recognize the consequences of interconnected European markets. In one memorandum, Clay noted that "further borrowing in New York or Paris ... would be difficult owing to the loss of confidence in sterling, and futile if the underlying causes of the weakness of sterling are not removed."[195] This perspective emphasized the international dimensions to the crisis, namely how Britain's unfavorable trade position and heavy foreign borrowing had put the country at a disadvantage. Clay was, in this regard, one of the few expert voices at the Bank who placed less blame on the budgetary imbalance and was mistakenly less concerned with party politics. "If the pound goes," he simply wrote, "the currencies of half the countries in Europe will go too."[196]

At the same time, the Bank had limited room for maneuver in this realm, as forcing foreign central banks to part with their gold reserves was not within its capability. On August 24, the same day that the Labour government fell, Addis reported that the central bank could only last "two or three days more" after reporting losses of £10 million.[197] The Bank was able to sustain itself longer than this projection, largely due to the supplementary credit of £80 million raised in Paris and New York on August 28.[198] Nevertheless, experts understood that the

[192] Harry A. Siepmann, Memo, August 14, 1931, BoE G1/457.

[193] Sprague to Harrison, July 20, 1931, BoE G1/438.

[194] Committee of Treasury, Minutes, August 18 and 22, 1931, BoE G8/60; Kunz, *The Battle for Britain's Gold Standard*, 100–101.

[195] Henry Clay, "The Threat to the Gold Standard," August 22, 1931, BoE EID4/102.

[196] Henry Clay, "The Pound and the Gold Standard," August 25, 1931, NRS Lothian Papers.

[197] Charles Addis, Diary, August 24, 1931, SOAS Addis Papers Box 5.

[198] Committee of Treasury, Minutes, August 25, 1931, BoE G8/60; George Harrison, "Telephone Conversation with Mr. Lacour Gayet," August 28, 1931, CUL Harrison Papers Box 21, Binder 45; J.P. Morgan & Co. to Morgan Grenfell & Co., September 19, 1931, BoE G1/459; Sayers, *The Bank of England, vol.* 2, 400; James Ashley Morrison, "Shocking Intellectual Austerity:

loan did nearly nothing to address the declining confidence in the pound. "The only way to stop it is to balance the budget," Clay opined.[199]

A final appeal to the government came in what would be the last month of the crisis. On September 3, Harvey and Peacock announced to the Cabinet that the Bank was unable to meet the demands for additional gold.[200] Restoring confidence at home by way of a balanced budget, according to this view, could have stopped the export of gold. Despite the credits from the US and French central banks, the prospect of an exchange-rate crisis depended on the outcome of political developments outside the Bank's direct control. While correct on this matter, Harvey, in the course of his meetings with politicians, did not mention the possibility of raising the Bank Rate out of concern that such a policy would have only raised more questions. Doing so could have also revealed that the Bank was, at least in part, culpable for monetary mismanagement.

That same day, MacDonald urged the Cabinet to consider fiscal retrenchment, although his main suggestion to the Bank centered on raising investors' confidence by communicating with the press.[201] In effect, he tried to buy the government more time to formulate a plan. Behind-the-scenes negotiations with Morgan Grenfell (London) resulted in the Bank procuring $200 million in credits from J.P. Morgan (New York) and another $200 million from a consortium of French banks.[202] Nevertheless, the weakness in the pound persisted because the emergency loan did not address the fundamental distrust in the currency following the May report.

A run on the Bank's reserves began as foreign investors sold Treasury bills en masse. On September 17, the Bank acknowledged that the existing lines of foreign credits were insufficient.[203] Sprague then told the German Embassy in London that heightened uncertainty and anxieties from the new election would

The Role of Ideas in the Demise of the Gold Standard in Britain," *International Organization* 70, no. 1 (2016), 190. Keynes described the credits as Britain's version of the "Dawes Loan" and wondered "whether we shall be content with this or whether we shall have to raise a Young Loan"; Keynes to Stamp, August 27, 1931, in *The Collected Writings of John Maynard Keynes, vol. 20: Activities 1929–1931: Rethinking Employment and Unemployment Policies*, ed. Donald Moggridge (Cambridge: Cambridge University Press, 1981): 595.

199 Henry Clay, Note, August 25, 1931, NRS Lothian Papers.

200 "Cabinet 53(31)," September 3, 1931, TNA CAB23/68; "Secretary's Notes of a Conversation between Sir Ernest Harvey and Mr. Peacock and Members of the Cabinet on Thursday, September 3rd 1931 at 3 p.m.," TNA CAB23/68 and T172/1756.

201 "Secretary's Notes of a Conversation between Sir Ernest Harvey and Mr. Peacock and Members of the Cabinet on Thursday, September 3rd 1931 at 3 p.m.," TNA CAB23/68 and T172/1756; Boyce, *The Great Interwar Crisis*, 322.

202 "C.P. 230(31)," September 15, 1931, TNA CAB24/223; "Cabinet 57(31)," September 16, 1931, TNA CAB23/68; Kunz, *The Battle for Britain's Gold Standard*, 103; Kunz, "American Bankers," 43; Mouré, *Managing the Franc Poincaré*, 68; Williamson, *National Crisis and National Government*, 421; Horn, *J.P. Morgan & Co.*, 141.

203 Committee of Treasury, Minutes, September 17, 1931, BoE G8/60; George Harrison, "Bank of England," September 17, 1931, CUL Harrison Papers Box 21, Binder 45.

make maintaining sterling's current rate impossible.[204] The rapid depletion of its gold and foreign-exchange reserves, coupled with the exhaustion of almost all its credits, forced the Committee of Treasury to arrive at the decision to abandon the gold standard on Saturday, September 19.[205] Deputy Governor Harvey wrote to MacDonald that it was "in the national interest" for the government to suspend the 1925 Gold Standard Act.[206] Heeding the Bank's warnings, the Labour government drafted a bill to relieve the Bank of such pressures.[207]

On September 20, the Treasury circulated a press notice on how the withdrawal of an estimated £200 million since July had forced the government "to protect the economy of this country by the only means at our disposal."[208] An array of additional precautionary pressures followed. The Committee of Treasury aimed to prevent further capital outflows by raising the Bank Rate to 6 percent. At the City's recommendation, the Cabinet also agreed to close the London Stock Exchange the following day, and the Bank hoped to see those in Paris, Berlin, and Amsterdam do the same.[209] The Big Five communicated to their branches that the impending collapse of the gold standard was "purely an external problem," as the "position of British Banking is beyond question."[210] To a certain degree, they were correct, as only the merchant banks (rather than the clearing banks) were affected by the financial turmoil. Still, attempts to calm markets embodied the possibility that declining confidence in sterling might have instigated debilitating capital outflows regardless of Britain's actual financial exposure to Central Europe. That day, Chancellor Snowden appeared before Parliament to introduce the Gold Standard (Amendment) Bill, describing it merely as a "temporary" expedient.[211] Although the idea of departing from gold itself incurred much controversy, exemplified by Arthur Henderson's campaign calling for Labour to abstain from the vote, the Bill still received Parliamentary approval.[212] On September 21, 1931, the United Kingdom officially abandoned the gold standard.

204 Johann Heinrich von Bernstorff [German Embassy in London] to the German Foreign Office, "Unterredung mit Dr. Sprague, dem amerikanischen Berater der Bank von England," September 17, 1931, PA AA RZ 207/243954.

205 Committee of Treasury, Minutes, September 19, 1931, BoE G8/60; Charles Addis, Diary, September 19, 1931, SOAS Addis Papers Box 5.

206 Harvey to MacDonald and Snowden, September 19, 1931, BoE G1/459 and TNA CAB23/68; "Cabinet 60(31)," September 20, 1931, TNA CAB23/68.

207 MacDonald and Fisher to Snowden, September 19, 1931, BoE G1/459.

208 "Press Notice," September 20, 1931, TNA T163/68/18; "[Appendix to] Cabinet 60(31)," September 20, 1931, TNA CAB23/68.

209 "Cabinet 60(31)," September 20, 1931, TNA CAB23/68.

210 F.A. Beane and G.E. Abell to Managers, September 20, 1931, LGA HO/GM/Bea/11; Edwin Fisher, H.T. Mitchell, A.W. Tuke, and N.S. Jones to Managers, September 21, 1931, BGA 0080-3255.

211 HC Deb, September 21, 1931, vol. 256 cc. 1289–1409.

212 Andrew Thorpe, *The British General Election of 1931* (Oxford: Clarendon Press, 1991), 147; Williamson, *National Crisis and National Government*, 428–430.

STABILITY AFTER GOLD

In the months after the crisis, the Bank's advisers acquired more prominent roles in debates over exchange-rate management. They might have little influence on the decision to depart from gold, but their subsequent discussions revolved around maintaining investors' confidence in sterling. In part, officials were increasingly concerned about the image of the central bank abroad. The loss of faith in sterling might have continued to hamper a chance at economic recovery. As one expert reported to the Belgian central bank, "of all the consequences of our going off the Gold Standard none was more distressing … than the effect upon our Central Banking friends."[213]

Nevertheless, discussions over the future of monetary management were mostly national in focus. On September 23, the Bank convened the first meeting of an internal Currency Committee to assess its future exchange-rate priorities. Members of the Bank's Old Guard, including Lubbock and Addis, sought to identify new measures to prevent a potential inflationary crisis by consulting the advisers who were active during the crisis. However, many advisers were unable to provide definitive conclusions in the immediate days after the crisis. Two days after the abandonment of the gold standard, Sprague claimed that the Bank was effectively "powerless to prevent inflation" and the responsibility largely lay with the commercial banks.[214] Because the factors that caused the gold standard's demise were outside the Bank's direct control, there seemed to be little need to enact sweeping reform. More evidently, the Bank could not reveal its own weaknesses and risk undermining its authority.

Yet the inability to offer an immediate solution did not deter the Bank from continuing to consult its experts. On the contrary, the Old Guard now felt that economic knowledge was even more necessary for restoring balance to the global order. In October, Josiah Stamp delivered a broadcast on the importance of using technical advice to devise a new monetary system:

> The nations together are giving the gold standard an impossible job to do. Devise a better machine or improve the machine, but it can still only work according to the limits set by its own constitution, and not how you would like it. The gold standard is not worked merely by bankers; everybody, politicians, workers, employers, all unconsciously take at a hand, and a special attitude of any section or nation may make it unworkable. There is nothing political in this – it is bare economics.[215]

213 Harry A. Siepmann, "Note of a Conversation with Monsieur van Zeeland Held at the Bank of England on 22nd September 1931," BNB P584.

214 "Currency Committee," September 23, 1931, BoE G15/30. Sprague later argued that the abandonment of the gold standard was decided "only after great efforts had been made to remain on gold," such as additional taxes; O.M.W. Sprague, *Recovery and Common Sense* (Boston and New York: Houghton Mifflin Company, 1934), 45.

215 Josiah Stamp, "What is the Gold Standard?," October 1931, in *The Financial Aftermath of the War* (New York: Charles Scribner's Sons, 1932), 148.

These sentiments reflected the Bank's evolving perspective on economic governance. Having returned to the Bank in late September, Governor Norman proposed that representatives from the Treasury and the Bank initiate an "academic study" of exchange rates.[216] In December 1931, he revived the Exchange Committee, a group of representatives from the Bank, City, and Treasury for weekly Friday meetings.[217] While serving on the committee, Sprague was able to make broad recommendations about the direction of monetary policy and a possible return to the gold standard.[218] Because he had proven his capacity as a financial expert through the Macmillan Committee, the Committee of Treasury invited him to begin attending its weekly meetings concerning the Bank Rate.[219]

In contrast to the Bank, the Treasury was more hesitant to believe that a return to the gold standard was possible. Many civil servants still viewed the maldistribution of gold reserves and unsuccessful negotiations with foreign nations as the main obstacles to financial stability. Hawtrey, for instance, criticized countries that had accepted gold inflows without proportionally increasing lines of credit, undoing "whatever tendency to revival there may have been."[220] Yet he also found faults with decisions made at home. "While France was to blame for absorbing gold, and the United States for not parting with gold," he maintained, "it was through England that the process of credit restriction ... took place."[221]

The Bank was committed to defending its own actions during the crisis. Beginning in September 1931, the Foreign Exchange Committee initiated a series of discussions on the City's exchange-rate priorities.[222] Members of the group sought to devise measures that would prevent a sudden outflow of capital, while at the same time not adversely affecting investors' confidence in sterling. They weighed the benefits of imposing greater restrictions on conversions out of sterling, known then as exchange control. Yet although there were widespread fears in the banking community around speculation in foreign-exchange markets, many were reluctant to devise a strict regime of economic governance similar to those in other countries, such as Germany and

[216] Clay, *Lord Norman*, 402.

[217] Montagu Norman, Diary, December 3, 1931, BoE ADM34/20; Committee of Treasury, Minutes, December 16, 1931, BoE G8/60.

[218] Committee of Treasury, Minutes, September 9, 1931, BoE G8/60.

[219] Committee of Treasury, Minutes, November 4, 1931, BoE G8/60; Committee of Treasury, Minutes, November 25, 1931, BoE G8/60.

[220] R.G. Hawtrey, "Public Expenditure and Trade Depression," *Journal of the Royal Statistical Society* 96, no. 3 (1933), 453.

[221] R.G. Hawtrey, *The Art of Central Banking* (London: Longmans, Green & Co., 1932), 245.

[222] "Report of the Meeting of the Foreign Exchange Committee and the Bankers' Exchange Experts held on the 23rd September 1931," BoE C43/98; Sayers, *The Bank of England, vol. 2*, 407–409.

Argentina.[223] According to Sprague, any form of exchange control "should be removed," and the Bank should instead opt to manage sterling through its foreign-currency reserves.[224]

As a result, the Bank prioritized the stability of sterling through indirect regulation. Some experts argued that addressing existing issues with the currency could help spur a trade-based industrial recovery.[225] Clay, for instance, did not believe that leaving the gold standard alone would necessarily improve Britain's balance of payments, nor was he convinced that growth could come without the implementation of a tariff.[226] For another one of the Bank's experts, Francis Rodd, it was similarly important to facilitate trade with Latin America through the Bank's existing relationships with the Anglo-South American Bank and the Bank of London and South America.[227] After serving in the Royal Field Artillery and the Arab Bureau in Damascus, Rodd had worked in various positions in the Foreign Office and the City before joining the Bank in January 1929.[228] Given his experience in foreign countries, he sought to improve the Bank's foreign economic relations, exemplified by his work with the Creditanstalt stabilization in Vienna and on the League Loans Committee.[229]

At the Bank, Rodd emphasized the importance of overseas trade. In February, he, along with Clay and Sprague, met with representatives from the Manchester Chamber of Commerce. The business association was particularly worried about the difficulties facing British exporters, especially after countries in Latin America had imposed "rigorous exchange control measures."[230] One representative asked whether Britain would be prepared to return to a type of modified gold standard in South Africa, while another questioned whether

223 "Meeting of Clearing Bankers at the Bank of England," September 18, 1931, BoE C43/98.

224 Committee on Foreign Exchange, "Report of the Meeting Held on the 10th November 1931," BoE C43/98.

225 Henry Clay, "Sterling and the Gold Standard," August 26, 1931, BoE EID4/102; Clay to Siepmann, September 30, 1931, BoE SMT5/3; Henry Clay, "Some Aspects of the World Depression, Lecture III," December 2, 1931, *Journal of the Institute of Bankers* LIII, no. 1 (1932), 26.

226 Clay to Cannan, September 22, 1931, LSE Cannan Papers; Barry J. Eichengreen, "Sterling and the Tariff, 1929–32," *Princeton Studies in International Finance*, no. 48 (1981), 23; Kunz, *The Battle for Britain's Gold Standard*, 131.

227 Francis Rodd, "Memorandum," February 16, 1932, BoE OV188.1.

228 Kathleen Burk, "Rodd, Francis James Rennell, second Baron Rennell," September 23, 2004, ODNB; Philip Boobbyer, *The Life and World of Francis Rodd, Lord Rennell (1895–1978): Geography, Money and War* (London: Anthem Press, 2021), 40–42; Per H. Hansen, *There Will Be the Devil to Pay: Central Bankers, Uncertainty and Sensemaking in the European Financial Crisis of 1931* (Cambridge: Cambridge University Press, 2025), 22–24.

229 Toniolo, *Central Bank Cooperation*, 91–93; Marcus, *Austrian Reconstruction*, 306–311.

230 "Note of a Meeting Held on 11th February 1932 between the Bank of England and the Representatives of the Manchester Chamber of Commerce," February 12, 1932, BoE OV188/1.

these reforms might also involve extending additional loans. From an outsider's perspective, the Bank appeared as the main authority that could lead such a recovery, leveraging the network of foreign central banks and other international contacts, which it had established in the 1920s.

However, British officials, not wanting to abandon their views on economic orthodoxy, instead focused their efforts on exchange-rate stability through less interventionist means. On April 19, the Treasury established the Exchange Equalisation Account (EEA) to stabilize sterling in the long run while also keeping it sufficiently low for a recovery in the short run.[231] The fund managed approximately £20 million in reserves, along with the option to borrow up to £150 million.[232] Conceptualized by Sir Frederick Phillips, the EEA gained broad support from Treasury officials, including Hopkins and Hawtrey, who sought to target a depreciated exchange rate.[233] Under this system, the United Kingdom oversaw a managed float of sterling at \$3.40, a rate that could encourage domestic investment and avoid instigating reactionary competitive devaluations by other countries.[234] By virtue of its operations, the EEA helped consolidate power at the Treasury, which was to decide the fund's priorities, while the Bank was primarily expected to conduct day-to-day operations.[235] Its policy of "cheap money" could engender a general economic recovery by spurring domestic investment and raising employment levels.[236]

Volatile capital flows continued to threaten sterling's future. Precisely because they could have been so "speedily withdrawn," short-term capital was no longer solely attracted to the traditional financial centers of London or New York

[231] Finance Act 1932, 22 & 23 Geo. 5 c. 25; Walter A. Morton, *British Finance, 1930–1940* (Madison: The University of Wisconsin Press, 1943), 236–239; Susan Howson, "The Management of Sterling, 1932–1939," *The Journal of Economic History* 40, no. 1 (1980), 56; Susan Howson, "Sterling's Managed Float: The Operations of the Exchange Equalisation Account, 1932–39," *Princeton Studies in International Finance*, no. 46 (November 1980), 4; Williamson, *National Crisis and National Government*, 500; Boyce, *The Great Interwar Crisis*, 398; Capie, *The Bank of England*, 59; Naef, *An Exchange Rate History*, 66–70.

[232] Leonard Waight, *The History and Mechanism of the Exchange Equalisation Account* (Cambridge: Cambridge University Press, 1939), 15; Bank of England, "The Exchange Equalisation Account: Its Origins and Development," *Bank of England Quarterly Bulletin* 8, Q4 (1968), 377–378; Howson, "Sterling's Managed Float," 9; Peden, *The Treasury*, 256; Allen, *The Bank of England and the Government Debt*, 34; Max Harris, *Monetary War and Peace: London, Washington, Paris, and the Tripartite Agreement of 1936* (Cambridge: Cambridge University Press, 2021), 66.

[233] Frederick Phillips, "The Present Position of the Pound," February 25, 1932, TNA T175/58.

[234] Howson, "The Management of Sterling," 55–56; Howson, "Sterling's Managed Float," 22.

[235] Howson, *Domestic Monetary Management*, 87; Howson, "The Management of Sterling," 53–54; Tomlinson, *Public Policy and the Economy*, 101; Middleton, *Government Versus the Market*, 359; Peden, *The Treasury*, 255–256; Harris, *Monetary War and Peace*, 65.

[236] Howson, *Domestic Monetary Management*, 86–89; Howson, "Sterling's Managed Float," 4; Cairncross and Eichengreen, *Sterling in Decline*, 89; Collins, *Money and Banking*, 291–304.

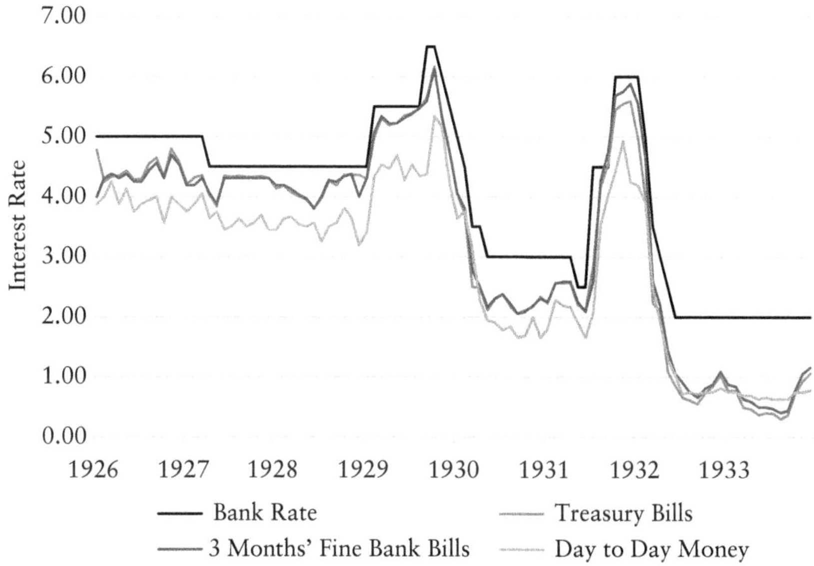

FIGURE 4.2 Interest Rates, 1926–1933
Source: Bank of England, *Statistical Summary*, various years.

but instead found profitable investment opportunities elsewhere.[237] High interest rates in Berlin, for instance, appeared no longer as a "symptom of weakness," but rather as a profitable investment.[238] Conversely, the Bank's repeated efforts to repatriate lost funds with its own high Bank Rate, raised to 6 percent in October 1931, did little to incentivize investors (Figure 4.2). In response, Sprague suggested that an international credit bureau could provide additional loans, potentially alongside the Bank for International Settlements, for industrial recovery. He believed that such a centralized institution could even serve an informational role by collecting information on conditions in markets abroad.[239]

Although restricted in their ability to enact major reforms, the Bank's advisers were granted access to new channels of influence. Even before the sterling crisis in September 1931, they found themselves privy to negotiations regarding the nature of international monetary cooperation. Governor Norman assigned both Siepmann and Sprague to meet with officials from the Banque de France to discuss the future of central bank cooperation.[240] Following the

[237] O.M.W. Sprague, "Statistical Data on Foreign Short-Term Funds: Their Collection and Use," May 1932, BoE OV4/27 and BIS Special Reports HS.23. See also O.M.W. Sprague, "The American Gold Problem and World Trade," *Proceedings of the Academy of Political Science* 19, no. 1 (1940): 80–87.

[238] O.M.W. Sprague, "Statistical Data on Foreign Short-Term Funds: Their Collection and Use," May 1932, BoE OV4/27 and BIS Special Reports HS.23.

[239] Pierre Quesnay, Note, May 11, 1932, BIS Quesnay Papers 20200106-2375.2.

[240] Siepmann to Lacour-Gayet, April 28, 1931, BoE OV45/82; Montagu Norman, Diary, April 29, 1931, BoE ADM34/20.

abandonment of the gold standard, the Bank's body of experts transformed from an ad hoc advisory group to a regularly consulted body. In debates over exchange-rate policy, the Old Guard turned to those who had been involved in the 1931 crisis. By March 1932, Deputy Governor Harvey approved sharing information "regarded as most secret" with the Bank's advisers, including Niemeyer, Siepmann, and Sprague.[241] He later revised the list to include the staff in the Bank's research department as well.[242]

The long-term pursuit of exchange-rate stability since the First World War had facilitated the institutionalization of economic expertise at the Bank. Throughout the relatively short life of the interwar gold standard, the debates over monetary policy overlapped with broader concerns related to central bank independence, industrial stagnation, and the political economy of finance. As the central bank grappled with such questions, it drew on technical advice to defend the decision to return to the prewar parity. Experts were particularly vital in explaining Bank Rate policy to its many critics, notably those on the Macmillan Committee, and they emerged as economic diplomats in their negotiations abroad. What effectively transpired in the aftermath of the 1931 crisis was an elevated role for technical advisers in domestic governance. By addressing the dearth of technical knowledge in the state apparatus, the central bank established a reputation as a leading intellectual authority.

[241] Ernest Harvey, "Memorandum for the Chief Cashier," March 21, 1932, BoE G14/135.
[242] Ernest Harvey, "Memorandum to the Chief Cashier," June 3, 1932, BoE G14/135.

5

Henry Clay and Industrial Reform

> There is no set pattern of rationalisation that can be applied to any and every industry. What is wanted in each case is to find the kind of organisation best suited to the technical and commercial conditions of the industry.[1]
>
> — Henry Clay, 1930

> There are few of our bankers indeed in my opinion who really know a great deal about industry. True they can never and should never be industrial experts.[2]
>
> — Robert Brand, 1930

> The very fact that economic advisers were appointed shows that a knowledge of economics had to be imported from outside, that those in charge of the Bank did not consider themselves adequately equipped.[3]
>
> — Paul Einzig, 1935

The First World War and its economic consequences – unprecedented levels of national debt, foreign-exchange volatility, and the ensuing British slump – prompted a series of discussions on the role of the state in industrial affairs. In the interwar years, academic economists, including Sir William Beveridge, Edwin Cannan, and Arthur Cecil Pigou, debated the actions needed from a government to address rising unemployment and social unrest. Their findings built upon the foundation of neoclassical theory established by Alfred Marshall at Cambridge, while also incorporating new perspectives based on prevailing economic conditions. One scholar in this group was Henry Clay,

[1] Henry Clay, "Note on Initiative in Rationalisation," April 14, 1930, BoE SMT2/60 and SMT5/11.

[2] Committee on Finance and Industry, "Memorandum by the Hon. R.H. Brand, C.M.G.," August 14, 1930, BLO Brand Papers 29/2.

[3] Einzig, *Bankers, Statesmen and Economists*, 64.

an economist who pioneered theories on unemployment, wages, and industrial performance. Identifying his contributions to both the academic discipline and the policymaking realm is the focus of this chapter.

Clay was one of the first economists employed at the Bank. Born in Germany to a family in the dye-manufacturing business, he moved to Yorkshire, England, where he attended Bradford Grammar School (1902) and, later, University College, Oxford (1906). He then worked as a lecturer at the Workers' Educational Association (1909–1917) and as a civil servant in the Ministry of Labour (1917–1919). Shortly thereafter, he returned to academia and joined New College, Oxford, as a fellow, a position that allowed him to devote much of his time to the study of unemployment. At the University of Manchester, he served as the Stanley Jevons Professor of Political Economy (1922–1927) and chair in social economics (1927–1930).

In January 1930, Clay became an adviser at the Bank, where he subsequently directed its interventionist policies. While the central bank had once confined much of its work to monetary policy and reconstruction, largely being uninvolved in the affairs of domestic industry, the unresolved problems of the First World War compelled the Bank to search for new solutions. Governor Montagu Norman acknowledged his own interest in assisting industry but initially noted that such an intervention "was entirely outside the normal sphere of the Bank of England."[4] Only with Clay's arrival did the project of industrial reform become an integral part of the central bank's agenda. His theories were rooted in a fundamental belief in rationalization, a program that encompassed a broad set of interventions, including extending or facilitating loans; closing, selling, or buying unproductive factories; and amalgamating smaller firms to achieve greater economies of scale. By the 1930s, the policy had gained widespread appeal not only because of its promises of economic efficiency but also due to its association with scientific modernization and cultural advancement.[5]

The Bank devised its industrial policy in response to broader political developments. Over the course of the interwar years, the national government debated and implemented numerous measures to support domestic industry.[6] Yet alongside politicians and civil servants, central bankers and their experts were able to enact sweeping reorganization programs due to their technical

4 "Lancashire Cotton Corporation," December 5, 1928, BoE SMT2/240.

5 Charles S. Maier, "Between Taylorism and Technocracy: European Ideologies and the Vision of Industrial Productivity in the 1920s," *Journal of Contemporary History* 5, no. 2 (1970): 27–61; Jo-Anne Pemberton, "New Worlds for Old: The League of Nations in the Age of Electricity," *Review of International Studies* 28, no. 2 (2002): 311–336.

6 On the Treasury's interventions, see Booth, "Britain in the 1930s," 500–505; Peden, *The Treasury*, 269–275; Lewis Johnman and Hugh Murphy, "Subsidy and Treasury: The Trade Facilities Act and the UK Shipbuilding Industry in the 1920s," *Contemporary British History* 22, no. 1 (2008): 89–110; Valerio Cerretano, "The Treasury, Britain's Postwar Reconstruction, and the Industrial Intervention of the Bank of England, 1921–9," *The Economic History Review* 62, no. S1 (2009): 80–100.

knowledge. Amidst the collapse of prices and ensuing slump, they sought to assist the armaments, cotton, shipbuilding, and aluminum industries in response to challenges to its hegemonic position abroad. Improvements in efficiency and Fordist-style production tactics in Nazi Germany and the Soviet Union further heightened global competition.[7] In contrast, liberal democracies, such as the United Kingdom, implemented policies that adhered to a market-oriented approach to reform, underpinned by the principles of classical liberalism from the prewar years. With the fracturing of the global economy in the 1930s, the Bank envisaged a policy that maintained these ideals, while also accounting for the broader challenges to the international order.

This argument thus challenges the view that industrial intervention emerged primarily in opposition to the idea of nationalization.[8] Such was a claim made by Governor Norman himself.[9] After the Labour Party's first electoral success in 1924, there was even a proposal in circulation about the prospect of nationalizing the central bank itself.[10] Yet as this chapter shows, what stands as the primary reason for industrial reform was not the political threat of nationalization given that, throughout the early and mid-1930s, the fragile National Government coalition under Prime Minister Ramsay MacDonald struggled to define its own policies and was usually divided by the interests of its many factions.[11] Nationalization, having little significant institutional traction even if desired by some Members of Parliament (MPs), was a verbal threat made by those on both the left and the right. Rather, it was the prominence of economic expertise that justified efforts to close unproductive firms, increase employment, and expand the role of the state in economic affairs. As Peter Sloman has shown, the Liberal Party often used expertise as a means of

7 Stefan J. Link, *Forging Global Fordism: Nazi Germany, Soviet Russia, and the Contest Over the Industrial Order* (Princeton and Oxford: Princeton University Press, 2020).

8 As argued in Steven Tolliday, *Business, Banking, and Politics: The Case of British Steel, 1918–1939* (Cambridge, MA, and London: Harvard University Press, 1987), 270–273; J.H. Bamberg, "The Rationalization of the British Cotton Industry in the Interwar Years," *Textile History* 19, no. 1 (1988), 97–98; Tomlinson, *Public Policy and the Economy*, 83–84; Williamson, *National Crisis and National Government*, 72–73; W.R. Garside and J.I. Greaves, "The Bank of England and Industrial Intervention in Interwar Britain," *Financial History Review* 3, no. 1 (1996), 76; Philip L. Cottrell, "Finance and the Germination of the British Corporate Economy," in *Finance in the Age of the Corporate Economy*, ed. P.L. Cottrell, A. Teichova, and T. Yuzawa (Aldershot: Ashgate, 1997), 29; Philip L. Cottrell, "The Financial System of the United Kingdom in the Twentieth Century," in *International Banking and Financial Systems: Evolution and Stability*, ed. Luigi de Rosa (Aldershot: Ashgate, 2003), 49; Julian Greaves, *Industrial Reorganization and Government Policy in Interwar Britain* (Aldershot: Ashgate, 2005), 55.

9 Committee of Treasury, Minutes, April 29, 1931, BoE G8/60.

10 During the campaign for the 1935 general election, Labour MP Clement Attlee proclaimed, "If the Labour Party secured power the first thing they would invade would be the 'Temple of the Golden Calf' in Threadneedle Street – the Bank of England"; quoted in "City Notes," *The Times* 47195, October 15, 1935, 21.

11 "Informal Court Records," May 1, 1931, BoE G14/55.

lending legitimacy to its own political goals.[12] Given the growing influence of technical analysis, the Bank similarly employed advisers to help identify the benefits of rationalization, a policy able to adapt to the rapid evolution in the global economy. "No revolutionary programme is necessary in this country," Clay asserted, as the expansion of public-works loans and the mobilization of "idle capital" would instead be part of the Bank's response.[13] State intervention was as much a product of political necessity as one of supposed economic rationality.

In this environment, Clay considered how Britain's export capabilities could be adapted to changing industrial circumstances. He developed the idea of a "post-war unemployment problem," a theory that explained the high industrial unemployment brought about by the First World War and served as a guide for rationalization. These findings also aligned with those of the waning Liberal Party, the views of which were entrenched in the *Liberal Industrial Inquiry* (1928). Clay's subsequent employment at the Bank afforded him an opportunity to implement these ideas. Initially an adviser to one of the Bank's subsidiaries, the Securities Management Trust (SMT), he was officially promoted to the position of Adviser to the Governors in 1933. By examining Clay's early contributions to the discipline of economics and his policy recommendations, this chapter shows how the Bank's industrial interventions redefined state–business relations in an age of industrial unrest.

INDUSTRY AND UNEMPLOYMENT AFTER THE FIRST WORLD WAR

The rationale for industrial reform emerged from debates over British economic performance. During the First World War, manufacturing firms had diverted their resources to new industries in response to shifting needs. Following the establishment of the Ministry of Munitions in July 1915, the government was able to secure control over the supply chain of vital weaponry.[14] It poured its resources into the shipping and armaments industry, counterbalancing these expenditures with funding from additional taxation and the McKenna duties. Yet the wartime stimulus had been unevenly distributed. Funding for the steel, munitions, and shipbuilding industries, which all faced significantly higher demand, came at the expense of many public works, such as railway maintenance and road construction.[15]

[12] Peter Sloman, *The Liberal Party and the Economy, 1929–1964* (Oxford: Oxford University Press, 2015), 13, 48.

[13] Henry Clay, Memorandum, July 12, 1933, BoE ADM22/1.

[14] Stephen Broadberry and Peter Howlett, "The United Kingdom during World War I: Business as Usual?," in *The Economics of World War I*, ed. Stephen Broadberry and Mark Harrison (Cambridge: Cambridge University Press, 2005), 213–214.

[15] Henry Clay, "Some Aspects of the World Depression, Lecture II," November 25, 1931, *Journal of the Institute of Bankers* LIII, no. 1 (1932), 10.

Compared to its continental counterparts, the British wartime economy may have been better equipped at mobilizing for war due to its access to cheaper capital and a more progressive tax system. A temporary postwar boom (1919–1920) also initially sustained demand for short-time employment in some of the leading manufacturing industries – cotton, coal, iron, steel, and linen – thereby providing continual employment to the workforce.[16] Nevertheless, the transition to a peacetime economy was anything but direct. The return of troops initially proved overwhelming for domestic labor markets. Workers struggled to find reliable, long-term employment in export-reliant sectors, which had suffered from declining prices. Moreover, the longer-term consequences of the war manifested themselves in the lack of adjustment to wages, a phenomenon Clay attempted to study in greater depth. Although prior to the war, the wage-rate system reflected the "normal commercial needs" of industry, the increased demands of wartime production led to an unsustainable rise in the cost of labor.[17] These factors characterized a postwar recession that placed even greater strains on the unemployment system. Compared to 2.5 million in 1911, around 12 million insured workers were without work by 1920.[18]

The 1920 Unemployment Insurance Act might have provided insurance to all manual and nonmanual workers below a certain income.[19] It assisted individuals who faced periodic unemployment, such as those in the public sector or railway industry. Yet reported abuses in the system led to declining trust in social programs and efforts to curtail public spending in line with the Geddes Axe. The legislation stipulated that beneficiaries had to prove that they were "genuinely seeking work" and, for those married to an employed person, that the refusal of benefits would cause serious difficulties.[20]

Following this legislation, new proposals in favor of state intervention emerged. Pigou and Keynes wrote about the possible mechanisms for incentivizing firms to employ more workers.[21] Both their theories represented a "middle-way" approach to government involvement. At the same time,

[16] W.R. Garside, *British Unemployment, 1919–1939: A Study in Public Policy* (Cambridge: Cambridge University Press, 1990), 88–89.

[17] Henry Clay, "The Post-War Wages Problem–(I)," September 1923, in *The Problem of Industrial Relations and Other Lectures* (London: Macmillan, 1929), 75.

[18] Skidelsky, *Politicians and the Slump*, 21.

[19] Unemployment Insurance Act 1920, 10 & 11 Geo. 5. c. 30.

[20] Parliament enacted several "tests" to ensure the scheme of unemployment insurance was not being abused. A "genuinely seeking work" test was adopted in March 1921, while a "means test" for determining needs was introduced in February 1922; Stephanie Ward, *Unemployment and the State in Britain: The Means Test and Protest in 1930s South Wales and North-East England* (Manchester and New York: Manchester University Press, 2013), 40; Boyer, *The Winding Road*, 226.

[21] Skidelsky, *John Maynard Keynes, vol.* 2, 183–185; Ian Kumekawa, *The First Serious Optimist: A.C. Pigou and the Birth of Welfare Economics* (Princeton and Oxford: Princeton University Press, 2017), 138–144, 147–150.

economists were increasingly divided over how to respond to the rise of organized labor. Cannan, for instance, contended that "[g]eneral unemployment appears when asking too much is a general phenomenon," hinting at the responsibility of workers and trade unions for elevating real wages.[22] In contrast, socialist theorists, such as Sidney and Beatrice Webb of the Fabian Society, felt that unions needed to push even further in their negotiations to overcome widespread corruption and corporate mismanagement.[23]

Amidst these calls for reform, Clay offered another solution to industrial problems. He attempted to identify the underlying causes of unemployment, which had increased from 10.3 percent in 1924 to 11.3 percent in 1925.[24] Although high wages had come "at the expense of increasing employment," economic stagnation also needed to be explained from the perspective of industry-specific differences. There was, in other words, a disequilibrium between wages and industrial productivity in many of the key wartime industries.[25] The conflict, Clay conjectured, had "dislocate[d] this system and destroy[ed] its stability, with the result we have been forced to face the problem of wages as a whole."[26] To be sure, employers were not to blame for all these systemic inefficiencies, as many businesses "were equally without guidance as to what they could concede, since commercial conditions were so hard to judge."[27] Still, unrest in labor markets instigated fears of a complete collapse in Britain's share of global trade.

Indeed, Clay formulated these theories in a time of growing social and political upheaval. Throughout Stanley Baldwin's second premiership, the Conservative Party repeatedly sought to confront rising unemployment, the rate of which had now risen to 14.2 percent by 1926.[28] Subsequent measures to combat the crisis were met with public censure from party members who wanted to decrease government spending, as well as from the Labour opposition. Yet committed to the principles of economic orthodoxy, the Baldwin government placed more onerous restrictions on the highly controversial means test and required unemployed workers to demonstrate that they were "genuinely seeking work," as outlined in the 1927 Unemployment Insurance

[22] Edwin Cannan, "The Demand for Labour," *The Economic Journal* 42, no. 167 (1932), 367.

[23] Sidney Webb and Beatrice Webb, *The History of Trade Unionism, 1666–1920* (London: Longmans, Green & Co., 1920), 711–714.

[24] "Memorandum by Professor Henry Clay on Unemployment since the War," July 3, 1930, BLO Brand Papers 28/B/1 and NRS Lothian Papers GD40/17/135; "Professor Henry Clay," July 23, 1930, in Macmillan Committee, *Minutes of Evidence, vol.* 2, 252.

[25] Henry Clay, "The Public Regulation of Wages in Great Britain," *The Economic Journal* 39, no. 155 (1929), 326; Keith Hancock, "Unemployment and the Economists in the 1920s," *Economica* 27, no. 108 (1960), 312; Meredith M. Paker, "Normal Science and Anomaly: Responding to Unemployment in Economics in the 1920s" (MPhil thesis, University of Oxford, 2018), 53.

[26] Clay, "The Post-War Wages Problem–(I)," 75.

[27] Clay, "The Post-War Wages Problem–(I)," 77.

[28] "Summary of Statistics for the United Kingdom," January 1929, BoE EID2/3.

Act.[29] The benefits conferred under the amendments to unemployment insurance were largely insufficient to cover living expenses, leading many unemployed individuals to rely on support from the antiquated Poor Laws.[30] For women and workers under twenty-one, the weekly unemployment benefits were even lower.[31]

Ongoing political debates compelled Clay to investigate the causes of the unemployment problem. Early in his career, he had asserted that the wartime industries dedicated to munitions, industry, and manufacturing – supported by "ever-extending State control" – could not serve the needs of peacetime Britain: "With the merchants and manufacturers, not the Government, rests the duty of finding new civilian markets to replace the Government's war demand of adapting plant and organisation now engaged on war work to production for civilian consumption."[32] The urgency of reform heightened following the miners' lock-out and the General Strike, both in 1926. In May, between 1.5 and 3 million workers protested the proposed reductions in public wages. A delegation from the Trades Union Congress sought to end the dispute by obtaining assurances over mutually agreeable wage negotiations with the government, although the strike ended without such arrangements being accepted.[33]

Neither the strikes nor their failure resolved underlying economic issues. The Board of Trade estimated that the conflict had decreased the total volume of foreign trade by £71 million from the previous year, while the Bank noted

[29] Garside, *British Unemployment*, 46–48; Ward, *Unemployment and the State in Britain*, 43. The means test had also been temporarily abolished between 1924 and 1925; Lavinia Clare Elizabeth Mitton, "The Objectives and Outcomes of Means Testing under the British Welfare State" (PhD diss., London School of Economics, 2014), 71–73.

[30] Helen Leland Witmer, "Some Effects of the English Unemployment Insurance Acts on the Number of Unemployed Relieved Under the Poor Law," *The Quarterly Journal of Economics* 45, no. 2 (1931), 287–288.

[31] Marianne Sakmann, "Unemployment and Health Insurance in Great Britain, 1911–1937," in *Bureau of Research and Statistics*, edited by Social Security Board (Washington, DC: United States Government Printing Office, 1938), 9.

[32] Henry Clay, "Industrial Reconstruction and the Government," *The Round* Table 9, no. 33 (1918), 138. On the reception of Clay's textbook, *Economics: An Introduction for the General Reader* (1916), see Midori Wakamori, "Henrī Kurei ni okeru sangyō, soshiki kyōgyō, 1916–1929," *Annual Report of the Society for the History of Economic Thought*, no. 44 (2003): 45–58; Roger E. Backhouse and Tamotsu Nishizawa, "Welfare Economics, Old and New," in *No Wealth but Life: Welfare Economics and the Welfare State in Britain, 1880–1945*, ed. Roger E. Backhouse and Tamotsu Nishizawa (Cambridge: Cambridge University Press, 2010), 226–227; Steven Kates, "The Hundredth Anniversary of Clay's *Economics*: The Best Introduction to Economics Ever Written," *History of Economics Review* 64, no. 1 (2016): 27–41.

[33] Keith Laybourn, *The General Strike: Day by Day* (Stroud: Alan Sutton, 1996), 112–126; Derek H. Aldcroft and Michael J. Oliver, *Trade Unions and the Economy, 1870–2000* (Aldershot: Ashgate, 2000), 76–81; Anne Perkins, *A Very British Strike: 3 May–12 May, 1926* (London: Macmillan, 2006), 232–240; Sue Bruley, *The Women and Men of 1926: A Gender and Social History of the General Strike and Miners' Lockout in South Wales* (Cardiff: University of Wales Press, 2010), 2–3.

how the general strike had led to a severe decline in the pound's purchasing power abroad.[34] Observing the escalation of tensions between workers and employers, the central bank became even more concerned with devising a response to the British slump. In reaction to an earlier labor dispute in the coal-mining industry, one of the Bank's directors, Sir Josiah Stamp, attempted to understand the views of both sides. He acknowledged the grievances of workers who had been subject to low wages, while also seeking ways of spurring a general economic recovery.[35] The central bank, he believed, needed to play a more active role in addressing the structural problems facing industry.

While still at the University of Manchester, Clay resigned from his position as the Stanley Jevons Professor of Political Economy in order to serve as the chair of social economics in 1927. From this post, he advanced the notion that the future of recovery lay not in the nationalization of major industries, but rather in the actions of "the management of the individual firms" themselves.[36] These findings challenged those of other academic economists who questioned the efficacy of industrial reform. At Cambridge, Pigou proposed several measures for decreasing unemployment without lowering wages. A scheme of protective subsidies could include a new tax being imposed on the income or land value, and the subsequently generated profits would then be distributed in the form of subsidies to laborers.[37] Grants needed to be selectively applied to workers in industries with declining exports. With regard to funding, Pigou's calculations showed how annual costs were set to decrease as the program expanded: £50 million until 1931, £18.4 million from 1931 to 1936, and £8 million from 1936 to 1941.[38]

Clay, however, challenged the simplicity of Pigou's analysis, particularly the "inadequate consideration" given to the distribution of labor as a critical function of both wages and unemployment.[39] Coupled with "the burden of taxation ... [that] handicapped industry," inflexibly high wages were a key driver for falling industrial profits.[40] High taxation also coincided with the years of worsening unemployment.[41] From one perspective, Pigou's dataset limited the

34 R.E.H. Allport, "The British Iron and Steel Industry," March 13, 1929, BoE EID9/23; "The U.K. Balance of Trade (Board of Trade Figures to 'Balance Apart from Gold')," April 11, 1930, BoE EID3/1.

35 Josiah Stamp, "The Coal Mining Deadlock in Great Britain," *Foreign Affairs* 4, no. 4 (1926), 549–551.

36 Clay, "Industrial Reconstruction and the Government," 138.

37 A.C. Pigou, "Wage Policy and Unemployment," *The Economic Journal* 37, no. 147 (1927), 362–366.

38 Pigou, "Wage Policy and Unemployment," 367.

39 Henry Clay, "Unemployment and Wage Rates," *The Economic Journal* 38, no. 149 (1928), 2. Later republished in *The Problem of Industrial Relations and Other Lectures* (London: Macmillan, 1929).

40 Clay, "Some Aspects of the World Depression, Lecture III," 26.

41 "Burdens of Industry: Professor Henry Clay on Taxation and Unemployment," *The Scotsman (Edinburgh)* 27233, September 9, 1930, 9.

scope of his analysis: The index of weekly wage rates and unemployment rates did not give appropriate weights to each industry, asserted Clay.[42] Instead, Pigou offered a more theoretical approach to economic policy, often concerned with questions of ethics and well-being. Abstract and hypothetical methodologies also characterized Pigou's later work, *The Theory of Unemployment* (1933).[43] It was primarily in capital-intensive industries – coal, iron, steel, shipbuilding, and engineering – where severe unemployment proliferated. Although these industries comprised less than one-fifth of the workforce, they accounted for one-third of the unemployment population.[44]

DEVISING A LIBERAL ECONOMIC POLICY

Debates among Britain's most influential economists shaped the trajectory of public policy.[45] Similar to Keynes and Pigou, Clay sought to reconcile the interrelated problems of unemployment, stagnant wages, and industrial underperformance with evolving liberal ideas in the late 1920s. At the center of his priorities was the question of state involvement. How could economic intervention be reconciled with the party's long-established views on a limited government?

To some extent, the prewar Liberal Party had already acknowledged the need for a more active state in the economy. The banner of New Liberalism, departing from the priorities associated with Gladstonian liberalism of free trade and limited government, sought to address the major social issues of unemployment and poverty.[46] Following a landslide victory in 1906, the Liberal Party altered its economic policy to reflect these new objectives. It introduced a series of sweeping changes known as the Liberal welfare reforms (1906–1914), which included the introduction of national insurance and the establishment of trade boards. Through regionally based campaign strategies, especially in Lancashire, the party was able to mobilize additional voters in subsequent elections.[47]

Even though the Liberal Party had long struggled with internal divisions – most notably concerning Irish Home Rule, which had led to the formation of an opposing faction, the Liberal Unionist Party, in 1886 – it was during the First World War when its parliamentary dominance began to falter. Both Asquith

[42] Clay, "Unemployment and Wage Rates," 4.

[43] Kumekawa, *The First Serious Optimist*, 140.

[44] Clay, "Unemployment and Wage Rates," 6.

[45] Mark Casson, *Economics of Unemployment: An Historical Perspective* (Oxford: Martin Robertson & Company, 1983), 37–53.

[46] Michael Freeden, *The New Liberalism: An Ideology of Social Reform* (Oxford: Clarendon Press, 1978); David Powell, "The New Liberalism and the Rise of Labour, 1886–1906," *The Historical Journal* 29, no. 2 (1986): 369–393.

[47] P.F. Clarke, *Lancashire and the New Liberalism* (Cambridge: Cambridge University Press, 1971).

and Lloyd George had formed wartime coalition governments that relied on cooperation with the Conservatives. Although the results of the 1918 "coupon election" allowed Lloyd George to remain prime minister, his cooperation with the Unionists, in addition to a split with the Asquithian Liberals, severely damaged his credibility with the left.[48] The party's continued ideological disputes in the interwar years over its economic priorities, as well as later challenges from the rise of Labour and a prolonged recession, damaged its future electoral prospects.[49]

In this politically charged environment, economic reforms might not only have addressed the unemployment question, but they could have also unified the fractured Liberal Party. Clay's own research often adhered to a version of Gladstonian liberalism, emphasizing free trade, low taxation, and minimal state intervention. The proper function of the government, according to Gladstone's maxim, "was to govern not to trade."[50] At the same time, the stagnation of British industry seemed to justify some type of reform. Clay had called for a refashioning of classical liberalism, one that clung to the old ambitions of free trade and competition, while still adapting to the view that government intervention could be of value for both economic and electoral reasons.[51] "The problem of Liberalism for a generation past," he wrote in 1926, "has been to find a domestic policy ... that will satisfy the democratic sentiment of the new electorate."[52]

Rationalization thus offered a "middle-way" solution between socialism and laissez-faire capitalism in an age of democracy. It was increasingly acceptable to many economists, industrialists, and politicians whose idea of stability rested on the resurrection of a pre-1914 liberal economic order. Some Liberal MPs, to be sure, were hesitant to endorse radical forms of government involvement, especially when it threatened to spur inflation.[53] As a result, Clay devised proposals that highlighted the importance of maintaining an unobtrusive state. A program of industrial reorganization and reductions in wages were two such measures that could tackle the problem of unemployment without leading to a rise in price levels. Both stood in contrast to existing

48 Kenneth O. Morgan, *Consensus and Disunity: The Lloyd George Coalition Government, 1918–1922* (Oxford: Clarendon Press, 1979), 31.

49 On the divisions in and decline of the Liberal Party, see George Dangerfield, *The Strange Death of Liberal England* (New York: H. Smith & R. Haas, 1935); Trevor Wilson, *The Downfall of the Liberal Party, 1914–1935* (London: Collins, 1966); J.A. Thompson, "The Historians and the Decline of the Liberal Party," *Albion: A Quarterly Journal Concerned with British Studies* 22, no. 1 (1990): 65–83; Keith Laybourn, "The Rise of Labour and the Decline of Liberalism: The State of the Debate," *History* 80, no. 259 (1995), 209–210.

50 Henry Clay, "Irresponsibility in Economic Life," *Political Quarterly* 2, no. 1 (1931), 76.

51 Henry Clay, "Liberalism, Laissez Faire and Present Industrial Conditions," *The Hibbert Journal* 24, no. 4 (1926), 732–733.

52 Henry Clay, "A Word for 'Laissez Faire,'" July 1926, in *The Problem of Industrial Relations and Other Lectures* (London: Macmillan, 1929), 307.

53 Sloman, *The Liberal Party and the Economy*, 96.

collective-bargaining measures, which Clay argued had only elevated wages and prices.[54]

Yet the contentious landscape of British interwar politics produced stark divides on the left on the viability of market capitalism. Although many Liberal MPs were willing to work with policies that preserved existing structures of power, the Labour Party seemingly threatened to undermine many proposals. According to Clay, "Socialist and Labour critics are fond of referring to the post-war depression and unemployment as proof of the failure of private enterprise. It would be reasonable to refer to it as proof of the failure of Government, since it was caused by the war and the war was the work of Governments."[55] Defending a market-based approach, he criticized Liberals who advocated radical proposals that called "for nationalising railways, coal and land ... as an opportunist attempt to steal the Labour Party's thunder."[56]

Clay may have misunderstood the realities of electoral strategy, and he only had a few direct connections to politicians through the Liberal Summer School. Still, his writings indicated that he was attuned to some of the broader issues of inadequate economic governance. He noted, for instance, the flaws with a complete free-market approach to industrial recovery, referring to a pure laissez-faire doctrine as "disreputable superstition" that "deserves the contempt into which it has fallen."[57] Political tensions also seemed to hinder the resolution of industrial issues. In November 1930, he expounded this argument in a public lecture:

> The confusion of responsibility for economic policy may account for the persistent failure to make the readjustments in British industry which are called for by the changes wrought by the war. Successive Governments take office pledged to remedy unemployment; having realised by experience that industry is not yet completely directed and controlled by the State, they proceed either to chide industry for its inefficiency or to complain that they are not permitted to apply the certain remedy – State Socialism or Protection or Inflation, as the case may be – on which they relied to do the trick. The business men retaliate by forming Councils of Industry to teach the politicians how to govern.[58]

Although the idea of industrial reform rested heavily on the political debates surrounding unemployment, Clay aimed to show how drawing on technical expertise would help the major parties with their electoral prospects.

It was in this setting that the value of statistics became increasingly evident. By "restrict[ing] the discussion very largely to elements of which there is a statistical measure," Clay believed that he could devise a more

54 Henry Clay, "The Authoritarian Element in Distribution," *The Economic Journal* 37, no. 145 (1927), 7.

55 Henry Clay, *The Post-War Unemployment Problem* (London: Macmillan, 1929), 189–190.

56 Clay, "Liberalism, Laissez Faire and Present Industrial Conditions," 733.

57 Clay, "Liberalism, Laissez Faire and Present Industrial Conditions," 733.

58 Clay, "Irresponsibility in Economic Life," 76.

JANUARY 1933 9

XVI—EMPLOYMENT IN MANUFACTURING INDUSTRIES SINCE 1923

Compiled from Ministry of Labour Gazette

	Number (Thousands)		Index (1923 = 100)								
End of June	1923	1932	1924	1925	1926*	1927	1928	1929	1930	1931	1932
Silk and Artificial Silk	35	57	114·2	125·0	129·7	148·5	197·0	199·6	179·4	151·2	167·1
Electrical Equipment	132	201	113·5	121·2	122·7	127·0	132·3	143·2	149·6	147·5	155·1
Printing and Paper	326	375	103·9	105·8	107·7	110·6	113·0	116·7	116·9	114·9	117·6
Motor Vehicles and Aircraft	174	196	109·4	116·4	116·0	126·8	126·3	134·4	125·2	115·5	114·4
Sawmilling, Furniture and Woodwork	172	182	103·1	105·8	106·1	115·4	117·4	120·6	117·3	112·1	110·0
Food, Drink and Tobacco	455	465	102·5	105·3	106·4	107·0	105·9	107·2	106·1	103·5	104·5
Chemicals etc.	192	186	101·8	101·9	97·6	103·6	109·4	110·3	105·3	97·5	100·1
Metal Trades other than Electrical	341	329	103·5	107·7	103·7	111·9	111·0	115·7	109·9	99·6	99·4
Clothing	538	524	100·3	101·1	99·2	104·3	101·4	102·9	100·4	99·9	99·0
Manufacturing Industries not separately specified	631	588	104·9	107·1	94·1	112·8	112·1	116·9	111·3	99·2	96·0
Textile Trades not separately specified	386	341	104·9	98·8	91·8	107·5	104·7	106·9	92·4	86·4	91·2
Cotton Preparing, Spinning, Weaving etc.	445	351	108·9	117·7	96·8	118·9	109·7	109·0	75·1	74·4	79·8
General Engineering	526	391	101·5	103·9	94·6	103·2	104·2	105·8	98·7	81·6	77·3
Woollen and Worsted	251	170	98·0	81·7	75·5	89·8	88·7	85·2	75·3	66·4	70·7
Iron and Steel	265	146	101·3	89·1	53·2	95·2	91·6	92·3	82·4	59·6	57·3
Ship Building and Repairs	151	68	119·5	103·6	85·1	109·1	101·1	108·9	97·5	58·3	46·4
All Manufacturing Industries	**5020**	**4570**	**104·4**	**104·2**	**96·1**	**108·9**	**107·8**	**110·4**	**102·1**	**93·3**	**93·5**

FIGURE 5.1 Excerpt from the *Statistical Summary*, January 1933
Source: Bank of England Archive, EID2/7.

appropriate policy.[59] His research identified how high-wage earners had little effect on the overall unemployment rate, which was instead more represented by low-wage workers who were once employed *en masse* in major export industries.[60] According to the Bank's monthly *Statistical Summary*, the rate of employment had actually increased in many of the nonindustrial and manufacturing sectors, such as silk and paper (Figure 5.1). Other expanding industries included the trades, engineering, motor manufacturing, and silk production.

Among the sectors that had experienced the highest levels of unemployment were those in the major wartime industries of iron, steel, and shipbuilding (Figure 5.2). As businesses had inaccurately estimated the amount of goods demanded by the market, overproduction of what could have been sold at an anticipated price forced them to operate at a loss. By the following business cycle, firms reported lower overall profits.[61] Building on these findings, Clay's magnum opus, *The Post-War Unemployment Problem* (1929), highlighted a key driver of unemployment, namely the problem of economic adjustment. Domestic firms had seen roughly six years of continuously rising demand during the war and the postwar boom, both periods in which they employed more workers and invested in new machinery.[62] With the decline in demand and limited access to markets abroad, many industries failed to make proper adjustments to their production costs. This argument resonated with Clay's prior theories on the intra-industrial factors that took into

[59] Henry Clay, "Unemployment," *Journal of the Royal Society of Arts* 78, no. 4065 (1930), 1211.
[60] Clay, "Unemployment and Wage Rates," 5–6.
[61] Clay, "Unemployment," 1212.
[62] Clay, *The Post-War Unemployment Problem*, 87–92.

XX—EMPLOYMENT IN EXPANDING AND CONTRACTING INDUSTRIES
UNITED KINGDOM

July to July	1923 to 1927 (*a*)		1927 to 1929 (*b*)		*1923 to 1929*	July, 1923 (*a*)	July, 1927 (*a*)	July, 1929 (*b*)
Principal Expanding Industries	Increase in Number Insured	Increase per Cent.	Increase in Number Insured	Increase per Cent.	*Increase in Number Insured*	Unemployment Percentage		
Distributive Trades	327,090	26·1	126,360	8·1	*453,450*	5·9	4·4	5·4
Building and Construction	173,200	20·5	20,790	2·1	*193,990*	13·1	8·4	10·4
Road Transport	49,840	19·4	38,270	12·8	*88,110*	11·3	6·5	6·8
Motor Manufacture etc.	41,030	21·4	15,280	6·6	*56,310*	9·6	7·9	7·2
Printing etc.	28,770	12·6	10,750	4·3	*39,520*	5·6	4·3	3·8
Silk and Artificial Silks	17,770	47·6	20,280	37·8	*38,050*	6·7	6·6	7·7
Brick, Cement etc.	35,680	40·5	1,120	·9	*36,800*	8·9	6·0	8·1
Furniture	20,390	21·7	10,320	9·4	*30,710*	7·7	4·6	5·7
Electrical Engineering	18,340	30·1	6,630	8·5	*24,970*	7·2	4·8	3·8
Shipping Service and Fishing	18,730	12·3	1,360	·8	*20,090*	17·6	13·6	14·3
ALL EXPANDING INDUSTRIES	**1,036,360**	**15·6**	**436,760**	**5·9**	**1,473,120**			
Principal Contracting Industries	Decrease in Number Insured	Decrease per Cent.	Decrease in Number Insured	Decrease per Cent.	*Decrease in Number Insured*	Unemployment Percentage		
Coal Mining	44,590	3·6	89,670	7·7	*134,260*	3·0	21·5	18·9
Shipbuilding	53,940	20·0	3,980	1·9	*57,920*	43·2	22·3	23·0
National Government	44,680	24·7	12,030	9·2	*56,710*	11·1	5·3	6·2
Railways	41,550	21·8	5,890	4·1	*47,440*	6·0	4·3	4·4
Iron and Steel	16,440	7·8	9,270	4·9	*25,710*	20·9	18·2	19·9
Woollen and Worsted	20,240	7·5	770	·3	*21,010*	9·3	9·5	15·8
Dress and Mantle	11,420	9·7	1,560	1·5	*12,980*	6·3	4·0	3·4
Carriages, Carts etc.	7,230	25·7	1,390	6·9	*8,620*	13·4	8·2	8·8
Watches, Clocks etc.	4,410	8·9	2,140	4·9	*6,550*	13·6	7·8	7·1
Lace	3,050	14·4	390	2·3	*3,440*	25·1	7·1	9·2
ALL CONTRACTING INDUSTRIES	**391,160**	**8·1**	**126,760**	**2·9**	**517,920**			

FIGURE 5.2 Employment by Industry, 1928–1930
Source: Bank of England Archive, EID2/4.

account regional differences and the composition of industry itself. Wage rates in "heavy" industries were more stagnant than those in "equally depressed" industries, such as textiles.[63]

This research further demonstrated how the "older and greater export industries," unable to correct their production levels after the postwar boom, drove unemployment.[64] Widespread was the idea that inefficient business practices explained the lack of industrial competitiveness of British goods in a changing global economy.[65] For instance, the coal industry, one of the "older" industries with a highly rigid production structure, suffered from severe excess capacity after the war.[66] Even for the "essential" industries of railways, mining, and manufacturing, rising demand during and after the war created false confidence that wages could have continued to increase.[67] Clay estimated that around 200,000 "superfluous workers" had made those firms less profitable

[63] Clay, "The Public Regulation of Wages," 333.

[64] Clay, *The Post-War Unemployment Problem*, 102.

[65] David Greasley, "The Coal Industry: Images and Realities on the Road to Nationalisation," in *The Political Economy of Nationalisation in Britain, 1920–1950*, ed. Robert Millward and John Singleton (Cambridge: Cambridge University Press, 1995), 50.

[66] Arthur Salter, Josiah Stamp, John Maynard Keynes, Basil Blackett, Henry Clay, and W.H. Beveridge, *The World's Economic Crisis and the Way of Escape, Halley Stewart Lecture, 1931* (London: Allen & Unwin, 1932), 138.

[67] Henry Clay, "The Post-War Wages Problem–(II)," November 1927, in *The Problem of Industrial Relations and Other Lectures* (London: Macmillan, 1929), 92.

as they faced increased competition abroad.[68] These circumstances led to both an increase in unemployment and, for those that remained employed, a more "precarious and uncertain tenure."[69]

His views increasingly aligned with the ideas forwarded by Lloyd George's faction of the Liberal Party. In July 1926, a public enquiry aimed to investigate the causes of Britain's unemployment and industrial decline. The committee, chaired by Walter Layton, editor of *The Economist*, made a series of proposals that encouraged greater state intervention but also ensured the continuation of the capitalist system. Over the ensuing years, Liberal MPs and economists agreed to a general set of policies that addressed the unemployment problem. Many of their discussions took place at the Liberal Summer School, originally established by Manchester Liberals and later convened in alternating years at Cambridge and Oxford.[70]

The result of these deliberations was *Britain's Industrial Future* (1928). Known as the Yellow Book, the plan involved the transition to "a new industrial order" based on the idea of industrial self-government through state encouragement and guidance.[71] Specific proposals included the creation of trade boards and industrial councils designed for advising production in Britain's staple industries.[72] Clay spoke highly of the publication, noting its "admirable collection of statistical material" and its "penetrating, original and constructive" assessment of British industry.[73] It was, in short, "the most elaborate unofficial survey of post-war industry."[74] Even so, contemporaries also identified the many shortcomings of the report. For one, it failed to identify a politically attractive solution, thereby spurring criticism from both economists of the Labour Party (G.D.H. Cole and J.A. Hobson) and politicians of the Conservative Party (Churchill and Lord Birkenhead).[75] Even Clay,

[68] Henry Clay, "Export Trades and Unemployment," April 1928, in *The Problem of Industrial Relations and Other Lectures* (London: Macmillan, 1929), 128.

[69] Clay, *The Post-War Unemployment Problem*, 148.

[70] Peter Clarke, *Liberals and Social Democrats* (Cambridge: Cambridge University Press, 1978), 239–241; Michael Freeden, *Liberalism Divided: A Study in British Political Thought, 1914–1939* (Oxford: Clarendon Press, 1986), 78–126; Richard S. Grayson, *Liberals, International Relations and Appeasement: The Liberal Party, 1919–1939* (London and New York: Routledge, 2001), 59–64; Sloman, *The Liberal Party and the Economy*, 30–43. Clay had previously contributed a paper to the Liberal Summer School on property tax; Henry Clay, "Property and Inheritance," *The New Way Series* 1, no. 5 (1923): 3–30.

[71] Liberal Industrial Inquiry, *Britain's Industrial Future, Being the Report of the Liberal Industrial Inquiry* (London: Ernest Benn, 1928), 205.

[72] Liberal Industrial Inquiry, *Britain's Industrial Future*, 207–213, 418–421; Sloman, *The Liberal Party and the Economy*, 44.

[73] Henry Clay, "The Liberal Industrial Report," *The Economic Journal* 38, no. 150 (1928), 195–196.

[74] Clay, *The Post-War Unemployment Problem*, 167.

[75] Churchill to Grigg, February 26, 1928, CAC Chartwell Papers 18/87; Lord Birkenhead to Lord Irwin, April 5, 1928, in *Conservative Politics in National and Imperial Crisis: Letters from*

admitting that "[t]he report never faces the difficulty in adjusting the relations of State and industry," called for another inquiry into which parts of the "Governmental machine" needed to be reformed.[76]

Nevertheless, interwar liberalism, as a bridge between free-market individualism and socialism, proved popular among Britain's leading economists, including Clay, Keynes, Hubert Henderson, and Dennis Robertson. The publication of *Britain's Industrial Future* signaled the Liberal Party's willingness to consider expert-approved solutions. A proposed Council of Industry would include representatives from labor and employers to advise a newly created Ministry of Industry, while a Board of National Investment could oversee public-spending programs. These groups would ensure that any future industrial reform would be based on technical analysis, rather than on political whims.

Yet the results of the 1929 general election demonstrated how there was no clear consensus on the future of industrial policy. Although Labour returned to power in May, albeit without a parliamentary majority, the Liberal Party under Lloyd George was able to win some of its previously lost seats. It aimed to resolve the unemployment question, which was addressed in the "We Can Conquer Unemployment" pamphlet. Moreover, MacDonald's government faced not only Conservative and Liberal opposition but also a worsening economic slump. By October 1930, unemployment had reached 2.2 million.[77] In turn, government expenditures arising from unemployment insurance were projected to increase from £14 million in 1930 to £46 million the following year.[78]

To identify ways of reducing these costs in the upcoming budget, the prime minister endeavored to procure additional evidence from experts.[79] Over the next two years, Clay served on a royal commission tasked with assessing the system's need for fiscal reform. The structure of the state-run Unemployment Insurance Scheme, Parliament had noted, "suffers from a rigidity which makes it difficult readily to adjust its provisions to the varying needs of the unemployed workers and of industry."[80] An initial report, published in June of the following year, proposed placing restrictions on the insurance program: an increase in the amount of contributions to the Unemployment Fund from the worker, the employer, and the Treasury, along with a limit of twenty-six weeks

Britain to the Viceroy of India, 1926–31, ed. Stuart Ball (London and New York: Routledge, 2016), 217; Clarke, *Liberals and Social Democrats*, 240–242.

[76] Clay, "The Liberal Industrial Report," 202–203.

[77] Williamson, *National Crisis and National Government*, 60.

[78] Williamson, *National Crisis and National Government*, 77. On the cost of unemployment insurance, see Ursula K. Hicks, *The Finance of British Government, 1920–1936* (London: Oxford University Press, 1938), 193–205.

[79] HC Deb, vol. 246, December 9, 1930, cc. 222–223; *Report of the Ministry of Labour for the Year 1930*, Cmd. 3859 (London: H.M. Stationery Office, 1931), 65.

[80] Royal Commission on Unemployment Insurance, *First Report*, Cmd. 3872 (London: H.M. Stationery Office, 1931), 5.

for benefit receivers.[81] These reforms might have placed less strain on the budget, although members of the commission largely believed that further analysis was required to assess the "social and economic effects of the Scheme."[82]

According to the report, there were three overlapping types of sectors that experienced unemployment differently: (1) those that witnessed significantly less demand for production in peacetime than in wartime (most notably, iron, steel, shipbuilding, and coal); (2) those dependent on exports, which suffered due to declining demand in overseas markets (textile and coal); and (3) those that had begun expanding under state-run programs (public works, roads, and docks).[83] The existence of "exceptional unemployment" could be seen most pervasively in the first two groups, as Britain's declining share of world exports further undermined the chance of recovery.[84] While on the commission, Clay reiterated his views on a readjustment problem. The failure of British industries to adapt to the changing needs of the global economy was clear from the performance of the coal-mining sector, which had once been a lucrative venture in the prewar years, but had by now become displaced by the growing prominence of electricity.[85] In addition, a contraction among large-scale industries, including shipbuilding and cotton, had caused many bank loans to become illiquid. On these trends, the commission's final report recommended that, in order to keep the Unemployment Fund solvent, there needed to be a reduction in the period during which benefits were paid, an increase in contributions to the Fund, and a decrease in the percentage of benefits.[86]

To be sure, Clay did have some sympathies with the plight of workers. It was the government's "public obligation" to meet "some standards of social need."[87] Already in 1918, he had called for the negotiation of an "industrial peace," in which unions would no longer threaten to use strikes or boycotts in exchange for the government pledging to maintain wage rates at stable levels.[88] Yet the 1920s witnessed a resurgence in organized strikes and protests. Across the United Kingdom, membership in trade unions had increased from 2 million in 1900 to over 6.5 million by 1918, again rising to 8.3 million by 1920.[89] Observing these trends, Clay became increasingly critical of labor unions, as

[81] Royal Commission on Unemployment Insurance, *First Report*, 14, 50.

[82] Royal Commission on Unemployment Insurance, *First Report*, 51.

[83] Royal Commission on Unemployment Insurance, *First Report*, 9.

[84] Royal Commission on Unemployment Insurance, *First Report*, 9.

[85] "Lays Britain's Woes to Export Policies: English Expert Says She Must Cut Costs to World Levels or Shift Labor to Home Fields," *The New York Times* LXXX, 26645, January 6, 1931, 11.

[86] Royal Commission on Unemployment Insurance, *Final Report*, Cmd. 4185 (London: H.M. Stationery Office, 1932), 351.

[87] Henry Clay, "The Economic Limits to Expenditure on Social Services," *The Manchester School of Economic and Social Studies* 3, no. 2 (1932), 104.

[88] Clay, "Industrial Reconstruction and the Government," 141.

[89] Henry Clay, "The Whitley Reports and the Machinery of Conciliation," November 29, 1927, in *The Problem of Industrial Relations and Other Lectures* (London: Macmillan, 1929), 143.

he believed that their power had placed undue stress on the government-run scheme of unemployment insurance.[90] Collective bargaining elevated wages, especially in sectors that were already on the verge of bankruptcy. While technological innovation might have helped certain industries, Clay recognized that frictions in the wage mechanism compounded difficulties, especially for the working class.[91] In either case, unemployment had persisted due to the failures of industry.

THE REFORM OF THE INDUSTRIAL ENTERPRISE

On April 14, 1930, Clay wrote to Governor Norman on the need for industrial intervention: "You asked me to consider the question of initiative in rationalisation and of finding ways of inducing people in industry itself to come forward with schemes … . The difficulty is that most people in industry look at the problem of depression from the point of view of their own firm, and not from the point of view of the industry as a whole. It is necessary, therefore, to give the impulse to any consideration of an industry's problems from outside."[92] Many officials at the Bank had become increasingly concerned with economic stagnation. Governor Norman had regularly met with industrialists throughout 1930, as his diary entries suggest, aiming to procure ideas from some of the leading experts of the day.[93]

The rise of economic expertise at the Bank can partly be explained by convenience. Clay's prior research on unemployment had directly aligned with the ongoing effort to reform the structure of industry, and a subsequent invitation to the Bank helped to foster new ideas on rationalization and credit. While the Bank had been willing to offer some support to industry prior to the First World War, the scale of these early activities had been minimal. Only in the interwar years did the Bank intervene in industrial affairs in a systematic manner. One such project in 1927 had concerned the merger of Armstrong Whitworth, a steel manufacturer, and Vickers, an engineering firm, following a loan from the Bank.[94] The project complied with the recommendations of the (Balfour) Committee on Industry and Trade, members of which advocated the rationalization of domestic

[90] Clay, "The Public Regulation of Wages," 335.

[91] Henry Clay, "Some Aspects of the World Depression, Lecture I," November 5, 1931, *Journal of the Institute of Bankers* LII, no. 9 (1931), 516–518.

[92] Clay to Norman, April 14, 1930, BoE SMT2/60 and SMT5/11.

[93] Montagu Norman, Diary, 1930, BoE ADM34/19.

[94] "Vickers-Armstrongs Ltd.," n.d., CUA Vickers Papers Doc. 775; Montagu Norman, Diary, July 28, 1927, BoE ADM34/16; Committee of Treasury, Minutes, August 3, 1927, BoE G8/57; Tolliday, *Business, Banking, and Politics*, 192–197; Valerio Cerretano, "Economic Crises and the Development of the Industrial State: The Industrial Intervention of the Bank of Italy and the Bank of England, 1918–1939," *Review of Keynesian Economics*, 1, no. 3 (2013), 319; Kumekawa, "Imperial Schemes," 184; Joanna Spear, *The Business of Armaments: Armstrongs, Vickers and the International Arms Trade, 1855–1955* (Cambridge: Cambridge University Press, 2023), 141–149.

industries based on "a thorough process of re-conditioning" that restored "the competitive power of British trade in overseas markets."[95] The goal was to identify a precedent for future industrial interventions. Questioning 240 witnesses in the process, the committee had also gathered extensive data on British trade to arrive at a market-based conclusion.[96]

Throughout the Vickers-Armstrongs negotiations, the Bank had prioritized identifying technical solutions to industrial problems. Its Committee of Treasury might have recognized the inherent difficulty in simultaneously seeking "to bring about the rationalisation of the iron and steel industry and to avoid the increase of unemployment and disturbance of labour" resulting from closed firms.[97] Yet even if officials wanted to assist domestic industry, they tacitly acknowledged their inability to implement reforms on their own. By June 1929, the Committee of Treasury concluded that it would be advantageous to "call on the services of experts" to advise on the future of rationalization.[98] Among the directors, Norman most strongly supported the idea of securing "the services of a leading world expert – on the technical side – in the iron and steel industry."[99] Shortly thereafter, he offered Clay an advisory post at one of the Bank's subsidiaries.

Following his arrival at the Bank in January 1930, Clay became the primary intellectual force behind industrial policy. He defined rationalization as a process that involved reorganizing the existing structure of domestic industry. Through mergers and acquisitions, the closure of unproductive firms, the standardization of equipment and information, the promotion of innovative techniques, and the centralization of purchasing plans, industrial reform aimed to halt the decline of British industry.[100] According to Clay, the central bank would be particularly vital to this work, since its existing connections allowed it to conduct detailed studies of industrial output and production, while its influence in the City provided it a channel for implementing change.[101] The development of its own industrial policy would help the Bank adapt to the realities of the post-First World War global economy: "New processes, new

[95] Committee on Industry and Trade, *Final Report*, Cmd. 3282 (London: H.M. Stationery Office, 1929), 297.

[96] Barry Supple, "Official Economic Inquiry and Britain's Industrial Decline: The First Fifty Years," in *The State and Economic Knowledge: The American and British Experiences*, ed. Mary O. Furner and Barry Supple (Washington, DC: Woodrow Wilson International Center for Scholars and Cambridge: Cambridge University Press, 1990), 342–344.

[97] Committee of Treasury, Minutes, August 24, 1927, BoE G8/57. Otto Niemeyer, who had been privy to discussions of the Vickers-Armstrongs case, accepted a position as one of its directors in November; Committee of Treasury, Minutes, November 4, 1927, BoE G8/57; "Vickers Limited," November 18, 1927, CUA Vickers Papers Doc. 561.

[98] Committee of Treasury, Minutes, June 19, 1929, BoE G8/58.

[99] Committee of Treasury, Minutes, September 4, 1929, BoE G8/58.

[100] Henry Clay, "Some Aspects of Rationalisation," October 8, 1930, BoE SMT2/60.

[101] Henry Clay, "Note on Initiative in Rationalisation," April 14, 1930, BoE SMT2/60 and SMT5/11.

materials, new demands, new markets, offer new openings for enterprise in the wide sense, and the businesses that are the first to take them are commonly described as 'enterprising.'"[102]

Viewed in this light, industrial rationalization was a product of economic advice, not of overt political pressures. Although Labour and radical Liberals may have been willing to use the threat of nationalization as a tool to achieve political change, both groups were too deeply divided to engage in a large-scale takeover of Britain's major industries. The Labour Party itself suffered from internal factionalism, as many of its leaders – Clement Attlee, Ernest Bevin, and George Lansbury, among them – condemned MacDonald for his "betrayal" of the party through spending cuts.[103] Liberal MPs, too, frequently questioned the efficacy of the National Government's policies.[104] Moreover, none of the established political parties faced a credible electoral threat from the smaller, more radical ones. Rationalization may have been one of the central features of the failed Mosley memorandum in 1930.[105] Yet even if both the British Communist Party (formed in 1920) and the British Union of Fascists (1932) called for major economic reform, neither was significant enough in pure electoral terms to affect the nation's industrial policy.[106]

MacDonald's Labour government and the successive National Government, reluctant to enforce mergers or amalgamations due to the political and financial resources needed, were willing to allow the Bank to lead such projects. Rationalization, for one, aligned with existing efforts to reduce unemployment. Labour politicians who were in the coalition government were even supportive of industrial reform, which they expressed in private conversations. After meeting with Governor Norman in September 1929, Chancellor Philip Snowden stated that he was a strong advocate of rationalization and "would

102 Henry Clay, "The Financing of Industrial Enterprise," *Transactions of the Manchester Statistical Society* 20 (1932), 206. Also located in NCO Clay Papers 68/16.

103 David J. Wrench, "'Cashing In': The Parties and the National Government, August 1931–September 1932," *Journal of British Studies* 23, no. 2 (1984), 140; Nick Smart, *The National Government, 1931–40* (New York: St. Martin's Press, 1999), 9–20; David Howell, *MacDonald's Party: Labour Identities and Crisis, 1922–1931* (Oxford: Oxford University Press, 2002), 1, 5.

104 Sloman, *The Liberal Party and the Economy*, 97–99.

105 Robert Skidelsky, *Oswald Mosley* (London: Macmillan, 1975), 192–196, 199–206; Daniel Ritschel, *The Politics of Planning: The Debate on Economic Planning in Britain in the 1930s* (Oxford: Clarendon Press, 1997), 51–70; Neil Riddell, *Labour in Crisis: The Second Labour Government, 1929–1931* (Manchester and New York: Manchester University Press, 1999), 152–157; Richard Toye, *The Labour Party and the Planned Economy, 1931–1951* (Suffolk: Boydell & Brewer, 2003), 36–39; David Powell, *British Politics, 1910–35: The Crisis of the Party System* (London and New York: Routledge, 2004), 161.

106 Richard Thurlow, "The Failure of British Fascism," in *The Failure of Political Extremism in Inter-War Britain*, ed. Andrew Thorpe (Exeter: University of Exeter Press, 1989), 71–77; Andrew Thorpe, *The British Communist Party and Moscow, 1920–43* (Manchester and New York: Manchester University Press, 2000), 15–17.

himself at all times support it."[107] While there may have been desires to bring the Bank closer to the state apparatus, the link between nationalization and rationalization was tenuous.

The formulation of an expert-led industrial policy marked the Bank's transformation from a private central bank to a de facto public institution. This evolution was far from direct, as the Bank was primarily concerned with industrial performance insofar as it protected British financial interests. Indeed, Clay's recommendations often centered on defending the actions of the City, such as when he argued that "banking policy necessarily follows, not leads industry."[108] Yet rationalization was also the primary tool for the state to combat unemployment, thereby addressing the needs of the mass electorate. Although the Bank might have been divided over its public responsibilities since the days of Walter Bagehot, intervention emerged as a concrete possibility in the aftermath of the First World War when it could accomplish multiple goals. For Sir Richard Hopkins at the Treasury, rationalization would help restore the competitive position of older industries abroad.[109] So, too, was the League of Nations keen on espousing the language and logic of international scientific management as a means of responding to global economic instability.[110]

In November 1929, the Bank established a subsidiary called Securities Management Trust.[111] Originally a holding company for the Bank's investments in private companies (including Armstrong Whitworth and the Lancashire Cotton Corporation [LLC]), SMT oversaw the subsequent program of rationalization.[112] Advised primarily by Clay, it extended loans to domestic firms, in addition to offering support services for employers by providing them with "up-to-date information" on market developments and training "in modern methods."[113] Following a successful public issue of £1.75 million for a steel merger in south Lancashire, SMT became the main entity through which the Bank conducted its industrial policy.[114] By 1931, it effectively acted as a

[107] "Memorandum Dated 4th September 1929 of an Interview between the Governor (Mr. Norman) and the Chancellor of the Exchequer (Mr. Snowden)," BoE G14/55.

[108] Henry Clay, "Memorandum on Unemployment since the War for the Finance & Industry Committee," n.d., BoE SMT2/60.

[109] Howson and Winch, *The Economic Advisory Council*, 27.

[110] Fior, *Institution globale et marchés financiers*, 197.

[111] Committee of Treasury, Minutes, November 20, 1929, BoE G8/58; "The City's Aid to Industry: Prof. H. Clay's Appointment," *The Manchester Guardian (Manchester)* 26022, January 27, 1930, 9; Carol E. Heim, "Limits to Intervention: The Bank of England and Industrial Diversification in the Depressed Areas," *The Economic History Review* 37, no. 4 (1984), 544; Kynaston, *The City of London, vol. 3*, 190; Kynaston, *Till Time's Last Sand*, 315.

[112] Taylor to Norman, "Proposed New Holding & Investigating Company," October 17, 1929, BoE G15/406.

[113] E.H.D. Skinner, "Industrial Securities Limited," November 6, 1929, BoE G15/406.

[114] Garside and Greaves, "The Bank of England," 72; Greaves, *Industrial Reorganization*, 58.

"consultant, adviser, draughtsman; accounting assistance can be offered, and technical reports called for."[115]

With Clay's support, Governor Norman had been personally involved in the project of industrial reform. He had, according to one contemporary, been "devoting his whole mind to rationalisation in the cotton and the heavy trades," even if there was "little immediate prosperity to come from his schemes."[116] Given the perceived success of SMT, as well as the ideology that underpinned its operations, Norman sought to use SMT as the foundation for industrial interventions. Before the Macmillan Committee, a government commission tasked with identifying the causes of the British slump, he announced his goal of establishing "another company which will unite the City as a whole in showing a willingness ... to assist industry towards the goal of rationalisation."[117]

Through these interventions, the Bank was able to maintain a strict adherence to the tenets of economic orthodoxy. Already in February 1929, Norman had assured the Committee of Treasury that the Bank would only oversee rationalization projects that were "established on an economic and profitable basis."[118] By the following January, he assigned an internal committee, chaired by Sir Josiah Stamp, to identify specific projects to which the Bank should offer its financial assistance.[119] This measured, market-based intervention allowed the central bank to provide credit-granting facilities for certain firms, while neither committing to a regulatory policy nor violating the terms of the gold standard through direct spending. Because SMT operated as a separate legal entity, the Bank was also able to avoid overcommitting its own resources to the projects it created. Far less interventionist than direct takeovers, rationalization had emerged as an increasingly popular policy in orthodox circles. "Amalgamation is the blessed word of the day," proclaimed one leading Bank official.[120] Norman similarly wrote in his diary, "Rationalisation is in the air."[121]

Facilitating mergers of unproductive firms provided a convenient middle-ground solution that aligned with ongoing efforts by the Liberal Party to identify an industrial policy, while at the same time securing a place for the Bank at the center of future reforms. On April 15, 1930, the Bank established the Bankers' Industrial Development Corporation (BIDCo), a private syndicate designed to support the reorganization of larger firms. Initially funded by £6 million in paid-in capital, it organized funding schemes by coordinating loans between merchant banks and targeting specific sectors that were unable to

115 Henry Clay, "Note on Initiative in Rationalisation," April 14, 1930, BoE SMT2/60 and SMT5/11.

116 Grenfell to Morgan, February 6, 1931, MLM ARC 1195 Box 5, Folder 19.

117 "The Right Hon. Montagu Collet Norman, D.S.O.," March 26, 1930, in Macmillan Committee, *Minutes of Evidence, vol. 1*, 212.

118 Committee of Treasury, Minutes, February 20, 1929, BoE G8/58.

119 Committee of Treasury, Minutes, January 22, 1930, BoE G8/59.

120 Josiah Stamp, *Industrial and Railway Amalgamations* (London: London General Press, 1928), 5.

121 Montagu Norman, Diary, January 8, 1930, BoE ADM34/19.

raise capital on their own.[122] With the backing of the banking and industrial communities, the new entity worked alongside SMT on additional rationalization programs.[123] The framework underlying the operation fundamentally altered the central bank's relationship with domestic industry. As one financial journalist, Paul Einzig, then described, BIDCo was "[t]he most revolutionary breach with the traditions of the Bank."[124]

The contours of industrial reform thus lay decisively with Norman and his advisers. At one level, their projects aimed to address the controversial industry–finance divide. The so-called "Macmillan gap" denoted the growing disconnect between the lending practices of British banks and the particular needs of domestic industries, specifically small- and medium-sized firms.[125] It was before the Macmillan Committee where Keynes attributed the unemployment problem to monetary policy. While he acknowledged many of the ongoing efforts to improve industrial efficiency through rationalization, he questioned whether employment could drastically improve under existing circumstances without a fundamental change in ideas.[126] To him, the blame lay firmly in the financial sector:

> Industry has no orthodoxies; industry is changing all the time, industry is not governed by wise sayings and traditions, it is all the time experimenting; it is opportunist, it is always trying new things; but the extraordinary character of finance is the extent to which it is governed by orthodoxy, it is kept back by maxims and orthodoxies and things handed down and things that were established as being sound a long time ago.[127]

[122] Clay, *Lord Norman*, 329; Garside and Greaves, "The Bank of England," 72; Carnevali, *Europe's Advantage*, 24. An earlier proposal suggested providing the company with £4 million in capital; "Memorandum," February 10, 1930, BoE SMT2/53.

[123] "The Bankers' Industrial Development Company, Limited," April 15, 1930, BoE EID9/22; "Industry," June 1930, TNA BT56/37/1770.

[124] Einzig, *Montagu Norman*, 35.

[125] On the debate over the Macmillan gap, see Raymond Frost, "The Macmillan Gap, 1931–53," *Oxford Economic Papers* 6, no. 2 (1954), 181–182; Leslie Hannah, *The Rise of the Corporate Economy* (London: Methuen & Co., 1976), 75; W.A. Thomas, *The Finance of British Industry, 1918–1976* (London: Methuen & Co., 1978), 24–25; Michael H. Best and Jane Humphries, "The City and Industrial Decline," in *The Decline of the British Economy*, ed. Bernard Elbaum and William Lazonick (Oxford: Clarendon Press, 1986), 236–237; Sidney Pollard, *The Development of the British Economy, 1914–1990*, 4th ed. (London: Edward Arnold, 1992), 116–117; Dieter Ziegler, "The Origins of the 'Macmillan Gap': Comparing Britain and Germany in the Early Twentieth Century," in *Finance in the Age of the Corporate Economy: The Third Anglo-Japanese Business History Conference*, ed. P.L. Cottrell, A. Teichova, and T. Yuzawa (Aldershot: Ashgate, 1997), 188–200; Lucy Newton, "Government, the Banks and Industry in Inter-War Britain," in *Business and Politics in Europe, 1900–1970: Essays in Honour of Alice Teichova*, ed. Terry Gourvish (Cambridge: Cambridge University Press, 2003), 159–160; Greaves, *Industrial Reorganization*, 92; Peter Scott and Lucy Newton, "Jealous Monopolists? British Banks and Responses to the Macmillan Gap during the 1930s," *Enterprise & Society* 8, no. 4 (2007), 883–885.

[126] Committee on Finance and Industry, Notes on Discussion, February 28, 1930, TNA T200/4/3.

[127] Committee on Finance and Industry, Notes on Discussion, October 30, 1930, TNA T200/5/4.

Clay's employment allowed the Bank to provide an intellectual defense of the Bank View in response to Keynes' criticism. On July 23, he went before the Macmillan Committee to provide testimony on the nonmonetary causes of the trade depression.[128] A wide range of factors determined industrial performance. In addition to overproduction and corporate mismanagement, high wartime spending exacerbated the subsequent collapse in demand of many exports.[129] These arguments directly built on Clay's prior research on unemployment. He further suggested microeconomic reforms that would combat the depression by "by getting ... prices down, by reducing costs ... [or by] finding new outlets for the employment of labour."[130]

Clay's rationale before the Macmillan Committee justified the Bank's rationalization initiatives, now viewed as imperative to economic recovery. Both SMT and BIDCo worked in tandem to support varying projects. For instance, the once-dominant Wigan Coal & Iron Company under Chairman Lord Crawford had been suffering severe financial losses and paid no dividends since the late 1920s.[131] SMT acquired shares in the Lancashire Steel Corporation, which now owned Wigan's iron and steel business. Meanwhile, in coordination with a merchant bank, J. Henry Schroder & Co., which had extended a loan of £1.25 million, BIDCo oversaw Wigan's amalgamation with other major steel companies, such as Partington Steel & Iron Co., Pearson & Knowles Ltd., and Rylands Brothers Ltd.[132] Initially meant to be a temporary measure lasting five years, BIDCo was involved with these types of projects until its liquidation in 1945.[133]

Despite the Bank's interventions, Britain's export-dependent industries continued to stagnate due to global developments outside its control. "The chief influence accentuating the depression and apparently accounting for its recent aggravation," Clay argued, "is the collapse in the world prices of agricultural staples."[134] Rubber manufacturers, for instance, had produced an "excessive capacity" of goods and now faced the threat of bankruptcy due to a lack of

[128] "Professor Henry Clay," July 23, 1930, *Committee on Finance and Industry, vol.* 2, 266; Sayers, *The Bank of England, vol.* 1, 367.

[129] "Memorandum by Professor Henry Clay on Unemployment since the War," July 3, 1930, BLO Brand Papers 28/B/1 and NRS Lothian Papers GD40/17/135.

[130] "Professor Henry Clay," July 23, 1930, *Committee on Finance and Industry, vol.* 2, 256. At a meeting of the Birmingham Chamber of Commerce, Clay further described the burden that often fell upon British industry to search for new export markets and identify other cost-cutting measures; "Professor Henry Clay: Britain's Need for New Product, New Methods, New Markets," *The Scotsman (Edinburgh)* 27266, October 17, 1930, 12.

[131] Cannadine, *The Decline and Fall of the British Aristocracy*, 124.

[132] "Steel Merger," January 24, 1930, BoE SMT2/132; J. Henry Schröder & Co. to the Directors of Pearson & Knowles Ltd. and Wigan Coal & Iron Co., February 27, 1930, BoE SMT2/132.

[133] Michael Collins, *Banks and Industrial Finance in Britain, 1800–1939* (Cambridge: Cambridge University Press, 1995), 79.

[134] Quoted in International Chamber of Commerce, "Summary of Business Conditions in the United Kingdom," May 2, 1930, BoE SMT5/12.

global demand.[135] In 1928, a parliamentary act established the Agricultural Mortgage Corporation, with Niemeyer as a board member.[136] Receiving £200,000 in initial capital from the Bank, the corporation offered long-term loans to farmers and other rural businesses.

Yet perhaps no other trend caused more anxiety at the Bank than the one facing the cotton industry. Throughout the 1920s, the overall decline in world trade and the British share of that trade had increased the number of unproductive cotton-textile manufacturers.[137] Already in 1921, the industry had lost a quarter of its pre-1914 market share.[138] Foreign import duties, such as those in India, further jeopardized British exports, particularly from manufacturers in the industrial towns of Blackburn and Oldham.[139] As Clay viewed, there was "an urgent need ... to attempt a re-organisation of the industry as a whole."[140]

The region most in need of reform was Lancashire, where manufacturers had been one of the world's leading sources of cotton.[141] Under the Bank's direction, BIDCo planned to reorganize the cotton-spinning aspects of production through

[135] Clay to C.P. Mahon, September 30, 1931, BoE SMT5/3.

[136] "The Agricultural Mortgage Corporation, Ltd.," *The Times* 45507, May 8, 1930, 21; "Sir Otto E. Niemeyer, G.B.E., K.C.B.," June 4, 1930, in Macmillan Committee, *Minutes of Evidence, vol.* 2, 102; Clay, *Lord Norman*, 351; Capie, *The Bank of England*, 323.

[137] Greaves, *Industrial Reorganization*, 181–184.

[138] Henry Clay, "Unemployment: B.B.C. Talk, 5th January 1931," BoE SMT2/60.

[139] "The British Cotton Industry," January 14, 1931, BoE SMT5/16; Henry Clay, "Banking & Industry," June 15, 1934, BoE ADM22/1.

[140] Henry Clay, "The Cotton Industry," September 20, 1930, BoE BID1/26.

[141] On the interwar Lancashire cotton industry, see M.W. Kirby, "The Lancashire Cotton Industry in the Inter-War Years: A Study in Organizational Change," *Business History* 16, no. 2 (1974): 145–159; Lars G. Sandberg, *Lancashire in Decline: A Study in Entrepreneurship, Technology, and International Trade* (Columbus: The Ohio State University Press, 1974), 121–130, 175–181; William Lazonick, "Industrial Organization and Technological Change: The Decline of the British Cotton Industry," *Business History Review* 57, no. 2 (1983): 195–236; Marguerite Dupree, "Fighting against Fate: The Cotton Industry and the Government during the 1930s," *Textile History* 21, no. 1 (1990): 101–117; John Singleton, *Lancashire on the Scrapheap: The Cotton Industry, 1945–1970* (Oxford: Oxford University Press, 1991), 11–20; Marguerite Dupree, "Foreign Competition and the Interwar Period," in *The Lancashire Cotton Industry: A History since 1700*, ed. Mary B. Rose (Preston: Lancashire County Books, 1996): 265–295; Geoffrey Timmins, *Made in Lancashire: A History of Regional Industrialisation* (Manchester and New York: Manchester University Press, 1998), 273–277, 280–282; Stephen Broadberry and Andrew Marrison, "External Economies of Scale in the Lancashire Cotton Industry, 1900–1950," *Economic History Review* 55, no. 1 (2002): 51–77; Julian I. Greaves, "Competition, Collusion, and Confusion: The State and the Reorganization of the British Cotton Industry, 1931–1939," *Enterprise & Society* 3, no. 1 (2002): 48–79; Sven Beckert, *Empire of Cotton: A Global History* (New York: Alfred A. Knopf, 2014), 381–383, 406–408; David Higgins and Steve Toms, "Financial Distress, Corporate Borrowing, and Industrial Decline: The Lancashire Cotton Spinning Industry, 1918–38," in *British Cotton Textiles: Maturity and Decline*, ed. David Higgins and Steven Toms (London and New York: Routledge, 2017): 105–130.

the LCC, established in January 1929.[142] The Bank extended cash advancements, originally totaling £300,000, to those that joined LCC, while also underwriting £2 million in debentures.[143] Specifically, the volume of advances was determined on a per-spindle basis, originally set at 1s., but later increased to 1s. 6d. and then again to 2s.[144] Such an intervention was essential for making Lancashire cotton manufacturers more profitable amidst heightened foreign competition.[145] Tasked with the amalgamation of six million spindles, LCC eventually acquired nearly ten million spindles at more than 100 firms.[146]

Clay viewed the difficulties facing Lancashire as more than a temporary dislocation that could be resolved through a simple credit stimulus. Instead, structural problems plagued many of the export-dependent industries: "We are still dependent to a large extent on export markets," he argued, "[and] our chief overseas customers are the great agricultural countries, who are all depressed."[147] The issues endemic to the Lancashire cotton industry also threatened to undermine the financial sector, which had extended loans to the now-failing businesses.[148] In response, contemporaries devised various proposals for addressing the concerns of domestic firms. A system of imperial preference, in which the countries of the British Empire agreed to a reduction in bilateral tariffs, might have assisted some British exporters. Supporting this reform, Clay argued that "it is clear that India offers openings mainly for those British manufacturing industries that are least affected by unemployment, while the depressed industries of cotton and iron and steel must look elsewhere for relief from the unemployment which Indian developments have caused."[149]

Global trade conditions appeared to limit the efficacy of rationalization at home. For one, Japan's competitive currency devaluations after 1931 allowed

[142] Catterns to Sir Kenneth D. Stewart [Chairman, Lancashire Cotton Corporation], January 29, 1929, BoE SMT2/240; Committee of Treasury, Minutes, January 30, 1929, BoE G8/58; Clay, *Lord Norman*, 336; Steven Toms, *Financing Cotton: British Industrial Growth and Decline, 1780–2000* (Woodbridge: The Boydell Press, 2020), 221–232.

[143] Committee of Treasury, Minutes, January 30, 1929, BoE G8/58; Sayers, *The Bank of England, vol. 1*, 320.

[144] Committee of Treasury, Minutes, May 7, 1930, BoE G8/59; Committee of Treasury, Minutes, September 3, 1930, BoE G8/59.

[145] Henry Clay, "Note on the Lancashire Cotton Industry," March 28, 1930, BoE BID1/26.

[146] Henry Clay, "Memorandum: The Financial Requirements of the Lancashire Cotton Corporation," July 30, 1930, BoE SMT5/26; Lancashire Cotton Corporation, "Memorandum Reporting Progress and Financial Requirements," August 22, 1930, BoE SMT2/243; J.I. Greaves, "'Visible Hands' and the Rationalization of the British Cotton Industry, 1925–1932," *Textile History* 31, no. 1 (2000), 106.

[147] Henry Clay, "The Recent Movement of Prices: Address to be Given to the Birmingham Chamber of Commerce on Thursday, 16th October, 1930," BoE SMT2/60.

[148] Sayers, *The Bank of England, vol. 1*, 314; Cerretano, "The Treasury," 81.

[149] Henry Clay, "Note on Sir George Schuster's Memorandum," July 12, 1934, BoE ADM22/1.

it to "undercut any European country by from 20 to 60 per cent."[150] Clay contended that the British cotton producers needed to be rationalized and concentrated in "two or three large merchanting units to operate on the scale of the three largest Japanese exporting houses."[151] Rationalization alone meant little if firms were unable "to find an increasing outlet abroad for its product."[152] There were additional strains due to developments in US and European markets. Competition with Germany, coupled with the growing dominance of security markets in the United States, appeared to undermine British industry and its ability to obtain credit. Contemporaries believed that the devaluation of currencies in both Belgium and France had given them an unfair advantage over the relatively more expensive British goods. In response to these trends, Clay wrote to the German economist, Moritz Julius Bonn, about the idea of Britain joining the recently formed Austro-German Customs Union.[153]

As currency wars and competitive devaluations revealed the risks associated with economic globalization, old ideas for industrial reform began to reemerge. For instance, the Empire Economic Union campaigned for a program of imperial protection to address industrial stagnation.[154] The proposal found support among government officials and civil servants, including Leo Amery, Lord Beaverbrook, and Sir Robert Horne. In July 1931, several meetings with the Federation of British Industries and Manchester-based industrialists revealed a similarly strong interest in greater trade coordination with the empire.[155] However, Clay warned of the potential inflationary consequences of these more radical recommendations. He suggested that the Bank instead needed to focus its efforts on existing rationalization projects and not to overextend its involvement.[156]

Less concerned with improving industrial performance as an end in itself, Clay believed that such interventions aligned with the City's prevailing interests. Since the late nineteenth century, the Big Five banks, with Midland and Barclays as the largest among them, had extended loans to local Lancashire banks and companies.[157] Although they aimed to recuperate their illiquid investments, the leading commercial banks hesitated to support the Bank's interventions. Additional

150 Clay to Siepmann, February 1, 1934, BoE ADM22/1.

151 Henry Clay, "Report on the Position of the English Cotton Industry," October 20, 1931, BoE SMT5/18.

152 Clay to Stamp, October 23, 1933, BoE ADM22/27.

153 Clay to Bonn, July 17, 1931, BoE SMT5/3.

154 Boyce, *British Capitalism*, 230–231; Williamson, *National Crisis and National Government*, 123; W.R. Garside, "Party Politics, Political Economy and British Protectionism, 1919–1932," *History* 83, no. 269 (1998), 54.

155 "Minutes of the Meeting of the Empire Currency Committee Held at the Offices of the Federation of British Industries," July 8, 1931, MRC FBI F/3/E1/14/1; "Memorandum of Discussion on the Cotton Report at Manchester," July 15, 1931, BoE SMT5/17.

156 Clay to Lubbock, September 30, 1931, BoE SMT5/3.

157 Bamberg, "The Rationalization of the British Cotton Industry," 85.

lending would have certainly reduced the level of liquidity reported on their balance sheets.[158] Instead, their goal "was simply a desire to get a portion of the capital invested out of the Cotton Industry."[159] Without support from the private banks, Governor Norman endeavored to implement schemes that were less costly for the Bank. He advocated a merger of Lancashire banks that had been overly invested in the cotton industry, a project that would not directly expose the central bank to an area's localized issues.[160] Far from a program of economic planning, the Bank's agenda centered on a self-regulating, rationalized Lancashire industry that received loans only when they could be repaid.

In other instances, a comprehensive industrial policy appeared to run counter to the City's existing goals. Although the Bank may have wished to take into account the goals of the financial sector in its reforms, it continually maintained a strained relationship with the clearing banks. A representative from District Bank acknowledged the value of some industrial support but still felt that the Bank failed to recognize the rights of creditors who had owned large shares of cotton companies.[161] Because the private banks were themselves unwilling to intervene, the Bank found it had to rely on its own resources for its new initiatives.

It may still be difficult to assess a counterfactual scenario in which rationalization had not taken place. Many contemporaries, such as Edwin Cannan, questioned the value of mergers, acquisitions, and wage reductions in helping long-term unemployment.[162] Nevertheless, the Bank's numerous subsidies embodied the ways in which economic advice could alter the structure of interwar governance. Both the centrality of the Bank to the domestic financial system and the unwillingness of other institutions (the clearing banks, the national government, or international organizations) to intervene determined the scope of industrial policy. Even if it absorbed the majority of LCC's losses in its first two years, the Bank referred to its amalgamation plans as "[t]he most revolutionary scheme undertaken."[163] By 1934, the Bank was able to claim that both SMT and BIDCo "have continued to show ample justification for their formation."[164]

[158] Stephen Broadberry, *Market Services and the Productivity Race, 1850–2000: British Performance in International Perspective* (Cambridge: Cambridge University Press, 2006), 267.

[159] Henry Clay, "Rationalisation: The Cotton Trade," *Lloyds Bank Limited Monthly Review* 2, no. 13 (1931), 89.

[160] Geoffrey Jones, "Competition and Competitiveness in British Banking, 1918–71," in *Competitiveness and the State: Government and Business in Twentieth-Century Britain*, ed. Geoffrey Jones and Maurice Kirby (Manchester and New York: Manchester University Press, 1991), 122.

[161] N. Shepherd to Clay, March 7, 1931, BoE SMT5/1.

[162] Edwin Cannan, "The Post-War Unemployment Problem," *The Economic Journal* 40, no. 157 (1930), 50; Martin Daunton, "Britain and Globalisation since 1850: II. The Rise of Insular Capitalism, 1914–1939," *Transactions of the Royal Historical Society* 17 (2007), 27.

[163] Economics & Statistics Section, "The Bank of England and Industry: An Account of Securities Management Trust, Ltd. (S.M.T.) and Bankers' Industrial Development Company, Ltd. (B.I.D.Co.)," March 1935, BoE EID9/22.

[164] "The Bank and Industry, Report No. 2," August 28, 1934, BoE G14/55.

These circumstances led the Bank to consider reforms in other sectors. As with producers in the cotton industry, those in the shipbuilding and manufacturing industry reported having excess capacity and suffered from high rates of unemployment. In early 1930, the Committee of Treasury recommended the closure of "obsolete and uneconomic shipbuilding yards" and the refinancing of more profitable ones through additional loans.[165] Its own deflationary monetary policies might have hampered recovery in sectors that relied heavily on debt financing.[166] Particularly vital, then, was the establishment of the National Shipbuilders Securities, which addressed overproduction in the shipbuilding industry by purchasing producers and closing unproductive ones.[167] To oversee these projects, the Bank hired Charles Bruce-Gardner, an English industrialist with experience as the chairman of the British Iron and Steel Federation, as another adviser.[168] Through BIDCo, the Bank arranged a debenture issue of £2 million in 1930 and an additional £1 million the following year.[169]

Technical analysis lay at the heart of these industrial projects. In October 1931, Clay wrote a report on the long-term decline of the cotton industry. He detailed the specific practices that needed to be undertaken by the British authorities for assisting domestic industry: lowering costs by reducing the amount of equipment, using existing equipment as collateral for future loans, concentrating firms into more productive units to achieve economies of scale. "Before the war," he remarked, "the steady growth of the English industry, which dominated all the export markets, was supported by the steady growth in the world's consumption of cotton manufactures, and permitted a simultaneous, if smaller, growth of other countries' industries. This dominating position has been lost."[170] Commercial overexpansion to meet wartime demands had caused prices to decline in the years thereafter.[171] By building on the technical findings of government commissions, the report effectively cemented the Bank's monopoly over industrial affairs.

Clay and other experts continually aimed to mobilize support for industrial intervention. One of the Bank's in-house statisticians, James Selwyn, showed

[165] Committee of Treasury, Minutes, January 15, 1930, BoE G8/59.

[166] Martin Daunton, *Wealth and Welfare: An Economic and Social History of Britain, 1851–1951* (Oxford: Oxford University Press, 2007), 179.

[167] "Conversation between the Governor and Sir Andrew Duncan," February 6, 1930, BoE SMT2/132; Sayers, *The Bank of England, vol. 1*, 321; Tolliday, *Business, Banking, and Politics*, 238–239; Cain and Hopkins, *British Imperialism*, 449.

[168] Clay, *Lord Norman*, 320–321, 327; Sayers, *The Bank of England, vol. 1*, 325; Tolliday, *Business, Banking, and Politics*, 200–210; Cairncross, "The Bank of England and the British Economy," 68; Greaves, *Industrial Reorganization*, 55.

[169] Committee of Treasury, Minutes, September 17, 1930, BoE G8/59; Committee of Treasury, Minutes, January 7, 1931, BoE G8/59; Garside and Greaves, "The Bank of England," 72; Greaves, *Industrial Reorganization*, 59.

[170] Henry Clay, "Report on the Position of the English Cotton Industry," October 20, 1931, BoE SMT5/18.

[171] Henry Clay, "Report on the Position of the English Cotton Industry," October 20, 1931, BoE SMT5/18.

how smaller firms were unable to issue shares due to the relatively higher costs of equity financing.[172] Even companies that were able to raise funds on the London Stock Exchange found themselves unable to persuade investors to buy their securities if they reported significant losses.[173] The Bank, seeking to provide capital when ordinary funding sources appeared unavailable, established the Industrial Credit Bank in March 1934. Later renamed Credit for Industry, the subsidiary provided capital for firms that were too small to justify a public issue.[174] Companies financed by Credit for Industry had to demonstrate their profitability for at least three years, and small businesses were usually only able to procure a loan of no more than £50,000.

Subsidiaries offered the Bank a financial stake in the revival of domestic industry without exposing its own assets to risk. Credit for Industry was a subsidiary of United Dominions Trust (UDT), a company that offered hire-purchase services. In January 1930, the Bank had purchased £250,000 in ordinary shares in UDT.[175] In alignment with the Bank's strategy, J. Gibson Garvie, the managing director of UDT, promised to extend funding "to any applicant in a position to justify his application for finance," which culminated in nearly £300,000 being granted to around forty businesses.[176] The last major industrial engagement of the interwar years was the Special Areas Reconstruction Association. Established in June 1936, the initiative offered to extend £1 million in short-term loans to depressed regions, including many parts of northern England and South Wales.[177] It was able to provide loans of up to £10,000 for firms when advances from local banks proved insufficient. Debt financing, rather than equity financing, offered companies another means to acquire much-needed capital.

EXPERTS AND INDUSTRIAL POLICY

When Clay was formally appointed as an Adviser to the Governors in 1933, he had already defined the Bank's industrial policy. He officially succeeded

[172] Scott and Newton, "Jealous Monopolists?," 896.

[173] Michie, *The London Stock Exchange*, 260.

[174] "Minutes of Meetings of Directors of United Dominions Trust Limited," May 8, 1934, LGA S/10/B/2; Clay, *Lord Norman*, 352; Heim, "Limits to Intervention," 547; Newton, "British Retail Banking," 192.

[175] Committee of Treasury, Minutes, November 13, 1929, BoE G8/58; Sue Bowden and Michael Collins, "The Bank of England, Industrial Regeneration, and Hire Purchase between the Wars," *The Economic History Review* 45, no. 1 (1992), 126; Newton, "British Retail Banking," 193.

[176] J. Gibson Garvie [Managing Director, United Dominions Trust] to Norman, March 13, 1934, BoE SMT2/7 and LGA S/10/B/2; "Credit for Industry, Ltd.," 1934, BoE SMT2/7.

[177] Sayers, *The Bank of England, vol. 2*, 548; Carol E. Heim, "Industrial Organization and Regional Development in Interwar Britain," *The Journal of Economic History* 43, no. 4 (1983), 937–941; Tolliday, *Business, Banking, and Politics*, 151–152; Garside, *British Unemployment*, 259; Scott and Newton, "Jealous Monopolists?," 902; Newton, "British Retail Banking," 192–193.

Sprague as Norman's chief adviser, earning a salary of £4,000 per year.[178] While expert arguments provided an initial justification, their continued intervention cemented the role of the central bank in industrial affairs.

Through his advisory work, Clay effectively made rationalization a policy that could be studied and improved. In one memorandum, he argued that "in order to lift industry out of depression, something must be done to stimulate the use of the existing large supplies of credit. Central Banks, beyond keeping it cheap, cannot help, because they have no direct influence on the use or direction of credit."[179] Identifying a clear industrial policy was also necessary due to "a great deal of redundant machinery in the industry which is never likely to be employed."[180] Many of the Bank's existing initiatives – Credit for Industry, National Shipbuilders Securities, LCC, and UDT – targeted particular industries, providing both technical knowledge and financial support for small- and medium-sized firms. Meanwhile, SMT and BIDCo oversaw broader changes to the export-dependent sectors. By extending loans or closing unproductive firms, these initiatives would not only help to resolve industrial stagnation but also ensure that the Bank remained at the center of future reforms.

Even so, Clay's findings were, at times, less than practical. One example was his proposal to move workers from more densely populated areas to sparsely populated cities: "An effort should be made to organise Manchester, Leeds, Cardiff, Newcastle, and Glasgow as metropolitan areas offering similar attractions to the London area."[181] Investment in public works, housing, and infrastructure (further supported by the Bank's low interest rates) might encourage migration to areas where "highly specialised communities like weaving villages in N.E. Lancashire, coal-mining villages in Glamorgan, or ship-building centres on the N.E. Coast and the Clyde" dominated, thereby helping to "relieve congestion in the metropolitan area."[182] In the mid- to late 1930s, parliamentary efforts and royal commissions provided additional aid for economic development in areas with high unemployment.[183] Nevertheless, the Bank, itself having little role in these political initiatives, had no practical means of encouraging mass migration, and Clay's technical recommendations on such matters went largely unnoticed.

[178] Committee of Treasury, Minutes, May 24, 1933, BoE G8/61; Montagu Norman, Diary, May 29, 1933, BoE ADM34/22; Committee of Treasury, Minutes, May 31, 1933, BoE G8/61; "Informal Court Records," May 31, 1933, BoE G14/55; "Memorandum," June 1, 1933, BoE ADM33/13; "Named Bank Adviser: Henry Clay Succeeds Prof. Sprague at the Bank of England," *The New York Times* LXXXII, 27541, June 20, 1933, 27; "New Adviser to Bank," *The Daily Telegraph* 24362, June 20, 1933, 13; "Prof. Henry Clay: New Economic Adviser to the Bank," *The Manchester Guardian (Manchester)* 27076, June 20, 1933, 11.

[179] Henry Clay, "Credit Policy and Price Levels," June 30, 1933, BoE ADM22/1.

[180] Clay to Stamp, October 23, 1933, BoE ADM22/27.

[181] Henry Clay, "The Government & Unemployment," January 3, 1935, BoE SMT2/61.

[182] Henry Clay, "The Government & Unemployment," January 3, 1935, BoE SMT2/61.

[183] Sloman, *The Liberal Party and the Economy*, 129.

In other instances, institutions appeared reluctant to overcommit their own resources to projects with no clear path toward success. Throughout the 1920s, the Bank had opposed providing its own capital in industries that were already on the verge of bankruptcy.[184] Norman acknowledged the inherent risk associated with industrial intervention, leading him to proclaim "just as we must now go into Industry so we must be sure that we get out of it!"[185] Deputy Governor Ernest Harvey similarly maintained that "it is no part of the Central Bank's duty to keep a permanent interest in industry, and we should like to be out of it."[186] In many respects, these views demonstrated the persistence of the Old Guard's aversion to intervention. It would have been difficult to enforce mergers or impose new business models on private firms that did not want to be regulated, either by a central bank or the national government. The central bank's own institutional design – a private entity beholden to its shareholders – further limited its ability to enact widespread public-sector reform.

Yet the Bank, however much it rejected academic theory and state control, began to accept the need for a middle-way intervention based on prevailing advice. Experts argued that any attempt to change or overturn the existing politico-economic system would incur substantial pushback and could instigate "a profound distrust among the traditionally independent leaders of industry of all schemes of re-organisation."[187] A more active industrial policy would need to have the blessings of both industrialists and politicians. In June 1934, Norman instructed Clay to give evidence on behalf of the Bank to the Trade and Industry Committee in the House of Commons.[188] There, several MPs had complained of the apathy from both the commercial banks and the central bank toward the needs of industry.[189] In response to these criticisms, the Bank was willing to enforce other types of indirect regulation. There were ensuing discussions surrounding the appointment of another economic adviser to assist with industrial reform in Scotland, a committee to study "the defence of the Banking System against ill-informed attacks," and another committee to organize additional financial support to industry.[190] Recognizing the dire impact of industrial stagnation on the international financial system, Stamp therefore acknowledged the importance of bringing nonquantifiable "technical knowledge" to the Bank:

184 Heim, "Limits to Intervention," 546; Tolliday, *Business, Banking, and Politics*, 189–197; Cain and Hopkins, *British Imperialism*, 451.

185 Quoted in Kynaston, *The City of London, vol.* 3, 192.

186 "The Right Hon. Ernest Musgrave Harvey, K.B.E.," December 14, 1929, in Macmillan Committee, *Minutes of Evidence, vol.* 1, 55.

187 Economics & Statistics Section, "The Bank of England and Industry: An Account of Securities Management Trust, Ltd. (S.M.T.) and Bankers' Industrial Development Company, Ltd. (B.I.D.Co.)," March 1935, BoE EID9/22.

188 Committee of Treasury, Minutes, June 13, 1934, BoE G8/62.

189 Committee of Treasury, Minutes, June 20, 1934, BoE G8/62.

190 Committee of Treasury, Minutes, July 4, 1934, BoE G8/62.

There is not a plentiful supply of people; they are scarce; but ... technical knowledge is a thing which is capable of being passed on to intelligent men. The kind of experience required in consolidating an industry, to know which factories should be shut, and the evidence upon which they could be shut, is a thing which ... can be passed from industry to industry, and given men of the requisite knowledge and intelligence, that experience can be cumulative, that type of man can be gradually evolved. Just as the old management required certain qualities, force of character, so the new management which is rather different, can also be educated for it.[191]

The Bank's advisers, Clay among them, were able to maintain influence policy due to the support they received from high-ranking officials. Although ambivalent toward economics and statistics, the Old Guard acknowledged the dearth of technical knowledge on industrial affairs, an area in which few directors specialized. Norman thus claimed that the Bank's directors "should be experts, ... and there should be at least one to deal with Industrial questions."[192]

Apprehensions over the country's weakening industrial capacity prompted an interest in the study of economics throughout the British government. In line with a recommendation published in *Britain's Industrial Future*, Prime Minister MacDonald proposed the creation of an economic general staff in December 1929.[193] Persuaded by Keynes' argument that such a committee needed to comprise "[p]rofessional economists" who had "a language and a method of their own," the government subsequently established the Economic Advisory Council (EAC) in January 1930.[194] The group collected information on economic trends to make general recommendations on public policy. One of its subcommittees focused on the drivers of unemployment by procuring evidence from an array of experts, including Clay, who provided a broad overview of the Bank's industrial interventions in the cotton, woolen, and textile industries.[195] Although later mired in internal disputes and disagreements, the EAC bridged the gap between politicians ("men in authority") and economists ("[those] with intimate knowledge").[196]

Due to his participation on government commissions and advisory groups, Clay earned a reputation as a leading economist. With his early contributions to academia, he had been invited to join the London School of Economics as the Chair of Political Economy in 1929 and to work on the government's

[191] "Sir Josiah Stamp, G.B.E.," April 10, 1930, in Macmillan Committee, *Minutes of Evidence, vol. 1*, 271.

[192] "Notes on the Governor's Evidence," January 4, 1932, BoE G15/204.

[193] Liberal Industrial Inquiry, *Britain's Industrial Future*, 116–120; Skidelsky, *Politicians and the Slump*, 135; Boyce, *British Capitalism*, 229; Garside, *British Unemployment*, 364; Williamson, *National Crisis and National Government*, 66; Riddell, *Labour in Crisis*, 84.

[194] Quoted in Clarke, *The Keynesian Revolution*, 120; Howson, *Lionel Robbins*, 179.

[195] A.F. Hemming [Secretary, Economic Advisory Council] to Clay, October 8, 1931, BoE SMT5/5; Clay to A.F. Hemming, January 13, 1932, BoE SMT5/5.

[196] MacDonald to Peacock, April 15, 1931, BoE G1/455.

Committee on Trade and Employment in 1932.[197] He accepted neither post, however, due to the workload associated with a full-time position at the Bank. Subsequent advisory responsibilities with SMT helped him earn additional recognition abroad. In 1935, the League of Nations recommended him for the new post of Director of the Economic Relations Section, an offer that he also declined.[198]

Still, the growing prominence of economic experts in government was not lost on contemporaries. Among them, British bankers and officials debated the amount of trust that they could have placed in the dismal science. In early 1932, the London Chamber of Commerce questioned the assumptions made in statistical models and asserted that economists needed to consider the rigidity of wages as they sought to define a post-gold standard monetary policy.[199] Others were more concerned with the political implications, with Chancellor Snowden and the Treasury believing that the EAC had accumulated far too much influence over the prime minister.[200] These views indicated the general anxieties surrounding the value of economics to confront the ongoing slump. As one of the members of the EAC, Sir Frederick Leith-Ross, wrote, "I do not think that any of the reports produced gave a clear and unqualified guidance to Ministers in regard to economic policy."[201]

Yet the desire to rely on expert opinion on technical matters led to the institutionalization of economics within the state apparatus. The Labour government, increasingly interested in tailoring technical expertise to its needs, established even more specialized advisory boards. Chaired by Keynes, the Committee of Economists aimed to study even more academic theories to resolve Britain's industrial problems. In this forum, several economists, including Henderson, Pigou, and Stamp, debated the causes and consequences of the depression.[202] To outsiders, the dependence of the government on such groups had become well known. As *The Economist* declared, the meeting was an "association of economists of high standing with the Government and the Bank ... [which] may be of immense practical importance in guiding economic policy."[203]

Through their policy interventions, experts became integral to the structure of interwar economic governance. At the Bank, Clay described how Governor Norman effectively "collected a small staff of experts through whom he could

[197] Beveridge to Clay, June 11, 1929, NCO Clay Papers 76/8/11; Clay to MacDonald, October 29, 1932, BoE SMT5/9.

[198] Committee of Treasury, Minutes, March 20, 1935, BoE G8/62.

[199] "Memorandum on Currency: A Report of the Committee Appointed by the London Chamber of Commerce," January 5, 1932, CAC Chartwell Papers 2/186.

[200] Skidelsky, *Politicians and the Slump*, 206.

[201] Leith-Ross, *Money Talks*, 147.

[202] Howson and Winch, *The Economic Advisory Council*, 46–58, 359; Moggridge, *Maynard Keynes*, 497; Skidelsky, *John Maynard Keynes*, *vol. 2*, 364.

[203] "Economists at the Bank," *The Economist* 110, 4510, February 1, 1930, 228.

assist in the necessary task of liquidating frozen assets, arranging mergers and financing new enterprises in some of the depressed export industries."[204] Industrial intervention, once virtually uncharted territory for the central bank, emerged as an area of pressing concern to many officials. Before the Macmillan Committee, Norman opined that "the process of rationalisation ... has been defined in many varying ways, but ... I am a strong adherent, and it is towards the goal of rationalisation ... that I hope the Bank of England will contribute as much as it can over the times to come."[205] Although Clay had not been elected to a highly coveted directorship position due to opposition from other directors, he was nevertheless able to offer practical applications behind the scenes.

In 1944, Clay returned to academia as Warden of Nuffield College, Oxford. He continued to offer advice on matters of unemployment and rationalization while serving as deputy chairman (1938–1940), chairman (1940–1949), and president (1949–1952) of the National Institute of Economic and Social Research. With support from the University of Manchester, where Clay had once been employed, the institute pioneered projects on the collection of wartime statistics. It led several projects of major interest to contemporary economists, conducting empirical research on unemployment and wages. The professionalization of the economic discipline, coupled with the unresolved problems from the First World War, created the institutional circumstances for expert-led governance to flourish. For his contributions, Clay was knighted in 1946 and worked as an economic adviser at Unilever (1949–1954). He believed that the study of economics, however flawed, could redefine the nation's industrial policy. As the *Daily Telegraph* reported when he joined the Bank, Clay was "an academic idealist with a severely practical mind."[206]

[204] Henry Clay, "Lord Norman: An Appreciation," March 1950, IAS Director's Office Box 22.

[205] "The Right Hon. Montagu Collet Norman, D.S.O.," March 26, 1930, in Macmillan Committee, *Minutes of Evidence, vol. 1*, 211.

[206] "An Economist at the Bank," *The Daily Telegraph* 23309, January 28, 1930, 12.

6

The Niemeyer Missions

> You can always balance a Budget if you have the guts.[1]
>
> —Otto Niemeyer, 1930

Otto Ernst Niemeyer was a name synonymous with orthodoxy (Figure 6.1). Born in London, he studied at St Paul's School and obtained first-class honours in classics (*literae humaniores*) from Balliol College, Oxford. When in 1906, John Maynard Keynes placed second on the civil service exam and accepted a post in the India Office, Niemeyer placed first and thus received the more coveted position: a second-class clerkship at the Treasury.[2] As Controller of Finance at the Treasury from 1922 to 1927, he joined a cohort of financial experts, including Ralph Hawtrey and Frederick Leith-Ross, who advocated fiscal restraint, free trade, and a return to the gold standard. The views espoused by the "Treasury knights" determined the economic priorities of the British government for much of the interwar years.

In the 1930s, Niemeyer undertook a series of overseas advisory missions, during which he consulted foreign bankers, politicians, and economists; conducted interviews on the local economy; relayed information to London; and proposed plans for financial reform, often by way of a new central bank. Joining the Bank as one of its advisers in 1927, he defended the interests of the City in

[1] Niemeyer to Leslie Melville, November 13, 1930, BoE OV9/289.

[2] "The Civil Service Competition of 1906," November 7, 1906, KCC Keynes Papers IA/1; Stanley Leathes [Civil Service Commission] to Niemeyer, October 2, 1906, TNA CSC11/204; Clarke, *The Keynesian Revolution*, 29; Susan Howson, "Niemeyer, Sir Otto Ernst (1883–1971)," September 23, 2004, ODNB; G.C. Peden, "Introduction," in *Keynes and His Critics: Treasury Responses to the Keynesian Revolution, 1925–1946* (Oxford: Oxford University Press, 2004), 13.

FIGURE 6.1 Sir Otto Niemeyer, December 1962
Source: Bank of England Archive, PN-005561.

his negotiations with foreign governments.[3] In the countries he visited, he also sought to gain the approval of influential economists, such as Raúl Prebisch in Argentina, Eugênio Gudin in Brazil, Douglas Copland in Australia, and Albert Tocker in New Zealand. These connections helped legitimize Niemeyer's recommendations, which were adjusted to each country's particular needs.

Traditional interpretations of the Niemeyer missions have primarily focused on the efforts of foreign governments to obtain loans in exchange for the imposition of stringent measures, while case studies of each country have led historians to place the missions along a success–failure distinction.[4]

[3] For instance, even after his resignation as Finance Minister, Alberto Hueyo continued to correspond with Niemeyer; Hueyo to Niemeyer, December 15, 1933, BoE OV102/4.

[4] Marcelo de Paiva Abreu, "A missão Niemeyer," *Revista de Administração de Empresas* 14, no. 4 (1974), 21; Bernard Attard, "The Bank of England and the Origins of the Niemeyer Mission, 1921–30," *Australian Economic Review* 32, no. 1 (1992), 82; William Coleman, Selwyn Cornish, and Alf Hagger, *Giblin's Platoon: The Trials and Triumph of the Economist in Australian Public Life* (Canberra: ANU E Press, 2006), 112–114; Millmow, *The Power of Economic Ideas*, 66–67; André Villela, "Las funciones de banca central antes del banco central: el caso del Banco de Brasil," in *Orígenes de la globalización bancaria: experiencias de España y América Latina*, ed. Daniel Díaz Fuentes, Andrés Hoyo Aparicio, and Carlos Marichal

Efforts to institutionalize economic orthodoxy via balanced budgets and a return to the gold standard were also linked to the work of an economics professor at Princeton University, Edwin Kemmerer.[5] At the same time, the Niemeyer missions should be understood beyond standard analyses of "money doctoring" or dollar diplomacy because they instigated fundamental changes to the interwar system of economic governance.[6] As the exigencies of war exacerbated concerns over globalization and cross-border linkages, financial experts were able to establish their authority by using highly technical language and tailoring their messages for various foreign governments. Niemeyer aimed to promote uniformity throughout disparate national banking systems – Argentina, Brazil, and New Zealand with no central bank,

(Santander: Genueve Ediciones, El Colegio de México, 2017), 442; John Singleton, "Central Banks in the British Dominions in the Interwar Period," in *The Spread of the Modern Central Bank and Global Cooperation, 1919–1939*, ed. Barry Eichengreen and Andreas Kakridis (Cambridge: Cambridge: University Press, 2023), 363.

5 Robert N. Seidel, "American Reformers Abroad: The Kemmerer Missions in South America, 1923–1931," *The Journal of Economic History* 32, no. 2 (1972): 520–545; Banco Central de Reserva del Perú, *La Misión Kemmerer en el Perú: informes y propuestas, Tomo 1* (Lima: Banco Central de Reserva del Perú, 1997), 29–45; Paul W. Drake, *The Money Doctor in the Andes: The Kemmerer Missions, 1923–1933* (Durham and London: Duke University Press, 1989); Rebeca Gomez Betancourt, "Edwin Walter Kemmerer: Money Theorist and Money Doctor" (PhD diss., Université Paris 1 Panthéon-Sorbonne, 2008), 95–102; Eric Helleiner, "Central Bankers as Good Neighbours: US Money Doctors in Latin America During the 1940s," *Financial History Review* 16, no. 1 (2009): 5–25; Marcelo de Paiva Abreu and Pedro Carvalho Loureiro de Souza, "'Palatable Foreign Control': British Money Doctors and Central Banking in South America, 1924–1935," *Pontifícia Universidade Católica do Rio de Janeiro, Texto para discussão*, no. 597 (2011), 12–13; Juan Flores Zendejas, "Money Doctors and Latin American Central Banks at the Onset of the Great Depression," *Journal of Latin American Studies* 53, no. 3 (2021): 429–463.

6 On money doctoring, see Stephen A. Schuker, "Money Doctors between the Wars: The Competition between Central Banks, Private Financial Advisers, and Multilateral Agencies, 1919–39," in *Money Doctors: The Experience of International Financial Advising, 1850–2000*, ed. Marc Flandreau (London and New York: Routledge, 2005): 49–77; Juan Flores Zendejas and Gianandrea Nodari, "Latin American Experiments in Central Banking at the Onset of the Great Depression," in *The Spread of the Modern Central Bank and Global Cooperation, 1919–1939*, ed. Barry Eichengreen and Andreas Kakridis (Cambridge: Cambridge: University Press, 2023): 320–351; Andrés Álvarez, Vincent Bignon, Anders Ögren, and Masato Shizume, eds., *Money Doctors around the Globe: A Historical Perspective* (Singapore: Springer, 2024); Gerold Krozewski, "Capitalism," in *The Interwar World*, ed. Andrew Denning and Heidi J.S. Tworek (Abingdon: Routledge, 2024), 464–465. On dollar diplomacy, see Dana G. Munro, *Intervention and Dollar Diplomacy in the Caribbean, 1900–1921* (Princeton: Princeton University Press, 1964); Carlos Marichal, *A Century of Debt Crises in Latin America: From Independence to the Great Depression, 1820–1930* (Princeton: Princeton University Press, 1989), 171–184; Cyrus Veeser, *A World Safe for Capitalism: Dollar Diplomacy and America's Rise to Global Power* (New York: Columbia University Press, 2002); Emily Rosenberg, *Financial Missionaries to the World: The Politics and Culture of Dollar Diplomacy, 1900–1930* (Durham: Duke University Press, 2003); Ellen D. Tillman, *Dollar Diplomacy by Force: Nation-Building and Resistance in the Dominican Republic* (Chapel Hill: The University of North Carolina Press, 2016).

Australia with a quasi-central bank – thereby bringing stability to an international order destabilized by the war.

Through its overseas missions, the Bank primarily sought to promote British financial interests through the establishment of new central banks around the world. As a direct extension of imperialism, the "chain of empire central banks" in the Dominions and India sustained the sterling area, a group of countries that maintained a peg to sterling after 1931.[7] The new system also effectively transferred jurisdiction over national credit from a network of private commercial banks to a single central bank. By using his connections at the League and the Treasury, Niemeyer sought to promote reconstruction efforts through monetary reform.

Blurring the distinction between the borders of the "formal" and "informal" empires, the Niemeyer missions shed light on the changing nature of British imperialism. John Darwin's concept of a British world system proves particularly useful in describing the extent of overseas influence wielded by the City's elite.[8] Throughout the nineteenth and early twentieth centuries, imperial and colonial banks had issued currencies, funded construction projects, and profited immensely from overseas trade in the first age of globalization. Yet the aftermath of the war reconfigured the global order, notably with the emergence of the Dominions as semi-independent entities within the British Empire.[9] Their status as "self-governing communities," outlined in the 1926 Balfour Report and later enshrined by the 1931 Statute of Westminster, granted them greater political sovereignty, although their economic independence remained much less clear. The war also disrupted British commercial interests in Latin America. In the 1920s, the volume of trade and direct investments from London remained consistently lower than its pre-1914 levels.

The backlash against the arrival of a foreign financial expert further determined the limits of monetary reform, as Niemeyer's presence spurred frequent criticism and controversy. Anti-Semitism pervaded the New Zealand press, which accused Niemeyer of being in collaboration with "those great Jewish houses, who for centuries have formed a powerful and exclusive

[7] A.F.W. Plumptre, *Central Banking in the British Dominions* (Toronto: University of Toronto Press, 1940), 193. Also cited in Dayer, *Finance and Empire*, 248; Helleiner, *The Making of National Money*, 150; Martin, *South Africa and the World Economy*, 83.

[8] John Darwin, *The Empire Project: The Rise and Fall of the British World-System, 1830–1970* (Cambridge: Cambridge University Press, 2009).

[9] A.S.J. Baster, *The Imperial Banks* (London: P.S. King & Son, 1929), 215–219; Bernard Attard, "Imperial Central Banks? The Bank of England, the London & Westminster Bank, and the British Empire before 1914," in *Les banques centrales et l'État-nation*, ed. Olivier Feiertag and Michel Margairaz (Paris: Presses de Sciences Po, 2016): 187–212; Cain and Hopkins, *British Imperialism*, 510–511.

hierarchy, dominating the money markets of the world."[10] Other editorials disputed whether he was "an English Jew" or "a German Jew."[11] The German Foreign Office indicated that he was likely pro-German, yet could have also simply been an objective voice.[12] Moreover, Niemeyer's past experience in diplomatic negotiations might have usually impressed those in British circles, but it often proved a hindrance abroad. A socialist Argentine newspaper, *La Vanguardia*, denounced him as an "arms agent" for his work in the amalgamation of Vickers-Armstrongs, a major weapons producer.[13] Contemporary opinions were therefore divided over whether a "money doctor" could diagnose and cure a nation's ailing economy. "Sir Otto is in finance what a consulting physician is in medicine," wrote the *Sydney Morning Herald* admiringly. "No one could be better equipped for the role in qualifications and special training."[14]

Public controversies notwithstanding, the Niemeyer missions constituted an integral part of an interwar state-building process, as the invitation of an expert brought additional legitimacy to many foreign governments. For the nations that Niemeyer consulted, neither the prospect of a loan nor the severity of the Great Depression alone can explain the implementation of orthodox monetary and fiscal reforms. Rather, national governments turned to expertise for the political benefits it conferred, mainly concerning internal social stability and legitimacy. For Australia and New Zealand, the goal was to assert greater economic independence from the imperial metropole (and from one another), while Brazil and Argentina sought to gain recognition in an era of political turmoil following their coups d'état, both in 1930. Although independent central banks may not have immediately materialized in all the countries that Niemeyer visited, his eponymous missions institutionalized the authority of both unelected experts and the foreign governments they advised.

NIEMEYER AT THE TREASURY

Early in his career at the Treasury, Niemeyer had been involved in international monetary relations. Formative years in the civil service influenced his

[10] "People and Their Doings," *Star (Christchurch)* 19136, July 31, 1930, 8.

[11] "Causes of the Depression," *Otago Daily Times (Dunedin)* 21307, April 11, 1931, 9; "Lively Meeting," *Press (Christchurch)* LXXVI, 22922, January 19, 1940, 10.

[12] Gerhard Köpke to the German Embassy in London, September 17, 1926, PA AA RZ 209/96834.

[13] "¿Sir Otto Niemeyer es Agente Armamentista? Una revelación importante," *La Vanguardia (Buenos Aires)* XLII, 10350, January 13, 1936, 1.

[14] "Sir Otto Niemeyer," *Sydney Morning Herald* 28974, December 14, 1930, 10. The medical analogy was commonly used, as *The Daily Telegraph* similarly noted: "Sir Otto Niemeyer has made just the impression in Australia that he was expected to make by his admirers, here – that of a cool expert, able to diagnose a case with precision and ready to prescribe fearlessly"; "London Day by Day," *The Daily Telegraph* 23485, August 22, 1930, 8.

nascent views on economic orthodoxy. Often more an observer than a participant, he learned how negotiations and concessions in the realm of domestic politics determined the prospect of reform abroad.

In the 1920s, the Treasury may have predominantly focused on aspects of domestic policy, such as taxation and the gold standard. Yet it could ignore broader colonial and foreign developments if it sought to confront the threat of inflation at home. Central to this endeavor was managing British economic priorities. While advising the Conservative government during the onset of a postwar recession, Niemeyer first asked what were the Treasury's goals: "Is it (1) to do something for present unemployment, (2) to do something to gratify the Dominions, or (3) generally to embark on a scheme for state-aided Development of the Empire?"[15] In this final scenario, Niemeyer was willing to offer some form of state intervention to address the economic dislocations of the 1920s, but he hesitated to commit the Treasury to any credit programs or aid packages for the Dominions. In June 1923, he wrote to the Chancellor and the Financial Secretary about how Britain's existing financial support to the empire of £71 million in the 1922/1923 fiscal year had been more than adequate. It seemed to him that the "United Kingdom continues to provide them with the cheapest capital in the world ... which they [the Dominions] could get nowhere else."[16]

Niemeyer thus searched for other ways of promoting economic recovery at home and abroad, while also limiting the Treasury's own financial involvement. One potential solution manifested itself in the Irish Free State. Under the first President of the Executive Council, W.T. Cosgrave, the government of the self-governing Dominion initially claimed autonomy in both domestic affairs and political power.[17] Yet securing financial independence presented more difficulties for the new nation. Eight joint-stock banks, with most of their assets invested in the London money market, dominated the financial sector in both Irish states.[18] Although the Bank of England's notes were no longer considered legal tender after independence, they continued to circulate alongside Irish banknotes in the Irish Free State.[19]

[15] Niemeyer to Baldwin, April 27, 1923, TNA T176/11.

[16] Niemeyer to Baldwin and Joynson-Hicks, "Empire Development," June 20, 1923, TNA T176/11.

[17] D.W. Harkness, *The Restless Dominion: The Irish Free State and the British Commonwealth of Nations, 1921–31* (London: Macmillan, 1969), 27–29; Mo Moulton, *Ireland and the Irish in Interwar England* (Cambridge: Cambridge University Press, 2014), 168.

[18] Cormac Ó Gráda, *Ireland: A New Economic History, 1780–1939* (Oxford: Clarendon Press, 1994), 365–366; Cormac Ó Gráda, "Money and Banking in the Irish Free State, 1921–1939," in *Banking, Currency, and Finance in Europe between the Wars*, ed. Charles H. Feinstein (Oxford: Clarendon Press, 1995), 414–415.

[19] This feature distinguished the Irish Currency Commission from other currency boards in the crown colonies; Chief Cashier's Office, "Bank Notes and Currency Notes as Legal Tender in the Crown Colonies," September 13, 1927, BoE OV50/3; "Currency," n.d., BoE OV50/3.

Initially, Niemeyer assessed the Irish Free State's economy and deemed the threat of monetary mismanagement to be low. The economically conservative Cosgrave administration seemed to have shown no signs of excessive spending, nor was the banking sector lending at unsustainable rates. Niemeyer asserted that any type of reform would therefore need to come from Irish officials themselves: "The Free State is now a dominion. It must make its own experience in currency matters as in others."[20] Proposals for reconstruction initially came from conversations with Joseph Brennan, a leading civil servant and financial expert. After studying at University College Dublin and Christ's College, Cambridge, Brennan worked in the Department of Finance and assisted in the early drafting of the Government of Ireland Act (1920) and the Anglo-Irish Treaty (1921).[21] This experience provided Brennan with a channel for influencing economic policy. In one memorandum, Brennan argued that the government needed to curb its own public spending to avoid exacerbating an already precarious situation: "Government borrowing generally must have a strong tendency to bring about a condition of inflation and an adverse exchange."[22] While Niemeyer had little direct knowledge of Irish credit needs and even less about industrial matters, he backed Brennan's proposals, claiming that they rested "entirely on sound lines."[23]

Niemeyer also endorsed Brennan's vision of a centralized monetary authority.[24] When in 1926, Finance Minister Ernest Blythe initiated a public investigation into the conditions necessary for reform, neither UK Treasury experts nor Bank of England officials were directly privy to the negotiations of the subsequent Commission of Inquiry into Banking and the Issue of Note.[25] It might have thus appeared that the politics of currency reform in the newly independent nation rested entirely with civil servants and bankers based in the Irish Free State. However, the tenets of economic orthodoxy, as idealized by London's monetary authorities, were already shared by many

[20] Otto Niemeyer, Memo, May 9, 1923, TNA T176/12.

[21] Leon Ó Broin, "Joseph Brennan, Civil Servant Extraordinary," *Studies: An Irish Quarterly Review* 66, no. 261 (1977), 30; Eoin Drea and Frank Berry, "A Reappraisal of Joseph Brennan and the Achievements of Irish Banking and Currency Policy, 1922–1943," *Financial History Review* 28, no. 1 (2021), 47.

[22] Seosamh Ua Braonán [Joseph Brennan], Memo, July 3, 1923, TNA T176/12.

[23] Niemeyer to Brennan, July 25, 1923, TNA T176/12.

[24] Joseph Brennan, "Notes on the Currency Situation in the Saorstát Éireann," August 15, 1924, NLI Brennan Papers 26214.

[25] Maurice Moynihan, *Currency and Central Banking in Ireland, 1922–1960* (Dublin: Gill and Macmillan, 1975), 39; Ronan Fanning, *The Irish Department of Finance, 1922–58* (Dublin: Institute of Public Administration, 1978), 177–178; Leon Ó Broin, *No Man's Man: A Biographical Memoir of Joseph Brennan: Civil Servant & First Governor of the Central Bank* (Dublin: Institute of Public Administration, 1982), 136; David Blaazer, *Forging Nations: Currency, Power, and Nationality in Britain and Ireland since 1603* (Oxford: Oxford University Press, 2023), 258.

officials in the Irish Free State. The commission's majority report recommended the creation of a Free State (*Saorstát*) pound, tied at a 1:1 ratio to the British pound.[26] To maintain this rate, the 1927 Currency Act established a currency board, to be chaired by Brennan and run by private bankers.[27] These changes initially sparked backlash from the Catholic press and Irish nationalists, such as Éamon de Valera.[28] Nevertheless, the establishment of the new Currency Commission represented the triumph of the Brussels consensus based on expert opinion.

The debate over currency reform seemed to demonstrate the extent to which countries were willing to adopt stringent austerity measures if they promised direct economic benefits. Financial stability did not require additional government funding or an externally raised loan, but it necessitated a commitment to economic orthodoxy. Appointed a member of the League's Financial Committee in 1923 (and chairman in 1927), Niemeyer was able to lead similar stabilization programs abroad. He took part in various League reform projects in Austria, Bulgaria, Estonia, Greece, Portugal, Romania, and Yugoslavia over the course of the 1920s.[29] In these countries, he aimed to apply a standardized

[26] *Final Reports of the Banking Commission* (Dublin: The Stationery Office, 1927), 22. This policy came into effect with the passing of the 1927 Currency Act; "Irish Banking Commission," *The Economist* 105, 4401, December 31, 1927, 1184; "Our Money," *Irish Independent (Dublin)* 37, 214 September 7, 1928, 7; F.G. Hall, *The Bank of Ireland, 1783–1946* (Dublin: Hodges Figgis & Co., 1949), 354–358; Mary E. Daly, *Industrial Development and Irish National Identity, 1922–1939* (Syracuse: Syracuse University Press, 1992), 18; Honohan, *Currency, Credit and Crisis*, 29–30.

[27] Willis to Brennan, October 31, 1927, NLI Brennan Papers 26018; G.A. Duncan, "Banking in Ireland," in *Banking in the British Commonwealth*, ed. R. S. Sayers (Oxford: Clarendon Press, 1952), 307–308; Ó Broin, "Joseph Brennan," 26; Fanning, *The Irish Department of Finance*, 190; Ó Broin, *No Man's Man*, 136–137.

[28] See, for instance, "New Currency Proposals," *The Cork Examiner (Cork)* 22808, January 22, 1927, 9–10; "The Report of the Banking Commission," *Irish Independent (Dublin)* 36, 20, January 24, 1927, 4; "Mr. de Valera in Drogheda: Banking Report Criticised," *The Irish Times* LXIX, 21774, January 31, 1927, 8. De Valera's opposition to closer economic ties with the United Kingdom later manifested during the Anglo-Irish Trade War, in which the Irish government responded to economic sanctions on Irish exports with retaliatory tariffs of its own. On the Economic War, see Paul Canning, *British Policy towards Ireland, 1921–1941* (Oxford: Clarendon Press, 1985), 132; J. Peter Neary and Cormac Ó Gráda, "Protection, Economic War and Structural Change: The 1930s in Ireland," *Irish Historical Studies* 27, no. 107 (1991): 250–266; Kevin O'Rourke, "Burn Everything British but Their Coal: The Anglo-Irish Economic War of the 1930s," *Journal of Economic History* 51, no. 2 (1991), 358; Daly, *Industrial Development and Irish National Identity*, 156–163; Gerard McCann, "Protectionism and the 'Economic War' in Interwar Ireland," *The Journal of European Economic History* 43, no. 3 (2014): 39–68.

[29] Niemeyer to Churchill, July 26, 1927, TNA T176/24; Comité financier, "Rapport au conseil sur les travaux de la vingt-neuvième session du comité," November 29–December 7, 1927, LoN R345/10/63781/11519; Niemeyer to Ivens Ferraz [Acting Finance Minister, Portugal], March 10, 1928, LoN R2927/10E/2644/203; Niemeyer to Emmanouil Tsouderos [Deputy Governor, Bank of Greece], July 11, 1928, GR IATE A3S1Y1F33T24; Niemeyer to Marcus Wallenberg

model of banking reform centered on the principles of orthodox finance. The backing of both the League and the Bank provided the legitimacy needed to stabilize foreign currencies.

Niemeyer's reputation attracted the attention of officials at the Bank. In November 1926, the Court of Directors appointed a special committee to assess the structure of the central bank's organization. One concern was whether to employ an individual who could manage relations with other central banks. There had certainly been some reluctance to invite outsiders into the close-knit circle of the Old Guard. As the committee noted, "it may be in the interests of the Bank for further men of special knowledge and experience to be appointed," although it was also possible that "the creation of a body of specialists ... might in the course of time acquire so considerable a control of the Bank's affairs as to usurp the functions and diminish the authority of the Committee of Treasury."[30]

Nevertheless, in 1927, Niemeyer arrived at the Bank as an Adviser to the Governors.[31] It was the overarching goal of the Court of Directors to ensure that the "greatest Banking institution in the world" was led by "a man competent to deal with experts in finance as is the practice in other Central Banks."[32] While not an economist, Niemeyer was well versed in theory and had extensive knowledge of foreign countries from his work at the League of Nations. His prior experience at the Treasury, one Bank official described, provided him with "exceptional qualification for examining budgetary and fiscal questions."[33]

Norman's invitation to Niemeyer thus came at a time when the Bank endeavored to play a greater role in the global economic order. To preserve the City's prestige, the Bank facilitated stabilization loans and implemented reform programs abroad. These projects represented a way to instill confidence in foreign economies, as countries viewed Niemeyer's expertise as a way of raising investors' confidence. "You will have all the advantages of League support and of a foreign expert at your Bank," he promised the central bank of Greece.[34] Even if the financiers and merchants based in the City represented a multiplicity

[Financial Committee, League of Nations], June 13, 1928, BoE OV9/257. On Niemeyer at the League, see Orde, *British Policy and European Reconstruction*, 284–292; Helleiner, *The Making of National Money*, 147; Bakić, "Diplomacy and Loans," 631–653; Martin, *The Meddlers*, 135–156.

30 "Special Committee on the Future Government and Administration of the Bank," June 14, 1927, BA Revelstoke Papers 203251 and BoE G15/253.

31 Committee of Treasury, Minutes, April 13 and April 27, 1927, BoE G8/57; "Civil Service Changes," *The Times* 44589, May 24, 1927, 16.

32 "A Meeting of the Directors at the Bank on Monday, the 21st May, 1928," BA Revelstoke Papers 203251.

33 Harvey to Gibson, May 22, 1930, BoE G1/291.

34 Niemeyer to Tsouderos, April 12, 1928, GR IATE A3S1Y1F33T36.

FIGURE 6.2 The Commonwealth Bank of Australia, 1933
Source: Reserve Bank of Australia Archives, PN-000967.

of institutions, the Bank espoused a singular version of economic orthodoxy through its technical advisers.

AUSTRALIA AND ITS BUDGET

In 1911, the Commonwealth Bank of Australia (CBA) had been established as a state-owned trading bank (another term for commercial bank), with its operations commencing the following year (Figure 6.2). The Labor-majority government had resolved to create a financial institution that resembled the Bank of England, although one that remained firmly under political control.[35] Established due to the government's efforts to address accusations of collusion in the domestic banking sector, the CBA initially supported the nation's evolving commercial needs.[36] After the First World War, the CBA gradually adopted more responsibilities associated with central banking: the financing of military expenditures during the conflict; the

[35] J.S.G. Wilson, "The Commonwealth Bank of Australia," in *Banking in the British Commonwealth*, ed. R.S. Sayers (Oxford: Clarendon Press, 1952), 40.

[36] Darwin, *The Empire Project*, 282; Andrew Dilley, *Finance, Politics, and Imperialism: Australia, Canada, and the City of London, c. 1896–1914* (Basingstoke: Palgrave Macmillan, 2012), 77–78; Cain and Hopkins, *British Imperialism*, 532.

issuance of Australian banknotes after 1920; and the separation of its savings department in 1927.[37]

Yet the onset of the global Great Depression threatened to destabilize Australia's export-dependent economy. In 1929, a collapse in export prices by 30 percent culminated in a crisis of confidence that caused foreign investors to withdraw their funds from the country.[38] A severe balance-of-payments crisis followed as the current-account deficit also rose to 10 percent of GDP by the following year.[39] Under Prime Minister James Scullin, the new Labor government responded by imposing additional tariffs and abandoning the sterling parity in December 1929. Between June 1928 and June 1931, average nominal wages fell rapidly in each of Australia's federal states: New South Wales by 7 percent, Queensland by 9 percent, South Australia by 15 percent, Tasmania by 10 percent, Victoria by 14 percent, and Western Australia by 8 percent.[40]

Amidst the crisis, the Australian government considered different ways of reorganizing its economy with the help of foreign experts.[41] Officials had previously devised some of their own reforms, such as the 1924 Commonwealth Bank Bill that provided the CBA a monopoly of note issue. A subsequent attempt at monetary reform occurred in 1927 when Ernest Harvey, then Comptroller of the Bank of England, spent eight months in Australia to restructure the country's banking system.[42] He concluded that the largest commercial bank, the CBA, needed to be reconstituted as a more public-oriented monetary authority, a reform that the CBA's own chairman, Sir Robert Gibson, approved.[43] Although Harvey's proposal was rejected by the government, it opened a debate on the need for broad changes to the financial system. The Bank continually endeavored to strengthen economic

37 D.B. Copland, "The Commonwealth Bank of Australia," December 1924, NLA Copland Papers Series 90.

38 Alex Millmow, *The Power of Economic Ideas: The Origins of Keynesian Macroeconomic Management in Interwar Australia, 1929–1939* (Canberra: ANU E Press, 2010), 33.

39 M.W. Butlin and P.M. Boyce, "Monetary Policy in Depression and Recovery," in *Recovery from the Depression: Australia and the World Economy in the 1930s*, ed. R.G. Gregory and N.G. Butlin (Cambridge: Cambridge University Press, 1989), 195.

40 "General Conditions," April 4, 1932, RBA C.3.15.10.7.

41 "Sir O. Niemeyer's Visit to Australia," *The Times* 45546, June 23, 1930, 13.

42 Committee of Treasury, Minutes, August 4, 1926, BoE G8/57; Harvey to Norman, March 10, 1927, BoE G1/289; "Sir Ernest Harvey in Australia," *The Old Lady of Threadneedle Street* IV, no. 27, September 1927, 116–117. The CBA had requested that Norman arrange "for an expert Banker to visit Australia to advise our Board in connection with the constitution of a Reserve Bank"; J.S. Scott [Manager, Commonwealth Bank of Australia] to Norman, February 8, 1926, RBA BRL-15-1.

43 "Interview with Sir Robert Gibson, Chairman of the Board of Directors of the Commonwealth Bank," September 27, 1927, NLA Copland Papers Series 90; C.B. Schedvin, *Australia and the Great Depression: A Study of Economic Development and Policy in the 1920s and 1930s* (Sydney: Sydney University, 1970), 123–124.

FIGURE 6.3 Sir Otto Niemeyer, Sir Robert Gibson, and Ernest Riddle (left to right), July 11, 1930
Source: Reserve Bank of Australia Archives, PN-002050.

relations between Britain and its Dominions. After briefly considering the aid of the Governor of the South African Reserve Bank, William Clegg, the Committee of Treasury dispatched Niemeyer to address Australia's economic instabilities.[44]

On July 14, Niemeyer landed in the port city of Fremantle. From there, he left for Sydney, where he planned to meet with Scullin five days later to discuss a program for rehabilitating the national economy.[45] During his trip, he toured the country and met with an array of civil servants and private bankers (Figure 6.3). Publicity was a key aspect of the mission since legitimacy was vital for raising investors' confidence in Australia's fiscal capacity. As a former member of the League's Financial Committee, Niemeyer was able to offer the government advice that had appeared workable in other countries. Because of his past work, *The Times* reported on the potential value of Niemeyer's

[44] Committee of Treasury, Minutes, December 9, 1925, BoE G8/56; Harvey to Gibson, May 22, 1930, BoE G1/291 and RBA S-C-16; "A Mission to Australia," *The Economist* 110, 4531, June 28, 1930, 1440.

[45] James Collins [Treasury, Australia] to Harvey, June 6, 1930, BoE G1/291; "Sir Otto Niemeyer in Melbourne," *The Times* 45570, July 21, 1930, 21; John Robertson, *J.H. Scullin: A Political Biography* (Nedlands: University of Western Australia Press, 1974), 261.

recommendations: "His mission to assist the Australian authorities in their endeavours to solve the grave financial problems with which they are confronted. His wide experience should enable him to give valuable aid in so far as sound advice and recommendations can be of service to Australia."[46] *The New York Times* similarly claimed that "[f]ew men have had such wide experience as Niemeyer with the particular kind of problems that now face Australia."[47]

Accompanied by the Bank's Australian-born adviser (Raymond N. Kershaw) and a professor of economics (Theodore Gregory), Niemeyer planned to conduct a thorough examination of public finance following his meetings with government officials. For, although Governor Norman himself remained thoroughly active in the establishment of these Commonwealth banks, reportedly displaying an "intimate knowledge of Australian affairs," he entrusted his advisers to conduct reforms on his behalf.[48] As he wrote to Scullin in September 1930, "Sir Otto Niemeyer has of course kept me fully advised regarding his investigations and conversations in Australia on behalf of the Bank of England and has informed me in confidence of the seriousness of the disclosures made to him regarding the financial position. His advices seem to indicate that prompt and drastic action by the Commonwealth and States Governments is needed if the position is to be corrected or even protected against further deterioration."[49]

Kershaw, who was less interested in attracting publicity, conducted interviews with representatives from Australia's major banks to assess their liquidity positions.[50] He concentrated his efforts on identifying the requirements needed for raising an external loan. Improving investors' confidence was the main hurdle, as Australia, according to one contemporary, was still viewed as "the bad boy of the British Commonwealth" due to its public spending.[51] Both Kershaw and Niemeyer recognized the difficulties of imposing austerity measures, particularly as many countries already struggled to manage their wartime debts. Lessons from other countries therefore informed many of their discussions. Whereas Australia, similar to the United Kingdom, had primarily funded the conflict through a combination of taxation, bonds, and savings, other countries, notably Germany, France, and the Soviet Union faced more destabilizing crises after the war because of their high public debts.[52]

[46] "Empire Banking," *The Times* 45574, July 25, 1930, 18.

[47] "Bank of England to Aid Australia," *The New York Times* LXXIX, 26445, June 20, 1930, 38.

[48] Jackson to Thomas Bradshaw [Dominion Bank], September 6, 1935, UTA Jackson Papers B2004-0019/010 (05).

[49] Norman to Scullin, September 26, 1930, BoE G1/291.

[50] R.N. Kershaw, "Notes on Conversation with Mr. [Alexander] Jobson, Director of the A.M.P.," July 28, 1930, BoE G1/291.

[51] Lyndhurst Falkiner Giblin, *The Growth of a Central Bank: The Development of the Commonwealth Bank of Australia, 1924–1945* (Melbourne: Melbourne University Press, 1951), 84.

[52] R.N. Kershaw, "Some Notes on the Situation in France, 1919–1930," 1930, BoE G1/291; Otto Niemeyer, Memorandum on Australian Credit, n.d., BoE G1/291.

Seeking to gauge Australia's creditworthiness, Kershaw aimed to assess the budgetary and monetary situation as a whole. Prior to his arrival, he had already found that "the Australian Government must come to the Bank of England for help" due to its projected trade imbalance.[53] Subsequent meetings with government officials and bankers confirmed this view. Using estimates provided by the CBA, the Bank determined that a foreign loan of around £20 million was needed to cover a potential deficit.[54] More structural measures, according to Kershaw, would be necessary to overcome persistent balance-of-payments issues. He advocated an increase in tariffs, which, although "unfavourable to Britain," might have stimulated the Australian economy.[55] Simultaneously trying to bear the Bank's interests in mind, Kershaw also suggested curtailing non-British imports through a special licensing system to ensure British goods still remained in demand.[56]

During their visit, the Bank's advisers met with government officials and reported their findings back to London. They remained particularly aware of ongoing political events that might lead to their recommendations being rejected. Because of the controversy surrounding their arrival, foreign dignitaries appeared largely unwilling to accept austerity measures, such as the severely unpopular reductions in public wages.[57] Niemeyer recognized the difficulty of divorcing economic advice from domestic politics, even if he aimed to do so. As he wrote to Norman in September 1930, it was best to remain "as far as possible out of the political issues which the New South Wales Election arouses."[58] He felt particularly threatened by a radical faction within the Labor Party led by Jack Lang, who denounced expert opinion and the intervention of an imperial entity.[59] Norman, responding to Niemeyer's apprehensions, believed that the "Victory of Lang [in the upcoming election] would without question be a severe blow to the policy formulated by you."[60]

Opposition to monetary reform had also come from the leading commercial banks. In 1927, the Bank of New South Wales had written a petition against a central bank for fear it could have succumbed to political interference, while at the same time unfairly competing with other commercial

53 R.N. Kershaw, "Australian Funds in London," March 25, 1930, BoE G1/291.

54 R.N. Kershaw, "London Financial Position of Australian Government by 1st October 1930," March 13, 1930, BoE G1/291.

55 R.N. Kershaw, "Australian Funds in London," March 25, 1930, BoE G1/291.

56 R.N. Kershaw, "Australian Funds in London," March 25, 1930, BoE G1/291.

57 Gibson to Harvey, May 16, 1930, BoE G1/291.

58 Niemeyer to Norman, September 24, 1930, BoE G1/291 and G1/335.

59 Peter Love, *Labour and the Money Power: Australian Labour Populism, 1890–1950* (Carlton: Melbourne University Press, 1984), 104–107; Frank Cain, *Jack Lang and the Great Depression* (Melbourne: Australian Scholarly Publishing, 2005), 117–118.

60 Norman to Niemeyer, October 22, 1930, BoE G1/291.

banks.[61] Other financial institutions would have rejected any proposal that involved a central bank acting as a potential competitor. By early 1929, sentiments among commercial banks shifted due to the changing economic landscape. From the bankers' perspective, unfavorable trade conditions in 1929 and 1930 made Niemeyer's intervention increasingly necessary. Harvey was then able to convince the CBA Governor, Ernest Riddle, to rally support for monetary reform in the banking community.[62] The result was that even before Niemeyer's arrival, the Bank had been able to gain the tacit approval of Melbourne bankers, who were reportedly "not very confident about anything else."[63]

Yet expert advice continually invited criticism from politicians. The idea of foreign mediation deeply divided government officials at the Melbourne Conference of Commonwealth and State Ministers in August 1930.[64] In the press, Labor MPs, most notably Lang and John Eldridge, launched a series of vehement attacks against Niemeyer and the acquiescing Scullin government. They referred to him as a "bushranger" whose "advice would betray the people of Australia" and would turn the country into a "chattel nation."[65] Austerity measures were hardly made more appealing when Niemeyer's criticisms of recent economic policy had been made public, such as one statement that suggested Australia had been living far beyond its means.[66] So controversial was Niemeyer in the public eye that even British politicians began to distance themselves from the Bank's affairs abroad, with one Labour MP condemning the mission entirely.[67]

61 Norman to Harvey, July 14, 1927, RBA C.3.15.10.7.

62 Harvey to Riddle, January 3, 1929, RBA C.3.15.10.7.

63 Peter Love, "Niemeyer's Australian Diary and Other English Records of His Mission," *Historical Studies* 20, no. 79 (1982), 267.

64 Schedvin, *Australia and the Great Depression*, 184; Peter Cook, "The Scullin Government, 1929–1932" (PhD diss., Australian National University, 1971), 228; Love, *Labour and the Money Power*, 97–101; Alex Millmow, "Niemeyer, Scullin and the Australian Economists," *Australian Economic History Review* 44, no. 2 (2004), 151; Millmow, *The Power of Economic Ideas*, 72; Neville Kirk, *Labour and the Politics of Empire: Britain and Australia 1900 to the Present* (Manchester and New York: Manchester University Press, 2011), 124–125; Era Dabla-Norris and Marina Marinkov, "Whom Do You Rescue? Honored Debts and Selective Defaults in Four British Dominions," in *Debt and Entanglements between the Wars*, ed. Era Dabla-Norris (Washington, DC: International Monetary Fund, 2019), 98.

65 "Mr. Lang Criticises Sir Otto Niemeyer," *The Evening News (Rockhampton)* 2838, October 4, 1930, 9; "The Public's Interest," *Sydney Morning Herald* 28953, October 21, 1930, 8; "Attack by Mr. Eldridge on Sir Otto Niemeyer," *The Barrier Miner (Broken Hill)* XLIII, 12944, November 22, 1930, 1; Darwin, *The Empire Project*, 451.

66 Otto Niemeyer, "The Melbourne Conference, July and August, 1930. (a) Sir Otto Niemeyer's Statement," in *The Crisis in Australian Finance, 1929 to 1931: Documents on Budgetary and Economic Policy*, ed. E.O.G. Shann and D.B. Copland (Sydney: Angus & Robertson, 1931), 27; Schedvin, *Australia and the Great Depression*, 181–182.

67 HC Deb, February 16, 1933, vol. 274, cc. 1327–1328.

The visit to Australia was thus a heavily politicized affair. Not working in his favor, Niemeyer's few sympathies for Australia were widely known. He referred to it as a "poor country" that was "probably over populated."[68] Ever hubristic, he expected to be awarded a medal for his "pioneer work in savage countries."[69] Following a meeting with state officials, he wrote to a former Treasury colleague, "This is an odd country, full of odd people and odder theories."[70] As he continued:

> The petty feuds on every conceivable subject are unlimited both in number and in bitterness. The ignorance of different sections of the population of one another's real feelings, problems and objects, the jealousies between political parties and between different wings of the same political party, and between the States ... with the Commonwealth could hardly be equalled in a small cathedral town ... . There is very little to work on and very few people with whom you can work, and the political leaders in general are listless and frightened, and quite incapable of giving a lead.[71]

Yet the dependence on Niemeyer (as an expert) overrode the distrust in Niemeyer (as a central banker). Despite the disparaging comments, Australian officials were willing to accept some degree of intervention when it aligned with their national interests. Among business associations, such as the Melbourne Chamber of Commerce, there was support for Niemeyer's plan revolving an independent central bank that remained "free from political control and influence."[72] Politicians similarly expressed their approval of some elements of the report.[73]

Niemeyer's arrival also coincided with a decade in which economists began to play more prominent roles in public policy.[74] One such figure was Douglas Copland, a New Zealand-born professor at the University of Melbourne. As the Sidney Myer Chair of Commerce, as well as a founding member and the first president of the Economic Society of Australia and New Zealand (1925–1928), Copland believed that economic theory played a crucial role in shaping

[68] Niemeyer to Harvey, August 14, 1930, BoE G1/291.

[69] Niemeyer to J. van Walré de Bordes [League of Nations], October 25, 1930, LoN S71/21/4.

[70] Niemeyer to Hopkins, September 1, 1930, BoE G1/291. Also quoted in Kosmas Tsokhas, "'A Pound of Flesh': War Debts and Anglo-Australian Relations, 1919–1932," *Australian Journal of Politics & History* 38, no. 1 (1992), 20; Michael Roe, *Australia, Britain and Migration, 1915–1940: A Study of Desperate Hopes* (Cambridge and New York: Cambridge University Press, 1995), 148; Millmow, *The Power of Economic Ideas*, 70–71.

[71] Niemeyer to Norman, September 1, 1930, BoE G1/291.

[72] "Central Reserve Bank Bill: Evidence Tendered on Behalf of the Melbourne Chamber of Commerce," April 16, 1930, NLA Copland Papers Series 90.

[73] Love, *Labour and the Money Power*, 101.

[74] Neville Cain, "Australian Economic Advice in 1930: Liberal and Radical Alternatives," *Australian National University Working Papers in Economic History*, no. 78 (1987), 2; Coleman, Cornish, and Hagger, *Giblin's Platoon*, 71–73; Alex Millmow, *A History of Australasian Economic Thought* (London and New York: Routledge, 2017), 66–67; Millmow, *The Power of Economic Ideas*, 79–80.

policy debates, particularly concerning the management of the money supply. "Every important country has found an elastic note issue and a central bank essential to sound trading conditions," Copland wrote in 1926. "Australia cannot long neglect such reforms, the need for which are emphasized by the present exchange situation, and the inelasticity of the note issue."[75]

The need for austerity, controversially tied to Niemeyer's image, continued to pervade policy discussions because of its direct implications on Australia's balance of payments. Although electoral rivalries and a general distrust in foreign advice initially prevented the implementation of the Bank's recommendations, Australian officials supported the broad tenets of economic orthodoxy embedded within Niemeyer's plan. For instance, the Niemeyer-inspired Melbourne Agreement offered the government a way of balancing the budget at the cost of extensive cuts to spending.[76] Reductions in both public- and private-sector wages were also to come into effect. By November, the Acting Federal Treasurer proposed a resolution to balance the budget with £3.2 million in spending reductions and £4.8 million in new taxation.[77]

The Bank was, to be sure, reluctant to issue a line of credit in the event that spending cuts were not implemented. During one meeting, Governor Norman alluded only to the possibility of a loan, but he did not want to commit to one until Australia accepted a plan.[78] Niemeyer, too, sought to prevent the main lending agency, the Australian Loan Council, from obtaining more foreign credits. As a result, he objected to the model of a central bank proposed by Australian economists, including Copland and another Melbourne-based economist, Lyndhurst Giblin. Both individuals, to his mind, had only been "producing the well worn arguments of the inflationist school with not ... much appreciation of the dangerous nature of what they are saying."[79] What the Bank instead desired was a full commitment to a balanced budget. Scullin, with little success, could only offer his verbal reassurance that although "Australia runs great risk of being driven into default," the Bank should ignore the "few irresponsible extremists" who tried to use debt repudiation as a threat.[80]

Niemeyer's proposals gained even more attention when Australian economists began to advocate economic orthodoxy. In May 1931, the (Copland) Committee of Under-Treasurers and Economists prepared a report for another conference in Melbourne. The meeting, known as the Premiers' Conference,

[75] D.B. Copland, *Monetary Policy and its Application to Australia* (Melbourne: Melbourne University Press, 1926), 523–524.

[76] H.J. Sheehan, "Conference of Commonwealth and State Governments in Melbourne 18th to 21st August 1930," BoE G1/291; Norman to Hopkins, October 23, 1930, BoE G1/291.

[77] "Australian Budget Statement," *The Times* 45663, November 6, 1930, 13.

[78] Norman to Niemeyer, October 3, 1930, BoE G1/291.

[79] Niemeyer to Melville, November 13, 1930, BoE OV9/289.

[80] "Australia," October 2, 1930, BoE G1/291.

saw delegates build on the 1930 Melbourne Agreement with additional reforms to public finance. An estimated deficit of £39 million in 1931/1932 could have been corrected by an increase in taxation (leading to a net contribution of £7.5 million), a reduction in interest rates (£6.5 million), and other measures.[81] Income tax, property tax, and corporate tax rates were all set to increase.[82] While the majority of the committee members argued that balanced budgets would not have been achievable within the next three years, the final report, known as the Premiers' Plan, outlined the cuts needed to government expenditures to accelerate closing the deficit.[83] The report also recommended increasing the level of overall spending cuts to 20 percent (below 1928 levels), alongside specific reductions to Australian bondholders (22.5 percent) and pensioners (12.5 percent).[84] There was some hope that a future trade surplus could have been used to cover interest payments on the national debt amounting to around £28 million.[85]

Australia's subsequent adoption of deflationary measures did not derive from any particular ideological pressure. Fiscal tightening during financial crises had long been compatible with a wide variety of political regimes, both on the left and on the right, over the twentieth century.[86] Nor was it the prospect of a loan that entirely led to austerity measures. Instead, the deliberations and, by extension, the possible configurations of monetary reform were determined by an institutionalized dependence on economic expertise. Politicians were willing to accept a program of severe cost-cutting measures when it came from trusted technical specialists, whose public image might help raise investors'

[81] State Governments of Australia, "Report of the Premiers' Conference, Adopted 10th June, 1931," in *The Battle of the Plans: Documents Relating to the Premiers' Conference, May 25th to June 11th, 1931*, ed. E.O.G. Shann and D.B. Copland (Sydney: Angus & Robertson, 1931), 132.

[82] "Australian Budget," *The Times* 45872, July 11, 1931, 12.

[83] Douglas Copland, *Australia in the World Crisis, 1929–1933* (New York: Macmillan, 1934), 133–136; Douglas Copland, "The Premiers' Plan in Australia: An Experiment in Economic Adjustment," *International Affairs (Royal Institute of International Affairs, 1931–1939)* 13, no. 1 (1934), 83–86; Kosmas Tsokhas, "Sir Otto Niemeyer, the Bankrupt State and the Federal System," *Australian Journal of Political Science* 30, no. 1 (1995), 22; Coleman, Cornish, and Hagger, *Giblin's Platoon*, 117–130; Millmow, *The Power of Economic Ideas*, 87–94; John Robert Hawkins, "The Australian Treasurers: Managers and Reformers in an Evolving Role" (PhD diss., Australian National University, 2017), 123.

[84] Parliament of the Commonwealth of Australia, *Conference of Commonwealth State Ministers, Held at Melbourne, 25th May to 11th June, 1931: Proceedings and Decisions of Conference*, C. 6744 (Canberra: H.J. Green, 1931), 173; Schedvin, *Australia and the Great Depression*, 248–249; Bernard Attard, "Financial Diplomacy," in *Between Empire and Nation: Australia's External Relations from Federation to the Second World War*, ed. Carl Bridge and Bernard Attard (Melbourne: Australian Scholarly Publishing, 2000), 125.

[85] R.N. Kershaw, "Notes on Professor Brigden's Telegram of 3rd March, 1930," March 12, 1930, BoE G1/291.

[86] Cristian Capotescu, Oscar Sanchez-Sibony, and Melissa Teixeira, "Austerity without Neoliberals: Reappraising the Sinuous History of a Powerful State Technology," *Capitalism: A Journal of History and Economics* 3, no. 2 (2022): 379–420.

confidence. Both the Niemeyer mission and the Premiers' Plan embodied such a strategy. At the 1931 Conference, Prime Minister Scullin might have acknowledged the influential role of apolitical expert recommendations in helping Australia respond to the Great Depression.[87] Yet the reality was that Niemeyer and Kershaw had learned how to manage the political controversy surrounding their mission.[88]

The Bank's advisers succeeded in influencing Australian fiscal reform. During his farewell speech, Niemeyer reiterated his claims as a seemingly apolitical voice: "Whatever views I expressed, whatever else they may have been, they were not political views. When I came to Australia I honestly didn't know the names of the various political parties."[89] He emphasized his "practical experience of currency," given that "Europe has had a great deal of experience during the last 10 years" of currency fluctuations.[90] While the CBA retained its commercial business, it also gained a greater degree of independence, free from political pressure in "its difficult technical functions," as Niemeyer desired.[91] Expertise, despite its limitations, presented a cogent and convincing solution to Australia's woes.

NEW ZEALAND UNCHAINED

Similar to that of Australia, the monetary system of New Zealand heavily depended on the operations of private commercial banks. Throughout the nineteenth and early twentieth centuries, British multinational banks had funneled capital into the country.[92] Their investments supported a range of technological improvements, from refrigeration to farming, which further raised agricultural output.[93]

Yet the dislocations engendered by the First World War and its aftermath led to the rapid contraction of international economic trade. With an agricultural sector heavily reliant on exports, New Zealand was particularly susceptible to these strains. A sharp decline in commodity prices induced a drop in the value of its exports from £49.8 million in 1929 to £40.4 million in 1930.[94] Driven by the availability of cheap credit in the 1920s, land speculation further

87 Parliament of the Commonwealth of Australia, *Conference of Commonwealth State Ministers*, 1.

88 Niemeyer to Gibson, January 26, 1931, BoE G1/291.

89 "Sir Otto Niemeyer," *Sydney Morning Herald* 28974, December 14, 1930, 10.

90 Niemeyer to Melville, November 13, 1930, BoE OV9/289.

91 Otto Niemeyer, "Observations on the Commonwealth Bank Bill (1930)," BoE G1/291.

92 Jones, *British Multinational Banking*, 30–40; Michie, *The London Stock Exchange*, 90–95.

93 James Belich, *Replenishing the Earth: The Settler Revolution and the Rise of the Anglo-World, 1783–1939* (Oxford and New York: Oxford University Press, 2009), 488; Darwin, *The Empire Project*, 175.

94 Department of Overseas Trade, *Economic Conditions in the Dominion of New Zealand* (London: H.M. Stationery Office, 1931), 35–36.

FIGURE 6.4 Sir Otto Niemeyer (fourth from left) and Raymond Kershaw (third from right) in Rotorua, 1930
Source: Archives New Zealand (Te Rua Mahara o te Kāwanatanga), Francis Bernard Dwyer Papers (AAZI) 19575, Box 1, Record Number 5, Item Code R6903195.

contributed to a rise in defaults on mortgage payments among farmers.[95] The importance of agriculture for New Zealand was internationally recognized, demonstrated by the numerous reports and publications by the League of Nations on nutrition, hunger, and farming.[96] In 1927, a parliamentary act offered financial support in the form of advances to farmers, with additional funding legislated in 1930.

A precipitous decline in agricultural prices further instigated calls for some form of government intervention. Although in the late nineteenth century, debates in the New Zealand Parliament had concerned the possibility of establishing a state-owned bank of issue, more detailed proposals only began to circulate in the interwar years after Niemeyer's arrival.[97] Initially motivated by an effort to retain a substantial market share for New Zealand's exports abroad, government officials tentatively suggested inviting a foreign expert to offer additional advice. Once the Bank proposed the idea of a clandestine

[95] G.R. Hawke, *The Making of New Zealand: An Economic History* (Cambridge: Cambridge University Press, 1985), 143; Dabla-Norris and Marinkov, "Whom Do You Rescue?," 104.

[96] Clavin, *Securing the World Economy*, 165–168.

[97] G.R. Hawke, *Between Governments and Banks: A History of the Reserve Bank of New Zealand* (Wellington: A.R. Shearer, Government Printer, 1973), 31–41; Malcolm McKinnon, *Treasury: The New Zealand Treasury, 1840–2000* (Auckland: Auckland University Press, 2003), 126; Matthew Wright, "The Policy Origins of the Reserve Bank of New Zealand," *Reserve Bank of New Zealand Bulletin* 69, no. 3 (2006), 7.

trip to New Zealand on June 30, Prime Minister George Forbes immediately agreed to make the necessary arrangements for a visit.[98]

Upon his arrival in Wellington, Niemeyer met with officials who informed him of the ongoing political and economic situation (Figure 6.4). In contrast to Australia, New Zealand had maintained balanced budgets, and, as a result, its overseas borrowing costs had not been prohibitively high.[99] As he then reported to Norman:

> New Zealand is a very different story from Australia. It makes a general appearance of solidity – almost in fact stodginess – and is full of sane people who inspire confidence, perhaps because the leading race are the Scotch and not, as in Australia, the Irish. The representatives of the six Banks, all of whom I saw frequently, are level headed people. The Treasury Officials ... are competent and have things well in hand; and even the political people, though not great men, have a sound foundation of sense. The country itself looks immeasurably more attractive than Australia, not merely scenically – and some of the scenery is very fine – but economically.[100]

Despite the comparatively better position of New Zealand, fundamental changes were needed to combat the decline in agricultural prices. One way to promote trade was stabilizing the New Zealand pound via a peg to the British pound. A "single effective rate of exchange between New Zealand and Australia" would be the primary means of preventing capital outflows.[101] Managing the sterling-exchange standard would have been the responsibility of a new currency board, although such an arrangement "would imply that ultimately London would have to support New Zealand['s] currency."[102]

Related to exchange-rate problems were questions about the banking sector as a whole. In New Zealand, six commercial banks managed the nation's access to credit and issued legal tender.[103] Given the lack of a central bank, the volume of credit was thus proportional to the notes in circulation. Initial discussions with Oliver Sprague, one of the Bank's economists, led to the idea of separating the New Zealand and Australian banking systems through tax incentives or political pressure.[104] Four of the six main commercial banks in New Zealand were based in Australia, and contemporaries argued that the dependence on (or a lack of access to) Australian credit had exacerbated the severity of the Great Depression.[105] Unchaining New Zealand from Australia might even allow it to develop its own money market.

98 Harvey to Wilford, June 30, 1930, BoE G1/335; Forbes to Wilford, July 2, 1930, BoE G1/335.

99 "Finances of New Zealand," *The Times* 45635, October 4, 1930, 9.

100 Niemeyer to Norman, September 28, 1930, BoE G1/335.

101 Niemeyer to Kershaw, January 31, 1931, BoE G1/335.

102 Niemeyer to Harvey, July 25, 1930, BoE G1/335.

103 Otto Niemeyer, *Banking and Currency in New Zealand*, B.–3 (Wellington: W.A.G. Skinner, Government Printer, 1931), 1.

104 "Proposals Regarding New Zealand Exchange," February 11, 1931, BoE OV59/15.

105 "Finances of New Zealand," *The Times* 45635, October 4, 1930, 9; D.A.S. Campbell, "The Report of the New Zealand Parliamentary Monetary Committee," *The Australian Quarterly*

Part of the Bank's success in influencing economic policy came from its ability to demonstrate how monetary reform was fundamentally in New Zealand's interests. If the ties to the Australian banking system had been the cause of the weakening exchange rate, then severing such links would have abated a future crisis. In a meeting with Finance Minister Downie Stewart, Governor Norman argued that a reserve bank would therefore allow New Zealand to function as an economically independent country: "were they to be dragged at the tail of Australia or to face their own affairs[?]"[106] In their discussions with government officials, experts also emphasized the benefits of a private and "non-political" reserve bank.[107] Niemeyer then suggested that the country should instead establish its own reserve bank, inspired by the Bank of England's proven model, which had already "been adopted by all modern countries."[108] Following his return to London, Niemeyer shared the main features of his final report, published in July 1931, with Prime Minister Forbes: a recommendation to adopt the sterling-exchange standard and to establish an independent central bank.[109]

The proposal for monetary reform was based on a standard set of principles: a note-issuing reserve bank, a commitment to fixed exchange rates, and the centralization of the nation's gold reserves.[110] Many recommendations in the report, such as the emphasis on control of government expenditures, echoed the language usually employed by the New Zealand Treasury. Extending additional concessions to the Treasury, the Bank agreed to additional provisions related to the reserve bank's prerogatives. The new reserve bank would be required to cooperate with the Treasury to manage public spending, in addition to managing the national debt.[111]

Yet the delay in the establishment of an independent reserve bank can partly be attributed to the government's prioritization of public finance over monetary

6, no. 24 (1934), 127; David Greasley and Les Oxley, "Regime Shift and Fast Recovery on the Periphery: New Zealand in the 1930s," *The Economic History Review* 55, no. 4 (2002), 702; Helleiner, *The Making of National Money*, 153; Wright, "The Policy Origins of the Reserve Bank of New Zealand," 7; Frank Decker, "The Monetary Union of Australia, New Zealand and the United Kingdom – Its Operation, Fragmentation and Break-Up," *Jahrbuch für Wirtschaftsgeschichte* 63, no. 2 (2022), 390.

106 Montagu Norman, Note, September 19, 1932, BoE G1/335.

107 Niemeyer to Norman, September 24, 1930, BoE G1/291 and G1/335.

108 Otto Niemeyer, "New Zealand," 1930, BoE OV59/15.

109 Niemeyer to Forbes, February 19, 1931, BoE OV59/15.

110 "New Zealand Finance," *The Times* 45889, July 31, 1931, 12; McKinnon, *Treasury*, 126–127; Singleton, *Central Banking in the Twentieth Century*, 64; Cain and Hopkins, *British Imperialism*, 510–511; Gary Hawke and John Singleton, "State and Central Bank in New Zealand," in *Les banques centrales et l'État-nation*, ed. Olivier Feiertag and Michel Margairaz (Paris: Presses de Sciences Po, 2016), 217; Singleton, "Central Banks in the British Dominions," 369.

111 Niemeyer to A.D. Park [Treasury, New Zealand], September 22, 1931, BoE OV59/15; Niemeyer, *Banking and Currency in New Zealand*, 10.

stabilization. On December 1, Norman learned of New Zealand's continued difficulties in refinancing short-term Treasury bills, estimated at around £6 or 7 million.[112] His calculations showed that, by the following April, the government would owe £3.2 million on its short-term debt, with an additional £3.57 million in interest payments.[113] Only £3 million was expected to be covered by New Zealand banks.[114] Moreover, the public coffers had already been struggling to service the state's debt payments. In 1922, the national debt had amounted to £219 million, while ten years later it had reached £282 million.[115] Norman, nevertheless, rejected the proposal to extend a temporary advance to the New Zealand government for fear of raising anxieties in the City. Only under several stringent conditions would he accept the terms of a loan: New Zealand would have to refrain from short-term borrowing on the London money market, it needed to plan to repay its "London commitments during the next twelve months," and it had to ensure the remittance through New Zealand banks.[116] The New Zealand government accepted these proposals a few days later.[117]

Still, the reform involving a new reserve bank did not primarily involve a loan negotiation but instead broadly concerned the place of New Zealand within the global economic system. While chairing the Committee on Methods of Economic Co-operation at the 1932 Ottawa Conference, the former Prime Minister, Gordon Coates, announced that his country "is willing and anxious to co-operate in any steps which London may devise with a view to remedying matters. Such co-operation might include the co-ordination of our banking system under a central reserve bank and the charging of such a bank with the duty of maintaining the sterling exchange system."[118] Electoral incentives further accelerated the prospect of institutional change. After 1931, the United and Reform parties formed a coalition government that became increasingly interested in using expert advice to combat the Great Depression, particularly as they wanted to take credit for any ensuing economic recovery. By September, Prime Minister Forbes decided to propose new banking legislation based on the combined recommendations of Niemeyer, Coates, and Walter W. Stewart (another one of the Bank's economists).[119]

112 Norman to Hopkins, December 1, 1931, BoE G1/335.
113 Basil G. Catterns, "Memorandum: New Zealand," December 4, 1931, BoE G1/335.
114 Basil G. Catterns, "Memorandum: New Zealand," December 4, 1931, BoE G1/335.
115 H. Belshaw, "Crisis and Readjustment in New Zealand," *Journal of Political Economy* 41, no. 6 (1933), 752.
116 Basil G. Catterns, "Memorandum: New Zealand," December 4, 1931, BoE G1/335; Catterns to Wilford, December 7, 1931, BoE G1/335.
117 Wilford to Norman, December 10, 1931, BoE G1/335; Leslie Lefeaux, "Memorandum: New Zealand," March 10, 1932, BoE G1/335; Montagu Norman, Diary, March 10 and 15, 1932, BoE ADM34/21.
118 "Statement by the Leader of the Delegation for New Zealand (The Rt. Hon. J.G. Coates)," in *Imperial Economic Conference, 1932*, A.–6 (Wellington: W.A.G. Skinner, Government Printer, 1932), 99.
119 "Central Reserve Bank for New Zealand," *The Times* 46248, September 26, 1932, 20.

Economists in Australia and New Zealand suggested additional measures to promote a general economic recovery. Douglas Copland (University of Melbourne) viewed a lower exchange rate as vital for supporting domestic agriculture.[120] The depreciation of the New Zealand pound promised to strengthen the country's ability to export, thereby promoting economic growth.[121] Horace Belshaw (Auckland University College) largely agreed, further asserting that a devaluation could spur an export-based recovery.[122] At the same time, he thought that a reserve bank, while conferring long-term benefits to the country, needed to be established in times of better political and economic circumstances. Both the absence of a domestic short-term money market and the unclear delineation between the proposed reserve bank and the government were his main reasons.[123] In contrast, Niemeyer's report argued the reverse causality: that a reserve bank would be precisely the means of creating a short-term money market and that a well-developed one was not a prerequisite for a reserve bank.[124]

Although economic advisers identified varying reasons for identifying the causes of the crisis, their views converged on the idea of a new reserve bank in some form. Both Niemeyer and the Economic Committee (on which both Copland and Belshaw served) believed that the United Kingdom might return to a new gold parity at a future date. Establishing a reserve bank would accelerate that prospect. Another influential expert on the Economic Committee was Bernard Ashwin, a New Zealand-born, Cambridge-educated Treasury official. He was interested in demonstrating the adverse impact of Australia's links to New Zealand during the crisis.[125] It was New Zealand's financial independence from Australia, rather than from the United Kingdom, that could aid in its recovery from the depression.

Niemeyer's recommendations, long after his mission had concluded, continued to pervade public discourse. With the backing of New Zealand economists, his proposal to create an independent reserve bank gained additional support in later years. Belshaw served on various advisory committees concerned with economic policy, and he later joined Tocker as one of Coates' economic advisers. In lectures and testimonies before government commissions, both Belshaw and Ashwin underscored the many benefits of an independent

[120] D.B. Copland, "New Zealand's Economic Difficulties and Expert Opinion," *The Economic Journal* 42, no. 167 (1932), 375; Greasley and Oxley, "Regime Shift and Fast Recovery on the Periphery," 705; Wright, "The Policy Origins of the Reserve Bank of New Zealand," 12.

[121] Otto Niemeyer, "Cablegram to A.D. Park, Esq.," March 9, 1932, BoE OV59/16.

[122] Belshaw, "Crisis and Readjustment in New Zealand," 763; McKinnon, *Treasury*, 139; Millmow, *A History of Australasian Economic Thought*, 76.

[123] "Central Bank Plan: Cases for and Against," *New Zealand Herald (Auckland)* LXIX, 21328, November 1, 1932, 13.

[124] Niemeyer, *Banking and Currency in New Zealand*, 4.

[125] Greasley and Oxley, "Regime Shift and Fast Recovery on the Periphery," 703.

reserve bank.[126] While commercial banks focused on generating profits for their shareholders, a reserve bank might serve the "general social interest" by financing public expenditures in times of crisis.[127] The Niemeyer report, despite its many shortcomings, had crafted a proposal that appealed to New Zealand's national interests.

BRAZIL AFTER ITS REVOLUTION

Shortly after his mission to Australia, Niemeyer accepted an invitation to design another reform plan in Brazil. The new government under President Getúlio Vargas sought assistance on a range of issues, including the elimination of the deficit, the stabilization of the exchange rate, and the overall reduction in foreign borrowing. Addressing these problems, he believed, would have lent greater legitimacy to the new regime. For the Bank, the revolution offered an opportunity to establish an independent central bank, which would hold a monopoly of note issue and resemble the structure of the British monetary authority. Although an existing commercial bank, the Banco do Brasil, already issued gold-backed notes and set its own discount rate, its priorities were often contradictory to the government's goals, as it continued to profit from lending operations.[128]

Prior efforts to shape Brazil's financial system had led to little change. The most recent attempt had occurred in 1923 when the country's request for a loan of £25 million led the Rothschilds to sponsor an overseas mission to assess the proposal. Led by Edwin Montagu, a Liberal MP and former Secretary of State for India, the mission produced a set of recommendations that included extensive budgetary reform and a reorganization of the railway system.[129] Although the Brazilian government accepted the terms of the

[126] Horace Belshaw, "Lecture 7: Foreign Exchanges," n.d., UAL Belshaw Papers 7/2/6; "Notes of Evidence Given before the Government Monetary Committee at Wellington on Thursday 19th April, 1934 at 10 A.M.," MBL Tocker Papers 1/4; Monetary Committee, *Minutes of Evidence*, B.–3 (Wellington: W.A.G. Skinner, Government Printer, 1934), 16.

[127] Horace Belshaw, "Lecture 6: Reserve Banks and the Control of Credit," n.d., UAL Belshaw Papers 7/2/5.

[128] "Cable Received from Sir Henry Lynch," June 25, 1930, RAL XI/111/398B; F.C. de Oliveira Botelho [Finance Minister] to the Banco do Brasil, October 11, 1930, FGV Aranha Papers No. 495; Steven Topik, "State Enterprise in a Liberal Regime: The Banco do Brasil, 1905–1930," *Journal of Interamerican Studies and World Affairs* 22, no. 4 (1980), 416; Steven Topik, *The Political Economy of the Brazilian State, 1889–1930* (Austin: University of Texas Press, 1987), 42; Maxfield, *Gatekeepers of Growth*, 123.

[129] Abreu, "A missão Niemeyer," 12; Mircea Buescu, "A missão inglesa de 1924," *Revista de informação legislativa* 21, no. 82 (1984): 173–186; Winston Fritsch, "The Montagu Financial Mission to Brazil and the Federal Economic Policy Changes of 1924," *Brazilian Economic Studies* 9 (1985): 263–325; Dayer, *Finance and Empire*, 161–162; Winston Fritsch, *External Constraints on Economic Policy in Brazil, 1889–1930* (Pittsburgh: University of Pittsburgh Press, 1988), 86–98; Ferguson, *The House of Rothschild*, vol. 2, 460–461; Caroline Shaw,

plan in February 1924, the mission failed due to Britain's subsequent embargo on foreign loans.[130]

In 1929, Brazil found itself again pressed to acquire a line of credit. The country was dependent on the export of agricultural products, such as coffee, as well as the earnings from its foreign-exchange dealings.[131] With the collapse in commodity prices following the Wall Street crash, the value of Brazil's exports fell drastically. Social unrest during the ensuing economic downturn, as well as allegations of public corruption, led to a coup d'état that forced President Washington Luís into exile on October 24, 1930. While the establishment of a provisional government under Vargas in November brought an end to the political vacuum, the emergency powers he used made British observers apprehensive about the future of the economy under a provisional government. As a result, the City's leading merchant banks threatened to withdraw their investments "unless Brazil invited some outside expert to investigate and reorganise financial methods."[132]

The Bank, seeking to promote the City's interests abroad, envisioned leading efforts to reshape the monetary system. Already in March 1930, Governor Norman had met with Lionel de Rothschild to discuss the prospect of sending an advisory mission to Brazil.[133] After the coup raised anxieties in the City, Norman was further convinced that a proper examination of Brazilian public finance was essential. In particular, he remarked how "the present financial difficulties" provided the Bank with an opportunity to "achieve orthodoxy for the Central Bank," while simultaneously resolving the problem of "large foreign indebtedness."[134] While still divided over the strategic goals of an intervention, the Bank preemptively received a formal invitation from the Brazilian government, inviting Niemeyer to Rio de Janeiro in early 1931.[135]

From Brazil's perspective, it was not solely the possibility of a loan that culminated in Niemeyer's mission. In January, a London syndicate of bankers – facilitated by N.M. Rothschild & Sons – had agreed to arrange

"Rothschilds and Brazil: An Introduction to Sources in the Rothschild Archive," *Latin American Research Review* 40, no. 1 (2005), 174; Cain and Hopkins, *British Imperialism*, 570–571.

130 "Aide-Mémoire Left with the President of Brazil," January 29, 1924, RAL XI/111/309; "Report by the British Financial Mission to Brazil," March 19, 1924, RAL XI/111/309.

131 Fiona Gordon-Ashworth, "Agricultural Commodity Control under Vargas in Brazil, 1930–1945," *Journal of Latin American Studies* 12, no. 1 (1980), 88.

132 As reported in Sir William Seeds [British Ambassador, Brazil] to Arthur Henderson [Secretary of State for Foreign Affairs], August 27, 1930, BoE OV103/1.

133 Montagu Norman, Diary, March 26, 1930, BoE ADM34/19.

134 Norman to Leon Fraser [Bank for International Settlements], January 7, 1931, BoE OV103/69.

135 Committee of Treasury, Minutes, January 7, 1931, BoE G8/59; Regis de Oliveira [Brazilian Ambassador to the Court of St James's] to Norman, January 8, 1931, BoE OV103/1 and RAL XI/111/437.

for Brazil to receive an emergency credit of £7 million ($35 million).[136] Concerned with the broader relationship between the economy and the state, the Vargas administration sought to establish its own legitimacy after a coup in October 1930. Government officials aimed to procure advice from an expert to implement and legitimize their post-revolutionary reforms.[137] There had already been an expansion of the state's jurisdiction in economic affairs, exhibited through its support for import-substitution industrialization, a policy of increasing prominence throughout Latin America. For Brazil in particular, a highly publicized visit from an international financial expert might have given the new regime political legitimacy. "[T]he new Government," *The Economist* declared, "is anxious to set its financial house in order."[138]

On February 13, Niemeyer arrived in Rio de Janeiro, where he was personally greeted by President Vargas.[139] Prepared for the political spectacle, the press closely his journey. The Rio-based *Correio da Manhã* reported that Niemeyer had "a name of great prestige in the circles of world finance," in addition to being "a sympathetic and jovial figure of charming simplicity."[140] Another newspaper, *O Jornal*, wrote that Niemeyer's mission came "with unprecedented probability of success." It seemed to promise Brazil "our first central bank built in accordance with the rules approved by universal experience on this matter."[141]

After his first few meetings with bankers, politicians, and industrialists, Niemeyer began to relay his findings back to London. Privately, he was not convinced that politicians would willingly accept his recommendations. Although another foreign loan depended on whether Brazil agreed to "pursue a firm financial policy," political blockages would likely hinder significant progress from being made.[142] He claimed that the finance minister's "ideas are entirely vague on details" and complained about the lack of reliable and readily available statistics on Brazilian public finance.[143]

Still, foreign expertise could offer, to a certain degree, concessions that might help the plan garner support. Niemeyer thus recommended a series of reforms, including balancing the budget, increasing taxes, and, most importantly,

136 "Brazil Gets London Loan," *The New York Times* LXXX, 26656, January 17, 1931, 28; "Memorandum," January 23, 1931, RAL XI/111/437; "City Notes," *The Times* 45729, January 24, 1931, 17.

137 "Várias Notícias," *Jornal do Commercio (Rio de Janeiro)* 104, 9, January 10, 1931, 5.

138 "Sir Otto Niemeyer's New Task," *The Economist* 112, 4560, January 17, 1931, 107.

139 "Sir Otto Niemeyer in Brazil," *The Times* 45748, February 16, 1931, 12.

140 "Sir Otto Niemeyer," *Correio da Manhã (Rio de Janeiro)* 30, 11092, February 14, 1931, 1.

141 "A missão de Sir Otto Niemeyer," *O Jornal (Rio de Janeiro)* XIII, 3734, January 13, 1931, 4.

142 Niemeyer to N.M. Rothschild & Sons, March 22, 1931, RAL XI/111/437.

143 Niemeyer to N.M. Rothschild & Sons, March 22, 1931, RAL XI/111/437; Abreu, "A missão Niemeyer," 15.

establishing an independent central bank.[144] The report also emphasized centralized state management, from railways and telegraph services, which formed part of a general framework of political economy that appealed to the Vargas regime.[145] In this scenario, the central bank would serve an important function in maintaining the stability of the currency and maintaining the sole right of note issue.[146] One implication of these changes was that the Banco do Brasil would be left entirely to its private business of commercial banking. Not only would it have been difficult to separate the operations of a commercial bank from those of a central bank, but the Banco do Brasil seemed to play too vital a role in the nation's economic development. When, for instance, the nationally important coffee sector began reporting low cash reserves in late 1930, the Provisional Government of São Paulo directly requested the assistance of the Banco do Brasil.[147]

Niemeyer's final report initially received the approval of various interest groups due to its quid pro quo arrangements. A group of private bankers agreed to back the plan in exchange for a temporary suspension of debt payments, as well as the opportunity to select the central bank's first president. Mário Brant, the president of the Banco do Brasil, welcomed this role for his institution: "The new Republic will rehabilitate financially the country, redeeming the former errors of the first Republic."[148] Another private banker similarly described how foreign expertise was "of great value" to Brazil because it accelerated "the urgent and painful task of rebuilding our financial edifice on solid foundations."[149] In the public eye, most government officials wanted to express support for a program, which would help raise international confidence in the economy. In March, Finance Minister José Maria Whitaker reported to the press that Brazil might have found itself in a dire situation, but the general guidelines for reforming the nation's currency and credit system were now "being duly studied with the valuable collaboration of Sir Otto Niemeyer."[150]

These comments, intended to be delivered to the public, were political tools that primarily aimed to raise overall trust in Brazil's economy. In

[144] Niemeyer to Whitaker, September 25, 1931, FGV Vargas Papers No. 0469–0470/2; Otto Niemeyer, *Reorganização das finanças brasileiras. Relatório apresentado ao Governo Brasileiro* (Rio de Janeiro: Imprensa Nacional, 1931), 23–30.

[145] "Balanced Budget for Brazil," *The Daily Telegraph* 23771, July 25, 1931, 9.

[146] Niemeyer, *Reorganização das finanças brasileiras*, 26–27; Zendejas and Nodari, "Latin American Experiments," 343.

[147] João Alberto Lins de Barros [Gabinete do Presidente do Estado de S. Paulo] to Vargas, December 20, 1930, FGV Vargas Papers No. 0248/1–2; "Exposição sobre a situação do Estado de São Paulo," December 30, 1930, FGV Vargas Papers No. 0250/1–2.

[148] Quoted in "Financial Reform in Brazil," *The Times* 45886, July 28, 1931, 12.

[149] "A situação financeira do paiz através das impressões do sr. Gudesteu Pires," *O Jornal (Rio de Janeiro)* XIII, 3787, March 15, 1931, 16.

[150] "A situação e os seus problemas mais transcendentes," *O Jornal (Rio de Janeiro)* XIII, 3782, March 10, 1931, 1.

reality, officials understood the many unresolved fiscal issues that threatened to undermine the plan. Even though Niemeyer "continues to be in good spirits," Whitaker claimed that "absolutely nothing will be possible to achieve without first obtaining a balanced budget."[151] In London, the Bank was unable to identify a source for the loan, which Niemeyer guessed needed to be at least $80 million.[152] It also remained to be seen whether such a loan could have covered both federal and state debts.[153] Given that City bankers had only earlier that year issued a loan, it was unlikely that a line of credit twice the previous amount could have been extended. Had public expenditures continued to remain high, the currency would have been placed under considerable strain, thereby risking the possibility of a devaluation or a default.

Although Niemeyer's initial version of a central bank seemed popular in theory, he was unable to gain support from Brazil's leading experts. One such figure was Eugênio Gudin, who had served on the 1931 Commission for the Financial and Economic Studies of States and Municipalities, a technical body of experts commissioned by the Ministry of Finance.[154] After studying civil engineering at the Polytechnic School of Rio de Janeiro, Gudin began publishing in economic journals and taught courses in economics at his alma mater. In addition to writing articles for *O Jornal*, where he served as a director, Gudin worked in the Bank Mobilization Fund (*Caixa de Mobilização Bancária*), an entity created by the government in 1932 to extend credits to the agricultural and industrial sector.[155] In these areas, Gudin sought to portray himself as a financial expert to gain influence in shaping public policy. While his adherence to free-market ideas characterized his later research on the problems of state-led industrialization, some of his earlier contributions to the field of economics focused on the question of central banking.[156]

151 Whitaker to Vargas, March 4, 1931, FGV Vargas Papers No. 0306–0307/1.

152 "Finds Central Bank Needed in Brazil: Sir Otto Niemeyer Suggests System Patterned after Our Federal Reserve," *The New York Times* LXXX, 26845, July 25, 1931, 22.

153 Whitaker to Aranha, July 8, 1931, FGV Aranha Papers No. 419.

154 República Federativa do Brasil, "Decreto no. 20.631 – de 9 de novembro de 1931," in República dos Estados Unidos do Brasil, *Coleção das leis de 1931, vol. 1* (Rio de Janeiro: Imprensa Nacional, 1931), 469–470; Maria Angélica Borges, *Eugênio Gudin: capitalismo e neoliberalismo* (São Paulo: EDUC, 1996), 307; Maria Rita Garcia Loureiro, *Os economistas no Governo: gestão econômica e democracia* (Rio de Janeiro: Fundação Getulio Vargas Editora, 1997), 51.

155 Sebastião Carlos Velasco e Cruz, *Empresariado e Estado na transição brasileira: um estudo sobre a economia política do autoritarismo, 1974–1977* (Campinas: Editora da Unicamp, 1995), 39–40; Borges, *Eugênio Gudin*, 153–154; Villela, "Las funciones de banca central antes del banco central," 442; Ivan Colangelo Salomão and Victoria Silva Oliveira, "Banco do Brasil: de autoridade monetária a banco comercial," *Revista Brasileira de História & Ciências Sociais* 15, no. 31 (2024), 451–452.

156 Marcelo de Paiva Abreu, "A economia brasileira, 1930–1964," *Pontifícia Universidade Católica do Rio de Janeiro Working Paper*, no. 585 (2010), 20; Marco Ludwik Patrício Krebs,

Gudin might have acknowledged the influential work of Niemeyer, referring to him, if disparagingly, as the "eminent British financier."[157] He certainly understood that the Banco do Brasil played a key role in sustaining the nation's economic, industrial, and agricultural development. Yet, far more skeptical of Niemeyer than his contemporaries, he opposed the prospect of foreign intervention in economic affairs. On August 3, 1931, Gudin met with Niemeyer at the Hotel Gloria to discuss the specifics of his plan.[158] Using the press to his advantage, he was able to ask incisive questions about the shortcomings of Niemeyer's proposals: If the new central bank held the government account, would all its reserves be used to meet the demands of foreign creditors? And would the public-spending reductions during a crisis, in reality, lower investors' confidence in Brazil's economy?[159] This targeted line of questioning was a tactical strategy that aimed to cause public anxiety over foreign encroachment and instill faith in Brazil's existing form of governance.

As a result, the proposal to create a central bank did not receive enough support, and one would only be established three decades later. From one perspective, City bankers were unwilling to offer a loan before the introduction of major structural changes.[160] Confidence in the Bank's plan severely diminished after the budget deficit had become publicly known. In December, Lionel de Rothschild wrote to Niemeyer about the accuracy of the government's books: "The [Finance] Minister's estimates of a deficit ... [appear] to be wildly exaggerated. I am quite sure he must have mixed up his figures."[161]

Along with fiscal issues, public opinion remained strongly divided over the report. Because of Gudin's questioning, widespread opposition from political elites and other commercial banks proliferated, thereby halting the creation of a new independent central bank in line with the Bank's policy prescription.[162] Niemeyer's plan came under scrutiny because it forced Brazil to accept the terms of a future loan given by foreign creditors.[163] The political influence of São Paulo's industrial interests, as well as the financial interests represented by the Banco do

"Os cinquenta anos do banco central do Brasil" (PhD diss., Universidade Federal do Rio de Janeiro, 2016), 17; Victor Cruz e Silva, Marco Cavalieri, and Marcelo Curado, "On the Transmission of Keynes' and Keynesian Ideas in Brazil through Eugênio Gudin's *Principles of Monetary Economics*," *The European Journal of the History of Economic Thought* 28, no. 1 (2021), 2.

[157] Eugênio Gudin, "O relatório de Sir Otto Niemeyer," *O Jornal (Rio de Janeiro)* XIII, 3903, July 29, 1931, 2.

[158] "Sir Otto Niemeyer responde às objeções feitas ao seu relatório através das colunas dos 'Diários associados' matutinos," *O Jornal (Rio de Janeiro)* XIII, 3907, August 2, 1931, 1.

[159] "Como Sir Otto Niemeyer responde às dúvidas e objeções que levantou o seu relatório, na opinião brasileira," *O Jornal (Rio de Janeiro)* XIII, 3908, August 4, 1931, 1.

[160] Sayers, *The Bank of England, vol.* 2, 523.

[161] Lionel de Rothschild to Niemeyer, December 5, 1931, BoE OV103/1.

[162] "Recent Developments in Central Banking Statutes and Technique, 1929–1937," 1937, BoE G1/502 and OV44/96.

[163] Vargas to Borges de Medeiros, October 17, 1931, FGV Vargas Papers No. 0489/2–0489/3.

Brasil, similarly threatened the encroachment of foreign financial interests.[164] These obstacles, the Bank later reported, "prevent[ed] any action being taken to set up the central bank recommended by Sir O.E. Niemeyer."[165]

ARGENTINA AT A CROSSROADS

Even before the conclusion of the mission to Brazil, the Bank's advisers had been reluctant to intervene in Argentina. Debilitating outflows of gold in November 1929 led to a sharp reduction in bank deposits, followed by the abandonment of the gold standard on December 16, 1929.[166] Amidst the ensuing depression, the Argentine government continued to oppose procuring the opinion of foreign experts. "Any movement in this direction [for the creation of a central bank]," Niemeyer wrote in January 1930, "must come from Argentine circles themselves."[167]

Yet a coup d'état in September 1930 instigated a radical shift in priorities. The overthrow of President Hipólito Yrigoyen commenced the "infamous decade" (*década infame*) in Argentine politics. While the nationalists had gained power under the leadership of the de facto president, General José Félix Uriburu, they only held minority power in the coalition government.[168] Instead, under Agustín P. Justo, the former war minister, the conservatives were able to consolidate electoral power after aligning with three left-wing parties and winning a highly contested general election in November 1931.[169] To resolve the country's pressing financial issues, the Justo administration planned to obtain an initial line of credit by issuing the so-called Patriotic Loan (*Empréstito Patriótico*), which amounted to 500 million Argentine pesos.[170] The government also aimed to discuss the prospect of long-term stability. In November 1932, Finance Minister Alberto Hueyo suggested procuring the assistance of an external expert to advise Argentina on its economic situation.[171] After the rejection of his own advisory board's recommendations,

[164] Maxfield, *Gatekeepers of Growth*, 123–124.

[165] "Review of Statutes of Central Banks, 1929–1937," May 1937, BoE G1/502.

[166] Banco de la Nación Argentina, Circular no. 364(b), November 27, 1929, AGN BNA01 Topogr. 27, Tomo VI.

[167] Niemeyer to T.K. Bewley [Treasury], January 6, 1930, BoE OV9/3.

[168] David Rock, *Argentina, 1516–1987: From Spanish Colonization to Alphonsín* (Berkeley: University of California Press, 1987), 216.

[169] Justo won a plurality, though not a majority, of seats and was able to win the support of the *Concordancia* alliance (the *Partido Demócrata Nacional*, *Partido Socialista Independiente*, and *Unión Cívica Radical*); Jorge A. Nállim, *Transformations and Crisis of Liberalism in Argentina, 1930–1955* (Pittsburgh: University of Pittsburgh Press, 2012), 37.

[170] Jorge A. Lorenzutti, *Dinero, política y bancos: historia del Banco Central de la República Argentina, 1935–1995* (Buenos Aires: Ediciones Dunken, 1996), 55.

[171] Hueyo to Manuel Malbrán [Argentine Ambassador, Court of St. James's], August 19, 1932, BoE G1/402; Alberto Hueyo, *El Banco Central: aspectos fundamentales y antecedentes de su implantación en la República Argentina* (Buenos Aires: Francisco A. Colombo, 1958), 28.

which led to the resignation of five civil servants, he extended a secret invitation to Niemeyer to visit Argentina.[172]

Niemeyer's planned visit had been one of a series of attempts to protect the City's interests in Latin America. The British government had previously dispatched advisory missions to Argentina, including one in 1899 and another in 1911. A more recent mission, undertaken in 1929 by Lord Viscount D'Abernon, a former British MP, came at the invitation of President Yrigoyen, who was interested in strengthening economic links between the two countries.[173] These efforts resulted in little diplomatic improvements and offered even less in trade benefits. Upon his return, D'Abernon predicted major challenges in maintaining future commercial arrangements with Argentina, suggesting the need for "a more active and more energetic policy."[174]

The Niemeyer mission, however, was more strategic in its timing after a political revolution and amidst an economic depression. On January 13, 1933, the Bank's experts arrived in Buenos Aires where they planned to meet with leading officials.[175] Extensive coverage by the press compelled the finance minister to report that Niemeyer was due to receive "no remuneration nor official status" during his visit since nominally he was only to be in negotiation with the commercial banks.[176] He was assigned to work with another one of the Bank's advisers, Henry Clay, to examine the Argentine economy and identify possible reforms.

A highly politicized affair, the intervention featured a multitude of stakeholders: the Bank, the City, and a cohort of Argentine economists, bankers, and civil servants. In general, British officials believed that there needed to be an independent central bank that issued notes and avoided commercial-banking activities.[177] The City was particularly concerned with the profitability of

[172] "Argentina Employs Briton as Adviser: Sir Otto Niemeyer Will Study Finances and Suggest Steps for Economic Remedies," *The New York Times* LXXXII, 27336, November 27, 1932, 25. The invitation had been sent on behalf of the Banco de la Nación to mitigate public speculation; Pedro Etchegaray [President, Banco de la Nación] and José Luis de Irigoyen [Secretary-General, Banco de la Nación] to Norman, November 10, 1932, BoE G1/402.

[173] Roger Gravil, *The Anglo–Argentine Connection, 1900–1939* (Boulder: Westview Press, 1985), 165–170; David Rock, *The British in Argentina: Commerce, Settlers and Power, 1800–2000* (Basingstoke: Palgrave Macmillan, 2019), 267, 273; Gaynor Johnson, "The D'Abernon Trade Mission to South America, 1929: Context and Reappraisal," in *Britain and the Growth of US Hegemony in Twentieth-Century Latin America: Competition, Cooperation and Coexistence*, ed. Thomas C. Mills and Rory M. Miller (Cham: Palgrave Macmillan, 2020): 105–125.

[174] Viscount D'Abernon, "The Economic Mission to South America," *Journal of the Royal Institute of International Affairs* 8, no. 6 (1929), 571.

[175] Niemeyer to Carlos Indalecio Gómez [Ministro Haciendo de la Plata], January 31, 1933, BoE OV102/208.

[176] "Sir Otto Niemeyer," *The Daily Telegraph* 24203, December 14, 1932, 11.

[177] "English Bank Link Aim of Argentina," *The New York Times* LXXXII, 27337, November 28, 1932, 5; Clay to Niemeyer, February 20, 1933, NCO Clay Papers 71/3.

British-owned Argentine railways, which was the largest single category of foreign investment in Latin America.[178] Any reform would have prioritized restructuring the country's outstanding foreign debts as well.

Yet a truly independent central bank – as the Bank envisioned – would need to appropriate existing powers from other state institutions: the Rediscount Committee (*Comisión de Redescuentos*), the Foreign Exchange Office (*Oficina de Control de Cambios*), and the Currency Board (*Caja de Conversión*).[179] Acknowledging the important function that each of these entities had, Niemeyer remained convinced that the current system was outdated. At the outbreak of the First World War, the Currency Board had "generally ceased to function as soon as the emergency arose ... which it was precisely called to face."[180] Instead, it was the nation's leading state bank, the Banco de la Nación Argentina, that had already adopted some of the responsibilities associated with an interventionist central bank.[181] Along with issuing notes and managing domestic credit, the Banco de la Nación had provided liquidity to the market through its rediscounting operations, seen notably during the crisis of 1913–1914.[182] The sustainability of the banking sector might have depended on the cooperation of multiple state institutions, but its proper functioning seemed to rely on private institutions.

[178] Of the £306 million invested in Argentina, the Bank estimated approximately £119 million were connected to the railway industry; Overseas & Foreign Department, "British Investments in Argentina," May 31, 1935, BoE OV102/5.

[179] Henry Clay, Memorandum, 1933, BoE OV102/207; Patricio Catriel Liddle and Juan José Pita, "Historia de la creación del Banco Central de la República Argentina," *Ensayos económicos*, no. 64 (2010), 127; Mónica Gómez, "El fin de la Caja de Conversión y el nacimiento del Banco Central. Argentina en la Gran Depresión, 1929–1935," in *Orígenes de la globalización bancaria: experiencias de España y América Latina*, ed. Daniel Díaz Fuentes, Andrés Hoyo Aparicio, and Carlos Marichal (Santander: Genueve Ediciones, El Colegio de México, 2017), 392–400; Mónica Gómez, *Avatares de un sistema monetario: la primera Caja de Conversión argentina y su transformación final en Banco Central (1890–1935)* (Buenos Aires: Teseo, 2018), 166–169.

[180] Otto Niemeyer, *Informe y proyectos* (Buenos Aires: Ministerio de Hacienda de la Nación, 1933), 9.

[181] Banco de la Nación Argentina, Circular no. 416(b), November 17, 1930, AGN BNA01 Topogr. 27, Tomo VI; Andrés M. Regalsky, "Estado, banca pública y crisis: los créditos del Banco de la Nación Argentina durante la coyuntura de 1914–15," in *Historia bancaria y monetaria de América Latina (siglos XIX y XX): nuevas perspectivas*, ed. Carlos Marichal and Thiago Gambi (Santander: Editorial de la Universidad de Cantabria, 2017), 261; Andrés Regalsky, "En los preámbulos de la Banca Central 1914–1930: el Banco de la Nación Argentina y sus nuevas orientaciones a partir de la Primera Guerra Mundial," in *Historia necesaria del Banco Central de la República Argentina: entre la búsqueda de la estabilidad y la promoción del desarrollo*, ed. Marcelo Rougier and Florencia Sember (Buenos Aires: Lenguaje Claro-Ciccus, 2018), 42.

[182] Gerardo della Paolera and Alan M. Taylor, *Straining at the Anchor: The Argentine Currency Board and the Search for Macroeconomic Stability, 1880–1935* (Chicago and London: The University of Chicago Press, 2001), 174.

Niemeyer, seeking to raise trust in the Argentine economy for City investors, suggested amalgamating these duties in a single institution, albeit one with more independence.[183] His report presented an extensive program of reform: balanced budgets, stable exchange rates, and an independent central bank.[184] While these recommendations aligned with his standard protocol, there were also some changes specific to Argentina's debt situation. In line with the City's interests, the report urged the national government to continue servicing its short-term debt payments, mostly owed to commercial banks and British creditors, over its long-term ones.[185] This recommendation would effectively secure seniority for foreign creditors, especially banks based in London. The Bank similarly recommended that Argentina continue to maintain its debt services in full, lest it risk the possibility of capital flight, which would have worsened an already precarious exchange-rate position.[186]

Given these stipulations, Niemeyer sought to find others who could support his plan. Alejandro Bunge, a prominent Argentine economist, was one potential candidate. In his prior role as the country's first Director General of National Statistics, Bunge had written about the need for economic reform in the aftermath of the First World War.[187] Whereas the inefficient organization of credit and unresolved political debates (mainly over wartime reparations) had plagued postwar Europe, Argentina and other export-driven economies in Latin America suffered from the lack of access to foreign loans.[188] He hinted at the need for the Argentine government to create a bank of its own, one that provided "generous credits" and rediscounted commercial bills.[189] While he had not yet referred to it as a "central bank" in 1922, he highlighted the government's key role in restoring national credit. By September 1931, Bunge announced before the National Academy of Economic Sciences his intention to

[183] Niemeyer, *Informe y proyectos*, 27–28; Lorenzutti, *Dinero, política y bancos*, 54.

[184] Otto Niemeyer, *Report Presented to the Argentine Government* (London: S.B. Chamberlain, 1933).

[185] James, *The End of Globalization*, 148.

[186] Siepmann to Bunge, October 13, 1932, BoE OV102/2.

[187] On Bunge, see Jorge F. Pantaleón, "El surgimiento de la nueva economía argentina: el caso Bunge," in *Intelectuales y expertos: la constitución del conocimiento social en la Argentina*, ed. Federico Neiburg and Mariano Plotkin (Buenos Aires: Paidós, 2004): 175–201; Claudio Belini, "El grupo Bunge y la política económica del primer peronismo, 1943–1952," *Latin American Research Review* 41, no. 1 (2006): 27–50; Javier Villanueva, "Alejandro E. Bunge: una visión de la Argentina," *Revista Cultura Económica* 28, no. 77/78 (2010): 73–77; Florencia Sember, "The Reception of Irving Fisher in Argentina: Alejandro Bunge and Raúl Prebisch," *The European Journal of the History of Economic Thought* 20, no. 2 (2013), 386–393; Eric Helleiner, *The Neomercantilists: A Global Intellectual History* (Ithaca and London: Cornell University Press, 2021), 98–99, 348–349.

[188] Alejandro E. Bunge, "Die Rohstoffe und der wirtschaftliche Wiederaufbau Europas, unter besonderer Berücksichtigung Argentiniens," *Weltwirtschaftliches Archiv* 18 (1922), 336–337.

[189] Bunge, "Die Rohstoffe und der wirtschaftliche Wiederaufbau Europas," 339.

continue his study on a proposal for a central bank.[190] Projecting a potential deficit of 160 million pesos in 1932, he sought to prioritize budgetary reform, particularly as a way of helping Argentine trade. Doing so would have corrected the balance-of-payments shortfalls. A general rise in the price of raw materials, Bunge hoped, might have further initiated an economic recovery.[191]

Niemeyer, however, was less optimistic about the prospect of an immediate recovery: "The good banks unduly liquid: the bad banks, including for this purpose the Banco de la Nación, entirely frozen. Up-country debtors, who of course are largely over borrowed, unable to pay their full mortgage interest ... . Politically a Government which is really in the minority, subject to pressure from its right wing followers."[192] Where Niemeyer and Bunge's proposals did converge was over the idea of a central bank. Partly to prevent "American financial carpet baggers" who profited from Argentine woes, as well as to limit the influence of radical proposals for monetary reform within Argentina, an independent central bank was the *sine qua non* of financial stability.[193] According to Niemeyer's report, the bank's main purpose would be to instill confidence in the national economic system: "Commercial banks, both national and foreign, will take considerable advantage of the establishment of a sound monetary system and the benefits offered by a central-banking organization."[194]

Orthodox views espoused by both the Bank's advisers and Argentine economists thereafter determined the nature of reform. Upon his departure, Niemeyer had convinced the Argentine government to accept the benefits of orthodox policies. On April 7, 1933, Finance Minister Hueyo thanked Governor Norman for offering Niemeyer's insights: "I have pleasure in writing to express the gratitude of the Argentine Government for the special consideration shown by the Bank of England in sending one of their most distinguished members, accompanied by qualified experts." Hueyo continued by praising the value of an expert in the process: "[T]he Mission [was] undertaken and completed with wonderful diligence and skill ..., and the opinions pronounced by Sir Otto Niemeyer are characterised by particular accuracy from a technical point of view."[195] Deputy Governor Harvey, responding on Norman's behalf, believed there was great value to this "legislative reform" in Argentina, further noting the Bank "will watch with keen interest any developments in this direction."[196]

190 As reported in Academia de Ciencias Económicas, "La academia de ciencias económicas inició las sesiones del corriente año," *Revista de economía argentina* 27, no. 157 (1931): 304.

191 Alejandro E. Bunge, "Sobre el problema del cambio en Argentina," September 30, 1932, BoE OV102/2.

192 Niemeyer to Hambro, February 27, 1933, BoE G1/402 and OV102/208.

193 Niemeyer to Hambro, February 27, 1933, BoE G1/402 and OV102/208.

194 Niemeyer, *Informe y proyectos*, 49.

195 Translated by the Bank; Hueyo to Norman, April 7, 1933, BoE OV102/3.

196 Harvey to Hueyo, April 20, 1933, BoE G1/402 and OV102/3.

Even after his mission, Niemeyer continued to shape debates over banking legislation in Argentina. He corresponded with Raúl Prebisch, a professor of political economy at the University of Buenos Aires and the later Executive Secretary of the United Nations' Economic Commission for Latin America and the Caribbean, whom Hueyo had previously assigned to review Niemeyer's proposals.[197] Prebisch had already begun drafting a charter for a central bank to replace the existing currency board. Pressed by the Bank, Niemeyer wanted to convince Prebisch that Argentina needed to return to the gold standard "as quickly as practicable."[198] That same day, Hueyo delivered a speech before the Argentine Senate on how following the advice of foreign experts might help to achieve a budgetary surplus.[199] As he reported,

> I will do all in my power to ensure that our country is freed as soon as possible from a system under which issues of notes depend [on] political bodies and I would hand this power over in statutory form to an institution of a mixed character which carries out the functions of a Central Reserve Bank, on the lines of those already existing in countries which have perfected their banking systems.[200]

The finance minister thus heavily relied on the advice of both Niemeyer and Prebisch. He denounced the members of the banking community "with mistaken pride and great lack of vision" for attempting to reject a proposal that was expected to fix "our defective banking system."[201] The government was able to circumvent private opposition and enact legislation for a new central bank in May 1935. With the government's backing, Niemeyer had effectively entrenched the tenets of economic orthodoxy in Argentina.

THE BRITISH MODEL OF CENTRAL BANKING

Throughout the interwar years, Britain led a multitude of efforts to reproduce institutions at home throughout the empire. From the system of honorifics to structures of colonial administration, officials aimed to replicate their own

[197] Joseph L. Love, Berta Brambila, and Andrea Martínez Baracs, "Raúl Prebisch y los orígenes de la doctrina del intercambio desigual," *Revista Mexicana de Sociología* 42, no. 1 (1980), 378; Fajardo, *The World That Latin America Created*, 35–36. Along with Bunge and several others, Prebisch offered advice on economic policies throughout the 1930s and 1940s while serving on the "brain trust" (*el trust de los cerebros*); Hernán Otero, *Estadística y nación: una historia conceptual del pensamiento censal de la Argentina moderna, 1869–1914* (Buenos Aires: Prometeo libros, 2006), 224; Jimena Caravaca and Mariano Plotkin, "Crisis, ciencias sociales y elites estatales: la constitución del campo de los economistas estatales en la Argentina, 1910–1935," *Desarrollo Económico* 47, no. 187 (2007), 419–420.

[198] Niemeyer to Prebisch, June 30, 1933, BoE OV102/3.

[199] "Summary of Dr. Hueyo's Speech Before Congress," July 11, 1933, BoE OV102/3.

[200] Quoted in "Summary of Dr. Hueyo's Speech Before Congress," July 11, 1933, BoE OV102/3.

[201] Hueyo to Niemeyer, August 20, 1933, BoE OV102/3.

hierarchies abroad, while at the same time adapting such modes of governance to local customs and traditions.[202]

Attempts to export the British model of central banking abroad served as the initial impetus behind the Bank's overseas missions.[203] At one level, the Bank endeavored to maintain influence over monetary policy by selecting its own officials to lead the newly established central banks. The Bank's Deputy Chief Cashier (Leslie Lefeaux) became the first Governor of the Reserve Bank of New Zealand, the Chief Accountant (William Clegg) became the first Governor of the South African Reserve Bank, and the former Secretary (J.A.C. Osborne) became the first Deputy Governor of the Bank of Canada. These appointments allowed the Bank to maintain the City's influence in financial centers across the empire. As one Bank director reported, the emerging Commonwealth of Nations was "more than a geographical expression," but the basis upon which "Empire finance" was built.[204]

Nevertheless, such employment practices and institutional changes needed to occur alongside more structural changes as well. The Niemeyer missions established a dependence on economic expertise abroad. Technical arguments surrounding the importance of fixed exchange rates and independent monetary policies had aligned with the vision of central banking that the Bank had long propounded. Since 1931, the CBA had gradually adopted the functions of a monetary authority as outlined in the plans forwarded by Niemeyer and Australian experts. During their private meetings, the Bank's advisers acknowledged the importance of identifying Australian economists who shared their views. Doing so would help policymakers accept cost-cutting measures without generating public controversy that was often associated with foreign interference.[205]

New Zealand's experts were even more directly involved in the planning of their own central bank.[206] At the 1933 World Economic Conference in London, Albert H. Tocker, a professor of economics at Canterbury College, represented his country in debates over monetary reform. During a series of meetings, the Bank's advisers convinced Tocker and other representatives from

202 David Cannadine, *Ornamentalism: How the British Saw Their Empire* (Oxford and New York: Oxford University Press, 2001), 61–66, 85–94.

203 Plumptre, *Central Banking*, 162; Sayers, *The Bank of England, vol. 1*, 201–210; Singleton, *Central Banking in the Twentieth Century*, 61–67; Cain and Hopkins, *British Imperialism*, 530–531; Stockwell, *The British End of the British Empire*, 40–42.

204 Josiah Stamp, *Central Banking as an Imperial Factor* (Nottingham: University College, 1934), 1.

205 "Commonwealth Bank: Central Banking Functions during 1931," January 21, 1932, RBA C.3.15.10.7.

206 On the role of New Zealand economists in public policy, see A.M. Endres, "The Development of Economists' Policy Advice in New Zealand, 1930–34: With Particular Reference to Belshaw's Contribution," *Australian Economic History Review* 30, no. 1 (1990): 64–78; Millmow, *A History of Australasian Economic Thought*, 34–35; Geoffrey T.F. Brooke, Anthony M. Endres, and Alan J. Rogers, "The Economists and Monetary Thought in Interwar New Zealand: The Gradual Emergence of Monetary Policy Activism," *History of Economics Review* 73, no. 1 (2019): 14–46.

the New Zealand government that there were many benefits to the proposed arrangements. They reported that Prime Minister Forbes appeared "much impressed [with] discussions on Central Banks and usefulness of such an institution in New Zealand."[207] Because "they had no expert to help them to champion the cause of Central Banking," he agreed to consult Tocker, Norman, Clegg, Kershaw, and Niemeyer to draft an outline for a new central bank.[208]

What the Bank offered New Zealand was a track record of seemingly successful Empire Central Banks. The topic of one meeting concerned Clegg's recent governorship (1920–1931) of the South African Reserve Bank. Although private bankers had once been "bitterly opposed" to monetary reform, the Bank was able to offer them numerous concessions that led to a "complete change" in their views.[209] Experts also emphasized the importance of central bank independence. According to Niemeyer, the new monetary authority needed to have representation from the industrial, commercial, and banking groups in the country, while Clegg noted the South African Reserve Bank was successfully managed by private shareholders (with only a minority being nominated by the government).[210] These stipulations further ensured that the City's interests would be maintained. After Forbes' departure from London, Norman stated that his "greatest wish is to help you by all means in our power – especially towards an early Central Bank."[211]

By 1933, more formalized reports for a central bank in New Zealand materialized. Before Parliament in February 1933, Forbes presented a bill that would reorganize the national banking system in accordance with Niemeyer's recommendations.[212] The legislation proposed an initial capital base of £500,000, a rotating directorship led by a Governor and Deputy Governor, and a prohibition on civil servants in Parliament or the Treasury serving on the board of directors. In the months thereafter, Tocker argued that the justification for a reserve bank had become clear. Any system that lacked centralized reserves was ill-equipped to deal with exchange-rate volatility, as "greater economic and efficiency of reserves might be obtained if they were concentrated under

207 Quoted in Kershaw to Norman, July 14, 1933, BoE G1/335.

208 "Notes on Discussion on Central Banking at Bank of England," July 11, 1933, MBL Tocker Papers 1/6; "Note of a Meeting Held to Discuss Some Points Raised Regarding the Establishment of a Reserve Bank," July 13, 1933, BoE OV59/16; Montagu Norman, Diary, July 11, 1933, BoE ADM34/22.

209 "Note of a Meeting Held to Discuss Some Points Raised Regarding the Establishment of a Reserve Bank," July 13, 1933, BoE OV59/16.

210 "Notes on Discussion on Central Banking at Bank of England," July 11, 1933, MBL Tocker Papers 1/6.

211 Norman to Forbes, August 3, 1933, BoE G1/335.

212 "City Notes," *The Times* 46367, February 13, 1933, 19; G.W. Forbes, *Financial Statement (in Committee of Supply, 4th October, 1932)*, B.–6 (Wellington: W.A.G. Skinner, Government Printer, 1932), 3–4; A.H. Tocker, "The Reserve Bank of New Zealand," *Economic Record* 10, no. 18 (1935), 88–89.

centralised control."[213] Yet Tocker also believed that such an institution needed to remain independent of the national government. As he insisted, "currency and banking policy is a technical matter, requiring highly specialised knowledge. Parliament is not organised to devise such a policy in detail."[214] For the Bank, this reform promised to create another institution in the empire that would uphold the principles of economic orthodoxy without direct oversight. Niemeyer envisioned the reserve bank acting as "a body of men who can give advice to the Government."[215] With the passing of the Reserve Bank of New Zealand Act in December, the government had institutionalized a shareholder bank in line with the vision of both Niemeyer and Coates.[216]

Elsewhere, there was a similarly strategic component to Niemeyer's missions. In Latin America, British capital had long funded infrastructure projects, particularly in railway construction. After a constitutional crisis led to the resignation of Finance Minister Hueyo in August 1933, British officials sought to identify a policy that would serve domestic investors based in London. Many believed that a central bank that was de jure independent from the government would help protect their overseas investments.[217] In December, the Bank received second-hand information that, due to strong opposition from the commercial banks, including the Banco de la Nación, the prospect of a new monetary authority would be increasingly unlikely.[218]

Nevertheless, support for reform from political circles was far more essential for subsequent reforms. The new finance minister, Federico Pinedo, who had once rejected the idea of a central bank, now accepted the policy.[219] Underlying economic conditions motivated his initial acceptance of the project. Both the collapse in prices of raw materials and a sudden stop in foreign lending raised the likelihood of a balance-of-payments crisis after 1933. Even more compelling was the ability to use expert advice as a political tool for justifying state intervention.[220] Niemeyer's central bank could set a precedent for future

213 A.H. Tocker, "The New Zealand Central Reserve Bank Proposal," September 15, 1933, MBL Tocker Papers 1/4.

214 A.H. Tocker, "The New Zealand Central Reserve Bank Proposal," September 15, 1933, MBL Tocker Papers 1/4.

215 "Notes of a Conversation with Sir Otto Niemeyer with Regard to the Establishment of New Central Banks in a Number of Countries," January 2, 1934, BoE OV50/7.

216 Malcolm McKinnon, *The Broken Decade: Prosperity, Depression and Recovery in New Zealand, 1928–39* (Dunedin: Otago University Press, 2016), 263; Singleton, "Central Banks in the British Dominions," 370.

217 Cain and Hopkins, *British Imperialism*, 567–569.

218 "Banking Reform in Argentina," December 12, 1933, BoE OV102/3. Niemeyer had also written to Pinedo, stating "I hope you may be accounted among the adherents of a Central Bank plan"; Niemeyer to Pinedo, April 3, 1933, BoE OV102/208.

219 Carlos Marichal and Daniel Díaz-Fuentes, "The Emergence of Central Banks in Latin America: Are Evolutionary Models Applicable?," in *The Emergence of Modern Central Banking From 1918 to the Present*, ed. Carl-Ludwig Holtfrerich, Jaime Reis, and Gianni Toniolo (Aldershot: Ashgate, 1999), 295; Nállim, *Transformations and Crisis of Liberalism in Argentina*, 79.

220 On Prebisch and Pinedo, see Joseph L. Love, "Economic Ideas and Ideologies in Latin America since 1930," in *The Cambridge History of Latin America, vol. 6, Latin America since*

government intervention under the new, three-party *Concordancia* alliance. As Pinedo later admitted, "the adoption of ... government initiatives would be facilitated if we could present them as coinciding in great part with the advice of the foreign expert."[221]

The inauguration of the Central Bank of the Argentine Republic (*Banco Central de la República Argentina*) in 1935 was thus a product of foreign expertise spurred by domestic politics. Debates in the Argentine Senate over the structure of the new institution directly drew on Niemeyer's report, as well as additional evidence procured from leading Argentine economists, such as Prebisch, Pedro Baiocco, and Luis Roque Gondra.[222] The final legislation proposed by the Bank contained several changes introduced by Prebisch.[223] In contrast to Niemeyer's initial version for a central bank with more "limited powers apart from money supply," Prebisch's framework offered the institution greater prerogatives, such as the ability to conduct open-market operations. This responsibility would have addressed specific concerns over deflation in the 1920s. According to Prebisch, the activities of the central bank had already existed among various institutions, and it fell upon the government to combine them into a single institution.[224] Further departing from Niemeyer's recommendations, the legislation also allowed the national government to be a shareholder of the central bank.

Still, the Bank was able to influence the broader structure of monetary governance. It appointed one of its officials, F.F.J. Powell, as a technical adviser at the new central bank. Joining the Bank in 1910, Powell had been Assistant Chief to the Overseas and Foreign Department prior to his trip to Buenos Aires.[225] He was welcomed at the Banco Central in 1935 by its president,

1930: Economy, Society and Politics, ed. Leslie Bethell (Cambridge: Cambridge University Press, 1994), 407–410; Edgar J. Dosman, *The Life and Times of Raúl Prebisch, 1901–1986* (Montreal and Kingston: McGill-Queen's University Press, 2008), 88–107, 124–129; Alejandro Blanco and Darlan Praxedes Barboza, "Raúl Prebisch y Federico Pinedo: técnica y política en la 'década infame,'" *Desarrollo Económico* 60, no. 232 (2021): 314–337; Juan Carlos de Pablo, *Pinedo y Prebisch: Vida, obra y gestión de dos economistas argentinos* (Buenos Aires: Sudamericana, 2022).

221 Quoted in Robert A. Potash, *The Army & Politics in Argentina, 1928–1934: Yrigoyen to Perón* (Stanford: Stanford University Press, 1969), 84.

222 Ley 12.160, May 18, 1935, AGN BNA01 Topogr. 82; Lorenzutti, *Dinero, política y bancos*, 71.

223 Florencia Sember, "Challenging a Money Doctor: Raúl Prebisch vs. Sir Otto Niemeyer on the Creation of the Argentine Central Bank," in *Research in the History of Economic Thought and Methodology: Including a Symposium on Latin American Monetary Thought: Two Centuries in Search of Originality*, ed. Luca Fiorito, Scott Scheall, and Carlos Eduardo Suprinyak (Bingley: Emerald Publishing, 2019), 56; Florencia Sember, "El banco mixto (1935–1945): entre la ortodoxia y la búsqueda de un nuevo sendero de crecimiento," in *Historia necesaria del Banco Central de la República Argentina: entre la búsqueda de la estabilidad y la promoción del desarrollo*, ed. Marcelo Rougier and Florencia Sember (Buenos Aires: Lenguaje Claro-Ciccus, 2018), 85–88.

224 "Extract from 'The South American Journal,' Dated 4th May 1935," BoE OV102/99.

225 P. Ashley Cooper to Powell, May 7, 1935, BoE OV102/99; Committee of Treasury, Minutes, May 8, 1935, BoE G8/62; Zendejas and Nodari, "Latin American Experiments," 339.

Ernesto Bosch, who recognized his "knowledge of practical banking."[226] Similar to its British counterpart, the Banco Central retained a high degree of independence from the government, as it was prohibited from engaging in excessive lending. From a regulatory perspective, the new institution began collecting information from the banking sector, including details on "the moral and material solvency of certain firms" in collaboration with the Banco de la Nación.[227] It also consolidated the functions of the former Currency Board, the Rediscount Committee, and the Exchange Control Board into a single institution. Further emulating the British model, a new Foreign Currencies Fund (similar to the British Exchange Equalisation Account) focused on the stabilization of exchange rates.[228]

In contrast to Argentina, Brazil largely opposed the model of British economic governance. The Vargas government expressed some interest in the idea of monetary reform but rejected the scheme crafted by the Bank. In early 1933, Niemeyer returned to Brazil to advise the government on how to consolidate the country's foreign-denominated debt. The invitation of an expert, rather than a banker or politician, was a deliberate attempt on the part of the Bank to influence the nation's economic policies. As Norman observed, the Rothschilds, as the government's financial advisers, wanted a compromise to be devised by "some accepted expert."[229] Yet there was little confidence that Brazil would be able to lower public spending to repay its foreign debts. Fiscal mismanagement led Niemeyer to report "Budget 1932 obviously unbalanced and much doubt if 1933 seriously balanced."[230]

By 1934, the debt plan faced even greater opposition from the Vargas government, now more hostile than during the previous mission. The sudden resignation of Finance Minister Oswaldo Aranha did little to assuage uncertainty in the City. "I suppose we must wait and see what the next development in Brazil is," Niemeyer wrote to Anthony de Rothschild. "It doesn't look good."[231] There was significant backlash from other economic experts as well. Gudin, who had worked at the Banco do Brasil, stated that Brazil needed to confront its exchange-rate problems and learn from the recent devaluations in the United States and United Kingdom.[232] Budget deficits were a threat to the stability of the currency. In assessing the benefits and costs of another devaluation, and while citing the most important factors to be the promotion of exports and the suppression of inflation, experts took into account past

226 Bosch to Niemeyer, July 12, 1935, BoE G14/91 and OV102/99.

227 Banco de la Nación Argentina, Circular no. 85(b), June 23, 1936, AGN BNA01 Topogr. 82.

228 Robert B. Stewart, "Anglo-Argentine Trade Agreements," *The Canadian Journal of Economics and Political Science/Revue canadienne d'Économique et de Science politique* 2, no. 1 (1936), 23.

229 Norman to Niemeyer, February 1, 1933, BoE G1/402 and RAL XI/111/637.

230 Niemeyer to N.M. Rothschild & Sons, January 19, 1933, RAL XI/111/637.

231 Niemeyer to Anthony de Rothschild, January 2, 1934, RAL XI/111/509.

232 Eugênio Gudin Filho, *Câmbio e café, 1933–1934* (Rio de Janeiro: Oficinas Graphicas 'Almanak Laemmert,' 1934), 11.

examples of monetary reform. Gudin described the urgent need to avoid the hyperinflation that afflicted postwar Europe: "It appears that the creation of prosperity by depreciation of the currency is nothing more than a chimera, not least because, if it were not so, all the exchange rates would be zero."[233] Even if Niemeyer's proposal for a new central bank did not materialize, his views on debt restructuring gained support because they prioritized the interests of British investors. The plan ultimately submitted to Aranha, despite its many controversies, was subsequently approved.[234]

From this perspective, the political distrust of foreign intervention alone is not enough to explain why Brazil did not follow the same line of reform that Argentina did. There were many structural similarities between the Argentine and Brazilian economic systems. Both depended on the services of prominent, London-based merchant banks: Barings Bank, the British agent of the Argentine government, conducted transactions mainly through its main fiscal agent, the Banco de la Nación, to sustain overseas trade, while in Brazil, N.M. Rothschild & Sons had served as the government's banker since the mid-nineteenth century.[235] They, along with multinational banks in London, helped to finance the export of various commodities, ranging from Argentine beef and wool to Brazilian coffee and rubber.[236] In both countries, there were also similar institutions in place to ensure exchange-rate stability. To minimize gold losses, the Banco do Brasil used a Stabilization Fund (*Caixa de Estabilização*) to sterilize gold inflows, an operation similar to the responsibilities undertaken by the Argentine Currency Board.[237]

Moreover, Argentina had equally as many, if not more, reasons to oppose foreign intervention. The controversial signing of the Roca–Runciman Treaty in May 1933 caused a political crisis due to terms that favored British exporters and culminated in Hueyo's resignation.[238] Whereas Argentina was permitted to export beef to the United Kingdom and the Commonwealth at 1932 price levels, only the United Kingdom would receive additional concessions: legal benefits for British companies, exceptions from certain labor laws, and

[233] Gudin, *Câmbio e café*, 5–6, 15–17.

[234] Marichal, *A Century of Debt Crises in Latin America*, 221–222.

[235] Overseas & Foreign Department, "Banco Central de la República Argentina," July 17, 1935, BoE OV102/99.

[236] Robert Greenhill, "Merchants and the Latin American Trades: An Introduction," in *Business Imperialism, 1840–1930: An Inquiry Based on British Experience in Latin America*, ed. D.C.M. Platt (Oxford: Clarendon Press, 1977), 178–191; Jones, *British Multinational Banking*, 83.

[237] Henry Clay, "Notes on the Conditions of Effective Credit Control in the Argentine," 1933, BoE SMT5/15 and NCO Clay Papers 71/3; Eichengreen, *Golden Fetters*, 238.

[238] "Argentina in Crisis on British Treaty," *The New York Times* LXXXII, 27569, July 18, 1933, 1; Darwin, *The Empire Project*, 437; Rock, *The British in Argentina*, 277–282; David Rock, "The Roca–Runciman Treaty of 1933: Defending Which British Interests?," in *Britain and the Growth of US Hegemony in Twentieth-Century Latin America: Competition, Cooperation and Coexistence*, ed. Thomas C. Mills and Rory M. Miller (Cham: Palgrave Macmillan, 2020), 149.

reduced tariffs on British imports to Argentina.[239] Although initially backed by Prebisch, one of the vice president's economic advisers, the treaty embodied a public humiliation for decades.

What explains the creation of a central bank in Argentina and the lack thereof in Brazil was neither the economic circumstances of the Great Depression nor domestic politics alone, but rather the evolution of an expert-based interwar order. Niemeyer's ability to work with other economists, including Bunge and Prebisch, made his proposals more acceptable in Argentina, a country seeking to establish its own authority following a coup d'état. In New Zealand, recently granted Dominion status, Niemeyer's intervention also succeeded because it drew a link between monetary reform and political independence. Yet in Brazil, Niemeyer was unable to receive the backing of influential Brazilian economists, such as Gudin. The existing commercial bank, the Banco do Brasil, amassed significant power in its own right, and any interference with its operations proved to be less than effective. While the Vargas government may have desired greater political authority in the aftermath of its own revolution, it was not convinced that Niemeyer could provide such legitimacy.

It was therefore not solely the discontent of foreign intervention that explained the limits of the Niemeyer missions. In all these countries, as well as others, British intervention spurred backlash from nationalist movements, labor parties, and commercial banks that questioned foreign encroachment. Yet it was the opportunity to gain political legitimacy, as defined by the mutually supportive endeavors of Niemeyer and other experts, that determined the varying degrees of success. In Australia, Niemeyer secured the approval of the Scullin administration, notably when Australian economists advocated the orthodox Premiers' Plan. Elsewhere, Niemeyer's reputation continually presented an opportunity to help establish a new regime's authority. After the left-wing Radical Party under Juan Esteban Montero came to power in Chile in 1931, Niemeyer received an invitation to visit the country, although he declined the invitation and admitted, "I know nothing about the Chilean position except that it is infernally complicated both in itself and internationally, and I should be very reluctant to butt in there without fuller knowledge."[240]

By implementing extensive reforms across Latin America and the British Empire, Niemeyer effectively transformed the system of global economic governance. In the years that followed, he continued to advocate British interests in his overseas missions, such as those to India and China.[241] As a member of

[239] Rock, *Argentina*, 224–225; Cain and Hopkins, *British Imperialism*, 567.

[240] Niemeyer to S.D. Waley, December 20, 1932, BoE OV102/208.

[241] Otto Niemeyer, "Representation of the Government of the Central Provinces and Berar on the Questions Included within the Scope of the Financial Enquiry," n.d., BL IOR/L/F/9/23; Otto Niemeyer, *Indian Financial Enquiry: Report*, Cmd. 5163 (London: H.M. Stationery Office, 1936); Philip Richardson, "'Plucking the China Brand from the Burning': Britain's Economic Assistance to China and Sir Otto Niemeyer's Mission, 1940–42," *The China Quarterly*, no. 125 (1991): 86–108.

the governing committee of the National Bank of Egypt, he negotiated a new charter with the finance minister, Ahmed Abdel Wahab Pasha, in 1936. His public notoriety notwithstanding, Niemeyer gained a reputation as the leading international financial expert of his day. As governments and central banks grappled with their own roles in the wake of a global depression, they turned to the counsel of outside specialists who were able to interpret the technical dimensions of monetary policy. Even in countries where Niemeyer's efforts to create a new central bank were not adopted, such as in Brazil, his legacy came in the form of expert-led reforms, seen in the years after his departure. Through these engagements, the Bank gained influence by appealing to a multitude of interests: for the City, the priority was to ensure a timely repayment of loans previously extended; for economists, exchange-rate stability offered the foundation for a steady recovery in export-dependent countries; for foreign governments, political negotiations and concessions configured into public debates over their legitimacy; and for Niemeyer, the sanctity of economic orthodoxy, a goal held since his time at the Treasury, necessitated the establishment of independent central banks abroad.

7

The Empire Central Banks

> [I]t is surely the part of wisdom to insist upon the maintenance of the British tradition in Canada; to take the evolution of the Bank of England during the nineteenth century as our model; and as far as possible to reproduce, in a Canadian Central Bank, the simple principles upon which the Bank of England is conducted.[1]
>
> —Bank of England, 1933

> Doubtless the Bank of England itself has fostered the impression that India will need considerable guidance in her monetary affairs for some time … . [I]t would be a thousand pities if India refrained from drawing upon the vast knowledge and experience of the Bank of England.[2]
>
> —*The Economist*, 1933

The collapse of the gold standard in September 1931 culminated in a search for monetary stability. Across the British Empire, civil servants, industrialists, and bankers sought to ensure a steady economic recovery from the Great Depression through empire-based cooperation. They debated ways of raising prices to their prewar levels, promoting the use of sterling in international payments, and implementing external tariffs to help the export-based economies of the empire. These recommendations were the basis of discussions prior to and during the 1932 Ottawa Conference. Following subsequent bilateral trade agreements, the United Kingdom, the Dominions, and India had introduced a system of preferential tariffs known as imperial preference.

Concerned with more than trade arrangements alone, the delegates of the conference also devised a new type of monetary policy along imperial lines. The

[1] "A Central Bank for Canada," September 24, 1933, BoE OV58/14.
[2] "The Indian Reserve Bank Bill," *The Economist* 117, 4712, December 16, 1933, 10.

foundation of such a transformation came from the so-called Empire Central Banks. Initially established by the Bank of England in the 1920s and 1930s, these institutions aimed to reinforce the economic ties between Britain and the empire. As a result, they have often been viewed as attempts at financial recolonization and extensions of indirect political control.[3] Yet rather than a manifestation of imperial expansion, or even an outcome of the Great Depression, the Empire Central Banks derived from direct efforts to refashion economic governance. They allowed the Bank of England to maintain its priorities in the City by replicating the British model of political economy abroad. As Sir Henry Strakosch, one of the Bank's unofficial advisers, declared at Ottawa: "It is clear that the measure of harmony of the interests of the United Kingdom and the rest of the Empire is much greater than any possible divergence in regard to the particular price level to be aimed at. In these circumstances it should not be difficult to devise a common policy which would suit the requirements both of the United Kingdom and [of] the rest of the Empire."[4]

Prior histories of central bank cooperation have predominantly emphasized the relations among the British, French, German, and US central banks. It was the establishment of the Bank for International Settlements in 1930, as envisioned by Governors Montagu Norman and Hjalmar Schacht, that institutionalized coordination in a more formalized setting.[5] Yet a shift in focus from a transatlantic lens to an imperial one offers a different set of insights. New central banks in India, Canada, South Africa, and New Zealand, imbued with the tenets of economic orthodoxy from their foundation, helped to promote exchange-rate stability. They offered a channel for sustaining the City's financial interests in response to the volatility of the interwar years. As the world's major industrialized economies of France and the United States turned toward their own gold bloc and dollar area, and as Germany and Japan retreated into autarky, closer cooperation with the Dominions and India became part of a strategic policy after the end of the gold standard.

An analysis of the Empire Central Banks must also be placed in the longer-term evolution of British imperialism. Efforts to strengthen Commonwealth relations

[3] See, for instance, Plumptre, *Central Banking in the British Dominions*, 192–201; W.F. Crick, "The Framework of Inter-Relations," in *Commonwealth Banking Systems*, ed. W.F. Crick (Oxford: Clarendon Press, 1965), 9; P.J. Cain, "Gentlemanly Imperialism at Work: The Bank of England, Canada, and the Sterling Area, 1932–1936," *The Economic History Review* 49, no. 2 (1996), 336–337; Cain and Hopkins, *British Imperialism*, 550; G. Balachandran, "Central Banking and Colonial Control: India, 1914–1939," in *The Spread of the Modern Central Bank and Global Cooperation, 1919–1939*, ed. Barry Eichengreen and Andreas Kakridis (Cambridge: Cambridge University Press, 2023), 383.

[4] Committee on Monetary and Financial Questions, "Introductory Statement by Sir Henry Strakosch (India)," July 28, 1932, BL IOR/L/F/9/12.

[5] Clay, *Lord Norman*, 364–367; Toniolo, *Central Bank Cooperation*, 29–60; Erin E. Jacobsson, *A Life for Sound Money: Per Jacobsson, His Biography* (Oxford: Clarendon Press, 1979), 95–103; Stephen Fay, *Portrait of an Old Lady: Turmoil at the Bank of England* (Harmondsworth: Viking, 1987), 131; Martin, *The Meddlers*, 119–120; Clement, "Institutionalizing Central Bank Cooperation," 81.

had many earlier precedents, such as the campaign for tariff reform led by Joseph Chamberlain at the turn of the century.[6] After the First World War, debates over imperial relations heightened as the idea of self-governing Dominions gained momentum.[7] Yet despite the legislative independence of the British Dominions set forth by the Balfour Report of 1926, the metropole and the empire remained commercially intertwined. Contrary to other parts of the "formal" and "informal" empire, where each country invited a financial expert to create a central bank, India and Canada were seemingly too important to entrust to a single adviser. One, the largest nation of the empire by population, and the other, the largest Dominion by area, were vital to the Bank's vision of economic recovery. Both countries resisted British imperial influence throughout the 1930s, a period in which rising nationalism led to calls for varying degrees of self-rule, greater autonomy, or independence. However, the collective pressure of economic dislocations, coupled with the continued prominence of the City as a financial center, compelled the Empire Central Banks to turn to experts for monetary reform.

Thus, neither a set of "gentlemanly values," as argued by P.J. Cain and A.G. Hopkins, nor a planned strategy of imperial dominance alone determined interwar monetary relations.[8] Rather, the concerted efforts to establish central banks abroad constituted part of a broader program to restructure the interwar order. Negotiations between national governments and the Bank's advisers – Henry Clay, Raymond Kershaw, Otto Niemeyer, Oliver Sprague, and Henry Strakosch – focused on strengthening economic relations with the empire. Further arising from the failure of transatlantic cooperation in the early 1930s, the Empire Central Banks provided a venue for institutionalized coordination on pressing financial issues, ranging from price levels to interest rates, and even affected other economic concerns, such as overseas trade and tariffs. An imperial monetary policy with independent central banks offered a means of appeasing nationalist sentiments, while still affirming the Bank's centrality to the global economic system.

THE MONETARY CONSEQUENCES OF OTTAWA

In the summer of 1932, representatives across the British Empire convened in Ottawa for the Imperial Economic Conference. Ensuing negotiations

[6] Guy Arnold, *Economic Co-operation in the Commonwealth* (Oxford: Pergamon Press, 1967), 6–10; Ian M. Drummond, *Imperial Economic Policy, 1917–1939: Studies in Expansion and Protection* (Toronto: University of Toronto Press, 1974), 25–26; Anthony Howe, *Free Trade and Liberal England, 1846–1946* (Oxford: Clarendon Press, 1997), 233–244; Frank Trentmann, *Free Trade Nation: Commerce, Consumption, and Civil Society in Modern Britain* (Oxford: Oxford University Press, 2008), 29–31; David Thackeray, *Forging a British World of Trade: Culture, Ethnicity, and Market in the Empire–Commonwealth, 1880–1975* (Oxford: Oxford University Press, 2019), 18–19.

[7] Darwin, *The Empire Project*, 393–395.

[8] Cain and Hopkins, *British Imperialism*, 487–495.

focused on the prospect of an export-based recovery from the Great Depression through the institutionalization of imperial preference.

At one level, the Ottawa Conference provided Britain with an opportunity to defend its overseas commercial interests. Already in February of that year, Chancellor of the Exchequer Neville Chamberlain introduced the Import Duties Act, which had established a general tariff on foreign (nonempire) imports. During the conference in July, he reiterated his vision of tariff policy as the basis for imperial cooperation.[9] Other politicians, including former Secretary of State for the Colonies Leo Amery, had long been staunch advocates of imperial preference.[10] Lowering or eliminating such barriers to trade might further help British and British Empire-based producers compete with their foreign competitors.[11]

While the conference emerged as a pivotal moment for both imperial relations and international trade, its negotiations also determined the trajectory of monetary policy.[12] In attendance was one of the Bank's leading advisers on imperial matters, Raymond Newton Kershaw. Having served in the Australian Imperial Force during the First World War, Kershaw read history at New College, Oxford, before working in the Minorities Section at the League of Nations. He then received an invitation from Governor Norman – who

[9] Neville Chamberlain, "Diary of the Ottawa Conference," July 27, 1932, UBL Chamberlain Papers 2/17.

[10] Leo Amery, "Notes on the Monetary Situation," n.d., CAC Amery Papers 1/5/21; R.F. Holland, *Britain and the Commonwealth Alliance, 1918–1939* (London: Macmillan, 1981), 19; Steiner, *The Lights that Failed*, 667; Thackeray, *Forging a British World of Trade*, 116; Liane Hewitt, "The World in Blocs: Leo Amery, the British Empire and Regionalist Anti-Internationalism, 1903–1947," *Journal of Global History* 18, no. 2 (2023), 241; Marvin Suesse, *The Nationalist Dilemma: A Global History of Economic Nationalism, 1776–Present* (Cambridge: Cambridge University Press, 2023), 126–128.

[11] R.N. Kershaw, "The Ottawa Conference," May 31, 1932, BoE OV44/37.

[12] For analyses of the 1932 Ottawa Conference, particularly concerning trade and imperial preference, see Ian M. Drummond, *British Economic Policy and the Empire, 1919–1939* (London: George Allen and Unwin, 1972), 89–104; Robert B. Bryce, *Maturing in Hard Times: Canada's Department of Finance through the Great Depression* (Kingston and Montreal: McGill-Queen's University Press, 1986), 79–81; Andrew Fenton Cooper, *British Agricultural Policy, 1912–36: A Study in Conservative Politics* (Manchester and New York: Manchester University Press, 1989), 143–151; Tim Rooth, *British Protectionism and the International Economy: Overseas Commercial Policy in the 1930s* (Cambridge: Cambridge University Press, 1991), 71–100; Francine McKenzie, *Redefining the Bonds of Commonwealth, 1939–1948: The Politics of Preference* (Basingstoke: Palgrave Macmillan, 2002), 20–27; Norman Miners, "Industrial Development in the Colonial Empire and the Imperial Economic Conference at Ottawa, 1932," *The Journal of Imperial and Commonwealth History* 30, no. 2 (2002): 53–76; David S. Jacks, "Defying Gravity: The 1932 Imperial Economic Conference and the Reorientation of Canadian Trade," *Explorations in Economic History* 53, no. 1 (2014): 19–39; Francine McKenzie, "Imperial Solutions to International Crises: Alliances, Trade and the Ottawa Imperial Economic Conference of 1932," in *The Foreign Office, Commerce and British Foreign Policy in the Twentieth Century*, ed. John Fisher, Effie G.H. Pedaliu, and Richard Smith (London: Palgrave Macmillan, 2016): 165–187.

allegedly stated during the interview, "I need help; I don't know how to talk to these people from the Dominions" – to join the Bank.[13] Because of his nationality, Kershaw was initially assigned to work on improving relations with the Dominions.[14] He was later appointed an Adviser to the Overseas and Finance Department (1932) and Adviser to the Governors (1935). Able to offer additional insights from his experience at the League, he was, according to one contemporary, "blessed (or cursed) with an acute analytical mind."[15]

Kershaw's diary entries offer a glimpse into the role of expertise in shaping international relations. At the conference, he espoused a vision of intraimperial trade and commerce that would aid empire-based producers confront the worldwide drop in agricultural prices.[16] Ensuing meetings with officials representing New Zealand agriculture, Canadian commerce, and the Australian financial sector in July and August allowed Kershaw to describe these concerns with compelling insights. During these discussions, he tried to make the idea of an Empire Central Bank compatible with the priorities of each delegation's nationally oriented agenda. His subsequent appointment as an adviser demonstrated the Bank's commitment to economic diplomacy through expert reforms.

The value of technical advice derived from its ability to encourage imperial alignment while also recommending concrete steps toward national economic recovery. During the conference, the delegates aimed to devise a coordinated response to the crisis that they collectively faced. A continued decline in agricultural price levels threatened each of the Dominions with a balance-of-payments crisis. In light of the general "feeling of anxiety" over politically charged discussions and controversial trade restrictions, such as tariffs and quotas, the Bank may have felt that its options were limited.[17] Yet it was able to devise an exchange-rate policy with the countries of the sterling area – a group of countries with currencies tied, either strictly or loosely, to the British pound – in response to the failure of the interwar gold standard.

Along with Kershaw, the Bank dispatched another one of its experts, Henry Clay, to Ottawa as an industrial adviser.[18] For him, the proceedings of the conference made a clear delineation between each country's ability to respond to the crisis with its own fiscal and commercial policies and its willingness to recognize "the common aim of expanding the volume of trade and

[13] R.N. Kershaw, "Montagu Norman: Some Personal Recollections," 1960, BoE G1/257.

[14] Committee of Treasury, Minutes, January 9, 1929, BoE G8/58; Montagu Norman, Diary, January 9, 1929, BoE ADM34/18; James Cotton, *The Australians at Geneva: Internationalist Diplomacy in the Interwar Years* (Carlton: Melbourne University Press, 2022), 75.

[15] Clay to Friedrich Hayek, June 11, 1936, BoE OV50/9.

[16] "R.N. Kershaw's Diary of Events and Discussions Before and During the Imperial Economic Conference in Ottawa, 21 July–20 August 1932," July 26, 1932, BoE G1/390.

[17] "Record of Interview with Representatives of the Bank of England on Wednesday, 8th June 1932," BoE G1/390.

[18] Committee of Treasury, Minutes, June 15, 1932, BoE G8/61.

industry."[19] Such a recovery would come from attempts to raise international price levels, while any generally acceptable resolution needed to include provisions for "the restoration of a satisfactory international monetary standard" and a commitment to "sound finance."[20]

Owing to the collapse in export prices, Canadian Prime Minister R.B. Bennett highlighted the importance of entrusting the "monetary authorities" with future reform efforts.[21] Amery also envisioned linking his project of imperial preference with the ongoing efforts to strengthen a sterling-based monetary system.[22] What seemed to prevent even greater cooperation, however, was the absence of any centralized institution or formal set of arrangements. As Kershaw contended:

> [A] "concerted monetary policy" implies effective substantial and unified authorities to act in concert. They might point out that there is no such authority in New Zealand, that there is no such authority in Canada, that there is only to a partial extent such an authority in India and that until strong and independent Central Banks are established in all the Dominions the machinery of co-operation must remain imperfect.[23]

To be sure, each nation's problems vastly diverged and needed to be taken into account. Politicians from Canada expressed anxieties over the influx of British manufactured goods that competed with their own domestic firms, exacerbated no less by a now depreciated pound.[24] Meanwhile, exporters from Australia and New Zealand believed that both their countries, largely agricultural and heavily indebted, had suffered significantly more than others from sterling's sudden devaluation.[25] These trends only seemed to confirm the pervasiveness of issues unique to each nation. A representative from the Council of India noted that "[India's] mere size makes our problems more serious, while the conditions of the people and the present political situation import considerations which are not present in the case of the other Empire countries."[26]

Nevertheless, the delegations began to recognize that their concerns often overlapped. For one, the collapse in prices had devastated the export-dependent economies of the empire. In Canada, the price of raw and partly manufactured goods fell by 47.3 percent since August 1929, with wheat experiencing

19 Henry Clay, Memorandum, July 12, 1933, BoE ADM22/1.

20 *Imperial Economic Conference at Ottawa, 1932: Summary of Proceedings and Copies of Trade Agreements*, Cmd. 4174 (London: H.M. Stationery Office, 1932), 12.

21 "Statement by the Prime Minister of Canada (The Right Hon. R.B. Bennett)," in *Imperial Economic Conference, Ottawa*, A.–6 (Wellington: W.A.G. Skinner, Government Printer, 1932), 94.

22 Leo Amery, "A Sterling Monetary System," 1932, CAC Amery Papers 1/5/21.

23 R.N. Kershaw, "Monetary Questions at Ottawa: An Architectural Survey," July 1, 1932, BoE G1/390 and OV44/85.

24 "The Imperial Conference and a Rise in Sterling Prices," July 20, 1932, BoE G1/390.

25 "The Imperial Conference and a Rise in Sterling Prices," July 20, 1932, BoE G1/390.

26 "Statement Made by Sir George Schuster," July 1932, BL IOR/L/F/9/12.

the sharpest decline of 63.3 percent.[27] Other Dominions, similarly exposed to reductions in their national income, were willing to cooperate with one another to address unemployment. Some of the leading economic advisers – Leslie Melville from Australia, John Holloway from South Africa, and William Clifford Clark from Canada – believed that a potential solution could be found in increased monetary cooperation. Following the five meetings of the Committee on Monetary and Financial Questions in early August, economists advocated the implementation of an "orderly monetary policy" that might induce a general rise in prices, while at the same time limiting uncontrolled inflation "within the limits of sound finance."[28]

What emerged thereafter was an agreed-upon vision of imperial monetary policy. Experts aimed to address the collapse of global trade through mutually beneficial arrangements. The committee's work, far from "meaningless," directly addressed the seemingly universal problem of unstable prices and volatile exchange rates.[29] As a representative of the Indian delegation, Strakosch presented additional rationale for such measures:

> [T]he question of Imperial Preference is bound up with that of monetary cooperation within the Empire ... [and] the absence of an appropriate and uniform monetary policy within the Empire is likely to frustrate the advantages that Imperial Preference is designed to give ... . The measures for Empire cooperation in the monetary field must therefore be regarded as no more than a preliminary stage to alleviate the position and pave the way to the restoration of an international monetary standard.[30]

For Strakosch, the global depression engendered "a crisis of confidence" that "threaten[ed] to destroy the very foundations of the Credit system; i.e., the system upon which our modern economic and social organization rests." In this way, imperial monetary cooperation offered a practical means of raising prices to sustainable levels. Subsequent reforms were based not on direct domination or control from the imperial metropole, but rather on the institutionalization of independent central banks, further aligned by a shared vision of economic orthodoxy.

The Bank certainly faced opposition to this idealized vision of imperial affairs. More radical proposals, for instance, came from the joint report of the Federation of British Industries and the Empire Economic Union. Both groups envisioned the establishment of a Central Bank of Empire (or a Bank of the British Empire), one that would collectively manage monetary policy for the entire empire.[31] Their report had echoed even earlier calls for Commonwealth

[27] Committee on Monetary and Financial Questions, "Canada," 1932, BL IOR/L/F/9/12.

[28] *Imperial Economic Conference, Ottawa*, A.–6 (Wellington: W.A.G. Skinner, Government Printer, 1932), 26.

[29] Drummond, *Imperial Economic Policy*, 228.

[30] Committee on Monetary and Financial Questions, "Introductory Statement by Sir Henry Strakosch (India)," July 28, 1932, BL IOR/L/F/9/12.

[31] "An Empire Currency Scheme," *The Economist* 113, 4602, November 7, 1931, 855; Federation of British Industries and the Empire Economic Union, *Report on Empire Monetary and*

reform, notably forwarded by John F. Darling, the erstwhile manager at Midland Bank.[32] His idea of uniting the Dominions and India under a single "Empire currency" was the topic of ensuing discussions. At the Bank, the project appeared politically unfeasible. Governor Norman believed that the administration of an Empire currency, even if such a proposal were to ignore the political and social backlash, would be economically chaotic.[33] Kershaw similarly argued that "sterling already serves as an Imperial money of exchange."[34] It was deemed neither practical nor desirable to structure monetary policy around a single currency: "The British Empire is not an economic unit," he later declared, and a monetary union would not address both the "different economic needs ... [and] different social and political theories" throughout the Dominions.[35]

At the other extreme, anti-British sentiments threatened to undermine the Bank's authority abroad. Although some of the Dominion governments favored stronger (not weaker) ties to the City of London in order to retain access to capital markets, tensions had heightened after the Ottawa Conference when the question of imperial oversight became an issue.[36] Some officials had expressed their dissatisfaction with the lack of an adequate British consumer market, which could have spurred an export-led recovery from the depression.[37] This grievance led several delegations to demand greater financial independence from the London money market. Canada, for instance, had pushed for federation status since the mid-nineteenth century.[38] The continued attractiveness of US financial markets, as well as the geographic proximity to New York, made British capital seem even less necessary for facilitating domestic growth.

Even so, the Ottawa Conference made imperial monetary reform possible because it addressed specific and mutual discontents. Since the end of the First World War, economists across the empire had proposed a wide range of reforms to their national banking systems. In Australia, Douglas Copland (University of Melbourne) declared that the existing commercial bank appeared to have

Financial Policy (London: Federation of British Industries, 1931), 21; D.D. Seligman [Seligman Brothers] to James Lithgow [Federation of British Industries], January 4, 1932, MRC FBI F/3/E1/4/2.

32 See various proposals, including J.F. Darling, "Currency Co-operation in the British Empire," December 4, 1922, BLO Brand Papers 35; J.F. Darling, "Empire Currency Bills," October 1923, BLO Brand Papers 38/1 and TNA T160/550; J.F. Darling, *Economic Unity of the Empire: Gold and Credit* (London: P.S. King & Son, 1926).

33 "Record of a Meeting Held at the Bank of England on the 8th June 1932," BoE G1/390.

34 R.N. Kershaw, "Monetary Questions at Ottawa: An Architectural Survey," July 1, 1932, BoE G1/390.

35 R.N. Kershaw, "Some Comments on Mr. Darling's Schemes," August 14, 1931, BoE oA48/1 and OV44/85.

36 Darwin, *The Empire Project*, 449–450; Attard, "Imperial Central Banks?," 192–193.

37 Holland, *Britain and the Commonwealth Alliance*, 145–148; Cain and Hopkins, *British Imperialism*, 507.

38 Belich, *Replenishing the Earth*, 284–285.

already adopted an important public-oriented role: "The [Commonwealth] Bank [of Australia] ... does not realize the enormous powers it now possesses for guiding Australia along the present course of credit creation to avoid unnecessary deflation."[39] Similarly, Albert Tocker (Canterbury College) submitted a report to the New Zealand Prime Minister that detailed the urgent need for a central bank in his country as well.[40] His proposal presented a standardized monetary system across the empire while still preserving a degree of national autonomy.

In South Africa, where a central bank had been established in 1921, experts made the case for reforming the national banking system in line with recent changes in the global economy. Before a government commission in 1924, John Holloway (Transvaal University College) had previously argued that the South African Reserve Bank needed to see its responsibilities expanded to managing exchange rates: "it [the central bank] should do foreign bill business to carry out its duty of maintaining the true value of the South African pound."[41] After attending the Ottawa Conference, he reiterated these concerns and argued that an independent central bank was now even more necessary for controlling widespread exchange-rate fluctuations.[42] Managing this volatility could help raise the country's share of overseas trade.

Attempts at reform coincided with the structural rebuilding of the Bank under Herbert Baker, a leading architect who had designed new buildings in South Africa, India, and other parts of the empire (Figure 7.1). With its own stately façade nearing completion, the Bank strived to shape economic affairs throughout the empire. Before the Committee of Treasury in October 1933, Governor Norman noted how the Ottawa Conference provided an opportune occasion to reconsider "the need for and the possibilities of developing and strengthening co-operation amongst Dominion Central Banks."[43] Still, officials recognized that imperial dominance was not something that could or should be implemented. As Kershaw maintained,

> So far as the relation of the Dominion currencies to Sterling are concerned, it is the responsibility of each Dominion ... to adjust its internal policy as to fortify the relation of its currency to Sterling at whatever level seems practicable, and having chosen that level to endeavour to minimise short-term exchange fluctuations ... . The difficulties of the past three years have shown the vital importance of the existence of a strong and independent Central Bank, both in regulating internal monetary conditions and in defending the external value of a currency ... . [I]t may confidently be asserted that no better instrument for cooperation will be found than independent but allied and

39 D.B. Copland, "Australian Banking Policy in the Crisis," *The Economic Journal* 42, no. 168 (1932), 587.

40 A.H. Tocker, "The New Zealand Central Reserve Bank Proposal," September 15, 1933, MBL Tocker Papers 1/4.

41 "Professor John Edward Holloway, D.Sc.," December 18, 1924, in *Report Submitted by Dr. Edwin Walter Kemmerer and Dr. Gerard Vissering*, 150.

42 J.E. Holloway, "The Bank's Rate of Exchange," 1932, UFS Holloway Papers 1/G2/53.

43 Committee of Treasury, Minutes, October 4, 1933, BoE G8/61.

FIGURE 7.1 The New Bank of England, 1933
Source: *The Old Lady of Threadneedle Street* IX, no. 51, September 1933.

friendly Central Banks applying a reasonably similar monetary policy in the various self-governing portions of the Empire.[44]

Given the economic and political importance of India and Canada to the empire, the Bank wanted to produce an acceptable version of monetary reform to national governments abroad. It was Kershaw's conviction that the depreciation of the pound since 1931 had heightened desires for "imperial monetary-cooperation," and the Bank needed to take advantage of the opportunity, transient as it may have been.[45] The effort to establish additional central banks throughout the empire thus heralded a new post-gold standard monetary era. "We can face the dark future of international financial relations with greater confidence," maintained one Bank official, "and the difficult task of securing the best interests of every branch of the Empire with real assurance, if the goal of co-operation forms at the outset one of the aims of our Imperial Central Banks."[46]

[44] R.N. Kershaw, "The Interrelation of Sterling and Dominion Currencies," July 1, 1932, BoE OV44/37.

[45] R.N. Kershaw, "Monetary Policy at Ottawa," April 21, 1932, BoE G1/390 and OV44/85.

[46] Stamp, *Central Banking as an Imperial Factor*, 32.

INDIA AND MONETARY REFORM

The Reserve Bank of India was a product of economic expertise in an imperial setting. Contentious disagreements over whether to create a state or private bank, as well as the exchange rate it would need to maintain (the so-called rupee–ratio controversy), had long characterized debates over the structure of the Indian monetary system.[47] Still, a central bank that held a monopoly of note issue and acted as a lender of last resort had yet to be established.

Prior to the Ottawa Conference, debates over the need for a central bank had arisen in response to the repeated crises of the prewar years. The Bank's interest-rate policy during the Panic of 1907, exacerbated by a devastating famine that same year, put pressure on the Indian rupee to devalue. This strain accompanied a worsening balance-of-payments deficit.[48] Observing the crisis, John Maynard Keynes, then a clerk in the India Office, wrote about the need for a state bank. He suggested that one based on the model of central banks in Europe would be enough to control the "wide fluctuations in her [India's] prosperity and trade."[49] While serving on the (Chamberlain) Royal Commission on Indian Finance and Currency (1913–1914), he aimed to identify a practical solution to exchange-rate volatility.[50] In committee's final report, the commission recommended the stabilization of the Indian rupee on a

[47] See, for instance, R.G. Hawtrey, *Currency and Credit* (London: Longmans, Green & Co., 1919), 321–343; G. Findlay Shirras, *Indian Finance and Banking* (London: Macmillan, 1920), 190–235; Herbert Stanley Jevons, *The Future of Exchange and the Indian Currency* (London: Oxford University Press, 1922), 7–20; Phillips to Hopkins and Fergusson, November 20, 1933, TNA T175/84. The rupee had been valued at 1s. 4d. prior to the First World War, 2s. briefly after the war, and 1s. 6d. from 1924 onward; B.P. Adarkar, "India's Monetary Muddle," *Sankhyā: The Indian Journal of Statistics (1933–1960)* 3, no. 4 (1938), 357–361; Ian M. Drummond, *The Floating Pound and the Sterling Area, 1931–1939* (Cambridge: Cambridge University Press, 1981), 28–29; Anand Chandavarkar, *Keynes and India: A Study in Economics and Biography* (London: Macmillan, 1989), 57–58, 82–83; G. Balachandran, *John Bullion's Empire: Britain's Gold Problem and India Between the Wars* (Richmond: Curzon Press, 1996), 124–130; Aditya Mukherjee, *Imperialism, Nationalism and the Making of the Indian Capitalist Class, 1920–1947* (New Delhi: Sage Publications, 2002), 79–95, 107–109; David Sunderland, *Financing the Raj: The City of London and Colonial India, 1858–1940* (Woodbridge: The Boydell Press, 2013), 147–152.

[48] John Maynard Keynes, "Recent Economic Events in India," *The Economic Journal* 19, no. 73 (1909), 51–52.

[49] John Maynard Keynes, *Indian Currency and Finance* (London: Macmillan, 1913), 193. See also "Mr. Keynes' Memorandum on a State Bank and Connected Matters," November 1913, KCC Keynes Papers ID/1; Skidelsky, *John Maynard Keynes, vol. 1*, 274–283; Balachandran, *John Bullion's Empire*, 200–201.

[50] Royal Commission on Indian Finance and Currency, Minutes of Evidence, June 5, 1913, in *The Collected Writings of John Maynard Keynes, vol. 15: Activities 1906–1914, India and Cambridge*, ed. Elizabeth Johnson (Cambridge: Cambridge University Press, 1971), 101–106; Chandavarkar, *Keynes and India*, 65–67.

gold-exchange standard but also prioritized flexibility by allowing paper currency to remain in circulation.[51]

After the war, these concerns resurfaced during the proceedings of another government commission, the (Hilton Young) Royal Commission on Indian Currency and Finance (1925–1926). Keynes, this time as a witness, again suggested the creation of a state bank dedicated to exchange-rate management.[52] Such remarks gained the attention of other experts serving on the commission. B.R. Ambedkar, a leading jurist and the later drafter of the constitution, had previously advocated the adoption of a pure gold standard, as opposed to the gold-exchange standard previously proposed by Keynes.[53] Doing so would have effectively prioritized price stability over exchange-rate stability, as the gold standard effectively limited the further expansion of the money supply. Before the commission in December 1925, Ambedkar built on some of his past research to craft a comprehensive plan of reform: adopting a gold standard, devaluing the rupee, and augmenting the domestic supply of gold reserves.[54]

Both Keynes and Ambedkar provided critical analysis of potential issues arising from currency mismanagement. Since the war, the main monetary controversy surrounded the maintenance of a fixed exchange rate at 1 rupee to 1 pound 6 shillings (1s. 6d.). Whereas devaluing the currency to the prewar rate of 1 rupee to 1s. 4d. might have assisted Indian exporters, the existing rate helped British exporters sell goods more cheaply in India. The latter was of particular interest to British officials at the Bank, the Treasury, and the India Office, which aimed to prevent the depreciation of the Indian rupee, as well as to those in the Government of India, which feared the potential inflationary consequences of a devaluation.[55] Keynes then suggested a compromise to these issues. He conceived of a new state bank that would remain "free to depart from the present level of exchange if it is in the interests of the internal stability for managing the exchange rate."[56]

[51] Royal Commission on Indian Finance and Currency, *Final Report of the Commissioners*, Cd. 7236 (London: H.M. Stationery Office, 1914), 53–55. Exchange-rate management was also the focus of the (Babington Smith) Committee on Indian Exchange and Currency (1919–1920); R.S. Sayers, "The Indian Exchange Problem, 1919–20," *Economica* 34 (1931), 454; S.L.N. Simha, *History of the Reserve Bank of India (1935–51)* (Bombay: Reserve Bank of India, 1970), 51–53; Chandavarkar, *Keynes and India*, 73–80.

[52] "Mr John Maynard Keynes," March 22, 1926, in Royal Commission on Indian Currency and Finance, *Minutes of Evidence Taken in India, vol. 5* (London: H.M. Stationery Office, 1926), 153–154; Simha, *History of the Reserve Bank of India*, 22–23; Chandavarkar, *Keynes and India*, 81, 106–108; Moggridge, *Maynard Keynes*, 227–229; Rebeca Gomez Betancourt, "John Maynard Keynes's *Indian Currency and Finance*," *History of Economics Review* 58, no. 1 (2013), 88.

[53] B.R. Ambedkar, *The Problem of the Rupee: Its Origin and Its Solution* (London: P.S. King & Son, 1923), 118–163.

[54] "Dr B.R. Ambedkar," December 15, 1925, in Royal Commission on Indian Currency and Finance, *Minutes of Evidence, vol. 4*, 313–322.

[55] Balachandran, *John Bullion's Empire*, 96–100; Cain and Hopkins, *British Imperialism*, 593.

[56] "Mr John Maynard Keynes," March 22, 1926, in Royal Commission on Indian Currency and Finance, *Minutes of Evidence, vol. 5*, 151.

Bankers continued to campaign for a higher exchange rate by deploying their advisers to counter Keynes' proposal. While on the Hilton Young Commission, the Secretary of State for India, F.E. Smith, 1st Earl of Birkenhead, initially suggested procuring the advisory services of Sir Henry Strakosch, a leading expert on international finance.[57] Strakosch viewed an undervalued rate of 1s. 4d., as envisioned by Keynes and other members of the commission, as highly inflationary.[58] Although a devalued rate might have been able to facilitate an export-led recovery, the ensuing loss of trust from international investors would have worsened an already precarious situation. The Bank instead wanted to design an independent central bank that would bring stability to the rupee at the existing rate.[59] As Strakosch explained, "the goal to be aimed at is the unification of the control of currency and credit in the hands of a single authority. That authority should be a Central Bank in the true sense of the word."[60]

Additional impetus behind reform came at the behest of Basil Blackett, a former Treasury official and the Finance Member of the Viceroy's Executive Council. His proposal centered on converting the existing commercial bank, the Imperial Bank of India, into a reserve bank that amalgamated the country's reserves and oversaw a gold-based currency.[61] In alignment with the orthodox Treasury View, these measures could appease Indian officials of the benefits of a reserve bank "as a big step towards Financial *Swaraj*," or self-rule.[62] Blackett's proposal also found support from other experts on the commission, including Sir Jehangir Cooverji (J.C.) Coyajee, a professor of political economy and philosophy at Presidency College, Calcutta. A graduate of Elphinstone College, Bombay, and Caius College, Cambridge, he earned a reputation as a leading economist, which had once led Alfred Marshall to remark "Coyajee will add one more to the now not inconsiderable number of natives of India who may claim to rank with the ablest and most thorough students of economics in any country."[63] As the only trained economist on the Hilton Young Commission, Coyajee provided additional justification for Blackett's version of a shareholders' bank that maintained an exchange rate of 1s. 6d.[64] Because

[57] F.E. Smith to Stanley Baldwin, June 26, 1925, CAC Chartwell Papers 18/8.

[58] Strakosch to Blackett, September 28, 1925, BoE OV56/84 and TNA T176/25B.

[59] Committee of Treasury, Minutes, October 20, 1926, BoE G8/57; Strakosch to Louis Kershaw [India Office], December 15, 1926, NAI Nos. 8(XXIX)-F.

[60] Strakosch to Blackett, September 28, 1925, BoE OV56/84 and TNA T176/25B.

[61] Blackett to Strakosch, August 5, 1925, and October 11, 1925, TNA T176/25B; Basil Blackett, "The Indian Currency System," November 15, 1925, TNA T176/25B.

[62] Blackett to Strong, December 21, 1927, FRBNY Strong Papers 1111.1.

[63] Quoted in Atul Chatterjee, "Jahangir Cooverjee Coyajee," *The Economic Journal* 53, no. 212 (1943), 454; Aditya Balasubramanian and Srinath Raghavan, "Present at the Creation: India, the Global Economy, and the Bretton Woods Conference," *Journal of World History* 29, no. 1 (2018), 73.

[64] J.C. Coyajee, *India's Currency and Exchange Problems, 1925–1927* (Calcutta: The Book Company, 1927), 41.

central banks in "all advanced countries" maintained boards free from "direct political representation," the Indian banking system could benefit from a similar framework.[65]

Yet neither the Bank nor the India Office wanted to see Blackett and Coyajee's proposals materialize. Similar to how they challenged Keynes in the years prior, they again deployed their economic experts to launch a verbal attack against their suggestions. The key point of disagreement lay in the structure of the new entity. Sir Otto Niemeyer, although still at the Treasury, denounced Blackett's plan to establish an "incompetent Central Bank."[66] Governor Norman also argued that such a version of a pure gold standard (as opposed to a gold-exchange standard) would not have been sustainable. Given the problem of gold hoarding among the countries of Europe, India appeared to lack the reserves needed to support a gold-backed currency. As Norman continued, the reform "involves an element of danger, in that the unconditional offer to exchange the legal tender money into gold bars may lead to silver hoards being converted into gold."[67]

Through its intervention in imperial affairs, the Bank effectively challenged the influence of Keynes and the once-dominant Treasury in economic affairs. On March 29, Norman and Addis provided testimony to the Hilton Young Commission that shaped the ensuing debate. They sought to address the possibility of gold being withdrawn from circulation, thereby leading to a decline in the supply of available credit worldwide. Because India held its reserves in London, the Bank would then have been responsible for exporting gold. The possibility that the accumulation of gold in India would contribute to a global shortage motivated the Bank to respond.[68] Although Addis might have claimed that he did not want to undermine the commission's intent to debate such policies or deny "the people of India [the right] to determine the kind of currency which they were in a position effectively to demand," he also maintained that it was primarily "their duty to point out the economic consequences" of the gold standard.[69]

Meanwhile, Norman contended that "[n]either the Indian members of the Commission nor public opinion in India would believe it if they were told by Englishmen in London that India cannot have the gold circulation," as Blackett might have suggested.[70] By enlisting the aid of other central banks, he hoped to

65 J.C. Coyajee, "Money Reconstruction in India (1925–27)," *The Annals of the American Academy of Political and Social Science* 145, no. 2 (1929), 110.

66 Niemeyer to Blackett, October 19, 1925, TNA T176/25B.

67 "Note of a Conversion with the Governor of the Bank of England & Sir Charles Addis Regarding the Indian Currency Question," March 9, 1926, BoE OV56/84.

68 G. Balachandran, "Gold, Silver, and India in Anglo-American Monetary Relations, 1925–1933," *The International History Review* 18, no. 3 (1996), 580–581; Singleton, *Central Banking in the Twentieth Century*, 66; Balachandran, "Central Banking and Colonial Control," 385.

69 Underlining in the original; Charles Addis, "Memorandum," April 1, 1926, BoE OV56/84 and FRBNY Strong Papers 1116.6, Part 2.

70 Norman to Strong, March 9, 1926, BoE OV56/84 and FRBNY Strong Papers 1116.6, Part 2.

identify other experts who could provide an intellectual defense of the Bank's authority. After Gerard Vissering of the Dutch central bank declined – "[I] am afraid [of] not being sufficiently familiar with [the] very intricate problem [of the] Indian currency."[71] – Norman asked Benjamin Strong at the Federal Reserve Bank of New York to see if "American evidence" could convince the commission of his views.[72]

Before the commission in May, two economists (Oliver Sprague of Harvard Business School, who later joined the Bank, and Jacob Hollander of Johns Hopkins University) continued the campaign against Blackett's gold-standard proposal.[73] Following their testimony and the rejection of the 1927 Reserve Bank Bill in the Legislative Assembly, Norman expressed deep gratitude to the economists for their testimony to the commission. "My Colleagues and your friends on the Court have directed me to write to the Professors and say how public-spirited they have been to come all this way to give evidence," he wrote to Strong. "Old acquaintances and great esteem and affection give you the right to ask help from us and us to ask it from you … . For the present we look forward to the time when you will come back and live among us again."[74] While it is unclear how much influence the central bankers' testimonies had on the legislative deliberations, they appeared to prove to contemporaries the value of expert opinion. Following the debates, the Bank asserted its intention to resolve "the Reserve Bank question."[75]

Fundamental disagreements over technicalities – a private or public reserve bank; a devalued exchange rate; a monopoly of note issue – continued to delay the establishment of a reserve bank.[76] Initially, the Bank was more focused on setting the rate at which the Indian rupee would be tied to the pound sterling rather than the project of a new reserve bank. Beginning in 1930, a currency crisis led to debilitating capital outflows that strained the existing 1s. 6d. exchange

[71] Vissering to Norman, April 16, 1926, BoE OV56/84.

[72] Norman to Strong, March 9, 1926, BoE OV56/84; Balachandran, *John Bullion's Empire*, 149.

[73] "Mr Benjamin Strong, Dr Jacob H. Hollander and Dr Oliver M.W. Sprague," May 7, 1926, in Royal Commission on Indian Currency and Finance, *Minutes of Evidence, vol. 5*, 274–318; Balachandran, "Gold, Silver, and India," 584.

[74] Norman to Strong, May 19, 1926, FRBNY Strong Papers 1116.6, Part 2.

[75] Norman to Kisch, January 9, 1929, BoE G14/96.

[76] "Summary of the Proceedings of the Joint Committee on the Reserve Bank of India Bill," 1927, NAI Nos. 8-XVII/F/1927; Rajul Mathur, "The Delay in the Formation of the Reserve Bank of India: The India Office Perspective," *The Indian Economic and Social History Review* 25, no. 2 (1988), 144; Aditya Mukherjee, "Controversy over Formation of Reserve Bank of India, 1927–35," *Economic and Political Weekly* 27, no. 6 (1992), 229–231; Balachandran, *John Bullion's Empire*, 204–215; G. Balachandran, "Towards a 'Hindoo Marriage': Anglo-Indian Monetary Relations in Interwar India, 1917–35," *Modern Asian Studies* 28, no. 3 (1994), 631–636; Mukherjee, *Imperialism, Nationalism and the Making of the Indian Capitalist Class*, 118–133; Bakhtiar Dadabhoy, *Barons of Banking: Glimpses of Indian Banking History* (Noida: Random House India, 2013), 134–143; Balachandran, "Central Banking and Colonial Control," 396–400.

rate.[77] Bank officials used the crisis as a pretext to justify additional coordination over economic policy. "The maintenance of the ratio must be secured beyond any peradventure," Norman urgently wrote to Strakosch, "and prudent management of currency and credit are an essential factor. For this latter we must rely on an efficient Reserve Bank and it will at all costs be necessary to ensure that such a Bank will be entirely free from political control as regards both its policy and operations."[78] What the Bank's experts ultimately aimed to achieve was a firm commitment to economic orthodoxy. By November 1932, Strakosch had joined the Council of India, where he continued to recommend sweeping reforms: "My advice is: Stand fast on the Sterling Standard, turn it into a help instrument, and refuse to be bribed, cajoled or threatened into returning to the Gold Standard or any other international standard until you are certain that it is going to work safely and satisfactorily."[79]

The Bank was particularly pressed to devise a solution before others could. In 1929, the Finance Department, also seeking to address the capital-flight crisis, requested that the commission investigate the structural problems of the domestic banking system. Chaired by the Indian High Commissioner to the United Kingdom, B.N. Mitra, the Indian Central Banking Enquiry Committee included industrialists, bankers, civil servants, and economists. Its final report, published two years later, detailed the benefits of a reserve bank for regulating the national system of credit, supporting agricultural development, and managing foreign-exchange reserves on behalf of commercial banks.[80] In the course of these discussions, experts offered a range of proposals. A.D. Shroff, an industrialist and a later representative at the 1944 Bretton Woods Conference, offered testimony specifically focused on national credit. He suggested establishing industrial banks in each of the major provinces or creating a single central bank that could provide credit to India's major export commodities, such as cotton and iron. Doing so, he argued, would provide the country an opportunity to spur its own economic growth and be less influenced by "the advice and guidance of foreign experts."[81]

Although the committee's deliberations did not directly lead to the creation of a central bank, their views largely aligned with the general view on monetary reform established at the Ottawa Conference. Delegates, and particularly those affiliated with the Bank, imagined greater imperial coordination

[77] B.R. Tomlinson, "Britain and the Indian Currency Crisis, 1930–2," *The Economic History Review* 32, no. 1 (1979), 97; Drummond, *The Floating Pound*, 32–33; G. Balachandran, "Gold and Empire: Britain and India in the Great Depression," *Journal of European Economic History* 20, no. 2 (1991), 249–250; Balachandran, *John Bullion's Empire*, 171–190.

[78] Norman to Strakosch, July 7, 1931, BoE G14/96.

[79] "Address Delivered by Sir Henry Strakosch, G.B.E.," November 28, 1932, BoE OV48/10.

[80] *The Indian Central Banking Enquiry Committee, vol. 1: Part I, Majority Report* (Calcutta: Government of India Central Publication Branch, 1931), 512.

[81] "Reserve Bank Needed: Indian Finance," *The Times of India (Bombay)* 74, XCIII, March 27, 1930, 13.

via a network of Empire Central Banks. "One of the most remarkable and impressive features of the discussions at Ottawa," announced Strakosch, "was the similarity of the problems which are facing agriculture in Australia, New Zealand and India."[82] The empire's collective challenges related to international trade appeared to require a technical solution. For India, the matter of exchange-rate stability had long been imperative to recovery. Kershaw was particularly anxious to ensure that the preeminence of sterling was maintained: "The situation in India … is more complex than in the other Dominions … . [F]rom the point of view of trade settlements and borrowing Sterling remains for India the paramount currency."[83] After 1932, he continually reiterated these views while serving as Governor Norman's replacement on an advisory committee of the Imperial Bank of India.[84]

The possible configurations of economic governance depended on the contours of imperial relations. Between 1930 and 1932, the Round Table Conferences brought the future of sovereignty and constitutional law into question. During the first and second conferences in London, British and Indian officials briefly debated the legal challenges to establishing a reserve bank.[85] M.R. Jayakar, a lawyer and member of the Legislative Assembly, wanted such a "Reserve Bank … [to] be started as soon as possible," while Lord Reading, the former Viceroy and Governor-General of India, argued that the bank "should manage the exchange and currency" and operate on "non-political lines" as "an independent bank to which India could look to act merely in the interests of India and considering nothing else."[86] These deliberations revealed the dependence of monetary reform on constitutional, as well as structural, conditions. Although members from one subcommittee deemed it essential to ensure "confidence in the management of Indian credit and currency," they noted the lack of "necessary gold and sterling reserves" that would support the Indian rupee.[87] Nevertheless, the prime minister's statement at the final meeting concluded that a reserve bank needed to be included in India's new constitution, as "[i]t is of vital interest to all parties."[88] By the third Round Table Conference in late 1932, Sir Samuel Hoare, the Secretary of State for

[82] "Address Delivered by Sir Henry Strakosch, G.B.E.," November 28, 1932, BoE OV48/10.

[83] R.N. Kershaw, "The Interrelation of Sterling and Dominion Currencies," July 1, 1932, BoE OV44/37.

[84] "Minutes of a Meeting of the London Advisory Committee of the Imperial Bank of India Held at the Bank of England on Wednesday the 13th January 1932," BoE OV56/53; London Advisory Committee, "Report for [the] Meeting of 6th January 1933," BoE OV56/53; London Advisory Committee, "Report for [the] Meeting of 29th September 1932," BoE OV56/53.

[85] Mukherjee, *Imperialism, Nationalism and the Making of the Indian Capitalist Class*, 78.

[86] *Indian Round Table Conference, 12th November, 1930–19th January, 1931: Proceedings*, Cmd. 3778 (London: H.M. Stationery Office, 1931), 276, 282.

[87] *Indian Round Table Conference, Proceedings*, 215–216.

[88] *Indian Round Table Conference, 12th November, 1930–19th January, 1931 (Sub-Committees' Reports; Conference Resolution; and Prime Minister's Statement)*, Cmd. 3772 (London: H.M. Stationery Office, 1931), 81.

India, reaffirmed the principles of independent central banking: "We feel that, if confidence is to be maintained in the financial stability and credit of India, a Reserve Bank must be in effective operation."[89]

With this political momentum, the India Office began to produce plans for a new central bank with assistance from the Bank. In February 1933, Hoare declared his intention "to appoint a small Departmental Committee to advise me on the subject," particularly with those who had "experience acquired outside India."[90] Norman then agreed to offer the services of two officials, Deputy Governor Ernest Harvey and William H. Clegg (the former governor of the South African Reserve Bank).[91] Both officials subsequently arranged meetings with the India Office's Finance Department to design new legislation that affirmed the reserve bank' prerogatives in centralizing India's sterling reserves.[92] This cooperation stemmed from a mutual interest in supporting the existing peg to sterling of 1s. 6d.[93]

In July, the London Committee, known as the Committee on Indian Reserve Bank Legislation, convened civil servants from the India Office, Indian industrialists, and Bank officials to review the details of the new central bank: its initial capital, the role of shareholders, and the responsibilities of directors.[94] Hoare opened the proceedings with a vision of a central bank formed along orthodox lines:

> [I]t is more than ever important that India should fall into line with other countries and that the control of the currency and credit should be concentrated in a properly organised central bank, the policy of which would be governed by financial and not political considerations. The Bank must be independent of day to day changes in the political situation, as otherwise that continuity of policy in the financial field which is so necessary to the wellbeing of the country could not be ensured.[95]

After discussions with the Bank and Finance Department, the Committee published its final report in August. Both Indian and British committee members, including Strakosch, advocated the immediate establishment of an orthodox reserve bank, especially one that was free from political oversight.[96] Although

[89] *Indian Round Table Conference (Third Session) (17th November, 1932–24th December, 1932)*, Cmd. 4238 (London: H.M. Stationery Office, 1933), 143.

[90] Hoare to Norman, February 6, 1933, BoE G1/313.

[91] Norman to Hoare, February 8, 1933, BoE G1/313.

[92] G.H. Baxter, "Note on Reserve Bank Requirements," February 6, 1933, BoE G1/313; G.H. Baxter, "Proposed Reserve Bank for India," February 7, 1933, BoE G1/313.

[93] "The Exchange Position of the Rupee," September 14, 1933, BoE OV56/2.

[94] "Committee on Indian Reserve Bank Legislation, First Meeting," February 20, 1933, BoE G1/313; "Committee on Indian Reserve Bank Legislation, Second Meeting," February 24, 1933, BoE G1/313.

[95] Reserve Bank Committee, Meeting Notes, July 5, 1933, TNA T/160/475/1.

[96] India Office, *Report of the Committee on Indian Reserve Bank Legislation* (London: India Office, 1933), 3; Simha, *History of the Reserve Bank of India*, 38; Dadabhoy, *Barons of Banking*, 145.

one industrialist, Purshotamdas Thakurdas, submitted a dissent, primarily over the rupee-to-sterling ratio, the majority's views served as the basis for the 1933 Reserve Bank Bill.[97]

To challenge such criticisms, the Bank deployed its own advisers to offer additional justification for a new reserve bank. Replying to Thakurdas, Kershaw sought to convince him that the more important question surrounded the structure of the reserve bank itself, not the technicalities of exchange-rate management. "Our Committee is not a Currency Committee," he wrote, "but one set up to advise on Reserve Bank legislation."[98] During private deliberations at the Bank as well, Kershaw intended to commit the Dominions and India to joining a network of "friendly Central Banks" with "a reasonably similar monetary policy in the various self-governing portions of the Empire."[99] His technical study of the Indian financial system, which described the structural differences between money markets in Calcutta and in Bombay, as well as the types of lenders specific to each region, aimed to present the idea of monetary reform as economically necessary even if politically controversial.[100]

This intellectual defense fully justified the creation of an independent central bank. In September, Sir George Schuster, Blackett's successor as Finance Minister, submitted draft legislation to the Legislative Assembly. Opposition to the plan initially centered on its many shortcomings. Ralph Hawtrey, a financial expert at the UK Treasury, noted the multitude of problems with the arrangements, such as its lack of clarity as to whether the directors or the governor would have more power.[101] Yet the Bank, in response, urged the Treasury to accept the existing terms, however imperfect they may have been, as they could have been revised later.

Following the expansion of the Legislative Council in accordance with the 1919 Governor of India Act, British officials felt compelled to offer certain concessions. The Legislative Assembly had proposed establishing a branch of the Reserve Bank in London to help access more foreign funds.[102] Initially reluctant, Governor Norman believed that such an arrangement had "not been judged on financial grounds but has been governed by political bias."[103] By March, however, he had been convinced otherwise. Strakosch, who had represented India at the 1933 World Economic Conference, joined a committee of the India Office

97 Purshotamdas Thakurdas, Note, 1933, BoE G1/313; Mukherjee, *Imperialism, Nationalism and the Making of the Indian Capitalist Class*, 130; Dadabhoy, *Barons of Banking*, 148–149.

98 Kershaw to Thakurdas, July 21, 1933, BoE G1/313.

99 R.N. Kershaw, "The Interrelation of Sterling and Dominion Currencies," July 1, 1932, BoE G1/390.

100 R.N. Kershaw, "Notes on India," November 22, 1933, BoE OV56/2.

101 Waley to Phillips, April 3, 1933, TNA T177/16; R.G. Hawtrey, "Indian Reserve Bank," April 29, 1933, TNA T177/16.

102 "Home Treasury Finance and the Reserve Bank: Report of Committee Appointed by the Secretary of State," August 1, 1934, BoE G1/314.

103 Norman to Kisch, February 20, 1934, BoE G1/314.

to decide whether the new central bank needed a London office.[104] Expert intervention ultimately convinced Norman to acquiesce to the proposal if it meant the reserve bank project as a whole succeeded.

Following the India Office's announcement, the Bank appointed Osborne Smith, an Australian banker, as the first governor.[105] Selecting a non-Bank (and non-British) official addressed many of the anti-British sentiments that had proliferated since the original legislation. In doing so, the Bank could appear uninvolved in such negotiations as part of its antipublicity campaign. Yet it was directly involved in the negotiations behind the scenes, as the structure of the Reserve Bank of India mirrored that of the Bank of England, notably through the separation of the Issue Department and the Banking Department. The Bank would work exclusively with the new reserve bank, terminating existing agreements with the Imperial Bank of India and other private commercial banks.[106] Through these changes, experts were able to establish a common monetary framework across the empire.

After Smith's appointment at the central bank, Governor Norman searched for an in-house specialist who was more well versed in Indian finance. Evelyn James Bunbury was one such figure. Born in 1888 and educated at The Queen's College, Oxford, he had also worked at the Bombay Telephone Company and Forbes, Forbes, Campbell & Co.[107] Prior to his arrival at the Bank, he had corresponded with other officials on the proper valuation of the Indian rupee.[108] The Bank, prioritizing the City's financial interests, was particularly keen to work with such experts who could support additional reform efforts. "[S]trengthening India's sterling reserves is," Kershaw wrote to Bunbury, "of the first importance."[109]

At some point, Bunbury became interested in an advisory position at the Bank. It was particularly helpful that he and Thakurdas alternated between the positions of president and vice president of the Imperial Bank of India. Through this link, the Bank would be able to maintain a connection to the private sector. In December 1934, the Court of Directors discussed and approved

104 "Economic Conference Committees: Indian Representatives," *The Times of India (Bombay)* 143, XCVI, June 17, 1933, 13; Kisch to Strakosch, March 8, 1934, BL IOR/L/F/7/327; Kisch to Norman, May 9, 1934, BoE G1/314.

105 India Office, "Communiqué," October 3, 1934, BoE G1/314; Committee of Treasury, Minutes, October 24, 1934, BoE G8/62; Drummond, *The Floating Pound*, 49; Balachandran, *John Bullion's Empire*, 203–204; Anand Chandavarkar, "Central Bank and Government: An Untold Story from RBI's Early History," *Economic and Political Weekly* 35, no. 34 (2000), 3049.

106 R.N. Kershaw, "Relations with Indian Reserve Bank," July 25, 1934, BoE G1/314; R.N. Kershaw, "India," October 23, 1934, BoE G1/314.

107 R.N. Kershaw, "E.J. Bunbury," January 11, 1933, BoE OV45/2; "Mr. Evelyn J. Bunbury," *The Times* 56375, July 16, 1965, 18; Dietmar Rothermund, *India in the Great Depression, 1929–1939* (New Delhi: Manohar, 1992), 46; Edwin Green and Sara Kinsey, *The Paradise Bank: The Mercantile Bank of India, 1893–1984* (Aldershot: Ashgate, 1999), 81.

108 Bunbury to Kershaw, November 7 and December 24, 1932, BoE OV45/2.

109 Kershaw to Bunbury, January 12, 1933, BoE OV45/2.

Bunbury's appointment as an Adviser to the Governors, a position set to begin the following year.[110] In the ensuing months, Bunbury emphasized the importance of centralizing India's sterling reserves and offered the Imperial Bank's seal of approval on the new legislation for a reserve bank.[111] He also supported the Bank's other engagements abroad. As the Bank's representative on the Iraq Currency Board, previously established in 1931, Bunbury advocated the creation of a new currency, the Iraqi dinar, to replace the Indian rupee previously in circulation. Through economic diplomacy, the Bank was able to address contentious political feuds and rising nationalism throughout the empire.

Prior efforts to create a reserve bank in India had thus failed due to a lack of adequate justification and compromise. Yet expert analysis, coinciding with broader political debates over constitutional reform and imperial preference, made the idea of a reserve bank compatible with existing national priorities. By April 1935, the Reserve Bank of India began its operations. In line with the terms of the 1935 Government of India Act, it was made legally independent of the Legislative Assembly, as the Bank's advisers had recommended. The new entity acted neither as a fully independent central bank with a lender-of-last-resort function nor as a state bank designed to lend extensively to the government, but rather as an institution that issued bank notes and maintained the 1s. 6d. exchange rate.[112] Niemeyer insisted that each institution established thereafter should be instilled with such orthodox ideals: "What I believe is vitally important is that there should be in every country a bank primarily concerned with central banking and primarily thinking in that direction."[113] Adding another link in the chain of Empire Central Banks reconfigured international economic governance along imperial lines.

CANADA AFTER THE GREAT DEPRESSION

In line with the principles of the 1926 Balfour Declaration, the 1931 Statute of Westminster ratified the political independence of the self-governing Dominions. Yet many officials across the empire saw economic benefits to continued imperial cooperation. At the Ottawa Conference, delegates from Canada and the United Kingdom convened to address the prospect of a recovery in international trade. Rapid fluctuations of the Canadian dollar,

110 Committee of Treasury, Minutes, December 27, 1934, BoE G8/62.

111 "Agreement between the Reserve Bank of India and the Imperial Bank of India," 1935, NAI Nos. 7(69)-F.

112 "Agreement between the Reserve Bank of India and the Imperial Bank of India," 1935, NAI Nos. 7(69)-F; Government of India Act 1935, 26 Geo. 5. c. 2; Reserve Bank of India, *Functions and Workings of the Reserve Bank of India* (Bombay: Reserve Bank of India, 1941), 7–13, 37; Cain and Hopkins, *British Imperialism*, 594–595.

113 Underlining in the original; Otto Niemeyer, "Central Banks Undertaking Commercial Business," October 8, 1935, BoE OV50/9.

which had destabilized the export-dependent economy, left unanswered the question of the future exchange-rate policy.[114]

During these deliberations, Prime Minister Bennett's chief technical adviser was William Clifford Clark, an economics professor and the Deputy Minister of the Department of Finance. Educated at Harvard and Queen's University, Clark had corresponded with officials over the need for monetary stability throughout the early 1930s.[115] Whereas Canadian politicians and civil servants debated the usefulness of imperial coordination and the imposition of tariffs, experts such as Clark believed that interventionist measures were necessary for a national economic recovery. He was, as a result, one of the most highly regarded Canadian economists in British banking circles. According to Kershaw, "he [Clark] seemed to me to be not an inflationist – but rather a 'managed currency' man (genre Strakosch)."[116] "[V]ery able and a good fellow," another contemporary reported.[117]

Responsible for the initial catalyst behind monetary reform, Canadian officials created the political momentum to which the Bank could respond. In November 1932, two months after the conclusion of the Ottawa Conference, Clark suggested forming a government commission to discuss the possibility of currency reform. He envisioned procuring the testimony of several economists, such as Walter W. Stewart, an American academic and former Bank adviser, and Sir Josiah Stamp, another Bank official.[118] Bennett, however, chose to consult another representative from the Bank, Sir Charles Addis.[119] Regardless of the particular individuals invited, the Bank and its experts were able to shape the debates of the (Macmillan) Royal Commission on Banking and Currency when it convened the following year.[120] Even the chairman of the commission, Hugh Macmillan, might not have appeared to be "unduly influenced by [the]

[114] Leo Amery, "Stable Exchange Essential to External Trade: Should the Canadian Dollar Be Brought to a Parity with Sterling?," n.d., CAC Amery Papers 1/5/20; C.A. Curtis, "The Canadian Monetary Situation," *Journal of Political Economy* 40, no. 3 (1932), 314; Harry A. Siepmann, "Reasons for Depreciation of Canadian Dollar," February 2, 1933, BoE OV58/1.

[115] R.B. Bryce, "William Clifford Clark, 1889–1952," *The Canadian Journal of Economics and Political Science/Revue canadienne d'Économique et de Science Politique*, 19, no. 3 (1953), 415; Drummond, *The Floating Pound*, 53; Bryce, *Maturing in Hard Times*, 81; Barry Ferguson, *Remaking Liberalism: The Intellectual Legacy of Adam Shortt, O.D. Skelton, W.C. Clark, and W.A. Mackintosh, 1890–1925* (Montreal and Kingston: McGill-Queen's University Press, 1993), 32; Eric Helleiner, *Towards North American Monetary Union? The Politics and History of Canada's Exchange Rate Regime* (Montreal and Kingston: McGill-Queen's University Press, 2006), 54–57; P.B. Waite, *In Search of R.B. Bennett* (Montreal and Kingston: McGill-Queen's University Press, 2012), 137, 172–173.

[116] Underlining in the original; Kershaw to Osborne, November 29, 1932, BoE OV58/1.

[117] J.L. Fisher, "Some Personalities in Canada," November 14, 1934, BoE OV58/1.

[118] Robert Wardhaugh, *Behind the Scenes: The Life and Work of William Clifford Clark* (Toronto: University of Toronto Press, 2010), 76–77.

[119] Dayer, *Finance and Empire*, 248–249; Singleton, "Central Banks in the British Dominions," 372.

[120] Not to be confused with the (Macmillan) Committee on Finance and Industry (1929–1931).

Bank of England," although he, too, had corresponded with Governor Norman on the priority of establishing a new central bank in Canada.[121]

Monetary reform would have entailed upending the existing financial system. In Canada, a highly concentrated banking sector, comprising ten major banks with branches across the country, contrasted with those of other countries, such as Germany with its universal banks or the United States with a unit-banking system of independent financial institutions.[122] During the Great Depression, Canada experienced no major bank failures and fared comparatively well due to the intervention of the Canadian Bankers' Association.[123] Alongside its structural differences, the Canadian financial system had also been less exposed to foreign capital than its counterparts in Central Europe throughout the 1920s.[124] Even so, the country had not escaped the full onslaught of the depression. Whereas the banking sector had fared comparatively better than its European counterparts, domestic exporters suffered immensely from the consequences of declining agricultural prices. Real economic growth remained negative until 1934.[125]

These and other factors served as the basis of the commission's discussions, which drew on the evidence procured from various experts. Clark, for one, campaigned for the establishment of a monetary authority that stabilized exchange rates and facilitated cooperation between commercial banks.[126] After abandoning the gold standard in October 1931, Canada had adopted a floating exchange rate, which exposed it to more volatility than the other Dominions that had pegged their currencies to the pound sterling. Moreover, the existing system of credit proved largely insufficient for managing public finance. The 1914 Finance Act had allowed the Dominion to issue unbacked

121 As reported in Macmillan to Norman, July 23, 1933, BoE G1/233; J.L. Fisher to Kershaw, September 6, 1933, BoE OV58/1.

122 J.L. Fisher, "Canadian Banking," June 17, 1933, BoE OV58/1; Ben Bernanke and Harold James, "The Gold Standard, Deflation, and Financial Crisis in the Great Depression: An International Comparison," in *Essays on the Great Depression*, ed. Ben Bernanke (Princeton: Princeton University Press, 2000), 95; Charles W. Calomiris and Stephen H. Haber, *Fragile by Design: The Political Origins of Banking Crisis & Scarce Credit* (Princeton and Oxford: Princeton University Press, 2014), 284–286.

123 Charles W. Calomiris and Gary Gorton, "The Origins of Banking Panics: Models, Facts, and Bank Regulation," in *U.S. Bank Deregulation in Historical Perspective*, ed. Charles W. Calomiris (Cambridge: Cambridge University Press, 2000), 154; Michael D. Bordo, Angela Redish, and Hugh Rockoff, "Why Didn't Canada Have a Banking Crisis in 2008 (Or in 1930, or 1907, Or...)?," *Economic History Review* 68, no. 1 (2015), 227.

124 Ian M. Drummond, "Why Canadian Banks Did Not Collapse in the 1930s," in *The Role of Banks in the Interwar Economy*, ed. Harold James, Håkan Lindgren, and Alice Teichova (Cambridge: Cambridge University Press, 1991), 235.

125 Alan G. Green and Gordon R. Sparks, "A Macro Interpretation of Recovery: Australia and Canada," in *Recovery from the Depression: Australia and the World Economy in the 1930s*, ed. R.G. Gregory and N.G. Butlin (Cambridge: Cambridge University Press, 1988), 89, 109.

126 Bryce, *Maturing in Hard Times*, 136–137; Helleiner, *Towards North American Monetary Union?*, 55–62.

notes, effectively ending the first iteration of the gold standard. However, Clark wanted to see a revival of the prewar system through the creation of a currency commission that set a fixed exchange rate and controlled the money supply.[127]

Expert analysis further convinced politicians that extensive reform could resolve persistent economic problems. Some of the early suggestions for a central bank had initially come from Canadian economists, predominantly those affiliated with Queen's University. Even though Canada did not experience bank failures as severe as those in the United States and continental Europe, the failure to address volatile agricultural and commodity prices hampered the chance of an economic recovery. Several proposals by C.A. Curtis had therefore cited the importance of proper exchange-rate management. He described the inability of the Department of Finance, a government department, to devise an adequate monetary policy free from political pressure.[128] Instead, an independent institution would be more adept at imposing restrictions on credit and, by extension, acting as a check on inflation.[129] Other economists at Queen's, such as F.A. Knox, argued that the creation of a central bank was not in itself sufficient. What the national authorities also needed to consider was how to promote domestic investment, prevent foreign speculation, and ensure the overall stability of the Canadian dollar.[130]

The various projects that threatened to alter the existing system faced backlash from Canada's leading commercial banks. Many opponents claimed that the country simply lacked the appropriate banking expertise, and some took note of the recent policy failures of the Federal Reserve in the United States.[131] Yet with the political momentum for monetary reform, notably after Bennett's intervention at Ottawa, bankers pivoted to a strategy of backing monetary reform that aligned with their own interests. A private institution, one that was owned and operated by shareholders, was the model they often advocated.[132] In September 1933, one banker even suggested establishing

[127] R.N. Kershaw, "Note of a Conversation with Professor W.C. Clark," August 17, 1932, BoE G1/390.

[128] C.A. Curtis, "Canada and the Gold Standard," *Queen's Quarterly* 38, no. 1 (1931), 117; Irving Brecher, *Monetary and Fiscal Thought and Policy in Canada, 1919–1939* (Toronto: University of Toronto Press, 1957), 144–146; Derek Chisholm, "La Banque du Canada était-elle nécessaire?," *L'actualité économique* 59, no. 3 (1983), 551; George S. Watts, *The Bank of Canada: Origins and Early History*, ed. Thomas K. Rymes (Ottawa: Carleton University Press, 1993), 7.

[129] C.A. Curtis, "Memorandum on Currency Proposals," n.d., QUA Curtis Papers Box 6, File 33.

[130] F.A. Knox, "The Nation's Money," *Queen's Quarterly* 41, no. 3 (1934), 305.

[131] Milton L. Stokes, *The Bank of Canada: The Development and Present Position of Central Banking in Canada* (Toronto: The Macmillan Company, 1939), 169–170; James Powell, *A History of the Canadian Dollar* (Ottawa: Bank of Canada, 2005), 48.

[132] Laurence B. Mussio, *Whom Fortune Favours: The Bank of Montreal and the Rise of North American Finance, A Dominion of Capital, 1817–1945, vol. 1* (Montreal and Kingston: McGill-Queen's University Press, 2020), 281.

an institution founded in "the British tradition ... a private Central Bank like the Bank of England, and not an official Central Bank like those of the United States."[133]

At the behest of Canadian politicians, and with the reluctant support of bankers, the Bank deployed its experts to craft a plan for a new central bank. One official urgently wrote to Kershaw that his testimony would be imperative for assisting the commission's deliberations: "[W]e ... need all the expert advice possible."[134] Upon his arrival in Ottawa on September 15, Kershaw proposed a structure of a central bank that bore many similarities to the Bank of England, a private central bank with a monopoly of note issue. Members of the Royal Commission largely backed the proposed structure.[135] The entity that Kershaw envisioned would be "the banker of the Dominion Government" by managing its accounts, in addition to acting as a "financial adviser" on economic conditions.[136]

Kershaw's involvement in the project provided politicians with the technical assistance they required. Because of his time in Ottawa, he was, more than the Queen's economists, recognized as a key expert on international finance. According to Addis, "Kershaw has been a godsend. His balanced mind, his sobriety of statement and his authority barn of knowledge have been invaluable."[137] Notably, experts found ways of framing their reforms as a venture of national importance. The proliferation of Canadian nationalism in domestic politics, exemplified by a "Canada First" tariff policy and the "Made in Canada" advertising campaign, rarely represented a fundamental threat to the Bank's monetary agenda.[138] Prime Minister Bennett believed that a central bank, as proposed by the Bank, could deflect some of the blame targeting his party for the depression without fully committing to any specific policies.[139] Doing so might have also allowed the Conservatives to take credit for any ensuing economic recovery.

By 1933, there had been widespread interest throughout the political establishment for some type of centralized monetary authority. Rising nationalism

133 Underlining in the original; "A Central Bank for Canada," September 24, 1933, BoE OV58/14.

134 J.L. Fisher to Kershaw, September 6, 1933, BoE OV58/1.

135 Charles Addis, Diary, September 15, 1933, SOAS Addis Papers Box 5; *Report of the Royal Commission on Banking and Currency in Canada*, Order in Council P.C. 1562 (Ottawa: J. O. Patenaude, 1933), 98; "Creation of Central Bank is Urged on Government," *Toronto Daily Star (Toronto)* 216446, November 13, 1933, 2; Michael D. Bordo and Angela Redish, "Why Did the Bank of Canada Emerge in 1935?," *The Journal of Economic History* 47, no. 2 (1987), 409; John Chant, "La construction d'une politique monétaire adaptée à la réalité canadienne," *Revue de la Banque du Canada*, Numéro spécial (2005/2006), 30.

136 *Report of the Royal Commission*, 98–100.

137 Addis to Norman, September 23, 1933, BoE G1/233.

138 James, *The End of Globalization*, 121; Darwin, *The Empire Project*, 454–457.

139 Cain, "Gentlemanly Imperialism at Work," 345; Helleiner, *Towards North American Monetary Union?*, 62.

and subsequent demands for greater sovereignty played a key role.[140] Both parties were interested, albeit to varying degrees, in a central bank that could manage the national credit system and maintain investors' confidence in the currency. How to achieve these objectives became the focal point of subsequent discussions between Canadian and Bank officials, particularly as the latter had begun to recognize the low likelihood of either country returning to the gold standard.[141] In November, the Macmillan Commission published its majority report in favor of a central bank, although there were two minority reports written in opposition.[142] Building on the framework set by experts at the 1922 Genoa Conference, the commission's majority report detailed the need for a central bank to regulate Canadian credit and currency, to promote central bank cooperation, and to act as "a source of skilled financial advice" for the government.[143] Thirteen of the seventeen economists who provided testimony also approved the proposal for a new central bank in Canada, and those from Queen's were among the supporters.[144] By demonstrating how a new monetary authority was an institution devised by Queen's economists and designed for Canada's own economic recovery, the Bank was able to frame reform as a fundamentally national project.

Before the House of Commons in February 1934, Finance Minister E.N. Rhodes proposed a bill that directly drew on the recommendations of the Macmillan Commission.[145] The plan involved the creation of a central bank that could independently buy or sell securities. Conservative MPs largely supported the idea of a privately owned central bank, especially one sufficiently distant from state oversight. Kershaw's own impression of the bill was also generally favorable, but he suggested that the proposal should include additional clauses that would help it remain fully independent from the national government.[146] Still, if the central bank were granted a monopoly of note issue, then chartered banks, such as the Royal Bank of Canada, would lose one of

[140] Bordo and Redish, "Why Did the Bank of Canada Emerge in 1935?," 415; Angela Redish, "British Financial Imperialism after the First World War," in *Gentlemanly Capitalism and British Imperialism: The New Debate on Empire*, ed. Raymond E. Dumett (London: Longman, 1999), 132.

[141] R.N. Kershaw, "Notes of a Conversation with Professor W.C. Clark," August 17, 1932, BoE G1/390.

[142] Macmillan, *A Man of Law's Tale*, 197; *Report of the Royal Commission*, 85–91, 95–97; Bank for International Settlements, *Fourth Annual Report: April 1, 1933–March 31, 1934* (Basle: Bank for International Settlements, 1934), 32.

[143] *Report of the Royal Commission*, 61–69.

[144] Watts, *The Bank of Canada*, 7–8; Bordo and Redish, "Why Did the Bank of Canada Emerge in 1935?," 416; Wardhaugh, *Behind the Scenes*, 84; Hugh Grant, *W.A. Mackintosh: The Life of a Canadian Economist* (Montreal and Kingston: McGill-Queen's University Press, 2015), 137–138.

[145] "Provisions of New Central Bank Bill Outlined by Rhodes," *Winnipeg Free Press (Winnipeg)* 59, 200, February 23, 1934, 2; "Central Bank in Canada," *The Times* 46686, February 23, 1934, 13; "Central Bank Bill Is Given to Parliament," *The Gazette (Montreal)* CLXIII, no. 47, February 23, 1934, 6.

[146] Kershaw to Clark, March 13, 1934, BoE OV58/14.

their main functions. Before the Committee on Banking and Commerce, Clark defended the existing version of the legislation, writing rebuttals to the arguments made by private banks.[147]

Among the bill's most vocal opponents were Liberal MPs. As the press reported, former Prime Minister (William Lyon) Mackenzie King denounced the project for offering no provisions for the control or management of national credit.[148] Gerry McGeer, the Liberal MP for Vancouver–Burrard, also opposed the idea of creating a central bank similar to the Bank, instead advocating the creation of a larger institution that provided social services and offered direct relief for domestic agriculture.[149] He was particularly critical of the Bank of England's behind-the-scenes negotiations, perhaps motivated by an attempt to create another "link in the chain of Central Banks under which international bankers now aim to control the money and credit wealth of the world."[150] Despite this attack, the Conservative majority, with substantial Liberal backing, was able to win enough support for the bill, which received royal assent in July 1934.

What the press and Parliament, save for a few politicians, did not know was the true extent to which the Bank of England had been responsible for creating the new central bank. In 1921, Governor Norman had suggested that a Canadian-born banker, Edward Peacock (later, Sir Edward), be invited to become a Bank director in an effort to promote closer ties with the Dominion. "If the time should arrive for the establishment of a Central bank in each Dominion," one of the Bank's memoranda stated, "Mr. Peacock's connection with our own Central institution should help towards the establishment of friendly relations in at least one direction."[151] Upon the resignation of Lord Hollenden in 1921, the Committee of Treasury subsequently agreed to his election as a director. By 1934, Governor Norman suggested that Peacock be considered for the position of Governor of the Bank of Canada. Despite the Bank's campaign, the public controversy surrounding its intervention proved to be too great, and Norman quietly abandoned the proposal.[152] Instead, Prime Minister Bennett appointed a Canadian banker, Graham F. Towers, as the first governor.[153]

Nevertheless, the Bank was able to maintain imperial influence in less overt ways. It may have been unable to appoint one of its own officials to lead the

[147] Bryce, *Maturing in Hard Times*, 138–139.

[148] "Private Money Monopoly," *The Vancouver Sun (Vancouver)* XCI, 249, July 26, 1934, 3.

[149] "'Stone Thrown to Drowning Man': G.G. McGeer, K.C., Raps Bank of Canada Plan," *The Vancouver Sun (Vancouver)* XCI, 125, February 24, 1934, 4; "G.G. McGeer Has Full Day Castigating Money System," *The Financial Post (Toronto)* XXVIII, May 12, 1934, 12.

[150] "McGeer's Fight for Credit Reform: 'London Will Dominate Canada's Central Bank,'" *The Vancouver Sun (Vancouver)* XCI, 197, May 23, 1934, 5.

[151] Memo, February 25, 1921, BoE OV50/1.

[152] "'Adjunct to Bank of England': Liberal View of Central Bank," *The Vancouver Sun (Vancouver)* XCI, 221, June 22, 1934, 4.

[153] Douglas H. Fullerton, *Graham Towers and His Times* (Toronto: McClelland and Stewart, 1986), 53–54.

new central bank, in contrast to what had transpired in South Africa and New Zealand. Yet having acquired experience from its interventions elsewhere, the Bank's advisers were able to build close links with the prospective central bank. They initially floated the idea of a £2 million line of credit being extended to the Bank of Canada in its first year of operations.[154] On the relationship between the two central banks, Clark wrote to Kershaw about the possibility of aligning operations.[155] The organization of the Bank of Canada largely resembled that of the Bank of England, with a Board of Directors that oversaw various divisions, a Chief Accountant who maintained regular valuations of the Bank's holdings, a Foreign Exchange Division that stabilized the exchange rate, and a Research Division with statisticians and economists. This structure ensured a high degree of communication between the two central banks, able to speak on similar terms in a similar language. Both Norman and Towers came to believe that they were able to consult each other confidentially on "matters of banking and monetary policy."[156]

Following the establishment of the Bank of Canada in March 1935, officials stressed the importance of continued connections between the two central banks. Governor Norman intended to identify a technical specialist to London who could keep him aware of events in Ottawa. One economist, Gilbert E. Jackson, appeared to have "the sort of knowledge and experience which would be useful to us in the Dominion field."[157] Born and educated in England, Jackson had moved to Canada in 1911 to join the department of economics at the University of Toronto. In addition to working as a lecturer, he represented private businesses on various government commissions and became the first economist of the Bank of Nova Scotia.[158] In February 1935, Jackson officially joined the Bank as an Adviser to the Governors. Over the next several years, he informed Norman about ongoing developments in Canadian politics, acting "as a guide to co-operation in general and with Dominion Central Banks in particular."[159] He also informally advised King, the recently elected Canadian Prime Minister.[160]

154 D. Gordon [Secretary, Bank of Canada] and Towers to Peppiatt, May 29, 1935, BoE OV58/15.

155 Clark to Kershaw, July 4, 1934, BoE OV58/14.

156 Committee of Treasury, Minutes, November 7, 1934, BoE G8/62.

157 Norman to Lefeaux, October 10, 1933, BoE G1/339.

158 Gilbert E. Jackson, "The World in Which Our Central Bank Will Work," April 11, 1934, in *The Canadian Economy and its Problems: Papers and Proceedings of Study Groups of Members of the Canadian Institute of International Affairs, 1933–1934*, ed. H.A. Innis and A.F.W. Plumptre (Toronto: Canadian Institute of International Affairs, 1934), 309; Drummond, *The Floating Pound*, 56; Bryce, *Maturing in Hard Times*, 34–36; Don Nerbas, "Managing Democracy, Defending Capitalism: Gilbert E. Jackson, the Canadian Committee on Industrial Reconstruction, and the Changing Form of Elite Politics in Canada," *Histoire sociale/Social History* XLVI, no. 9 (2013), 180.

159 Norman to Stamp, January 9, 1935, BoE G1/513; Jackson to Norman, January 10, 1936, BoE G1/234; Norman to Jackson, January 18, 1936, BoE G1/234.

160 Jackson to King, October 17, 1935, UTA Jackson Papers B2004-0019/010 (06).

For the Bank of Canada's Deputy Governor, experts now seemed to hold even greater influence in economic policymaking: "Central banks should give expert advice on government financing and carry out the mechanical part of such operations."[161] Still, fostering coordination depended not only on the individuals involved but also on the exchange of information. Jackson shared his own statistical findings on trade, finance, and production with other officials in the Dominions, including Johannes Postmus (the new governor of the South African Reserve Bank) and D.A. Ewen (a director at the Reserve Bank of New Zealand).[162] He and the Bank's other experts distributed the so-called Empire Letter, a fortnightly (and, later, monthly) circular sent to each of the Empire Central Banks since 1928.[163] In the other direction, the Bank dispatched one of its advisers, J.A.C. Osborne, to become the new central bank's Deputy Governor.[164] Osborne, who had been at the Bank for 32 years, was similarly highly regarded in Canada due to his experience working with other central banks and organizing the research department. For him, a central bank that prioritized exchange-rate stability would not only support foreign trade but also might help lower the burden of foreign-denominated debt, a persistent goal in Canada's banking and political establishment.[165]

Beyond its monetary responsibilities, the Bank of Canada developed a public-oriented purpose. At the first general meeting of shareholders in February 1936, officials defined the chief functions of the new authority in regulating credit, stabilizing the value of the Canadian dollar, cooperating with other central banks, and offering "skilled and impartial advice at the disposal of the Government."[166] Practically, too, the Bank of Canada served a regulatory role. In the national clearing system, the ten major commercial banks would settle their cash balances no longer with one another, but rather directly with the central bank.[167] Following its full nationalization in 1938, the central

[161] "Bank of Canada: An Address Given by Mr. J.A.C. Osborne, the Deputy Governor, to a Group of the Professional Institute in Ottawa," January 15, 1936, QUA Deutsch Papers Box 67, File 475.

[162] Jackson to H.P. van Gelder [Canadian Bank of Commerce], June 27, 1935, UTA Jackson Papers B2004-0019/010 (02); Jackson to A.M.M. Kirkpatrick [Canadian Bank of Commerce], August 22, 1935, UTA Jackson Papers B2004-0019/010 (04).

[163] Committee of Treasury, Minutes, November 21, 1928, BoE G8/58; Otto Niemeyer, "Empire Letter," December 21, 1928, BoE OV181/1; Overseas & Foreign Department, "Empire Letter," June 3, 1936.

[164] Committee of Treasury, Minutes, October 24, 1934, BoE G8/62; "Britisher in Canada Bank Post," *The Wall Street Journal* CIV, no. 99, October 27, 1934, 2; Watts, *The Bank of Canada*, 24; Cottrell, "The Bank of England in its International Setting," 107; Wardhaugh, *Behind the Scenes*, 157.

[165] J.A.C. Osborne, "Central Banking," 1936, QUA Deutsch Papers Box 67, File 475.

[166] Bank of Canada, *First Annual General Meeting of Shareholders* (Ottawa: Bank of Canada, 1936), 11.

[167] "Clearing System Between Banks in Canada," July 15, 1935, QUA Deutsch Papers Box 67, File 481.

bank became responsible for managing public debt on behalf of the government.[168] Although the Bank of England had long opposed the idea of nationalization, it had nevertheless succeeded in creating another orthodox institution as part of its imperial project.

THE CONFERENCE OF EMPIRE CENTRAL BANKS

The Empire Central Banks represented the culmination of the Bank's efforts to reshape imperial economic governance. By 1937, South Africa, New Zealand, India, and Canada had established central banks, while a de jure private bank in Australia effectively functioned as one. The work of the Bank's advisers, in agreement with the conclusion of the 1932 Ottawa Conference, laid the foundation for an imperial order based on a common monetary policy.

The most direct manifestation of these efforts came from the Conference of Empire Central Banks in 1937.[169] Under the auspices of the Bank, the conference had been several years in the making. Already in 1934, Governor Norman had written to Governor Claude Reading of the Commonwealth Bank of Australia on the new arrangements: "Australia with New Zealand, India and, for all practical purposes, South Africa, is now on a sterling exchange standard. You therefore have a vital interest in the successful management of sterling and [the Bank of England] have a responsibility in that we are the guardians of the international validity of your principal, if not your only, external reserves."[170] There existed a strong belief that to uphold the principles of economic orthodoxy and maintain international financial stability, the Bank had to implement its own policies in coordination with the Empire Central Banks.[171] With the establishment of new central banks in India, Canada, and New Zealand, the Bank was able to generate institutional interest in monetary cooperation. "Central Banks," Kershaw declared, "should be able and ready to apply to each other for information

168 W.C. Clark, "Financial Administration of the Government of Canada," *The Canadian Journal of Economics and Political Science/Revue canadienne d'Économique et de Science politique* 4, no. 3 (1938), 411.

169 On the Conference of Empire Central Banks, see Sayers, *The Bank of England, vol.* 2, 525–527; Philip L. Cottrell, "Established Connections and New Opportunities: London as an International Financial Centre, 1914–1958," in *London and Paris as International Financial Centres in the Twentieth Century*, ed. Youssef Cassis and Éric Bussière (Oxford: Oxford University Press, 2005), 171; Kynaston, *Till Time's Last Sand*, 365; Stockwell, *The British End of the British Empire*, 41; Sarah Stockwell, "Banking on a Commonwealth Future," in *Commonwealth History in the Twenty-First Century*, ed. Saul Dubow and Richard Drayton (Cham: Palgrave Macmillan, 2020), 317; Harris, *Monetary War and Peace*, 65.

170 Norman to Reading, June 27, 1934, BoE G14/90.

171 Committee of Treasury, Minutes, April 25, 1934, BoE G8/62.

regarding facts and tendencies in the confident expectation of receiving useful assistance."[172]

Yet therein lay a potential problem. Central bankers, backed by their technical advisers, believed they were immune to rising militarism and geopolitical tensions. Writing to the governors of each Empire Central Bank, Norman stated that the intent of his conference was to avoid resolving the crisis through a "political and formal line of approach," but instead to focus on "the usefulness of a frank and informal examination – as between Empire Central Bankers – of our joint and several monetary and financial problems."[173] He reported that discussions of important economic trends needed to be kept separate from the "official and therefore political meetings" with elected politicians.[174] Both Canada and New Zealand had recently elected new governments in late 1935, while the 1935 Government of India Act mandated that provincial elections were to be held the following year. Not only would the Bank be confronting a new landscape of central banks, but it also had to contend with nationalist forces.

Still, the positive responses from the Empire Central Banks indicated the growing interest in initiating some form of dialogue. In response to Norman's suggestion, the Governor of the Reserve Bank of New Zealand, Leslie Lefeaux, reported his enthusiasm for the meeting: "I cannot imagine any more helpful method of promoting the successful and beneficial development of Empire Central Banking than an informal exchange of information and views."[175] So, too, did representatives from the Bank of Canada express a similar desire to commence unofficial meetings with their British counterparts.[176] With this momentum, the Bank shared a series of potential topics on the agenda. As one described,

> In a world of rapidly increasing complexity, financial and especially monetary problems are constantly arising in great variety. Many of them are new, so that experience of the past may not give the key to their solution; yet similar problems frequently arise in different circumstances and in different places. There is, as yet, no science of Central Banking, and the help to be obtained from theoretical economists is often insufficient, partly because their science may be said still to be in an inconclusive state and partly because theory generally lags somewhat behind practice. We are, then, pioneers in a new field, breaking new ground every day; moreover, we approach our problems from a quite peculiar angle. For while most of those who are engaged in finance have a simple test to apply to any proposition … we have to consider not only the immediate reaction upon ourselves but the remoter reactions upon other people.

172 R.N. Kershaw, "Some Observations on Co-operation," January 1935, BoE ADM29/1 and 0A48/1.

173 Underlining in the original; Norman to Reading, October 1, 1936, BoE G1/501.

174 Committee of Treasury, Minutes, September 2, 1936, BoE G8/63.

175 Lefeaux to Norman, October 22, 1936, BoE G1/501.

176 Committee of Treasury, Minutes, November 25, 1936, BoE G8/63.

Whatever may be our nationality, that is our point of view and it is shared by every member of the profession.[177]

Contemporary proposals suggested that the discussion could range from relevant monetary developments to general economic trends, all with specific instructions not to have a political dimension.[178] An emphasis on only technical aspects ensured that no central banker or economic adviser would feel politically alienated or ignored.

The 1937 Imperial Conference thus emerged as a key moment in international monetary relations. It followed the coronation of King George VI in May, a ceremony that the prime ministers of the Dominions planned to attend. The various heads of government gathered to examine matters of pressing geopolitical importance, namely foreign policy and appeasement. Yet because the meetings' agenda featured no monetary items, the Bank viewed the occasion as an opportune time to organize the first Conference of Empire Central Banks.[179] With delegates already in London for the Imperial Conference, the Bank was able to construct a moment of imperial unity not seen since Ottawa five years prior. Contemporaries were also enthusiastic to attend a meeting during the highly decorative coronation, an event that symbolically linked the nations of the British Empire. The display of monarchical grandeur supported the Bank's endeavors to foster closer connections with the Dominions and India in response to rising nationalism. In turn, the Dominions dispatched their own economists as representatives: Douglas Copland, Lyndhurst Giblin, and Leslie Melville from Australia; Bernard Ashwin from New Zealand; and J.A.C. Osborne from Canada.[180]

The conference was the first major meeting of officials from various parts of the empire in half a decade, and three new central banks had recently been established. Because the delegations comprised both the governors and economic advisers of the Empire Central Banks, the overall proceedings could focus on technical matters.[181] Commencing the proceedings, Clay planned to give a paper on economic conditions in the United Kingdom since 1929, followed by lectures given by Jackson on recent trends in the empire, Niemeyer on the Bank for International Settlements, R.E.H. Allport on overseas lending, and H.C.B. Mynors on the US economic position.[182] Siepmann's presentation on gold and foreign-exchange reserves offered additional recommendations on how to promote central bank cooperation after the collapse of the gold

177 "Empire Central Banking Co-operation in Practice," 1937, BoE OV44/96.

178 "Preliminary Notes on the Imperial Conference, 1937," June 23, 1936, BoE OV44/66.

179 Kershaw to Norman, September 17, 1936, BoE G1/501.

180 Lefeaux to Norman, February 15, 1937, BoE G1/335; Reading to Norman, March 11, 1937, BoE G1/501; Jackson to Norman, April 19, 1937, BoE OV44/66.

181 Committee of Treasury, Minutes, September 2, 1936, BoE G8/63; "Empire Central Banks – Meeting in London 1937," November 25, 1936, BoE G14/34; "Heads of Banks of Empire Scan Gold Situation," *The Gazette (Montreal)* CLXVI, 122, May 22, 1937, 1.

182 Montagu Norman, "Meeting of Empire Central Bankers," January 20, 1937, BoE G14/34.

standard. Through these meetings, the Bank hoped to offer a display of transparency that might encourage other banks to do the same. As they asserted,

(a) A central bank has an interest in seeing that such public discussion as there may be of economic conditions in its own country is not misinformed.
(b) An impartial summary of information may be useful to government officials and men of affairs ...
(c) The central bank is a natural place in which current information, the details of which are confidential, may be compiled ... A statistical publication is a natural outlet.[183]

Promoting financial stability with the Dominions became the primary goal. In this endeavor, the Bank's advisers – Allport, Clay, Jackson, Mynors, Niemeyer, and Siepmann – emphasized the importance of standardized statistical information among the Empire Central Banks on a regular basis. The newly created Reserve Bank of India and Bank of Canada would begin sharing their monthly reports, similar to those already compiled in Australia, New Zealand, and South Africa.[184]

Through this network, the Bank determined the future of economic governance. Its experts used the newly established "chain of Empire Central Banks" as a channel for coordinating monetary policy.[185] As their respective governments gradually became more open to the idea of reform, technical advisers working within each country were able to demonstrate how monetary intervention could be compatible with the goal of national economic recovery. Subsequent proposals sought to track and measure global economic conditions through the application of statistics, which provided additional legitimacy to their reports. Although the Bank faced certain limitations, demonstrated by the nationalization of many Empire Central Banks, their recommendations nevertheless institutionalized economic orthodoxy abroad.

Thus, the conference embodied the transformation of the interwar order along imperial lines. Representatives may have been initially focused on statistical matters pertaining to exchange rates, the distribution of gold, and overseas lending patterns. Yet the conference's more substantial legacy included providing a set of arrangements for stable monetary governance in the ensuing years. At the outbreak of the Second World War, the Empire Central Banks maintained direct lines of communication with one another, connections that proved vital for preserving the stability of the pound. Close ties to the City of London via the Bank influenced later debates over the accumulation of sterling balances in the postwar era. While once outside the purview of a central bank, managing imperial and foreign relations had become a new responsibility for the Bank and its counterparts.

183 "The Publication of Statistical and Other Information," 1937, BoE G1/502.

184 Overseas & Foreign Department, "Co-operation: Exchange of Information," June 3, 1937, BoE OV44/66; "Supply of Information to Empire Central Banks," June 10, 1937, BoE ADM33/18.

185 R.N. Kershaw, Memo, September 13, 1934, BoE G14/34.

8

The Road to Exchange Control

> The successful operation of exchange control requires an extremely high degree of State interference with and control of every branch of economic life. It means the complete regimentation of the economic system and its progressive subordination to the State.[1]
>
> —Frederick Phillips, 1938

> The control of foreign trade, involving as it does the questions of trading with the enemy, blockade, maintenance of industries dependent on imported materials, and maintenance of commercial relations with overseas markets, as well as the primary question of ensuring essential food and munition requirements from overseas, will be one of the most important functions of the Government in another war.[2]
>
> —Henry Clay, 1938

> The best way to ensure the future of sterling as an international currency is to win the war, and the working of our system of exchange control should therefore be guided with that all-embracing objective in view to the exclusion of all others.[3]
>
> —*The Economist*, 1940

On August 24, 1939, Parliament enacted the Emergency Powers (Defence) Act.[4] Over the ensuing months, a series of orders would lead to the full implementation of exchange control, a practice that encompassed varying prohibitions on the currency: limits on foreign-exchange conversions, barriers to the export of sterling, and restrictions on the possession of various foreign

[1] Phillips to Hopkins, June 22, 1938, BoE EC4/1.
[2] Henry Clay, "Exchange Control & Control of Foreign Trade," April 21, 1938, BoE EC4/1.
[3] "Towards Real Exchange Control," *The Economist* 138, 5051, July 15, 1940, 14.
[4] Emergency Powers (Defence) Act 1939, 2 & 3 Geo. 6 c. 62. An amended version of the legislation appeared as the Emergency Powers (Defence) Act (No. 2) 1940, 3 & 4 Geo. 6 c. 45.

currencies. These constraints primarily aimed to avert a "flight of capital," the scenario in which investors rapidly sold their holdings of sterling, thereby depreciating its value.[5] With the declaration of war on Germany arriving in less than a fortnight, the powers granted under the new provisions would support the country financially throughout an impending conflict of unknown duration.

Scholars have argued that the prospect and eventual outbreak of war made capital and exchange control a fundamental necessity.[6] It was a policy that conserved financial resources in preparation for a military conflict, in addition to aligning the economic priorities of Britain and the empire.[7] Yet as this chapter shows, there were numerous institutional obstacles to the enactment of exchange control. That the administrative requirements for sustaining such a system would fall upon an already-strained state apparatus seemed an increasingly possible scenario. For these reasons, exchange control sparked much controversy throughout the national government.[8] Contemporaries often discussed how to reconcile it with the prevailing views of classical liberalism and whether it was a practice too closely associated with authoritarian regimes. Others wanted to avoid imposing controls on sterling altogether, particularly if they proved too cumbersome to manage or had adverse effects on investors' confidence.

Above all, exchange control originated from attempts to combat the persistent instability that had characterized the global order since the First World War. When Britain entered the conflict in August 1914, the need for wartime expenditures and threats to the nation's reserves compelled the Bank to abandon the gold standard. Again in 1931, the country departed from a system of fixed exchange rates and toward a regime based on a managed float of sterling. As long-standing problems, such as industrial stagnation and a high public debt, continued to place a heavy burden on the national economy, the Bank designed an exchange-rate policy that could shield the country from the effects of foreign speculation. It represented a compromise arising from protracted debates over the state's capabilities and resources. Even if City bankers did not recognize that exchange control was in their own interests, the new policy could, in fact, protect London's status as a financial center at the outbreak of a future war.

[5] Ralph Hawtrey, "Sterling under War Conditions," October 3, 1939, CAC Hawtrey Papers 1/63.

[6] G. Clayton, "The Development of British Exchange Control 1939–45," *The Canadian Journal of Economics and Political Science/Revue canadienne d'Économique et de Science politique* 19, no. 2 (1953): 161–173; Eric Helleiner, *States and the Reemergence of Global Finance: From Bretton Woods to the 1990s* (Ithaca and London: Cornell University Press, 1994), 31; Peden, *The Treasury*, 330.

[7] R.S. Sayers, *Financial Policy, 1939–45* (London: H.M. Stationery Office and Longmans, Green & Co., 1956), 18–19.

[8] Sayers, *The Bank of England, vol. 2*, 567; Hennessy, *A Domestic History of the Bank of England*, 83–85.

From this perspective, the Bank View diverged considerably from the orthodox Treasury View. Long beholden to the tenets of classical economic liberalism, the Treasury had been the main bulwark against the practice of exchange control. Criticism came from leading officials and experts, including Ralph Hawtrey, Richard Hopkins, Frederick Leith-Ross, Frederick Phillips, and Sigismund David (S.D.) Waley, all of whom questioned the practicality and necessity of new regulations. Any limits placed on capital flows conflicted with the framework of liberal governance, often associated with the stability of the late Victorian and Edwardian eras. The Treasury, in this regard, found much in common with international organizations, including the League of Nations and the Bank for International Settlements, which viewed exchange control as a hindrance to a recovery in world trade.[9] Even John Maynard Keynes had once been a strong opponent of such restrictions, reporting that "[i]t is difficult for an exchange controller to have the necessary knowledge" for managing the system.[10]

Despite the opposition, expert knowledge was critical for justifying, constructing, and implementing a new regime of economic governance. Over the course of the 1930s, the Bank crafted an economically viable and legally sound argument in favor of exchange control, distinguishable from the illiberal practices associated with authoritarian regimes. Its advisers had technical knowledge of foreign-exchange markets and international finance, as well as direct insights into sterling's volatility from foreign central banks. In contrast to politicians, economists, and civil servants, who were often preoccupied with the more politically visible concerns of unemployment and rearmament, the Bank's experts emerged as the primary defenders of exchange control. Overseeing the logistics of the system was, as one adviser contended, a topic that "can only be answered by expert knowledge."[11]

In subsequent negotiations and debates, the Bank was able to identify a myriad of compelling reasons for the use of exchange restrictions. Both Harry A. Siepmann (a former Treasury official) and George Bolton (a former foreign-exchange dealer) agreed that the adoption of exchange control was necessary for maintaining the value of sterling abroad.[12] One of the Bank's economists, Henry Clay, who was more perceptive to the needs of industry, similarly argued that the "control of exchange transactions" was "the only means of safeguarding an adequate war-reserve."[13] With these arguments, the Bank was able to convince the national government of the need for direct

[9] "Séance du Conseil et 4e Assemblée générale annuelle de la B.R.I.," May 13 and 14, 1934, BIS Quesnay Papers 20200106-2375.1; League of Nations, *Report on Exchange Control* (Geneva: League of Nations, 1938).

[10] John Maynard Keynes, "Notes on Exchange Control," September 24, 1939, KCC Keynes Papers W/3 and TNA T177/45.

[11] Siepmann to Bolton, March 28, 1938, BoE EC4/1.

[12] As mentioned in Cobbold to Norman, August 31, 1939, BoE EC4/70.

[13] Clay, Note, June 19, 1939, BoE EC4/6.

intervention. Once committed to "the freedom of financial and commercial markets," the Treasury, by 1939, agreed that the war necessitated "a complete and sudden change of system."[14]

From a broader perspective, the implementation of exchange control marked the collapse of the interwar economic order. The policy offered tangible benefits, such as defending the nation's export capabilities, financing rearmament, and addressing stalled negotiations between the United States and France. It also required abandoning the standard vision of returning to a pre-1914 version of exchange-rate management. As the continued strains of the Great Depression, the rise of Nazism and communism, and the prospect of another world war raised new anxieties, exchange control appeared to present a viable means of preserving the City's status as an international financial center. In this regard, the global context was as important as the domestic one. Increasingly stringent forms of regulation found in Latin America and Central Europe made British officials question the viability of their own system of free capital movements. They instead sought to coordinate financial resources with the Dominions, the self-governing entities in accordance with the Statute of Westminster. Because the operations of exchange control extended to the nations of the sterling area, the Bank effectively became the manager of the new economic system. The interwar order had thus evolved into one fundamentally defined by exchange control, persisting for decades until its abolition in 1979 under Prime Minister Margaret Thatcher.[15]

OPPOSITION TO EXCHANGE CONTROL

In the aftermath of the 1931 financial crisis, countries throughout Central Europe, Eastern Europe, and Latin America devised new exchange-control measures.[16] These restrictions had a devastating effect on an already stagnant British economy. According to the Committee on Economic Information, the regulations imposed by the countries of South America, while aiming to correct their own balance-of-payment deficits by limiting the reliance on foreign

[14] Harry A. Siepmann, "Emergency Measures," February 28, 1939, BoE EC4/3.

[15] Capie, *The Bank of England*, 766–772; Duncan Needham, *UK Monetary Policy from Devaluation to Thatcher, 1967–82* (Basingstoke: Palgrave Macmillan, 2014), 141–143; Aled Davies, *The City of London and Social Democracy: The Political Economy of Finance in Britain, 1959–1979* (Oxford: Oxford University Press, 2017), 142; James, *Making a Modern Central Bank*, 37–42; Copley, *Governing Financialization*, 100–109.

[16] In Europe: Germany (July 13), Hungary (July 17), Greece (September 28), Czechoslovakia (October 2), Yugoslavia (October 7), Latvia (October 8), Austria (October 9), Bulgaria (October 15), Estonia (October 23), and Denmark (November 18). In Latin America: Chile (July 30), Uruguay (September 7), Colombia (September 24), Brazil (September 29), Argentina (October 13), Nicaragua (November 13), Ecuador (May 2, 1932), and Paraguay (June 28, 1932); Kris James Mitchener and Kirsten Wandschneider, "Capital Controls and Recovery from the Financial Crisis of the 1930s," *Journal of International Economics* 95, no. 2 (2015), 191.

imports, had caused a decline in British exports by 67 percent in 1931 compared to two years prior.[17] Viewing these trends, the Treasury predicted that as long as these restrictions proliferated, "British export trade in particular is bound to suffer severely … . Nothing that we can do will alter this."[18]

Across Europe, both government officials and economists had criticized the bureaucratic governance that a regime of exchange control would have entailed. "Attempts to limit fluctuations in Exchange by imposing artificial control on Exchange operations are futile and mischievous," declared one committee at the 1920 Brussels Conference.[19] This view was shared by international organizations as well. Alongside quota systems, bilateral clearing agreements, and retaliatory tariffs, exchange restrictions were one of the main barriers to trade that threatened the global economy. The League of Nations opposed interventions on exchange markets for practical reasons as well. For the director of the Economic and Financial Section, Alexander Loveday, the reform would give central banks "a function in the realm of commercial policy which is not and should not be theirs," in addition to being "not particularly effective."[20]

British officials similarly protested the imposition of exchange control. For the Treasury, the abandonment of the gold standard in 1931 had already been deemed "a great disaster," and any additional restrictions might have only brought more instability.[21] Although speculation caused capital outflows that brought the current account from a surplus of £44 million to a projected deficit of £70 million by year's end, the depreciation of the pound would "produce automatically a certain adjustment in the negative balance."[22] Moreover, historical evidence seemed to show the limits of artificial regulations on markets. According to a 1931 report, the piecemeal implementation of exchange control during the Great War had largely been a failure. The War Trade Department had overseen the blockade against enemy countries; the Treasury had approved applications for import and export licenses; and the London Exchange Committee, formed in November 1915 and composed of the clearing banks and central bank, had restricted capital issues and amassed US dollars to fund the war effort.[23] These temporary protocols, far from being sustainable in the long run, were developed in an ad hoc nature only after the beginning of the war.

[17] Committee on Economic Information, "Second Report: Survey of the Economic Situation," March 1932, TNA CAB 24/228/46.

[18] Waley to Kershaw, "Exchange Restrictions Abroad," January 18, 1932, BoE OV49/2.

[19] Committee on Currency and Exchange, "Report," 1920, LoN R502/10A/392/392.

[20] Alexander Loveday, "Note on Trade and Exchange Situation," February 4, 1931, BoE OV49/2.

[21] Cecil Kisch [India Office], "The Suspension of Gold Payments," September 26, 1931, TNA T188/20.

[22] "The Deficiency in the British Balance of Payment and the Influence of Speculation," December 8, 1931, TNA T188/20.

[23] "Exchange Control during the War," 1931, BoE OV49/2 and TNA T160/435.

Examinations of other countries made British officials even more unwilling to depart from the prevailing orthodoxy of the interwar years. One Treasury report had characterized exchange control as "ineffective" when adopted by the French government in 1926 (although it offered little explanation as to why).[24] France had achieved the de facto stabilization of the franc by enacting legislation that allowed its central bank to purchase foreign-exchange reserves abroad on behalf of its own Treasury.[25] In contrast, the British authorities deferred prerogatives to the Exchange Committee, an informal group of Treasury, Bank, and City officials, which advised on the purchases and sales of foreign currencies to stabilize the currency.[26] Such transient measures offered a more controlled policy of exchange-rate management that purposely did not entrust regulatory power to any single institution. There was a widespread belief in the City that disrupting the existing free exchange of sterling would severely harm public confidence in the currency. Even while confronting "the grave and threatening position in Eastern Europe and South America," Governor Montagu Norman conceded that any radical announcement might give markets "a false impression as to the situation."[27]

Comparisons to Germany's system of exchange control sparked even more controversies. On July 18, 1931, the German government issued an emergency ordinance (*Notverordnung*) that required all individuals (and later, all companies) to report their foreign-exchange dealings, while legislation on August 1 placed additional limits on the purchase of foreign currencies and securities.[28] The Brüning cabinet was advised by various experts who made the imposition of greater control over the economy seem unavoidable.[29] In contrast to these developments abroad, Britain opposed implementing similar policies at home. According to the Treasury, there was "very little evidence to show that these

24 "Restrictions on Exchange Dealings and Export of Capital," 1931, TNA T188/20.

25 Hubert Bonin, "The Challenged Competitiveness of the Paris Banking and Finance Markets, 1914–1958," in *London and Paris as International Financial Centres in the Twentieth Century*, ed. Youssef Cassis and Eric Bussière (Oxford: Oxford University Press, 2005), 185.

26 Committee of Treasury, Minutes, September 30, 1931, BoE G8/60. The group's composition in December 1931 included the Deputy Governor, Hambro, Sprague, Beaumont Pease, C.J. Whigham, and Treasury officials; Committee of Treasury, Minutes, December 16, 1931, BoE G8/60.

27 Committee of Treasury, Minutes, November 4, 1931, BoE G8/60.

28 "Verordnung des Reichspräsidenten gegen die Kapital- und Steuerflucht," *Reichsgesetzblatt*, no. 35 (July 18, 1931): 373–376; "Verordnung des Reichspräsidenten über die Devisenbewirtschaftung," *Reichsgesetzblatt*, no. 48 (August 1, 1931): 421–425; James, *The German Slump*, 388.

29 "Nr. 424: Besprechung mit Wirtschaftssachverständigen am 31. Juli 1931, 17 Uhr," in *Die Kabinette Brüning I u. II, Band* 2, 1483–1497; "Nr. 509: Besprechung mit den präsidierenden Mitgliedern der Länderregierungen über Sanierungsmaßnahmen vom 6. Oktober 1931, 11 Uhr," in *Die Kabinette Brüning I u. II, Band* 2, 1812–1815; Friedrich Döhlemann [Director, Bayerische Gemeindebank] to Brüning, October 19, 1931, GStA PK, I. HA Rep. 77, Tit. 32, Nr. 41.

decrees have in fact been effective. They have evidently caused great inconvenience to those engaged in foreign trade and have led to numerous protests."[30] Although Keynes and Sir Josiah Stamp suggested the idea of some degree of exchange-rate intervention, Sir Frederick Leith-Ross and Deputy Governor Ernest Harvey dismissed such ideas.[31] Again in August 1931, two of the Bank's advisers, Oliver M.W. Sprague and Walter W. Stewart, hinted that such restrictions might be inevitable if Europe experienced additional currency troubles. Their proposals amounted to no immediate change.[32]

Indeed, the Bank itself had not yet been fully convinced of the need for exchange control in 1931. Its Committee of Treasury intended to ensure that "no definitive restrictions should at present be imposed on dealings in Foreign Exchange."[33] Members of the Old Guard were willing to accept a range of other possible measures, from wage cuts to indirect and luxury taxes, which could secure confidence in the currency.[34] Yet they disapproved of more radical measures that were not in the interests of the City. The business community was similarly committed to the tenets of economic orthodoxy and, as a result, rejected the implementation of controls on principle. Such measures were fundamentally "a symptom of the world crisis," as a meeting of the International Chamber of Commerce in March 1932 concluded.[35]

For others, the enactment of exchange restrictions threatened to reduce their profits on overseas activities.[36] In November 1932, the London Chamber of Commerce proposed an alternative scheme that might be able to spur international trade. Under this plan, clearing houses could allow British traders to circumvent onerous exchange restrictions by denominating transactions in a new currency ("Bartex") with exchange rates set by the Bank.[37] The arrangement would have avoided the stringent forms of exchange control later proposed by the Bank. Nevertheless, the Bartex plan lacked institutional endorsement from other business associations, which denounced a managed currency, and from government ministries, which feared its unintended consequences. The Board of Trade suggested that one potential outcome of the Bartex plan might have been the proliferation of an unofficial market for sterling (a "black bourse"). Rather than facilitate trade, a black-market exchange rate "might create a hampering uncertainty" and hinder economic recovery.[38]

[30] "Restrictions on Exchange Dealings and Export of Capital," 1931, TNA T188/20.
[31] Leith-Ross, *Money Talks*, 140; Moggridge, *Maynard Keynes*, 527; Helen Johnson, "Frederick Leith-Ross: The Career of an Economic Diplomat" (DPhil diss., University of Oxford, 2008), 48.
[32] Sayers, *The Bank of England, vol.* 2, 411.
[33] Committee of Treasury, Minutes, September 19, 1931, BoE G8/60.
[34] Harry A. Siepmann, "Memorandum," August 14, 1931, BoE OV48/9.
[35] "Foreign Exchange Control," *The Times* 46079, March 11, 1932, 13.
[36] Jones, *British Multinational Banks*, 193.
[37] "Bartex," November 17, 1932, BoE OV49/2; The London Chamber of Commerce, "Exchange Restrictions," November 19, 1932, BoE OV49/2.
[38] E. Hale [Board of Trade] to Waley, November 21, 1932, BoE OV49/2.

What instead emerged from the collapse of the gold standard in 1931 was a form of economic governance revolving around the sterling bloc (or sterling area). The group comprised countries that, to varying degrees, followed the movement of the British pound on foreign-exchange markets, such as India, Egypt, and many of the Dominions, excluding Canada and Newfoundland.[39] According to Ralph Hawtrey at the Treasury, the sterling area was a temporary expedient for promoting the use of sterling abroad, "pending our restabilisation on gold."[40] By this argument, maintaining the value of the currency effectively made a regulatory policy unnecessary. Contemporaries were even keen to convince countries outside the sterling area that indirect exchange-rate management offered many benefits. Writing to the Canadian prime minister, Chancellor of the Exchequer Neville Chamberlain boasted of the benefits of the sterling area with its "intermediate position between gold currencies and [the] United States dollars," thereby allowing it to retain "complete freedom of movement without attaching ourselves to either camp."[41]

Over the course of the 1930s, exchange control became an increasingly controversial policy, not least due to its continued association with authoritarian states. In Germany, the regulations enacted by the government were particularly onerous. Under the auspices of the Reich Office for Foreign Exchange Management (*Reichsstelle für Devisenbewirtschaftung*), prohibitions on foreign-currency transactions aimed to punish so-called "currency profiteers" (*Devisenschieber*) who undermined the stability of the RM.[42] The legislation most directly persecuted Jews and political dissidents, such as former Finance Minister Rudolf Hilferding.[43] Other victims included citizens of neutral countries, such as one Swiss national who faced the prospect of a fine of 100,000 RM and the maximum penalty of ten years of penal servitude.[44] Even naturalized

39 The term "sterling area" often refers to the post-1945 countries pegged to the British pound, while the term "sterling bloc" relates to the less-formalized set of arrangements after the collapse of the gold standard in 1931. However, contemporaries seemed to use the term sterling area in place of the sterling bloc; Economics & Statistics Section, "U.K. Balance of Payments with Non-Sterling Area," November 14, 1934, BoE EID3/4; Economics & Statistics Section, "Balance of Payments: Sterling Area with Rest of World," February 8, 1935, BoE EID3/4.

40 Hawtrey to Chamberlain, December 8, 1931, TNA T188/20.

41 Chamberlain to Bennett, January 1934, TNA T175/84.

42 Axel Drecoll, *Der Fiskus als Verfolger. Die steuerliche Diskriminierung der Juden in Bayern 1933–1941/42* (Munich: R. Oldenbourg, 2009), 126–146; Christoph Raichle, *Die Finanzverwaltung in Baden und Württemberg im Nationalsozialismus* (Stuttgart: W. Kohlhammer, 2019), 80–81.

43 Drecoll, *Der Fiskus als Verfolger*, 140–141; Dieter Ziegler, "'A Regulated Market Economy': New Perspectives on the Nature of the Economic Order of the Third Reich, 1933–1939," in *Business in the Age of Extremes: Essays in Modern German and Austrian Economic History*, ed. Hartmut Berghoff, Jürgen Kocka, and Dieter Ziegler (Cambridge: Cambridge University Press, 2013), 140.

44 "Exchange Evasion in Germany," *The Times* 46580, October 20, 1933, 11.

UK citizens, such as a Berlin-based agent of a London bank who had been arrested on charges of trying to convert one million RM, were targeted.[45]

Instead of setting harsh punishments similar to those in Germany, Britain stabilized exchange rates through alternative means. One measure involved placing limits on the issuance of foreign securities in the City. The logic followed that British investors, fleeing lower interest rates at home, had been investing more funds abroad, thereby raising demand for foreign currencies at the expense of sterling. In the summer of 1932, Chamberlain issued a statement calling for an embargo on new capital issues.[46] The protocol, while temporarily enacted in preparation for the 1932 conversion of wartime debt, embodied the government's commitment to indirect regulation.

Less direct, yet no less effective, were the operations of the Exchange Equalisation Account (EEA). Established by the Treasury in July 1932, the EEA offered a viable alternative to state intervention. With its initial capital of £150 million, in addition to £20 million in reserves, it allowed the Bank to maintain sterling's value through the purchase of Treasury bills.[47] British officials sought to use the EEA to keep sterling at a low rate, thereby providing a source of "cheap money" to encourage investment.[48] The mechanism also provided the Treasury a way of concealing information on gold inflows and outflows.[49]

Yet even if Chamberlain's embargo and the EEA could provide a degree of temporary stability, officials began to recognize the need to assess the limitations and inadequacies with the existing system in the long run. In January 1933, the Treasury predicted that the upward trend of sterling relative to other currencies would lead to an increased inflow of gold into the country.[50] While a concomitant influx of capital might have been beneficial in theory, Norman noted several concerns. A rise in demand for sterling, for instance, could have prevented the maintenance of a rate under $3.50, which then would have required the EEA to expand its base to £170 million.[51] The Treasury advised taking a more conservative approach by maintaining an artificially high value of sterling and even limiting the EEA to £140 million.[52] Proper exchange-rate management

45 "German Exchange Regulations," *The Times* 46038, January 23, 1932, 9.

46 "The Embargo on New Issues," *The Times* 46216, August 19, 1932, 11; "New Capital Issues," *The Times* 46225, August 30, 1932, 10; Sayers, *The Bank of England, vol. 2*, 439–440; Kindleberger, *The World in Depression*, 242; Wormell, *The Management of the National Debt*, 617; Allen, *The Bank of England and the Government Debt*, 31.

47 Howson, "Sterling's Managed Float," 9; Peden, *The Treasury*, 256; Naef, *An Exchange Rate History*, 66.

48 Howson, "The Management of Sterling," 54–55.

49 Hopkins to Fisher and Chamberlain, "Exchange Position," January 21, 1933, TNA T172/2082.

50 Phillips to Hopkins, Fisher, and Chamberlain, January 28, 1933, TNA T175/71; Hopkins to Fisher, January 30, 1933, TNA T175/71.

51 Phillips to Hopkins, Fisher, and Chamberlain, January 28, 1933, TNA T175/71.

52 Hopkins to Fisher, January 30, 1933, TNA T175/71.

could counter the need for government regulation. Even so, Hopkins told Chamberlain that both "[b]udget developments in France" and "a new fit of waves" of bankruptcy in New York would create problems for sterling, since now "[d]ollars and francs are both being thrown at us in large volume."[53]

Both domestic and international threats to stability raised concerns about the British system of indirect regulation. At the World Economic Conference in 1933, representatives from the United Kingdom, the United States, and France convened to discuss a plan for stabilizing exchange rates. Efforts to cancel inter-Allied war debts demonstrated the limits of economic diplomacy and the national priorities of each country.[54] Indeed, the unresolved negotiation over debts owed to the United States only further worsened exchange-rate volatility. The Bank may have once considered taking such proactive steps to set aside some foreign-exchange reserves for debt repayments to the United States.[55] Yet President Roosevelt's announcement of a bank holiday in March 1933 did little to assuage the Treasury's apprehensions. Hopkins claimed that investors were now beginning to scramble to sell their foreign currencies in exchange for the safe asset of gold.[56] Additional memoranda by Treasury officials revealed a renewed desire to keep "sterling reasonably stable at a level suitable to industrial interests and likely to assist in inducing that rise in sterling prices which is so vital an object though so difficult in present world conditions to attain."[57] The Bank, meanwhile, largely accepted this argument.

CHALLENGING LIBERAL ORTHODOXY

In *Exchange Control* (1934), Paul Einzig traced the historical use of exchange control, "the most neglected action of the science of currency, banking, and finance."[58] A leading financial journalist, Einzig predicted the importance of exchange-rate management in determining the future of the international economic order. As he wrote,

> Exchange Control has become a factor of importance in international politics. It has been used as a means for exerting political pressure and as a bargaining counter. Its significance in internal politics is beginning to be realised by those who are desirous of establishing new régimes and initiating new experiments, the success of which stands

53 Hopkins to Chamberlain, January 26, 1933, TNA T175/71.

54 Patricia Clavin, "The World Economic Conference 1933: The Failure of British Internationalism," *Journal of European Economic History* 20, no. 3 (1991): 489–527; Eichengreen, *Golden Fetters*, 317–337; Cottrell, "The Bank of England in its International Setting," 108–109; Daunton, *The Economic Government of the World*, 31–49.

55 Committee of Treasury, Minutes, October 26, 1932, BoE G8/61.

56 Hopkins to Chamberlain, March 4, 1933, TNA T175/71.

57 See, for instance, "Treasury Note Dated 4 March 1933 on the Recent Position of the Sterling Exchange up to the Date of the New York Banking Moratorium," TNA T175/71.

58 Paul Einzig, *Exchange Control* (London: Macmillan, 1934), vii.

or falls on the extent to which the flight of capital can be prevented. It is the dream of both Socialists and Fascists in various countries to secure complete control over the international movements of funds in the interest of their political and economic plans.[59]

Indeed, opponents of such policies often rallied on ideological grounds against the authoritarian elements of exchange control. While Einzig's analysis acknowledged the growing controversy surrounding such measures, he also understood how the once-dominant tenets of economic orthodoxy were now being undermined. The question that officials, bankers, and economists had to confront was whether there existed an alternative exchange-rate policy.

To varying degrees, British officials sought to uphold the principles of liberal orthodoxy, acknowledging that such policies were necessary for spurring an economic recovery. With the US departure from the gold standard in March 1933 and renewed rumors of the collapse of the gold bloc in 1934, the Treasury considered different ways of limiting the depreciation of foreign currencies against sterling without resorting to exchange control. Doing so would have helped to stabilize the exchange rate without committing significant government resources to intervention. One proposal included "the maintenance of the pretended gold standard," similar to France's gold bloc, while another suggested "a uniform devaluation" of countries on gold along the lines discussed at the World Economic Conference.[60] Either framework would have helped to stabilize sterling, but both risked lowering investors' trust in the currency. However, neither proposal gained significant traction because the Treasury opposed any policy that would restrict market forces. As Sir Frederick Phillips asserted, "any important sacrifice of our own freedom would ... perhaps be too high a price to pay."[61]

Ensuing debates over different forms of economic intervention led officials to evaluate the legislation adopted in other countries. Since 1931, Argentine importers were required to obtain licenses from the Control Commission, a regulatory body that maintained the peso's peg to sterling by limiting the volume of currency that could be converted.[62] Those who did not obtain permits and purchased foreign currencies at market prices faced a fine.[63] Meanwhile, Germany had developed an even more stringent form of exchange control. Alongside Reichsbank President Hjalmar Schacht's New Plan, clearing agreements with Latin America and Southeastern Europe intended to conserve resources and impose restrictions on the volume of imports.[64]

59 Einzig, *Exchange Control*, 8.

60 Frederick Phillips, "Future Exchange Problems," February 15, 1934, TNA T175/71.

61 Frederick Phillips, "Future Exchange Problems," February 15, 1934, TNA T175/71.

62 Frederick Leith-Ross, "Exchange Control and Clearing," December 16, 1932, TNA T188/57; Overseas & Foreign Department, "Government Exchange Profits," May 10, 1935, BoE OV102/5.

63 Overseas & Foreign Department, "Foreign Exchange Control," May 25, 1935, BoE OV102/5.

64 Howard S. Ellis, "German Exchange Control, 1931–1939: From an Emergency Measure to a Totalitarian Institution," *The Quarterly Journal of Economics* 54, no. 4 (1940), 54–59; Frank

In light of the policy responses in Germany and Argentina, a series of bilateral agreements helped to sustain Britain's overseas trade. The 1933 Anglo-Argentine Convention (Roca–Runciman Treaty) established minimum quotas for Argentine beef imported into the United Kingdom in exchange for duty-free access for British goods imported into Argentina. Companies greatly benefited from the "benevolent treatment" clause that granted them a favorable exchange rate on remittances to the United Kingdom.[65] Other agreements aimed to ease trade restrictions in Europe. The Anglo-German Exchange Agreement of August 1934 ensured that German businesses were able to import British goods by accessing foreign-exchange reserves via a special account (*Sondermark*) at the Bank of England. Meanwhile, the Anglo-German Payments Agreement, signed in November, ensured the prompt repayment of British creditors after the Bank of England offered the Reichsbank a line of credit amounting to £750,000.[66] The motivation behind these negotiations was to see the German government continue to make payments on its commercial debt.[67] Moreover, the maintenance of sterling as the currency used for international transactions could have helped to sustain demand and, by extension, the exchange rate. "So long as the exchange agreement exists," Leith-Ross wrote to Governor Norman, "we are committed to doing all we can to help it to operate successfully."[68]

Nevertheless, the main obstacle surrounding the implementation of exchange control continued to be its association with authoritarian regimes, often inimical to the free movement of capital. A financial adviser at the British Embassy in Berlin highlighted "the brutal effects of exchange control" on the German economy.[69] Publicly, too, the press noted the growing difficulties that German citizens faced in obtaining permits to travel on trips requiring more than 200

C. Child, *The Theory and Practice of Exchange Control in Germany: A Study of Monopolistic Exploitation in International Markets* (The Hague: Martinus Nijhoff, 1958), 133–149; Zara Steiner, *The Triumph of the Dark: European International History, 1933–1939* (Oxford: Oxford University Press, 2011), 269; Adam Tooze, *The Wages of Destruction: The Making and Breaking of the Nazi Economy* (London: Allen Lane, 2006), 86–96.

65 Sember, "Challenging a Money Doctor," 67.

66 Committee of Treasury, Minutes, August 8, 1934, BoE G8/62; HC Deb, December 11, 1934, vol. 296, cc. 199–201; *Anglo-German Exchange Agreement Relating to Commercial Payments*, Cmd. 4673 (London: H.M. Stationery Office, 1934); *Anglo-German Payments Agreement*, Cmd. 4726 (London: H.M. Stationery Office, 1934); League of Nations, *Commercial Banks, 1929–1934* (Geneva: League of Nations, 1935), 50; Neil Forbes, *Doing Business with the Nazis: Britain's Economic and Financial Relations with Germany, 1931–1939* (London: Frank Cass, 2000), 101–104, 110–115.

67 As expressed by Hopkins and Walter Runciman, President of the Board of Trade; HC Deb, November 1, 1934, vol. 293, cc. 358–362; Hopkins to Fisher and Chamberlain, January 22, 1934, TNA T175/84.

68 Leith-Ross to Norman, September 10, 1934, BoE G14/110.

69 G.H.S. Pinsent, "A Short Note on the Economic Outlook in Germany at the End of July 1934," July 31, 1934, TNA T188/83.

RM.[70] Stringent measures enacted by the Nazi government fundamentally destabilized the prevailing economic order. In response to declining reserves, Germany opted to enact a complete moratorium on foreign-debt repayments in June.[71]

These restrictions, if similarly adopted in the United Kingdom, could have greatly harmed the City's reputation. The Bank's experts understood the risks associated with such measures and recognized several issues with importing a seemingly foreign model of exchange-rate management. For one, there were far fewer institutions dedicated to regulation in the United Kingdom than in either Germany or Argentina. In the comparatively more liberal British market, the institutions that did exist themselves seemed to have little direct control over the economy. According to one of the Bank's economists, Henry Clay, "[c]ommercial Banks cannot make people borrow if they do not want to, and Central Banks cannot make Clearing Banks lend, merely by putting larger cash resources at their disposal."[72] There was also an operational complexity to the tight regime of regulation in Germany that the Bank was unwilling to implement:

> At 5 o'clock each day representatives from the Reichswirtschaftsministerium [the Ministry of Economics] come to the Reichsbank [the central bank] to decide how much exchange is to be allotted to the various applicants. Requests have first to be graded into order of importance; essential raw-materials and food-stuffs being given preference over luxury goods. Then pro-rata allocations, differing for each type of import, have to be made. This lasts till 7 o'clock when the Government officials retire. The unsatisfied applications turn up again at the next allotment, so that the whole process grows in complexity from day to day.[73]

Logistically, the German system had gradually become more complicated with the creation of twenty-five new government offices assigned to issue currency certificates for imports.[74] Given the shortage of both foreign-exchange reserves and raw materials, the Reichsbank and other government bodies pursued an aggressive program of economic recovery through import substitution, exchange control, and other trade restrictions.[75] Following his meeting with Schacht, Leith-Ross predicted future problems with an economic regime centered on stimulating internal trade and encouraging certain imports, which came at the cost of a continued depletion of foreign-currency reserves.[76]

70 "The Economics of Hitlerism," *The Times* 46525, August 17, 1933, 11.

71 Franz Döring, "Das deutsche Devisenproblem," September 1934, BArch R2501/6441, ff. 390–398.

72 Henry Clay, "Banking & Industry," June 15, 1934, BoE ADM22/1.

73 Overseas & Foreign Department, "A Visit to Berlin 17th–24th July 1934," August 3, 1934, BoE G14/110.

74 Eric Phipps [British Ambassador to Germany] to John Simon [Foreign Secretary], September 12, 1934, TNA T188/82.

75 Steiner, *The Triumph of the Dark*, 96–97; Tooze, *The Wages of Destruction*, 106–112.

76 "Committee on Exchange Restrictions," July 11, 1934, TNA T188/82; Leith-Ross, "Note of Conversation with Dr Schacht," September 22, 1934, TNA T188/83.

It was in this context that informal pressure on British banks and commercial agreements with foreign countries remained the preferred model of governance. For one, a steady and promising economic recovery had already been underway. Reginald McKenna of Midland Bank believed that there was "a striking benefit resulting from our departure from gold," and he favored the existing "cheap money" policy that was supporting international trade.[77] Additionally, the Treasury suggested different ways of transitioning the system back to a regime of fixed exchange rates. In one note, Phillips advocated the restoration of some form of an international gold standard to bring currencies in line with one another, a goal shared by government officials throughout the Commonwealth.[78] Even though it was well known that the pound was undervalued against the dollar and overvalued against the franc, the government continued to advocate "a more liberal economic policy" that rejected a draconian system of exchange control and import restrictions.[79]

Yet the Bank began to express reluctance that such arrangements could bring lasting stability. Its advisers initially discussed the possibility of using the EEA to peg sterling to a new parity. Humphrey Mynors, the Bank's recently appointed Secretary, questioned whether it was possible to return to the gold standard at the current devalued rate.[80] A lower exchange rate would have greatly benefited the industries most dependent on exports, such as cotton and shipbuilding. Yet although a second devaluation could have helped these industries, it would not have counteracted protectionist policies abroad.[81] The EEA seemed to be the main mechanism for "limit[ing] fluctuations in the exchange value of sterling," Clay wrote, but "the big movements have been beyond our control."[82]

Ongoing concerns over exchange-rate instability led Bank officials to search for additional expertise. As early as 1926, they had considered the possibility of employing an "exchange expert" given that "[n]o official of the Bank has the intimate knowledge or experience required."[83] Following the creation of the EEA in 1932, the Bank found more reasons to hire a technical specialist, as officials aimed to reassert their authority over the Treasury in economic affairs. The following January, the Bank hired George Bolton, a foreign-exchange expert from the City, to assist with the EEA's operations.[84] Although in nominal

[77] "Chairman's Speech: Annual General Meeting," January 24, 1935, CAC McKenna Papers 7/6.

[78] Frederick Phillips, Note, January 30, 1934, TNA T175/84.

[79] Committee on Economic Information, "Fourteenth Report: Survey of the Economic Situation," December 1934, TNA CAB24/251/74.

[80] Humphrey Mynors, "Stabilisation," May 31, 1934, BoE ADM22/18.

[81] Henry Clay, "Note on the State of Trade," October 23, 1934, BoE EID9/40.

[82] Henry Clay, Note, December 4, 1934, BoE G14/133; Geoffrey Jones, "Bolton, Sir George Lewis French (1900–1982)," September 23, 2004, ODNB.

[83] "Exchange Expert," November 1926, BoE ADM16/4.

[84] Hennessy, *A Domestic History of the Bank of England*, 86–87; Roberts, *Schroders*, 372; Kynaston, *The City of London, vol. 3*, 385, 399; Harris, *Monetary War and Peace*, 67; Daunton, *The Economic Government*, 200.

agreement with the Treasury View on the importance of the free movement of capital, Bolton and the other experts understood London's fragile position and the insufficient gold reserves it held. They thus worked to institute a type of exchange-rate regime that would protect sterling from foreign speculation, yet still allow for some degree of flexibility.

Ongoing discussions centered on the prospect of institutional reforms. In March 1932, Harry A. Siepmann proposed the establishment of a new entity that could have processed foreign-exchange conversions with partner correspondent banks abroad.[85] Doing so would have allowed the Bank to work closely with private banks in New York, where speculation appeared to be at its greatest. Internal deliberations emphasized how information on the market could only be accessed through regular contact with foreign commercial banks. By November, Clay was able to propose a more elaborate plan for the creation of a "permanent Council" or a "new regulating authority," comprising the issuing houses and the Bank. Under this system, limits on outflows of capital would have prevented rapid fluctuations in the currency. Clay further believed that any form of "Government control would be dangerous" due to the possibility of political influence in regulating overseas lending, warning that "Government interference is inevitable, if nothing is done."[86]

Yet these suggestions could not be enacted in the political environment of the early 1930s. For those outside the United Kingdom, the shortcomings of such arrangements were clear. A meeting of the Bank for International Settlements led to the conclusion that the interconnectedness of foreign-exchange markets would continue to threaten the pound: "The current fall of the pound sterling appears as a consequence not only of the English internal political malaise and of the fears which may have aroused the speculative position of recent weeks, but also as an indirect development of the American decisions on the gold clause."[87] It was particularly troublesome that foreign countries had been accumulating vast amounts of sterling balances (UK-based liabilities owed to foreign countries), which could have been easily redeemed at the sign of the next crisis.[88] The consensus that underpinned the Basel View, espoused by the Bank for International Settlements, vehemently opposed controls in all its forms. As its chief economist, Per Jacobsson, later opined, exchange control represented "not only a loss of trade but [also] a danger of moral isolation."[89]

The Bank thus struggled to justify state intervention, especially as the particular variant of capital control and pervasive racial discrimination in Germany became more apparent. A capital-flight tax (*Reichsfluchtsteuer*), first introduced

85 Harry A. Siepmann, "Memorandum: Exchange Control," March 31, 1932, BoE G14/307.
86 Henry Clay, "Regulation of Foreign Lending," November 10, 1932, NCO Clay Papers 67/1/12.
87 "Séance de mars du Conseil de la Banques des Règlements Internationaux," March 10 and 11, 1935, BIS Quesnay Papers 20200106-2375.1.
88 Drummond, *The Floating Pound and the Sterling Area*, 201.
89 Quoted in Toniolo, *Central Bank Cooperation*, 291.

in 1931 and raised to 25 percent in 1933, had targeted "non-Aryans" under the Nazi regime, which expropriated domestic assets at arbitrary penalty rates.[90] In collaboration with several merchant banks, the Bank established the Advance and Transfer Corporation to help German citizens who wanted to transfer their savings abroad.[91] Yet the program was severely underfunded, offering too little relief to those persecuted by the Nazi government. By 1935, the Reichsbank and other government departments planned to exert complete control over capital transfers by conducting extensive tax audits of Germany's major banks.[92] When Winston Churchill had learned through Leonard Montefiore, who led both the Anglo-Jewish Association and the Central British Fund for German Jewry, of the increasingly restrictive laws on German Jews through the Nuremberg laws, he called for the government to intervene.[93] He also urged the Treasury to consider helping Baroness Goldschmidt-Rothschild, a German aristocrat and actress, acquire British nationality and transfer "an enormous fortune" from her estates in Germany and Poland to the United Kingdom.[94] Hopkins, while acknowledging the stringent forms of exchange restrictions in Germany, nevertheless stated that "it is not a matter on which the Treasury can give any help."[95]

The inability of the British authorities to mitigate the consequences of repeated crises became more apparent following the collapse of the gold bloc. Belgium had already abandoned the parity to gold in March 1935, while Poland banned the export of gold the following April. Further hindering an economic recovery was the electoral victory of France's socialist Popular Front in May 1936. Its leader, Léon Blum, had initially campaigned on a promise of exchange control despite the warnings of former Finance Minister Paul Reynaud.[96] Although Blum ultimately opted for a devaluation instead of exchange control to avoid alienating the other Western democracies, the prospect of another major European power imposing financial regulations – the

[90] Dorothee Mußgnug, *Die Reichsfluchtsteuer 1931–1953* (Berlin: Duncker & Humblot, 1993), 19–23; Saul Friedländer, *Das Dritte Reich und die Juden. Die Jahre der Verfolgung 1933–1939* (Munich: C.H. Beck, 1998), 76; Susanne Meinl and Jutta Zwilling, *Legalisierter Raub. Die Ausplünderung der Juden im Nationalsozialismus durch die Reichsfinanzverwaltung in Hessen* (Frankfurt am Main and New York: Campus Verlag, 2004), 298–301; Ramona Bräu, *Die Plünderung Polens. Die Reichsfinanzverwaltung in den Jahren der Besatzung (1939–1945)* (Berlin: De Gruyter Oldenbourg, 2022), 68–73.

[91] Committee of Treasury, Minutes, August 19, 1936, BoE G8/63.

[92] "Sitzungsbericht über die Sitzung im Reichsfinanzministerium am 28. August 1935," BArch R3101/15568.

[93] Martin Gilbert, *Churchill and the Jews: A Lifelong Friendship* (New York: Henry Holt, 2007), 106.

[94] Churchill to Hopkins, November 20, 1936, CAC Chartwell Papers 2/260.

[95] Hopkins to Churchill, November 27, 1936, CAC Chartwell Papers 2/260.

[96] Jean Bouvier, "Contrôle des changes et politique économique extérieure de la SFIO en 1936," *Relations internationales*, no. 13 (1978), 112; Mouré, *Managing the Franc Poincaré*, 242; Steiner, *The Triumph of the Dark*, 276.

debate for which reemerged in 1938 – made Whitehall increasingly nervous.[97] Economic nationalism would further hamper cooperative efforts. Even after the signing of the Tripartite Agreement in September 1936, the collapsing value of the franc and the oversupply of gold made policymakers apprehensive over the stability of the international monetary system.[98]

To contemporaries, a reprisal of a 1931 crisis appeared certain. As the Committee on Economic Information noted, a general recovery in international trade was contingent upon resolving exchange-rate issues:

> [T]he heart of these problems lies in the extreme mobility of capital between different international centres, in circumstances in which the movement of goods between nations is circumscribed by every kind of restriction. Movements of capital have taken a great variety of forms, the piling up of short-term liabilities, the sale of securities, and participation in stock exchange speculation. But in the event they have led to the subordination of internal credit policy to the exigencies of a dangerous exchange situation.[99]

Other officials recognized the inherent weaknesses of existing arrangements. For the Bank, the shortage of reserves held by the EEA had caused "some embarrassment."[100] The Committee of Treasury's understatement misjudged the situation. With the resignation of Blum's first short-lived administration in June 1937, the EEA began to experience a rapid accumulation of capital, including £41 million in gold from France alone.[101] Predominantly destabilized by investor speculation, the franc depreciated from over 130 francs to the pound to around 150 by October.[102] What the ordeal revealed was how destabilizing capital inflows could have undermined the stability of the pound, as they had done to the franc.

DECENTRALIZED MODELS OF GOVERNANCE

With both war and crisis becoming more likely, the Bank considered ways of institutionalizing a robust system of economic management. Its advisers observed developments abroad and became convinced that major reform was necessary to prevent capital flight. In March 1937, Siepmann suggested

97 Vansittart to the Foreign Office, October 2, 1935, TNA T177/33.

98 Howson, *Domestic Monetary Management*, 126–127; Stephen V.O. Clarke, "Exchange-Rate Stabilization in the Mid-1930s: Negotiating the Tripartite Agreement," *Princeton Studies in International Finance*, no. 41 (1977), 51–52; Drummond, *The Floating Pound*, 225–233; Harris, *Monetary War and Peace*, 142–149.

99 Committee on Economic Information, "Twentieth Report: Survey of the Economic Situation," June 1936, TNA CAB24/263/3.

100 Committee of Treasury, Minutes, December 9, 1936, BoE G8/63.

101 Harry A. Siepmann, "Increase of the E.E.A.," July 7, 1937, BoE ADM22/21.

102 Conseil général, "Procès-verbal de la séance du jeudi 7 octobre 1937," BdF 1069201116/65; Committee on Economic Information, "Twenty-Third Report: Survey of the Economic Situation," October 1937, TNA CAB24/273/12.

devising "a defensive measure of militant nationalism," which could, "in the event of war, be converted from a defensive to an offensive weapon."[103] The implementation of "half measures" that only partially committed the country to exchange control would have been insufficient given the realities of the current economic system.[104] What the Bank aimed to do was to alter the perception of exchange control as an illiberal policy.

Drawing on past examples proved to be a useful intellectual exercise. "We ought to be studying the German and Russian systems of industrial and currency control," asserted Clay, "since they are organising now on the lines on which we should have to organize in war-time."[105] To contemporaries, Germany seemed far more financially prepared for war. In 1937, the Reichsbank had already employed an estimated 650 staff members in its foreign-exchange department.[106] Its elaborate system of financial regulation involved the circulation of foreign-exchange vouchers being used in exchange for RM at rates set by the central bank.[107] While Siepmann acknowledged that "the English still do not take kindly to the system, having an obstinate and misguided likely for individualism and personality," he nevertheless outlined a series of conditions needed for Britain's wartime mobilization:

(i) [A]ll foreign exchange transactions prohibited, except with the Bank of England.
(ii) [A]ll foreign securities in private possession to be registered, deposited[,] and taken over by the control.
(iii) The Bullion market to be closed and the import or export of gold for private account[s] forbidden.
(iv) All exchange rates to be fixed by the authorities and varied at their discretion.
(v) Agents to be appointed in neutral and allied countries to transact exchange business (not necessarily only for sterling) for [the] account of the authorities.
(vi) All foreign lending to be prohibited.
(vii) All Empire mined gold to be bought at the source.
(viii) Gold to be secured for [the] account of the control wherever and whenever possible.
(ix) No allied currencies to be purchased or held by the control.[108]

103 Siepmann to Catterns, March 25, 1937, BoE EC4/1.
104 Siepmann to Catterns, March 25, 1937, BoE EC4/1.
105 Clay to Catterns, March 13, 1937, BoE EC4/1.
106 Siepmann to Catterns, March 25, 1937, BoE EC4/1.
107 Hans Hartenstein, "Runderlasse der Reichsstelle für Devisenbewirtschaftung," January 9, 1937, GStA PK, I. HA Rep. 151, IC, Nr. 9385; Tooze, *The Wages of Destruction*, 84–86.
108 Siepmann to Catterns, March 25, 1937, BoE EC4/1.

Based on the advice of experts, Deputy Governor Basil Catterns contacted the Treasury concerning a draft of an Emergency Powers Bill. The new legislation presented a plan for preparing the country's economy for a war. Catterns explained that, "judging from the lessons of the Great War," Britain needed to take all the necessary precautions for another conflict, while also ensuring that "[t]he function of the exchange control would be purely technical and monetary in scope."[109] He further emphasized the centrality of the Bank to the future system: "It would probably be convenient in practice, where such a technical subject as gold and exchange is concerned, to employ for the purpose of this control the machinery already available in the shape of the Foreign Exchange Department of the Bank of England."[110]

Still, it remained to be seen whether the Bank's proposals could be made compatible with the tenets of economic orthodoxy. There was a strong possibility that the private banks, rather than the central bank, would be the institutions primarily responsible for exchange-rate stability. One proposal came in response to the threat that Egypt would leave the sterling area. A local Barclays director based in Alexandria, seeking "to be fully prepared in the event of dissociation of the Pound Egyptian from the Pound Sterling," outlined a framework of limited exchange control.[111] In a scenario in which Egypt abandoned its peg to sterling, Barclays could control the flight from the currency through its own private Exchange Control Office.[112] If all of Barclays' branches in Egypt kept detailed records of the purchase and sale of sterling, the main branch in Alexandria could then reconcile these figures for its London office.[113] Although hypothetical, the proposal found support from senior management. Recognizing that local bankers had far more technical knowledge of overseas markets than the London office, the Chief Accountant encouraged the Alexandria branch to be operationally responsible for maintaining a favorable exchange rate with the Egyptian pound.[114] Changes in exchange rates would then be determined by the Alexandria branch, while branches in other cities, such as Cairo or Assiut, could offer additional assistance.[115] This form of economic governance would permit the continued existence of a system of indirect regulation in which private commercial banks effectively managed the currency.

Others within the political establishment were even more opposed to any form of control, especially one with the Bank in command. The Treasury was

[109] Catterns to Phillips, July 8, 1937, BoE EC4/1.
[110] Catterns to Phillips, July 8, 1937, BoE EC4/1.
[111] Barclays Local Director to the General Managers, "Exchange Control," March 24, 1938, BGA 0011-0348.
[112] "General Remarks," n.d., BGA 0011-0348.
[113] "Outline of the General Working of the Scheme," November 15, 1937, BGA 0011-0348.
[114] E.L. Neynoe [Chief Accountant] to the Local Directors, Alexandria, "Exchange Control," June 15, 1938, BGA 0011-0348.
[115] "Outline of the General Working of the Scheme," November 15, 1937, BGA 0011-0348.

particularly vocal and, until 1937, denounced the Bank's attempts to manipulate exchange rates. As Sir Frederick Phillips wrote to the Bank, "there are very great advantages in a free market ... [and] there is everything to be said for controlling imports and for leaving exchanges free."[116] He found support from politicians in Westminster. In April, several British officials attended a session of the International Studies Conference in Paris, where they blamed the "great financial difficulties which a certain number of countries had to face since 1930" on bilateral exchange agreements and commercial restrictions, such as quotas.[117] An ensuing parliamentary discussion reiterated many of these concerns, with one Conservative MP declaring that "exchange control is an evil."[118]

The Bank's advisers responded to these comments with great frustration. Siepmann, for instance, noted how "[t]he debate in the House was only remarkable as a display of incomprehension."[119] Indeed, experts believed that such criticisms represented a fundamental misunderstanding of the technical needs of exchange-rate policy. The true nature of the economic situation, namely how unprepared Britain was for war, seemed to be lost on those who would block the implementation of much-needed reforms. Even if the Treasury could be convinced, major political obstacles stood in the way of assuring a reform, as "Parliament would hardly tolerate a system allowing [the banks] any measure of control unless they were subjected to a strong central authority answerable to Parliament."[120] With declining trust in sterling, followed by the support for economic autarky and other nationalist policies abroad, Britain might have had to confront the consequences of "[a] panic flight from sterling" and "[h]oarding demand for commodities thus increasing the strain on the exchange."[121]

Yet opposition continued to come from those who extolled the benefits of economic orthodoxy. Liberal economists, such as Lionel Robbins, argued that the stabilization of exchange rates was fundamentally "the first condition of permanent recovery."[122] Similarly, Paul van Zeeland, a Belgian economist and the former Prime Minister, believed that illiberal policies would only foster a dangerous form of economic nationalism.[123] As Chamberlain (now the Prime Minister) sought to identify steps for spurring a trade-based recovery, he turned to a 1938 report published by van Zeeland, who firmly denounced the use of exchange control. According to the document, "[r]estrictions regarding

116 Phillips to Catterns, September 3, 1937, BoE EC4/1.

117 Conférence permanente des hautes études internationales, Xème session, "Mémoire sur les aspects monétaires du problème des matières premières par Michel A. Heilperin," April 1937, LoN R4014/5B/25952/2381.

118 HC Deb, June 28, 1937, vol. 325 c. 1723.

119 Harry A. Siepmann, "Increase of the E.E.A.," July 7, 1937, BoE ADM22/21.

120 Phillips to Catterns, May 9, 1938, BoE EC4/1.

121 G.F.C. Bolton, "War Measures," March 25, 1938, BoE EC4/1.

122 Lionel Robbins, *The Great Depression* (London: Macmillan, 1934), 164.

123 Clavin, *Securing the World Economy*, 187.

the transfer of funds, even when they are limited to movements of a financial character, deprive international trade of the essential assistance of credit facilities whether on short, middle or long term, without which such trade cannot develop fully and with certainty."[124]

The Bank might have recognized the value in some of the suggestions made in the van Zeeland report, particularly those on reducing tariffs and building on the Tripartite Agreement. However, experts criticized the readability of the document, its logical flaws, and the "economic mumbo-jumbo" on which it relied.[125] Above all, the report was unable to show how exchange-rate stability could be achieved without exchange control. Van Zeeland seemed to have intentionally obscured or ignored many of the pressing realities endemic to the British economy, which could have only been known to insiders. For instance, capital flight from sterling was increasingly likely due to recent estimates of rearmament spending.[126] From this perspective, van Zeeland's document resembled less of a policy prescription and more of "a model of economic diplomacy," only seeking to influence "high foreign officials" and inspire "a certain amount of hope."[127]

Still, the Bank found itself blocked by political misunderstandings and institutional challenges. At one level, they faced numerous challenges from central banks that had long remained committed to economic liberalism. An official at the Belgian central bank, where van Zeeland had been serving as Vice Governor, observed with great anxiety how its British counterpart could even consider "abandoning the ways of orthodoxy" and learning from "the example of totalitarian countries."[128] Nazi Germany had also been continually expanding its system of exchange control since 1933. Under the Third Reich, the economic and finance ministries were able to maintain strict control over capital investments and foreign credits, and severe penalties for noncompliance were also widespread.[129]

On the other extreme of the political spectrum, socialist governments throughout Europe began to impose greater restrictions on trade and commerce. In France, an ideological shift within the Socialist Party had led to the support for exchange restrictions as a necessary policy "to save democracy."[130]

124 Paul van Zeeland, "Annex: Report on the Possibility of Obtaining a General Reduction of the Obstacles to International Trade," December 24, 1937, TNA CAB24/274/10, 8. See also *Report Presented by Monsieur van Zeeland to the Governments of the United Kingdom and France*, Cmd. 5648 (London: H.M. Stationery Office, 1938).

125 Cameron Cobbold, "Van Zeeland Report – First Thoughts," January 31, 1938, BoE G1/205.

126 Henry Clay, "Van Zeeland Report," February 9, 1938, BoE G1/205.

127 Overseas & Foreign Department, "The Van Zeeland Report: Foreign Press Comment," February 2, 1938, BoE G1/205.

128 François Cracco [Department of Economic Studies, National Bank of Belgium] to Georges Janssen [Governor, National Bank of Belgium], January 16, 1939, BNB O151.

129 Tooze, *The Wages of Destruction*, 133–134.

130 Quoted in Julian Jackson, *The Popular Front in France: Defending Democracy, 1934–38* (Cambridge: Cambridge University Press, 1990), 186.

When Prime Minister Camille Chautemps was forced to resign after losing the confidence of the governing Popular Front in March 1938, a flight of capital from France precipitated due to investors foreshadowing the implementation of exchange control. The collapse in confidence in the French franc provoked a response from the monetary authorities. Since at least January, the Banque de France had requested that private French banks abstain from trading on foreign-exchange markets and asked if the Bank of England would consider making a similar announcement in London.[131] The Bank hesitated to respond because it had been secretly selling francs in anticipation of a socialist victory.

The exchange-rate crisis in France could also be used as a pretext for future reforms. Over the ensuing months, various memoranda at the Bank began to hint at the idea that currency restrictions would soon be inevitable.[132] Officials prepared a list of recommendations on how to quell a mass sell-off of sterling. In July 1938, Catterns claimed that exchange control might help "to avoid such a panic flight from sterling as would lead to an uncontrollable depreciation."[133] Viewing events in France with apprehension, the Bank's advisers realized that Britain was not immune to currency instability. It had become even more vulnerable due to the global interconnectedness of the London money market. As Bolton noted, the goals of the Bank were multifaceted: first, to deter "the unregulated outflow of foreign exchange from the British economic system," and second, to protect "all present and future reserves."[134] The choice was not simply between complete control and no control, but rather a decision on how to address the different regulatory priorities of a managed economy.

To justify exchange control, experts needed to prove that such a system was feasible, valuable, and sustainable. Bolton sought to show how "[c]omplete control on the lines of a totalitarian state" could be avoided.[135] Due in part to its existing financial status in the world, Britain would not need to enact overly burdensome regulation. As he surmised, "London is the centre of a vast system of trade and credit," and as such, could find a middle ground "between the two extremes of freedom and regimentation."[136] Yet internal disagreements persisted. Siepmann, himself more forward than Bolton, wrote an outline of one potential scheme of government intervention, which included a complete prohibition on the sale of foreign assets, the export of securities, and the volume of loans available to nonresidents of the

131 Harry A. Siepmann, "14th January 1938," BoE ADM 22/21; George Bolton, Diary, January 14, 1938, BoE C160/10.

132 Cameron Cobbold, "War Measures: Sir F. Phillips' Memo," May 9, 1938, BoE EC4/1; Clay to Catterns, May 12, 1938, BoE EC4/1; Catterns to Phillips, May 23, 1938, BoE EC4/1.

133 Catterns to Hopkins, July 8, 1938, BoE EC4/1.

134 G.F.C. Bolton, "Foreign Exchange Regulations," May 24, 1938, BoE EC4/1.

135 G.F.C. Bolton, "War Measures," March 25, 1938, BoE EC4/1.

136 G.F.C. Bolton, "War Measures," March 25, 1938, BoE EC4/1.

United Kingdom.[137] For him, the implementation of exchange control was an all-or-nothing proposition.

Heightened economic tensions with France over exchange-rate negotiations compelled the Bank to search for additional solutions. In April 1933, Cameron Cobbold, a banker with experience working in the gold bloc countries of France and Italy, joined the Bank.[138] Promoted to the position of adviser in 1935, he was able to apply his foreign-exchange expertise to assist the Bank with its overseas relations. In accordance with the 1936 Tripartite Agreement, the British and French central banks established reciprocal convertibility arrangements between the two currencies, the operations of which were overseen by Cobbold.[139] Negotiations initially helped to stabilize exchange rates between the "core" countries. Having also accompanied Governor Norman on several trips to the Bank for International Settlements, he was then appointed a Bank director in 1938 at the age of thirty-four.

After being rapidly promoted within the Bank's hierarchy, Cobbold strived to construct an adequate rationale for a system of exchange control. He first advanced the notion that a wartime central bank needed to act as the sole institution responsible for the purchase and sale of foreign currencies. In April 1938, he wrote to the Treasury about the need for a bank holiday at the beginning of a future conflict, whereupon the Bank could introduce an array of exchange control and foreign-trade restrictions.[140] Both these measures seemed justifiable given the failure of piecemeal policies implemented during the First World War. The Treasury, however, remained ideologically committed to the orthodox principles that had long worked in its favor. Phillips described the potential burden of "a very great degree of interference in the existing free institutions in the City of London. Every country which has applied exchange control has found that it can only be made effective by following up every individual export as well as by subjecting to official permission every individual transaction in foreign exchange."[141] Instead, he suggested a less stringent form of state intervention based on "the market for voluntary abstention from unnecessary purchases of foreign exchange."[142] London could avert a crisis simply due to its historic status as an international financial center.

In many respects, the Treasury remained an intellectual powerhouse in its own right. Its officials drew on the examples of other countries to justify their own arguments. As a result, many of them believed that maintaining the

137 Harry A. Siepmann, "War Measures," May 25, 1938, BoE EC4/1.

138 "The Bankers' Magazine Profile: The Bank Governor," *The Bankers' Magazine* CLXXXVIII, 1959, 186; Fforde, *The Bank of England and Public Policy*, 38; Capie, *The Bank of England*, 42–43; Peter Taylor, "Cobbold, Cameron Fromanteel, first Baron Cobbold (1904–1987)," May 26, 2005, ODNB.

139 Harris, *Monetary War and Peace*, 137.

140 "War Measures: Gold & Foreign Exchange Markets," April 27, 1938, BoE EC4/1.

141 Phillips to Catterns, May 9, 1938, BoE EC4/1.

142 "War Measures," May 17, 1938, BoE EC4/1.

existing system rested on underscoring its differences with more centralized, restrictive forms of economic governance. While Germany, Austria, and Italy were able to reorganize their economies around comprehensive exchange control, the United Kingdom might have been able to avoid "the most strenuous efforts" associated with "such a system with all its enormous disadvantages."[143] Nevertheless, the Bank, with its own technical knowledge of international finance and exchange rates, argued that more controls were needed. It was certainly possible for the country to avoid creating "a complicated machinery of control at the centre on the model of the totalitarian countries."[144] In July, Catterns wrote to the Treasury on how the Bank's proposals were more calculated and a far cry from the highly restrictive "German system."[145] His priority was simply to institute preemptive reforms so as to avoid "having to introduce control step by step, as happened in the last war."[146]

Phillips again disagreed with the Bank's logic. Germany's bureaucratic system was, in fact, "the only possible system of efficient exchange control," and such arrangements would be unavoidable if Britain wanted to implement a regulatory policy.[147] This view was confirmed by his regular conversations with German leaders. During one meeting with Reichsbank President Schacht in late 1938, the Treasury learned that a return to "a free system of currency in Germany" was highly improbable with Hitler in power, even though some officials within the administration secretly wanted to "enable trade and finance to resume their normal operations."[148] Phillips thus concluded that it would be "a great mistake except in face of the clearest necessity to set up a bureaucracy and to interfere with every business transaction at a time of crisis and difficulty, when it is essential to maintain trade, and especially export trade. What is the object of this vast and vexatious bureaucracy?"[149]

Sustaining a less restrictive form of exchange-rate management was certainly in the vested interest of the Treasury. Its stronghold over domestic governance could only be ensured if the Bank had a secondary role in influencing exchange rates and, by extension, financial policy. In August, Phillips reported on the importance of "patriotic appeal" and noted how it should be "the duty of everyone to exercise self-restraint and to abstain from contributing or causing an excessive demand for foreign money, foreign securities and gold."[150] Both British individuals and institutions, according to the Treasury, would seek to

[143] Phillips to Hopkins, June 22, 1938, BoE EC4/1.
[144] Harry A. Siepmann, "Emergency Measures," February 28, 1939, BoE EC4/3.
[145] Catterns to Hopkins, July 8, 1938, BoE EC4/1.
[146] Catterns to Hopkins, July 8, 1938, BoE EC4/1.
[147] Phillips to Hopkins, July 14, 1938, TNA T231/184.
[148] Frederick Leith-Ross, Note, December 16, 1938, TNA T188/227.
[149] Phillips to Hopkins, July 14, 1938, TNA T231/184.
[150] Phillips to Cobbold, August 4, 1938, BoE EC4/2. See also Frederick Phillips, "The Actual Steps Necessary on the Occurrence of an Emergency," August 26, 1938, BoE EC4/2; Waley to Hopkins, "Exchange Control," September 14, 1938, TNA T231/184.

support sterling because such stability was in the national interest. Hopkins similarly agreed with this sentiment, claiming that "British nationals ... will be put on their honour (in Wartime) not to [sell sterling]."[151]

Yet the Bank remained unconvinced. Britain could not rely on a laissez-faire style of economic governance during a military conflict, nor could it manage a wartime bureaucracy based solely on patriotic zeal. Experts were again drawn to historical lessons from the previous war. Having worked at the Treasury from 1912 to 1915, Siepmann recognized that the current administration was again unprepared for war. Without the anchor of the gold standard, exchange-rate stability had been mistakenly abandoned as a priority: "The difference between our pre-war exchange policy and our present policy is that before the war we were prepared to make whatever adjustments in the direction of our trade and in our costs to maintain a fixed rate, while now are not."[152] Temporary expedients might have only been possible in the short run. The Bank considered opening discussions with foreign central banks to gain access to the gold reserves held in Ottawa (£65 million), Pretoria (£60 million), Buenos Aires (£15 million), and Bombay (£10 million).[153]

On the political obstacles to exchange control, officials repeatedly sought to find ways to circumvent them. "Perhaps what we need is not a Treasury ruling at all," wrote Siepmann, "but a decision of policy by the Government."[154] He continued:

> Our plans contemplate a totalitarian war. The Treasury appear to contemplate business as usual. When it comes to objecting that our plans would increase the administrative costs of doing business, or might hamper private initiative, it is quite clear that we are not speaking the same language as the Treasury ... . The idea that sterling is an intrinsically strong and stable currency supports the Treasury's hankerings after liberty. Our view is that, in war conditions, sterling is flotsam and jetsam, unless it can be brought under complete control by methods which are necessarily troublesome, costly, and in direct opposition to the traditions and precedents of the past. But if we were far stronger than we are, the Treasury's attitude would still be either reckless or frivolous.[155]

Siepmann, as a result, looked elsewhere for support. He first considered an indirect form of regulation that involved cooperation with the private commercial banks. Arrangements with London's clearing banks, which had already formed their own committee, could have been an ersatz regulatory policy.

Yet the Bank struggled to address criticism from bankers who desired a more decentralized system of governance. Charles Lidbury, a director at Westminster, one of the Big Five clearing banks, believed "the contemplated

[151] Richard Hopkins, Note, July 25, 1938, TNA T231/184.
[152] Harry A. Siepmann, "Sterling," October 31, 1938, BoE EC4/3.
[153] Cobbold, "Gold Abroad," June 22, 1938, BoE EC4/1; Catterns to Michiel Hendrik de Kock [South African Reserve Bank], July 12, 1938, BoE EC4/2.
[154] Siepmann to Cobbold, June 24, 1938, BoE EC4/1.
[155] Siepmann to Cobbold, June 24, 1938, BoE EC4/1.

emergency half measures will be useless and will merely lead to a loss of exchange."[156] Barclays also shared a list of grievances over the logistics of exchange control.[157] In general, although less unified in their opposition than the Treasury, private bankers remained devotees of economic liberalism. Upon receiving an initial draft of new legislation, a committee of clearing banks noted numerous issues, such as a prohibition on the use of checks for foreign payment and the lack of references to the potential export of gold.[158]

Meanwhile, criticism from the Treasury became even more forceful. Because "gold is freely available in London," Phillips believed it was important to avoid "put[ting] obstacles in the way of its leaving."[159] Any announcement indicating otherwise might have given a dangerous signal to investors that sterling was unable to maintain its value, thereby leading to a mass selloff.[160] Rather than follow with regulatory proposals of their own, the Treasury wanted to consider alternative measures, such as tying the British pound to other European currencies. Such was the topic of talks with Leith-Ross, van Zeeland (Belgium), Schacht (Germany), and former Finance Minister Constantin Argetoiano (Roumania).[161] Waley, the Treasury's specialist in overseas finance, envisioned even less interventionist schemes. The goal was to prevent the mass withdrawal of foreign capital in London if the government declared war. Of high priority, then, was the estimated £100 million in French-owned balances, "which the owners would want to convert into dollars in the event of war."[162]

In contrast to their counterparts at the Treasury and in the City, the Bank continued to push for comprehensive controls in an effort to prepare for an impending crisis.[163] Experts wanted control over foreign-exchange transactions to apply "as widely as possible to British subjects."[164] In October 1938, Siepmann produced a note in which he asserted that "unless there is an almost miraculous change in international politics," a European war was possible "within two to three years."[165] He was particularly aware that recent foreign-exchange losses of some £89 million over the past two months threatened not only the stability of the pound itself but also future access to US dollars at the outbreak of war.[166]

156 Charles Lidbury, "Foreign Exchange Control," August 4, 1938, BoE EC4/2.

157 Frederick Cecil Ellerton, "Skeleton of a Scheme for Foreign Exchange Control," September 15, 1938, BoE EC4/2; Frederick Cecil Ellerton to Bolton, September 16, 1938, BoE EC4/2.

158 "Committee of London Clearing Bankers," September 21, 1938, BoE EC4/2.

159 Phillips to Hopkins, July 18, 1938, TNA T231/184.

160 Richard Hopkins, Note, July 25, 1938, TNA T231/184.

161 Leith-Ross, *Money Talks*, 233–237.

162 Waley to Phillips, September 30, 1938, TNA T231/185.

163 Cameron Cobbold, "War Measures," August 10, 1938, BoE EC4/2.

164 "Note of a Meeting Held at the Bank on Thursday, 15th September 1938," September 16, 1938, BoE EC4/2.

165 Harry A. Siepmann, "Crisis Measures," October 12, 1938, BoE EC4/3.

166 Harry A. Siepmann, "Summary," October 12, 1938, BoE EC4/3.

The challenge was convincing the Treasury to approve a plan of exchange control in peacetime, which would "look like a confession of technical weakness even in supposedly normal conditions."[167] With Siepmann's calculations, Cobbold reported to Phillips the urgency of reaching an agreement with the Treasury and the Empire Central Banks over exchange control.[168]

It was this line of argument that convinced the Treasury to accept some of the Bank's recommendations. One discussion concerned the question of which department would enforce prohibitions on travelers (both UK and non-UK residents) who brought gold, foreign currencies, and securities out of the country (a measure known as Regulation 86). Waley suggested that it could be a matter for the Customs Office, as he wanted these restrictions to operate "without any change in the wording of the Regulation" and "in the most efficient and cheapest way possible."[169] The Bank agreed with the suggestion, but noted that Customs could deliver "any detained article to their ordinary banker for our account."[170] Still, more prominent figures at the Treasury continued to oppose ceding jurisdiction over economic affairs to another government office. Because Waley's proposal would do little to correct future foreign-exchange problems, Hopkins claimed that "a regulation of this kind, once introduced, may create apprehension in the minds of non-residents."[171] Phillips echoed these sentiments and wanted to reaffirm his belief that "no restraint should be placed on sterling balances owned by non-residents," noting "the psychological effect" of this course of action.[172]

The structural dislocations caused by inefficient exchange-rate management had become more widely known abroad. Both the French and the Belgian authorities acknowledged the fundamental weaknesses of sterling on international markets.[173] To the British authorities as well, continued losses of gold reserves via the EEA in late 1938 appeared to confirm such pessimism. As the City's reputation as a financial center had come increasingly under question, the Bank convinced both the Treasury and the City of the need to adopt some version of exchange control. If war were to occur, it would have been unlikely

[167] Harry A. Siepmann, "Crisis Measures," October 12, 1938, BoE EC4/3.

[168] Cobbold to Catterns, "War Measures: Points Outstanding with the Treasury," October 14, 1938, BoE EC4/3.

[169] Waley to R.J. Lloyd [H.M. Customs and Excise], October 5, 1938, TNA T231/185.

[170] Cobbold to Waley, October 19, 1938, TNA T231/185.

[171] Hopkins to Fisher, October 19, 1938, TNA T175/104 and T231/185. Waley countered these suggestions by noting the difficulty of distinguishing between residents and non-residents, particularly British companies that had offices both at home and overseas; Waley to Phillips, "Exchange Control," February 15, 1939, TNA T231/185.

[172] Phillips to Catterns, "Emergency Measures," December 29, 1938, TNA T231/185.

[173] "La politique monétaire anglaise," *Le Temps (Paris)* 28270, February 6, 1939, 3; Banque nationale de Belgique, Service des études économiques, "Les perspectives de la livre sterling," June 15, 1939, BNB Y188.

that Britain would be able to ship gold to the United States in exchange for an emergency loan denominated in dollars.[174]

By November, the Bank preemptively circulated a draft of new exchange-control legislation. The scheme allowed the clearing banks to authorize each individual transaction for residents who submitted requests for foreign currencies.[175] Such a prerogative was vital for preventing the unsustainable export of gold and other securities by British residents overseas and, more importantly, gaining the support of the commercial banks.[176] Siepmann stated that there was no intention "to requisition gold and foreign exchange balances belonging to U.K. residents" as of yet, but did not wholly eliminate the possibility.[177]

It was largely the effort to defend the City's status as a financial center that convinced the Treasury to accept the idea of regulation. By December, they were willing to engage in negotiations over trade and import controls with the Bank of England and the Empire Central Banks.[178] The imposition of these restrictions necessitated even more coordination with other government departments. Both the Ministry for Economic Warfare and the Ministry of Labour drafted a list of civil servants who were able to assume additional responsibilities, while the Board of Trade was to differentiate between restricted and unrestricted types of imports.[179] Under this system, domestic exporters would be required to obtain a license to export goods, in addition to reporting the type and amount thereof.[180] "Much as I dislike interfering with the freedom of the market," the Chancellor hesitatingly wrote to Governor Norman, "I feel that the time has now come when the embargo should be restored in full force."[181]

THE END OF THE INTERWAR ECONOMIC ORDER

Exchange control was critical to defending the City from economic turmoil. It was the primary means by which the value of sterling could be secured, thereby keeping imports cheap and prices stable. If the UK financial system faced a

174 Catterns to Phillips, "Emergency Measures," October 19, 1938, BoE EC4/3 and TNA T231/185.

175 "Relations between the Bank of England and Authorised Agents," November 2, 1938, BoE EC4/3; Lidbury to Cobbold, November 2, 1938, BoE EC4/3.

176 G.F.C. Bolton, "Defence Regulation 86: Certificates and Evidence of Non-Residence," February 23, 1939, BoE EC4/3.

177 Harry A. Siepmann, Note, December 30, 1938, BoE EC4/3.

178 Hopkins to Norman, December 23, 1938, BoE EC4/3.

179 Cobbold to Catterns, February 14, 1939, BoE EC4/3; Cobbold to Waley, February 14, 1939, BoE EC4/3; "Import and Export Control," February 16, 1939, BoE EC4/3; Chief Foreign Manager, Midland Bank, to Managers of the Branches, November 1, 1939, HSBC, Midland Bank UK 0030-0085.

180 "Outline of Plan for Ensuring that Proceeds of All Exports are Sold to the Exchange Control," February 9, 1939, BoE EC4/3 and EC4/14.

181 Simon to Norman, January 2, 1939, LGA HO/GM/Off/44.

crisis similar to that seen in 1914 or 1931, the Bank intended to maintain free movement of capital among the nations of the sterling area, while restricting it elsewhere. This exchange-rate policy effectively called for the abandonment of the liberal economic order, a model that the Bank long extolled, in favor of a managed currency with bureaucratic supervision.

Convinced of the Bank's arguments, the Committee on Economic Information reported in its December 1938 report that there were few existing tools for achieving general stability "[u]nless and until we are prepared to impose a general exchange control."[182] With the effective approval from the UK government, exchange control marked the beginning of a new economic order. Two of the Bank's advisers, Clay and Cobbold, served on the Committee on Exchange Difficulties and Essential Materials (later, the Exchange Requirements Committee), created in January 1939 to oversee the accumulation of commodities and gold.[183] The sheer complexity associated with the new system led to no shortage of anxieties, with Cobbold acknowledging he was "frightened" by "the administrative complications" of certain clauses.[184] For this reason, it was important for the Bank's leadership, namely the Governor and the Deputy Governor, to be informed of the technical work undertaken by the new Exchange Control Department. By February, a group of Bank officials and experts planned to convene regularly, with Bolton assigned to coordinate cross-departmental communication.[185]

In advocating these reforms, the Bank repeatedly challenged the Treasury as the main intellectual voice on economic matters. One of its reports on exchange control noted that "[i]ts chief purpose is to conserve financial resources for national use, by preventing them from escaping out of the country," leading Phillips to comment in the marginalia, "I hope so, but I doubt it."[186] Nevertheless, experts were able to devise a sound argument for exchange control as an effective and beneficial system. In one confrontational meeting with the Treasury, the Bank insisted that exchange restrictions needed to apply to foreign residents of the United Kingdom and only with some exceptions for those from neutral countries.[187] An additional exemption would be granted to clearing banks, which were able to submit applications for conversions up to a £10,000 limit, an amount that Westminster Bank still deemed "far too small."[188]

182 Committee on Economic Information, "Twenty-Sixth Report: Survey of the Economic Situation," December 1938, TNA CAB24/281/22, 10.

183 J.A.C. Osborne and Ronald Allport, "Unpublished War History (Part 2 Exchange Control) – Chapter 9," 1950, BoE M5/536, 966; Scott Newton, *Profits of Peace: The Political Economy of Anglo-German Appeasement* (Oxford: Clarendon Press, 1996), 139.

184 Cobbold to Waley, March 1, 1939, BoE EC4/3 and TNA T231/185.

185 "War Measures: The Management of Exchange Control," February 21, 1939, BoE EC4/3.

186 Note, March 2, 1939, TNA T231/185.

187 Waley to Phillips, "Exchange Regulation," March 8, 1939, TNA T231/185.

188 Lidbury to Cobbold, "Emergency Measures: Sub-Committee of London Clearing Bankers on Foreign Exchange Control," March 29, 1939, BoE EC4/4.

Even more vital to the proper functioning of exchange control was increased coordination with the nations within the sterling area. Transactions outside the sterling area were to be restricted, while those within the sterling area were effectively allowed to remain open.[189] The main challenge with the focus on the sterling area (rather than the empire) was confronting the potential "leaks" in the system among independent nations. For instance, residents of the Republic of Ireland (Éire) would theoretically have been able to circumvent foreign-exchange laws if they could convert freely between British pounds and foreign currencies. In this scenario, Catterns proposed "treating Irishmen as if they were residents, although their currency is called foreign."[190] In short, Irish residents would be subject to the same regulations as UK residents. Waley suggested that Britain needed to "get the Government of Eire to impose the same exchange restrictions as we do," especially to conserve the US dollars needed for war.[191] After additional negotiations with private banks, the Bank and the Treasury decided to include the Republic of Ireland with the other Dominions, "whose currencies are to be treated as assimilated to sterling."[192]

Coordination with other financial centers would be even more difficult to maintain. In March, Siepmann estimated that the EEA's assets held abroad were far below the ideal amounts needed for funding a war: Ottawa (£31 million), Pretoria (£29 million), New York (£9 million), and Bombay (£7 million).[193] To raise confidence in the stability of sterling, the Bank considered how to draw on these funds in an efficient manner. They initiated discussions with government officials across the empire, especially in Canada because of the large volume of reserves held there. Yet Canada, a self-governing Dominion, lay outside the sterling area. Since the Treasury estimated that more than £100 million would be needed in the first year of war alone, closer relations with the Bank of Canada and the Canadian government seemed even more urgent.[194] Deputy Governor Catterns concurred with the urgency of the "shortage of Canadian dollars" and the need for a "drastic revision" of imperial arrangements.[195]

Ensuing negotiations rested with one of the Bank's experts, J.A.C. Osborne. After having served as the Deputy Governor of the Bank of Canada (1935–1938), Osborne briefly returned to the Bank to work as an adviser to Governor Norman. A few months later, he was dispatched back to Canada to convince

[189] G.F.C. Bolton, "Colonial Empire & Dependencies," February 8, 1939, BoE EC4/15; Sayers, *The Bank of England, vol.* 2, 569; "The U.K. Exchange Control: A Short History," *Bank of England Quarterly Bulletin* 7, Q3 (1967), 246.

[190] Catterns to Waley, "Eire," April 14, 1939, BoE EC4/10.

[191] Waley to Catterns, "Eire," April 17, 1939, BoE EC4/10.

[192] Cobbold to Waley, August 28, 1939, BoE EC4/10.

[193] Siepmann to Catterns, "E.E.A. Assets Abroad," March 22, 1939, BoE EC4/4.

[194] Phillips to Catterns, March 23, 1939, BoE EC4/4.

[195] Catterns to Phillips, March 28, 1939, BoE EC4/4.

government officials that Britain's requisition of foreign currencies, including Canadian dollars, would be "in Canada's interest."[196] Bank officials were aware that they had little direct control over the political decisions of the independent Dominion governments. Their attempts to purchase the Bank of Canada's reserves, however, were unsuccessful, leading Osborne to suggest several other measures for promoting financial coordination.[197] As he reported, the Canadian government did not appear even remotely interested in such matters.[198] Other issues, namely budgetary policy and wheat exports, took precedence, while an upcoming election in which a democratic socialist party, the Co-operative Commonwealth Federation, would gain many seats was "not likely to be helpful."[199] Similar efforts to convince the governments of India and South Africa to accept the terms of exchange control subsequently failed.[200]

Yet through more informal arrangements, Britain could achieve a reasonable degree of financial coordination with the Dominions. After discussions with the Empire Central Banks, the Bank began compiling a list of banks abroad that would be authorized agents in foreign-exchange transactions.[201] A preliminary list included the London-based clearing banks, as well as several Scottish and Northern Irish banks. Later, an expanded series included prominent overseas banks as the Bank of British West Africa, and the Bank of London & South America.[202] At the same time, an overhaul of the existing system of governance required the cooperation of private commercial banks and their respective national governments. There was the possibility that some countries might be willing to hold (or hoard) British pounds during the war, while other countries – such as South Africa, Denmark, and the Netherlands – were deemed "Doubtful Adherents."[203]

By late April 1939, the Bank's advisers were able to circulate a nearly complete version of draft legislation. A list of authorized dealers, alongside the central bank, were allowed to engage in gold and foreign-exchange operations; the purchase, export, and transfer of gold and foreign-exchange reserves were all prohibited without government permission; and all transactions were to be reported directly to the Bank.[204] These new arrangements effectively put

196 Waley to W. Bankes Amery [Dominions Office], March 30, 1939, BoE EC4/4.

197 Committee of Treasury, Minutes, April 12, 1939, BoE G8/64; "Mr Osborne's Mission to Canada," May 19, 1939, TNA DO35/543/7.

198 Osborne to Phillips, May 10, 1939, TNA DO35/543/7.

199 Osborne to Phillips, May 10, 1939, TNA DO35/543/7.

200 Cobbold to Phillips, July 20, 1939, BoE ADM26/8.

201 G.F.C. Bolton, "Authorised Dealers," April 26, 1939, BoE EC4/5; Cameron Cobbold, "War Measures: Authorised Dealers," April 28, 1939, BoE EC4/5.

202 Catterns to Phillips, May 8, 1939, BoE EC4/5; "Banks Authorised to Deal in Certain Colonial and Dominion Currencies," 1939, BoE EC4/5; "Banks Authorised to Deal in Certain Foreign Currencies," 1939, BoE EC4/5.

203 G.F.C. Bolton, "Exchange Control: Sterling Standard Currencies," April 12, 1939, BoE EC4/4.

204 "Defence Regulations," 1939, BoE EC4/5; "Memorandum to Authorised Dealers in Foreign Exchange," 1939, BoE EC4/5; Catterns to Lord Wardington [Lloyds Bank], April 26, 1939,

an end to the indirect model of regulation that had undergirded the national monetary system. In its place was a regime of tight control and close financial monitoring with the Bank at its center.

It was then when the last of the Bank's interwar experts arrived. Educated at King's College, Cambridge, Lucius Thompson (later, Thompson-McCausland) had worked in the City and in financial journalism before joining the Bank's Exchange Control Department in October 1939. He was initially employed as a temporary clerk in response to the Bank's employment needs during the war. Rising through the ranks as an Assistant Adviser in 1941 and an Adviser to the Governors in 1949, Thompson played a more important role in the post-war years by serving on various internal committees concerning interest rates and the sterling area.[205] He also accompanied Keynes to the Bretton Woods Conference in 1944 and represented Britain at the Havana Conference in 1947–1948, which culminated in the General Agreement on Tariffs and Trade.

Thompson and other experts represented the Bank in ensuing negotiations with the national government. In mid-April, the Treasury agreed to allow the Bank to run the Foreign Exchange Committee if it could appoint a liaison officer as its representation.[206] A continuation of a 1936 group, the committee had been tasked with promoting coordination between the government and the private banks, along with two foreign banks (Chase National and the Federal Reserve).[207] It included representatives from the London accepting houses, as well as private banks in Austria, Canada, France, Scotland, and the United States.[208] Through an existing body, the Bank was able to devise a system in which it shared control with the Treasury and the City. New departments, from the Dealing and Accounts Office to the Securities Control Office, also increased internal communication, thereby supporting the functioning of its exchange-rate policy (Figures 8.1 and 8.2).

Throughout the summer of 1939, the terms of exchange control came under careful scrutiny. Experts at the Bank and the Treasury accepted the fact that there needed to be a provision to block the sale of securities without acquiring the permission of either institution (Regulation 94).[209] Doing so would have relieved them of some administrative burdens. Another requirement was the

LGA HO/S/Gen/4; John Atkin, *The Foreign Exchange Market of London: Development since 1900* (London and New York: Routledge, 2005), 92–93.

205 Fforde, *The Bank of England and Public Policy*, 88, 370.

206 Phillips to Catterns, April 14, 1939, BoE EC4/4 and TNA T231/186. On the Foreign Exchange Committee, see Hennessy, *A Domestic History of the Bank of England*, 110–111; Atkin, *The Foreign Exchange Market*, 87; Harris, *Monetary War and Peace*, 60.

207 Ernest Sykes, "Foreign Exchange Committee," December 13 and 22, 1938, TLA CLC/B/029/MS32026/001; "New Group Formed Here," *The New York Times* LXXXVIII, no. 29799, August 26, 1939, 6.

208 Ernest Sykes, "The Foreign Exchange Committee," September 29, 1936, TLA CLC/B/029/MS32063/001.

209 Waley to R.W.A. Speed [Treasury Solicitor's Department], June 10, 1939, TNA T231/187.

FIGURE 8.1 Dealing and Accounts Office, 1942
Source: Bank of England Archive, 15A13/1/1/42/1.

prohibition of transfers from residents to nonresidents that might have allowed people to bypass this and other restrictions (Regulation 97).[210] Technical arrangements generally saw little disagreement among Treasury and Bank officials who were able to submit an initial draft to the Office of the Parliamentary Counsel by August.[211]

Yet how these standards could be configured into Britain's broader imperial policy, particularly with the Dominions, remained to be decided. The government warned that any effort to pressure a foreign government into adopting exchange control could prove counterproductive. As the Dominions Office wrote in August, "[t]he Union Government [of South Africa] have shown themselves strongly adverse on political grounds from taking any action that could be construed as binding them in any way to co-operation with the United Kingdom in war."[212] Rather than exert pressure through a position of strength, the British authorities, at times, chose to express their

210 "Notes for Meeting on Defence Regulations," June 19, 1939, TNA T231/187.

211 Harold Chorley [Office of the Parliamentary Counsel] to Waley, August 2, 1939, TNA T231/188; "Draft Defence (Finance) Regulations, 1939," TNA T231/188.

212 Dominions Office, "Exchange Control in Time of War: The Position vis-à-vis the Union of South Africa," August 21, 1939, TNA DO35/543/8.

FIGURE 8.2 Securities Control Office, 1944
Source: Bank of England Archive, 15A13/1/1/23/6.

relative weakness in preparation for war. A telegram sent to the Dominion governments highlighted the wide array of strains on British finance, including limited sources of capital, poor market conditions, and a hike to the Bank Rate up to 4 percent.[213] This strategy of moral suasion was met with mixed success. The High Commissioner of Australia shared the news that the Australian Prime Minister would be willing to grant the Treasurer "control of all overseas exchange transactions," while the private banks were designated as agents much like their London counterparts.[214] New Zealand expressed its willingness to offer support "to the greatest possible extent."[215] Less convinced were South African officials who planned to concentrate their investments in domestic machinery and manufacturing. Yet they, too, were not wholly

[213] "Telegram to the Governments of Canada, Commonwealth of Australia, New Zealand, Union of South Africa, Eire, Southern Rhodesia, and Newfoundland," August 24, 1939, TNA DO35/543/8.

[214] Quoted in "Australia: Monetary Control Regulations," August 28, 1939, TNA DO35/543/8.

[215] High Commissioner of the United Kingdom in New Zealand to the Dominions Office, July 29, 1939, TNA DO35/543/7.

dismissive of the idea of exchange control "at some stage ... [although not] before or necessarily immediately after outbreak of war in Europe."[216]

Above all, the fundamental stability of the pound rested on the proper functioning of foreign-exchange management with the Dominion governments. There were concerns that a "black market" for sterling might develop, thereby undermining national control over the financial system.[217] At the Treasury, Waley mentioned that it was "very difficult to be consistent in our decisions about exchange control," particularly because of the access to foreign exchange on the "Black Bourse."[218] Following the German invasion of Poland on September 1, the unofficial market for sterling displayed signs of pessimism. The pound, once valued between $4.02 and $4.06, dropped to a value of $3.75 in New York by mid-September. Einzig denounced this mishandling of the system as "the worst of both worlds": London had failed to maintain "her reputation for freedom," while still suffering "the loss of gold" to foreign speculators.[219]

Embarrassed by its initial mishandling of its own currency, the government began to implement policies in line with the Bank's overall recommendations. Through a series of Statutory Rules and Orders (SRO), the Treasury was prepared to exercise its prerogatives over the use of sterling in international transactions. On September 3, the Currency Restrictions Exemption Order had already given the Treasury the power to grant authorizations and exemptions in applications.[220] The next day, Chancellor John Simon announced the full institutionalization of exchange control to maintain the exchange rate "at just about 4 Dollars to the Pound."[221] As he reported to the House of Commons, the legislation would help enforce other wartime restrictions – import purchases by the Ministries of Supply and Food; control of shipping by the Ministry of Shipping – to align with the "comprehensive and co-ordinated direction of the economic activity of this country."[222]

Although Treasury officials mostly acknowledged the importance of exchange control, they continued to debate whether the system was tenable for a war of unknown length. "It is obvious," Phillips remarked, "that we are in grave danger of our gold reserves being exhausted at a rate that will render

[216] High Commissioner of the United Kingdom in the Union of South Africa to the Dominions Office, August 26, 1939, TNA DO35/543/8.

[217] Harry A. Siepmann, "Emergency Measures," February 17, 1939, BoE EC4/3.

[218] Waley to Phillips, September 22, 1939, TNA T177/45.

[219] Paul Einzig, "The Unofficial Market in Sterling," *The Economic Journal* 49, no. 196 (1939), 673.

[220] Sayers, *Financial Policy*, 235. "The Currency Restrictions Exemption (No. 3) Order 1939, no. 1168" was replaced later on December 20, 1939; "The Currency Restrictions Exemption (No. 4) Order 1939, no. 1843," in *Statutory Rules and Orders, 1939, vol. 1* (London: H.M. Stationery Office, 1940), 975–976.

[221] "War Cabinet 2(39)," September 1939, TNA CAB65/1/2.

[222] HC Deb, March 5, 1940, vol. 358, cc. 204–205.

us incapable of waging war if war is prolonged."[223] Keynes also believed that the monetary authorities should be wary of designing a system that too closely resembled the regulatory measures enacted by foreign countries. As he confessed, "[o]ur international position is so totally different from Germany's that their technique does not offer a good model for us."[224]

Yet the Bank's advisers, who had already gone to great lengths to see exchange control implemented, were committed to showing how the arrangements were "something entirely different in structure and in purpose."[225] Exchange control required all resources and departments for its proper functioning, as any major "leakages" in the system would undermine the entire government's policy. In coordinating this policy, the Governor insisted that the Bank should act as the mediator between the clearing banks and the government. Doing so ensured that "banking interests as a whole" would be secured.[226] Others emphasized the importance of the nation. Writing to the Treasury, Cobbold underscored the value of clarity and authority when designing regulation. As he warned, "so long as there is only a trifling discrepancy between the official and the free rate, some foreign holders of sterling ... escape us without penalty, so that our present regulations are made to look ineffective."[227]

Convinced by this argument, the government was willing to enact greater restrictions on private corporations that wanted to send their profits (via dividends) overseas. Any indication of a noncommittal exchange-rate regime could appear as a sign of fragility to foreign holders of sterling. Still, concessions were possible. The Treasury wanted to grant residents access to sterling "for reasonable personal needs."[228] This rationale was applied to other cases, such as for a "woman suffering from ill-health" who "wished to live in the South of France" and needed to acquire francs.[229] Arrangements with the corresponding French authorities concerned whether it was possible to permit foreign remittances and relax some restrictions between the two countries on small transactions. After a brief negotiation with the Bank, the Treasury promised to be "liberal but not extravagant in the allotment of French francs," only for approved "personal purposes."[230]

Experts successfully convinced the government of the need for exchange control. As they crafted new exchange-control measures, no immediate

[223] Frederick Phillips, Note, September 7, 1939, BoE EC4/70 and TNA T177/48.

[224] John Maynard Keynes, "Notes on Exchange Control," September 24, 1939, KCC Keynes Papers W/3 and TNA T177/45.

[225] Cobbold to Waley, October 27, 1939, BoE ADM26/8 and TNA T177/45.

[226] Committee of London Clearing Bankers, Minutes, September 14, 1939, TLA CLC/B/029/MS32027/078.

[227] Cobbold to Waley, October 27, 1939, BoE ADM26/8 and TNA T177/45.

[228] "Daily Meeting between Mr. Waley and Mr. Rowe-Dutton," September 15, 1939, TNA T231/64.

[229] "Exchange Control – Treasury," November 24, 1939, TNA T231/64.

[230] "Exchange Control – Treasury," December 29, 1939, TNA T231/64.

currency crisis befell the City in September 1939. Still, the continued strain on sterling that persisted well into early 1940, in addition to the fall of France in June, compelled officials to impose greater restrictions on foreign-exchange markets. Siepmann feared the likely scenario where "the German occupation and control of France ... might lead to the large stocks of Bank of England notes hoarded in France [an estimated £11 million] passing into German hands."[231] This possibility – that "the Germans will get value for their loot" – seemed likely because there were no safeguards in place to distinguish between banknotes at home and those stored abroad.[232]

Many bankers continued to insist that the United Kingdom should avoid designing an overly burdensome system of regulation.[233] Yet the Bank, nevertheless, viewed such measures as necessary for securing the nation's financial interests. Additional trade- and exchange-related regulations were subsequently introduced on June 7 and July 17, 1940.[234] One new requirement known as "dollar invoicing" stipulated that exports to a group of select countries had to be invoiced in an approved local currency rather than in sterling.[235] The goal of this particular reform was to force exporters to accept payments at the official sterling–dollar rate, which was more costly to them than the free-floating rate.[236]

Britain had thus developed a bureaucratic system of economic control that permitted some flexibility, yet proved uncompromising in other circumstances. Although Vera Brittain, a nurse during the First World War and author of *Testament of Youth* (1933), had previously earned approximately $2,000 from her lecture tours in the United States, the Treasury retroactively required her to surrender her earnings.[237] The charge was partly due to her support for socialism or, as the Treasury described, her affiliation "with certain political and quasi-political organisations."[238] When she had not complied, the Bank ordered that the dollar-denominated funds be transferred to a UK-based bank.

[231] "Bank of England Notes," July 25, 1940, BoE EC4/333.

[232] "Bank of England Notes," July 25, 1940, BoE EC4/333.

[233] Intelligence Department, "The British Exchange Control: A Survey of the First Six Months' Operations," March 18, 1940, HSBC, Midland Bank UK 0030-0085; Hennessy, *A Domestic History of the Bank of England*, 85.

[234] SRO (1940) No. 892, in *Statutory Rules and Orders, 1940, vol.* 2 (London: H.M. Stationery Office, 1941), 202–204; SRO (1940) No. 1254, in *Statutory Rules and Orders, vol.* 2, 206–213. Also cited in Clayton, "The Development of British Exchange Control," 169; Sayers, *Financial Policy*, 250; Hennessy, *A Domestic History of the Bank of England*, 95.

[235] SRO (1940) No. 291, in *Statutory Rules and Orders, vol.* 2, 197–200. Also cited in Sayers, *Financial Policy*, 241.

[236] Rosella Cappella Zielinski, *How States Pay for Wars* (Ithaca and London: Cornell University Press, 2016), 70.

[237] "Exchange Control – Treasury," June 4, 1940, TNA T231/64.

[238] "Exchange Control – Treasury," April 30, 1940, TNA T231/64.

By the summer of 1940, sterling had effectively ceased to be a free-trading currency. The Bank's Exchange Control Office, a successor to its Foreign Exchange Section, had employed approximately 1,000 staff members to oversee restrictions on the sale and holding of sterling.[239] These institutional changes dealt the final blow to the interwar variant of economic governance, one in which the central bank upheld the principles of prewar orthodoxy. Instead, the prospect of exchange-rate volatility compelled officials to endorse an increasingly burdensome system of controls. New restrictions on the currency allowed the Bank to achieve its concurrent goals of protecting the status of the City of London as an international financial center and ensuring its centrality in any future framework of economic management. Both the lessons learned from the First World War and the existing arrangements in other countries had compelled the Bank to create their own rules of economic governance in the interest of national security.

In the postwar years, the priority of British officials, amidst two catastrophic devaluations, remained fixated on the stabilization of the pound.[240] Maintaining the existing restrictions on conversions out of sterling had not only been a means of preparing for war but also could be a new alternative to the liberal orthodoxy that had prevailed in the prewar and interwar years. Even with the challenges to the status of sterling as an international reserve currency, technical advisers continued to shape exchange-rate policy in the Bretton Woods era. Through their interventions, the Bank and the Treasury were able to determine the future of sterling.

239 "The Exchange Control Office," November 13, 1940, BoE G14/130.

240 Schenk, *The Decline of Sterling*, 31; Naef, *An Exchange Rate History*, 19–21, 144–147.

9

Authority Maintained

> If I had to sum up my impression of the work of an economic adviser in a single sentence I should describe it as either highly frustrating, or maddeningly humdrum, or furiously active, or all three at once.[1]
>
> —Alec Cairncross, 1955

> [T]he central bank is the natural and proper direction to which the various organs of Government should look, at any rate in the first place, for expert advice on technical financial problems connected directly or indirectly with the central bank's daily operations.[2]
>
> —Radcliffe Committee, 1959

> Sir Humphrey Appleby: Well, didn't you read the *Financial Times* this morning?
> Sir Desmond Glazebrook: Never do.
> Appleby: Well, you're a banker. Surely you read the *Financial Times*?
> Glazebrook: Can't understand it. Full of economic theory.
> Appleby: Why do you buy it?
> Glazebrook: Oh, you know, it's part of the uniform.[3]
>
> —*Yes, Minister*, 1981

The actions and ambitions of the interwar Bank of England set a precedent for its evolution in the ensuing decades. Between the meetings of the Central Economic Information Service and the negotiations at the Bretton Woods

[1] Alec Cairncross, "On Being an Economic Adviser," *Scottish Journal of Political Economy* 2, no. 2 (1955), 197.

[2] Committee on the Working of the Monetary System, *Report*, Cmnd. 827 (London: H.M. Stationery Office, 1959), 116.

[3] *Yes, Minister*, "The Quality of Life," March 30, 1981, *British Broadcasting Corporation*, directed by Peter Whitmore, written by Antony Jay and Jonathan Lynn, www.bbc.co.uk/programmes/b0074rh7.

Conference, expert knowledge had come to underpin contemporary debates over wartime economic governance. In the postwar years, central banks reemerged as leading authorities, albeit in different forms. They adopted new responsibilities in the provision of credit, the regulation of security markets, and the maintenance of high employment.[4] A regime of fixed-but-adjustable exchange rates, in which currencies were pegged to the gold-backed US dollar, might have forced many countries to forego capital mobility, as dictated by the monetary trilemma. Yet these arrangements also granted central banks greater autonomy, particularly with the ability to set discretionary monetary policies.

Far from a linear process, the extent to which an institutional dependence on expertise would define the structures of governance in the postwar years was neither predetermined nor known to contemporaries. At the Bank, newly hired economists often felt their opinions challenged, their reports disregarded, and their motivations questioned. They also confronted macroeconomic impediments, such as Britain's persistent balance-of-payments deficits and the decline of sterling as an international reserve currency. In response, the Bank continually adapted its priorities to changing economic conditions. Although officials frequently oscillated and contradicted themselves on the importance of economic data for setting policy, they relied on the input of technical advisers to inform them of ongoing developments. Through their negotiations with bankers and government officials, experts played a key role in maintaining the Bank's reputation as a monetary authority throughout the twentieth century.

ECONOMISTS AND THE SECOND WORLD WAR

At the outbreak of war, the national government sought to test the usefulness of expert advice. In October 1939, one of the Cabinet's internal committees requested that Sir Josiah Stamp (Bank) and Sir Horace Wilson (Treasury) bring together a group of technical specialists to advise the government on its most pressing economic questions. The subsequently formed Central Economic Information Service helped to improve the government's access to economic knowledge by providing a constant source of information. With the aid of Hubert Henderson and Henry Clay, the division became a hub for Britain's leading economists and statisticians, including Lionel Robbins, James Meade, John Jewkes, Austin Robinson, and Ely Devons.[5] Due to differences

[4] Éric Monnet, *Controlling Credit: Central Banking and the Planned Economy in Postwar France, 1948–1973* (Cambridge: Cambridge University Press, 2018), 283.

[5] Robert Skidelsky, *John Maynard Keynes, vol. 3: Fighting for Britain, 1937–1946* (London: Macmillan, 2000), 46, 139; Alec Cairncross, *Austin Robinson: The Life of an Economic Adviser* (Basingstoke: Macmillan, 1993), 78–83; Susan Howson, *Lionel Robbins* (Cambridge: Cambridge University Press, 2011), 354–356, 387; Keith Tribe, *The Economy of the Word: Language, History, and Economics* (Oxford: Oxford University Press, 2015), 104.

in priorities, the group split into the Central Statistical Office and the Economic Section in 1941.[6] Nevertheless, the latter continued to work on matters related to the distribution of food, industrial production, and wages. As in the interwar years, the exigencies of another crisis compelled the state to turn to experts for guidance.

Yet concerned with more than information alone, the government also searched for ways of restructuring economic governance. Prime Minister Neville Chamberlain had asked Stamp to run another group focused on broader policy matters.[7] From June 1939 onward, the (Stamp) Survey of Financial and War Plans complemented the statistical work of the Central Economic Information Service by offering additional recommendations to the Cabinet on how to run a wartime economy.[8] Its main task was to provide details on the necessary allocation of resources and the needs of national production, with one of the survey's early projects involving the measurement of the country's wartime balance of payments.[9] Partly established to quell public demands for a Minister of Economic Co-ordination (a proposal that Chamberlain opposed), the Stamp Survey offered a politically acceptable project to the Conservative government. It certainly reflected the growing interests of the state to avail itself of statistical data that informed policy, while at the same time not over-committing its resources to an entirely new government department.[10] There was also an interest in assessing the long-term consequences of the conflict, such as taxation and management of sterling balances, topics that demanded more information-sharing with the empire.[11]

[6] R.L. Marris, "The Position of Economics and Economists in the Government Machine," *The Economic Journal* 64, no. 256 (1954), 775–776; Howson and Winch, *The Economic Advisory Council*, 2–3; Alan Booth, "Economic Advice at the Centre of British Government, 1939–1941," *The Historical Journal* 29, no. 3 (1986), 657–659; Alec Cairncross and Nita Watts, *The Economic Section, 1939–1961: A Study in Economic Advising* (London: Routledge, 1989), 15, 43–49; Fourcade, *Economists and Societies*, 141.

[7] "Economic Co-ordination," *The Economist* 137, 5016, October 14, 1939, 44; Howson and Winch, *The Economic Advisory Council*, 151; Booth, "Economic Advice at the Centre of British Government," 657; Toye, *The Labour Party*, 89.

[8] Alec Cairncross, "Ely Devons: A Memoir," in *Papers on Planning and Economic Management*, ed. Alec Cairncross (Manchester: Manchester University Press, 1970), 5; Alan Booth and A.W. Coats, "Some Wartime Observations on the Role of the Economist in Government," *Oxford Economic Papers* 32, no. 2 (1980), 178; Cairncross and Watts, *The Economic Section*, 11; Peden, *The Treasury*, 312.

[9] See, for instance, the files in NCO Clay Papers 69.

[10] "Co-ordination and Policy," *The Economist* 138, 5031, January 27, 1940, 133.

[11] On the problem of postwar sterling balances, see Susan Strange, *Sterling and British Policy: A Political Study of an International Currency in Decline* (London and New York: Oxford University Press, 1971); Gerold Krozewski, *Money and the End of Empire: British International Economic Policy and the Colonies, 1947–58* (Basingstoke: Palgrave, 2001); Catherine Schenk, *Britain and the Sterling Area: From Devaluation to Convertibility in the 1950s* (London and New York: Routledge, 1994).

The Bank invested even more of its resources into economic research. In April 1937, officials had reaffirmed the responsibilities of the in-house research division, the Economics & Statistics Section. Its purpose was "to supply information to the Governors, Officials and Advisers of the Bank on general financial and economic subjects and on conditions in the United Kingdom."[12] Statistics proved vital in helping the Bank remain an indispensable source of information on wartime exchange-rate policy. In April 1941, the Committee of Treasury expressed an interest in "applying economic science to practical affairs" by committing £1,000 for the annual Stamp Memorial Lectures.[13] Later that year, Humphrey Mynors, the Bank's Secretary, recommended the merging of the Economics & Statistics Office with the similarly named Statistical Office (which supplied statistical information, albeit in a less organized manner) and the Exchange Economy Section.[14] These changes helped to streamline statistical research and avoid redundant work among the central banks of the empire. "Co-ordination and economy of resources," Clay declared, "are as essential to Economic Defence as to Imperial Defence."[15]

During the early years of the war, the Bank was generally regarded as a reliable source of information for private bankers.[16] After the implementation of exchange controls, the Bank continued to make decisions based on technical advice. In August 1941, Governor Montagu Norman appointed a group of advisers who would discuss wartime priorities, particularly to manage the volatility of capital outflows. The subsequently established Post-War Exchange Policy Committee, which included three of the Bank's advisers (Clay, George Bolton, and Harry A. Siepmann), was tasked with assessing the financial needs of domestic industry.[17] Their primary concern was ensuring that the Bank's gold and foreign-exchange holdings were sufficient to last not only the war but also the initial postwar years.

Yet as the war progressed, the Bank recognized that it had to confront other pressing issues. Many officials lived through the contentious interwar debates over the Macmillan gap, a term that highlighted the inadequacy of financial support for domestic industry. From 1943 onward, four of the Bank's advisers (Clay, Mynors, Raymond Kershaw, and Otto Niemeyer) served on

[12] "Economics & Statistics Section – Bank of England," April 9, 1937, BoE EID8/1.

[13] Committee of Treasury, Minutes, July 9, 1941, BoE G8/65.

[14] Humphrey Mynors, "Statistics," December 5, 1941, BoE EID8/1.

[15] Henry Clay, "Appendix I(D)," May 15, 1939, BoE M5/533, in J. A. C. Osborne and Ronald Allport, "The Bank of England, 1939–45 (Unpublished War History) – Volume 1, Internal Finance," 1950, BoE M5/533, 71.

[16] "Reply to Midland Bank's Memorandum on Foreign Exchange Control," March 8, 1940, HSBC, Midland Bank UK 0252-0086; Schroder to Norman, October 4, 1940, SA Schroder Papers 1936–1963.

[17] "Members of Sundry Committees," September 9, 1941, BoE EC4/80; Howson, *British Monetary Policy*, 54; Gary Burn, *The Re-Emergence of Global Finance* (Basingstoke: Palgrave Macmillan, 2006), 74.

the Committee on Post-War Domestic Finance.[18] Examining the necessary allocation of capital to support industry, an ensuing report highlighted the inadequacy of existing channels to provide the necessary provisions of credit for domestic industry.[19] In line with these findings, officials advocated the establishment of a new organization with £1 million in working capital to support small businesses in collaboration with London's major clearing banks.[20] Through this initiative, the Bank could avert a repeat of the criticisms that it faced from some of its most ardent critics.

It was, however, the election of John Maynard Keynes as Bank director in 1941 that symbolized the complete acceptance of expertise. In the years prior to his appointment, Keynes had started to work on a plan for managing the transition from a peacetime to a wartime economy. Beginning in April 1939, he wrote more than a dozen articles in *The Times* on the need for coordination among the various government departments.[21] The subsequently compiled manifesto, entitled *How to Pay for the War: A Radical Plan for the Chancellor of the Exchequer* (1940), proposed a range of reforms that included rationing, price controls, and savings campaigns, all of which might suppress consumer spending.[22] Its broader goal was to offer a unified framework for running a wartime economy: "A Government, which has control of the banking and currency system, can always find the cash to pay for its purchases of home-produced goods."[23]

While *How to Pay for the War* might have been heavily censured by some directors, such as Sir Robert Kindersley, it nevertheless attracted the attention of officials at the Bank and the Treasury.[24] The document seemed to offer a novel means of quelling inflationary pressures, an objective that the orthodox monetary authorities had long shared. Keynes also benefited from

[18] Lucius Thompson-McCausland, "Committee on Post-War Domestic Finance," April 8, 1943, BoE C40/775; Mynors to Norman, October 25, 1943, BoE G14/155; J.A.C. Osborne and Ronald Allport, "The Bank of England, 1939–45 (Unpublished War History) – Volume 1, Internal Finance," 1950, BoE M5/533, 252; J.A.C. Osborne and Ronald Allport, "Unpublished War History (Part 2 Exchange Control) – Chapter 10," 1950, BoE M5/536, 996–997; Howson, *British Monetary Policy*, 56–57; Fforde, *The Bank of England and Public Policy*, 320, 705–709.

[19] Committee on Post-War Domestic Finance, Report, October 19, 1943, BoE G14/155.

[20] J.A.C. Osborne and Ronald Allport, "The Bank of England, 1939–45 (Unpublished War History) – Volume 1, Internal Finance," 1950, BoE M5/533, 253.

[21] See, for instance, John Maynard Keynes, "Crisis Finance," *The Times* 48281, April 17, 1939, 13; John Maynard Keynes, "Crisis Finance," *The Times* 48282, April 18, 1939, 15.

[22] John Maynard Keynes, *How to Pay for the War: A Radical Plan for the Chancellor of the Exchequer* (London: Macmillan, 1940), 51–52, 57–61.

[23] Keynes, *How to Pay for the War*, 61.

[24] Moggridge, *Maynard Keynes*, 633; Skidelsky, *John Maynard Keynes, vol. 3*, 56–58; Alan Bollard, *Economists at War: How a Handful of Economists Helped Win and Lose the World Wars* (Oxford: Oxford University Press, 2020), 129; Sebastian Teupe, "Keynes, Inflation and the Public Debt: *How to Pay for the War* as a Policy Prescription for Financial Repression?," *Financial History Review* 27, no. 2 (2020), 196.

his reputation as a public intellectual. Having acquired a national image that none of the Bank's advisers could claim to match, he was able to present workable (and even appealing) arrangements to those in circles of influence.[25] As Governor Norman admitted, "I do not pretend to understand the inwardness of your solution or the technical methods by which it might be carried out. But it has my sympathy and I do not doubt that a drastic solution will be necessary."[26]

In March 1940, ten years after the contentious proceedings of the Macmillan Committee, Keynes arranged a meeting with Norman to explain how his recommendations in *How to Pay for the War* might be compatible with the Bank's priorities.[27] Several factors help to explain the complete reversal of Norman's stance on Keynes. R.S. Sayers noted how the "wondrous alliance of Norman and Keynes, unthinkable ten or fifteen years earlier," was due in part to shifting views at the Bank.[28] There was, indeed, an ideological alignment between Keynes and some of the Bank's leading advisers, most notably Catterns, Clay, Cobbold, and Siepmann, who had called for more interventionist policies throughout the 1930s. With the implementation of exchange control in 1939, the Bank had acknowledged the need for a coordinated economic policy to manage wartime expenditures. At the same time, Keynes, as the more knowledgeable of the pair, was able to convince Norman that inaction might have had even more drastic consequences. According to the summary of one meeting, Keynes had warned of the potential for "shop-shortages, queues and general discontent," which would force the UK government "to take some drastic action, and might be forced into general rationing – the German and Russian Solution – with extreme administrative inconvenience and great waste."[29] The threat of political disorder due to another world war likely convinced the Bank to follow Keynes' advice.

As the Bank had initially turned to experts after the First World War, it now depended even more on technical solutions at the outbreak of the Second World War. "He must come again," Governor Norman wrote shortly after the visit.[30] Keynes unexpectedly returned to the Bank to replace Stamp, who had

25 H.C.B. Mynors, "J.M. Keynes on Crisis Finance," April 20, 1939, BoE ADM22/24; Henry Clay, "Borrowing in War-Time," April 26, 1939, BoE ADM22/24; Clay to Siepmann, January 4, 1940, BoE ADM22/24.

26 Norman to Keynes, February 28, 1940, in *The Collected Writings of John Maynard Keynes, vol. 22: Activities 1939–1945, Internal War Finance*, ed. Donald Moggridge (Cambridge: Cambridge University Press, 1978), 104.

27 Montagu Norman, Diary, March 8, 1940, BoE ADM34/29; Henry Clay, "Note of Conversation 8th March 1940," March 9, 1940, NCO Clay Papers 52/50.

28 Sayers, *The Bank of England, vol. 2*, 591.

29 Henry Clay, "Note of Conversation 8th March 1940," March 9, 1940, NCO Clay Papers 52/50.

30 Quoted in Sayers, *The Bank of England, vol. 2*, 591; Skidelsky, *John Maynard Keynes, vol. 3*, 76; Kynaston, *Till Time's Last Sand*, 382.

died in April 1941 during the Blitz.[31] Thereafter, he consulted the Governor and directors on technical matters through his participation on various committees concerning exchange-rate management and a postwar currency.[32] The ensuing meetings of the Exchange Control Conference (1940–1943), a group of Treasury and Bank officials, allowed Keynes to shape wartime exchange-rate policy.[33] Although his views may have once alienated the Bank's Old Guard – chief among its proponents, Norman himself – the effects of the war led to an even greater reliance on economic knowledge.

Keynes' most famous wartime contribution occurred at the Bretton Woods Conference in July 1944. Throughout the negotiations, he offered his expert opinion on foreseeable monetary issues, and he relayed information back to the Chancellor, Sir John Anderson, and the Bank's new Governor, Lord Catto.[34] Keynes envisioned a multilateral trading and payments system that could avoid the risks associated with tariffs, quotas, and devaluations of the interwar years.[35] An International Clearing Union (ICU) could hold foreign currencies and manage national accounts, allowing central banks to buy and sell their own currencies in the new reserve unit, the *bancor* ("bank gold").[36] The ICU proposal would have also involved a quota system of credits and debits for each member country, thereby permitting increased public spending while still adhering to a fixed exchange rate.

Keynes might have been a Bank director, but he aimed to represent the interests of the United Kingdom. At the conference, the Bank's advisers questioned Keynes' proposal, although they did not offer any of their own. For them, the priority lay in domestic economic policy, rather than in the management of international capital flows. They had written about the need for the adoption of exchange-control measures and therefore continued to argue that such policies were more than capable of securing postwar prosperity on their own: "The case for Exchange Control as a means of anticipating and meeting the strains and responsibilities of our position would be decisive," they described.[37] On

[31] Peden, *The Treasury*, 311–312; Moggridge, *Maynard Keynes*, 663; Skidelsky, *John Maynard Keynes, vol. 3*, 203.

[32] John Maynard Keynes, "Post-War Currency Policy," September 8, 1941, BoE OV38/1; Keynes to Norman, September 16, 1941, BoE OV38/41; "Post-War Economic Talks," October 26, 1942, BoE OV38/2.

[33] Hennessy, *A Domestic History of the Bank of England*, 123; Moggridge, *Maynard Keynes*, 638; Skidelsky, *John Maynard Keynes, vol. 3*, 79.

[34] Steil, *The Battle of Bretton Woods*, 217, 223–224, 244.

[35] Steil, *The Battle of Bretton Woods*, 142–143.

[36] John Maynard Keynes, "Proposals for an International Clearing Union," August 1941, KCC Keynes Papers W/6/1; Skidelsky, *John Maynard Keynes, vol. 3*, 225–228, 231–232; Daunton, *The Economic Government of the World*, 147–155.

[37] "Post-War Trade and Financial Policy," October 17, 1941, BoE M5/537, in J.A.C. Osborne and Ronald Allport, "The Bank of England, 1939–45 (Unpublished War History) – Volume 5, Relations with Certain Overseas Countries," 1950 BoE M5/537, 1116.

Keynes' plan, the Bank was divided between those who believed it had some merit (Catto and Clay) and those who saw it as technically impractical (Bolton) or unfavorable to the sterling area (Siepmann).[38]

Yet the Bank View had no direct influence on the debates and negotiations at the Bretton Woods Conference, which determined the structure of the international monetary order over the next several decades. It was, instead, Harry Dexter White, a Treasury official and the main US representative, who led the discussion. Initially, he had recognized the inherent challenges of reconciling each nation's economic objectives with the broader goal of global monetary order.[39] Similar to Keynes' plan, his proposal advocated the creation of a multilateral clearing system to address balance-of-payment issues among member countries. Seeing the inherent value of a stable monetary system based on a fixed unit, White, however, envisaged a regime in which the dollar would play the defining role in the international financial system.[40] The plan involved the United States committing only $2 billion to the fund, in contrast to Keynes' proposal of $23 billion.[41] At the same time, the Treasury suggested that its aim should be to encourage private capital investments through a new International Stabilization Fund.[42]

Whereas Britain had once shaped the contours of economic governance in the interwar years, the exigencies of the Second World War forced the Bank to balance its own national interests with those of a changing international monetary system. As a result, the postwar priorities shifted to managing imperial relations, with a strong emphasis on sterling balances and exchange control. The Bank's research department strove to build on the work of the national government and Keynes, who had compiled preliminary estimates of wartime sterling balances.[43] It also fostered closer ties with the newly established Empire Central Banks.

Some officials continued to recognize the lack of direct political power they wielded, often instead conceding decisions to the US Treasury and Federal Reserve. At times, Keynes' presence at the Bank divided officials more than the views of their US counterparts. As the Deputy Governor wrote, "[i]t is scarcely possible that we can obtain formal American blessing for any joint statement of policy for the immediate post-war period within the framework outlined above. We therefore agree in principle with Keynes' view that we shall

[38] Fforde, *The Bank of England and Public Policy*, 39–43; Skidelsky, *John Maynard Keynes, vol. 3*, 213–214.

[39] Steil, *The Battle of Bretton Woods*, 130.

[40] Steil, *The Battle of Bretton Woods*, 132–134.

[41] Steil, *The Battle of Bretton Woods*, 151–152; Eichengreen, *Globalizing Capital*, 90.

[42] Henry Morgenthau Jr. [Secretary of the Treasury] to Marriner Eccles [Chairman of the Federal Reserve], December 7, 1943, FRBNY Eccles Papers Box 32, Folder 22, Item 1.

[43] John Maynard Keynes, "Notes on the Bank of England's Proposals for the Sterling Area," February 15, 1944, in *The Collected Writings of John Maynard Keynes, vol. 24: Activities 1944–1946, The Transition to Peace*, ed. Donald Moggridge (Cambridge: Cambridge University Press, 1979): 19–22.

do better to state the facts and the limitations which are imposed upon us by these facts, and then seek American comment and co-operation in working out a scheme of longer range and wider scope."[44]

THE POSTWAR STATE OF ECONOMIC ADVICE

In the immediate years following the war, the role of expert advice remained in a state of uncertainty. The transition from a wartime to a peacetime economy invited new questions on the priorities of politico-economic governance.[45] Following the 1945 election, the New Labour government became even more cautious of the influence that outside experts had acquired. Prime Minister Clement Attlee was generally suspicious of Norman, now retired from the Bank, and he disliked the bitter ideological battles that had taken place on the government's Economic Advisory Council.[46] Chancellor Hugh Dalton, a former reader in economics at the London School of Economics (LSE), also felt that there was little need for economic advisers outside the Treasury.[47] While he had employed Keynes as an adviser for eight months, the relationship was strained by their divergent ideological views.[48] In turn, many prominent economists developed a deep distrust of the radical policies forwarded by Labour MPs. W. Arthur Lewis (Manchester) claimed that "Socialist planning has had no principles for dealing with money, investment, foreign trade, mobility, or private enterprise," and Roy Harrod (Nuffield College, Oxford) more sharply decried that "[t]he Socialists had put everything out of balance and had prepared the ground for the worst slump in history."[49]

[44] Underlining in the original; J.A.C. Osborne and Ronald Allport, "The Bank of England, 1939–45 (Unpublished War History) – Volume 5, Relations with Certain Overseas Countries," 1950, BoE M5/537, 1112.

[45] On postwar planning, see John Hackett and Anne-Marie Hackett, *L'Économie britannique : problèmes et perspectives* (Paris: Armand Colin, 1966); Jacques Leruez, *Planification et politique en Grande-Bretagne, 1945–1971* (Paris: Armand Colin, 1972); Alec Cairncross, *Years of Recovery: British Economic Policy, 1945–51* (London and New York: Routledge, 1985); Martin Chick, *Industrial Policy in Britain, 1945–1951: Economic Planning, Nationalisation, and the Labour Governments* (Cambridge: Cambridge University Press, 1998).

[46] John Bew, *Clement Attlee: The Man Who Made Modern Britain* (New York: Oxford University Press, 2017), 149–150.

[47] Alec Cairncross, "Economic Advisers in the United Kingdom," *Contemporary British History* 13, no. 2 (1999), 234. On economic advisers in postwar Britain, see P.D. Henderson, "The Use of Economists in British Administration," *Oxford Economic Papers* 13, no. 1 (1961): 5–26; Alec Cairncross, "The Work of an Economic Adviser," November 6, 1967, in *Essays in Economic Management* (London: George Allen & Unwin, 1971), 189–193; A.W. Coats, "Britain: The Rise of the Specialists," *History of Political Economy* 13, no. 3 (1981): 365–404; Thomas Wilson, "James Meade and the Role of Economic Advisers," *Contemporary British History* 11, no. 2 (1997): 143–145; Glen O'Hara, *Governing Post-War Britain: The Paradoxes of Progress, 1951–1973* (Basingstoke: Palgrave Macmillan, 2012), 125–130.

[48] Skidelsky, *John Maynard Keynes, vol. 3*, 144.

[49] Quoted in T.W. Hutchison, *Economics and Economic Policy in Britain* (London: Routledge, 2003), 84, 86.

At the Bank, the future of economic expertise was also an unsettled question. On March 1, 1946, the government nationalized the central bank with a vote in the House of Commons of 351 to 152.[50] The legislation had little effect on day-to-day operations, although the Governor would no longer be elected by a vote of the Court of Directors and instead be directly appointed by the Chancellor.[51] What more ostensibly limited the dynamism of the postwar central bank was its own decision to abandon economic research. In 1946, the monthly *Statistical Summary* ceased publication and was effectively replaced by the government's Central Statistical Office's *Statistical Digest*.[52] With Governor Norman's departure from the governorship in 1944, the Bank had become more reluctant to engage its technical advisers.[53] A special committee briefly considered the appointment of five assistants to support the advisers, but their employment remained tenuous at best.[54]

The revival of economic research at the Bank occurred through a gradual process of reform and relearning. Throughout the 1950s, Governor Cameron Cobbold (later, 1st Baron Cobbold) repeatedly expressed his disappointment with the state of technical training at the central bank.[55] The research department had largely been neglected, while London's banking sector as a whole struggled to attract university-level talent. As a former adviser to Governor Norman, Cobbold envisioned elevating the central bank's reputation in economic research. Unable to convince Dennis Robertson (Trinity College, Cambridge) to join, the Bank subsequently employed Maurice Allen (LSE) as an Assistant Adviser in 1950 and, later, as an Adviser to the Governors in 1954. Another economist, John Fforde (Nuffield College, Oxford), was recruited to revive economic studies in accordance with the recommendations of a government commission.[56] By October 1959, Cobbold was able to revitalize the Bank with a new division: the Central Banking Information Department (CBID).[57]

The Bank had yet to reestablish itself as a leading source of economic knowledge with the same amount of authority as its interwar predecessor. In November, Cobbold had written about the importance of academic research to public policy: "Our economic advisory services have ... been much developed

50 HC Deb, October 29, 1945, vol. 415, cc. 43–167.

51 Fforde, *The Bank of England and Public Policy*, 4; Capie, *The Bank of England*, 61; Singleton, *Central Banking in the Twentieth Century*, 117–118; Wansleben, *The Rise of Central Banks*, 90–91.

52 Committee of Treasury, Minutes, November 21, 1945, BoE G8/67; Hennessy, *A Domestic History of the Bank of England*, 317.

53 Fforde, *The Bank of England and Public Policy*, 318–320; Wood, *A History of Central Banking*, 301.

54 "Assistant Advisers and Acting Assistant Advisers," January 3, 1950, BoE G15/276.

55 Hennessy, *A Domestic History of the Bank of England*, 313; Capie, *The Bank of England*, 54.

56 Hennessy, *A Domestic History of the Bank of England*, 320; Capie, *The Bank of England*, 51.

57 "Central Banking Information," *The Economist* 193, 6062, October 31, 1959, 445; Hennessy, "The Governors, Directors and Management of the Bank of England," 207; Capie, *The Bank of England*, 128.

in recent years … . The more complete the picture of statistics and information, the better … ."[58] Statistics and economics, to his mind, were not discrete disciplines, but instead overlapping areas in which the Bank needed to focus on its future research. Siepmann, a former Adviser and current Executive Director, similarly believed that the Bank needed to alter its priorities in light of geopolitical changes. Advisers, he imagined, could work on improving relations with the Dominions, as well as "Russia and the Iron Curtain countries."[59] The potential value of expert opinion gradually became apparent to others at the Bank. It was perhaps true, as Forrest Capie has argued, that Deputy Governor Mynors "made no effort to advance the use of economics in the Bank."[60] However, as Mynors himself explained to Cobbold, there was a case to be made for the introduction of more advisers by "discarding tradition and recruiting a small number of the right type – if we can get them – *as economists*."[61]

The institutionalization of expertise at the Bank coincided with a similar shift in the national government. In 1947, Robert Hall (later, Baron Roberthall) became the Director of the Economic Section, the first full-time group of government economic advisers.[62] As the Chief Economic Adviser to the Treasury from 1953 onward, he consulted the chancellor on ways of coordinating monetary and fiscal policy to address the persistent threat of inflation.[63] With their promotions, Hall and other newly employed advisers gradually became integral components of the bureaucratic apparatus in Whitehall. According to Cairncross,

> A Government department when it recruits an economic adviser … always feels tempted to thrust on him the unappetising responsibilities which every other member of the department shuns. He will be asked, for example, to write speeches for his Minister … . He will be asked to draft lengthy reports which are a standing responsibility of the department, but which senior officials are too busy to undertake. Added to all this, he may find that while he is an adviser, no-one particularly wants to be advised. He may be left without access to the person in authority who ought to have the benefit of his advice.[64]

58 Quoted in Hennessy, *A Domestic History of the Bank of England*, 321–322.
59 Siepmann to Mynors, January 22, 1954, BoE G15/276.
60 Capie, *The Bank of England*, 44.
61 Quoted in Capie, *The Bank of England*, 129.
62 Robert Hall, "The Place of the Economist in Government," *Oxford Economic Papers* 7, no. 2 (1955), 135; Ely Devons, *Essays in Economics* (London: George Allen & Unwin, 1961), 46; Alec Cairncross, "Preface," in *The Robert Hall Diaries, 1947–1953*, ed. Alec Cairncross (London: Unwin Hyman, 1989), vii–viii; Alec Cairncross, "The United Kingdom," in *The Role of the Economist in Government: An International Perspective*, ed. Joseph A. Pechman (New York and London: Harvester Wheatsheaf, 1989), 32–38; Kit Jones, *An Economist among Mandarins: A Biography of Robert Hall, 1901–1988* (Cambridge: Cambridge University Press, 1994), 70.
63 Jones, *An Economist among Mandarins*, 143–152.
64 Cairncross, "On Being an Economic Adviser," 186.

Many politicians wanted to have the benefits of economic advisers without conceding their own power to them. During the 1950s and early 1960s, Whitehall supported the employment of economic advisers, albeit with major limitations on the positions they held.[65] Although economists might have been greater in number, their roles in the postwar state were mostly "operational" and often only as "personal confidants of ministers."[66] That they had become more normalized figures within existing structures of governance is clear. This assertion, however, eludes the fact that technical specialists became the source of knowledge for questions and topics that politicians were unable to answer on their own. The quantification of economics provided a greater degree of legitimacy to their claims.

Such a view was established during the proceedings of the (Radcliffe) Committee on the Working of the Monetary System (1958–1959). Expert testimony procured from the Bank, Treasury, and the City investigated the functioning of the UK monetary system and the central bank's place within it. The deliberations concluded that the Bank had not only emerged as an important mediator in domestic affairs, such as managing the government accounts and trading Treasury bills, but it had also begun to represent British interests on the international stage. Officials wanted to see the government employ economic advisers who could converse with the Bank on increasingly technical topics as well. Most vocally, Hugh Gaitskell, the leader of the Labour Party and a former Chancellor, suggested that the Treasury should consider the procurement of "more technical expertise" to help foster "a convention of closer relations between the Bank and the Treasury."[67]

The Radcliffe discussions thus highlighted the severe underinvestment in economic advice. "Many of the Bank's operations are, however, highly technical and must be handled exclusively by men who are experts in the techniques of operation and management," the final report read.[68] Because of its important role, the Bank needed to draw on technical specialists who could lead negotiations with foreign central banks and international organizations. The committee concluded that this form of governance – with the Bank as the central institution for setting monetary policy – seemed ideal for the realities of the postwar economy. As the committee's report continued, the desire "to

[65] M.C. Fessey, "Some Developments in Economic Statistics since 1934," *Journal of the Royal Statistical Society* 19, no. 2 (1969), 114–117; Glen O'Hara, "Towards a New Bradshaw? Economic Statistics and the British State in the 1950s and 1960s," *The Economic History Review* 60, no. 1 (2007), 12–13, 21; Fourcade, *Economists and Societies*, 169–172; Tomlinson, *Managing the Economy*, 174–176.

[66] A.W. Bob Coats, "Economic Policy Advice: Opportunities and Limitations," in *The Transfer of Economic Knowledge*, ed. Ernst Mohr (Cheltenham: Edward Elgar, 1999), 77–78.

[67] "The Rt. Hon. H.T.N. Gaitskell, C.B.E., M.P.," December 18, 1958, in Committee on the Working of the Monetary System, *Minutes of Evidence* (London: H.M. Stationery Office, 1960), 850.

[68] Committee on the Working of the Monetary System, *Report*, 114.

strengthen further the research and intelligence side of the Bank's activities and so to assist the Bank to take the lead in promoting and inspiring the objective study of monetary and financial problems. The total volume of research that has been done upon them up to now, inside and outside the bank, appears to us to be insufficient."[69]

After the 1964 general election, the Labour government under Harold Wilson established a permanent body of professional economists. Headquartered in the Treasury, the Government Economic Service (GES) recruited economic graduates in line with Gaitskell's earlier proposals.[70] Yet in contrast with the wartime Economic Section, which had only employed experts on a temporary basis with undefined roles, the postwar GES created a cohort of economists employed on a permanent basis and trained specifically for working within the government apparatus.[71] It offered opportunities to economists as civil servants, thereby seeking to develop an in-house model of expert knowledge.[72]

In its first five years, the GES was led by Sir Alec Cairncross, the official economic adviser to the UK government. Born in Scotland, Cairncross had studied at Glasgow and Trinity College, Cambridge, before working in various government agencies and institutions, including the Treasury, Board of Trade, and Organisation for European Economic Co-operation. His diary entries offer a portrait of a government bureaucracy that had gradually become open to economic expertise. For instance, in the days leading to the 1967 devaluation of the pound, Cairncross had close contact with elected officials – Defence Secretary Denis Healey, Chancellor James Callaghan, and Prime Minister Wilson among them – which proved vital to subsequent negotiations with the International Monetary Fund (IMF).[73] Active participation on the Treasury's steering committee allowed him to act as the mediator between Bank officials and politicians, even if there was disagreement over the logistics of the devaluation.

The Bank, too, underwent its own institutional transformation in these years. In 1964, its CBID was dissolved and replaced with the Economic Intelligence Department at the behest of Governor Rowland Baring, 3rd Earl of

69 Committee on the Working of the Monetary System, *Report*, 301.

70 Geoffrey Kingdon Fry, *Statesmen in Disguise: The Changing Role of the Administration Class of the British Home Civil Service, 1853–1966* (London: Macmillan, 1969), 232–235; G.C. Peden, "Economic Knowledge and the State in Modern Britain," in *The Boundaries of the State in Modern Britain*, ed. S.J.D. Green and R.C. Whiting (Cambridge: Cambridge University Press, 1996), 177–178; Roger Middleton, *Charlatans or Saviours? Economists and the British Economy from Marshall to Meade* (Cheltenham: Edward Elgar, 1998), 99–101; Brian Harrison, *Seeking a Role: The United Kingdom, 1951–1970* (Oxford: Clarendon Press, 2009), 268.

71 Fourcade, *Economists and Societies*, 169–171.

72 Phyllis Colvin, *The Economic Ideal in British Government: Calculating Costs and Benefits in the 1970s* (Manchester: Manchester University Press, 1985), 56.

73 Alec Cairncross, Diary, November 15, 1967, in *The Wilson Years: A Treasury Diary, 1964–1969* (London: Historians' Press, 1997), 246–247.

Cromer. This decision indicated the Bank's transition from being a source of technical information to one of general economic knowledge. Such an institutional shift, *The Economist* reported, represented "the coming of age of economic intelligence in the Bank as a department able to stand alone in its own right."[74] Over the ensuing decades, rapid organizational changes were part of a wider campaign to elevate the Bank's status in international affairs. Executive Director and future Governor Leslie O'Brien (later, Baron O'Brien) specifically wanted to strengthen the ties between the Bank's technical experts and the overseas department.[75] Doing so would prove useful not only for statistical research but also for pressing foreign economic developments, such as decolonization or European economic integration.

Indeed, the role of a central bank in international affairs had rarely been static or well defined. In contrast to the interwar years, the postwar years saw the Bank unable to challenge or command authority over the central banks of Europe or the Commonwealth. Instead, a significant proportion of its operations comprised domestic interventions in the rapidly expanding gilt-edged market of the 1950s and 1960s.[76] At the same time, the Bank greatly benefited from sterling's status as a reserve currency and, under Governor Cromer, leveraged its connections in the City and at the Bank for International Settlements to promote the use of sterling abroad.[77] By the 1970s, the Bank was able to maintain its reputation in international monetary affairs through its connections.[78] While its officials may have been unable to halt the Britain's economic volatility owing to the oil crisis and ensuing social unrest, the City continued to remain an important international financial center in these years.

The Bank's postwar transformation was also shaped by expert opinion. Those who had been advisers under Governor Norman in the interwar years became actively involved in the central bank's governance. Many of them were promoted to new positions at the Bank: Siepmann (who became a director in 1945), Bolton (director in 1948), Mynors (deputy governor in 1954), and Cobbold (governor in 1949). A few returned to academia, such as Clay, who served as Warden of

74 "Economists Ascendant?," *The Economist* 210, 6286, February 15, 1964, 632.

75 Leslie K. O'Brien, Note, March 3, 1964, BoE G15/276.

76 Jeremy Wormell, *The Gilt-Edged Market* (London: George Allen & Unwin, 1985), 22–26; David Gowland, "Debt Management in the United Kingdom and the London Gilt-Edged Market," in *International Bond Markets*, ed. David Gowland (London and New York: Routledge, 1990), 106–107; William A. Allen, *Monetary Policy and Financial Repression in Britain, 1951–59* (New York: Palgrave Macmillan, 2014), 55–62, 174–177; Allen, *The Bank of England and the Government Debt*, 77–82;

77 Philip L. Cottrell, "La Banque d'Angleterre, les crises de la livre sterling et l'Europe (1958–1967)," in *Politiques et pratiques des banques d'émission en Europe (XVIIe–XXe siècle) : le bicentenaire de la Banque de France dans la perspective de l'identité monétaire européenne*, ed. Olivier Feiertag and Michel Margairaz (Paris: Albin Michel, 2003): 787–803; Schenk, *The Decline of Sterling*, 184, 277; Naef, *An Exchange Rate History*, 46–47.

78 C.A.E. Goodhart, "The Changing Role of Central Banks," *Financial History Review* 18, no. 2 (2011), 140.

Nuffield College, Oxford, before joining the Institute for Advanced Study in Princeton. Others found their skills more useful in the private sector. Kershaw, after serving in various advisory positions, joined the Bank of New Zealand as its chairman in 1963. Meanwhile, Bolton served as chairman of the Bank of London & South America, where he was involved in the development of the Eurodollar market and still retained many connections at the Bank.[79]

Expertise had therefore set a precedent for the postwar institutionalization of economics at the Bank. The contributions of the interwar experts mirrored those of a new cohort of postwar advisers: Christopher (Kit) McMahon in 1964, Andrew Crockett in 1966, Leslie Dicks-Mireaux in 1967, and Charles Goodhart in 1968.[80] In these iterations, the value of economic advice became apparent. Efforts to reconcile the desire for an adequate response to inflationary pressures with the hopes of maintaining a market-based approach to regulation led to the implementation of Competition and Credit Control in September 1971. Based on an earlier consultative document, the new initiative – proposed by advisers within the Bank's Money Supply Group and spearheaded by Fforde, then the Executive Director for Home Finance – helped the central bank assert dominance over the clearing banks by limiting the volume of credit the latter could extend.[81] Its de jure abandonment two years later, however, demonstrated the necessity of constant negotiation and concessions to maintain influence over domestic economic policy.

THE BANK IN A GLOBALIZED ECONOMY

Repeated strikes to the UK economy, from the 1967 devaluation to the 1976 IMF loan, further weakened the central bank's authority.[82] Exacerbated by the

[79] On the Bank and the Eurodollar market, see Richard Fry, "Introduction," in *A Banker's World: The Revival of the City, 1957–1970: Speeches and Writings of Sir George Bolton*, ed. Richard Fry (London: Hutchinson, 1970), 27–28, 32–33; Geoffrey Jones, "Competitive Advantages in British Multinational Banking since 1890," in *Banks as Multinationals*, ed. Geoffrey Jones (London: Routledge, 1990), 52–54; David Kynaston, *The City of London, vol. 4: A Club No More, 1945–2000* (London: Chatto & Windus, 2001), 268–287; Catherine R. Schenk, "The New City and the State in the 1960s," in *The British Government and the City of London in the Twentieth Century*, ed. Ranald Michie and Philip Williamson (Cambridge: Cambridge University Press, 2004), 331; Burn, *The Re-Emergence of Global Finance*, 37, 102–107, 112–118; Daunton, *The Economic Government*, 609–610.

[80] Capie, *The Bank of England*, 130; Kynaston, *Till Time's Last Sand*, 481.

[81] Bank of England, "Copy of Bank of England Consultative Paper Issued in May 1971," in *The Banks and the Monetary System in the UK, 1959–1971*, ed. J.E. Wadsworth (London: Methuen & Co., 1973), 492–496; Geddes, *Inside the Bank of England*, 99–101; Middleton, *Government Versus the Market*, 551; Kynaston, *The City of London, vol. 4*, 436–439; Needham, *UK Monetary Policy*, 64–77; Davies, *The City of London*, 93–96; Kynaston, *Till Time's Last Sand*, 494–499; Copley, *Governing Financialization*, 81–87; Wansleben, *The Rise of Central Banks*, 94.

[82] Kathleen Burk and Alec Cairncross, *"Goodbye, Great Britain": The 1976 IMF Crisis* (New Haven and London: Yale University Press, 1992); Douglas Wass, *Decline to Fall: The Making*

oil crisis, the current-account deficit peaked at £3.2 billion in 1974. The Bank, hoping to address these issues while simultaneously defending its institutional independence, turned to quantitative methods. Introduced in the 1970s, large-scale macroeconomic models incorporated new forecasting techniques to help the research division simultaneously understand the impact of different policies in an era of stagflation.[83]

When the Bank searched for recommendations on how to combat stagflation, it employed Christopher Dow as the first chief economist in 1973. Although he was unable to have much direct influence on monetary policy, his presence represented a continued interest in expert opinion.[84] In later cases, too, Bank officials even acknowledged the apparent lack of trained economists. In October 1977, they commissioned a group of economists to debate the priorities of the authorities. The subsequently formed Panel of Academic Consultants included a dozen academics, Cairncross among them, who offered their recommendations to the Bank on a regular basis.[85]

Tensions between central bankers and economists continued through the age of neoliberalism. Throughout the 1970s and 1980s, political leaders experimented with monetarist ideas that might have promised to resolve inflation. As one Cambridge economist, Nicholas Kaldor (later, Baron Kaldor), wrote in 1985, "I know of no other instance where an utterly false doctrine concerning the causation of economic events had such a sweeping success in a matter of a few years."[86] The Medium-Term Financial Strategy, devised by Chancellor Geoffrey Howe in 1980, established a target range for £M3 growth, a program that most exemplified the interests in monetarist theory.[87] Identifying a causal link between the money supply and price levels, however, proved less convincing in discussions at the Bank. Its economists were hesitant to believe

of British Macro-Economic Policy and the 1976 IMF Crisis (Oxford: Oxford University Press, 2008); Niall Ferguson, Charles S. Maier, Erez Manela, and Daniel J. Sargent, eds., *The Shock of the Global: The 1970s in Perspective* (Cambridge, MA, and London: Harvard University Press, 2010).

83 John Whitley, "Economic Models and Policy-Making," *Bank of England Quarterly Bulletin* 37, Q2 (1997): 163–173; Capie, *The Bank of England*, 705–706; Juan Acosta, Beatrice Cherrier, François Claveau, Clément Fontan, Aurélien Goutsmedt, and Francesco Sergi, "Six Decades of Economic Research at the Bank of England," *History of Political Economy* 56, no. 1 (2024), 6–10.

84 Graham Hacche and Christopher Taylor, "Editors' Introduction," in *Inside the Bank of England: Memoirs of Christopher Dow, Chief Economist, 1973–84*, ed. Graham Hacche and Christopher Taylor (Basingstoke: Palgrave Macmillan, 2013), 8, 13–16.

85 Bank of England, "Panel of Academic Consultants," *Bank of England Quarterly Bulletin* 19, Q2 (1979), 195; Melvyn Westlake, "Bank of England Sets up Panel of Top Economists to Debate Policies," *The Times* 60124, October 3, 1977, 17; Capie, *The Bank of England*, 777.

86 N. Kaldor, "Lessons of the Monetarist Experiment," in *Monetary Conditions for Economic Recovery*, ed. C. van Ewijk and J.J. Klant (Dordrecht: Martinus Nijhoff, 1985), 243.

87 Needham, *UK Monetary Policy*, 146–153; Davies, *The City of London*, 183–187; James, *Making a Modern Central Bank*, 66–70; Copley, *Governing Financialization*, 117–124; Wansleben, *The Rise of Central Banks*, 116.

that traditional models could explain recent exchange-rate fluctuations, while a reliance on monetary targeting also seemed to be a futile endeavor.[88] The result was a central bank largely interested in the idea of economic advice, yet one still deeply divided over the application of theory.

Still, the Bank of the 1980s, similar to its interwar predecessor, saw value in technical advice for work outside its standard domain of knowledge. For one, improved foreign relations had been vital for promoting the stability of the British economy. Where Britain most depended on expert analysis was in its work on maintaining sterling's status as an international reserve currency. Following the de facto rejection of monetary aggregates by Chancellor Nigel Lawson, the Bank sought to define an exchange-rate policy in coordination with its foreign counterparts.[89] In September 1985, representatives from Britain, France, Germany, Japan, and the United States convened at the Plaza Hotel in New York City. The ensuing agreement demonstrated the convergent interests of central bankers as they aimed to counter threats to their independence from their respective national governments.[90]

In these international fora, central bankers relied on economists to help navigate the travails of the post-Bretton Woods system. The period from the mid-twentieth century onward represented the dominance of economic ideas in public policy and global governance. This "economists' hour," according to Binyamin Appelbaum, further coincided with the shift toward market-oriented reforms, such as deregulation and free trade.[91] It was in the later decades of the century when the Bank resembled a central bank dominated by economists. Deputy Governor George Blunden admitted that while the central bank might have once focused too much on the recruitment of generalist staff members and civil servants, by 1987, it had actively hired those with training in economics.[92]

If the beginning of the twentieth century saw the emergence of central bank expertise, then the end of the century witnessed its ascendency. After the United Kingdom withdrew from the European Exchange Rate Mechanism in September 1992, the Bank considered investing more resources into the study of economics. Its officials acknowledged the value of economists who were able to translate quantitative models into understandable language, particularly in the aftermath of Black Wednesday. One banker therefore claimed that the value in economists lay not in their ability to create complex econometric models, but rather in their knowledge of a wide range of practical issues.[93] Indeed, expert involvement was vital for policy debates over the institutional

[88] James, *Making a Modern Central Bank*, 99.

[89] James, *Making a Modern Central Bank*, 147.

[90] James, *Making a Modern Central Bank*, 152–153.

[91] Binyamin Appelbaum, *The Economists' Hour: False Prophets, Free Markets, and the Fracture of Society* (New York: Little, Brown and Company, 2019).

[92] James, *Making a Modern Central Bank*, 28–29.

[93] James, *Making a Modern Central Bank*, 348.

independence of the Bank, demonstrated by Goodhart's testimony before the Treasury and Civil Service Committee in 1993.[94] Alongside Whitehall's civil servants, Westminster's elected politicians, and the City's bankers, the Bank's advisers could claim to be a leading authority on economic concerns.

The operational independence of the central bank on May 6, 1997, fully cemented its status as a monetary authority. To protect it from the short-run pressures of the electoral cycle, the Chancellor of the Exchequer, Gordon Brown, announced that the Bank would be able to determine interest rates independently. The following year, the Bank of England Act of 1998 established a Monetary Policy Committee, which comprised the governor, four internal members, and four external "expert" members.[95] Although the governor and external posts were appointed by the chancellor, the group would thereafter be allowed to set monetary policy without direct intervention from the government, thereby providing the institution with greater jurisdiction over economic affairs. In exchange, the act outlined significant administrative reforms to the central bank. The publication of the Monetary Policy Committee's meeting minutes intended to enhance overall transparency, while additional adjustments to the Court of Directors reflected an overall commitment to a public-oriented mission. With changes that aimed to elevate public confidence and trust in an independent institution, the Bank secured its reputation as both a national and an international monetary authority.

[94] De Saint Seine, *La Banque d'Angleterre*, 260–263.
[95] James, *Making a Modern Central Bank*, 430.

Epilogue

The Bank of England reshaped the structure of economic governance. As the monetary authority of the United Kingdom, it enacted policies that defended the primacy of the City of London. In the interwar years, its operations expanded into domains unprecedented for a central bank at the time. An array of interventions in industrial policy, foreign affairs, and imperial relations primarily aimed to maintain the status of sterling as a world reserve currency. By assuming additional responsibilities beyond domestic monetary management, the Bank was able to establish itself as a mediator between the City and the state.

The interwar evolution of central banking parallels developments in the twenty-first century. At the turn of the new millennium, the Bank again confronted a range of pervasive issues. Although the ever-present threat of inflation remained its chief concern, other threats, such as rising asset prices and volatile exchange rates, also began to undermine the stability of the British economy. The Bank may have obtained operational independence from the national government in 1997, yet neither it nor the Treasury had regained the confidence lost on Black Wednesday.

In response, the Bank sought to employ more experts. Far from a design flaw, the integration of unelected advisers served a functional purpose, as academically trained specialists allowed the central bank to establish its legitimacy as an institution. Three decades after the appointment of the first chief economist, Mervyn King was appointed to lead the Bank in 2003. With a degree in economics, King aimed to reinvigorate the institution with new ideas. While not severing the important historical links to the City, he invited economists into the upper echelons of the Bank's hierarchy. As he was able to report in one interview, "We now recruit quite a large number of non-UK nationals to work in the Bank. Quite a lot of our masters and PhD economists are non-UK Europeans. We recruit the best in the world in the international marketplace. We have no qualms at all about going out there and approaching the best people. And not many central banks do that."[1]

King (later, Baron King of Lothbury) served as Governor throughout the global financial crisis (GFC) of 2007–2008. Amidst widespread threats to global capital markets, the British authorities endeavored to maintain the preeminence of the City abroad. At the onset of the crisis, the United Kingdom continued to maintain its standing as a center of international trade and finance. In 2007, London reported the highest volume of foreign-exchange trading at 34.6 percent globally, followed by New York at 17.4 percent.[2] The British pound also peaked at a dollar-sterling rate of 2.10 in November, the highest in more than two decades.

Because of its economic position, Britain had been relatively well placed to respond. Initially, the Bank responded by lowering interest rates from 5.75 percent in July 2007 to 4.5 percent after the collapse of Lehman Brothers, and later to 0.5 percent in March 2009. Although lowering the Bank Rate might have mainly been used to encourage domestic spending among consumers and businesses, its secondary effect was supporting a fragile banking system that needed access to more capital. Alongside the European Central Bank, the Federal Reserve, and the Bank of Japan, the Bank of England had crafted a stabilization plan loosely based on Bagehot's idea of a lender of last resort, while at the same time opting for unorthodox measures, such as forward guidance and quantitative easing. With the purchase of mortgage-backed securities and long-term assets, the balance sheets of the major central banks grew to unprecedented levels.[3]

In the years thereafter, the Bank was able to justify and maintain its expanded role in domestic governance, notably in the realm of regulation. In April 2013, it established the Prudential Regulation Authority to replace the government's Financial Services Authority. The new entity, led by a trained economist, represented a firm commitment to financial oversight amidst political pressures and public criticism. It worked with the Bank's Monetary Policy Committee and the G20's Financial Stability Board on practical, policy-oriented tasks, while the academically oriented Monetary Analysis group continued to publish technical reports on the crisis. Through its multitude of committees, the Bank acted as a mediator between public policy and academic research.

1 Quoted in Patience Wheatcroft, "'You Don't Play with the Traditions of an Institution like the Bank,'" *The Times* 67803, July 1, 2003, 22.

2 Ranald C. Michie, *Forex Forever: The City of London and the Foreign Exchange Market since 1850* (Oxford: Oxford University Press, 2024), 251.

3 Adam Tooze, *Crashed: How a Decade of Financial Crises Changed the World* (New York: Viking, 2018), 203, 285–286; Manuela Moschella, *Unexpected Revolutionaries: How Central Banks Made and Unmade Economic Orthodoxy* (Ithaca: Cornell University Press, 2024), 60. On central bank balance sheets over a longer term, see Niall Ferguson, Martin Kornejew, Paul Schmelzing, and Moritz Schularick, "The Safety Net: Central Bank Balance Sheets and Financial Crises, 1587–2020," *Hoover Institution Economics Working Papers*, no. 23102 (2023).

After Governor King left the Bank in 2013, a debate ensued over his potential successor. Whether academic economists would continue to hold the single most influential post in the City remained a key question. As *The Economist* remarked, "[The Bank] will have new powers to secure financial stability using 'macroprudential' tools, such as varying capital requirements for banks over the business cycle. And it will continue to set monetary policy to meet the government's inflation target. The new boss would ideally have expertise in all these areas; be able to explain clearly to politicians and the public how it is carrying out these complicated tasks; and have sufficient diplomatic skills."[4] The subsequent appointment of Mark Carney, the former Governor of the Bank of Canada (2008–2013), marked the permanence of this trend.

After the GFC, central banks gained a broader set of responsibilities not limited to the setting of interest rates, but instead concerned with overall economic policy.[5] Their operations included the continued purchases of government bonds and specialized lending facilities. At the same time, the long-term consequences of the GFC also included a heightened awareness of the Bank as an "anti-democratic" institution. Ensuing criticisms largely stemmed from the idea that central banks must constantly decide between protecting the interests of a private banking sector or serving the wider public good. The position of Governor, although appointed by an elected official (the Chancellor), was therefore called "the most powerful unelected job in Britain."[6] Meanwhile, a general distrust of central bankers as unelected officials in an already unelected institution sparked further controversy.[7]

In other instances, the Bank confronted censure when it seemed to overstep its institutional boundaries. Far from the apolitical entity it may wish to become, Bank officials repeatedly clashed with politicians and civil servants over their public remarks. During the 2016 Brexit campaign, Governor Carney noted the potential economic fallout from a departure from the European Union, a comment that Conservative MP Jacob Rees-Mogg claimed was "speculative and beneath the dignity of the Bank of England."[8] When other economists similarly voiced their disapproval of Brexit, Justice Secretary Michael Gove tersely responded, "people in this country have had enough of experts."[9]

4 "The England Job," *The Economist* 404, 8800, September 1, 2012, 12.

5 Neil Irwin, *The Alchemists: Three Central Bankers and a World on Fire* (New York: Penguin, 2013), 235–247.

6 Sam Coates, "The Job Interview That Came with a Caveat – No Experience, You've Got No Chance," *The Times* 70745, December 1, 2012, 73.

7 Stephen King, "Uneasy Is the Banker Who Wears the Crown," *The Times* 70506, February 27, 2012, 21.

8 Chris Giles and Emily Cadman, "Carney Supports Cameron's Deal with Brussels," *Financial Times*, March 8, 2016, www.ft.com/content/49969e4a-e524-11e5-a09b-1f8b0d268c39.

9 Henry Mance, "Britain Has Had Enough of Experts, Says Gove," *Financial Times*, June 3, 2016, www.ft.com/content/3be49734-29cb-11e6-83e4-abc22d5d108c.

It thus becomes apparent that any study of economic governance must take into account its political context. The end of the twentieth century could certainly be viewed as a moment of triumph for Europe's monetary authorities, which had once benefited from a decades-long bull market and relative freedom from political pressure.[10] Yet disputes with elected officials demonstrated the continued controversies surrounding the idea of central bank independence. While the Bank of England's actions during the GFC tested its institutional capabilities, the Brexit debate further added an ostensibly political dimension to its operations. Public clashes have illustrated the continued centrality of the Bank in contemporary discourse, as well as its flexibility in response to criticism.

The result has been an economic order that harkens back to its century-old counterpart. In both eras, central banks confronted a world destabilized by financial and political dislocations, further threatened by frequent wars and economic nationalism. For the interwar Bank of England, monetary policy and exchange-rate management might have historically been the most prioritized areas. The ability to set interest rates independently, free from the demands of the election cycle, was its standard mantra. Other responsibilities, such as industrial policy, postwar reconstruction, and foreign relations, increasingly fell under its purview.

Similarly, the crises of the twenty-first century induced extensive interventionist measures. Emergency-lending programs, swap agreements, and information-sharing via the Bank for International Settlements became the primary channels through which central banks could mitigate the risk of financial contagion. A resurgence in regulatory capabilities and a return to macroprudential policies have further embodied the post-GFC mandate for Europe's monetary authorities.[11]

Yet the global economic order has never been defined by the actions of central banks alone. Nor have the monetary authorities been blind to their own mistakes and fallibility. It was Andrew Haldane, the Bank's director of financial stability, who spoke of the "intellectual virus" plaguing the Bank during the GFC.[12] He admitted that existing statistical models failed to capture the complexity of the modern world economy. Even King, himself a trained economist, has been critical of the overreliance on the theory of rational expectations,

[10] "The Central Banker as God," *The Economist* 349, 8094, November 14, 1998, 25; "An Endangered Species," *The Economist* 352, 8138, September 25, 1999, 36–38.

[11] Andrew Baker, "Tower of Contrarian Thinking: How the BIS Helped Reframe Understandings of Financial Stability," in *Promoting Global Monetary and Financial Stability: The Bank for International Settlements after Bretton Woods, 1973–2020*, ed. Claudio Borio, Stijn Claessens, Piet Clement, Robert N. McCauley, and Hyun Song Shin (Cambridge: Cambridge University Press, 2020): 134–167; Matthias Thiemann, *Taming the Cycles of Finance? Central Banks and the Macro-Prudential Shift in Financial Regulation* (Cambridge: Cambridge University Press, 2023).

[12] "It Was Our Fault Too, Says Bank of England Economist," *The Times* 70694, October 3, 2012, 37.

embedded within the quantitative tools and normative assumptions of the economics discipline.[13]

Nevertheless, central banks have continually depended on technical expertise to confront pressing issues. Over the past century, they have relied on experts to defend their actions and maintain their legitimacy as monetary authorities.[14] Declining trust has convinced many central banks to craft reports and deliver speeches that appeal to a general public.[15] One component of their strategy has therefore been demonstrating the central bank's commitment to more transparent policies and objectives, such as with the publication of economic forecasts, policy decisions, and information regarding internal governance. Although the broad goal has been to raise public confidence, even these measures have led many central banks, especially the Federal Reserve, to wrestle with the dichotomy between increased visibility and strategic ambiguity.[16]

Rather than a history of decline, *The City's Defense* portrays British economic history as one of persistence and resilience.[17] In response to multitudes of crises, from decolonization and devaluation to Black Wednesday and Brexit, the City continued to maintain its position as one of the world's leading financial centers. Its adaptability has come to represent a certain dynamism to cataclysmic events as they unfolded.

For all their praise, criticism, and controversy, central banks have acquired a vast amount of influence over domestic and global economic governance. With a shift in public discourse that has focused on the issues of climate change, pandemics, and inequality, they have begun to confront a range of contemporary issues. Green-finance initiatives have set ambitious environmental goals, while collective social pressure has initiated some discussions over how to incorporate inequality targets into economic policy. Whether such work can

[13] Mervyn King, *The End of Alchemy: Money, Banking, and the Future of the Global Economy* (New York: W.W. Norton, 2016), 121–126, 301–309; John Kay and Mervyn King, *Radical Uncertainty: Decision-Making Beyond the Numbers* (New York: W.W. Norton, 2020), 371–373, 388–401.

[14] Paul Tucker, *Unelected Power: The Quest for Legitimacy in Central Banking and the Regulatory State* (Princeton and Oxford: Princeton University Press, 2018); Annelise Riles, *Financial Citizenship: Experts, Publics, and the Politics of Central Banking* (Ithaca and London: Cornell University Press, 2019).

[15] Benjamin Braun, "Speaking to the People? Money, Trust, and Central Bank Legitimacy in the Age of Quantitative Easing," *Review of International Political Economy* 23, no. 6 (2016): 1064–1092; Manuela Moschella, Luca Pinto, and Nicola Martocchia Diodati, "Let's Speak More? How the ECB Responds to Public Contestation," *Journal of European Public Policy* 27, no. 3 (2020): 400–418.

[16] Jacqueline Best, "Uncomfortable Knowledge in Central Banking: Economic Expertise Confronts the Visibility Dilemma," *Economy and Society* 51, no. 4 (2022): 559–583.

[17] Similar approaches can be found in Jim Tomlinson, "Inventing 'Decline': The Falling Behind of the British Economy in the Postwar Years," *The Economic History Review* 49, no. 4 (1996): 731–757; David Edgerton, *The Rise and Fall of the British Nation: A Twentieth-Century History* (London: Allen Lane, 2018).

engender significant change, particularly if it conflicts with the price-stability mandate, remains to be seen.[18] Yet if the authorities are serious about these projects, they should look outside their hierarchies for bright individuals with novel perspectives. Interwar central banks, themselves reluctant to expand their prerogatives into different areas, were once willing to venture outside the City for help. They confronted numerous controversies in their search for new ideas that were compatible with old traditions. Although evolving priorities, both in the interwar years and in more recent times, have continued to align with the City's interests, the ability to adapt to changing circumstances has affirmed the centrality of the Bank of England to the global economic order.

[18] Daniela Gabor, "Green Central Banking," in *Making the Great Turnaround Work: Economic Policy for a Green and Just Transition*, ed. Heinrich Böll Foundation, ZOE – Institute for Future-Fit Economies, and Finanzwende Recherche (Berlin: Heinrich-Böll-Stiftung, 2022), 39.

Appendix

BIOGRAPHIES OF THE BANK'S EXPERTS

Ronald Eric Harrison (R.E.H.) Allport (1887–1951)

Joined (1904), Superintendent, Statistical Section (1925–1933), Deputy Principal of the Economics & Statistics Section (1933–1938), Principal of the Economics & Statistics Section (1938–1947), Bank of England. Royal Field Artillery, British Army (1914–1918). Fellow, Royal Statistical Society (1934).

B.Mus. (1923), University of London

George Lewis French Bolton (1900–1982)

Trainee, Société Générale (1917). Foreign Exchange Department, Herbert, Wagg & Co. (1920–1933). Joined (1933), Deputy Principal, Foreign Exchange Section, Chief Cashier's Office (1934–1936), Principal, Foreign Exchange Section, Chief Cashier's Office (1936–1941), Adviser to the Governors (1941–1948), Director (1948–1957), Non-Executive Director (1957–1968), Bank of England. Executive Director (1946–1952), Alternate Governor (1952–1957), International Monetary Fund. Director, Bank for International Settlements (1949–1957). High Sheriff of the County of London (1952–1953, 1961–1962). Deputy Chairman (1957–1968), Chairman (1968–1980), Commonwealth Development Finance Corporation. Director, Sun Life Assurance Company of Canada (1957–1975). Chairman (1957–1970), President (1970–1982), Bank of London & South America (BOLSA). President, Overseas Bankers Club (1960–1961). Deputy Chairman, London United Investments (1971–1974). Deputy Chairman, Lonrho (1973–1982). Chairman, Premier Consolidated Oilfields (1974–1976).

Leyton County High School for Boys, Waltham Forest
KCMG (1950)

Charles Bruce-Gardner (1887–1960)

Director, John Summers & Sons (1913–1930). Member, Sheet Trade Board (1914–1930). Chairman, Galvanizing Conciliation Board (1920–1930). Member, Advisory Committee, Department of Overseas Trade (1929–1930). Adviser to the Governors, Bank of England (1935–1938). Managing Director, Bankers' Industrial Development Company (1930–1938). Chairman, London Iron and Steel Exchange (1936–1937). Member, Air Council Committee on Supply (1938–1939). Member, Industrial Advisory Panel, Secretary of State for Air (1938–1939). Executive Chairman, Society of British Aircraft Constructors (1938–1943). Member, Air Supply Board (1939–1941). Member, National Production Advisory Council (1942–1943). Controller of Labour Allocation and Supply, Ministry of Aircraft Production (1943–1944). Chief Executive for Industrial Reconversion, Board of Trade (1944–1946). Industrial Adviser, Board of Trade (1947). Chairman, British Iron & Steel Corporation (1953–1960).

St Dunstan's College and Battersea Technical College
Knight Bachelor (1938), Baronet (1945)

Evelyn James Bunbury (1888–1965)

Joined (1912), General Manager (1926–1935), Chairman (1934–1935), Forbes, Forbes, Campbell & Co. Bombay Volunteer Rifles, British Army (1914–1917). Grenadier Guards, British Army (1917–1918). Director (1920–1935), Chairman (1925–1935), Bombay Telephone Company. Director (1922–1933), President of the Bombay Local Board, Imperial Bank of India. Chairman, London Tin Corporation (1935–1937). Chairman, Anglo-Oriental Mining Corporation (1935–1937). Adviser to the Governors (1935–1937), Executive Director (1937–1938), Bank of England. Chairman, Oriental Telephone and Electric Co. (1936–1957). Director (1938–1965), Deputy Chairman (1938–1944), Chairman (1944–1965), Agricultural Mortgage Corporation. Director, Mercantile Bank of India (1943–1959).

The Oratory School
B.A., Modern History (1910), The Queen's College, Oxford
MC (1946), CBE (1952)

Henry Clay (1883–1954)

Warden, Neighbourhood Guild Settlement, Sheffield (1906–1909). Lecturer, Workers' Educational Association (1909–1917). Lecturer in Economics, Leeds University (1911–1912). Ministry of Labour (1917–1919). Fellow, New College, Oxford (1919–1921). Stanley Jevons Professor of Political Economy, University of Manchester (1922–1927). Council (1924–1954), Vice President (1949–1954), Royal Economic Society. Chairman, Economic and Wage Commission, Union of South Africa (1925). Chair and Professor of Social Economics, University of Manchester (1927–1930). Member, Royal Commission on Unemployment Insurance (1930–1931). Adviser, Securities Management Trust, a Bank of England subsidiary (1930–1933). Adviser to the Governors, Bank of England (1933–1944). Deputy Chairman (1938–1940), Chairman (1940–1949), President (1949–1952), National Institute of Economic and Social Research. Economic Adviser, Board of Trade (1941–1944). Warden, Nuffield College, Oxford (1944–1949). Member, Institute for Advanced Study (1949–1954).

Bradford Grammar School
B.A., Literae Humaniores (1906), M.A. (1913), University College, Oxford
Knight Bachelor (1946)

Cameron Fromanteel Cobbold (1904–1987)

Kemp, Chatteris & Co. (1925–1928). Excess Insurance Company (1928–1933). Adviser to the Governors (1933–1938), Executive Director (1938–1945), Deputy Governor (1945–1949), Governor (1949–1961), Bank of England. High Sheriff, County of London (1946–1947). Board Member, Bank for International Settlements (1949–1961). Fellow, Eton College (1951–1967). Chairman, Malaysia Commission (1961–1963). Lord Chamberlain (1963–1971).

Eton College (1923)
King's College, Cambridge (1923–1924)
PC (1959), Baronet (1960), GCVO (1963), KG (1970), DL (1972)

Jessie Iris (J.I.) Douglas (1893–1974)

Drafting Officer, Ministry of Food (1918–1919). Assistant Secretary, Bradford Girls' Grammar School (1919–1921). Assistant, Rowntree and Co., and Lecturer in Economics, Bootham School (1921–1928). Head of the Statistical Department, J. Walter Thompson & Co. (1928–1931). Economist, Bank of England (1931–1948). Fellow (1928), Council (1935–1961), Honorary Secretary (1952–1960), Council (1960–1961), Royal Statistical Society. Conference Secretary, International Federation of University Women (1950, 1953).

Bradford Girls' Grammar School and École normale d'Angers
B.A., Economics (1918), M.A. (1931), Girton College, Cambridge

Anthony Reay Mackay (A.R.M.) Geddes (1912–1998)

Economics & Statistics Section, Bank of England (1932–1935). Joined (1935–1937), Overseas Manager (1945–1947), Executive Director (1947–1957), Managing Director (1957–1968), Chairman (1968–1978), Dunlop Rubber

Company (later, Dunlop). Royal Air Force Volunteer Reserve (1937–1945). Deputy Director of Air Transport, Air Ministry (1945–1947). Chairman, International Road Federation (1955–1958). President, Society of Motor Manufacturers and Traders (1958–1959). Part-Time Member, United Kingdom Atomic Energy Authority (1960–1965). Founding Member, National Economic Development Council (1962–1965). Chair, Committee of Inquiry into the Shipbuilding Industry (1965–1955). Director (1967–1984), Deputy Chairman (1978–1984), Midland Bank. Director, Shell Transport and Trading Company (1968–1982). President, International Chamber of Commerce (1980). Chairman (1985–1990), President (1991–1993), Charities Aid Foundation.

Rugby School (1930)
Magdalene College, Cambridge (1930–1931)
OBE (1943), KBE (1968)

Gilbert Edward Jackson (1890–1959)

Lecturer in Economics (1911–1916), Assistant Professor (1919–1921), Associate Professor (1921–1927), Professor (1927–1935), University of Toronto. Member and Secretary, Ontario Commission on Unemployment (1915–1916). British Army (1916–1919). Editor, Canadian Forum (1920–1925). Chairman, Ontario Employment Service Council (1921–1926). Economist, Bank of Nova Scotia (1926–1935). Adviser to the Governors, Bank of England (1935–1939). Founder, Canadian York Finance Company (1939). Acting Director, School of Commerce, McGill University (1940). Member, Industrial Disputes Enquiry Commission (1941). Member, National War Labour Board (1942). Member, National Selective Service Advisory Board (1942–1945).

Denstone College
B.A., Economics (1911), M.A. (1958),
St John's College, Cambridge
OBE (1946)

Raymond Newton Kershaw (1898–1981)

Second Lieutenant, Australian Imperial Force (1916–1918). Health Section (1924), Minorities Section (1924–1929), Secretariat, League of Nations. Joined (1929), Adviser to the Overseas and Finance Department (1932–1935), Adviser to the Governors (1935–1953), Bank of England. Member, East African Currency Board (1932–1953). Adviser, Commonwealth Development Finance Company (1953–1955). Chairman, London Board, Commercial Banking Company of Sydney (1964–1966). Chairman, Bank of New Zealand (1963–1968).

Sydney Boys' High School
University of Sydney (1915–1916)
B.A., Modern History (1921), New College, Oxford
MC (1918), CMG (1947)

Humphrey Charles Baskerville (H.C.B.) Mynors (1903–1989)

Fellow and University Lecturer in Economics, Corpus Christi College, Cambridge (1926–1933). Member (1928–1964), Council (1954–1964), Treasurer (1946–1953), Royal Economic Society. Deputy Principal, Economics & Statistical Section (1933–1934), Principal, Economics & Statistical Section (1934–1938), Deputy Secretary (1938–1939), Secretary (1939–1944), Adviser to the Governors (1944–1949), Director (1949–1954), Deputy Governor (1954–1964), Bank of England. Member, Institute for Advanced Study (1937). Director, Commonwealth Development Finance Company (1953). Council of Management (1944–1959), Executive Committee (1945–1954), National Institute of Economic and Social Research. Joined as Director (1964) and Chairman (1967–1970), Finance Corporation for Industry. Chairman (1968–1969), Deputy Chairman (1969–1970), Panel on Takeovers and Mergers. Director, English Electric Company, Imperial Tobacco Group, Legal & General Assurance Society, Pilkington Brothers.

Marlborough College
B.A., Economics (1925), M.A. (1929),
Corpus Christi College, Cambridge
Baronet (1964)

Otto Ernst Niemeyer (1883–1971)

Assistant Principal (1906–1912), Principal (1912–1919), Assistant Secretary (1919–1920), Principal Assistant Secretary (1920–1921), Deputy Controller of Finance (1921–1922), Controller of Finance (1922–1927), Treasury. Member (1923–1937) and Chairman (1927–1928), Financial Committee, League of Nations. Adviser to the Governors (1927–1938), Director (1938–1952), Bank of England. Director (1932–1964), Chairman (1937–1940), Vice Chairman (1941–1964), Bank for International Settlements. Member (1935–1965), Vice President (1950–1955), President (1956–1965), Council of Foreign Bondholders. Chairman of the Court of Governors (1941–1957) and Governor (1941–1965), London School of Economics and Political Science. Board Member of Anglo-International Bank, the Agricultural Mortgage Company, Vickers Armstrong.

St Paul's School (1902)
B.A., Literae Humaniores (1906), Balliol College, Oxford
CB (1921), KCB (1924), GBE (1927)

John Arundel Caulfeild (J.A.C.) Osborne (1881–1971)

Joined (1902), Assistant Principal, Chief Cashier's Office (1921–1922), Deputy Principal, Chief Cashier's Office (1922–1923), Assistant Chief Cashier (1923–1929), Principal, Chief Cashier's Office (1929–1931), Principal, Statistical

Section (1931–1934), Secretary (1934), Adviser to the Governors (1938–1945), Bank of England. Member (1925), Fellow (1929), Royal Economic Society. Deputy Governor, Bank of Canada (1935–1938). Treasury Representative, British Air Mission to Canada (1939). Treasury Representative, British Supply Board in Canada and the United States (1940). Treasury Representative, British Technical Mission (1941–1942). Inspection Board of the United Kingdom and Canada (1941).

Charterhouse School

William Brian Reddaway (1913–2002)

Economics & Statistics Section, Bank of England (1934–1936). Tutor and Research Fellow in Economics, University of Melbourne (1936–1937). Fellow, Clare College, Cambridge (1938–2002). Economist, Statistics Division, Board of Trade (1940–1947). Director, Organisation for European Economic Co-operation (1951–1952). Director, Department of Applied Economics, University of Cambridge (1955–1969). Executive Committee (1957–1972), Council of Management (1958–1993), National Institute of Economic and Social Research. Economic Consultant, World Bank (1966). Fellow, British Academy (1967). Professor of Political Economy, University of Cambridge (1969–1980).

Oundle School
B.A., Economics (1934), King's College, Cambridge
CBE (1971)

Francis James Rennell Rodd (1895–1978)

Royal Field Artillery, British Army (1914–1915). Intelligence Officer, Italy (1916). Staff Officer, British Army (1917–1918). Staff Captain, Arab Bureau (1918–1919). Diplomatic Service (1919–1922). Foreign Office (1923–1924). Member, Buckmaster & Moore (1926–1929). Adviser to the Governors, Bank of England (1929–1932). Manager, Bank for International Settlements (1930–1931). Partner, Morgan Grenfell & Co. (1933–1961). Intelligence Department, Ministry of Economic Warfare (1939–1940). Colonel (1941–1942), Major-General (1942–1944), Brigadier (1944), Civil Affairs Administration in the Middle East, East Africa, and Italy. President, Royal Geographical Society (1945–1948). Deputy Lord Lieutenant (1948), Vice-Lord Lieutenant (1957–1973), Herefordshire. Visiting Fellow, Nuffield College, Oxford (1947–1959). Justice of the Peace (1950). Director, BOAC (1954–1965).

Eton College
Balliol College, Oxford (1913–1914)
CB (1943), KBE (1944), DL (1948)

James Bertram Selwyn (1910–1997)

Joined (1933), Deputy Principal, Economics & Statistics Section (1947–1957), Principal, Economics & Statistics Section (1957–1959), Deputy Chief of the Central Banking Information Department (1959–1964), Deputy Chief of the Economic Intelligence Department (1964–1965), Adviser (1965–1971), Bank of England. Royal Naval Volunteer Service (1939–1945). Commissioner for Securities, Hong Kong (1973–1977).

B.Sc., Economics (1932), London School of Economics

Harry Arthur Siepmann (1889–1963)

Treasury (1912–1915). Royal Field Artillery, British Army (1915–1919). Assistant to Keynes, Paris Peace Conference (1919). Buckmaster & Moore (1919–1923). Assistant to the Finance Member, Viceroy's Council of India (1923–1924). Adviser, National Bank of Hungary (1924–1926). Adviser to the Governors (1926–1945), Chief of Overseas and Foreign Department (1932–1935), Executive Director (1945–1954), Bank of England. Sheriff, County of London (1949–1950). Director, Mocatta & Goldsmid (1954–1963).

Cargilfield School, Rugby School
B.A., Literae Humaniores (1912), New College, Oxford

Oliver Mitchell Wentworth Sprague (1873–1953)

Instructor (1898–1904), Assistant Professor of Economics (1904–1905), Harvard University. Professor of Economics, Imperial University of Tokyo (1905–1908). Council of National Defense (1918). Assistant Professor of Banking and Finance (1908–1913), Edmund Cogswell Converse Professor of Banking and Finance (1913–1941), Acting Dean (1928–1929), Professor Emeritus (1941–1953), Harvard Business School. Editorial Board, *Quarterly Journal of Economics* (1909–1920). Adviser to the Governors, Bank of England (1930–1933). Special Assistant, Secretary of the Treasury (1933). President, American Economic Association (1937).

St Johnsbury Academy
A.B. in Political Science (1894), Harvard College
A.M. (1895), Ph.D. in Economics (1897),
Harvard University

Josiah Charles Stamp (1880–1941)

Clerk (1896–1900), Assistant Surveyor of Taxes (1900–1903), Surveyor of Taxes (1903–1914), Committee Clerk in the Secretaries' Office (1914–1916), Assistant Secretary (1916–1919), Board of Inland Revenue. B.Sc. in Economics, University of London (1911). D.Sc. in Economics, London School of Economics and Political Science (1916). Member, Royal Commission on Income Tax (1919). Secretary and Director, Nobel Industries Ltd. (1919–1926). Joint Secretary (1920–1930), President (1930–1932), Honorary Vice President (1932–1941), Royal Statistical Society. Member, Northern Ireland Finance Arbitration Committee (1923–1924). Member, Committee on Taxation and National Debt (1924). Member, (Dawes) Committee on German Currency and Finance (1924). Governor (1925–1941), Vice Chairman (1925–1935), Chairman of the Court of Governors (1935–1941), London School of Economics and Political Science. Chairman and President, London, Midland and Scottish Railway (1926–1941). Director, Imperial Chemical Industries (1927–1928). Chairman, Committee of Social Science Research (1928). Treasurer (1928–1935), President (1936), British Association for the Advancement of Science. Director, Bank of England (1928–1941). Member, Young Committee (1929). Member, Committee of Economists (1930). Member, Economic Advisory Council (1930–1939). Member, Prime Minister's Advisory Committee on Financial Questions (1931). Chairman, Committee on Economic Information (1931–1939). Chairman, Committee on Limits of Economic Policy (1932). Member, Committee on International Economic Policy (1932–1933). Mayor, Borough of Beckenham, Kent (1935). President, National Institute of Economic and Social Research (1937–1941). Chairman, (Stamp) Survey of Financial and Economic Plans (1939–1941). Co-Head (with Horace Wilson), Central Economic Information Service (1939–1941).

Bethany House School
CBE (1918), KBE (1920), GBE (1924),
GCB (1936), Baronet (1938)

Walter Winne Stewart (1885–1958)

Instructor of Economics (1910–1911), Assistant Professor of Economics (1913–1915), University of Missouri. Instructor of Economics, University of Michigan (1911–1913). Professor of Economics, Amherst College (1916–1922). Staff Member, War Industries Board (1918). Director, Division of Research and Statistics, Federal Reserve Board (1922–1925). Vice President (1926–1927), Chairman (1930–1937), President (1937–1938), Case, Pomeroy & Co. Fellow, American Statistical Association (1927). Adviser to the Governors, Bank of England (1927–1930). Fellow, Royal Statistical Society (1931). American Representative, Bank for International Settlements (1931). Trustee (1931–1950) and Chairman (1940–1950), Rockefeller Foundation. Trustee, Bennington College (1932–1938). Trustee (1933–1941) and Faculty (1938–1950), Institute for Advanced Study. Trustee, General Education Board (1933–1950). Adviser, Secretary of the Treasury (1939–1943). President, Council of Economic Advisers (1953–1955).

A.B. in Economics (1909), University of Missouri

Henry Strakosch (1871–1943)

Anglo-Austrian Bank of South Africa (1891–1895). Manager (1899–1902), Managing Director (1902–1942), Chairman (1924–1943), A. Goerz & Co. (later, Union Corporation). Chairman (1920–1921) and Member (1920–1937), Financial Committee, League of Nations. Member, Royal Commission on Indian Currency and Finance (1925–1926). Chairman, *The Economist* (1929–1943). Member, Council of India (1930–1937). Adviser, Secretary of State for India (1937–1942). Board Member of Anglo-International Bank, Burma Corporation, Geduld Proprietary Mines, Rand Agency.

Wasagymnasium, Vienna
Knight Bachelor (1921), KBE (1924), GBE (1927)

Lucius Perronet Thompson, later Thompson-McCausland (1904–1984)

Herbert, Wagg & Co. (1928–1929). *Financial News* (1929–1934). Joint Managing Director, Moody's Economist Services (1929–1939). Temporary Clerk (1939–1941), Assistant Adviser (1941–1949), Adviser to the Governors (1949–1965), Bank of England. Chairman, Governing Body of Repton School (1959–1971). Vice Chairman (1957–1964), Chairman (1964–1969), Corporation of Working Men's College, London. High Sheriff, Hertfordshire (1965–1966). Part-Time Consultant on International Monetary Problems, Treasury (1965–1968). Chairman, Tricentrol (1970–1976). Moody's Services (1970–1975).

Repton School
B.A., Literae Humaniores (1927),
King's College, Cambridge
CMG (1966)

Bibliography

Archives

Banks

Archives historiques de la Banque de France, Paris (BdF)
Direction des études (1370200401)
Direction des publications économiques (1397199403)
Direction du réseau (1064199002)
Procès-verbaux du Conseil général (1069201116)
Bank of England Archive, London (BoE)
Administration Department (ADM)
Bankers Industrial Development Co., Ltd. Papers (BID)
Cashier's Department (C)
Committee of Treasury Files (G14)
Economic Intelligence Department (EID)
Establishment Department (E)
Exchange Control Department (EC)
Governor's Files (G1)
Minutes of the Committee of Treasury (G8)
Minutes of the Court of Directors (G4)
Museum Holdings (M)
Museum Photographic Print Collection (15A13)
Overseas Department (OV)
Recruitment Brochures (4A156)
R.N. Kershaw: Personal Papers (0A48/1)
Secretary's Files (G15)
Securities Management Trust, Ltd. Papers (SMT)
Banque nationale de Belgique, Brussels (BNB)
Barclays Group Archives, Manchester (BGA)
General Manager's Office (0011)
General Manager's Office, Sir John Caulcutt Papers (0080)

Baring Archive, London (BA)
Private Papers, John Baring, second Baron Revelstoke (Revelstoke Papers)
C. Hoare & Co. Archive, London (HCA)
Partnership Files (HB/2)
Administration (HB/7)
Federal Reserve Bank of New York, New York (FRBNY)
Benjamin Strong Jr. Papers (Strong Papers)
Committee on the History of the Federal Reserve System (History Committee)
Marriner S. Eccles Papers (Eccles Paper)
Minutes of the Board of Governors of the Federal Reserve System (Board Minutes)
HSBC Archives, London (HSBC)
Midland Bank, Corporate Governance (UK 0009)
Midland Bank, Head Office, Overseas Branch Manager Files (UK 0252)
Midland Bank, Management Committee, Supporting Papers (UK 0030)
Midland Bank, Records of Edward Holden, War Finance Papers (UK 0158)
Midland Bank, Records of Edward Holden and Samuel Murray (UK 0558)
Lloyds Banking Group Archives, London (LGA)
Records of the Head Office (HO)
Records of United Dominions Trust Limited (S/10)
Morgan Library & Museum, New York (MLM)
Morgan Bank European and Argentinean Records (ARC 1221)
Records of the Morgan Firms (ARC 1195)
National Bank of Greece Historical Archives, Athens (GR IATE)
Archive of Emmanuel Tsouderos (A3)
Oesterreichische Nationalbank, Bankhistorisches Archiv, Vienna (OeNB)
Sitzungsprotokolle des Direktoriums (I/5a)
Sitzungsprotokolle des Generalrates (I/4b)
Reserve Bank of Australia, Sydney (RBA)
Branch Records London (BRL)
Correspondence (C)
Secretary's Department (S)
The Rothschild Archive, London (RAL)
Correspondence Department (XI)
Schroders Archive, London (SA)
J. Henry Schröder & Co., Partners & Directors, Helmut Schroder, JHS/PD/HS (Schroder Papers)
J. Henry Schröder & Co., Partners & Directors, Henry Frederick Tiarks, JHS/PD/HFT (Tiarks Papers)

International Organizations

Bank for International Settlements Archives, Basel (BIS)
Hors Série, CH-000583-8 A.BISA.9.1.003 (Special Reports)
Pierre Quesnay Papers, CH-000583-8 A.BISA.7.18.3 (Quesnay Papers)
League of Nations, Geneva (LoN)
Commission Files (C)
Registry Files (R)
Section Files (S)

National, State, and City Archives and Libraries

Archives nationales de France, Pierrefitte-sur-Seine (ANF)
Pierre Quesnay Fonds, 374AP (Quesnay Papers)
Archivo General de la Nación, Buenos Aires (AGN)
Banco de la Nación Argentina (BNA01)
British Library, London (BL)
India Office Records and Private Papers (IOR)
Bundesarchiv, Berlin-Lichterfelde (BArch)
Reichsbank (R2501)
Reichsfinanzministerium (R3101)
Geheimes Staatsarchiv Preußischer Kulturbesitz, Berlin-Dahlem (GStA PK)
Finanzministerium (I. HA Rep. 151)
Ministerium des Innern (I. HA Rep. 77)
The London Archives, London (TLA)
British Bankers' Association (CLC/B/029)
The National Archives, Kew (TNA)
Board of Trade (BT)
Cabinet (CAB)
Civil Service Commission (CSC)
Colonial Office (CO)
Dominions Office (DO)
Foreign Office (FO)
Home Office (HO)
Treasury Papers (T)
National Library of Australia, Canberra (NLA)
Papers of Douglas Berry Copland, MS 3800 (Copland Papers)
National Archives of India, New Delhi (NAI)
Finance Department (F)
National Archives of South Africa, Pretoria (NASA)
Secretary of Home Affairs (BNS)
Secretary of the Treasury (TES)
Oesterreichisches Staatsarchiv, Archiv der Republik, Vienna (OeStA)
Bundeskanzleramt, Auswärtige Angelegenheiten, Abteilung 14/Handelspolitik (BKA-AA HP)
Bundeskanzleramt, Auswärtige Angelegenheiten, Abteilung 15/Völkerrecht (BKA-AA VR)
Bundesministerium für Finanzen, Departement 17/Frieden (BMF Dept. 17)
Politisches Archiv des Auswärtigen Amts, Berlin (PA AA)
Länderabteilung III (RZ 207)
Referat Völkerbund (RZ 209)

Universities, Institutes, and Research Centers

Archive Centre, King's College, Cambridge (KCC)
The Papers of John Maynard Keynes, GBR/0272/JMK (Keynes Papers)
Bodleian Libraries, Oxford (BLO)
Archive of Herbert Henry Asquith, 1st Earl of Oxford and Asquith (Asquith Papers)

Archive of Robert Henry Brand, Baron Brand (Brand Papers)
Cambridge University Archives, Cambridge (CUA)
Stanley Baldwin Papers, GBR/0012/MS Baldwin (Baldwin Papers)
Vickers Ltd: Records, GBR/0012/MS Vickers (Vickers Papers)
Churchill Archives Centre, Cambridge (CAC)
Papers of Leopold Amery (Amery Papers)
Papers of Reginald McKenna (McKenna Papers)
Papers of Sir Ralph Hawtrey (Hawtrey Papers)
Papers of Sir Winston Churchill (Chartwell Papers)
Columbia University, Rare Book & Manuscript Library, New York (CUL)
George Leslie Harrison Papers, MS0561 (Harrison Papers)
Fundação Getulio Vargas, Centro de Pesquisa e Documentação de História Contemporânea do Brasil, Rio de Janeiro (FGV)
Getúlio Vargas, Correspondência (Vargas Papers)
Oswaldo Aranha, Correspondência política (Aranha Papers)
Harvard Business School, Baker Library Special Collections, Cambridge (HBS)
Faculty Publication Series
Thomas W. Lamont Collection, MS Eng 1417 (Lamont Papers)
Institute for Advanced Study, Shelby White and Leon Levy Archives Center, Princeton (IAS)
Director's Office Records: Member Files (Director's Office)
London School of Economics and Political Science, Archives, London (LSE)
Edwin Cannan Papers, Private Correspondence (Cannan Papers)
National Records of Scotland, Edinburgh (NRS)
Papers of Philip Kerr, 11th Marquess of Lothian (Lothian Papers)
Nuffield College Library Archives, Oxford (NCO)
Sir Henry Clay Papers, MSS.HC (Clay Papers)
Princeton University, Seeley G. Mudd Manuscript Library, Princeton (PUL)
Edwin W. Kemmerer Papers, MC146 (Kemmerer Papers)
Queen's University Archives, Kingston (QUA)
Clifford Austin Curtis Fonds, F01144 (Curtis Papers)
John James Deutsch Fonds, F01192 (Deutsch Papers)
School of Oriental and African Studies, Special Collections, London (SOAS)
Papers of Sir Charles Stewart Addis, PP MS 14 (Addis Papers)
University of Auckland, Libraries and Learning Services, Auckland (UAL)
Horace Belshaw Papers, MSS-Archives-A-3 (Belshaw Papers)
University of Birmingham, Cadbury Research Library, Special Collections, Birmingham (UBL)
Papers of Neville Chamberlain, NC (Chamberlain Papers)
University of Canterbury, Macmillan Brown Library, Christchurch (MBL)
Albert Tocker Papers, MB 1357 (Tocker Papers)
University of the Free State, Archive for Contemporary Affairs, Bloemfontein (UFS)
John Edward Holloway, PV515 (Holloway Papers)
University of Toronto, Archives and Records Management Services, Toronto (UTA)
Gilbert Edward Jackson Fonds, 1425 (Jackson Papers)
University of Warwick, The Modern Records Centre, Coventry (MRC)
Federation of British Industries, MSS 200 (FBI)
University of the Witwatersrand, Historical Papers Research Archive, Johannesburg (UWA)

Jan Christian Smuts Papers, A1337 (Smuts Papers)
Samuel Evans Papers, A619 (Evans Papers)

Online Sources

Hansard, House of Commons Parliamentary Debates (HC Deb)
Hansard, House of Lords Debates (HL Deb)
Oxford Dictionary of National Biography (ODNB)

Newspapers and Periodicals

Place of publication is London unless otherwise indicated.

The Banker
The Bankers' Magazine
The Barrier Miner (Broken Hill)
The Canadian Magazine (Toronto)
Correio da Manhã (Rio de Janeiro)
The Daily Telegraph
Deutschösterreichische Tages-Zeitung (Vienna)
The Economic World (New York)
The Economist
The Evening News (Rockhampton)
Evening Sentinel (Stoke-on-Trent)
The Financial Post (Toronto)
Financial Times
The Gazette (Montreal)
The Guardian
Jornal do Commercio (Rio de Janeiro)
The Manchester Guardian (Manchester)
The Nation & Athenæum
The New York Times (New York)
The New York Times Blog (New York)
Neue Freie Presse (Vienna)
New Zealand Herald (Auckland)
O Jornal (Rio de Janeiro)
The Old Lady of Threadneedle Street
Otago Daily Times (Dunedin)
Press (Christchurch)
Rand Daily Mail (Johannesburg)
The Scotsman (Edinburgh)
Star (Christchurch)
Supplement to the Economist
The Telegraph
Le Temps (Paris)
The Times
The Times of India (Bombay)
Toronto Daily Star (Toronto)
The Vancouver Sun (Vancouver)

La Vanguardia (Buenos Aires)
The Wall Street Journal (New York)
Wiener Allgemeine Zeitung (Vienna)
Winnipeg Free Press (Winnipeg)

Official Publications

Acts of Parliament are cited according to the standard convention, using the regnal year. For instance, the Bank of England Act 1946, 9 & 10 Geo. 6 c. 27 refers to the 27th Act passed during a parliamentary session that began in the 9th year and ended in the 10th year of King George VI. Command papers are cited as Cd. (1900–18), Cmd. (1919–56), or Cmnd. (1956–86).

Official government reports elsewhere are abbreviated as follows: in South Africa, Union Government (UG) or Select Committee (SC) are used; in Australia, command papers in this period are denoted with a (C) and parliamentary papers with a number; in New Zealand, the Appendices to the Journals of the House of Representatives are categorized by subject with (A) denoting reports related to legislative and foreign affairs and (B) denoting reports related to finance; in Canada, the Order in Council number is preceded by Privy Council (PC).

Primary Sources

Acts of Parliament

Bank Act 1892, 55 & 56 Vict. c. 48.
Bank Charter Act 1844, 7 & 8 Vict. c. 32.
Bank of England Act 1946, 9 & 10 Geo. 6 c. 27.
Currency and Bank Notes Act 1928, 18 & 19 Geo. 5 c. 13.
Currency and Bank Notes (Amendment) Act 1914, 4 & 5 Geo. 5 c. 72.
Emergency Powers (Defence) Act 1939, 2 & 3 Geo. 6 c. 62.
Emergency Powers (Defence) Act (No. 2) 1940, 3 & 4 Geo. 6 c. 45.
Finance Act 1932, 22 & 23 Geo. 5 c. 25.
Gold and Silver (Export Control, &c.) Act 1920, 10 & 11 Geo. 5 c. 70.
The Gold Standard Act 1925, 15 & 16 Geo. 5 c. 29.
Government of India Act 1935, 26 Geo. 5. c. 2.
Unemployment Insurance Act 1920, 10 & 11 Geo. 5. c. 30.

Government Publications

Akten der Reichskanzlei. Die Kabinette Brüning I u. II, Band 2. 30. März 1930 bis 10. Oktober 1931; 10. Oktober 1931 bis 1. Juni 1932, edited by Tilman Koops. Boppard am Rhein: Harald Boldt Verlag, 1982.

Anglo-German Exchange Agreement Relating to Commercial Payments. Cmd. 4673. London: H.M. Stationery Office, 1934.

Anglo-German Payments Agreement. Cmd. 4726. London: H.M. Stationery Office, 1934.

Committee on Finance and Industry. *Report*. Cmd. 3897. London: H.M. Stationery Office, 1931.

Committee on Industry and Trade. *Final Report*. Cmd. 3282. London: H.M. Stationery Office, 1929.

Committee on National Expenditure. *Report*. Cmd. 3920. London: H.M. Stationery Office, 1931.

Committee on the Working of the Monetary System. *Minutes of Evidence*. London: H.M. Stationery Office, 1960.

Committee on the Working of the Monetary System. *Report*. Cmnd. 827. London: H.M. Stationery Office, 1959.

Copy of Report of the Treasury Committee on Bank Amalgamations. Cd. 9052. London: H.M. Stationery Office, 1918.

Department of Overseas Trade. *Economic Conditions in the Dominion of New Zealand*. London: H.M. Stationery Office, 1931.

Documents on British Foreign Policy, 1919–1939, First Series, vol. 7, edited by Rohan Butler and J.P.T. Bury. London: H.M. Stationery Office, 1958.

Documents on British Foreign Policy, 1919–1939, First Series, vol. 15, edited by Rohan Butler, J.P.T. Bury, and M.E. Lambert. London: H.M. Stationery Office, 1967.

Documents on British Foreign Policy, 1919–1939, First Series, vol. 19, edited by W.N. Medlicott, Douglas Dakin, and M.E. Lambert. London: H.M. Stationery Office, 1974.

Documents on British Foreign Policy, 1919–1939, First Series, vol. 24, edited by W.N. Medlicott, Douglas Dakin, and Gillian Bennett. London: H.M. Stationery Office, 1983.

Final Report of the Committee on Currency and Foreign Exchange Rates after the War. Cmd. 464. London: H.M. Stationery Office, 1919.

Final Reports of the Banking Commission. Dublin: The Stationery Office, 1927.

First Interim Report of the Committee on Currency and Foreign Exchange Rates after the War. Cd. 9182. London: H.M. Stationery Office, 1918.

Forbes, G.W. *Financial Statement (in Committee of Supply, 4th October, 1932)*. B.–6. Wellington: W.A.G. Skinner, Government Printer, 1932.

Imperial Economic Conference, Ottawa. A.–6. Wellington: W.A.G. Skinner, Government Printer, 1932.

Imperial Economic Conference: Records of Proceedings and Documents. Cmd. 2009. London: H.M. Stationery Office, 1924.

Imperial Economic Conference at Ottawa, 1932: Summary of Proceedings and Copies of Trade Agreements. Cmd. 4174. London: H.M. Stationery Office, 1932.

India Office. *Report of the Committee on Indian Reserve Bank Legislation*. London: India Office, 1933.

The Indian Central Banking Enquiry Committee, vol. 1: Part I, Majority Report. Calcutta: Government of India Central Publication Branch, 1931.

Indian Round Table Conference, 12th November, 1930–19th January, 1931: Proceedings. Cmd. 3778. London: H.M. Stationery Office, 1931.

Indian Round Table Conference, 12th November, 1930–19th January, 1931 (Sub-Committees' Reports; Conference Resolution; and Prime Minister's Statement. Cmd. 3772. London: H.M. Stationery Office, 1931.

Indian Round Table Conference (Third Session) (17th November, 1932–24th December, 1932). Cmd. 4238. London: H.M. Stationery Office, 1933.

Macmillan Committee. *Minutes of Evidence Taken before the Committee on Finance and Industry, vol. 1*. London: H.M. Stationery Office, 1931.

Macmillan Committee. *Minutes of Evidence Taken before the Committee on Finance and Industry, vol. 2*. London: H.M. Stationery Office, 1931.

Monetary Committee. *Minutes of Evidence*. B.–3. Wellington: W.A.G. Skinner, Government Printer, 1934.

Niemeyer, Otto. *Banking and Currency in New Zealand*. B.–3. Wellington: W.A.G. Skinner, Government Printer, 1931.

Niemeyer, Otto. *Indian Financial Enquiry: Report*. Cmd. 5163. London: H.M. Stationery Office, 1936.

Niemeyer, Otto. *Reorganização das finanças brasileiras. Relatório apresentado ao Governo Brasileiro*. Rio de Janeiro: Imprensa Nacional, 1931.

Parliament of the Commonwealth of Australia. *Conference of Commonwealth State Ministers, Held at Melbourne, 25th May to 11th June, 1931: Proceedings and Decisions of Conference*. C. 6744. Canberra: H.J. Green, 1931.

Report of the Committee on the Currency and Bank of England Note Issues. Cmd. 2393. London: H.M. Stationery Office, 1925.

Report of the Ministry of Labour for the Year 1930. Cmd. 3859. London: H.M. Stationery Office, 1931.

Report of the Royal Commission on Banking and Currency in Canada. Order in Council P.C. 1562. Ottawa: J.O. Patenaude, 1933.

Report of the Select Committee on Embargo on Export of Specie. S.C. 2–'20. Cape Town: Government Printers, 1920.

Report Presented by Monsieur van Zeeland to the Governments of the United Kingdom and France. Cmd. 5648. London: H.M. Stationery Office, 1938.

Report Submitted by Dr. Edwin Walter Kemmerer and Dr. Gerard Vissering on the Resumption of Gold Payments by the Union of South Africa. U.G. 13–'25. Pretoria: The Government Printing and Stationery Office, 1925.

República Federativa do Brasil. "Decreto no. 20.631 – de 9 de novembro de 1931." In República dos Estados Unidos do Brasil. *Coleção das leis de 1931, vol. 1*. Rio de Janeiro: Imprensa Nacional, 1931.

Royal Commission on Indian Currency and Finance. *Minutes of Evidence Taken in India, vol. 4*. London: H.M. Stationery Office, 1926.

Royal Commission on Indian Currency and Finance. *Minutes of Evidence Taken in India, vol. 5*. London: H.M. Stationery Office, 1926.

Royal Commission on Indian Finance and Currency. *Final Report of the Commissioners*. Cd. 7236. London: H.M. Stationery Office, 1914.

Royal Commission on Unemployment Insurance. *Final Report*. Cmd. 4185. London: H.M. Stationery Office, 1932.

Royal Commission on Unemployment Insurance. *First Report*. Cmd. 3872. London: H.M. Stationery Office, 1931.

Statutory Rules and Orders, 1939, vol. 1. London: H.M. Stationery Office, 1940.

Statutory Rules and Orders 1940, vol. 2. London: H.M. Stationery Office, 1941.

Summarised Report of the Proceedings of the Gold Conference Held at the Union Buildings, Wednesday, 22nd October 1919. U.G. 18–'20. Cape Town: Cape Times, 1920.

"Verordnung des Reichspräsidenten gegen die Kapital- und Steuerflucht." *Reichsgesetzblatt*, no. 35 (July 18, 1931): 373–376.

"Verordnung des Reichspräsidenten über die Devisenbewirtschaftung." *Reichsgesetzblatt*, no. 48 (August 1, 1931): 421–425.

Other Primary Sources

Academia de Ciencias Económicas. "La academia de ciencias económicas inició las sesiones del corriente año." *Revista de economía argentina* 27, no. 157 (1931): 304.

Acres, W. Marston. *The Bank of England from Within*, vol. 2. London: Oxford University Press, 1931.

Adarkar, B.P. "India's Monetary Muddle." *Sankhyā: The Indian Journal of Statistics (1933–1960)* 3, no. 4 (1938): 355–368.

Ambedkar, B.R. *The Problem of the Rupee: Its Origin and Its Solution*. London: P.S. King & Son, 1923.

Arndt, E.H.D. *Banking and Currency Development in South Africa (1652–1927)*. Cape Town and Johannesburg: Juta, 1928.

Arndt, E.H.D., and C.S. Richards. "The Banking System of South Africa." In *Foreign Banking Systems*, edited by H. Parker Willis and B.H. Beckhart, 955–1010. New York: H. Holt and Company, 1929.

Arnold, Percy. *The Bankers of London*. London: The Hogarth Press, 1938.

Bagehot, Walter. *Lombard Street: A Description of the Money Market*. London: Henry S. King & Co., 1873.

Bagehot, Walter. "A New Standard of Value." *The Economic Journal* 2, no. 7 (1892): 472–477.

Bank for International Settlements. *Fourth Annual Report: April 1, 1933–March 31, 1934*. Basle: Bank for International Settlements, 1934.

Bank of Canada. *First Annual General Meeting of Shareholders*. Ottawa: Bank of Canada, 1936.

Bank of England. "Copy of Bank of England Consultative Paper Issued in May 1971." In *The Banks and the Monetary System in the UK, 1959–1971*, edited by J.E. Wadsworth, 492–496. London: Methuen & Co., 1973.

Bank of England. "The Exchange Equalisation Account: Its Origins and Development." *Bank of England Quarterly Bulletin* 8, no. Q4 (1968): 377–390.

Bank of England. "Panel of Academic Consultants." *Bank of England Quarterly Bulletin* 19, Q2 (1979): 195.

Bank of England. "The U.K. Exchange Control: A Short History." *Bank of England Quarterly Bulletin* 7, no. Q3 (1967): 245–260.

Bank of England. "The Work of the Economic Intelligence Department." *Bank of England Quarterly Bulletin* 16, no. Q4 (1976): 436–446.

Baster, A.S.J. *The Imperial Banks*. London: P.S. King & Son, 1929.

Belshaw, H. "Crisis and Readjustment in New Zealand." *Journal of Political Economy* 41, no. 6 (1933): 750–775.

Birkenhead, Lord to Lord Irwin. April 5, 1928. In *Conservative Politics in National and Imperial Crisis: Letters from Britain to the Viceroy of India, 1926–31*, edited by Stuart Ball, 217. London and New York: Routledge, 2016.

Bowley, A.L., and A.R. Burnett-Hurst. *Livelihood and Poverty: A Study in the Economic Conditions of Working-Class Households in Northampton, Warrington, Stanley and Reading*. London: G. Bell and Sons, 1915.

Bowley, A.L., and Josiah Stamp. *The National Income, 1924*. Oxford: Clarendon Press, 1927.

Bowley, A.L., and M.H. Hogg. *Has Poverty Diminished?* London: P.S. King & Son, 1925.

Boyle, Andrew. *Montagu Norman: A Biography*. London: Cassell & Company, 1967.

Brüning, Heinrich. *Memoiren, 1918–1934*. Stuttgart: Deutsche Verlags-Anstalt, 1970.

Bunge, Alejandro E. "Die Rohstoffe und der wirtschaftliche Wiederaufbau Europas, unter besonderer Berücksichtigung Argentiniens." *Weltwirtschaftliches Archiv* 18 (1922): 335–347.

Butler, Eric D. *The Enemy within the Empire: A Short History of the Bank of England*. Melbourne: New Times, 1941.

Cairncross, Alec. "On Being an Economic Adviser." *Scottish Journal of Political Economy* 2, no. 2 (1955): 181–197.

Cairncross, Alec. *The Wilson Years: A Treasury Diary, 1964–1969*. London: Historians' Press, 1997.

Campbell, D.A.S. "The Report of the New Zealand Parliamentary Monetary Committee." *The Australian Quarterly* 6, no. 24 (1934): 126–128.

Cannan, Edwin. "The Demand for Labour." *The Economic Journal* 42, no. 167 (1932): 357–370.

Cannan, Edwin. "The Post-War Unemployment Problem." *The Economic Journal* 40, no. 157 (1930): 45–55.

Chamberlain, Austen. *Down the Years*. London: Cassell and Company, 1935.

Churchill, Winston. "British Financial Policy." *Advocate of Peace through Justice* 87, no. 8 (1925): 493–496.

Clark, W.C. "Financial Administration of the Government of Canada." *The Canadian Journal of Economics and Political Science/Revue canadienne d'Économique et de Science politique* 4, no. 3 (1938): 391–419.

Clay, Henry. "The Authoritarian Element in Distribution." *The Economic Journal* 37, no. 145 (1927): 1–18.

Clay, Henry. "The Economic Limits to Expenditure on Social Services." *The Manchester School of Economic and Social Studies* 3, no. 2 (1932): 85–105.

Clay, Henry. "The Financing of Industrial Enterprise." *Transactions of the Manchester Statistical Society* 20 (1932): 205–227.

Clay, Henry. "Industrial Reconstruction and the Government." *The Round Table* 9, no. 33 (1918): 135–162.

Clay, Henry. "Irresponsibility in Economic Life." *Political Quarterly* 2, no. 1 (1931): 64–81.

Clay, Henry. "The Liberal Industrial Report." *The Economic Journal* 38, no. 150 (1928): 193–203.

Clay, Henry. "Liberalism, Laissez Faire and Present Industrial Conditions." *The Hibbert Journal* 24, no. 4 (1926): 731–741.

Clay, Henry. *Lord Norman*. London: Macmillan, 1957.

Clay, Henry. *The Post-War Unemployment Problem*. London: Macmillan, 1929.

Clay, Henry. *The Problem of Industrial Relations and Other Lectures* London: Macmillan, 1929.

Clay, Henry. "Property and Inheritance." *The New Way Series* 1, no. 5 (1923): 3–30.

Clay, Henry. "The Public Regulation of Wages in Great Britain." *The Economic Journal* 39, no. 155 (1929): 323–343.

Clay, Henry. "Rationalisation: The Cotton Trade." *Lloyds Bank Limited Monthly Review* 2, no. 13 (1931): 87–94.

Clay, Henry. "Some Aspects of the World Depression, Lecture I." *Journal of the Institute of Bankers* LII, no. 9 (1931): 515–523.
Clay, Henry. "Some Aspects of the World Depression, Lecture II." *Journal of the Institute of Bankers* LIII, no. 1 (1932): 5–19.
Clay, Henry. "Some Aspects of the World Depression, Lecture III." *Journal of the Institute of Bankers* LIII, no. 1 (1932): 19–28.
Clay, Henry. "Unemployment." *Journal of the Royal Society of Arts* 78, no. 4065 (1930): 1211–1216.
Conférence financière internationale. *Rapport de la conférence*. Brussels: League of Nations, 1920.
Copland, Douglas. *Australia in the World Crisis, 1929–1933*. New York: Macmillan, 1934.
Copland, D.B. "Australian Banking Policy in the Crisis." *The Economic Journal* 42, no. 168 (1932): 583–587.
Copland, D.B. *Monetary Policy and Its Application to Australia*. Melbourne: Melbourne University Press, 1926.
Copland, D.B. "New Zealand's Economic Difficulties and Expert Opinion." *The Economic Journal* 42, no. 167 (1932): 371–379.
Copland, Douglas. "The Premiers' Plan in Australia: An Experiment in Economic Adjustment." *International Affairs (Royal Institute of International Affairs, 1931–1939)* 13, no. 1 (1934): 79–92.
Courtney, Janet E. *Recollected in Tranquility*. London: William Heinemann, 1926.
Coyajee, J.C. *India's Currency and Exchange Problems, 1925–1927*. Calcutta: The Book Company, 1927.
Coyajee, J.C. "Money Reconstruction in India (1925–27)." *The Annals of the American Academy of Political and Social Science* 145, no. 2 (1929): 101–114.
Curtis, C.A. "Canada and the Gold Standard." *Queen's Quarterly* 38, no. 1 (1931): 104–120.
Curtis, C.A. "The Canadian Monetary Situation." *Journal of Political Economy* 40 no. 3 (1932): 314–337.
Dangerfield, George. *The Strange Death of Liberal England*. New York: H. Smith & R. Haas, 1935.
Darling, J.F. *Economic Unity of the Empire: Gold and Credit*. London: P.S. King & Son, 1926.
Douglas, Iris. "The American Census of Distribution, 1930." *Journal of the Royal Statistical Society* 94, no. 3 (1931): 432–437.
Douglas, Iris. "Retail Trade Statistics in Different Countries." *Journal of the Royal Statistical Society* 98, no. 3 (1935): 455–496.
D'Abernon, Viscount. "The Economic Mission to South America." *Journal of the Royal Institute of International Affairs* 8, no. 6 (1929): 568–582.
Einzig, Paul. *Bankers, Statesmen and Economists*. London: Macmillan, 1935.
Einzig, Paul. *Exchange Control*. London: Macmillan, 1934.
Einzig, Paul. *Montagu Norman: A Study in Financial Statesmanship*. London: Kegan Paul, Trench, Trubner & Co., 1932.
Einzig, Paul. "The Unofficial Market in Sterling." *The Economic Journal* 49, no. 196 (1939): 670–677.
Einzig, Paul. *World Finance since 1914*. London: Kegan Paul, Trench, Trubner & Co., 1935.

Evans, Samuel. *The Gold Premium: Paper Read before the Chemical, Metallurgical and Mining Society of South Africa on Saturday, 15th May, 1920*. Johannesburg: McKowen & Radford, 1920.

Federal Reserve Board. *Tenth Annual Report of the Federal Reserve Board, Covering Operations for the Year 1923*. Washington, DC: Government Printing Office, 1924.

Federation of British Industries and the Empire Economic Union. *Report on Empire Monetary and Financial Policy*. London: Federation of British Industries, 1931.

Fisk, Harvey E. *The Inter-Ally Debts: An Analysis of War and Post-War Public Finance 1914–1923*. New York and Paris: Bankers Trust Company, 1924.

Gregory, Theodore. "The 'Norman Conquest' Reconsidered." *Lloyds Bank Review*, no. 46 (1957): 1–20.

Grundy, C.H. "A Plea for the Poor South of the Thames." *The Church of England Pulpit, and Ecclesiastical Review XI*, no. 262 (1881): 231–233.

Gudin Filho, Eugênio. *Câmbio e café, 1933–1934*. Rio de Janeiro: Oficinas Graphicas 'Almanak Laemmert,' 1934.

Hawtrey, R.G. *The Art of Central Banking*. London: Longmans, Green & Co., 1932.

Hawtrey, R.G. *Currency and Credit*. London: Longmans, Green & Co., 1919.

Hawtrey, R.G. "The Genoa Resolutions on Currency." *The Economic Journal* 32, no. 127 (1922): 290–304.

Hawtrey, R.G. *The Gold Standard in Theory and Practice*. London: Longmans, Green & Co., 1927.

Hawtrey, R.G. "La situation monétaire européenne." *Revue de métaphysique et de morale* 28, no. 2 (1921): 205–231.

Hawtrey, R.G. "Public Expenditure and Trade Depression." *Journal of the Royal Statistical Society* 96, no. 3 (1933): 438–477.

Henderson, Hubert. "The Economy Report." August 7, 1931. In *The Inter-War Years and Other Papers: A Selection from the Writings of Hubert Douglas Henderson*, edited by Henry Clay, 71–77. Oxford: Clarendon Press, 1955.

Hueyo, Alberto. *El Banco Central: aspectos fundamentales y antecedentes de su implantación en la República Argentina*. Buenos Aires: Francisco A. Colombo, 1958.

Jackson, Gilbert E. "The World in Which Our Central Bank Will Work." April 11, 1934. In *The Canadian Economy and Its Problems: Papers and Proceedings of Study Groups of Members of the Canadian Institute of International Affairs, 1933–1934*, edited by H.A. Innis and A.F.W. Plumptre, 300–317. Toronto: Canadian Institute of International Affairs, 1934.

Jevons, Herbert Stanley. *The Future of Exchange and the Indian Currency*. London: Oxford University Press, 1922.

Kemmerer, E.W. "The Establishment of the Gold Exchange Standard in the Philippines." *The Quarterly Journal of Economics* 19, no. 4 (1905): 585–609.

Keynes, John Maynard. "Alfred Marshall, 1842–1924." *The Economic Journal* 34, no. 135 (1924): 311–372.

Keynes, John Maynard. "The British Balance of Trade, 1925–27." *The Economic Journal* 37, no. 148 (1927): 551–565.

Keynes, John Maynard. "The City of London and the Bank of England, August, 1914." *The Quarterly Journal of Economics* 29, no. 1 (1914): 48–71.

Keynes, John Maynard. "The Committee on the Currency." *The Economic Journal* 35, no. 138 (1925): 299–304.

Keynes, John Maynard. "An Economic Analysis of Unemployment." June 1931. In *The Collected Writings of John Maynard Keynes, vol. 13: The General Theory and After, Part I: Preparation*, edited by Donald Moggridge, 343–367. Cambridge: Cambridge University Press, 1973.

Keynes, John Maynard. *The Economic Consequences of Mr Churchill*. London: The Hogarth Press, 1925.

Keynes, John Maynard. "The Finance Experts at Genoa." April 15, 1922. In *The Collected Writings of John Maynard Keynes, vol. 17: Activities 1920–1922, Treaty Revision and Reconstruction*, edited by Elizabeth Johnson, 380–384. Cambridge: Cambridge University Press, 1977.

Keynes, John Maynard. *How to Pay for the War: A Radical Plan for the Chancellor of the Exchequer*. London: Macmillan, 1940.

Keynes, John Maynard. *Indian Currency and Finance*. London: Macmillan, 1913.

Keynes, John Maynard. "Mr McKenna on Monetary Policy." February 12, 1927. In *The Collected Writings of John Maynard Keynes, vol. 9: Essays in Persuasion*, edited by Donald Moggridge, 201. Cambridge: Cambridge University Press, 1972.

Keynes, John Maynard. "Note on the Financial Arrangements between the United Kingdom and the Allies." April 9, 1917. In *The Collected Writings of John Maynard Keynes, vol. 16: Activities 1914–1919, The Treasury and Versailles*, edited by Elizabeth Johnson, 226–238. Cambridge: Cambridge University Press, 1971.

Keynes, John Maynard. "Notes on the Bank of England's Proposals for the Sterling Area." February 15, 1944. In *The Collected Writings of John Maynard Keynes, vol. 24: Activities 1944–1946, The Transition to Peace*, edited by Donald Moggridge, 19–22. Cambridge: Cambridge University Press, 1979.

Keynes, John Maynard. "Recent Economic Events in India." *The Economic Journal* 19, no. 73 (1909): 51–67.

Keynes, John Maynard. "Relation of Finance to British Industry." October 15, 1925. In *The Collected Writings of John Maynard Keynes, vol. 19: Activities 1922–1929, The Return to Gold and Industrial Policy*, edited by Donald Moggridge, 200–206. Cambridge: Cambridge University Press, 1981.

Keynes, John Maynard. *A Tract on Monetary Reform*. London: Macmillan, 1924.

Keynes, John Maynard. *A Treatise on Money, vol. 1*. London: Macmillan, 1930.

Keynes, John Maynard. *A Treatise on Money, vol. 2*. London: Macmillan, 1930.

Keynes, John Maynard. "War and the Financial System, August, 1914." *The Economic Journal* 24, no. 95 (1914): 460–486.

Keynes to Stamp. August 27, 1931. In *The Collected Writings of John Maynard Keynes, vol. 20: Activities 1929–1931: Rethinking Employment and Unemployment Policies*, edited by Donald Moggridge, 595. Cambridge: Cambridge University Press, 1981.

King, W.T.C. *History of the London Discount Market*. London: Routledge, 1936.

Knox, F.A. "The Nation's Money." *Queen's Quarterly* 41, no. 3 (1934): 289–306.

Leaf, Walter. *Banking*. New York: Henry Holt and Company, 1927.

League of Nations. *Commercial Banks, 1929–1934*. Geneva: League of Nations, 1935.

League of Nations. *The Financial Reconstruction of Austria: General Survey and Principal Documents*. Geneva: League of Nations, 1926.

League of Nations. *Financial Reconstruction of Austria: Report of the Financial Committee of the Council*. London: Constable & Co., League of Nations, 1921.

League of Nations. *Interim Report of the Gold Delegation of the Financial Committee*. Geneva: League of Nations, 1930.

League of Nations. *International Financial Conference, vol. 1: Report of the Conference.* Brussels: League of Nations, 1920.

League of Nations. *International Financial Conference, vol. 2: Verbatim Record of the Debates.* Brussels: League of Nations, 1920.

League of Nations. *International Financial Conference, vol. 3: Proceedings of the Conference.* Brussels: League of Nations, 1920.

League of Nations. *Report on Exchange Control.* Geneva: League of Nations, 1938.

Leith-Ross, Frederick. *Money Talks: Fifty Years of International Finance.* London: Hutchinson & Co., 1968.

Liberal Industrial Inquiry. *Britain's Industrial Future, Being the Report of the Liberal Industrial Inquiry.* London: Ernest Benn, 1928.

Lloyd George, David. *War Memoirs of David Lloyd George, vol. 1.* London: Ivor Nicholson & Watson, 1933.

Macmillan, Lord. *A Man of Law's Tale: The Reminiscences of the Rt. Hon. Lord Macmillan.* London: Macmillan, 1952.

McKenna, Reginald. *Post-War Banking Policy: A Series of Addresses.* London: William Heinemann, 1928.

Moreau, Émile. *Souvenirs d'un Gouverneur de la Banque de France : histoire de la stabilisation du franc (1926–1928).* Paris: Librairie de Médicis, 1954.

Niemeyer, Otto. *Informe y proyectos.* Buenos Aires: Ministerio de Hacienda de la Nación, 1933.

Niemeyer, Otto. "The Melbourne Conference, July and August, 1930." In *The Crisis in Australian Finance, 1929 to 1931: Documents on Budgetary and Economic Policy*, edited by E.O.G. Shann and D.B. Copland, 18–29. Sydney: Angus & Robertson, 1931.

Niemeyer, Otto. *Report Presented to the Argentine Government.* London: S.B. Chamberlain, 1933.

Norman to Keynes. February 28, 1940. In *The Collected Writings of John Maynard Keynes, vol. 22: Activities 1939–1945, Internal War Finance*, edited by Donald Moggridge, 104. Cambridge: Cambridge University Press, 1978.

Patterson, Norman. "London: The Heart of the Empire." *The Canadian Magazine (Toronto) XXVI*, no. 1 (1905): 3–11.

Pigou, A.C. "Wage Policy and Unemployment." *The Economic Journal* 37, no. 147 (1927): 355–368.

Polanyi, Karl. *The Great Transformation.* New York and Toronto: Farrar & Rinehart, 1944.

Pownall, George H. "Bank Reserves, the Central Stock of Gold, and £1 Notes." January 27, 1892. In *Transactions of the Manchester Statistical Society*, edited by Manchester Statistical Society, 13–75. London: John Heywood, 1891–1892.

Pownall, George H. "The Insufficiency of Our Cash Reserves and of Our Central Stock of Gold." *The Economic Journal* 2, no. 7 (1893): 530–543.

Reserve Bank of India. *Functions and Workings of the Reserve Bank of India.* Bombay: Reserve Bank of India, 1941.

Richards, C.S. "The Kemmerer–Vissering Report and the Position of the Reserve Bank of the Union of South Africa." *The Economic Journal* 35, no. 140 (1925): 558–567.

Rist, Charles. "The International Consequences of the Present Distribution of Gold Holdings." February 11, 1931. In *The International Gold Problem, Collected Papers: A Record of the Discussions of a Study Group of Members of the Royal Institute of*

International Affairs, 1929–1931, edited by Royal Institute of International Affairs, 193–222. London: Oxford University Press, 1931.
Rist, Charles. "La question de l'or." *Revue d'économie politique* 44, no. 6 (1930): 1489–1518.
Robbins, Lionel. *The Great Depression*. London: Macmillan, 1934.
Rooksby Steele, H., and F.R. Yerbury. *The Old Bank of England, London*. London: Ernest Benn, 1930.
Royal Commission on Indian Finance and Currency. Minutes of Evidence. 5 June 1913. In *The Collected Writings of John Maynard Keynes, vol. 15: Activities 1906–1914, India and Cambridge*, edited by Elizabeth Johnson, 100–106. Cambridge: Cambridge University Press, 1971.
Sakmann, Marianne. "Unemployment and Health Insurance in Great Britain, 1911–1937." In *Bureau of Research and Statistics*, edited by Social Security Board. Washington, DC: United States Government Printing Office, 1938.
Salter, Arthur. "The Reconstruction of Austria." *Foreign Affairs* 2, no. 4 (1924): 630–643.
Salter, Arthur, Josiah Stamp, John Maynard Keynes, Basil Blackett, Henry Clay, and W.H. Beveridge. *The World's Economic Crisis and the Way of Escape, Halley Stewart Lecture, 1931*. London: Allen & Unwin, 1932.
Schoonover, Lynn Irvine. "O.M.W. Sprague." *Harvard Business School Alumni Bulletin* 7, no. 1 (1930): 15–19.
Schuster, Felix. *The Bank of England and the State: A Lecture Delivered on 14th November, 1905*. Manchester: Manchester University Press, 1906.
Shirras, G. Findlay. *Indian Finance and Banking*. London: Macmillan, 1920.
Siepmann, Harry. *Echo of the Guns: Recollections of an Artillery Officer, 1914–18*. London: Robert Hale, 1987.
Siepmann, H.A. "The International Financial Conference at Brussels." *The Economic Journal* 30, no. 120 (1920): 436–459.
"Sir Henry Strakosch." In *The Annual Register: A Review of Public Events at Home and Abroad for the Year 1943*, edited by M. Epstein, 441. London: Longmans, Green & Co., 1944.
Smuts to Keynes. September 27, 1920. In *Selections from the Smuts Papers, vol. 5: September 1919–November 1934*, edited by Jean van der Poel, 29–30. Cambridge: Cambridge University Press, 1973.
South African Reserve Bank. *First Ordinary General Meeting of Stockholders: Report of Proceedings*. Pretoria: South African Reserve Bank, 1921.
Sprague, O.M.W. "The Aldrich Plan for Monetary Legislation." *The American Economic Review* 1, no. 2 (1911): 262–271.
Sprague, O.M.W. "The American Gold Problem and World Trade." *Proceedings of the Academy of Political Science* 19, no. 1 (1940): 80–87.
Sprague, O.M.W. *Banking Reform in the United States: A Series of Proposals, Including a Central Bank of Limited Scope*. Cambridge, MA: Harvard University Press, 1913.
Sprague, O.M.W. *History of Crises under the National Banking System*. Washington, DC: Government Printing Office, 1910.
Sprague, O.M.W. "Major and Minor Trade Fluctuations." *Journal of the Royal Statistical Society* 94, no. 4 (1931): 540–563.
Sprague, O.M.W. "The Proposal for a Central Bank in the United States: A Critical View." *The Quarterly Journal of Economics* 23, no. 3 (1909): 363–415.

Sprague, O.M.W. "Proposals for Strengthening the National Banking System. III." *The Quarterly Journal of Economics* 25, no. 1 (1910): 67–95.

Sprague, O.M.W. *Recovery and Common Sense*. Boston and New York: Houghton Mifflin Company, 1934.

Sprague, O.M.W. "Statistics and Economics." *Journal of the American Statistical Association* 29, no. 185 (1934): 162–164.

Sprague, O.M.W. "The Working of the Gold Standard under Present Conditions." *Proceedings of the Academy of Political Science* 13, no. 4 (1930): 72–78.

Stamp, Josiah. *Central Banking as an Imperial Factor*. Nottingham: University College, 1934.

Stamp, Josiah. "The Coal Mining Deadlock in Great Britain." *Foreign Affairs* 4, no. 4 (1926): 547–555.

Stamp, Josiah. *The Financial Aftermath of the War*. New York: Charles Scribner's Sons, 1932.

Stamp, Josiah. *Industrial and Railway Amalgamations*. London: London General Press, 1928.

Stamp, Josiah. "The International Functions of Gold: Introductory Survey." December 5, 1929. In *The International Gold Problem, Collected Papers: A Record of the Discussions of a Study Group of Members of the Royal Institute of International Affairs, 1929–1931*, edited by Royal Institute of International Affairs, 1–17. London: Oxford University Press, 1931.

Stamp, Josiah. "The Report of the Macmillan Committee." *The Economic Journal* 41, no. 163 (1931): 424–435.

Stamp, Josiah. *Some Economic Factors in Modern Life*. London: P.S. King & Son, 1929.

Stamp, Josiah. *Studies in Current Problems in Finance and Government*. London: P.S. King & Son, 1924.

State Governments of Australia. "Report of the Premiers' Conference, Adopted 10th June, 1931." In *The Battle of the Plans: Documents Relating to the Premiers' Conference, May 25th to June 11th, 1931*, edited by E.O.G. Shann and D.B. Copland, 126–136. Sydney: Angus & Robertson, 1931.

Stewart, Robert B. "Anglo-Argentine Trade Agreements." *The Canadian Journal of Economics and Political Science/Revue canadienne d'Économique et de Science politique* 2, no. 1 (1936): 16–26.

Stewart, Robert B. "Instruments of British Policy in the Sterling Area." *Political Science Quarterly* 52, no. 2 (1937): 174–207.

Stone, N.I., W.C. Schluter, and Walter W. Stewart. "Controlling Business Cycles – Discussion." *The American Economic Review* 12, no. 1 (1922): 33–43.

Strakosch, Henry. "The Convention on Financial Assistance." *International Affairs* 10, no. 2 (1931): 208–222.

Strakosch, Henry. *The South African Currency and Exchange Problem*. Johannesburg: Central News Agency, 1920.

Strakosch, Henry. *The South African Currency and Exchange Problem Re-Examined*. Johannesburg: Central News Agency, 1922.

Strakosch, Henry. "The South African Reserve Bank." *The Economic Journal* 31, no. 122 (1921): 172–178.

Strakosch, Henry. *The Value of Gold in Our Economic System*. London: Crowther & Goodman, 1918.

Tocker, A.H. "The Reserve Bank of New Zealand." *Economic Record* 10, no. 18 (1935): 88–91.

Truptil, R.J. *British Banks and the London Money Market*. London: Jonathan Cape, 1936.

Van Walré de Bordes, J. *The Austrian Crown: Its Depreciation and Stabilization*. London: P.S. King and Son, 1924.

Webb, Sidney, and Beatrice Webb. *The History of Trade Unionism, 1666–1920*. London: Longmans, Green & Co., 1920.

Weber, Max. *Grundriß der Sozialökonomik, III. Abteilung: Wirtschaft und Gesellschaft*. Tübingen: Verlag von J.C.B. Mohr [Paul Siebeck], 1922.

Whitley, John. "Economic Models and Policy-Making." *Bank of England Quarterly Bulletin* 37, no. Q2 (1997): 163–173.

Witmer, Helen Leland. "Some Effects of the English Unemployment Insurance Acts on the Number of Unemployed Relieved Under the Poor Law." *The Quarterly Journal of Economics* 45, no. 2 (1931): 262–288.

Secondary Sources

"A8. Real Compromise/Balanced Estimates of GDP – 'GDP(a),' 1700–2016." In *A Millennium of Macroeconomic Data for the UK: The Bank of England's Collection of Historical Macroeconomic and Financial Statistics*, Version 3.1, 2018, www.bankofengland.co.uk/statistics/research-datasets.

Abbenhuis, Maartje, and Gordon Morrell. *The First Age of Industrial Globalization: An International History, 1815–1918*. London: Bloomsbury, 2020.

Abramson, Daniel M. *Building the Bank of England: Money, Architecture, Society, 1694–1942*. New Haven and London: Yale University Press, 2005.

Abreu, Marcelo de Paiva. "A economia brasileira, 1930–1964." *Pontifícia Universidade Católica do Rio de Janeiro Working Paper*, no. 585 (2010).

Abreu, Marcelo de Paiva. "A missão Niemeyer." *Revista de Administração de Empresas* 14, no. 4 (1974): 7–28.

Abreu, Marcelo de Paiva, and Pedro Carvalho Loureiro de Souza. "'Palatable Foreign Control': British Money Doctors and Central Banking in South America, 1924–1935." *Pontifícia Universidade Católica do Rio de Janeiro, Texto para discussão*, no. 597 (2011).

Accominotti, Olivier. "International Banking and Transmission of the 1931 Financial Crisis." *Economic History Review* 72, no. 1 (2019): 260–285.

Accominotti, Olivier. "London Merchant Banks, the Central European Panic, and the Sterling Crisis of 1931." *The Journal of Economic History* 72, no. 1 (2012): 1–43.

Accominotti, Olivier, Marc Flandreau, and Riad Rezzik. "The Spread of Empire: Clio and the Measurement of Colonial Borrowing Costs." *The Economic History Review* 64, no. 2 (2011): 385–407.

Accominotti, Olivier, Delio Lucena-Piquero, and Stefano Ugolini. "The Origination and Distribution of Money Market Instruments: Sterling Bills of Exchange during the First Globalization." *The Economic History Review* 74, no. 4 (2021): 892–921.

Ackrill, Margaret, and Leslie Hannah. *Barclays: The Business of Banking, 1690–1996*. Cambridge: Cambridge University Press, 2001.

Acosta, Juan, Beatrice Cherrier, François Claveau, Clément Fontan, Aurélien Goutsmedt, and Francesco Sergi. "Six Decades of Economic Research at the Bank of England." *History of Political Economy* 56, no. 1 (2024): 1–40.

Addison, Paul. *Churchill on the Home Front, 1900–1955*. London: Jonathan Cape, 1992.

Ahamed, Liaquat. *Lords of Finance: The Bankers Who Broke the World*. New York: Penguin, 2009.

Aldcroft, Derek H. "The Development of the Managed Economy before 1939." *Journal of Contemporary History* 4, no. 4 (1969): 117–137.

Aldcroft, Derek H., and Michael J. Oliver. *Trade Unions and the Economy, 1870–2000*. Aldershot: Ashgate, 2000.

Allen, William A. *The Bank of England and the Government Debt: Operations in the Gilt-Edged Market, 1928–1972*. Cambridge: Cambridge University Press, 2019.

Allen, William A. *Monetary Policy and Financial Repression in Britain, 1951–59*. New York: Palgrave Macmillan, 2014.

Ally, Russell. *Gold & Empire: The Bank of England and South Africa's Gold Producers, 1886–1926*. Johannesburg: Witwatersrand University Press, 2001.

Álvarez, Andrés, Vincent Bignon, Anders Ögren, and Masato Shizume, eds. *Money Doctors around the Globe: A Historical Perspective*. Singapore: Springer, 2024.

Amsler, Christine. "Keynes and Bank Rate Policy: Interest Rates Inconsistent with Full Employment." *Journal of Post Keynesian Economics* 15, no. 3 (1993): 409–425.

Andréadès, A. *Histoire de la Banque d'Angleterre : ses origines, sa fondation, son développement, Tome deuxième, 1819–1903*. Paris: Arthur Rousseau, 1904.

Appelbaum, Binyamin. *The Economists' Hour: False Prophets, Free Markets, and the Fracture of Society*. New York: Little, Brown and Company, 2019.

Arch, Linda. *The Regulation of the London Clearing Banks, 1946–1971: Stability and Compliance*. Cham: Palgrave Macmillan, 2018.

Arena, Lise. "From Economics of the Firm to Business Studies at Oxford: An Intellectual History (1890s–1990s)." DPhil diss., University of Oxford, 2011.

Arnold, Guy. *Economic Co-operation in the Commonwealth*. Oxford: Pergamon Press, 1967.

Artaud, Denise. *La reconstruction de l'Europe (1919–1929)*. Paris: Presses universitaires de France, 1973.

Arthmar, Rogério, and Michael McLure. "On Britain's Return to the Gold Standard: Was There a 'Pigou–McKenna School'?" *Economic Record* 92, no. S1 (2016): 1–14

Arthur, Simon James. "The Independence of the Bank of England: A Sociological Investigation." PhD diss., University of Warwick, 2022.

Atkin, John. *The Foreign Exchange Market of London: Development since 1900*. London and New York: Routledge, 2005.

Attard, Bernard. "The Bank of England and the Origins of the Niemeyer Mission, 1921–30." *Australian Economic Review* 32, no. 1 (1992): 66–83.

Attard, Bernard. "Financial Diplomacy." In *Between Empire and Nation: Australia's External Relations from Federation to the Second World War*, edited by Carl Bridge and Bernard Attard, 111–132. Melbourne: Australian Scholarly Publishing, 2000.

Attard, Bernard. "Imperial Central Banks? The Bank of England, the London & Westminster Bank, and the British Empire before 1914." In *Les banques centrales et l'État-nation*, edited by Olivier Feiertag and Michel Margairaz, 187–212. Paris: Presses de Sciences Po, 2016.

Avaro, Maylis. "Zombie International Currency: The Pound Sterling 1945–1971." *The Journal of Economic History* 84, no. 3 (2024): 917–952.

Backhouse, Roger E., and Tamotsu Nishizawa. "Welfare Economics, Old and New." In *No Wealth but Life: Welfare Economics and the Welfare State in Britain,*

1880–1945, edited by Roger E. Backhouse and Tamotsu Nishizawa, 223–235. Cambridge: Cambridge University Press, 2010.

Baker, Andrew. "Tower of Contrarian Thinking: How the BIS Helped Reframe Understandings of Financial Stability." In *Promoting Global Monetary and Financial Stability: The Bank for International Settlements after Bretton Woods, 1973–2020*, edited by Claudio Borio, Stijn Claessens, Piet Clement, Robert N. McCauley, and Hyun Song Shin, 134–167. Cambridge: Cambridge University Press, 2020.

Bakić, Dragan. *Britain and Interwar Danubian Europe: Foreign Policy and Security Challenges, 1919–1936*. London: Bloomsbury, 2017.

Bakić, Dragan. "Diplomacy and Loans: The Foreign Office, Economic Reconstruction, and Security in South-Eastern Europe in the 1920s." *The International History Review* 34, no. 4 (2012): 631–653.

Balachandran, G. "Central Banking and Colonial Control: India, 1914–1939." In *The Spread of the Modern Central Bank and Global Cooperation, 1919–1939*, edited by Barry Eichengreen and Andreas Kakridis, 383–405. Cambridge: Cambridge: University Press, 2023.

Balachandran, G. "Gold, Silver, and India in Anglo-American Monetary Relations, 1925–1933." *The International History Review* 18, no. 3 (1996): 573–590.

Balachandran, G. "Gold and Empire: Britain and India in the Great Depression." *Journal of European Economic History* 20, no. 2 (1991): 239–270.

Balachandran, G. *John Bullion's Empire: Britain's Gold Problem and India between the Wars*. Richmond: Curzon Press, 1996.

Balachandran, G. "Towards a 'Hindoo Marriage': Anglo-Indian Monetary Relations in Interwar India, 1917–35." *Modern Asian Studies* 28, no. 3 (1994): 615–647.

Balasubramanian, Aditya, and Srinath Raghavan. "Present at the Creation: India, the Global Economy, and the Bretton Woods Conference." *Journal of World History* 29, no. 1 (2018): 65–94.

Balderston, T. "War Finance and Inflation in Britain and Germany, 1914–1918." *The Economic History Review* 42, no. 2 (1989): 222–244.

Bamberg, J.H. "The Rationalization of the British Cotton Industry in the Interwar Years." *Textile History* 19, no. 1 (1988): 83–101.

Banco Central de Reserva del Perú. *La Misión Kemmerer en el Perú: informes y propuestas, Tomo 1*. Lima: Banco Central de Reserva del Perú, 1997.

Banholzer, Simon, and Tobias Straumann. "Why the French Said 'Non': A New Perspective on the Hoover Moratorium of June 1931." *Journal of Contemporary History* 56, no. 4 (2021): 1040–1060.

Bátonyi, Gábor. *Britain and Central Europe, 1918–1933*. Oxford: Clarendon Press, 1999.

Baughan, Emily. *Saving the Children: Humanitarianism, Internationalism, and Empire*. Oakland: University of California Press, 2022.

Bazot, Guillaume, Eric Monnet, and Matthias Morys. "Taming the Global Financial Cycle: Central Banks as Shock Absorbers in the First Era of Globalization." *The Journal of Economic History* 82, no. 3 (2022): 801–839.

Beckert, Sven. *Empire of Cotton: A Global History*. New York: Alfred A. Knopf, 2014.

Belich, James. *Replenishing the Earth: The Settler Revolution and the Rise of the Anglo-World, 1783–1939*. Oxford and New York: Oxford University Press, 2009.

Belini, Claudio. "El grupo Bunge y la política económica del primer peronismo, 1943–1952." *Latin American Research Review* 41, no. 1 (2006): 27–50.

Bemmann, Martin. "Das Chaos beseitigen. Die internationale Standardisierung forst- und holzwirtschaftlicher Statistiken in den 1920er und 1930er Jahren und der Völkerbund." *Jahrbuch für Wirtschaftsgeschichte* 57, no. 2 (2016): 545–587.

Bemmann, Martin. *Weltwirtschaftsstatistik. Internationale Wirtschaftsstatistik und die Geschichte der Globalisierung, 1850–1950*. Berlin and Boston: De Gruyter Oldenbourg, 2023.

Berman, Elizabeth Popp. *Thinking Like an Economist: How Efficiency Replaced Equality in U.S. Public Policy*. Princeton and Oxford: Princeton University Press, 2022.

Bernanke, Ben, and Harold James. "The Gold Standard, Deflation, and Financial Crisis in the Great Depression: An International Comparison." In *Essays on the Great Depression*, edited by Ben Bernanke, 33–68. Princeton: Princeton University Press, 2000.

Best, Jacqueline. "Uncomfortable Knowledge in Central Banking: Economic Expertise Confronts the Visibility Dilemma." *Economy and Society* 51, no. 4 (2022): 559–583.

Best, Michael H., and Jane Humphries. "The City and Industrial Decline." In *The Decline of the British Economy*, edited by Bernard Elbaum and William Lazonick, 223–239. Oxford: Clarendon Press, 1986.

Bew, John. *Clement Attlee: The Man Who Made Modern Britain*. New York: Oxford University Press, 2017.

Beyersdorf, Frank. "'Credit or Chaos'? The Austrian Stabilisation Programme of 1923 and the League of Nations." In *Internationalism Reconfigured: Transnational Ideas and Movements between the World Wars*, edited by Daniel Laqua, 135–157. London: I.B. Tauris, 2011.

Bignon, Vincent, Marc Flandreau, and Stefano Ugolini. "Bagehot for Beginners: The Making of Lender-of-Last-Resort Operations in the Mid-Nineteenth Century." *The Economic History Review* 65, no. 2 (2012): 580–608.

Billings, Mark, and Forrest Capie. "Financial Crisis, Contagion, and the British Banking System between the World Wars." *Business History* 53, no. 2 (2011): 193–215.

Billings, Mark, Simon Mollan, and Philip Garnett. "Debating Banking in Britain: The Colwyn Committee, 1918." *Business History* 63, no. 6 (2021): 944–965.

Bindseil, Ulrich. *Central Banking before 1800: A Rehabilitation*. Oxford: Oxford University Press, 2019.

Blaazer, David. "Finance and the End of Appeasement: The Bank of England, the National Government and the Czech Gold." *Journal of Contemporary History* 40, no. 1 (2005): 25–39.

Blaazer, David. *Forging Nations: Currency, Power, and Nationality in Britain and Ireland since 1603*. Oxford: Oxford University Press, 2023.

Black, Iain. "Imperial Visions: Building the Bank of England, 1919–39." In *Imperial Cities: Landscape, Display and Identity*, edited by Felix Driver and David Gilbert, 96–113. Manchester and New York: Manchester University Press, 1999.

Blanco, Alejandro, and Darlan Praxedes Barboza. "Raúl Prebisch y Federico Pinedo: técnica y política en la 'década infame.'" *Desarrollo Económico* 60, no. 232 (2021): 314–337.

Blaug, Mark. "Second Thoughts on the Keynesian Revolution." *History of Political Economy* 23, no. 2 (1991): 171–192.

Blyth, Mark. *Austerity: The History of a Dangerous Idea*. Oxford: Oxford University Press, 2013.

Bollard, Alan. *Economists at War: How a Handful of Economists Helped Win and Lose the World Wars*. Oxford: Oxford University Press, 2020.

Bonin, Hubert. "The Challenged Competitiveness of the Paris Banking and Finance Markets, 1914–1958." In *London and Paris as International Financial Centres in the Twentieth Century*, edited by Youssef Cassis and Eric Bussière, 183–204. Oxford: Oxford University Press, 2005.

Boobbyer, Philip. *The Life and World of Francis Rodd, Lord Rennell (1895–1978): Geography, Money and War*. London: Anthem Press, 2021.

Booker, John Michael Lloyd. "The Architecture of Banking: A Study of the Design of British Banks from the 18th Century to Modern Times." PhD diss., University of York, 1984.

Booth, Alan. "Britain in the 1930s: A Managed Economy?" *The Economic History Review* 40, no. 4 (1987): 499–522.

Booth, Alan. "Britain in the 1930s: A Managed Economy? A Reply to Peden and Middleton." *The Economic History Review* 42, no. 4 (1989): 548–556.

Booth, Alan. *British Economic Policy, 1931–49: Was There a Keynesian Revolution?* Hertfordshire: Harvester Wheatsheaf, 1989.

Booth, Alan. "Economic Advice at the Centre of British Government, 1939–1941." *The Historical Journal* 29, no. 3 (1986): 655–675.

Booth, Alan, and A.W. Coats. "Some Wartime Observations on the Role of the Economist in Government." *Oxford Economic Papers* 32, no. 2 (1980): 177–199.

Borchardt, Knut. "Wirtschaftspolitische Beratung in der Krise. Die Rolle der Wissenschaft." In *Die deutsche Staatskrise, 1930–1933. Handlungsspielräume und Alternativen*, edited by Heinrich August Winkler, 109–132. Munich: R. Oldenbourg Verlag, 1992.

Bordiss, Bradley, and Vishnu Padayachee. "'A Superior Practical Man': Sir Henry Strakosch, the Gold Standard and Monetary Policy Debates in South Africa, 1920–23." *Economic History of Developing Regions* 26, no. 1 (2011): 114–122.

Bordo, Michael D. "The Gold Standard: The Traditional Approach." In *A Retrospective on the Classical Gold Standard, 1821–1931*, edited by Michael D. Bordo and Anna J. Schwartz, 23–119. Chicago and London: The University of Chicago Press, 1984.

Bordo, Michael D. "The Lender of Last Resort: Alternative Views and Historical Experience." *Federal Reserve Bank of Richmond Economic Review* 76, no. 1 (1990): 18–29.

Bordo, Michael, Michael Edelstein, and Hugh Rockoff. "Was Adherence to the Gold Standard a 'Good Housekeeping Seal of Approval' during the Interwar Period?" In *Finance, Intermediaries, and Economic Development*, edited by Stanley L. Engerman, Philip T. Hoffman, Jean-Laurent Rosenthal, and Kenneth L. Sokoloff, 288–318. Cambridge: Cambridge University Press, 2003.

Bordo, Michael D., and Finn E. Kydland. "The Gold Standard as a Rule." In *The Gold Standard in Theory and History*, 2nd ed., edited by Barry Eichengreen and Marc Flandreau, 77–99. London and New York: Routledge, 1997.

Bordo, Michael D., and Angela Redish. "Why Did the Bank of Canada Emerge in 1935?" *The Journal of Economic History* 47, no. 2 (1987): 405–417.

Bordo, Michael D., Angela Redish, and Hugh Rockoff. "Why Didn't Canada Have a Banking Crisis in 2008 (Or in 1930, or 1907, Or ...)?" *Economic History Review* 68, no. 1 (2015): 218–243.

Bordo, Michael D., and Hugh Rockoff. "The Gold Standard as a 'Good Housekeeping Seal of Approval.'" *The Journal of Economic History* 56, no. 2 (1996): 389–428.

Borges, Maria Angélica. *Eugênio Gudin: capitalismo e neoliberalismo.* São Paulo: EDUC, 1996.

Bosmans, J.L.J. *De Nederlander. Mr. A.R. Zimmerman als commissaris-generaal van de Volkenbond in Oostenrijk 1922–1926.* Nijmegen: Drukkerij Gebr. Janssen N.V., 1973.

Bouvier, Jean. "Contrôle des changes et politique économique extérieure de la SFIO en 1936." *Relations internationales*, no. 13 (1978): 111–115.

Bowden, Sue, and Michael Collins. "The Bank of England, Industrial Regeneration, and Hire Purchase between the Wars." *The Economic History Review* 45, no. 1 (1992): 120–136.

Boyce, Robert. "The Bank of England in the First World War and Its Aftermath: The Price of Victory." In *Les banques centrales pendant la Grande Guerre*, edited by Olivier Feiertag, 225–248. Paris: Presses de Sciences Po, 2019.

Boyce, Robert. "La Banque de France et la Banque d'Angleterre dans l'entre-deux-guerres: origines et conséquences d'un conflit." In *Politiques et pratiques des banques d'émission en Europe (XVIIe–XXe siècle) : le bicentenaire de la Banque de France dans la perspective de l'identité monétaire européenne*, edited by Olivier Feiertag and Michel Margairaz, 451–474. Paris: Albin Michel, 2003.

Boyce, Robert W.D. *British Capitalism at the Crossroads, 1919–1932: A Study in Politics, Economics, and International Relations.* Cambridge: Cambridge University Press, 1987.

Boyce, Robert. "Creating the Myth of Consensus: Public Opinion and Britain's Return to the Gold Standard in 1925." In *Money and Power: Essays in Honour of L.S. Pressnell*, edited by P.L. Cottrell and D.E. Moggridge, 173–197. Basingstoke: Macmillan, 1988.

Boyce, Robert. "Government–City of London Relations under the Gold Standard 1925–1931." In *The British Government and the City of London in the Twentieth Century*, edited by Ranald Michie and Philip Williamson, 215–235. Cambridge: Cambridge University Press, 2004.

Boyce, Robert. *The Great Interwar Crisis and the Collapse of Globalization.* Basingstoke: Palgrave Macmillan, 2009.

Boyer, George R. *The Winding Road to the Welfare State: Economic Insecurity and Social Welfare Policy in Britain.* Princeton and Oxford: Princeton University Press, 2019.

Bräu, Ramona. *Die Plünderung Polens. Die Reichsfinanzverwaltung in den Jahren der Besatzung (1939–1945).* Berlin: De Gruyter Oldenbourg, 2022.

Braun, Benjamin. "Speaking to the People? Money, Trust, and Central Bank Legitimacy in the Age of Quantitative Easing." *Review of International Political Economy* 23, no. 6 (2016): 1064–1092.

Brecher, Irving. *Monetary and Fiscal Thought and Policy in Canada, 1919–1939.* Toronto: University of Toronto Press, 1957.

Breckenridge, Keith. "'Money with Dignity': Migrants, Minelords and the Cultural Politics of the South African Gold Standard Crisis, 1920–33." *The Journal of African History* 36, no. 2 (1995): 271–304.

Bridges, Edward. *Portrait of a Profession: The Civil Service Tradition.* Cambridge: Cambridge University Press, 1950.

Bridges, Mary. *Dollars and Dominion: US Bankers and the Making of a Superpower.* Princeton and Oxford: Princeton University Press, 2024.

Briggs, Asa, ed. "Cerberus and the Sphinx: Modern Greats in Oxford." In *Serious Pursuits: Communications and Education: The Collected Essays of Asa Briggs, vol. 3*, 320–326. Urbana: University of Illinois Press, 1991.

Broadberry, S.N. *The British Economy between the Wars: A Macroeconomic Survey.* Oxford: Basil Blackwell, 1986.

Broadberry, Stephen. *Market Services and the Productivity Race, 1850–2000: British Performance in International Perspective.* Cambridge: Cambridge University Press, 2006.

Broadberry, Stephen, and Mark Harrison. "The Economics of World War I: An Overview." In *The Economics of World War I*, edited by Stephen Broadberry and Mark Harrison, 3–40. Cambridge: Cambridge University Press, 2005.

Broadberry, Stephen, and Peter Howlett. "The United Kingdom during World War I: Business as Usual?" In *The Economics of World War I*, edited by Stephen Broadberry and Mark Harrison, 206–234. Cambridge: Cambridge University Press, 2005.

Broadberry, Stephen, and Andrew Marrison. "External Economies of Scale in the Lancashire Cotton Industry, 1900–1950." *Economic History Review* 55, no. 1 (2002): 51–77.

Brooke, Geoffrey T.F., Anthony M. Endres, and Alan J. Rogers. "The Economists and Monetary Thought in Interwar New Zealand: The Gradual Emergence of Monetary Policy Activism." *History of Economics Review* 73, no. 1 (2019): 14–46.

Bruley, Sue. *The Women and Men of 1926: A Gender and Social History of the General Strike and Miners' Lockout in South Wales.* Cardiff: University of Wales Press, 2010.

Bruner, Robert F., and Sean D. Carr. *The Panic of 1907: Lessons Learned from the Market's Perfect Storm.* Hoboken: John Wiley & Sons, 2007.

Bryce, Robert B. *Maturing in Hard Times: Canada's Department of Finance through the Great Depression.* Kingston and Montreal: McGill-Queen's University Press, 1986.

Bryce, Robert B. "William Clifford Clark, 1889–1952." *The Canadian Journal of Economics and Political Science/Revue canadienne d'Économique et de Science Politique*, 19, no. 3 (1953): 413–423.

Buescu, Mircea. "A missão inglesa de 1924." *Revista de informação legislativa* 21, no. 82 (1984): 173–186.

Burk, Kathleen. *Britain, America and the Sinews of War, 1914–1918.* London: G. Allen & Unwin, 1985.

Burk, Kathleen. "J.M. Keynes and the Exchange Rate Crisis of July 1917." *The Economic History Review* 32, no. 3 (1979): 405–416.

Burk, Kathleen. *Morgan Grenfell, 1838–1988: The Biography of a Merchant Bank.* Oxford: Oxford University Press, 1989.

Burk, Kathleen. "The Treasury: From Impotence to Power." In *In War and the State: The Transformation of British Government, 1914–1919*, 84–107. London: George Allen & Unwin, 1982.

Burk, Kathleen. "War and Anglo-American Financial Relations in the Twentieth Century." In *Anglo-American Attitudes: From Revolution to Partnership*, edited by Fred M. Leventhal and Roland Quinault, 243–260. Abingdon: Ashgate, 2000.

Burk, Kathleen, and Alec Cairncross. *'Goodbye, Great Britain': The 1976 IMF Crisis.* New Haven and London: Yale University Press, 1992.

Burn, Gary. *The Re-Emergence of Global Finance.* Basingstoke: Palgrave Macmillan, 2006.

Busch, Andreas. *Banking Regulation and Globalization.* Oxford: Oxford University Press, 2012.

Bussière, Éric. "L'Organisation économique de la SDN et la naissance du régionalisme économique en Europe." *Relations internationales*, no. 75 (1993): 301–313.

Butlin, M.W., and P.M. Boyce. "Monetary Policy in Depression and Recovery." In *Recovery from the Depression: Australia and the World Economy in the 1930s*, edited by R.G. Gregory and N.G. Butlin, 193–215. Cambridge: Cambridge University Press, 1989.

Bytheway, Simon James, and Mark Metzler. *Central Banks and Gold: How Tokyo, London, and New York Shaped the Modern World*. Ithaca and London: Cornell University Press, 2016.

Cain, Frank. *Jack Lang and the Great Depression*. Melbourne: Australian Scholarly Publishing, 2005.

Cain, Neville. "Australian Economic Advice in 1930: Liberal and Radical Alternatives." *Australian National University Working Papers in Economic History*, no. 78 (1987).

Cain, P.J. "Gentlemanly Imperialism at Work: The Bank of England, Canada, and the Sterling Area, 1932–1936." *The Economic History Review* 49, no. 2 (1996): 336–357.

Cain, P.J., and A.G. Hopkins. *British Imperialism, 1688–2015*, 3rd ed. London and New York: Routledge, 2016.

Cairncross, Alec. *Austin Robinson: The Life of an Economic Adviser*. Basingstoke: Macmillan, 1993.

Cairncross, Alec. "The Bank of England: Relationships with the Government, the Civil Service, and Parliament." In *Central Banks' Independence in Historical Perspective*, edited by Gianni Toniolo, 39–72. Berlin and New York: Walter de Gruyter, 1988.

Cairncross, Alec. "The Bank of England and the British Economy." In *The Bank of England: Money, Power and Influence, 1694–1994*, edited by Richard Roberts and David Kynaston, 56–82. Oxford: Clarendon Press, 1995.

Cairncross, Alec. "Economic Advisers in the United Kingdom." *Contemporary British History* 13, no. 2 (1999): 232–242.

Cairncross, Alec. "Ely Devons: A Memoir." In *Papers on Planning and Economic Management*, edited by Alec Cairncross, 1–16. Manchester: Manchester University Press, 1970.

Cairncross, Alec. "Preface." In *The Robert Hall Diaries, 1947–1953*, edited by Alec Cairncross, vii–ix. London: Unwin Hyman, 1989.

Cairncross, Alec. "The United Kingdom." In *The Role of the Economist in Government: An International Perspective*, edited by Joseph A. Pechman, 25–46. New York and London: Harvester Wheatsheaf, 1989.

Cairncross, Alec. "The Work of an Economic Adviser." November 6, 1967. In *Essays in Economic Management*, edited by Alec Cairncross, 184–196. London: George Allen & Unwin, 1971.

Cairncross, Alec. *Years of Recovery: British Economic Policy, 1945–51*. London and New York: Routledge, 1985.

Cairncross, Alec, and Barry Eichengreen. *Sterling in Decline: The Devaluations of 1931, 1949 and 1967*. Oxford: Basil Blackwell, 1983.

Cairncross, Alec, and Nita Watts. *The Economic Section, 1939–1961: A Study in Economic Advising*. London: Routledge, 1989.

Calomiris, Charles W., and Gary Gorton. "The Origins of Banking Panics: Models, Facts, and Bank Regulation." In *U.S. Bank Deregulation in Historical Perspective*, edited by Charles W. Calomiris, 93–163. Cambridge: Cambridge University Press, 2000.

Calomiris, Charles W., and Stephen H. Haber. *Fragile by Design: The Political Origins of Banking Crisis & Scarce Credit*. Princeton and Oxford: Princeton University Press, 2014.

Cannadine, David. *Aspects of Aristocracy: Grandeur and Decline in Modern Britain*. New Haven and London: Yale University Press, 1994.

Cannadine, David. *In Churchill's Shadow: Confronting the Past in Modern Britain*. Oxford and New York: Oxford University Press, 2003.

Cannadine, David. *The Decline and Fall of the British Aristocracy*. New Haven and London: Yale University Press, 1990.

Cannadine, David. *Ornamentalism: How the British Saw Their Empire*. Oxford and New York: Oxford University Press, 2001.

Cannadine, David. "Review Article: The Empire Strikes Back." *Past & Present* 147, no. 1 (1995): 180–194.

Canning, Paul. *British Policy towards Ireland, 1921–1941*. Oxford: Clarendon Press, 1985.

Capie, Forrest. *The Bank of England, 1950s to 1979*. Cambridge: Cambridge University Press, 2010.

Capie, Forrest, and Alan Webber. *A Monetary History of the United Kingdom, 1870–1982: vol. 1, Data, Sources and Methods*. London: George Allen & Unwin, 1985.

Capie, Forrest H., and Geoffrey E. Wood. "A European Lender of Last Resort? Some Lessons from History." In *International Monetary Systems in Historical Perspective*, edited by Jaime Reis, 209–229. London: Palgrave Macmillan, 1995.

Capie, Forrest, and Geoffrey Wood. "The Governance of Central Banks: With Some Examples and Some Implications for All." In *The Oxford Handbook of the Economics of Central Banking*, edited by David G. Mayes, Pierre L. Siklos, and Jan-Egbert Sturm, 99–128. Oxford: Oxford University Press, 2019.

Capotescu, Cristian, Oscar Sanchez-Sibony, and Melissa Teixeira. "Austerity without Neoliberals: Reappraising the Sinuous History of a Powerful State Technology." *Capitalism: A Journal of History and Economics* 3, no. 2 (2022): 379–420.

Cappella Zielinski, Rosella. *How States Pay for Wars*. Ithaca and London: Cornell University Press, 2016.

Caravaca, Jimena, and Mariano Plotkin. "Crisis, ciencias sociales y elites estatales: la constitución del campo de los economistas estatales en la Argentina, 1910–1935." *Desarrollo Económico* 47, no. 187 (2007): 401–428.

Carnevali, Francesca. *Europe's Advantage: Banks and Small Firms in Britain, France, Germany, and Italy since 1918*. Oxford: Oxford University Press, 2005.

Carr, E.H. *The Twenty Years' Crisis, 1919–1939: An Introduction to the Study of International Relations*. London: Macmillan, 1939.

Cassis, Youssef. "Bankers in English Society in the Late Nineteenth Century." *The Economic History Review* 38, no. 2 (1985): 210–229.

Cassis, Youssef. *Les banquiers de la City à l'époque Édouardienne (1890–1914)*. Geneva: Librairie Droz, 1984.

Cassis, Youssef. *Les capitales du capital: histoire des places financières internationales, 1780–2005*. Paris: Champion classiques, 2008.

Cassis, Youssef. "Merchant Bankers and City Aristocracy." *The British Journal of Sociology* 39, no. 1 (1988): 114–120.

Cassis, Youssef. "Private Banks and the Onset of the Corporate Economy." In *The World of Private Banking*, edited by Youssef Cassis and Philip L. Cottrell, 69–86. Farnham: Ashgate, 2009.

Cassis, Youssef, and Philip L. Cottrell. *Private Banking in Europe: Rise, Retreat, and Resurgence*. Oxford: Oxford University Press, 2015.

Casson, Mark. *Economics of Unemployment: An Historical Perspective*. Oxford: Martin Robertson & Company, 1983.

Catterall, Peter. "Churchill as Chancellor of the Exchequer (1924–9) and the Return to the Gold Standard." In *Winston Churchill: Politics, Strategy and Statecraft*, edited by Richard Toye, 35–48. London: Bloomsbury, 2017.

Cerretano, Valerio. "Economic Crises and the Development of the Industrial State: The Industrial Intervention of the Bank of Italy and the Bank of England, 1918–1939." *Review of Keynesian Economics*, 1, no. 3 (2013): 314–321.

Cerretano, Valerio. "The Treasury, Britain's Postwar Reconstruction, and the Industrial Intervention of the Bank of England, 1921–9." *The Economic History Review* 62, no. S1 (2009): 80–100.

Chandavarkar, Anand. "Central Bank and Government: An Untold Story from RBI's Early History." *Economic and Political Weekly* 35, no. 34 (2000): 3048–3060.

Chandavarkar, Anand. *Keynes and India: A Study in Economics and Biography*. London: Macmillan, 1989.

Chandler, Lester V. *Benjamin Strong, Central Banker*. Washington, DC: The Brookings Institution, 1958.

Chant, John. "La construction d'une politique monétaire adaptée à la réalité canadienne." In *Revue de la Banque du Canada*, Numéro spécial (2005/2006): 29–34.

Chapman, S.D. "Aristocracy and Meritocracy in Merchant Banking." *The British Journal of Sociology* 37, no. 2 (1986): 180–193.

Chapman, Stanley. *The Rise of Merchant Banking*. London: George Allen & Unwin, 1984.

Chatriot, Alain. *La démocratie sociale à la française : l'expérience du Conseil national économique 1924–1940*. Paris: La Découverte, 2013.

Chatterjee, Atul. "Jahangir Cooverjee Coyajee." *The Economic Journal* 53, no. 212 (1943): 453–456.

Chester, Norman. *Economics, Politics and Social Studies in Oxford, 1900–85*. Basingstoke: Macmillan, 1986.

Chick, Martin. *Industrial Policy in Britain, 1945–1951: Economic Planning, Nationalisation, and the Labour Governments*. Cambridge: Cambridge University Press, 1998.

Child, Frank C. *The Theory and Practice of Exchange Control in Germany: A Study of Monopolistic Exploitation in International Markets*. The Hague: Martinus Nijhoff, 1958.

Chisholm, Derek. "La Banque du Canada était-elle nécessaire?" *L'actualité économique* 59, no. 3 (1983): 551–574.

Clapham, John. *The Bank of England: A History, 1694–1797, vol. 1*. Cambridge: Cambridge University Press, 1944.

Clapham, John. *The Bank of England: A History, 1797–1914, vol. 2*. Cambridge: Cambridge University Press, 1944.

Clarke, Peter. "Churchill's Economic Ideas, 1900–1930." In *Churchill: A Major Reassessment of His Life in Peace and War*, edited by Robert Blake and Wm. Roger Louis, 79–95. Oxford: Clarendon Press, 1996.

Clarke, Peter. *The Keynesian Revolution in the Making, 1924–1936*. Oxford: Clarendon Press, 1988.

Clarke, P.F. *Lancashire and the New Liberalism*. Cambridge: Cambridge University Press, 1971.

Clarke, Peter. *Liberals and Social Democrats*. Cambridge: Cambridge University Press, 1978.

Clarke, Sabine. *Science at the End of Empire: Experts and the Development of the British Caribbean, 1940–62*. Manchester: Manchester University Press, 2018.

Clarke, Stephen V.O. *Central Bank Cooperation, 1924–31*. New York: Federal Reserve Bank of New York, 1967.

Clarke, Stephen V.O. "Exchange-Rate Stabilization in the Mid-1930s: Negotiating the Tripartite Agreement." *Princeton Studies in International Finance*, no. 41 (1977).

Clarke, Stephen V.O. "The Reconstruction of the International Monetary System: The Attempts of 1922 and 1933." *Princeton Studies in International Finance*, no. 33 (1973).

Clavin, Patricia. "The Austrian Hunger Crisis and the Genesis of International Organization after the First World War." *International Affairs* 90, no. 2 (2014): 265–278.

Clavin, Patricia. "The Ben Pimlott Memorial Lecture 2019: Britain and the Making of Global Order after 1919." *Twentieth Century British History* 31, no. 3 (2020): 340–359.

Clavin, Patricia. *The Failure of Economic Diplomacy: Britain, Germany, France and the United States, 1931–36*. Basingstoke: Macmillan, 1996.

Clavin, Patricia. "'The Fetishes of So-Called International Bankers': Central Bank Co-operation for the World Economic Conference, 1932–3." *Contemporary European History* 1, no. 3 (1992): 281–311.

Clavin, Patricia. "Habit Not Heredity: Central Banks and Global Order." In *The Spread of the Modern Central Bank and Global Cooperation, 1919–1939*, edited by Barry Eichengreen and Andreas Kakridis, 57–79. Cambridge: Cambridge: University Press, 2023.

Clavin, Patricia. "Men and Markets: Global Capital and the International Economy." In *Internationalisms: A Twentieth-Century History*, edited by Glenda Sluga and Patricia Clavin, 85–109. Cambridge: Cambridge University Press, 2017.

Clavin, Patricia. *Securing the World Economy: The Reinvention of the League of Nations, 1920–1946*. Oxford: Oxford University Press, 2013.

Clavin, Patricia. "The World Economic Conference 1933: The Failure of British Internationalism." *Journal of European Economic History* 20, no. 3 (1991): 489–527.

Clavin, Patricia, Giancarlo Corsetti, Maurice Obstfeld, and Adam Tooze, eds. *Keynes's Economic Consequences of the Peace after 100 Years: Polemics and Policy*. Cambridge: Cambridge University Press, 2024.

Clavin, Patricia, and Jens-Wilhelm Wessels. "Another Golden Idol? The League of Nations' Gold Delegation and the Great Depression, 1929–1932." *The International History Review* 26, no. 4 (2004): 765–795.

Clayton, G. "The Development of British Exchange Control 1939–45." *The Canadian Journal of Economics and Political Science/Revue canadienne d'Économique et de Science politique* 19, no. 2 (1953): 161–173.

Clement, Piet. "Institutionalizing Central Bank Cooperation: The Norman–Schacht Vision and Early Experience of the Bank for International Settlements, 1929–1933." In *The Spread of the Modern Central Bank and Global Cooperation, 1919–1939*, edited by Barry Eichengreen and Andreas Kakridis, 80–102. Cambridge: Cambridge: University Press, 2023.

Coats, A.W. "Britain: The Rise of the Specialists." *History of Political Economy* 13, no. 3 (1981): 365–404.

Coats, A.W. Bob. "Economic Policy Advice: Opportunities and Limitations." In *The Transfer of Economic Knowledge*, edited by Ernst Mohr, 74–89. Cheltenham: Edward Elgar, 1999.

Cohrs, Patrick O. *The New Atlantic Order: The Transformation of International Politics, 1860–1933*. Cambridge: Cambridge University Press, 2022.

Cohrs, Patrick O. *The Unfinished Peace after World War I: America, Britain and the Stabilisation of Europe 1919–1932*. Cambridge: Cambridge University Press, 2006.

Coleman, William, Selwyn Cornish, and Alf Hagger. *Giblin's Platoon: The Trials and Triumph of the Economist in Australian Public Life*. Canberra: ANU E Press, 2006.

Collins, Michael. *Banks and Industrial Finance in Britain, 1800–1939*. Cambridge: Cambridge University Press, 1995.

Collins, Michael. *Money and Banking in the UK: A History*. London: Croom Helm, 1988.

Collins, Michael, and Mae Baker. "Bank of England Autonomy: A Retrospective." In *The Emergence of Modern Central Banking from 1918 to the Present*, edited by Carl-L. Holtfrerich, Jaime Reis, and Gianni Toniolo, 13–33. Aldershot: Ashgate, 1999.

Colvin, Phyllis. *The Economic Ideal in British Government: Calculating Costs and Benefits in the 1970s*. Manchester: Manchester University Press, 1985.

Conti-Brown, Peter. *The Power and Independence of the Federal Reserve*. Princeton and Oxford: Princeton University Press, 2016.

Conze, Eckart. *Die große Illusion. Versailles 1919 und die Neuordnung der Welt*. Munich: Siedler, 2018.

Cook, Eli. *The Pricing of Progress: Economic Indicators and the Capitalization of American Life*. Cambridge, MA, and London: Harvard University Press, 2017.

Cook, Peter. "The Scullin Government, 1929–1932." PhD diss., Australian National University, 1971.

Cooper, Andrew Fenton. *British Agricultural Policy, 1912–36: A Study in Conservative Politics*. Manchester and New York: Manchester University Press, 1989.

Copley, Jack. *Governing Financialization: The Tangled Politics of Financial Liberalization in Britain*. Oxford: Oxford University Press, 2022.

Costigliola, Frank C. "Anglo-American Financial Rivalry in the 1920s." *The Journal of Economic History* 37, no. 4 (1977): 911–934.

Costigliola, Frank C. *Awkward Dominion: American Political, Economic, and Cultural Relations with Europe, 1919–1933*. Ithaca and London: Cornell University Press, 1984.

Cotton, James. *The Australians at Geneva: Internationalist Diplomacy in the Interwar Years*. Carlton: Melbourne University Press, 2022.

Cottrell, Philip L. "Austrian Reconstruction, 1920–1921: A Matter for Private Business or the League of Nations?" In *Business in the Age of Extremes: Essays in Modern German and Austrian Economic History*, edited by Hartmut Berghoff, Jürgen Kocka, and Dieter Ziegler, 59–75. Cambridge: Cambridge University Press, 2013.

Cottrell, Philip L. "The Bank of England in its International Setting, 1918–1972." In *The Bank of England: Money, Power and Influence, 1694–1994*, edited by Richard Roberts and David Kynaston, 83–139. Oxford: Clarendon Press, 1995.

Cottrell, Philip L. "La Banque d'Angleterre, les crises de la livre sterling et l'Europe (1958–1967)." In *Politiques et pratiques des banques d'émission en Europe*

(XVIIe–XXe siècle) : le bicentenaire de la Banque de France dans la perspective de l'identité monétaire européenne, edited by Olivier Feiertag and Michel Margairaz, 787–803. Paris: Albin Michel, 2003.

Cottrell, Philip L. *British Overseas Investment in the Nineteenth Century*. London: Macmillan, 1975.

Cottrell, Philip L. "Established Connections and New Opportunities: London as an International Financial Centre, 1914–1958." In *London and Paris as International Financial Centres in the Twentieth Century*, edited by Youssef Cassis and Éric Bussière, 153–182. Oxford: Oxford University Press, 2005.

Cottrell, Philip L. "Finance and the Germination of the British Corporate Economy." In *Finance in the Age of the Corporate Economy*, edited by P.L. Cottrell, A. Teichova, and T. Yuzawa, 5–36. Aldershot: Ashgate, 1997.

Cottrell, Philip L. "The Financial System of the United Kingdom in the Twentieth Century." In *International Banking and Financial Systems: Evolution and Stability*, edited by Luigi de Rosa, 43–71. Aldershot: Ashgate, 2003.

Cottrell, Philip L., "Norman, Strakosch and the Development of Central Banking: From Conception to Practice, 1919–1924." In *Rebuilding the Financial System in Central and Eastern Europe, 1918–1994*, edited by Philip L. Cottrell, 29–73. Aldershot: Ashgate, 1997.

Cox, Mary E. *Hunger in War and Peace: Women and Children in Germany, 1914–1924*. Oxford: Oxford University Press, 2019.

Coyle, Diane. *GDP: A Brief but Affectionate History*. Princeton and Oxford: Princeton University Press, 2014.

Crafts, Nicholas, and Terence C. Mills. "Self-Defeating Austerity? Evidence from 1930s' Britain." *European Review of Economic History* 19, no. 2 (2015): 109–127.

Crick, W.F., "The Framework of Inter-Relations." In *Commonwealth Banking Systems*, edited by W.F. Crick, 1–53. Oxford: Clarendon Press, 1965.

Crook, Tom, and Glen O'Hara, "The 'Torrent of Numbers': Statistics and the Public Sphere in Britain, c. 1800–2000." In *Statistics and the Public Sphere: Numbers and the People in Modern Britain, c. 1800–2000*, edited by Tom Crook and Glen O'Hara, 1–31. New York and London: Routledge, 2011.

Cruz e Silva, Victor, Marco Cavalieri, and Marcelo Curado. "On the Transmission of Keynes' and Keynesian Ideas in Brazil through Eugênio Gudin's *Principles of Monetary Economics*." *The European Journal of the History of Economic Thought* 28, no. 1 (2021): 83–102.

Cussó, Roser. "L'activité statistique de l'Organisation économique et financière de la Société des Nations : un nouveau lien entre pouvoir et quantification." *Histoire & mesure* 27, no. 2 (2012): 107–136.

Dabla-Norris, Era, and Marina Marinkov. "Whom Do You Rescue? Honored Debts and Selective Defaults in Four British Dominions." In *Debt and Entanglements between the Wars*, edited by Era Dabla-Norris, 81–120. Washington, DC: International Monetary Fund, 2019.

Dadabhoy, Bakhtiar. *Barons of Banking: Glimpses of Indian Banking History*. Noida: Random House India, 2013.

Dalgaard, Bruce Ronald. *South Africa's Impact on Britain's Return to Gold, 1925*. New York: Arno Press, 1981.

Daly, Mary E. *Industrial Development and Irish National Identity, 1922–1939*. Syracuse: Syracuse University Press, 1992.

Darwin, John. *The Empire Project: The Rise and Fall of the British World-System, 1830–1970*. Cambridge: Cambridge University Press, 2009.

Darwin, John. *Unfinished Empire: The Global Expansion of Britain*. New York: Bloomsbury Press, 2012.

Daunton, Martin. "Britain and Globalisation since 1850: II. The Rise of Insular Capitalism, 1914–1939." *Transactions of the Royal Historical Society* 17 (2007): 1–33.

Daunton, Martin. *The Economic Government of the World, 1933–2023*. London: Allen Lane, 2023.

Daunton, M.J. "Financial Elites and British Society, 1880–1950." In *Finance and Financiers in European History, 1880–1960*, edited by Youssef Cassis, 121–146. Cambridge: Cambridge University Press, 1992.

Daunton, Martin. "'Gentlemanly Capitalism' and British Industry 1820–1914." *Past & Present* 122, no. 1 (1989): 119–158.

Daunton, Martin. *Just Taxes: The Politics of Taxation in Britain, 1914–1979*. Cambridge: Cambridge University Press, 2002.

Daunton, Martin. *State and Market in Victorian Britain: War, Welfare and Capitalism*. Woodbridge: The Boydell Press, 2008.

Daunton, Martin. *Wealth and Welfare: An Economic and Social History of Britain, 1851–1951*. Oxford: Oxford University Press, 2007.

Davies, Aled. *The City of London and Social Democracy: The Political Economy of Finance in Britain, 1959–1979*. Oxford: Oxford University Press, 2017.

Day, A.C.L. "The South African Reserve Bank." In *Banking in the British Commonwealth*, edited by R.S. Sayers, 372–400. Oxford: Clarendon Press, 1952.

Dayer, Roberta Allbert. *Finance and Empire: Sir Charles Addis, 1861–1945*. Basingstoke: Macmillan, 1988.

Decker, Frank. "The Monetary Union of Australia, New Zealand and the United Kingdom – Its Operation, Fragmentation and Break-Up." *Jahrbuch für Wirtschaftsgeschichte* 63, no. 2 (2022): 375–407.

Decorzant, Yann. "Banques centrales, banques privées et Société des nations (1919–1929)." In *Les banques centrales et l'État-nation*, edited by Olivier Feiertag and Michel Margairaz, 355–377. Paris: Presses de Sciences Po, 2016.

Decorzant, Yann. "La Société des Nations et l'apparition d'un nouveau réseau d'expertise économique et financière (1914–1923)." *Critique internationale* 52, no. 3 (2011): 35–50.

Decorzant, Yann. *La Société des nations et la naissance d'une conception de la régulation économique internationale*. Brussels: Peter Lang, 2011.

Degive, Nicolas, and Kim Oosterlinck. "Independence and the Effect of Empire: The Case of 'Sovereign Debts' Issued by British Colonies." In *Sovereign Debt Diplomacies: Rethinking Sovereign Debt from Colonial Empires to Hegemony*, edited by Pierre Pénet and Juan Flores Zendejas, 94–118. Oxford: Oxford University Press, 2021.

Dehne, Phillip A. *After the Great War: Economic Warfare and the Promise of Peace in Paris 1919*. London: Bloomsbury, 2019.

Dekker, Erwin. *Jan Tinbergen (1903–1994) and the Rise of Economic Expertise*. Cambridge: Cambridge University Press, 2021.

De Kock, Gerhard. *A History of the South African Reserve Bank (1920–52)*. Pretoria: J.L. van Schaik, 1954.

Delalande, Nicolas. "The Financial Challenges of Total War." In *A World of Public Debts: A Political History*, edited by Nicolas Barreyre and Nicolas Delalande, 261–286. Cham: Palgrave Macmillan, 2020.

Della Paolera, Gerardo, and Alan M. Taylor. *Straining at the Anchor: The Argentine Currency Board and the Search for Macroeconomic Stability, 1880–1935*. Chicago and London: The University of Chicago Press, 2001.

De Pablo, Juan Carlos. *Pinedo y Prebisch: Vida, obra y gestión de dos economistas argentinos*. Buenos Aires: Sudamericana, 2022.

Deringer, William. *Calculated Values: Finance, Politics, and the Quantitative Age*. Cambridge, MA, and London: Harvard University Press, 2018.

De Saint Seine, Sylviane. *La Banque d'Angleterre : une marche erratique vers l'indépendance, 1977–2007*. Paris: Presses de Sciences Po, 2017.

Deutscher, Patrick. *R.G. Hawtrey and the Development of Macroeconomics*. Basingstoke: Macmillan, 1990.

Devons, Ely. *Essays in Economics*. London: George Allen & Unwin, 1961.

Devons, Ely. *An Introduction to British Economic Statistics*. Cambridge: Cambridge University Press, 1956.

Dilley, Andrew. *Finance, Politics, and Imperialism: Australia, Canada, and the City of London, c. 1896–1914*. Basingstoke: Palgrave Macmillan, 2012.

Dimand, Robert W. "What Keynesian Revolution? A Reconsideration Seventy Years after *The General Theory*." In *Keynes's General Theory after Seventy Years*, edited by Robert W. Dimand, Robert A. Mundell, and Alessandro Vercelli, 287–311. Basingstoke: Palgrave Macmillan, 2010.

Dohrn, Susanne. "Pioneers in a Dead-End Profession: The First Women Clerks in Banks and Insurance Companies." In *The White-Blouse Revolution: Female Office Workers since 1870*, edited by Gregory Anderson, 48–66. Manchester and New York: Manchester University Press, 1988.

Dosman, Edgar J. *The Life and Times of Raúl Prebisch, 1901–1986*. Montreal and Kingston: McGill-Queen's University Press, 2008.

Drake, Paul W. *The Money Doctor in the Andes: The Kemmerer Missions, 1923–1933*. Durham and London: Duke University Press, 1989.

Drea, Eoin, and Frank Berry. "A Reappraisal of Joseph Brennan and the Achievements of Irish Banking and Currency Policy, 1922–1943." *Financial History Review* 28, no. 1 (2021): 45–66.

Drecoll, Axel. *Der Fiskus als Verfolger. Die steuerliche Diskriminierung der Juden in Bayern 1933–1941/42*. Munich: R. Oldenbourg, 2009.

Drummond, Ian M. *British Economic Policy and the Empire, 1919–1939*. London: George Allen and Unwin, 1972.

Drummond, Ian M. *The Floating Pound and the Sterling Area, 1931–1939*. Cambridge: Cambridge University Press, 1981.

Drummond, Ian M. *Imperial Economic Policy, 1917–1939: Studies in Expansion and Protection*. Toronto: University of Toronto Press, 1974.

Drummond, Ian M. "Why Canadian Banks Did Not Collapse in the 1930s." In *The Role of Banks in the Interwar Economy*, edited by Harold James, Håkan Lindgren, and Alice Teichova, 232–250. Cambridge: Cambridge University Press, 1991.

Duchaussoy, Vincent, and Olivier Feiertag. "L'invention des banques centrales: organisation et gouvernance." *Histoire, économie & société* 4, no. 35 (2016): 4–7.

Duncan, G.A. "Banking in Ireland." In *Banking in the British Commonwealth*, edited by R.S. Sayers, 303–319. Oxford: Clarendon Press, 1952.

Dungy, Madeleine Lynch. *Order and Rivalry: Rewriting the Rules of International Trade after the First World War*. Cambridge: Cambridge University Press, 2023.

Düppe, Till. "Les origines historiques de l'expertise." In *Experts, sciences et sociétés*, edited by François Claveau and Julien Prud'homme, 23–37. Montréal: Les Presses de l'Université de Montréal, 2018.

Dupree, Marguerite. "Fighting against Fate: The Cotton Industry and the Government during the 1930s." *Textile History* 21, no. 1 (1990): 101–117.

Dupree, Marguerite. "Foreign Competition and the Interwar Period." In *The Lancashire Cotton Industry: A History since 1700*, edited by Mary B. Rose, 265–295. Preston: Lancashire County Books, 1996.

Dutilleul, Maxence. "From Technical to Academic Central Banking: The Scientization of the Banque de France." *Finance and Society* 11, no. 2 (2025).

Eddy, John. "The Technique of Government: Governing Mid-Victorian Australia." In *Government and Expertise: Specialists, Administrators, and Professionals, 1860–1919*, edited by Roy Macleod, 166–181. Cambridge: Cambridge University Press, 1988.

Edelstein, Michael. *Overseas Investment in the Age of High Imperialism: The United Kingdom, 1850–1914*. New York: Columbia University Press, 1982.

Edgerton, David. *Britain's War Machine: Weapons, Resources, and Experts in the Second World War*. Oxford and New York: Oxford University Press, 2011.

Edgerton, David. *The Rise and Fall of the British Nation: A Twentieth-Century History*. London: Allen Lane, 2018.

Eichengreen, Barry. "The Bank of France and the Sterilization of Gold, 1926–1932." *Explorations in Economic History* 23, no. 1 (1986): 56–84.

Eichengreen, Barry. "Conducting the International Orchestra: Bank of England Leadership under the Classical Gold Standard." *Journal of International Money and Finance* 6, no. 1 (1987): 5–29.

Eichengreen, Barry. *Elusive Stability: Essays in the History of International Finance, 1919–1939*. Cambridge: Cambridge University Press, 1990.

Eichengreen, Barry. *Exorbitant Privilege: The Rise and Fall of the Dollar*. Oxford: Oxford University Press, 2011.

Eichengreen, Barry. *Globalizing Capital: A History of the International Monetary System*, 3rd ed. Princeton and Oxford: Princeton University Press, 2019.

Eichengreen, Barry. *Golden Fetters: The Gold Standard and the Great Depression, 1919–1939*. New York and Oxford: Oxford University Press, 1992.

Eichengreen, Barry. "Sterling and the Tariff, 1929–32." *Princeton Studies in International Finance*, no. 48 (1981).

Eichengreen, Barry, and Marc Flandreau. "The Rise and Fall of the Dollar (or When Did the Dollar Replace Sterling as the Leading Reserve Currency?)." *European Review of Economic History* 13, no. 3 (2009): 377–411.

Eichengreen, Barry, and Andreas Kakridis. "Interwar Central Banks: A Tour d'Horizon." In *The Spread of the Modern Central Bank and Global Cooperation, 1919–1939*, edited by Barry Eichengreen and Andreas Kakridis, 3–39. Cambridge: Cambridge: University Press, 2023.

Eichengreen, Barry, Mark W. Watson, and Richard S. Grossman. "Bank Rate Policy under the Interwar Gold Standard: A Dynamic Probit Model." *The Economic Journal* 95, no. 379 (1985): 725–745.

Ekbladh, David. *Plowshares into Swords: Weaponized Knowledge, Liberal Order, and the League of Nations*. Chicago and London: The University of Chicago Press, 2022.

Ellis, Howard S. "German Exchange Control, 1931–1939: From an Emergency Measure to a Totalitarian Institution." *The Quarterly Journal of Economics* 54, no. 4 (1940): 1–158.

Endres, A.M. "The Development of Economists' Policy Advice in New Zealand, 1930–34: With Particular Reference to Belshaw's Contribution." *Australian Economic History Review* 30, no. 1 (1990): 64–78.

Esposito, Marie-Claude. "La Banque d'Angleterre et le financement de la Première Guerre mondiale." In *Les banques centrales pendant la Grande Guerre*, edited by Olivier Feiertag, 117–134. Paris: Presses de Sciences Po, 2019.

Evans, Chris. *Slave Wales: The Welsh and Atlantic Slavery, 1660–1850*. Cardiff: University of Wales Press, 2010.

Evans, Chris, and Louise Miskell. *Swansea Copper: A Global History*. Baltimore: Johns Hopkins University Press, 2020.

Fajardo, Margarita. *The World That Latin America Created: The United Nations Economic Commission for Latin America in the Development Era*. Cambridge, MA, and London: Harvard University Press, 2022.

Fanning, Ronan. *The Irish Department of Finance, 1922–58*. Dublin: Institute of Public Administration, 1978.

Farquet, Christophe. "'Le comité financier ne pense et ne travaille que pour le bien de l'Autriche.' Théories et pratiques budgétaires du comité financier de la Société des Nations lors de la stabilisation monétaire autrichienne des années 1920." In *Les crises de la dette publique : XVIIIe–XXIe siècle*, edited by Gérard Béaur and Laure Quennouëlle-Corre, 345–364. Paris: Comité pour l'histoire économique et financière de la France, 2019.

Farr, Martin. *Reginald McKenna: Financier among Statesmen, 1863–1916*. London and New York: Routledge, 2008.

Fay, Stephen. *Portrait of an Old Lady: Turmoil at the Bank of England*. Harmondsworth: Viking, 1987.

Feichtinger, Johannes. "On the Fraught Internationalism of Intellectuals: Alfons Dopsch, Austria, and the League's Intellectual Cooperation Programme." In *Remaking Central Europe: The League of Nations and the Former Habsburg Lands*, edited by Peter Becker and Natasha Wheatley, 167–190. Oxford: Oxford University Press, 2020.

Feiertag, Olivier. "Le signe des temps : l'invention de l'expert financier international dans l'entre-deux-guerres." In *Experts et expertises en diplomatie : la mobilisation des compétences dans les relations internationales du congrès de Westphalie à la naissance de l'ONU*, edited by Stanislas Jeannesson, Fabrice Jesné, and Éric Schnakenbourg, 275–289. Rennes: Presses universitaires de Rennes, 2018.

Feiertag, Olivier, ed. *Mesurer la monnaie : banques centrales et construction de l'autorité monétaire, XIXe–XXe siècle*. Paris: Albin Michel, 2005.

Feinstein, Charles H. *An Economic History of South Africa: Conquest, Discrimination, and Development*. Cambridge: Cambridge University Press, 2005.

Feldman, Gerald D. *The Great Disorder: Politics, Economics, and Society in the German Inflation, 1914–1924*. New York and Oxford: Oxford University Press, 1997.

Ferguson, Barry. *Remaking Liberalism: The Intellectual Legacy of Adam Shortt, O.D. Skelton, W.C. Clark, and W.A. Mackintosh, 1890–1925*. Montreal and Kingston: McGill-Queen's University Press, 1993.

Ferguson, Niall. *The House of Rothschild, vol. 1: Money's Prophets, 1798–1848*. New York: Viking, 1998.

Ferguson, Niall. *The House of Rothschild, vol. 2: The World's Banker, 1849–1999*. New York: Viking, 1999.

Ferguson, Niall. *The Pity of War*. London: Penguin, 1998.

Ferguson, Niall, Martin Kornejew, Paul Schmelzing, and Moritz Schularick. "The Safety Net: Central Bank Balance Sheets and Financial Crises, 1587–2020." *Hoover Institution Economics Working Papers*, no. 23102 (2023).

Ferguson, Niall, Charles S. Maier, Erez Manela, and Daniel J. Sargent, eds. *The Shock of the Global: The 1970s in Perspective*. Cambridge, MA, and London: Harvard University Press, 2010.

Ferguson, Niall, and Moritz Schularick. "The Empire Effect: The Determinants of Country Risk in the First Age of Globalization, 1880–1913." *The Journal of Economic History* 66, no. 2 (2006): 283–312.

Fessey, M.C. "Some Developments in Economic Statistics since 1934." *Journal of the Royal Statistical Society* 19, no. 2 (1969): 105–123.

Fforde, John. *The Bank of England and Public Policy, 1941–1958*. Cambridge: Cambridge University Press, 1992.

Fink, Carole. *The Genoa Conference: European Diplomacy, 1921–1922*. Chapel Hill: University of North Carolina Press, 1984.

Fink, Carole, Axel Frohn, and Jürgen Heideking, eds. *Genoa, Rapallo, and European Reconstruction in 1922*. Washington, DC: German Historical Institute and Cambridge: Cambridge University Press, 1991.

Fior, Michel. *Institution globale et marchés financiers : la Société des Nations face à la reconstruction de l'Europe, 1918–1931*. Bern: Peter Lang, 2008.

Flandreau, Marc. *Anthropologists in the Stock Exchange: A Financial History of Victorian Science*. Chicago and London: The University of Chicago Press, 2016.

Flandreau, Marc, and Stefano Ugolini. "Where It All Began: Lending of Last Resort at the Bank of England Monitoring During the Overend-Gurney Panic of 1866." In *The Origins, History, and Future of the Federal Reserve: A Return to Jekyll Island*, edited by Michael D. Bordo and William Roberds, 113–161. Cambridge: Cambridge University Press, 2013.

Flandreau, Marc, and Frédéric Zumer. *The Making of Global Finance, 1880–1913*. Paris: Development Centre of the Organisation for Economic Co-operation and Development, 2004.

Flores Zendejas, Juan. "Money Doctors and Latin American Central Banks at the Onset of the Great Depression." *Journal of Latin American Studies* 53, no. 3 (2021): 429–463.

Flores Zendejas, Juan, and Gianandrea Nodari. "Latin American Experiments in Central Banking at the Onset of the Great Depression." In *The Spread of the Modern Central Bank and Global Cooperation, 1919–1939*, edited by Barry Eichengreen and Andreas Kakridis, 320–351. Cambridge: Cambridge: University Press, 2023.

Forbes, Neil. *Doing Business with the Nazis: Britain's Economic and Financial Relations with Germany, 1931–1939*. London: Frank Cass, 2000.

Fourcade, Marion. *Economists and Societies: Discipline and Profession in the United States, Britain, and France, 1890s to 1990s*. Princeton and Oxford: Princeton University Press, 2009.

Freeden, Michael. *Liberalism Divided: A Study in British Political Thought, 1914–1939*. Oxford: Clarendon Press, 1986.

Freeden, Michael. *The New Liberalism: An Ideology of Social Reform*. Oxford: Clarendon Press, 1978.
Frieden, Jeffry A. *Global Capitalism: Its Fall and Rise in the Twentieth Century*. New York and London: W.W. Norton, 2006.
Friedländer, Saul. *Das Dritte Reich und die Juden. Die Jahre der Verfolgung 1933–1939*. Munich: C.H. Beck, 1998.
Friedman, Milton, and Anna Jacobson Schwartz. *A Monetary History of the United States, 1867–1960*. Princeton: Princeton University Press, 1963.
Friedman, Walter A. *Fortune Tellers: The Story of America's First Economic Forecasters*. Princeton and Oxford: Princeton University Press, 2014.
Fritsch, Winston. *External Constraints on Economic Policy in Brazil, 1889–1930*. Pittsburgh: University of Pittsburgh Press, 1988.
Fritsch, Winston. "The Montagu Financial Mission to Brazil and the Federal Economic Policy Changes of 1924." *Brazilian Economic Studies* 9 (1985): 263–325.
Frost, Raymond. "The Macmillan Gap, 1931–53." *Oxford Economic Papers* 6, no. 2 (1954): 181–201.
Fry, Geoffrey Kingdon. *Statesmen in Disguise: The Changing Role of the Administration Class of the British Home Civil Service, 1853–1966*. London: Macmillan, 1969.
Fry, Geoffrey K. "Three Giants of the Inter-War British Higher Civil Service: Sir Maurice Hankey, Sir Warren Fisher and Sir Horace Wilson." In *Bureaucrats and Leadership: Transforming Government*, edited by Kevin Theakston, 39–67. Basingstoke: Macmillan Press, 2000.
Fry, Richard. "Introduction." In *A Banker's World: The Revival of the City, 1957–1970: Speeches and Writings of Sir George Bolton*, edited by Richard Fry, 11–38. London: Hutchinson, 1970.
Fullerton, Douglas H. *Graham Towers and His Times*. Toronto: McClelland and Stewart, 1986.
Gabor, Daniela. "Green Central Banking." In *Making the Great Turnaround Work: Economic Policy for a Green and Just Transition*, edited by Heinrich Böll Foundation, ZOE – Institute for Future-Fit Economies, and Finanzwende Recherche, 39–45. Berlin: Heinrich-Böll-Stiftung, 2022.
Garside, W.R. *British Unemployment, 1919–1939: A Study in Public Policy*. Cambridge: Cambridge University Press, 1990.
Garside, W.R. "Party Politics, Political Economy and British Protectionism, 1919–1932." *History* 83, no. 269 (1998): 47–65.
Garside, W.R., and J.I. Greaves. "The Bank of England and Industrial Intervention in Interwar Britain." *Financial History Review* 3, no. 1 (1996): 69–86.
Gaukroger, Alan. "The Director of Financial Enquiries: A Study of the Treasury Career of R.G. Hawtrey, 1919–1939." PhD diss., University of Huddersfield, 2008.
Geddes, Philip. *Inside the Bank of England*. London: Boxtree, 1987.
Getachew, Adom. *Worldmaking after Empire: The Rise and Fall of Self-Determination*. Princeton and Oxford: Princeton University Press, 2019.
Giblin, Lyndhurst Falkiner. *The Growth of a Central Bank: The Development of the Commonwealth Bank of Australia, 1924–1945*. Melbourne: Melbourne University Press, 1951.
Gil Aguadó, Iago. "The Creditanstalt Crisis of 1931 and the Failure of the Austro-German Customs Union Project." *The Historical Journal* 44, no. 1 (2001): 199–221.

Gilbert, Martin. *Churchill and the Jews: A Lifelong Friendship*. New York: Henry Holt, 2007.

Giuseppe, Telesca. "Introduction." In *Financial Elites and European Banking: Historical Perspectives*, edited by Youssef Cassis and Giuseppe Telesca, 1–16. Oxford: Oxford University Press, 2018.

Giuseppi, John. *The Bank of England: A History from Its Foundation in 1694*. London: Evans Brothers, 1966.

Glasemann, Hans-Georg. *Deutschlands Auslandsanleihen, 1924–1945. Rückzahlungen nach der Wiedervereinigung von 1990*. Wiesbaden: Gabler, 1993.

Gómez, Mónica. *Avatares de un sistema monetario: la primera Caja de Conversión argentina y su transformación final en Banco Central (1890–1935)*. Buenos Aires: Teseo, 2018.

Gómez, Mónica. "El fin de la Caja de Conversión y el nacimiento del Banco Central. Argentina en la Gran Depresión, 1929–1935." In *Orígenes de la globalización bancaria: experiencias de España y América Latina*, edited by Daniel Díaz Fuentes, Andrés Hoyo Aparicio, and Carlos Marichal, 381–410. Santander: Genueve Ediciones, El Colegio de México, 2017.

Gomez Betancourt, Rebeca. "Edwin Walter Kemmerer: Money Theorist and Money Doctor." PhD diss., Université Paris 1 Panthéon-Sorbonne, 2008.

Gomez Betancourt, Rebeca. "John Maynard Keynes's *Indian Currency and Finance*." *History of Economics Review* 58, no. 1 (2013): 83–95.

Gomez Betancourt, Rebeca. "The Political Economy of a Modern Missionary: E.W. Kemmerer in the Philippines." *History of Political Economy* 54, no. 3 (2022): 483–505.

Goodhart, C.A.E. "The Bank of England, 1694–2017." In *Sveriges Riksbank and the History of Central Banking*, edited by Rodney Edvinsson, Tor Jacobson, and Daniel Waldenström, 143–171. Cambridge: Cambridge University Press, 2018.

Goodhart, C.A.E. "The Changing Role of Central Banks." *Financial History Review* 18, no. 2 (2011): 135–154.

Goodhart, Charles. *The Evolution of Central Banks*. Cambridge, MA, and London: The MIT Press, 1988.

Goodhart, C.A.E. "Myths about the Lender of Last Resort." *International Finance* 2, no. 3 (1999): 339–360.

Goodhart, Charles A.E., and Duncan J. Needham. "Historical Reasons for the Focus on Broad Monetary Aggregates in Post-World War II Britain and the 'Seven Years War' with the IMF." *Financial History Review* 24, no. 3 (2017): 331–356.

Gordon-Ashworth, Fiona. "Agricultural Commodity Control under Vargas in Brazil, 1930–1945." *Journal of Latin American Studies* 12, no. 1 (1980): 87–105.

Gorton, Gary B., and Ellis W. Tallman. *Fighting Financial Crises: Learning from the Past*. Chicago and London: The University of Chicago Press, 2018.

Gottlieb, Julie V., and Richard Toye, eds. *The Aftermath of Suffrage: Women, Gender, and Politics in Britain, 1918–1945*. Basingstoke: Palgrave Macmillan, 2013.

Gowland, David. "Debt Management in the United Kingdom and the London Gilt-Edged Market." In *International Bond Markets*, edited by David Gowland, 106–129. London and New York: Routledge, 1990.

Grant, Hugh. *W.A. Mackintosh: The Life of a Canadian Economist*. Montreal and Kingston: McGill-Queen's University Press, 2015.

Gravil, Roger. *The Anglo–Argentine Connection, 1900–1939*. Boulder: Westview Press, 1985.

Grayson, Richard S. *Liberals, International Relations and Appeasement: The Liberal Party, 1919–1939*. London and New York: Routledge, 2001.

Greasley, David. "The Coal Industry: Images and Realities on the Road to Nationalisation." In *The Political Economy of Nationalisation in Britain, 1920–1950*, edited by Robert Millward and John Singleton, 37–64. Cambridge: Cambridge University Press, 1995.

Greasley, David, and Les Oxley. "Regime Shift and Fast Recovery on the Periphery: New Zealand in the 1930s." *The Economic History Review* 55, no. 4 (2002): 697–720.

Greaves, Julian I. "Competition, Collusion, and Confusion: The State and the Reorganization of the British Cotton Industry, 1931–1939." *Enterprise & Society* 3, no. 1 (2002): 48–79.

Greaves, Julian. *Industrial Reorganization and Government Policy in Interwar Britain*. Aldershot: Ashgate, 2005.

Greaves, J.I. "'Visible Hands' and the Rationalization of the British Cotton Industry, 1925–1932." *Textile History* 31, no. 1 (2000): 102–122.

Green, Alan G., and Gordon R. Sparks. "A Macro Interpretation of Recovery: Australia and Canada." In *Recovery from the Depression: Australia and the World Economy in the 1930s*, edited by R.G. Gregory and N.G. Butlin, 89–112. Cambridge: Cambridge University Press, 1988.

Green, E.H.H. "The Influence of the City over British Economic Policy, c. 1880–1960." In *Finance and Financiers in European History, 1880–1960*, edited by Youssef Cassis, 193–218. Cambridge: Cambridge University Press, 1992.

Green, Edwin, and Sara Kinsey. *The Paradise Bank: The Mercantile Bank of India, 1893–1984*. Aldershot: Ashgate, 1999.

Green, Jeremy. *The Political Economy of the Special Relationship: Anglo-American Development from the Gold Standard to the Financial Crisis*. Princeton and Oxford: Princeton University Press, 2020.

Greenaway, John R. "Warren Fisher and the Transformation of the British Treasury, 1919–1939." *Journal of British Studies* 23, no. 1 (1983): 125–142.

Greenhill, Robert. "Merchants and the Latin American Trades: An Introduction." In *Business Imperialism, 1840–1930: An Inquiry Based on British Experience in Latin America*, edited by D.C.M. Platt, 159–197. Oxford: Clarendon Press, 1977.

Grossman, Richard S. *Unsettled Account: The Evolution of Banking in the Industrialized World since 1800*. Princeton and Oxford: Princeton University Press, 2010.

Grossman, Richard S., and Hugh Rockoff. "Fighting the Last War: Economists on the Lender of Last Resort." In *Central Banks at a Crossroads: What Can We Learn from History?*, edited by Michael D. Bordo, Øyvind Eitrheim, Marc Flandreau, and Jan F. Qvigstad, 231–279. Cambridge: Cambridge University Press, 2016.

Grytten, Ola Honningdal, and Arngrim Hunnes. "Price Stability in the Periphery during the International Gold Standard: Scandinavia." In *The Gold Standard Peripheries: Monetary Policy, Adjustment and Flexibility in a Global Setting*, edited by Anders Ögren and Lars Fredrik Øksendal, 58–80. London: Palgrave Macmillan, 2012.

Hacche, Graham, and Christopher Taylor. "Editors' Introduction." In *Inside the Bank of England: Memoirs of Christopher Dow, Chief Economist, 1973–84*, edited by Graham Hacche and Christopher Taylor, 1–33. Basingstoke: Palgrave Macmillan, 2013.

Hackett, John, and Anne-Marie Hackett. *L'Économie britannique : problèmes et perspectives*. Paris: Armand Colin, 1966.

Hall, F.G. *The Bank of Ireland, 1783–1946*. Dublin: Hodges Figgis & Co., 1949.
Hall, Robert. "The Place of the Economist in Government." *Oxford Economic Papers* 7, no. 2 (1955): 119–135.
Hall, Rodney Bruce. *Central Banking as Global Governance: Constructing Financial Credibility*. Cambridge: Cambridge University Press, 2008.
Hancock, Keith. "Unemployment and the Economists in the 1920s." *Economica* 27, no. 108 (1960): 305–321.
Hannah, Leslie. *The Rise of the Corporate Economy*. London: Methuen & Co., 1976.
Hansen, Per H. "Cooperate or Free Ride? The Scandinavian Central Banks, Bank for International Settlements and the Austrian Financial Crisis of 1931." *Scandinavian Journal of History* 37, no. 1 (2012): 87–107.
Hansen, Per H. *There Will Be the Devil to Pay: Central Bankers, Uncertainty and Sensemaking in the European Financial Crisis of 1931*. Cambridge: Cambridge University Press, 2025.
Harkness, D.W. *The Restless Dominion: The Irish Free State and the British Commonwealth of Nations, 1921–31*. London: Macmillan, 1969.
Harris, Max. *Monetary War and Peace: London, Washington, Paris, and the Tripartite Agreement of 1936*. Cambridge: Cambridge University Press, 2021.
Harrison, Brian. *Seeking a Role: The United Kingdom, 1951–1970*. Oxford: Clarendon Press, 2009.
Hawke, G.R. *Between Governments and Banks: A History of the Reserve Bank of New Zealand*. Wellington: A.R. Shearer, Government Printer, 1973.
Hawke, G.R. *The Making of New Zealand: An Economic History*. Cambridge: Cambridge University Press, 1985.
Hawke, Gary, and John Singleton. "State and Central Bank in New Zealand." In *Les banques centrales et l'État-nation*, edited by Olivier Feiertag and Michel Margairaz, 213–230. Paris: Presses de Sciences Po, 2016.
Hawkins, John Robert. "The Australian Treasurers: Managers and Reformers in an Evolving Role." PhD diss., Australian National University, 2017.
Heim, Carol E. "Industrial Organization and Regional Development in Interwar Britain." *The Journal of Economic History* 43, no. 4 (1983): 931–952.
Heim, Carol E. "Limits to Intervention: The Bank of England and Industrial Diversification in the Depressed Areas." *The Economic History Review* 37, no. 4 (1984): 533–550.
Helleiner, Eric. "Central Bankers as Good Neighbours: US Money Doctors in Latin America During the 1940s." *Financial History Review* 16, no. 1 (2009): 5–25.
Helleiner, Eric. *The Contested World Economy: The Deep and Global Roots of International Political Economy*. Cambridge: Cambridge University Press, 2023.
Helleiner, Eric. *The Making of National Money: Territorial Currencies in Historical Perspective*. Ithaca and London: Cornell University Press, 2003.
Helleiner, Eric. *The Neomercantilists: A Global Intellectual History*. Ithaca and London: Cornell University Press, 2021.
Helleiner, Eric. *States and the Reemergence of Global Finance: From Bretton Woods to the 1990s*. Ithaca and London: Cornell University Press, 1994.
Helleiner, Eric. *Towards North American Monetary Union? The Politics and History of Canada's Exchange Rate Regime*. Montreal and Kingston: McGill-Queen's University Press, 2006.
Henderson, P.D. "The Use of Economists in British Administration." *Oxford Economic Papers* 13, no. 1 (1961): 5–26.

Hennessy, Elizabeth. *A Domestic History of the Bank of England, 1930–1960*. Cambridge: Cambridge University Press, 1992.

Hennessy, Elizabeth. "The Governors, Directors and Management of the Bank of England." In *The Bank of England: Money, Power and Influence, 1694–1994*, edited by Richard Roberts and David Kynaston, 185–216. Oxford: Clarendon Press, 1995.

Herren, Madeleine. *Internationale Organisationen seit 1865. Eine Globalgeschichte der internationalen Ordnung*. Darmstadt: Wissenschaftliche Buchgesellschaft, 2009.

Hewitt, Liane. "The World in Blocs: Leo Amery, the British Empire and Regionalist Anti-Internationalism, 1903–1947." *Journal of Global History* 18, no. 2 (2023): 236–258.

Heyde, Philipp. *Das Ende der Reparationen. Deutschland, Frankreich und der Youngplan, 1929–1932*. Paderborn: F. Schöningh, 1998.

Hicks, Ursula K. *The Finance of British Government, 1920–1936*. London: Oxford University Press, 1938.

Hidalgo-Weber, Olga. "Expertise britannique à l'OIT dans l'entre-deux-guerres : enjeux politiques et transferts de savoirs." *Revue d'histoire de la protection sociale* 10, no. 1 (2017): 22–41.

Higgins, David, and Steve Toms. "Financial Distress, Corporate Borrowing, and Industrial Decline: The Lancashire Cotton Spinning Industry, 1918–38." In *British Cotton Textiles: Maturity and Decline*, edited by David Higgins and Steven Toms, 105–130. London and New York: Routledge, 2017.

Hitzler, Ronald, Anne Honer, and Christoph Maeder, eds. *Expertenwissen. Die institutionalisierte Kompetenz zur Konstruktion von Wirklichkeit*. Opladen: Westdeutscher Verlag, 1994.

Hodge, Joseph Morgan. *Triumph of the Expert: Agrarian Doctrines of Development and the Legacies of British Colonialism*. Athens: Ohio University Press, 2007.

Holland, R.F. *Britain and the Commonwealth Alliance, 1918–1939*. London: Macmillan, 1981.

Hömig, Herbert. *Brüning – Kanzler in der Krise der Republik. Eine Weimarer Biographie*. Paderborn: F. Schöningh, 2000.

Horn, Martin. *Britain, France, and the Financing of the First World War*. Montreal and Kingston: McGill-Queen's University Press, 2002.

Horn, Martin. *J.P. Morgan & Co. and the Crisis of Capitalism: From the Wall Street Crash to World War II*. Cambridge: Cambridge University Press, 2022.

Hotson, Anthony C. *Respectable Banking: The Search for Stability in London's Money and Credit Markets since 1695*. Cambridge: Cambridge University Press, 2017.

Howe, Anthony. *Free Trade and Liberal England, 1846–1946*. Oxford: Clarendon Press, 1997.

Howe, Anthony. "From 'Old Corruption' to 'New Probity': The Bank of England and Its Directors in the Age of Reform." *Financial History Review* 1, no. 1 (1994): 23–41.

Howell, David. *MacDonald's Party: Labour Identities and Crisis, 1922–1931*. Oxford: Oxford University Press, 2002.

Howson, Susan. *Domestic Monetary Management in Britain, 1919–38*. Cambridge: Cambridge University Press, 1975.

Howson, Susan. *Lionel Robbins*. Cambridge: Cambridge University Press, 2011.

Howson, Susan. "The Management of Sterling, 1932–1939." *The Journal of Economic History* 40, no. 1 (1980): 53–60.

Howson, Susan. "The Origins of Dear Money, 1919–20." *The Economic History Review* 27, no. 1 (1974): 88–107.

Howson, Susan. "Sterling's Managed Float: The Operations of the Exchange Equalisation Account, 1932–39." *Princeton Studies in International Finance*, no. 46 (1980).
Howson, Susan, and Donald Winch. *The Economic Advisory Council, 1930–1939: A Study in Economic Advice during Depression and Recovery*. Cambridge: Cambridge University Press, 1977.
Hutchison, T.W. *Economics and Economic Policy in Britain*. London: Routledge, 2003.
Hutchison, T.W. *On Revolutions and Progress in Economic Knowledge*. Cambridge: Cambridge University Press, 1978.
Hyam, Ronald. *Britain's Imperial Century, 1815–1914: A Study of Empire and Expansion*, 3rd ed. Basingstoke: Palgrave Macmillan, 2002.
Ikenberry, G. John. "The Political Origins of Bretton Woods." In *A Retrospective on the Bretton Woods System: Lessons for International Monetary Reform*, edited by Michael D. Bordo and Barry Eichengreen, 155–198. Chicago and London: The University of Chicago Press, 1993.
Ikenberry, G. John. *A World Safe for Democracy: Liberal Internationalism and the Crises of Global Order*. New Haven and London: Yale University Press, 2020.
Ingham, Geoffrey. *Capitalism Divided? The City and Industry in British Social Development*. Basingstoke: Macmillan, 1984.
Irwin, Douglas A. "La France a-t-elle causé la Grande Dépression ?" *Revue française d'économie* XXV, no. 4 (2010): 3–10.
Irwin, Neil. *The Alchemists: Three Central Bankers and a World on Fire*. New York: Penguin, 2013.
Jacks, David S. "Defying Gravity: The 1932 Imperial Economic Conference and the Reorientation of Canadian Trade." *Explorations in Economic History* 53, no. 1 (2014): 19–39.
Jackson, Julian. *The Popular Front in France: Defending Democracy, 1934–38*. Cambridge: Cambridge University Press, 1990.
Jackson, Peter, William Mulligan, and Glenda Sluga, eds. *Peacemaking and International Order after the First World War*. Cambridge: Cambridge University Press, 2023.
Jacobsson, Erin E. *A Life for Sound Money: Per Jacobsson, His Biography*. Oxford: Clarendon Press, 1979.
James, Harold. "The Causes of the German Banking Crisis of 1931." *The Economic History Review* 37, no. 1 (1984): 68–87.
James, Harold. *The End of Globalization: Lessons from the Great Depression*. Cambridge, MA, and London: Harvard University Press, 2001.
James, Harold. "Financial Flows across Frontiers during the Interwar Depression." *The Economic History Review* 45, no. 3 (1992): 594–613.
James, Harold. *The German Slump: Politics and Economics, 1924–1936*. Oxford: Clarendon Press, 1986.
James, Harold. *Making a Modern Central Bank: The Bank of England, 1979–2003*. Cambridge: Cambridge University Press, 2020.
James, Harold. "What Is Keynesian about Deficit Financing? The Case of Interwar Germany." In *The Political Power of Economic Ideas: Keynesianism across Nations*, edited by Peter A. Hall, 231–262. Princeton: Princeton University Press, 1989.
Janeway, William H. "The 1931 Sterling Crisis and the Independence of the Bank of England." *Journal of Post Keynesian Economics* 18, no. 2 (1995): 251–268.
Jenkins, Roy. *Churchill: A Biography*. New York: Farrar, Straus and Giroux, 2001.

Jobst, Clemens, and Hans Kernbauer. *Die Bank. Das Geld. Der Staat. Nationalbank und Währungspolitik in Österreich 1816–2016*. Frankfurt am Main: Campus Verlag, 2016.

Johnman, Lewis, and Hugh Murphy. "Subsidy and Treasury: The Trade Facilities Act and the UK Shipbuilding Industry in the 1920s." *Contemporary British History* 22, no. 1 (2008): 89–110.

Johnson, Gaynor. "The D'Abernon Trade Mission to South America, 1929: Context and Reappraisal." In *Britain and the Growth of US Hegemony in Twentieth-Century Latin America: Competition, Cooperation and Coexistence*, edited by Thomas C. Mills and Rory M. Miller, 105–125. Cham: Palgrave Macmillan, 2020.

Johnson, H. Clark. *Gold, France, and the Great Depression, 1919–1932*. New Haven and London: Yale University Press, 1997.

Johnson, Helen. "Frederick Leith-Ross: The Career of an Economic Diplomat." DPhil diss., University of Oxford, 2008.

Jones, Geoffrey. *British Multinational Banking, 1830–1990*. Oxford: Clarendon Press, 1993.

Jones, Geoffrey. "Competition and Competitiveness in British Banking, 1918–71." In *Competitiveness and the State: Government and Business in Twentieth-Century Britain*, edited by Geoffrey Jones and Maurice Kirby, 120–140. Manchester and New York: Manchester University Press, 1991.

Jones, Geoffrey. "Competitive Advantages in British Multinational Banking since 1890." In *Banks as Multinationals*, edited by Geoffrey Jones, 30–61. London: Routledge, 1990.

Jones, Kit. *An Economist among Mandarins: A Biography of Robert Hall, 1901–1988*. Cambridge: Cambridge University Press, 1994.

Jones, Stuart. *The Great Imperial Banks in South Africa: A Study of the Business of Standard Bank and Barclays Bank, 1861–1961*. Pretoria: University of South Africa, 1996.

Kacowicz, Arie M. "Global Governance, International Order, and World Order." In *The Oxford Handbook of Governance*, edited by David Levi-Faur, 686–698. Oxford: Oxford University Press, 2012.

Kaiga, Sakiko. *Britain and the Intellectual Origins of the League of Nations, 1914–1919*. Cambridge: Cambridge University Press, 2021.

Kaldor, N. "Lessons of the Monetarist Experiment." In *Monetary Conditions for Economic Recovery*, edited by C. van Ewijk and J.J. Klant, 243–262. Dordrecht: Martinus Nijhoff, 1985.

Kates, Steven. "The Hundredth Anniversary of Clay's *Economics*: The Best Introduction to Economics Ever Written." *History of Economics Review* 64, no. 1 (2016): 27–41.

Kay, John, and Mervyn King. *Radical Uncertainty: Decision-Making beyond the Numbers*. New York: W.W. Norton, 2020.

Kennedy, David. *A World of Struggle: How Power, Law, and Expertise Shape Global Political Economy*. Princeton and Oxford: Princeton University Press, 2016.

Kernbauer, Hans. "Central Bank Policy under Foreign Control: The Austrian National Bank in the 1920s." In *The Spread of the Modern Central Bank and Global Cooperation, 1919–1939*, edited by Barry Eichengreen and Andreas Kakridis, 105–138. Cambridge: Cambridge: University Press, 2023.

Kernbauer, Hans. *Währungspolitik in der Zwischenkriegszeit. Geschichte der Österreichischen Nationalbank von 1923 bis 1938*. Vienna: Oesterreichische Nationalbank, 1991.

Kindleberger, Charles P. *A Financial History of Western Europe*. London: George Allen & Unwin, 1984.
Kindleberger, Charles P. *The World in Depression, 1929–1939*, 2nd ed. Berkeley: University of California Press, 1986.
King, Mervyn. *The End of Alchemy: Money, Banking, and the Future of the Global Economy*. New York: W.W. Norton, 2016.
Kirby, M.W. "The Lancashire Cotton Industry in the Inter-War Years: A Study in Organizational Change." *Business History* 16, no. 2 (1974): 145–159.
Kirk, Neville. *Labour and the Politics of Empire: Britain and Australia 1900 to the Present*. Manchester and New York: Manchester University Press, 2011.
Knafo, Samuel. *The Making of Modern Finance: Liberal Governance and the Gold Standard*. London and New York: Routledge, 2013.
Kohlrausch, Martin, Katrin Steffen, and Stefan Wiederkehr, eds. *Expert Cultures in Central and Eastern Europe: The Internationalization of Knowledge and the Transformation of Nation States since World War I*. Osnabrück: Fibre Verlag, 2010.
Kohlrausch, Martin, and Helmuth Trischler. *Building Europe on Expertise: Innovators, Organizers, Networkers*. Basingstoke: Palgrave Macmillan, 2014.
Krebs, Marco Ludwik Patrício. "Os cinquenta anos do banco central do Brasil." PhD diss., Universidade Federal do Rio de Janeiro, 2016.
Krozewski, Gerold. "Capitalism." In *The Interwar World*, edited by Andrew Denning and Heidi J.S. Tworek, 461–477. Abingdon: Routledge, 2024.
Krozewski, Gerold. *Money and the End of Empire: British International Economic Policy and the Colonies, 1947–58*. Basingstoke: Palgrave, 2001.
Kumekawa, Ian. *The First Serious Optimist: A.C. Pigou and the Birth of Welfare Economics*. Princeton and Oxford: Princeton University Press, 2017.
Kumekawa, Ian. "Imperial Schemes: Empire and the Rise of the British Business-State, 1914–1939." PhD diss., Harvard University, 2020.
Kunz, Diane B. "American Bankers and Britain's Fall from Gold." In *The Role of Banks in the Interwar Economy*, edited by Harold James, Håkan Lindgren, and Alice Teichova, 35–48. Cambridge: Cambridge University Press, 1991.
Kunz, Diane. *The Battle for Britain's Gold Standard in 1931*. London: Croom Helm, 1987.
Kynaston, David. "The Bank of England and the Government." In *The Bank of England: Money, Power and Influence, 1694–1994*, edited by Richard Roberts and David Kynaston, 19–55. Oxford: Clarendon Press, 1995.
Kynaston, David. *The City of London, vol. 1: A World of Its Own, 1815–1890*. London: Chatto & Windus, 1994.
Kynaston, David. *The City of London, vol. 2: Golden Years, 1890–1914*. London: Chatto & Windus, 1995.
Kynaston, David. *The City of London, vol. 3: Illusions of Gold, 1914–1945*. London: Chatto & Windus, 1999.
Kynaston, David. *The City of London, vol. 4: A Club No More, 1945–2000*. London: Chatto & Windus, 2001.
Kynaston, David. *Till Time's Last Sand: A History of the Bank of England, 1694–2013*. London: Bloomsbury, 2017.
Laba, Agnes. "Akademisches Expertenwissen als Ressource für die Politik. Die 'Publikationsstelle Berlin-Dahlem' als Think Tank der nationalsozialistischen Expansions- und Vernichtungspolitik." In *Externe Experten in Politik und Wirtschaft*, edited by Felix Selgert, 95–122. Berlin: De Gruyter Oldenbourg, 2020.

Laidler, David. *Fabricating the Keynesian Revolution: Studies of the Inter-War Literature on Money, the Cycle, and Unemployment*. Cambridge: Cambridge University Press, 1999.

Lambert, Nicholas A. *Planning Armageddon: British Economic Warfare and the First World War*. Cambridge, MA, and London: Harvard University Press, 2012.

Landry, Julien. *Les think tanks et le discours expert sur les politiques publiques au Canada (1890–2015)*. Ottawa: Les Presses de l'Université d'Ottawa, 2021.

Laqua, Daniel. "Transnational Intellectual Cooperation, the League of Nations, and the Problem of Order." *Journal of Global History* 6, no. 2 (2011): 223–247.

Laybourn, Keith. *The General Strike: Day by Day*. Stroud: Alan Sutton, 1996.

Laybourn, Keith. "The Rise of Labour and the Decline of Liberalism: The State of the Debate." *History* 80, no. 259 (1995): 207–226.

Lazonick, William. "Industrial Organization and Technological Change: The Decline of the British Cotton Industry." *Business History Review* 57, no. 2 (1983): 195–236.

Leonhard, Jörn. *Der überforderte Frieden. Versailles und die Welt 1918–1923*. Munich: C.H. Beck, 2018.

Leruez, Jacques. *Planification et politique en Grande-Bretagne, 1945–1971*. Paris: Armand Colin, 1972.

Levy, Jonathan. *The Real Economy: History and Theory*. Princeton and Oxford: Princeton University Press, 2025.

Liddle, Patricio Catriel, and Juan José Pita. "Historia de la creación del Banco Central de la República Argentina." *Ensayos económicos*, no. 64 (2010): 117–139.

Link, Stefan J. *Forging Global Fordism: Nazi Germany, Soviet Russia, and the Contest over the Industrial Order*. Princeton and Oxford: Princeton University Press, 2020.

Link, Werner. *Die amerikanische Stabilisierungspolitik in Deutschland, 1921–32*. Düsseldorf: Droste Verlag, 1970.

Lojkó, Miklós. *Meddling in Middle Europe: Britain and the "Lands Between", 1919–1925*. Budapest and New York: Central European University Press, 2006.

Lorenzutti, Jorge A. *Dinero, política y bancos: historia del Banco Central de la República Argentina, 1935–1995*. Buenos Aires: Ediciones Dunken, 1996.

Lough, David. *No More Champagne: Churchill and His Money*. London: Head of Zeus, 2015.

Loureiro, Maria Rita Garcia. *Os economistas no Governo: gestão econômica e democracia*. Rio de Janeiro: Fundação Getulio Vargas Editora, 1997.

Love, Joseph L. "Economic Ideas and Ideologies in Latin America since 1930." In *The Cambridge History of Latin America, vol. 6, Latin America since 1930: Economy, Society and Politics*, edited by Leslie Bethell, 393–460. Cambridge: Cambridge University Press, 1994.

Love, Joseph L., Berta Brambila, and Andrea Martínez Baracs. "Raúl Prebisch y los orígenes de la doctrina del intercambio desigual." *Revista Mexicana de Sociología* 42, no. 1 (1980): 375–405.

Love, Peter. *Labour and the Money Power: Australian Labour Populism, 1890–1950*. Carlton: Melbourne University Press, 1984.

Love, Peter. "Niemeyer's Australian Diary and Other English Records of His Mission." *Historical Studies* 20, no. 79 (1982): 261–277.

Lumba, Allan E.S. *Monetary Authorities: Capitalism and Decolonization in the American Colonial Philippines*. Durham and London: Duke University Press, 2022.

Macher, Flora. "The Austrian Banking Crisis of 1931: A Reassessment." *Financial History Review* 25, no. 3 (2018): 297–321.

MacMillan, Margaret. *Paris 1919: Six Months That Changed the World*. New York: Random House, 2003.

Maier, Charles S. "Between Taylorism and Technocracy: European Ideologies and the Vision of Industrial Productivity in the 1920s." *Journal of Contemporary History* 5, no. 2 (1970): 27–61.

Maier, Charles S. *Recasting Bourgeois Europe: Stabilization in France, Germany, and Italy in the Decade after World War I*. Princeton: Princeton University Press, 1975.

Maier, Charles S. *In Search of Stability: Explorations in Historical Political Economy*. Cambridge: Cambridge University Press, 1987.

Mallet, Bernard, and C. Oswald George. *British Budgets, Third Series, 1921–22 to 1932–33*. London: Macmillan, 1933.

Maloney, John. *Marshall, Orthodoxy and the Professionalisation of Economics*. Cambridge: Cambridge University Press, 1985.

Manela, Erez. *The Wilsonian Moment: Self-Determination and the International Origins of Anticolonial Nationalism*. Oxford: Oxford University Press, 2007.

Marcus, Nathan. *Austrian Reconstruction and the Collapse of Global Finance, 1921–1931*. Cambridge, MA, and London: Harvard University Press, 2018.

Marcus, Nathan. "Les conseillers étrangers à la Banque nationale d'Autriche 1923–1929 : contrôle ou cooperation ?" *Histoire, économie & société* 35, no. 4 (2016): 8–20.

Marichal, Carlos. *A Century of Debt Crises in Latin America: From Independence to the Great Depression, 1820–1930*. Princeton: Princeton University Press, 1989.

Marichal, Carlos, and Daniel Díaz-Fuentes. "The Emergence of Central Banks in Latin America: Are Evolutionary Models Applicable?" In *The Emergence of Modern Central Banking from 1918 to the Present*, edited by Carl-Ludwig Holtfrerich, Jaime Reis, and Gianni Toniolo, 279–319. Aldershot: Ashgate, 1999.

Marris, R.L. "The Position of Economics and Economists in the Government Machine." *The Economic Journal* 64, no. 256 (1954): 759–783.

Martin, Jamie. *The Meddlers: Sovereignty, Empire, and the Birth of Global Economic Governance*. Cambridge, MA, and London: Harvard University Press, 2022.

Martin, Jamie. "Raw Materials and International Order from the Great War to the Crisis of 1920–21." In *Peacemaking and International Order after the First World War*, edited by Peter Jackson, William Mulligan, and Glenda Sluga, 266–285. Cambridge: Cambridge University Press, 2023.

Martin, Jamie. "Time and the Economics of the Business Cycle in Modern Capitalism." In *Power and Time: Temporalities in Conflict and the Making of History*, edited by Dan Edelstein, Stefanos Geroulanos, and Natasha Wheatley, 317–334. Chicago and London: The University of Chicago Press, 2020.

Martin, William G. *South Africa and the World Economy: Remaking Race, State and Region*. Rochester: University of Rochester Press, 2013.

Mathias, Peter. *The First Industrial Nation: The Economic History of Britain, 1700–1914*. London: Methuen & Co., 1969.

Mathur, Rajul. "The Delay in the Formation of the Reserve Bank of India: The India Office Perspective." *The Indian Economic and Social History Review* 25, no. 2 (1988): 133–169.

Mattei, Clara. *The Capital Order: How Economists Invented Austerity and Paved the Way to Fascism*. Chicago and London: The University of Chicago Press, 2022.

Mattei, Clara Elisabetta. "Hawtrey, Austerity, and the 'Treasury View,' 1918–25." *Journal of the History of Economic Thought* 40, no. 4 (2018): 471–492.

Mattei, Clara Elisabetta. "Treasury View and Post-WWI British Austerity: Basil Blackett, Otto Niemeyer and Ralph Hawtrey." *Cambridge Journal of Economics* 42, no. 4 (2018): 1123–1144.

Matthews, K.G.P. "Was Sterling Overvalued in 1925?" *The Economic History Review* 39, no. 4 (1986): 572–587.

Maxfield, Sylvia. *Gatekeepers of Growth: The International Political Economy of Central Banking in Developing Countries*. Princeton: Princeton University Press, 1997.

Mayer, Arno J. *The Persistence of the Old Regime: Europe to the Great War*. New York: Pantheon, 1981.

Mazower, Mark. *Governing the World: The History of an Idea*. London: Penguin, 2012.

McCann, Gerard. "Protectionism and the 'Economic War' in Interwar Ireland." *The Journal of European Economic History* 43, no. 3 (2014): 39–68.

McCarthy, Helen. *The British People and the League of Nations: Democracy, Citizenship and Internationalism, c. 1918–45*. Manchester and New York: Manchester University Press, 2013.

McCarthy, Helen. "Whose Democracy? Histories of British Political Culture between the Wars." *The Historical Journal* 55, no. 1 (2012): 221–238.

McKenzie, Francine. "Imperial Solutions to International Crises: Alliances, Trade and the Ottawa Imperial Economic Conference of 1932." In *The Foreign Office, Commerce and British Foreign Policy in the Twentieth Century*, edited by John Fisher, Effie G.H. Pedaliu, and Richard Smith, 165–187. London: Palgrave Macmillan, 2016.

McKenzie, Francine. *Redefining the Bonds of Commonwealth, 1939–1948: The Politics of Preference*. Basingstoke: Palgrave Macmillan, 2002.

McKercher, B.J.C. "Old Diplomacy and New: The Foreign Office and Foreign Policy, 1919–1939." In *Diplomacy and World Power: Studies in British Foreign Policy, 1890–1950*, edited by Michael Dockrill and Brian McKercher, 79–114. Cambridge: Cambridge University Press, 1996.

McKinnon, Malcolm. *The Broken Decade: Prosperity, Depression and Recovery in New Zealand, 1928–39*. Dunedin: Otago University Press, 2016.

McKinnon, Malcolm. *Treasury: The New Zealand Treasury, 1840–2000*. Auckland: Auckland University Press, 2003.

Meade, Ellen E. "The Governance of Central Banks." In *The Oxford Handbook of Governance*, edited by David Levi-Faur, 401–414. Oxford: Oxford University Press, 2012.

Meinl, Susanne, and Jutta Zwilling. *Legalisierter Raub. Die Ausplünderung der Juden im Nationalsozialismus durch die Reichsfinanzverwaltung in Hessen*. Frankfurt am Main and New York: Campus Verlag, 2004.

Meissner, Christopher M. *One from the Many: The Global Economy since 1850*. Oxford: Oxford University Press, 2024.

Meltzer, Allan H. *A History of the Federal Reserve, 1913–1951, vol. 1*. Chicago and London: The University of Chicago Press, 2003.

Michie, Ranald C. *The City of London: Continuity and Change, 1850–1990*. Basingstoke: Macmillan, 1992.

Michie, Ranald. "The City of London and the British Government: The Changing Relationship." In *The British Government and the City of London in the Twentieth*

Century, edited by Ranald Michie and Philip Williamson, 31–55. Cambridge: Cambridge University Press, 2004.

Michie, Ranald C. "The City of London as a Global Financial Centre, 1880–1939: Finance, Foreign Exchange, and the First World War." In *Centres and Peripheries in Banking: The Historical Development of Financial Markets*, edited by Phillip L. Cottrell, Even Lange, and Ulf Olsson, 41–79. Aldershot: Ashgate, 2007.

Michie, Ranald. "A Financial Phoenix: The City of London in the Twentieth Century." In *London and Paris as International Financial Centres in the Twentieth Century*, edited by Youssef Cassis and Éric Bussière, 15–41. Oxford: Oxford University Press, 2005.

Michie, Ranald C. *Forex Forever: The City of London and the Foreign Exchange Market since 1850*. Oxford: Oxford University Press, 2024.

Michie, Ranald C. *The London Stock Exchange: A History*. Oxford: Oxford University Press, 2001.

Middleton, Roger. "Britain in the 1930s: A Managed Economy? A Comment." *The Economic History Review* 42, no. 4 (1989): 544–547.

Middleton, Roger. *Charlatans or Saviours? Economists and the British Economy from Marshall to Meade*. Cheltenham: Edward Elgar, 1998.

Middleton, Roger. *Government versus the Market: The Growth of the Public Sector, Economic Management and British Economic Performance, c. 1890–1979*. Cheltenham: Edward Elgar, 1996.

Middleton, Roger. *Towards the Managed Economy: Keynes, the Treasury, and the Fiscal Policy Debate of the 1930s*. London and New York: Methuen, 1985.

Millmow, Alex. *A History of Australasian Economic Thought*. London and New York: Routledge, 2017.

Millmow, Alex. "Niemeyer, Scullin and the Australian Economists." *Australian Economic History Review* 44, no. 2 (2004): 142–160.

Millmow, Alex. *The Power of Economic Ideas: The Origins of Keynesian Macroeconomic Management in Interwar Australia, 1929–1939*. Canberra: ANU E Press, 2010.

Millmow, Alex. "W. Brian Reddaway (1913–2002)." *History of Economics Review* 36, no. 1 (2002): 177–179.

Miners, Norman. "Industrial Development in the Colonial Empire and the Imperial Economic Conference at Ottawa, 1932." *The Journal of Imperial and Commonwealth History* 30, no. 2 (2002): 53–76.

Mirwis, Arnold T. "Carl Jung and Lord Montagu Norman: A Failed Consultation." *American Imago* 44, no. 2 (1987): 159–169.

Mitchell, B.R. *British Historical Statistics*. Cambridge: Cambridge University Press, 1988.

Mitchell, Timothy. "Economists and Economy in the Twentieth Century." In *The Politics of Method in the Human Sciences: Positivism and Its Epistemological Other*, edited by George Steinmetz, 126–142. Durham: Duke University Press, 2005.

Mitchell, Timothy. "Fixing the Economy." *Cultural Studies* 12, no. 1 (1998): 82–101.

Mitchell, Timothy. *Rule of Experts: Egypt, Techno-Politics, Modernity*. Berkeley: University of California Press, 2002.

Mitchener, Kris James, and Kirsten Wandschneider. "Capital Controls and Recovery from the Financial Crisis of the 1930s." *Journal of International Economics* 95, no. 2 (2015): 188–201.

Mitton, Lavinia Clare Elizabeth. "The Objectives and Outcomes of Means Testing under the British Welfare State." PhD diss., London School of Economics, 2014.

Moggridge, D.E. *British Monetary Policy, 1924–1931: The Norman Conquest of $4.86*. Cambridge: Cambridge University Press, 1972.

Moggridge, D.E. *Maynard Keynes: An Economist's Biography*. London and New York: Routledge, 1992.

Moggridge, D.E. *The Return to Gold, 1925: The Formulation of Economic Policy and Its Critics*. Cambridge: Cambridge University Press, 1969.

Monnet, Éric. *Controlling Credit: Central Banking and the Planned Economy in Postwar France, 1948–1973*. Cambridge: Cambridge University Press, 2018.

Morgan, Kenneth O. *Consensus and Disunity: The Lloyd George Coalition Government, 1918–1922*. Oxford: Clarendon Press, 1979.

Morrison, James Ashley. *England's Cross of Gold: Keynes, Churchill, and the Governance of Economic Beliefs*. Ithaca and London: Cornell University Press, 2021.

Morrison, James Ashley. "Shocking Intellectual Austerity: The Role of Ideas in the Demise of the Gold Standard in Britain." *International Organization* 70, no. 1 (2016): 175–207.

Morton, Walter A. *British Finance, 1930–1940*. Madison: The University of Wisconsin Press, 1943.

Moschella, Manuela. *Unexpected Revolutionaries: How Central Banks Made and Unmade Economic Orthodoxy*. Ithaca: Cornell University Press, 2024.

Moschella, Manuela, Luca Pinto, and Nicola Martocchia Diodati. "Let's Speak More? How the ECB Responds to Public Contestation." *Journal of European Public Policy* 27, no. 3 (2020): 400–418.

Moschella, Manuela, and Catherine Weaver. "Global Economic Governance: Players, Power and Paradigms." In *Handbook of Global Economic Governance*, edited by Manuela Moschella and Catherine Weaver, 1–22. Abingdon: Routledge, 2014.

Moulton, Mo. *Ireland and the Irish in Interwar England*. Cambridge: Cambridge University Press, 2014.

Mouré, Kenneth. "French Money Doctors, Central Banks, and Politics in the 1920s." In *Money Doctors: The Experience of International Financial Advising, 1850–2000*, edited by Marc Flandreau, 138–165. London and New York: Routledge, 2005.

Mouré, Kenneth. *The Gold Standard Illusion: France, the Bank of France, and the International Gold Standard, 1914–1939*. Oxford: Oxford University Press, 2002.

Mouré, Kenneth. "Les banques centrales et l'étalon-or dans l'entre-deux-guerres." In *Politiques et pratiques des banques d'émission en Europe (XVIIe–XXe siècle) : le bicentenaire de la Banque de France dans la perspective de l'identité monétaire européenne*, edited by Olivier Feiertag and Michel Margairaz, 345–367. Paris: Albin Michel, 2003.

Mouré, Kenneth. *Managing the Franc Poincaré: Economic Understanding and Political Constraint in French Monetary Policy, 1928–1936*. Cambridge: Cambridge University Press, 1991.

Mouton, Marie-Renée. *La Société des Nations et les intérêts de la France (1920–1924)*. Bern and New York: P. Lang, 1995.

Moynihan, Maurice. *Currency and Central Banking in Ireland, 1922–1960*. Dublin: Gill and Macmillan, 1975.

Mseba, Admire. "Beyond Imperial Interests: Settler Regimes, Capital and Africans in Colonial Southern Africa's Currency Politics to 1920." In *Monetary Transitions: Currencies, Colonialism and African Societies*, edited by Karin Pallaver, 139–159. Cham: Palgrave Macmillan, 2022.

Mukherjee, Aditya. "Controversy over Formation of Reserve Bank of India, 1927–35." *Economic and Political Weekly* 27, no. 6 (1992): 229–234.

Mukherjee, Aditya. *Imperialism, Nationalism and the Making of the Indian Capitalist Class, 1920–1947*. New Delhi: Sage Publications, 2002.

Mulder, Nicholas. *The Economic Weapon: The Rise of Sanctions as a Tool of Modern War*. New Haven and London: Yale University Press, 2022.

Munro, Dana G. *Intervention and Dollar Diplomacy in the Caribbean, 1900–1921*. Princeton: Princeton University Press, 1964.

Murphy, Anne L. *Virtuous Bankers: A Day in the Life of the Eighteenth-Century Bank of England*. Princeton and Oxford: Princeton University Press, 2023.

Mußgnug, Dorothee. *Die Reichsfluchtsteuer 1931–1953*. Berlin: Duncker & Humblot, 1993.

Mussio, Laurence B. *Whom Fortune Favours: The Bank of Montreal and the Rise of North American Finance, A Dominion of Capital, 1817–1945, vol. 1*. Montreal and Kingston: McGill-Queen's University Press, 2020.

Naef, Alain. *An Exchange Rate History of the United Kingdom, 1945–1992*. Cambridge: Cambridge University Press, 2022.

Nállim, Jorge A. *Transformations and Crisis of Liberalism in Argentina, 1930–1955*. Pittsburgh: University of Pittsburgh Press, 2012.

Naylor, John F. *A Man and an Institution: Sir Maurice Hankey, the Cabinet Secretariat and the Custody of Cabinet Secrecy*. Cambridge: Cambridge University Press, 1984.

Neary, J. Peter, and Cormac Ó Gráda. "Protection, Economic War and Structural Change: The 1930s in Ireland." *Irish Historical Studies* 27, no. 107 (1991): 250–266.

Needham, Duncan. *UK Monetary Policy from Devaluation to Thatcher, 1967–82*. Basingstoke: Palgrave Macmillan, 2014.

Nerbas, Don. "Managing Democracy, Defending Capitalism: Gilbert E. Jackson, the Canadian Committee on Industrial Reconstruction, and the Changing Form of Elite Politics in Canada." *Histoire sociale/Social History* XLVI, no. 9 (2013): 173–204.

Newton, Lucy. "British Retail Banking in the Twentieth Century: Decline and Renaissance in Industrial Lending." In *Business in Britain in the Twentieth Century: Decline and Renaissance?*, edited by Richard Coopey and Peter Lyth, 189–206. Oxford: Oxford University Press, 2009.

Newton, Lucy. "Government, the Banks and Industry in Inter-War Britain." In *Business and Politics in Europe, 1900–1970: Essays in Honour of Alice Teichova*, edited by Terry Gourvish, 145–168. Cambridge: Cambridge University Press, 2003.

Newton, Scott. *Profits of Peace: The Political Economy of Anglo-German Appeasement*. Oxford: Clarendon Press, 1996.

Nützenadel, Alexander. *Stunde der Ökonomen. Wissenschaft, Politik und Expertenkultur in der Bundesrepublik 1949–1974*. Göttingen: Vandenhoeck & Ruprecht, 2005.

Ó Broin, Leon. "Joseph Brennan, Civil Servant Extraordinary." *Studies: An Irish Quarterly Review* 66, no. 261 (1977): 25–37.

Ó Broin, Leon. *No Man's Man: A Biographical Memoir of Joseph Brennan: Civil Servant & First Governor of the Central Bank*. Dublin: Institute of Public Administration, 1982.

Ó Gráda, Cormac. *Ireland: A New Economic History, 1780–1939*. Oxford: Clarendon Press, 1994.

Ó Gráda, Cormac. "Money and Banking in the Irish Free State, 1921–1939." In *Banking, Currency, and Finance in Europe between the Wars*, edited by Charles H. Feinstein, 414–433. Oxford: Clarendon Press, 1995.

O'Brien, D.P., and John Creedy. *Darwin's Clever Neighbour: George Warde Norman and His Circle*. Cheltenham: Edward Elgar, 2010.

O'Brien, Patrick K., and Nuno Palma. "Not an Ordinary Bank but a Great Engine of State: The Bank of England and the British Economy, 1694–1844." *The Economic History Review* 76, no. 1 (2023): 305–329.

O'Halpin, Eunan. *Head of the Civil Service: A Study of Sir Warren Fisher*. London and New York: Routledge, 1989.

O'Hara, Glen. *Governing Post-War Britain: The Paradoxes of Progress, 1951–1973*. Basingstoke: Palgrave Macmillan, 2012.

O'Hara, Glen. "Towards a New Bradshaw? Economic Statistics and the British State in the 1950s and 1960s." *The Economic History Review* 60, no. 1 (2007): 1–34.

O'Rourke, Kevin. "Burn Everything British but Their Coal: The Anglo-Irish Economic War of the 1930s." *Journal of Economic History* 51, no. 2 (1991): 357–366.

O'Rourke, Kevin H., and Jeffrey G. Williamson. *Globalization and History: The Evolution of a Nineteenth-Century Atlantic Economy*. Cambridge, MA, and London: The MIT Press, 1999.

O'Sullivan, Brian. *From Crisis to Crisis: The Transformation of Merchant Banking, 1914–1939*. Cham: Palgrave Macmillan, 2018.

Obstfeld, Maurice, and Alan M. Taylor. "Sovereign Risk, Credibility and the Gold Standard: 1870–1913 versus 1925–31." *The Economic Journal* 113, no. 487 (2003): 241–275.

Offner, Amy C. *Sorting Out the Mixed Economy: The Rise and Fall of Welfare and Developmental States in the Americas*. Princeton and Oxford: Princeton University Press, 2019.

Orde, Anne. *British Policy and European Reconstruction after the First World War*. Cambridge: Cambridge University Press, 1990.

Otero, Hernán. *Estadística y nación: una historia conceptual del pensamiento censal de la Argentina moderna, 1869–1914*. Buenos Aires: Prometeo libros, 2006.

Otte, T.G. "Introduction: British World Policy and the White Queen's Memory." In *British World Policy and the Projection of Global Power, c. 1830–1960*, edited by T.G. Otte, 1–23. Cambridge: Cambridge University Press, 2019.

Otto, Frank. *Die Keynesianische Revolution in Großbritannien (1929–1948). Zur Entwicklung der Finanzpolitik im Spannungsfeld von wirtschaftswissenschaftlicher Herausforderung, politischem Reformwillen und institutioneller Beharrungskraft*. Berlin: Duncker & Humblot, 1996.

Paish, F.W. "Note on Bank Window-Dressing." *Economica* 6, no. 24 (1939): 456–460.

Pak, Susie J. *Gentlemen Bankers: The World of J.P. Morgan*. Cambridge, MA, and London: Harvard University Press, 2013.

Paker, Meredith M. "Normal Science and Anomaly: Responding to Unemployment in Economics in the 1920s." MPhil thesis, University of Oxford, 2018.

Pantaleón, Jorge F. "El surgimiento de la nueva economía argentina: el caso Bunge." In *Intelectuales y expertos: la constitución del conocimiento social en la Argentina*, edited by Federico Neiburg and Mariano Plotkin, 175–201. Buenos Aires: Paidós, 2004.

Pauly, Louis W. *Who Elected the Bankers? Surveillance and Control in the World Economy*. Ithaca and London: Cornell University Press, 1997.

Peden, G.C. "Britain in the 1930s: A Managed Economy? A Comment." *The Economic History Review* 42, no. 4 (1989): 538–543.

Peden, G.C. "Economic Knowledge and the State in Modern Britain." In *The Boundaries of the State in Modern Britain*, edited by S.J.D. Green and R.C. Whiting, 170–187. Cambridge: Cambridge University Press, 1996.

Peden, G.C. "Introduction." In *Keynes and His Critics: Treasury Responses to the Keynesian Revolution, 1925–1946*, edited by G.C. Peden, 1–22. Oxford: Oxford University Press, 2004.

Peden, G.C. *Keynes, The Treasury and British Economic Policy*. Basingstoke: Macmillan, 1988.

Peden, G.C. "The Road to and from Gairloch: Lloyd George, Unemployment, Inflation, and the 'Treasury View' in 1921." *Twentieth Century British History* 4, no. 3 (1993): 224–249.

Peden, G.C. *The Treasury and British Public Policy, 1906–1959*. Oxford: Oxford University Press, 2000.

Peden, G.C. "The Treasury and the City." In *The British Government and the City of London in the Twentieth Century*, edited by Ranald Michie and Philip Williamson, 117–134. Cambridge: Cambridge University Press, 2004.

Peden, G.C. "The Treasury as the Central Department of Government, 1919–1939." *Public Administration* 61, no. 4 (1983): 371–385.

Peden, G.C. "The 'Treasury View' on Public Works and Employment in the Interwar Period." *The Economic History Review* 37, no. 2 (1984): 167–181.

Pedersen, Susan. "Back to the League of Nations." *The American Historical Review* 112, no. 4 (2007): 1091–1117.

Pedersen, Susan. *The Guardians: The League of Nations and the Crisis of Empire*. Oxford: Oxford University Press, 2015.

Pellew, Jill. "Law and Order: Expertise and the Victorian Home Office." In *Government and Expertise: Specialists, Administrators, and Professionals, 1860–1919*, edited by Roy Macleod, 59–72. Cambridge: Cambridge University Press, 1988.

Pemberton, Jo-Anne. "New Worlds for Old: The League of Nations in the Age of Electricity." *Review of International Studies* 28, no. 2 (2002): 311–336.

Perkin, Harold. *The Rise of Professional Society: England since 1880*. London and New York: Routledge, 1989.

Perkins, Anne. *A Very British Strike: 3 May–12 May, 1926*. London: Macmillan, 2006.

Peter, Matthias. *John Maynard Keynes und die britische Deutschlandpolitik. Machtanspruch und ökonomische Realität im Zeitalter der Weltkriege 1919–1946*. Munich: R. Oldenbourg, 1997.

Peterecz, Zoltán. *Jeremiah Smith, Jr. and Hungary, 1924–1926: The United States, the League of Nations, and the Financial Reconstruction of Hungary*. London: Versita, 2013.

Peterecz, Zoltán. "Hungary and the League of Nations." In *Remaking Central Europe: The League of Nations and the Former Habsburg Lands*, edited by Peter Becker and Natasha Wheatley, 145–166. Oxford: Oxford University Press, 2020.

Péteri, György. "Central Bank Diplomacy: Montagu Norman and Central Europe's Monetary Reconstruction after World War I." *Contemporary European History* 1, no. 3 (1992): 233–258.

Péteri, György. *Global Monetary Regime and National Central Banking: The Case of Hungary, 1921–1929*, translated by Mario D. Fenyo. Boulder: Social Science Monographs, 2002.

Péteri, György. "Sneaking Nationalization: Hungary and the Liberal Monetary Order, 1924–1931." In *The Spread of the Modern Central Bank and Global Cooperation, 1919–1939*, edited by Barry Eichengreen and Andreas Kakridis, 139–159. Cambridge: Cambridge: University Press, 2023.

Piétri, Nicole. *La Société des Nations et la reconstruction financière de l'Autriche, 1921–1926*. Geneva: Centre européen de la Dotation Carnegie pour la paix internationale, 1970.

Piller, Elisabeth, and Neville Wylie, eds. *Humanitarianism and the Greater War, 1914–24*. Manchester: Manchester University Press, 2023.

Plumptre, A.F.W. *Central Banking in the British Dominions*. Toronto: University of Toronto Press, 1940.

Pollard, Sidney. *The Development of the British Economy, 1914–1990*, 4th ed. London: Edward Arnold, 1992.

Pollard, Sidney. "Die Krise des Sozialismus in der Zwischenkriegszeit: Großbritannien." *Geschichte und Gesellschaft* 17, no. 2 (1991): 160–181.

Porter, Theodore M. *The Rise of Statistical Thinking, 1820–1900*. Princeton: Princeton University Press, 1986.

Porter, Theodore M. *Trust in Numbers: The Pursuit of Objectivity in Science and Public Life*. Princeton: Princeton University Press, 1995.

Postel-Vinay, Natacha, and Stéphanie Collet. "Hot Money Inflows and Bank Risk-Taking: Germany from the 1920s to the Great Depression." *The Economic History Review* 77, no. 2 (2024): 472–502.

Potash, Robert A. *The Army & Politics in Argentina, 1928–1934: Yrigoyen to Perón*. Stanford: Stanford University Press, 1969.

Powell, David. *British Politics, 1910–35: The Crisis of the Party System*. London and New York: Routledge, 2004.

Powell, David. "The New Liberalism and the Rise of Labour, 1886–1906." *The Historical Journal* 29, no. 2 (1986): 369–393.

Powell, James. *A History of the Canadian Dollar*. Ottawa: Bank of Canada, 2005.

Queralt, Didac. *Pawned States: State Building in the Era of International Finance*. Princeton and Oxford: Princeton University Press, 2022.

Raichle, Christoph. *Die Finanzverwaltung in Baden und Württemberg im Nationalsozialismus*. Stuttgart: W. Kohlhammer, 2019.

Raphael, Lutz. "Zwischen Sozialaufklärung und radikalem Ordnungsdenken. Die Verwissenschaftlichung des Sozialen im Europa der ideologischen Extreme." In *Europäische Wissenschaftskulturen und politische Ordnungen in der Moderne (1890–1970)*, edited by Gangolf Hübinger, 29–50. Munich: Oldenbourg Verlag, 2014.

Read, Charles. *Calming the Storms: The Carry Trade, the Banking School and British Financial Crises since 1825*. Cham: Palgrave Macmillan, 2023.

Redish, Angela. "British Financial Imperialism after the First World War." In *Gentlemanly Capitalism and British Imperialism: The New Debate on Empire*, edited by Raymond E. Dumett, 127–140. London: Longman, 1999.

Redmond, John. "The Sterling Overvaluation in 1925: A Multilateral Approach." *The Economic History Review* 37, no. 4 (1984): 520–532.

Regalsky, Andrés. "En los preámbulos de la Banca Central 1914–1930: el Banco de la Nación Argentina y sus nuevas orientaciones a partir de la Primera Guerra Mundial." In *Historia necesaria del Banco Central de la República Argentina: entre la búsqueda de la estabilidad y la promoción del desarrollo*, edited by Marcelo Rougier and Florencia Sember, 39–67. Buenos Aires: Lenguaje Claro-Ciccus, 2018.

Regalsky, Andrés M. "Estado, banca pública y crisis: los créditos del Banco de la Nación Argentina durante la coyuntura de 1914–15." In *Historia bancaria y monetaria de América Latina (siglos XIX y XX): nuevas perspectivas*, edited by Carlos Marichal and Thiago Gambi, 249–277. Santander: Editorial de la Universidad de Cantabria, 2017.

Renard, Didier. "*Technocracy*, ou la science contre l'économie : un mouvement américain des années 30." In *La question technocratique: de l'invention d'une figure aux transformations de l'action publique*, edited by Vincent Dubois and Delphine Dulong, 19–33. Strasbourg: Presses universitaires de Strasbourg, 1999.

Reynolds, David. *Britannia Overruled: British Policy and World Power in the 20th Century*. London and New York: Longman, 1991.

Richardson, Philip. "'Plucking the China Brand from the Burning': Britain's Economic Assistance to China and Sir Otto Niemeyer's Mission, 1940–42." *The China Quarterly*, 125 (1991): 86–108.

Riddell, Neil. *Labour in Crisis: The Second Labour Government, 1929–1931*. Manchester and New York: Manchester University Press, 1999.

Riles, Annelise. *Financial Citizenship: Experts, Publics, and the Politics of Central Banking*. Ithaca and London: Cornell University Press, 2019.

Ritschel, Daniel. *The Politics of Planning: The Debate on Economic Planning in Britain in the 1930s*. Oxford: Clarendon Press, 1997.

Ritschl, Albrecht. *Deutschlands Krise und Konjunktur 1924–1934. Binnenkonjunktur, Auslandsverschuldung und Reparationsproblem zwischen Dawes-Plan und Transfersperre*. Berlin: Akademie Verlag, 2002.

Robbins, Lord. "Montagu Norman: A 'Monarch' in the City." In *The Evolution of Modern Economic Theory and Other Papers on the History of Economic Thought*, 234–242. London: Palgrave Macmillan, 1970.

Roberts, Richard. "The Bank of England and the City." In *The Bank of England: Money, Power and Influence, 1694–1994*, edited by Richard Roberts and David Kynaston, 152–184. Oxford: Clarendon Press, 1995.

Roberts, Richard. "'How We Saved the City': The Management of the Financial Crisis of 1914." In *British Financial Crisis since 1825*, edited by Nicholas Dimsdale and Anthony Hotson, 94–115. Oxford: Oxford University Press, 2014.

Roberts, Richard. *Saving the City: The Great Financial Crisis of 1914*. Oxford: Oxford University Press, 2013.

Roberts, Richard. *Schroders: Merchants & Bankers*. Basingstoke: Macmillan, 1992.

Robertson, John. *J.H. Scullin: A Political Biography*. Nedlands: University of Western Australia Press, 1974.

Rock, David. *Argentina, 1516–1987: From Spanish Colonization to Alphonsín*. Berkeley: University of California Press, 1987.

Rock, David. *The British in Argentina: Commerce, Settlers and Power, 1800–2000*. Basingstoke: Palgrave Macmillan, 2019.

Rock, David. "The Roca–Runciman Treaty of 1933: Defending Which British Interests?" In *Britain and the Growth of US Hegemony in Twentieth-Century Latin America: Competition, Cooperation and Coexistence*, edited by Thomas C. Mills and Rory M. Miller, 127–150. Cham: Palgrave Macmillan, 2020.

Rockoff, Hugh. "O.M.W. Sprague (The Man Who 'Wrote the Book' on Financial Crises) Meets the Great Depression." *Jahrbuch für Wirtschaftsgeschichte* 63, no. 2 (2022): 527–557.

Roe, Michael. *Australia, Britain and Migration, 1915–1940: A Study of Desperate Hopes*. Cambridge and New York: Cambridge University Press, 1995.

Rollings, Neil. "British Budgetary Policy 1945–1954: A 'Keynesian Revolution'?" *The Economic History Review* 41, no. 2 (1988): 283–298.

Rooth, Tim. *British Protectionism and the International Economy: Overseas Commercial Policy in the 1930s*. Cambridge: Cambridge University Press, 1991.

Rosenberg, Emily. *Financial Missionaries to the World: The Politics and Culture of Dollar Diplomacy, 1900–1930*. Durham: Duke University Press, 2003.

Rosenboim, Or. *The Emergence of Globalism: Visions of World Order in Britain and the United States, 1939–1950*. Princeton and Oxford: Princeton University Press, 2017.

Rothermund, Dietmar. *India in the Great Depression, 1929–1939*. New Delhi: Manohar, 1992.

Rubinstein, W.D. *Men of Property: The Very Wealthy in Britain since the Industrial Revolution*. London: Croom Helm, 1981.

Salomão, Ivan Colangelo, and Victoria Silva Oliveira. "Banco do Brasil: de autoridade monetária a banco comercial." *Revista Brasileira de História & Ciências Sociais* 15, no. 31 (2024): 447–477.

Sandberg, Lars G. *Lancashire in Decline: A Study in Entrepreneurship, Technology, and International Trade*. Columbus: The Ohio State University Press, 1974.

Sargent, Thomas J. "The Ends of Four Big Inflations." In *Inflation: Causes and Effects*, edited by Robert E. Hall, 41–97. Chicago and London: The University of Chicago Press, 1982.

Savage, Gail. *The Social Construction of Expertise: The English Civil Service and Its Influence, 1919–1939*. Pittsburgh: University of Pittsburgh Press, 1996.

Sayers, R.S. *The Bank of England, 1891–1944, vol. 1*. Cambridge: Cambridge University Press, 1976.

Sayers, R.S. *The Bank of England, 1891–1944, vol. 2*. Cambridge: Cambridge University Press, 1976.

Sayers, R.S. *Bank of England Operations, 1890–1914*. London: P.S. King & Son, 1936.

Sayers, R.S. *Bank Rate in Keynes's Century: Keynes Lecture in Economics*. London: British Academy, Oxford University Press, 1979.

Sayers, R.S. *Central Banking after Bagehot*. Oxford: Clarendon Press, 1957.

Sayers, R.S. *Financial Policy, 1939–45*. London: H.M. Stationery Office and Longmans, Green & Co., 1956.

Sayers, R.S. "The Indian Exchange Problem, 1919–20." *Economica* 34 (1931): 450–462.

Sayers, R.S. *Modern Banking*. London: Oxford University Press, 1938.

Sayers, R.S. "The Return to Gold, 1925." In *Studies in the Industrial Revolution: Presented to T.S. Ashton*, edited by L.S. Pressnell, 313–327. London: University of London, The Athlone Press, 1960.

Sayward, Amy L. *The Birth of Development: How the World Bank, Food and Agriculture Organization, and World Health Organization Changed the World, 1945–1965*. Kent: The Kent State University Press, 2006.

Schabas, Margaret. "Constructing 'the Economy'." *Philosophy of the Social Sciences* 39, no. 1 (2009): 3–19.

Schedvin, C.B. *Australia and the Great Depression: A Study of Economic Development and Policy in the 1920s and 1930s*. Sydney: Sydney University, 1970.

Schenk, Catherine. *Britain and the Sterling Area: From Devaluation to Convertibility in the 1950s*. London and New York: Routledge, 1994.

Schenk, Catherine R. *The Decline of Sterling: Managing the Retreat of an International Currency, 1945–1992*. Cambridge: Cambridge University Press, 2010.

Schenk, Catherine R. "The New City and the State in the 1960s." In *The British Government and the City of London in the Twentieth Century*, edited by Ranald Michie and Philip Williamson, 322–339. Cambridge: Cambridge University Press, 2004.

Schmelzer, Matthias. *The Hegemony of Growth: The OECD and the Making of the Economic Growth Paradigm*. Cambridge: Cambridge University Press, 2016.

Schnabel, Isabel. "The German Twin Crisis of 1931." *The Journal of Economic History* 64, no. 3 (2004): 822–871.

Schneider, Sabine. "The Politics of Last Resort Lending and the Overend & Gurney Crisis of 1866." *The Economic History Review* 75, no. 2 (2022): 579–600.

Schubert, Aurel. *The Credit-Anstalt Crisis of 1931*. Cambridge: Cambridge University Press, 1991.

Schubert, Aurel. "The Emergence of National Central Banks in Central Europe after the Break-Up of the Austro-Hungarian Monarchy." In *The Emergence of Modern Central Banking From 1918 to the Present*, edited by Carl-Ludwig Holtfrerich, Jaime Reis, and Gianni Toniolo, 186–230. Aldershot: Ashgate, 1999.

Schui, Florian. *Austerity: The Great Failure*. New Haven and London: Yale University Press, 2014.

Schuker, Stephen A. "American Reparations to Germany, 1919–33: Implications for the Third World Debt Crisis." *Princeton Studies in International Finance*, no. 61 (1988).

Schuker, Stephen A. "Money Doctors between the Wars: The Competition between Central Banks, Private Financial Advisers, and Multilateral Agencies, 1919–39." In *Money Doctors: The Experience of International Financial Advising, 1850–2000*, edited by Marc Flandreau, 49–77. London and New York: Routledge, 2005.

Schulz, Gerhard. *Von Brüning zu Hitler. Der Wandel des politischen Systems in Deutschland 1930–1933*. Berlin and New York: Walter de Gruyter, 1992.

Schumann-Bacia, Eva. *Die Bank von England und ihr Architekt John Soane*. Zurich and Munich: Verlag für Architektur Artemis, 1989.

Schwabe, Klaus. *Versailles. Das Wagnis eines demokratischen Friedens 1919–1923*. Paderborn: F. Schöningh, 2019.

Scott, Peter, and Lucy Newton. "Jealous Monopolists? British Banks and Responses to the Macmillan Gap during the 1930s." *Enterprise & Society* 8, no. 4 (2007): 881–919.

Seidel, Robert N. "American Reformers Abroad: The Kemmerer Missions in South America, 1923–1931." *The Journal of Economic History* 32, no. 2 (1972): 520–545.

Sember, Florencia. "Challenging a Money Doctor: Raúl Prebisch vs. Sir Otto Niemeyer on the Creation of the Argentine Central Bank." In *Research in the History of Economic Thought and Methodology: Including a Symposium on Latin American Monetary Thought: Two Centuries in Search of Originality*, edited by Luca Fiorito, Scott Scheall, and Carlos Eduardo Suprinyak, 55–79. Bingley: Emerald Publishing, 2019.

Sember, Florencia. "El banco mixto (1935–1945): entre la ortodoxia y la búsqueda de un nuevo sendero de crecimiento." In *Historia necesaria del Banco Central de la*

República Argentina: entre la búsqueda de la estabilidad y la promoción del desarrollo, edited by Marcelo Rougier and Florencia Sember, 69–135. Buenos Aires: Lenguaje Claro-Ciccus, 2018.

Sember, Florencia. "The Reception of Irving Fisher in Argentina: Alejandro Bunge and Raúl Prebisch." *The European Journal of the History of Economic Thought* 20, no. 2 (2013): 372–398.

Shaw, Caroline. "Rothschilds and Brazil: An Introduction to Sources in the Rothschild Archive." *Latin American Research Review* 40, no. 1 (2005): 165–185.

Sicsic, Pierre, and Bertrand Villeneuve. "L'afflux d'or en France de 1928 à 1934." In *Du franc Poincaré à l'écu : colloque tenu à Bercy les 3 et 4 décembre 1992*, edited by Maurice Lévy-Leboyer, Alain Plessis, Michel Aglietta, and Christian de Boissieu, 21–55. Paris: Comité pour l'histoire économique et financière de la France, 1993.

Siegel, Jennifer. "Planning for International Financial Order: The Call for Collective Responsibility at the Paris Peace Conference." In *Peacemaking and International Order after the First World War*, edited by Peter Jackson, William Mulligan, and Glenda Sluga, 246–265. Cambridge: Cambridge University Press, 2023.

Simha, S.L.N. *History of the Reserve Bank of India (1935–51)*. Bombay: Reserve Bank of India, 1970.

Simmons, Beth A. *Who Adjusts? Domestic Sources of Foreign Economic Policy during the Interwar Years*. Princeton: Princeton University Press, 1994.

Singleton, John. *Central Banking in the Twentieth Century*. Cambridge: Cambridge University Press, 2011.

Singleton, John. "Central Banks in the British Dominions in the Interwar Period." In *The Spread of the Modern Central Bank and Global Cooperation, 1919–1939*, edited by Barry Eichengreen and Andreas Kakridis, 352–382. Cambridge: Cambridge: University Press, 2023.

Singleton, John. *Lancashire on the Scrapheap: The Cotton Industry, 1945–1970*. Oxford: Oxford University Press, 1991.

Skidelsky, Robert. *John Maynard Keynes, vol. 1: Hopes Betrayed, 1883–1920*. London: Macmillan, 1983.

Skidelsky, Robert. *John Maynard Keynes, vol. 2: The Economist as Saviour, 1920–1937*. London: Macmillan, 1992.

Skidelsky, Robert. *John Maynard Keynes, vol. 3: Fighting for Britain, 1937–1946*. London: Macmillan, 2000.

Skidelsky, Robert. "Keynes and the Treasury View: The Case for and against an Active Unemployment Policy, 1920–1929." In *The Emergence of the Welfare State in Britain and Germany, 1850–1950*, edited by W.J. Mommsen, 167–187. London: Croom Helm, 1981.

Skidelsky, Robert. *Money and Government: The Past and Future of Economics*. New Haven and London: Yale University Press, 2018.

Skidelsky, Robert. *Oswald Mosley*. London: Macmillan, 1975.

Skidelsky, Robert. *Politicians and the Slump: The Labour Government of 1929–1931*. London: Macmillan, 1967.

Slobodian, Quinn. *Globalists: The End of Empire and the Birth of Neoliberalism*. Cambridge, MA, and London: Harvard University Press, 2018.

Slobodian, Quinn. "How to See the World Economy: Statistics, Maps, and Schumpeter's Camera in the First Age of Globalization." *Journal of Global History* 10, no. 2 (2015): 307–332.

Sloman, Peter. *The Liberal Party and the Economy, 1929–1964*. Oxford: Oxford University Press, 2015.

Sluga, Glenda. *Internationalism in the Age of Nationalism*. Philadelphia: University of Pennsylvania Press, 2013.

Sluga, Glenda. *The Invention of International Order: Remaking Europe after Napoleon*. Princeton and Oxford: Princeton University Press, 2021.

Sluga, Glenda, and Patricia Clavin, eds. *Internationalisms: A Twentieth-Century History*. Cambridge: Cambridge University Press, 2016.

Smart, Nick. *The National Government, 1931–40*. New York: St. Martin's Press, 1999.

Spear, Joanna. *The Business of Armaments: Armstrongs, Vickers and the International Arms Trade, 1855–1955*. Cambridge: Cambridge University Press, 2023.

Speich, Daniel. "The Use of Global Abstractions: National Income Accounting in the Period of Imperial Decline." *Journal of Global History* 6, no. 1 (2011): 7–28.

Speich Chassé, Daniel. "Towards a Global History of the Marshall Plan: European Post-War Reconstruction and the Rise of Development Economic Expertise." In *Industrial Policy in Europe after 1945: Wealth, Power and Economic Development in the Cold War*, edited by Christian Grabas and Alexander Nützenadel, 187–212. Basingstoke: Palgrave Macmillan, 2014.

Steffek, Jens. *International Organization as Technocratic Utopia*. Oxford: Oxford University Press, 2021.

Steil, Benn. *The Battle of Bretton Woods: John Maynard Keynes, Harry Dexter White, and the Making of a New World Order*. Princeton and Oxford: Princeton University Press, 2013.

Steiner, Zara. *The Foreign Office and Foreign Policy, 1898–1914*. Cambridge: Cambridge University Press, 1969.

Steiner, Zara. *The Lights that Failed: European International History, 1919–1933*. Oxford: Oxford University Press, 2005.

Steiner, Zara. *The Triumph of the Dark: European International History, 1933–1939*. Oxford: Oxford University Press, 2011.

Stigler, Stephen M. *The History of Statistics: The Measurement of Uncertainty before 1900*. Cambridge, MA, and London: Harvard University Press, 1986.

Stockwell, Sarah. "Banking on a Commonwealth Future." In *Commonwealth History in the Twenty-First Century*, edited by Saul Dubow and Richard Drayton, 311–328. Cham: Palgrave Macmillan, 2020.

Stockwell, Sarah. *The British End of the British Empire*. Cambridge: Cambridge University Press, 2018.

Stokes, Milton L. *The Bank of Canada: The Development and Present Position of Central Banking in Canada*. Toronto: The Macmillan Company, 1939.

Stone, Irving. *The Global Export of British Capital, 1865–1914: A Statistical Survey*. Basingstoke: Macmillan, 1999.

Stone, Lawrence, and Jeanne C. Fawtier Stone. *An Open Elite? England, 1540–1880*. Oxford: Clarendon Press, 1984.

Strange, Susan. *Sterling and British Policy: A Political Study of an International Currency in Decline*. London and New York: Oxford University Press, 1971.

Straumann, Tobias. *1931: Debt, Crisis, and the Rise of Hitler*. Oxford: Oxford University Press, 2019.

Suesse, Marvin. *The Nationalist Dilemma: A Global History of Economic Nationalism, 1776–Present*. Cambridge: Cambridge University Press, 2023.

Sunderland, David. *Financing the Raj: The City of London and Colonial India, 1858–1940*. Woodbridge: The Boydell Press, 2013.

Supple, Barry. "Official Economic Inquiry and Britain's Industrial Decline: The First Fifty Years." In *The State and Economic Knowledge: The American and British Experiences*, edited by Mary O. Furner and Barry Supple, 325–353. Washington, DC: Woodrow Wilson International Center for Scholars and Cambridge: Cambridge University Press, 1990.

Susskind, Daniel, and David Vines. "Global Economic Order and Global Economic Governance." *Oxford Review of Economic Policy* 40, no. 2 (2024): 189–219.

Sutherland, Gillian. *In Search of the New Woman: Middle-Class Women and Work in Britain 1870–1914*. Cambridge: Cambridge University Press, 2015.

Szöllösi-Janze, Margit. "Politisierung der Wissenschaften – Verwissenschaftlichung der Politik. Wissenschaftliche Politikberatung zwischen Kaiserreich und Nationalsozialismus." In *Experten und Politik. Wissenschaftliche Politikberatung in geschichtlicher Perspektive*, edited by Stefan Fisch and Wilfried Rudloff, 79–100. Berlin: Duncker & Humblot, 2004.

Tabb, William K. *Economic Governance in the Age of Globalization*. New York: Columbia University Press, 2004.

Teichova, Alice. "Banking and Industry in Central-East Europe in the First Decades of the 20th Century." In *Bank Austria Creditanstalt. 150 Jahre österreichische Bankengeschichte im Zentrum Europas*, edited by Oliver Rathkolb, Theodor Venus, and Ulrike Zimmerl, 148–161. Vienna: Paul Zsolnay Verlag, 2005.

Teichova, Alice, and Penelope Ratcliffe. "British Interests in Danube Navigation after 1918." *Business History* 27, no. 3 (1985): 283–300.

Telesca, Giuseppe. "Myths and Memory: The Crisis of the Pound and the Political Use of the Memory of 1931 in the United Kingdom." In *Remembering and Learning from Financial Crisis*, edited by Youssef Cassis and Catherine R. Schenk, 57–81. Oxford: Oxford University Press, 2021.

Temin, Peter. *Lessons from the Great Depression: The Lionel Robbins Lectures for 1989*. Cambridge, MA, and London: The MIT Press, 1989.

Teupe, Sebastian. "Keynes, Inflation and the Public Debt: *How to Pay for the War* as a Policy Prescription for Financial Repression?" *Financial History Review* 27, no. 2 (2020): 187–209.

Thackeray, David. *Forging a British World of Trade: Culture, Ethnicity, and Market in the Empire–Commonwealth, 1880–1975*. Oxford: Oxford University Press, 2019.

Thane, Pat. "Private Bankers and Philanthropy: The City of London, 1880s–1920s." In *The World of Private Banking*, edited by Youssef Cassis and Philip L. Cottrell, 273–288. Farnham: Ashgate, 2009.

Thiemann, Matthias. *Taming the Cycles of Finance? Central Banks and the Macro-Prudential Shift in Financial Regulation*. Cambridge: Cambridge University Press, 2023.

Thomas, W.A. *The Finance of British Industry, 1918–1976*. London: Methuen & Co., 1978.

Thompson, F.M.L. *Gentrification and the Enterprise Culture: Britain, 1780–1980*. Oxford: Oxford University Press, 2001.

Thompson, J.A. "The Historians and the Decline of the Liberal Party." *Albion: A Quarterly Journal Concerned with British Studies* 22, no. 1 (1990): 65–83.

Thornton, Christy. *Revolution in Development: Mexico and the Governance of the Global Economy*. Oakland: University of California Press, 2021.

Thorpe, Andrew. *The British Communist Party and Moscow, 1920–43*. Manchester and New York: Manchester University Press, 2000.

Thorpe, Andrew. *The British General Election of 1931*. Oxford: Clarendon Press, 1991.

Thurlow, Richard. "The Failure of British Fascism." In *The Failure of Political Extremism in Inter-War Britain*, edited by Andrew Thorpe, 67–84. Exeter: University of Exeter Press, 1989.

Tilley, Helen. *Africa as a Living Laboratory: Empire, Development, and the Problem of Scientific Knowledge, 1870–1950*. Chicago and London: The University of Chicago Press, 2011.

Tillman, Ellen D. *Dollar Diplomacy by Force: Nation-Building and Resistance in the Dominican Republic*. Chapel Hill: The University of North Carolina Press, 2016.

Timmins, Geoffrey. *Made in Lancashire: A History of Regional Industrialisation*. Manchester and New York: Manchester University Press, 1998.

Tolliday, Steven. *Business, Banking, and Politics: The Case of British Steel, 1918–1939*. Cambridge, MA, and London: Harvard University Press, 1987.

Tomlinson, B.R. "Britain and the Indian Currency Crisis, 1930–2." *The Economic History Review* 32, no. 1 (1979): 88–99.

Tomlinson, Jim. *Churchill and Industrial Britain: Liberalism, Empire and Employment, 1900–1929*. London: Bloomsbury, 2024.

Tomlinson, Jim. "Inventing 'Decline': The Falling Behind of the British Economy in the Postwar Years." *The Economic History Review* 49, no. 4 (1996): 731–757.

Tomlinson, Jim. *Managing the Economy, Managing the People: Narratives of Economic Life in Britain from Beveridge to Brexit*. Oxford: Oxford University Press, 2017.

Tomlinson, Jim. *Public Policy and the Economy since 1900*. Oxford: Clarendon Press, 1990.

Toms, Steven. *Financing Cotton: British Industrial Growth and Decline, 1780–2000*. Woodbridge: The Boydell Press, 2020.

Toniolo, Gianni. *Central Bank Cooperation at the Bank for International Settlements, 1930–1973*. Cambridge: Cambridge University Press, 2005.

Tooze, Adam. *Crashed: How a Decade of Financial Crises Changed the World*. New York: Viking, 2018.

Tooze, Adam. *The Deluge: The Great War, America and the Remaking of the Global Order, 1916–1931*. New York: Viking, 2014.

Tooze, J. Adam. "Imagining National Economies: National and International Economic Statistics, 1900–1950." In *Imagining Nations*, edited by Geoffrey Cubitt, 212–228. Manchester and New York: Manchester University Press, 1998.

Tooze, J. Adam. *Statistics and the German State, 1900–1945: The Making of Modern Economic Knowledge*. Cambridge: Cambridge University Press, 2001.

Tooze, Adam. *The Wages of Destruction: The Making and Breaking of the Nazi Economy*. London: Allen Lane, 2006.

Tooze, J. Adam. "Weimar's Statistical Economics: Ernst Wagemann, the Reich's Statistical Office, and the Institute for Business-Cycle Research, 1925–1933." *Economic History Review* 52, no. 3 (1999): 523–543.

Tooze, Adam, and Ted Fertik. "The World Economy and the Great War." *Geschichte und Gesellschaft* 40, no. 2 (2014): 214–238.

Topik, Steven. *The Political Economy of the Brazilian State, 1889–1930*. Austin: University of Texas Press, 1987.

Topik, Steven. "State Enterprise in a Liberal Regime: The Banco do Brasil, 1905–1930." *Journal of Interamerican Studies and World Affairs* 22, no. 4 (1980): 401–422.

Toye, Richard. *The Labour Party and the Planned Economy, 1931–1951*. Suffolk: Boydell & Brewer, 2003.

Trentmann, Frank. *Free Trade Nation: Commerce, Consumption, and Civil Society in Modern Britain*. Oxford: Oxford University Press, 2008.

Tribe, Keith. *Constructing Economic Science: The Invention of a Discipline, 1850–1950*. Oxford: Oxford University Press, 2022.

Tribe, Keith. *Economic Careers: Economics and Economists in Britain 1930–1970*. London: Routledge, 1997.

Tribe, Keith. *The Economy of the Word: Language, History, and Economics*. Oxford: Oxford University Press, 2015.

Tsokhas, Kosmas. "'A Pound of Flesh': War Debts and Anglo-Australian Relations, 1919–1932." *Australian Journal of Politics & History* 38, no. 1 (1992): 12–26.

Tsokhas, Kosmas. "Sir Otto Niemeyer, the Bankrupt State and the Federal System." *Australian Journal of Political Science* 30, no. 1 (1995): 18–38.

Tucker, Paul. *Unelected Power: The Quest for Legitimacy in Central Banking and the Regulatory State*. Princeton and Oxford: Princeton University Press, 2018.

Turner, John D. *Banking in Crisis: The Rise and Fall of British Banking Stability, 1800 to the Present*. Cambridge: Cambridge University Press, 2014.

Ugolini, Stefano. *The Evolution of Central Banking: Theory and History*. London: Palgrave Macmillan, 2017.

Veeser, Cyrus. *A World Safe for Capitalism: Dollar Diplomacy and America's Rise to Global Power*. New York: Columbia University Press, 2002.

Velasco e Cruz, Sebastião Carlos. *Empresariado e Estado na transição brasileira: um estudo sobre a economia política do autoritarismo, 1974–1977*. Campinas: Editora da Unicamp, 1995.

Venn, Fiona. "In Pursuit of National Security: The Foreign Office and Middle Eastern Oil, 1908–39." In *The Foreign Office, Commerce and British Foreign Policy in the Twentieth Century*, edited by John Fisher, Effie G.H. Pedaliu, and Richard Smith, 69–87. London: Palgrave Macmillan, 2016.

Verhoef, Grietjie. "Financial Intermediaries in Settler Economies: The Role of the Banking Sector Development in South Africa, 1850–2000." In *Settler Economies in World History*, edited by Christopher Lloyd, Jacob Metzer, and Richard Sutch, 403–433. Leiden and Boston: Brill, 2013.

Vermeulen, Cobus. "One Hundred Years of Private Shareholding in the South African Reserve Bank." *Economic History of Developing Regions* 36, no. 2 (2021): 245–263.

Villanueva, Javier. "Alejandro E. Bunge: una visión de la Argentina." *Revista Cultura Económica* 28, no. 77/78 (2010): 73–77.

Villela, André. "Las funciones de banca central antes del banco central: el caso del Banco de Brasil." In *Orígenes de la globalización bancaria: experiencias de España y América Latina*, edited by Daniel Díaz Fuentes, Andrés Hoyo Aparicio, and Carlos Marichal, 437–457. Santander: Genueve Ediciones, El Colegio de México, 2017.

Wagner, Florian. *Colonial Internationalism and the Governmentality of Empire, 1893–1982*. Cambridge: Cambridge University Press, 2022.

Waight, Leonard. *The History and Mechanism of the Exchange Equalisation Account*. Cambridge: Cambridge University Press, 1939.

Waite, P.B. *In Search of R.B. Bennett*. Montreal and Kingston: McGill-Queen's University Press, 2012.

Wakamori, Midori. "Henrī Kurei ni okeru sangyō, soshiki kyōgyō, 1916–1929." *Annual Report of the Society for the History of Economic Thought*, no. 44 (2003): 45–58.

Wake, Jehanne. *Kleinwort, Benson: The History of Two Families in Banking*. Oxford: Oxford University Press, 1997.

Wandschneider, Kirsten. "The Stability of the Interwar Gold Exchange Standard: Did Politics Matter?" *The Journal of Economic History* 68, no. 1 (2008): 151–181.

Wansleben, Leon. *The Rise of Central Banks: State Power in Financial Capitalism*. Cambridge, MA, and London: Harvard University Press, 2023.

Ward, Stephanie. *Unemployment and the State in Britain: The Means Test and Protest in 1930s South Wales and North-East England*. Manchester and New York: Manchester University Press, 2013.

Wardhaugh, Robert. *Behind the Scenes: The Life and Work of William Clifford Clark*. Toronto: University of Toronto Press, 2010.

Warnock, Barbara Susan. "The First Bailout: The Financial Reconstruction of Austria 1922–1926." PhD diss., Birkbeck College, University of London, 2015.

Wass, Douglas. *Decline to Fall: The Making of British Macro-Economic Policy and the 1976 IMF Crisis*. Oxford: Oxford University Press, 2008.

Watts, George S. *The Bank of Canada: Origins and Early History*, edited by Thomas K. Rymes. Ottawa: Carleton University Press, 1993.

Weber, Fritz. *Vor dem großen Krach. Österreichs Banken in der Zwischenkriegszeit am Beispiel der Credit-Anstalt für Handel und Gewerbe*. Vienna: Böhlau Verlag, 2016.

Wehrheim, Lino. *Im Olymp der Ökonomen. Zur öffentlichen Resonanz wirtschaftspolitischer Experten von 1965 bis 2015*. Tübingen: Mohr Siebeck, 2021.

Wheatley, Natasha. *The Life and Death of States: Central Europe and the Transformation of Modern Sovereignty*. Princeton and Oxford: Princeton University Press, 2023.

Wiener, Martin J. *English Culture and the Decline of the Industrial Spirit, 1850–1980*. Cambridge: Cambridge University Press, 1981.

Wilkins, Mira. *The History of Foreign Investment in the United States, 1914–1945*. Cambridge, MA: Harvard University Press, 2005.

Williams, David. "Montagu Norman and Banking Policy in the Nineteen Twenties." *Bulletin of Economic Research* 11, no. 1 (1959): 38–55.

Williamson, Philip. "A 'Bankers' Ramp'? Financiers and the British Political Crisis of August 1931." *The English Historical Review* 99, no. 393 (1984): 770–806.

Williamson, Philip. *National Crisis and National Government: British Politics, the Economy and Empire, 1926–1932*. Cambridge: Cambridge University Press, 1992.

Wilson, Graham. "Governance after the Crisis." In *The Oxford Handbook of Governance*, edited by David Levi-Faur, 372–386. Oxford: Oxford University Press, 2012.

Wilson, J.S.G. "The Commonwealth Bank of Australia." In *Banking in the British Commonwealth*, edited by R.S. Sayers, 39–99. Oxford: Clarendon Press, 1952.

Wilson, Thomas. "James Meade and the Role of Economic Advisers." *Contemporary British History* 11, no. 2 (1997): 143–145.

Wilson, Trevor. *The Downfall of the Liberal Party, 1914–1935*. London: Collins, 1966.

Winch, Donald. “Britain in the ‘Thirties: A Managed Economy?” In *The Managed Economy: Essays in British Economic Policy and Performance since 1929*, edited by Charles Feinstein, 47–67. Oxford: Oxford University Press, 1983.

Winch, Donald. “Economic Knowledge and Government in Britain: Some Historical and Comparative Reflections.” In *The State and Economic Knowledge*, edited by Mary O. Furner and Barry Supple, 40–70. Washington, DC: Woodrow Wilson International Center for Scholars and Cambridge: Cambridge University Press, 1990.

Wolcott, Susan. “Keynes versus Churchill: Revaluation and British Unemployment in the 1920s.” *The Journal of Economic History* 53, no. 3 (1993): 601–628.

Wood, John Cunningham. *British Economists and the Empire*. London and Canberra: Croom Helm, 1983.

Wood, John H. *A History of Central Banking in Great Britain and the United States*. Cambridge: Cambridge University Press, 2005.

Wormell, Jeremy. *The Gilt-Edged Market*. London: George Allen & Unwin, 1985.

Wormell, Jeremy. *The Management of the National Debt of the United Kingdom, 1900–1932*. London and New York: Routledge, 2000.

Wrench, David J. “‘Cashing In’: The Parties and the National Government, August 1931–September 1932.” *Journal of British Studies* 23, no. 2 (1984): 135–153.

Wright, Matthew. “The Policy Origins of the Reserve Bank of New Zealand.” *Reserve Bank of New Zealand Bulletin* 69, no. 3 (2006): 5–22.

Wueschner, Silvano A. *Charting Twentieth-Century Monetary Policy: Herbert Hoover and Benjamin Strong, 1917–1927*. Westport and London: Greenwood Press, 1999.

Xu, Chenzi. “Reshaping Global Trade: The Immediate and Long-Run Effects of Bank Failures.” *The Quarterly Journal of Economics* 137, no. 4 (2022): 2107–2161.

Yee, Robert. “Stability in Numbers: Central Banks, Expertise and the Use of Statistics in Interwar Europe.” *Contemporary European History* 33, no. 3 (2024): 1038–1059.

Yee, Robert. “A State of Supervision: The Political Economy of Banking Regulation in Germany, 1900s–1930s.” *Business History Review* 97, no. 1 (2023): 93–125.

Yes, Minister. “The Quality of Life.” March 30, 1981. *British Broadcasting Corporation*, directed by Peter Whitmore, written by Antony Jay and Jonathan Lynn, www.bbc.co.uk/programmes/b0074rh7.

Yohe, William P. “The Mysterious Career of Walter W. Stewart, Especially 1922–1930.” *History of Political Economy* 14, no. 4 (1982): 583–607.

Young, Warren, and Frederic S. Lee. *Oxford Economics and Oxford Economists*. Basingstoke: Macmillan, 1993.

Zahra, Tara. *Against the World: Anti-Globalism and Mass Politics between the World Wars*. New York: W.W. Norton & Company, 2023.

Ziblatt, Daniel. *Conservative Parties and the Birth of Democracy*. Cambridge: Cambridge University Press, 2017.

Ziegler, Dieter. “The Origins of the ‘Macmillan Gap’: Comparing Britain and Germany in the Early Twentieth Century.” In *Finance in the Age of the Corporate Economy: The Third Anglo-Japanese Business History Conference*, edited by P.L. Cottrell, A. Teichova, and T. Yuzawa, 184–208. Aldershot: Ashgate, 1997.

Ziegler, Dieter. "'A Regulated Market Economy': New Perspectives on the Nature of the Economic Order of the Third Reich, 1933–1939." In *Business in the Age of Extremes: Essays in Modern German and Austrian Economic History*, edited by Hartmut Berghoff, Jürgen Kocka, and Dieter Ziegler, 139–152. Cambridge: Cambridge University Press, 2013.

Ziegler, Philip. *The Sixth Great Power: Barings, 1762–1929*. London: William Collins Sons & Co., 1988.

Index

For EU product safety concerns, contact us at Calle de José Abascal, 56–1°, 28003 Madrid, Spain or eugpsr@cambridge.org.

www.ingramcontent.com/pod-product-compliance
Ingram Content Group UK Ltd.
Pitfield, Milton Keynes, MK11 3LW, UK
UKHW040308020426
469595UK00013B/186
* 9 7 8 1 0 0 9 6 7 1 8 8 0 *